MASTER INDEX TO SUMMARIES OF CHILDREN'S BOOKS

Vol. II: Title and Subject Indexes

by

ELOISE S. PETTUS

with the assistance of
DANIEL D. PETTUS

The Scarecrow Press, Inc.
Metuchen, N.J., & London
1985

TITLE INDEX

NOTE: Numbers after each title refer to entry numbers, not page numbers.

A Apple Pie 7251
ABC, an Alphabet Book 11836
ABC Book 5655
ABC Bunny, The 6463
ABCDEFGHIJKLMNOPQRSTUVWXYZ 2677
ABCDEFGHIJKLMNOPQRSTUVWXYZ in English and Spanish 16634
A B C de Puerto Rico 14598
A, B, C: Go! 11723
ABC for the Library 10945
A B C Molly 14372
ABC of Bumptious Beasts, The 10083
ABC of Buses, The 15629
ABC of Cars and Trucks 255
ABC of Ecology 12198
ABC of Monsters 12843
ABC Science Experiments 12199
ABC Workbook 11596
ABC ... XYZ 9226
ABC's in English and Spanish see ABCDEFGHIJKLMNOPQRSTUVWXYZ in English and Spanish
ABC's of Black History 8520
ABC's of Ecology 731
ABC's of Origami, The 14912
ABC's of Space 732
ABC's of the Earth 733
ABC's of the Ocean 734
A for Angel 12372
A for the Ark 5175
A-Haunting We Will Go 8587
A Is for Africa 1870
A Is for Always 543
A Is for Annabelle 17028
A. J. Foyt (May) 11853
A. J. Foyt (Olsen) 13100
A. P. Giannini: Boy of San Francisco 7673
Aaron and the Green Mountain Boys 6670
Aaron's Door 12177
Abacus, The 4907
Abba 16265
Abbott's Michigan History Stories for Boys and Girls 16
Abby 2809
Abby Hoffman 11319
Abby Takes Over 10182
Abdul 17727
Abe Lincoln 12920
Abe Lincoln and the River Robbers 484
Abe Lincoln Gets His Chance 3184
Abe Lincoln Grows Up 14884
Abe Lincoln's Birthday 7930
Abe Lincoln's Hobby 9570
Abe Lincoln's Other Mother 879
Abe Martin's Back Country Sayings 8702
Abecedarian Book, The 5822
Abel's Island 16187
Abeto Vallente, El 4187
Abigail 16075
Abigail Adams (Kelly) 9668
Abigail Adams (Peterson) 13572
Abigail Adams (Wagoner) 17386
Abimbolu 9094
Abominable Swamp Man, The 7579
Aborigines of Australia 8698
About Animals 14984
About Dying 16202
About Garbage and Stuff 15408
About Glasses for Gladys 5527
About Handicaps 16203
About Measurement 6369
About Owls 6594
About the B'nai Bagels 9985
About Wise Men and Simpletons 7386
Abracadabra! 15362

1

Abraham Lincoln (Colver) 3883
Abraham Lincoln (Daugherty)
    4530
Abraham Lincoln (d'Aulaire)
    4543
Abraham Lincoln (Foster) 6139
Abraham Lincoln (Judson) 9417
Abraham Lincoln (Martin) 11741
Abraham Lincoln (Nolan) 12872
Abraham Lincoln (Ostendorf)
    13200
Abraham Lincoln in Peace and War
    12153
Abraham Lincoln's World 6140
Absolute Zero 4278
Absurd Alphabedtime Stories
    8774
Abu 17013
Abu Ali 17234
Accident, The 3068
Accomplice, The 14325
Achilles 11421
Achouna, Boy of the Arctic 4490
Ackson 1064
Acoma 9113
Acorns and Squash 605
Across Five Aprils 8748
Across the Barricades 10863
Across the Bridge 1334
Across the Meadow 15512
Across the Ocean Sea 14892
Across the Sea from Galway 5939
Across the Tracks 18445
Act It Out 2944
Act Now! 11230
Active-Enzyme Lemon-Freshened
    Junior High School Witch 8172
Actor in Exile 11576
Adam and Eve 14181
Adam and Eve Name the Animals
    15214
Adam and the Golden Cock 4452
Adam Bookout 15588
Adam Clayton Powell 7816
Adam of the Road 7202
Adam's ABC 5855
Adam's Key 10324
Adam's World 6234
Adamu and the Stolen Child
    18361
Adaptation 1413
Adassa and Her Hen 12834
Add-a-Line Alphabet 6255
Addie and the King of Hearts
    14496
Adlai Stevenson 17516
Adopted Daughter 3601

Adopted Jane 4497
Adu's Bicycle 16799
Advanced Tennis 12122
Adventure 9120
Adventure Across Africa 14066
Adventure in Addis Ababa 15554
Adventure in Bangkok 7676
Adventure in Black and White 6666
Adventure in Tunisia 11729
Adventures in an African Jungle
    204
Adventures in Fanti-Land 10491
Adventures in Paper Modelling
    13406
Adventures of A Apple Pie, The
    2647
Adventures of Aku, The 2457
Adventures of Arab, The 15837
Adventures of B. J., the Amateur
    Detective 16033
Adventures of Benjamin Pink, The
    17995
Adventures of Coalpot, The 137
Adventures of Dixie North 2721
Adventures of Don Quixote de la
    Mancha 3226
Adventures of George Washington,
    The 4577
Adventures of Hatim Tai 5474
Adventures of Hiawatha, The 17337
Adventures of Homer Fink, The
    13029
Adventures of Huckleberry Finn
    17082
Adventures of Isabel, The 12645
Adventures of Jimmy Poole, The
    343
Adventures of Kama Pua'a 2545
Adventures of K'Tonton, The
    17661
Adventures of Kwaku, The 13852
Adventures of Little Mouk, The
    7841
Adventures of Mr. Hyena, The
    4436
Adventures of Mr. Rabbit, The
    16438
Adventures of Ngondo, Mungai and
    Wangari, The 9497
Adventures of Obadiah, The 17056
Adventures of Olatunde in Ghana
    30
Adventures of Ookpik, The 7962
Adventures of Paddy Pork, The
    7035
Adventures of Paulo Mukasa, The
    8316

Adventures of Pinocchio, The
(Collodi) 3858
Adventures of Pinocchio, The
(Lorenzini) 11078
Adventures of Pongo and His
Uncle Talema, The 9476
Adventures of Sasa and Esi, The
13219
Adventures of Snowshoe Thomp-
son, The 3142
Adventures of So-Hi 1259
Adventures of Spider, The 630
Adventures of Strong Vanya
13905
Adventures of the Black Hand
Gang, The 13894
Adventures of the Greek Heroes
11445
Adventures of the Negro Cow-
boys, The 5165
Adventures of the Three Colors,
The 16882
Adventures of Tom Sawyer
17083
Adventures of Yemima ..., The
16045
Adventures of Yoo-Lah-Teen
13985
Adventures on the Airboat Trail
7815
Adventures with a Cardboard
Tube 12200
Adventures with a Paper Cup
12201
Adventures with Collage 1255
Advertising 13812
Aesop's Fables (Untermeyer)
17155
Aesop's Fables (White) 17778
Afo-A-Kom 5834
Africa (Allen) 358
Africa (Hatch) 7836
Africa (MacGregor-Hastie) 11384
Africa (Nielson) 12836
Africa and Asia 8202
Africa, Awakening Giant 10557
Africa Dream 7304
Africa in Perspective 15796
Africa Is People 12888
Africa Is Thunder and Wonder
12889
Africa 1966 5020
Africa 1968 5021
Africa 1973 5022
Africa 1974 5023
Africa 1975 5024
Africa 1976 5025

Africa, Past and Present 16830
Africa Through the Ages 15457
Africa Today 7367
African Adventure (Hostetler) 8643
African Adventure (Price) 13930
African Adventures 12777
African Animals Through African
Eyes 4470
African Apes 1301
African Art Today 153
African Cookbook, The 14898
African Crafts 9726
African Crafts for You to Make 4471
African Elephant, The 1486
African Episodes 16933
African Folk Tales (Guillot) 7474
African Folk Tales (Leslau) 10623
African Folk Tales (Nunn) 12966
African Hair Sculpture 1227
African Herdboy 1981
African Lion, The 4217
African Lions and Cats 1302
African Myths and Legends 673
African Myths, Together with
Proverbs 18251
African Nationalism 8496
African Night's Entertainment, An
5314
African Panorama, An 16061
African Poems and Love Songs
10624
African Poetry for Schools 14064
African Proverbs 10625
African Rhythm-American Dance
7732
African Safari 13352
African Shadows 12298
African Slavery 8695
African Songs 14566
African Stories 17744
African Success Story 1565
African Tales of Magic and Mystery
10004
African Traveler 16576
African Treehouse 16663
African Village Folktales 9546
African Wanderers or the Adven-
tures of Carlos and Antonio,
The 10492
African Wonder Tales 3050
Africans Knew, The 13678
Africa's Animals 5344
Africa's Large Animals 245
Africa's Living Arts 11707
Afro-American Contributors to
American Life 6209
Afro-American History 6239

Afro-Americans: Then and Now 8818

After Candlemas 685

After-Harvest Festival, The 606

After the Goat Man 2781

After the Sun Goes Down 1795

Afuera 9160; see also Watch Me Outdoors

Against a Crooked Sky 16306

Against Time! 9186

Agatha's Alphabet 6079

Age of Aquarius 2111

Aggrey of Achimota 12590

Agikuyu Folk Tales 12854

Agossou, Boy of Africa 4491

Agouhanna 790

Aguinaldos del Infante, Los 1722

Aguk of Alaska 17631

Ah, Man, You Found Me Again 7446

Ah-meek 556

Ah See and the Spooky House 16838

Ah Ucu and Itzo 13937

Ahdoolo! The Biography of Matthew A. Henson 12225

Aida 17283

Aiimu and His Ox, The 13858

Aikido Complete 18359

Aim for a Job in Appliance Service 9611

Aim for a Job in Automotive Service 2075

Air 99

Air Force Cadet 6109

Air Is All Around You 2112

Air of Mars ... 6841

Air Pollution 10429

Air-Raid-Pearl Harbor! 16710

Air Traffic Control 13088

Air We Breathe!, The 1790

Aircraft at Work 5390

Airport Builders, The 9664

Aise-ce-bon, a Raccoon 2085

Ajapa the Tortoise 1214

Ajayi the Bishop 208

Akavak 8655

Akua the Ebony Doll 7222

Akwasi Seeks Adventure 154

Al Kaline and the Detroit Tigers 2747

Alabama Mounds to Missiles 206

Alan and Naomi 10667

Alan and the Animal Kingdom 8466

Alan Mendelsohn, the Boy from Mars 13694

Alaska 2746

Alaska Bush Pilot 4025

Albert B. Cub and Zebra 14501

Albert Herbert Hawkins ... 4883

Albert Payson Terhune 17142

Albert the Albatross 8345

Alberto and His Missing Sock 6545

Albert's Toothache 17971

Alborada 13984

Album of Black Americans in the Armed Forces 12218

Album of Chinese Americans, An 16503

Album of Dinosaurs 11365

Album of Dogs 8061

Album of Irish Americans, An 12570

Album of Martin Luther King, Jr., An 14719

Album of New Netherland, An 4905

Album of North American Birds 5109

Album of Puerto Ricans in the United States, An 2090

Album of Sharks 11366

Album of the American Cowboy 11575

Album of the American Indian 18385

Album of the Civil War, An 9521

Album of the Fifties, An 10846

Album of the Italian-American An 10193

Album of the Jews in America, An 16444

Album of Women in American History, An 8900

Album of World War II, An 8538

Alcancia de los Sueños, La 16863

Alchemists, The 827

Alcohol (Fleming) 6025

Alcohol (Seixas) 15256

Alcohol and Alcoholism 5596

Alcohol and You 10483

Alcohol as a Crutch 15162

Alcoholism 15676

Aldar the Trickster 3533

Alec Majors, Trail Boss 454

Alec's Sand Castle 14779

Alegrias-poemas para niños 14591

Alexander and the Car with the Missing Headlight 6022

Alexander and the Terrible, Horrible No Good, Very Bad Day 17317

Alexander and the Wind-up Mouse 10872

Alexander Hamilton and Aaron Burr 4322

Alexander the Great (Gunther) 7499

Alexander the Great (Mercer) 12086

Alexander the Great, Scientist King 16440

Alexander von Humboldt 16822

Alexander, Who Used to Be Rich Last Sunday 17318

Alfalfa, Beans, and Clover 14082

Alfalfa Hill: Winter 13337

Alfie and Me and the Ghost of Peter Stuyvesant 11414

Alfombra Magica 17297

Alfred Goes Flying 1651

Alfred Hitchcock and the Three Investigators in the Mystery of the Screaming Clock 684

Alfred Hitchcock's Daring Detectives 8255

Alfred Hitchcock's Sinister Spies 8256

Alfred's Alphabet Walk 3335

Algodon de Azucar 14398

Algonkians of the Eastern Woodlands 14556

Ali 13129

Ali Goes Travelling 16800

Ali of Egypt 3190

Alice-All-By-Herself 3666

Alice Freeman Palmer 6026

Alice of Old Vincennes 16835

Alice Yazzie's Year 11544

Alice's Adventures in Wonderland 3098

All Aboard 5117

"All Aboard!" The Story of Passenger Trains in America 793

All About Archaeology 17779

All About Arthur 2920

All About Biology 6894

All About Cats 2645

All About Courts and the Law 2255

All About Dinosaurs 527

All About Eggs ... 15268

All About Electricity 6286

All About Famous Inventors and Their Inventions 13880

All About Fire 8439

All About Goldfish as Pets 4073

All About Great Rivers of the World 17780

All About Horses 8062

All About Houses 5107

All About Jewish Holidays and Customs 5485

All About Light and Radiation see Light and Radiation

All About Mountains and Mountaineering 17781

All About Rabbits as Pets 4074

All About Rockets and Space Flight 7059

All About Sailing 2454

All About Snakes 7992

All About Strange Beasts of the Past 528

All About the Arctic and Antarctic 16069

All About the Desert 5486

All About the Human Body 6895

All About the Human Mind 6991

All About the Planets 10342

All About the Symphony Orchestra and What It Plays 3912

All About the Wonders of Chemistry 6287

All About Us (Evans) 5581

All About Us (Kaufman) 9530

All Alone 1671

All Along the Way: Poetry 12394

All-American 17047

All-American Coeds, The 11513

All Around the Town 11334

All Around You 1414

All Butterflies 2369

All Day Long (Scarry) 14985

All Day Long (Whitlock) 17818

All Except Sammy 4288

All Falling Down 18586

All for Fall 9741

All in a Day's Work 1229

All in an African Lifetime 7340

All in Free but Janey 9257

All in Good Time 13172

All in the Morning Early 12815

All It Takes Is Practice 12167

All Kinds of Babies 15269

All Kinds of Bees 15630

All Kinds of Codes 851

All Kinds of Families 15724

All Kinds of Kings in Fact and Legend 9318

All Kinds of Mothers 2443

All Kinds of Seals 9964

All Kinds of Time 1314

All Men Are Brothers 15711

All My Troubles Were Little Ones
  12035
All-of-a-Kind Family 16703
All-of-a-Kind Family Downtown
  16704
All-of-a-Kind Family Uptown
  16705
All-of-a-Sudden Susan 3667
All Ready for School 82
All Ready for Winter 83
All-Stars of the Outfield 15431
All the Children Were Sent Away
  6623
All the Mowgli Stories 9841
All the Pretty Horses 9180
All the Summer Voices 4128
All the Way Home 15243
All the Way to Wit's End 7317
All This Wild Land 3479
All Together 239
All upon a Sidewalk 6732
All upon a Stone 6733
All Us Come Cross the Water
  3618
Allah, the God of Islam 5964
Allan Napier MacNab 1164
Allan Pinkerton (Anderson) 485
Allan Pinkerton (Borland) 1956
Alley, The 5576
Alligator 15495
Alligator and His Uncle Tooth,
  The 7915
Alligator Book, The 1482
Alligator Case, The 5078
Alligator Pie 10480
Alligator Smiling in the Sawgrass
  8927
Alligator Under the Bed 12850
Alligators All Around 15328
Alligators and Crocodiles 18535
Alligators and Music 5363
Alligator's Toothache 4666
Almena's Dogs 18253
Almost All-White Rabbity Cat,
  The 4671
Almost Ancestors 10105
Almost Big Enough 16641
Almost Brothers 3251
Almost Like Sisters 3191
Almost Year, The 14102
Alo Man, The 3231
Aloha from Bobby 16096
Alone Amid All This Noise 14229
Alone in the Wild Forest 15775
Along Came a Dog 4672
Along Our Country Road 17623
Along Sandy Trails 3480

Along the Forest Path 18286
Along the Niger River 9193
Along the Seashore 2474
Alphabeast Book, The 15086
Alphabet Art 5940
Alphabet Boat, The 12061
Alphabet Book, The (Eastman)
  5221
Alphabet Book (Peppe) 13497
Alphabet Symphony, The 11456
Alphabet Tale, The 6642
Alphabet Tree, The 10873
Alphabet World 12215
Alphabet Zoop 8001
Alphonse, That Bearded One 2954
Altogether, One at a Time 9986
Alvin Fernald, Foreign Trader
  8152
Alvin Fernald, Superweasel 8153
Always Movin' On 7817
Always Room for One More 12816
Am I a Bunny? 4803
Amahl and the Night Visitors
  12079
Amanda, Dreaming 17748
Amanda the Panda and the Redhead
  16752
Amanda's Choice 8467
Amateur Magician's Handbook, The
  7908
Amateur Zoologist's Guide to Turtles
  and Crocodilians, The 18495
Amazing 5172
Amazing Bee, The 6191
Amazing Bone, The 16188
Amazing Book of Birds, The 15714
Amazing Dandelion, The 15325
Amazing Miss Laura, The 3859
Amazing Mr. Prothero, The 701
Amazing Red Man, The 13314
Amazing Seeds, The 8844
Amazon, River Sea of Brazil, The
  16070
Amber Wellington, Camp Shadow
  6878
Amber Wellington, Daredevil 6879
Ambush at Fort Dearborn 6169
Amelia Bedelia 13282
Amelia Bedelia Helps Out 13283
Amelia Earhart (Davis) 4586
Amelia Earhart (Howe) 8684
Amelia Earhart (Mann) 11605
Amelia Earhart (Parlin) 13334
Amelia Earhart (Seibert) 15246
Amelia Mixed the Mustard ... 12741
Amelia Quackenbush 6985
Amelia's Flying Machine 7963

America and Its Indians 10473
America Becomes Free 10524
America Before Man 916
America Begins 4453
America Forever New 2213
America Goes to the Fair 13516
America Grows Up 9266
America Is Also Irish 17632
America Is Also Italian 11597
America Is Also Jewish 6993
America Is Also Scandinavian
  11574
America Is Not All Traffic Lights
  6027
America: Land of Wonders 18229
America: Red, White, Black,
  Yellow 5731
America Sings 2979
America Travels 4454
American Alligator, The (Adrian)
  139
American Alligator, The (Ricciuti)
  14296
American Badges and Insignia
  9736
American Cattle Trails East and
  West 13717
American Composers 13831
American Congress, The 17680
American Denim 1247
American Eagle, The 140
American Flag, The 13341
American Folk Songs for Children
  15237
American Folk Songs for Christmas
  15238
American Forts Yesterday and
  Today 7163
American Freedom and the Bill of
  Rights 18136
American Ghost, An 11
"American Girl" Book of Teenage
  Questions, The 393
American Heritage Book of Indians
  9393
American Heritage Pictorial His-
  tory of the Presidents of the
  United States, The 10539
American Heroes of the 20th Cen-
  tury 5632
American History in Art 3726
American Houses 8264
American Indian, The 6790
American Indian Artifacts see
  Collector's Guide to American
  Indian Artifacts, The
American Indian Dances 16104

American Indian Design and Decora-
  tion 597
American Indian Fairy Tales 3914
American Indian Food and Lore
  12838
American Indian 1492-1970, The
  4827
American Indian Story, The 11466
American Indian Tribes 7346
American Indian Women 7347
American Indians, The 6051
American Indians Sing 8379
American Indians Today 8699
American Indians Yesterday and
  Today 7164
American Inventors 8874
American Jews 7690
American Modern Dancers 11950
American Mother Goose, The 18242
American Neighbors 792
American Nightmare, The 7018
American Painter in Paris 18073
American Presidency 17681
American Riddle Book, The 18165
American Sokol Sings!, The 395
American Tall-Tale Animals 16390
American Tall Tales 16391
American Windmills 4184
American Women in Sports 8482
American Women of the Space Age
  8697
Americans All (Anthony) 578
Americans All (Leonard) 10601
Americans Before Columbus 917
Americans to the Moon 7506
America's Abraham Lincoln 11467
America's Ancient Treasures 6091
America's Buried Past 1002
America's Cup Yacht Race 11854
America's Endangered Birds 11243
America's Ethan Allen 8433
America's First Ladies 1789-1865
  2777
America's First Trained Nurse 982
America's First Woman Astronomer
  985
America's First World War 3150
America's Horses and Ponies 2078
America's Mark Twain 11468
America's Most Haunted Places
  14425
America's Paul Revere 6100
America's Reign of Terror 5841
America's Robert E. Lee 3908
Amiable Giant, The 15838
Amifika 3619
Amigo 15174

Amigo Chum 4379
Amigos! Amigos! Amigos! 9161;
  see also Friends! Friends!
  Friends!
Amin and the Robbers and the
  Two Friends 14906
Amina and the Moshi Makers 18388
Aminal, The 1018
Amish Family, An 12677
Amish Wedding 14722
Amistad Mutiny, The 9965
Among the Amish 8629
Among the Dolls 15828
Among the Plains Indians 5443
Among the Shoshones see White
  Indian Boy, The
Amos and Boris 16189
Amos Fortune, Free Man 18376
Amphibians and Reptiles in Kansas
  3852
Amphibians as Pets 18498
Amphibians of Illinois 13336
Amulets, Talismans, and Fetishes
  7326
Amuny, Boy of Old Egypt 15063
Amy 5894
Amy and Laura 14836
Amy and the Cloud Basket 13879
Amy and the New Baby 2413
Amy Loves Goodbyes 7072
Amy Moves In 14837
Amy's Dinosaur 8346
Amy's Goose 8517
Amy's Long Night 6549
Ana 15996
Ananse and the Wise Man 40
Ananse Stories 586
Ananse the Spider (Appiah) 589
Ananse the Spider (Brown) 2347
Anansi the Spider 11289
Anansi, the Spider Man 15543
Anastasia Krupnik 11126
Anatole 16886
Anatole and the Cat 16887
Anatole and the Thirty Thieves
  16888
Anatole in Italy 16889
Ancestral Roof, The 11277
Anchor Man 8999
Ancient Africa 74
Ancient Egypt 5815
Ancient Egypt from A to Z 13908
Ancient Greece 5636
Ancient Indians of the Southwest
  16639
Ancient Indonesia 17626
Ancient Rome 5637

Ancient Scrolls 4392
And All Between 15961
And All Her Paths Were Peace
  10554
And Everywhere Children! 3361
And I Mean It, Stanley 1902
And I Must Hurry for the Sea Is
  Coming In 12062
And It Came to Pass 15825
And It Is Still That Way 1233
And It Rained 14119
And Leffe Was Instead of a Dad
  16851
And My Mean Old Mother Will Be
  Sorry, Blackboard Bear 278
... And Now Miguel 10113
And Now We Are a Family 12087
And One Was a Wooden Indian 920
And So My Garden Grows 16084
And the Jackal Played the Masinko
  8605
And the Waters Prevailed 1119
And Then Mom Joined the Army
  7558
And Then the Harvest 13127
And Then There Were None 10505
And Then What Happened, Paul
  Revere? 6380
And This Is Laura 3931
And to Think That I Saw It on Mul-
  berry Street 15366
And What Do You Do? 430
And What of You, Josephine Char-
  lotte? 18157
Andanzas de Pepita Canela, Las
  12410
Andrew and the Alchemist 2796
Andrew Carnegie 11577
Andrew Carnegie and the Age of
  Steel 15564
Andrew Henry's Meadow 2662
Andrew Jackson 3774
Andrew Young 7818
Andrews Raid ..., The 5487
Andries 17225
Androcles and the Lion (Galdone)
  6497
Androcles and the Lion (Hawkins)
  7894
Andromedar SRI 14399
Andron and the Magician 11047
Andy (de Paola) 4715
Andy (Schick) 15042
Andy and Benny Catch a Thief
  11461
Andy and the Lion 4531
Andy and the Wild Worm 16779

Andy Buckram's Tin Men 2261
Andy Jackson and the Battle for
New Orleans 11187
Andy Jackson's Water Well 16165
Andy Panda Goes Fishing 10267
Andy's Dan'l Boone Rifle 607
Andy's Mountain 2057
Angel en Colombia 5831
Angel en España 5832
Angel in the Tower 5063
Angel of Appalachia 12597
Angel of Mercy 983
Angelita la Ballena Pequenita
14353
Angelo the Naughty One 6621
Angeles Albriciadores 12537
Angelita 9739
Angelito 17487
Angels and Other Strangers
13366
Angie 17109
Angles Are Easy as Pie 6399
Angry Moon, The 15829
Angry Waters 12423
Angus and the Ducks 5987
Animal Antics see Way It All
Began, The
Animal Babies 1191
Animal Camouflage (Carthy) 3132
Animal Camouflage (Shuttlesworth)
15631
Animal Disguises 5904
Animal Doctors (Curtis) 4414
Animal Doctors (Greene) 7263
Animal Fact/Animal Fable 15735
Animal Family, The 9155
Animal Fathers 6245
Animal Folk Songs for Children
15239
Animal Friends 5138
Animal Friends of Peng-U, The
2271
Animal Games 6246
Animal Grandstand see Running,
Jumping, Throwing, Sliding,
Racing, Climbing Book, The
Animal Homes 3134
Animal Hospital 1509
Animal House, The 4424
Animal Instincts 6249
Animal Invaders 15677
Animal Kingdom, The 7475
Animal Man, The 6312
Animal Migration 6368
Animal Stories from Africa 4989
Animal Stories the Indians Told
9259

Animal Tales 5019
Animal Territories 3743
Animal Tracks 11782
Animal Vision 11783
Animales Carpinteros, Los 6546
Animals and Plants That Trap
7017
Animals and Their Niches 13947
Animals Are Like This 10622
Animals Around My Block 14230
Animals as Parents 15270
Animals at My Doorstep 8567
Animals' Christmas, The 5228
Animals Come to My House 9651
Animals Do the Strangest Things
8620
Animals Everywhere 4544
Animals Grow 579
Animals in Clay 14368
Animals in the Zoo 14567
Animals in Winter 1041
Animals in Wood 14369
Animals Live Here 1175
Animals Made by Me 2407
Animals Mourn for Da Leopard and
Other West African Tales 5015
Animals of East Africa 4775
Animals of the Arctic 17298
Animals of the Bible 5901
Animals of the Polar Regions 9289
Animals of the Prairie 12242
Animals of the Sea 15271
Animals on the Farm 14568
Animals Should Definitely Not Wear
Clothing 1109
Animals That Changed the World
4607
Animals That Eat Nectar and Honey
8574
Animals That Help Us 5807
Anita's Choice 7645
Ann Aurelia and Dorothy 2955
Ann Can Fly 13645
Anna and Dula 17257
Anna Banana 8373
Anna's Silent World 18194
Anne and the Sand Dobbies 3716
Anne Bradstreet 5131
Anne of Green Gables 12368
Annemarie Proell 9056
Annie 14936
Annie and the Old One 12178
Annie Annie 3916
Annie, Bridget, and Charlie 16952
Annie Oakley (Graves) 7188
Annie Oakley (Wilson) 18074
Annie Oakley and the World of Her

Time 231
Annie Sullivan 11578
Annie Wauneka 12723
Annie's Rainbow 2318
Anno's Alphabet 569
Anno's Counting Book 570
Anno's Journey 571
Ann's Spring 4383
Ann's Surprising Summer 326
Another Day 5558
Another Place, Another Spring 9332
Anpao 8170
Answers to Your Questions About American Indians 17170
Ant and Bee Time 1053
Ant Is Born, An 4968
Ant Realm, The 8845
Antarctic Challenge 15415
Anteater Named Arthur, An 17357
Antelope Singer 17124
Anthony and Sabrina 13874
Antique Cars 9006
Anton Retaco--del ancho mundo 6708
Anton Retaco--el bautizo 6709
Anton Retaco--en Villavieja 6710
Anton Retaco--la funcion 6711
Anton Retaco--los niños tristes 6712
Anton Retaco--por los caminos 6713
Antonia's Surprise 7500
Antonio 13847
Antrim's Orange 16502
Ants Are Fun 12620
Ants Go Marching, The 6326
Any Me I Want to Be 10154
Anybody's Bike Book 4422
Apache Indians, The 1744
Apaches 8950
Aparecen los "Blok" 407
Ape in a Cape 5296
Appalachia 16935
Apple and Other Fruits, The 15272
Apple and the Arrow, The 2563
Apple and the Moth, The 11673
Apple Is Red, An see Manzana Es Roja, La
Apple Stone, The 7217
Apple Tree Cottage 17338
Apple War, The 12595
Applemouse 16825
Apples (Hogrogian) 8406
Apples (Hunt) 8747
Apples Every Day 14341

Apples to Zippers 14731
Appleseed Farm 5034
Appolonia's Valentine 12204
Approaches to Clay Modelling 15205
Approaches to Crayons, Chalks and Pastels 15190
Approaches to Painting 17474
Apricot ABC 12179
April Age, The 14780
April Fools 10016
April's Witches 4307
Apt. 3 9592
Aquanauts, The 15006
Aquarium Book for Boys and Girls 12434
Aquatic Insects 11244
Aqui Viene el Ponchado see Here Comes the Strikeout
Aquiii, Inosito! 11571
Arab World in the 20th Century, The 10947
Arabel's Raven 179
Arabian Nights, The (Colum) 3874
Arabian Nights (Lang) 10239
Arabs Knew, The 13679
Arbol Chico, El 17349
Arbor Day 5905
Archaeology (Besserat) 1613
Archaeology (Cooke) 4014
Archaeology of Ancient Egypt, The 9121
Archaeology of New York, The 16441
Archery 2028
Archy's Dream World 13664
Arco Iris, El 12326
Arctic Journey 2535
Arctic Tundra, The 6963
Ardillas Mellizas, Las 15354
Ardizzone's Hans Andersen 4167
Are All the Giants Dead? 12946
Are There Any More at Home Like You? 14623
Are You My Friend? 12063
Are You My Mother? 5222
Are You Square? 9742
Are You There God? It's Me, Margaret 1814
Area 16105
Aretha Franklin 13101
Arilla Sun Down 7658
Arithmetic Can Be Fun 10455
Arithmetic for Billy Goats 1100
Arithmetic in Verse and Rhyme 9031
Arizona (Carpenter) 2995
Arizona Highways Indian Arts and

Crafts 16649
Ark, The (Angel) 535
Ark, The (Benary-Isbert) 1390
Arkansas 2996
Arm of the Starfish, The 10545
Armed with Courage 11469
Armed with Love 1184
Armenian Cookbook 8415
Armenian Folk Songs 8664
Armor 12474
Arms and Armor in Africa 12826
Arnold Palmer 13102
Around and Around: LOVE 12168
Around Another Corner 7982
Around London 1900-1950 4385
Around the Corner 16023
Around the House That Jack Built 25
Around the World in Eighty Days 17286
Around the World with Nellie Bly 7559
Arriba capitan 14551
Arriba en el monte 8909
Arrow Book of Poetry 11346
Arrow to the Sun 11290
Arrunango 1966
Art and Archaeology 6909
Art and Artists of Indiana 2664
Art for Children 1580
Art for City Children 10096
Art from Found Objects 3901
Art of Africa, The 6910
Art of America from Jackson to Lincoln, The 6911
Art of America in the Gilded Age, The 6912
Art of America Since World War II, The 6913
Art of Ancient Egypt, The 6914
Art of Ancient Greece, The 6915
Art of Ancient Mexico, The 6916
Art of Ancient Peru, The 6917
Art of Ancient Rome, The 6918
Art of China, The 6919
Art of Choosing, The 3332
Art of Colonial America, The 6920
Art of Francis Lee Jaques, The 9152
Art of India, The 6921
Art of Japan, The 6922
Art of Lands in the Bible, The 6923
Art of Photography, The 6924
Art of the Comic Strip, The 6925

Art of the Eskimo, The 6926
Art of the Etruscans, The 6927
Art of the New American Nation, The 6928
Art of the North American Indian, The 6929
Art of the Northwest Coast Indians, The 6930
Art of the Old West, The 6931
Art of the Plains Indians, The 6932
Art of the Southwest Indians, The 6933
Art of the Spanish ..., The 6934
Art of the Woodland Indians, The 6935
Art of Walt Disney, The 5870
Arte Mexicano, El 5830
Arthur Ashe (May) 11855
Arthur Ashe (Morse) 12482
Arthur Ashe (Robinson) 14475
Arthur Mitchell 16895
Arthur the Kid 4150
Arthur's Christmas Cookies 8265
Arthur's Honey Bear 8266
Arthur's Pen Pal 8267
Arts and Crafts You Can Eat 3705
Arts of Clay 13909
Arts of Wood 13910
As I Walked Out One Evening 13743
As I Was Crossing Boston Common 5663
As Right as Right Can Be 14600
As Tall as a Spear 1872
Aseban 10511
Ash Road 16036
Ashanti Heroes 10168
Ashanti of Ghana, The 1745
Ashanti to Zulu 12589
Asi es nuestra casa 4516
Asi es nuestro hermano pequeño 4517
Asi es nuestro perro 4518
Asi pasamos el dia 4519
Asi somos nosotros 4520
Asi son los abuelos que viven cerca 4521
Asi son los abuelos que viven lejos 4522
Asi son los tios 4523
Asi son nuestros amigos 4524
Asi son papa y mama 4525
Asian Crafts 16124
Asiatic Land Battles 5157
Ask Me a Question 17130
Ask Me a Question About the Atom

14630
Ask Me Another Riddle   17127
Ask Me No Questions   16380
Ask Mr. Bear   5988
Assembling Automobiles at Oakville
   3119
Assignment: Sports   10900
Asteroids, The   12958
Astonishing Stereoscope   10259
Astrology and Foretelling the Fu-
   ture   828
Astronautas del "Mochuelo," Los
   16031
At Bat #3   7516
At Daddy's Office   12274
At Home in the Wild   18230
At Jesus' House   18180
At Last to the Ocean   14686
At Mary Bloom's   297
At Night   14257
At the Back of the North Wind
   11299
At the Center of the World   921
At the Hospital   18532
At the Mouth of the Luckiest
   River   7361
At the Top of My Voice   8500
At Work   14986
Atom, the Little Moon Monkey
   13623
Atomic Energy   100
Atomic Energy for Human Needs
   12143
Atoms and Molecules   110
Atoms Today and Tomorrow   8868
Atonement in the Sun   7476
Attack at Fort Lookout   14189
Attic of the Wind   11166
Attractive Universe, The   17181
Atu, the Silent One   9435
Atuk   4475
August Explains   14258
August the Fourth   5693
Auk, the Dodo and the Oryx,
   The   15665
Aunt America   1780
Aunt Flora   3668
Aunt Malissa's Memory Jug   662
Aunt Sally's Life   see   Victorian
   Doll Stories
Aunt Vinnie's Invasion   425
Aunt Vinnie's Victorious Six
   426
Aurora and Socrates   17295
Aurora, Brigida y Carlos   6426
Australia, Wonderland Down Under
   18063

Australian Aborigines   940
Australian Legendary Tales   13313
Australian Marsupials   4327
Authorized Autumn Charts of the
   Upper Red Canoe River Country
   3765
Auto Racing   4026
Auto Racing Highlights   2609
Autobiography of Miss Jane Pittman
   6480
Automobile Factory   1510
Autumn Harvest   16995
Autumn People, The   686
Automobile Racing   12823
Avalanche!   14807
Avalanche Dog   1153
Aventura en Australia   8252
Aventuras de Calaquito, Las   4276
Aventuras de Polichinela   8197
Averages   16106
Aviation   see   Contributions of
   Women: Aviation
Avril   5620
Awake and Ago   11264
Awake and Dreaming   18512
Away Goes Sally   3669
Away Is So Far   16624
Away to East Africa   12770
Away to Mexico   12771
Away Went the Balloons   7946
Awful Mess, The   14502
Awful Name to Live Up to, An
   8642
Awful Thursday   14728
Awkward Magic   1498
Axe-time, Sword-time   4129
Ayo   674
Azeet, Paratrooper Dog   7501
Aztec Indians of Mexico, The   1746

- B -

B Is for Bear   2448
"B" Is for Betsy   7947
Baba and Mr. Big   13252
Baba and the Flea   15189
Baba Yaga   15861
Baba Yaga's Geese and Other Rus-
   sian Stories   2918
Babar and the Wully-Wully   4648
Babar Comes to America   4649
Babar Loses His Crown   4650
Babar y el Papa Noel   4645

Babe Didrikson   4667
Babe Ruth   17292
Babe Ruth and Hank Aaron   7819
Baboon, The   6589
Baboushka and the Three Kings
   14422
Baby, The (Burningham)   2678
Baby (Manushkin)   11651
Baby Baboon   5403
Baby Elephant and the Secret
   Wishes   9394
Baby Elephant Goes to China
   9395
Baby Farm Animals   17996
Baby Island   2262
Baby Sister for Frances, A   8272
Baby Starts to Grow, A   15592
Babylon to Brasilia   8198
Baby's Lap Book, The   3387
Baby's Song Book, The   13838
Back Field Challenge   6678
Backbone of the King   2370
Backpacking   6784
Backstroke Swimming   14814
Backward Beasts from A to Z
   12213
Backward Day, The   10072
Backyard Astronomer, The   12959
Backyard Birds   14769
Backyard Trees   14770
Bad Bell of San Salvador, The
   1267
Bad Boy, Good Boy   5559
Bad Child's Book of Beasts, The
   1362
Bad Fairy and the Caterpillar,
   The   12075
Bad Fall   4251
Bad News Bears, The   18247
Bad Times of Irma Baumlein, The
   2263
Badu Goes to Kumasi   411
Bag Full of Nothing, A   18006
Bag of Tricks!   14169
Bagel Baker of Mulliner Lane,
   The   1742
Bagthorpes Unlimited   4279
Bailout   5193
Baja Run, The   15876
Bajun and the Sea, The   14671
Bake Bread!   16003
Baked Beans for Breakfast   3340
Bakers, The   86
Balarin's Goat   1597
Bald Eagles of the Chippewa
   Forest   340
Balder and the Mistletoe   1132

Baldur and the Mistletoe   8327
Ball for Little Bear, A   2324
Ball of Clay, A   7895
Ballad of the Burglar of Babylon,
   The   1686
Ballad of the Long-Tailed Rat, The
   13805
Ballad of William Sycamore, The
   1462
Ballads and Songs from Ohio   5252
Ballads and Songs from Utah   8703
Ballet   16761
Ballet Companion, The   11951
Ballet Dance for Two   17166
Ballet Family, The   318
Ballet for Beginners   5065
Ballet Shoes   16406
Ballooning Adventures of Paddy
   Pork, The   7036
Balloons   2626
Ballpoint Bananas and Other Jokes
   for Kids   9639
Baltimore Colts, The   11856
Baltimore Orioles   2182
Balto, Sled Dog of Alaska   486
Bambi   14866
Bamboo School in Bali, The   10307
Bamburu   5540
Baney's Lake   157
Bang Bang Family, The   18077
Bang, Bang, You're Dead   5978
Banji's Magic Wheel   15012
"Banner, Forward!"   14118
Banner in the Sky   17122
Bantam Trivia Quiz Book, The
   14867
Bantu Africans, The   9547
Bantu Civilization of Southern Afri-
   ca, The   12568
Bantu Folk Tales   8113
Bantu Folk Tales from Southern Af-
   rica   14956
Bantu Tales (Holladay)   8463
Bantu Tales (Price)   13927
Barbapapa's Voyage   16883
Barbarossa   7183
Barefoot Abe   11122
Barefoot in the Grass   647
Bargain for Frances, A   8273
Barkley   8347
Barkley Street Six-Pack, The
   15621
Barn, The   15100
Barnes Book of Nursery Verse, The
   8924
Barney Bipple's Magic Dandelions
   3268

Barney the Beard 2588
Barney's Adventure 798
Baron Munchausen 13169
Baron's Booty, The 9452
Baron's Hostage, The 16979
Barred Road, The 4694
Barrel, The 17862
Barry 8821
Bart Starr, Professional Quarter-
    back 11841
Barter, Bills and Banks 16657
Bartholomew, We Love You!
    13159
Barto Takes the Subway 2183
Base 5 93
Base Hit 7729
Baseball 12154
Baseball Bargain, The 4098
Baseball Brothers 14736
Baseball Flyhawk 3413
Baseball for Boys 14628
Baseball for Young Champions
    581
Baseball Hall of Fame 5488
Baseball Players Do Amazing
    Things 3213
Baseball Stories 13215
Baseball Talk for Beginners 617
Baseball Trick, The 4099
Baseball's Art of Hitting 16451
Baseball's Champion Pitchers
    2748
Baseball's Great Moments 6940
Baseball's Greatest Sluggers
    10759
Baseball's Hall of Fame 15916
Baseball's Home-Run Hitters
    14090
Baseball's Most Colorful Managers
    14479
Bashorun Oluyole 209
Basic Baseball Strategy 6307
Basic Football Strategy 4972
Basic Hockey Strategy 11194
Basic Ju-Jitsu Handbook 12704
Basic Karate Handbook 12705
Basic Sailing 6754
Basic Soccer Strategy 4839
Basil and Hilary 18488
Basil and the Pygmy Cats 16890
Basil Brush Goes Boating 5891
Basil Brush Goes Flying 5892
Basil Brush in the Jungle 5893
Basil in Mexico 16891
Basil of Baker Street 16892
Basket Counts, The 3414
Basket in the Reeds, A 14911

Basket of Guavas and Other Stories,
    The 6313
Basket That Flew over the Moun-
    tain, The 17609
Basketball (Allen) 333
Basketball (Kaplan) 9491
Basketball (Miers) 12155
Basketball Basics 12457
Basketball for Young Champions
    582
Basketball Girl of the Year 17421
Basketball Lingo 8489
Basketball My Way 17758
Basketball Players Do Amazing
    Things 3214
Basketball Skillbook, The 12355
Basketball Superstars 5571
Basketball Talk 10909
Basketball's Big Men 14091
Basketball's Greatest Teams 8240
Basque Girl 8938
Bassumtyte Treasure, The 4393
Basuto Fireside Tales 14957
Bat, The 10506
Bat Is Born, A 9156
Bat-Poet, The 9157
Bates Family, The 13203
Bathtub Ocean, The 13362
Bats (Lauber) 10343
Bats (Pitt) 13712
Bats and Balls 11064
Bats in the Dark 9538
Battle in the Arctic Seas 16711
Battle for Iwo Jima, The 10476
Battle of Britain, The 14279
Battle of Bubble and Squeak, The
    13424
Battle of Fallen Timbers, August 20,
    1794 16726
Battle of Lake Erie, The 11779
Battle of Lake Erie, September,
    1813, The 1124
Battle of Midway, The 8647
Battle of Mogori ..., The 9807
Battle of Reuben Robin and Kite
    Uncle John, The 2829
Battle of St. George Without, The
    11480
Battle of Tabkin Kwatto, The 2039
Battle of the Bulge 16911
Battle of the Wind Gods, The
    17243
Battle of Wednesday Week, The
    see Storm from the West
Battle of Wounded Knee, The 1884
Battle of Yorktown, The 6039
Battle of Zango, The 2040

Battlefield, The (Gatanyu) 6657
Battlefield, The (Mayne) 11952
Bayeux Tapestry, The 4836
Bayou Backwaters 5244
Bayou Boy (Lattimore) 10325
Bayou Boy (Smith) 15898
Bayou Boy and the Wild Dog
  15899
Bayou Suzette 10558
Bazar de Todas las Cosas, El
  6130
Be a Smart Shopper 6697
Be a Winner in Basketball 4027
Be a Winner in Football 4028
Be a Winner in Ice Hockey 4029
Be a Winner in Skiing 4030
Be a Winner in Soccer 4031
Be a Winner in Tennis 4032
Be a Winner in Track and Field
  4033
Be Brave, Charlie 11742
Be Good, Harry 3244
Be Nice to Josephine 8631
Be Nice to Spiders 7141
Beach Before Breakfast, The
  10129
Beach Bird 3069
Beachcombers, The 4280
Beachcomber's Book, The 9966
Beads as Jewelry 4582
Beady Bear 6256
Beanie 3110
Beany 5746
Beany and His New Recorder
  13271
Bear, a Bobcat and Three Ghosts,
  A 14503
Bear and the Fly, The 18121
Bear and the People, The 18580
Bear by Himself 7916
Bear Called Paddington, A 1873
Bear Circus 5079
Bear Detectives, The 1490
Bear Mouse 6327
Bear Party 5080
Bear Scouts 1491
Bear Tales 2333
Bear Teeth for Courage 15210
Bear Weather 3235
Bear Who Had No Place to Go,
  The 16285
Bear Who Liked Hugging People
  and Other Stories, The 196
Bear Who Saw the Spring, The
  10155
Bear Who Stole the Chinook and
  Other Stories, The 6232

Bear Who Wanted to Be a Bear, The
  16216
Bear, Wolf and Mouse 17393
Bearcat, The 9239
Bears 13749
Bears and I, The 10626
Bears Are Sleeping 18476
Bear's Bicycle, The 11447
Bear's Heart 16508
Bears' House, The 14838
Bears in the Night 1492
Bears Live Here 5236
Bears' Nature Guide, The 1493
Bears of Blue River, The 11563
Bears on Hemlock Mountain, The
  4455
Bears on Wheels 1494
Bear's Picture 13695
Bear's Toothache, The 11493
Bears Up Stairs, The 7538
Bear's Water Picnic, The 18390
Bears Who Went to the Seaside, The
  7341
Beast in Holger's Woods, The 4843
Beast of Lor, The 2549
Beast of Monsieur Racine, The
  17131
Beastly Boys and Ghastly Girls
  3808
Beastly Circus, A 13284
Beat It, Burn It and Drown It
  8205
Beat the Turtle Drum 7282
Beatinest Boy, The 16424
Beatrice and Vanessa 18391
Beautiful Christmas Tree, The
  18598
Beautiful Girl and the Snake, The
  2348
Beautiful Junk 11518
Beautiful Namirembe 11975
Beautiful Nyakiemo, The 11811
Beautiful Rat, The 18522
Beautiful Ship 13892
Beauty 11431
Beauty and the Beast 13425
Beauty Is No Big Deal 10412
Beauty Millionaire 5621
Beauty of Being Black 16339
Beauty of Birth, The 13827
Beauty Queen, The 13602
Beaver, The 14693
Beaver in Ontario, The 12964
Beaver Pond, The 16996
Beaver Trail 9669
Beaver Valley 5265
Beaver Year 2079

Beavers Live Here   5237
Bebedero de rocio   14717
Because I Promised   4289
Because of a Flower   12253
Because of the Sand Witches There
    16158
Bechuana Fireside Tales   14958
Becky   18086
Becky and the Bear   17235
Becky Landers   15806
Becky's Christmas   17029
Becky's Horse   11525
Bed Book, The   13732
Bed Just So, The   7714
Bed-Knob and Broomstick   12947
Bed-Stuy Beat   1804
Bedtime for Frances   8274
Bedtime Story, A   10655
Bee   3766
Bee Is Born, A   4969
Bee-Man of Orn, The   16329
Bee Tree and Other Stuff   13453
Beech Tree, The   2480
Beef for Beauregard   8554
Beef Stew   2184
Bees and Beelines   7884
Bees and Wasps   3635
Bees Can't Fly, but They Do
    9926
Beeswax Catches a Thief   9862
Beethoven   9033
Beethoven Medal, The   see   If I
    Ever Marry
Beetle Bush, The   9636
Beetles   2296
Beezus and Ramona   3554
Befana   14504
Before and After Dinosaurs   4505
Before the Colors Fade   17624
Before the Indians   11857
Before the Supreme Court   5146
Before You Came This Way   1234
Before You Were a Baby   15607
Before You Were Three   7790
Beggar in the Blanket ..., The
    7126
Beginner Under the Backboards
    8979
Beginner's Book of Needlepoint, A
    13327
Beginner's Guide to Building and
    Flying Model Airplanes   11058
Beginning Crafts for Beginning
    Readers   6816
Beginning Mobiles   13285
Beginning of the Earth, The
    2113

Beginning Stamp Collecting   13067
Beginning-to-Read Poetry   3634
Beginning-to-Read Riddles and
    Jokes   6817
Beginnings and Blunders   8397
Beginnings of Cities, The   17676
Behind the Back of the Mountain
    1
Behind the Magic Line   5536
Behind the Plate   17217
Behind the Scenes in a Car Factory
    7777
Behind the Scenes in a Department
    Store   7778
Behind the Scenes in an Oil Field
    3999
Behind the Scenes of Television
    Programs   7779
Behind the Sealed Door   16567
Behind the Wheel (Jackson)   9007
Behind the Wheel (Koren)   9998
Behold This Dream   4695
Being Alone, Being Together   1537
Being Born   16400
Being Green   14117
Bell for Ursli, A   3386
Bell Laboratories   7327
Bell That Rang for Freedom, The
    7627
Bella Abzug   5622
Belle Boyd   12873
Bellfounder's Son, The   7443
Belling the Tiger   16342
Bells of Bleecker Street, The   538
Below the Root   15962
Bemba, an African Adventure   3471
Ben and Annie   16665
Ben and Me   10419
Ben Franklin of Old Philadelphia
    4210
Ben Goes into Business   8230
Ben Hooper Tales   2334
Ben on the Ski Trail   15582
Beneath the Hill   4394
Beneath Your Feet   15736
Benedict Arnold   12874
Benefactors of the World   5586
Benin   5365
Benito   2550
Benjamin and Tulip   17728
Benjamin Banneker   10695
Benjamin Franklin (d'Aulaire)   4545
Benjamin Franklin (Fleming)   6040
Benjamin Franklin (Judson)   9418
Benjamin Franklin (Meadowcroft)
    11986
Benjamin West and His Cat Grimalkin

Big Orange Splot, The 13696
Big Pile of Dirt, The 3640
Big Push, The 922
Big Rain, The 6211
Big Red 9875
Big Red Barn, The 2590
Big Red Bus 9743
Big Road, The 3540
Big Sea, The 645
Big Sister and Little Sister 18599
Big Sister, Little Brother 1538
Big Sister Tells Me That I'm Black 124
Big Snow, The 7542
Big Snowstorm, The 13569
Big Star Fallin' Mama 9353
Big Stick, The 6679
Big Susan 9345
Big Tiger and Christian 12540
Big Tree 2537
Big Wave, The 2482
Big Wheels, The 8797
Big World and the Little House, The 10073
Bigfoot 1203
Bigfoot Wallace and the Hickory Nut Battle 14771
Bigger and Smaller 6400
Bigger Than an Elephant 1503
Bigger They Come, The 12317
Biggest and the Littlest Animals, The 13243
Biggest Bear, The 17514
Biggest Fish in the Sea, The 8911
Biggest House, The 9163
Biggest House in the World, The 10874
Biggest Riddle Book in the World 14626
Biggest Snowstorm Ever, The 13363
Biggest Victory, The 15850
Bigity Anne 4498
Bike Tripping 4423
Bike-Ways (101 Things to Do with a Bike) 6224; see also The Bicycle Book
Bikes 8051
Bill Bergson Lives Dangerously 10829
Bill Bergson, Master Detective 10830
Bill Cosby 13103
Bill Cosby's Personal Guide to Tennis Power ... 4172
Bill of Rights, The 5871
Bill Russell 4776

Bill Severn's Big Book of Magic 15389
Billie Jean King (Baker) 970
Billie Jean King (Church) 3441
Billie Jean King (May) 11858
Billie Jean King (Olsen) 13104
Billie Learns Karate 18152
Billion for Boris, A 14547
Billions of Bugs 13581
Billy and Blaze 455
Billy and Our New Baby 678
Billy Bedamned, Long Gone By 1268
Billy Beg and the Bull 4384
Billy Boll Weevil 11517
Billy Boy 3300
Billy Goat and His Well-Fed Friends 8407
Billy Goat in the Chili Patch, The 10438
Billy, the Littlest One 15064
Billy's Basketball 16766
Bim, the Little Donkey 13907
Bimby 2627
Binary Numbers 17563
Binky Brothers and the Fearless Four 10400
Binky Brothers, Detectives 10401
Biographies of Black Americans for All Americans 11735
Biographies of Great Composers 12702
Biography of a Buzzard 6330
Biography of a Cottontail 17020
Biography of a Desert Bighorn 16211
Biography of a Grizzly 15359
Biography of a Kangaroo Rat 16212
Biography of a Rhino 8575
Biography of a River 12618
Biography of a River Otter 7781
Biography of a Snowy Owl 8576
Biography of an Alligator 4417
Biography of an American Reindeer 8577
Biography of an Ant 8578
Biography of an Armadillo 8579
Biography of an Atom 15315
Biography of an Octopus 8580
Biography of an Ostrich 8581
Biography of Physics 6530
Biological Revolution, The 8976
Biombo infantil 14552
Bionics (Marteka) 11720
Bionics (Silverstein) 15678
Bird 15809

Bird Book, The 15502
Bird from the Sea, The 17709
Bird in the Family, A 2186
Bird Is Born, A 1967
Bird of Passage 16721
Bird of Time, The 18404
Bird Talk 6533
Bird That Swallowed the Stool and
    Other Stories, The 6080
Bird Watchers and Bird Feeders
    1796
Bird Watcher's Guide, The 3851
Bird Woman, The 9483
Birds, The (Peterson) 13580
Birds (Pluckrose) 13750
Birds and the Beasts Were There,
    The 3809
Birds and Their Beaks 5203
Birds and Their Nests 5204
Birds Are Flying 9539
Birds at Home 8064
Birds at Night 6534
Birds' Christmas Carol, The 17885
Birds Do the Strangest Things
    8621
Birds Eat and Eat and Eat 6535
Birds, Frogs, and Moonlight
    3147
Birds in the Street 11132
Birds in Your Backyard 5304
Birds of a Feather 1202
Birds of Algonquin Provincial
    Park 13140
Birds of Hano Village, The 16616
Birds of Prey 8401
Birds of the Crow Family 5205
Birds That Stopped Flying 797
Birds with Bracelets 17736
Bird's Woodland, The 5705
Birdstones, The 4395
Birkin 13632
Birth of a Forest 15274
Birth of an Island 15275
Birth of Sunset's Kittens, The
    16258
Birth of Texas, The 9301
Birth of the United States, 1763-
    1816 736
Birthday 16231
Birthday Candles Burning Bright
    2214
Birthday for Frances, A 8276
Birthday for the Princess, A 10986
Birthday Goat, The 17589
Birthday in Kishinev 16210
Birthday Tree, The 3835
Birthday Visitor, The 17090

Birthday Wish, The 8961
Birthdays 13378
Birthdays of Freedom 6141
Bisha of Burundi 3612
Bishop and the Devil, The 15346
Bits That Grow Big 17635
Bitter Herbs and Honey 3738
Bizarre Animals, The 2908
Black Africa on the Move see
    First Book of Africa on the
    Move, The
Black African Empires 9388
Black African Voices 12231
Black American Leaders 18452
Black and Blue Magic 15963
Black and Brave 10827
Black and White 634
Black Athlete 13185
Black B C's 3620
Black Bear's Story, A 10789
Black Beauty 15394
Black Bondage 7052
Black Book, The 7787
Black Cauldron, The 261
Black Champions of the Gridiron
    18438
Black Cop 6358
Black Courage 15111
Black Cowboy 3508
Black Crusaders for Freedom
    17614
Black Experiences in Michigan His-
    tory 10284
Black Fairy Tales 1539
Black Folk Tales 1581
Black Gems for His Crown 4970
Black Gold 8065
Black Folktales 10629
Black Frontiersman, The 7981
Black Hawk (Anderson) 487
Black Hawk (Beckhard) 1294
Black Hawk (Cleven) 3599
Black Heart of Indri, The 8400
Black Hearts in Battersea 180
Black Heroes in Our Nation's His-
    tory 5071
Black Images 12676
Black in America 9003
Black Is 2430
Black Is Beautiful 11347
Black Is Beautiful Beauty Book, The
    12234
Black Is Brown Is Tan 125
Black Jack 11245
Black Joke, The 12521
Black Literature in America 969
Black Magic, White Magic 9197

Black Man in America, 1619–1790, The 8993

Black Man in America, 1791–1861, The 8989

Black Man in America, 1861–1877, The 8990

Black Man in America, 1905–1932, The 8991

Black Man in America, 1932–1954, The 8992

Black Man in Art, The 3727

Black Means 7456

Black Mountain Boy 2978

Black Music in America 14739

Black Mustanger, The 18273

Black on White and Read All Over 1073

Black Panther of the Great Lakes 17766

Black Pearl, The 13010

Black Penny 5520

Black People of America, The 4830

Black Pilgrimage 5754

Black Pioneers of Science and Invention 7541

Black Politicians 2453

Black Power 2985

Black Pride 7772

Black Prince ..., The 18482

Black River, a Wisconsin Story 532

Black Roots 4563

Black Sheep, The 12108

Black Soldier 3529

Black Stallion 5688

Black Stallion and the Girl, The 5689

Black Stallion's Ghost, The 5690

Black Stars 2250

Black Stone Knife, The 11698

Black Struggle 6436

Black Sunshine 2702

Black Swamp Farm 7033

Black Symbol, The 9240

Black Tiger at Indianapolis 13002

Black Voyage 8680

Black Within and Red Without 12467

Black Wolf of Riverbend, The 17859

Black Wolf of the Steppes 4564

Black Woman 9513

Black Women of Valor 2703

Blackbeard's Ghost 16129

Blackberry Winter 11976

Blackbird in the Lilac 14202

Blackboard Bear 279

Blackbriar 15830

Blackie, the Gorilla 9238

Blackmail Machine, The 8501

Blackout 14528

Blacks in Bondage 16153

Blacks in Communications 16198

Blacksmiths, The 5941

Blah, The 9702

Blanche Neige / Snow White 10372

Blanford's Painting Book of National Costumes, No. 7 Africa 4603

Blaze and the Forest Fire 456

Blaze and the Gray Spotted Pony 457

Blaze and the Indian Cave 458

Blaze and the Lost Quarry 459

Blaze and the Mountain Lion 460

Blaze Finds Forgotten Roads 461

Blaze Shows the Way 462

Blazing Hills 7686

Blazing Star 6833

Bless This Day 17324

Blind Boy and the Loon ..., The 11545

Blind Colt, The 14694

Blind Connemara, The 463

Blind Men and the Elephant, The (Quigley) 14036

Blind Men and the Elephant, The (Saxe) 14975

Blok y la bicicleta fantasma, Los 408

Blood 18536

Blood Brothers 16252

Blood Feud 16518

Blood in the Snow 15647

Blood Red Belt 12988

Blood Royal 17671

Bloody Country, The 3843

Bloody Kansas, 1854–65 1125

Bloomers & Ballots 3530

Blossom on the Bough, The 5041

Blow Ye Winds Westerly 6724

Blowfish Live in the Sea 6177

Blubber 1815

Blue and Green Wonders ... 8714

Blue Caboose, The 7646

Blue Canyon Horse 3481

Blue Cat of Castle Town, The 3713

Blue Fin 16793

Blue Horse and Other Night Poems, The 6188

Blue in the Seed 8886

Blue Jackal, The 2371

Blue Jacket 5245

Blue Jeans 14625
Blue Lobster, The 3070
Blue Man, The 13735
Blue Mittens, The 14196
Blue Moose 13697
Blue Mystery 1391
Blue-Nosed Witch, The 5420
Blue Ribbons for Meg 4696
Blue Ridge Billy 10559
Blue Rose, The 9894
Blue Sea 9461
Blue Seed, A 12634
Blue Snow, The 14139
Blue Stars Watching 1269
Blue Stone, The 9690
Blue Tree, Red Sky 9904
Blue Valentine, The 15124
Blue Wampum 3972
Blue Whale, The 12290
Blue Willow 6658
Blueberries for Sal 11234
Blueberry 14889
Blueberry Corners 10560
Bluejay Boarders, The 9624
Bluenose Brainerd Stories 2335
Bluntstone and the Wildkeepers
  7412
Boat Handling 16868
Boat in the Reeds, The 16301
Boat for Peppe, A 13776
Boats on the River, The 5989
Bob Bodden and the Good Ship,
  Rover 3672
Bob Gibson 10892
Bob Hope 16696
Bob McAdoo 17080
Bob: Watchdog of the River 7597
Bobby Clarke 11859
Bobby Hull (May) 11860
Bobby Hull (Zalewski) 18491
Bobby Orr (Liss) 10910
Bobby Orr (May) 11861
Bobo's Dream 280
Bobsledding 7334
Bobwhite from Egg to Chick to
  Egg 15151
Bodach, The see Walking Stones,
  The
Bodies 2187
Body, Boots and Britches 16831
Body Snatchers, The 3744
Body Talk 6698
Boer War, The (Barbary) 1065
Boer War, The (Borer) 1946
Bogwoppit 18044
Bojabi Tree, The 14352
Bola and the Oba's Drummers

  15013
Bolivar the Liberator 16577
Bollerbam 9138
Boloji and Old Hippo 15402
Bone for Bone 4174
Bones 18537
Bonfires and Broomsticks see
  Bed-knob and Broomstick
Bongleweed, The 4281
Bongo Bradley 6887
Bonus Day 9494
Bonus of Redonda, The 34
Boo to a Goose 11112
Book About God, A 5965
Book About Pandas, A 7448
Book About Your Skeleton, A 7449
Book for Abe, A 17339
Book for Jodan, A 12783
Book of American Negro Spirituals,
  The 9287
Book of Americans, A 1461
Book of Animal Poems, A 3810
Book of Big Bugs, A 13582
Book of Bosh, A 10461
Book of Charms and Changelings,
  A 11627
Book of Christmas, The 1929
Book of Christmas Carols, A 15528
Book of Devils and Demons, A
  11628
Book of Dogs, The 3638
Book of Dragons, A 11629
Book of Enchantments and Curses,
  A 11630
Book of Expert Driving, The 5642
Book of Festivals and Holidays the
  World Over, The 8881
Book of Flying Saucers for You, A
  2115
Book of Ghosts and Goblins, A
  11631
Book of Giants, A 11632
Book of Greek Myths 4546
Book of Heroes 8009
Book of Holidays, The 11508
Book of Horses, The 989
Book of Hugh Flower, The 1310
Book of Indian Crafts and Costumes
  11778
Book of Indian Crafts and Indian
  Lore 14864
Book of Indian Life Crafts 12893
Book of Indians, The 8490
Book of Joyous Children, The
  14377
Book of Kings and Queens, A
  11633

Book of Magic Animals, A 11634
Book of Magical Horses, The 11964
Book of Monsters, A 11635
Book of Moon Rockets for You, A 2116
Book of Myths, A 2548
Book of Negro Folklore, The 8723
Book of Negro Humor, The 8715
Book of Nonsense (Lear) 10462
Book of Nonsense, A (Rhys) 14292
Book of Nursery and Mother Goose Rhymes 4629
Book of Planet Earth for You, A 2117
Book of Planets for You, A 2118
Book of Satellites for You, A 2119
Book of Snails, A 9650
Book of Sorcerers and Spells, A 11636
Book of Stars for You, A 2120
Book of the Dance, The 4714
Book of the Goat, The 15195
Book of the Milky Way Galaxy for You, A 2121
Book of Think (or How to Solve a Problem Twice Your Size), The 2687
Book of Three, The 262
Book of Time, A 3825
Book of Wishes and Wishmaking 5431
Book of Witches, A 11637
Book to Begin on Time, A 17466
Booker T. Washington (Graham) 7147
Booker T. Washington (Stevenson) 16271
Booker T. Washington (Wise) 18137
Books 7301
Books: A Book to Begin On 1145
Books for You to Make 13995
Boom Town Boy 10561
Boomba Lives in Africa 15774
Boomerang Hunter 9876
Boonmee and the Lucky White Elephant 7667
Border Hawk 263
Bordon y la estrella, El 171
Boris 16746
Boris Bad Enough 10054
Born Free 65

Born in a Barn 6725
Born on the Circus 13869
Born to Run 6168
Born to Trot 8066
Bornene pa Kuglen / The Children on the Globe 1547
Borribles, The 4693
Borrowed Boots 14009
Borrowed Canoe, The 5643
Borrowed House, The 17226
Borrowed Treasure 3884
Borrowers, The 12948
Borrowers Aloft, The 12949
Bosque Maravilloso, El 10825
Boss Cat 8775
Boss Chombale 8705
Botswana (Carpenter & Balow) 3041
Botswana (Hanson) 7708
Bottom of the Sea, The 6995
Bouboukar, Child of the Sahara 18282
Boundary Riders, The 13633
Bow in the Clouds, A 5656
Bow Island 2993
Bowie's Lost Mine see Jim Bowie's Lost Mine
Bowleg Bill 5773
Bowling Talk for Beginners 10911
Bows Against the Barons 16980
Box Full of Infinity, A 18007
Box of Daylight, The 8203
Box of Fire, A 203
Box Tied with a Red Ribbon, A 9164
Box with Red Wheels, The 13555
Boxcar Children, The 17524
Boxing for Boys 15662
Boxing's Heavyweight Champions 14092
Boy, The 13130
Boy, a Dog, a Frog and a Friend, A 11944
Boy, a Dog and a Frog, A 11925
Boy Alone 13204
Boy and a Battery, A 18381
Boy and a Pig, but Mostly Horses, A 9720
Boy and the Bird, The 6433
Boy and the Blind Storyteller, The 512
Boy Apprenticed to an Enchanter, The 3875
Boy at Bat 14239
Boy at the Window 13214
Boy Beyond the Moon 371
Boy Blue's Book of Beasts 15936

Boy Called Fish, A 12437
Boy Called Hopeless, A 12036
Boy Called Plum, A 14574
Boy Doctor, The 13057
Boy Drummer of Vincennes, The
  2980
Boy from Abilene, The 15549
Boy from Johnny Butte 14575
Boy from Nowhere, The 6893
Boy Had a Mother Who Bought
  Him a Hat, A 10156
Boy in Between, The 17743
Boy in the Moon, The 13097
Boy Named Paco, A 13373
Boy of Dahomey 10286
Boy of Nepal 10287
Boy of Old Prague, A 8943
Boy of Tache, A 1707
Boy of the Islands 10889
Boy of the Masai 5005
Boy of the Pyramids 9365
Boy on a White Giraffe 7617
Boy on Lincoln's Lap, The 1335
Boy on the Ox's Back ..., The
  16420
Boy on the Run 2058
Boy Once Lived in Nazareth, A
  16681
Boy, the Baker, the Miller and
  More, The 1598
Boy, the Rat, and the Butterfly,
  The 4733
Boy Travellers in the Far East,
  Part Fifth, The 9950
Boy Travellers on the Congo,
  The 9951
Boy Wanted 5788
Boy, Was I Mad! 8259
Boy Went Out to Gather Pears,
  A 8376
Boy Who Could Do Anything and
  Other Mexican Folk Tales, The
  2179
Boy Who Could Fly, The 12789
Boy Who Could Make Himself Dis-
  appear, The 13736
Boy Who Could Make Things,
  The 13896
Boy Who Could Sing Pictures
  10517
Boy Who Didn't Believe in Spring,
  The 3621
Boy Who Drew Sheep, The
  14506
Boy Who Had No Birthday, The
  8756
Boy Who Had Wings, The 18405

Boy Who Learnt a Lesson ..., The
  17035
Boy Who Loved Music, The 10295
Boy Who Made a Million, The
  13030
Boy Who Made Dragonfly, The 8199
Boy Who Played Tiger, The 6609
Boy Who Sailed Around the World
  Alone, The 7145
Boy Who Sang the Birds, The
  17762
Boy Who Tried to Cheat Death, The
  12164
Boy Who Was Followed Home, The
  11551
Boy Who Would Not Say His Name
  17354
Boy Who Wouldn't Talk, The 1992
Boy with a Pack 11981
Boy with a Problem, The 5709
Boy with an R in His Hand, The
  14173
Boy with Many Houses, The 14879
Boy with Three Names 6544
Boy Without a Name 10953
Boyhood of Grace Jones, The
  10260
Boyhood on the Upper-Mississippi
  10822
Boys and Girls Book About Divorce,
  The 6590
Boys and Girls, Girls and Boys
  12095
Boy's Book of Biking, The 11320
Boy's Book of Gun Handling, The
  9942
Boy's Book of Hiking, The 11321
Boy's Book of Indian Skills, The
  11322
Boy's Book of Insects, The see
  Junior Book of Insects, The
Boy's Book of Outboard Boating
  13346
Boy's Book of Science and Con-
  struction 12435
Boy's Book of Ships and Shipping
  13494
Boy's Own Book of Frontiersmen,
  The 2269
Brady 6381
Braid Craft 10806
Bratchets, The 4013
Brave Baby Elephant 9396
Brave Balloon of Benjamin Buckley,
  The 17749
Brave Cowboy, The 544
Brave Eagle's Account of the Fetter-

man Fight 6944
Brave Frontier, The 13188
Brave Gives Blood, The 5310
Brave Heritage 12308
Brave Janet Reachfar 5120
Brave Little Hummingbird 17340
Brave Riders, The 990
Bravest Babysitter, The 7256
Bravo, Burro! 5660
Bread-and-Butter Indian 3885
Bread-and-Butter Journey 3886
Bread and Jam for Frances 8277
Bread and Roses 12038
Bread Book, The 12123
Bread Dough Craft Book, The 16008
Break a Leg 13593
Break a Leg, Betsy Maybe! 9824
Break a Magic Circle 9258
Break Through in Science 737
Breakaway Back 8860
Breaking Branch, The 3348
Breaking In 11082
Breakthrough to the Big League 14467
Breaststroke Swimming 14815
Breath of Air and a Breath of Smoke, A 11695
Breed to Come 12931
Bremen Town Musicians, The 7387
Brendan the Navigator 6382
Brer Rabbit 7773
Brevet's North Dakota Historical Markers and Sites 2205
Brian Piccolo, a Short Season 12458
Brian Wildsmith's ABC 17914
Brian Wildsmith's Bible Stories 17071
Brian Wildsmith's Birds 17915
Brian Wildsmith's Circus 17916
Brian Wildsmith's Fishes 17917
Brian Wildsmith's Mother Goose 17918
Brian Wildsmith's 1, 2, 3's 17919
Brian Wildsmith's Puzzles 17920
Brian Wildsmith's the Twelve Days of Christmas 17921
Brian Wildsmith's Wild Animals 17922
Brian's Trip to the Hospital 13023
Bride Who Wanted a Special Present ..., The 13195
Bridge to Terabithia 13367

Bridges and How They Are Built 7026
Bridget 10614
Brief Biographies of Brave Texans 14351
Brigham Young 2704
Brigham Young and Me, Clarissa 17972
Bright and Morning Star, The 7791
Bright April 4630
Bright, Bright Morning 8449
Bright Eyes 18071
Bright Fawn and Me 10499
Bright High Flyer 976
Bright Sunset 17772
Brighty of the Grand Canyon 8067
Brimhall Turns to Magic 4814
Brink of Dawn 17179
Bristle Face 1026
British Americans 12951
British Isles 3548
Broderick 13173
Brogeen Follows the Magic Tune 11183
Broken Arrow 659
Broken Citadel, The 7329
Broken-Hand Fitzpatrick 6630
Broken Hoop, The 6729
Broken Spear, The 15225
Bronko 5295
Bronx Remembered, El 12314
Bronze Bow, The 16048
Bronzeville Boys and Girls 2309
Broomsticks and Other Tales 4685
Broomtail Bronc, The 11743
Brother, Can You Spare a Dime? 12039
Brothers and Sisters 126
Brothers and Sisters Are Like That! 3355
Brothers by Choice 14171
Brothers Lionheart, The 10831
Brothers of the Sea 15548
Brown Bear, Brown Bear, What Do You See? 11725
Brown Cow Farm 8912
Brown Is a Beautiful Color 1871
Brown Mouse and Vole 693
Brown Paper School Presents My Backyard History Book, The
  see My Backyard History Book
Brown Rabbit 12490
Brownies--Hush! 147
Brownies--It's Christmas! 148
Brownjohn's Beasts 2440
Bruce Carries the Flag 9419

Bruno   2289
Bruno Bear's Bedtime Book   4463
Bruno Munari's ABC   12554
Bruno Munari's Zoo   12555
Bruno, the Bear of Split Rock
   Island   15558
Brush Fire!   15927
Brush Goat, Milk Goat   16824
Brushland Bill   8865
Bubba and Babba   13804
Bubble, Bubble   11926
Bubblebath   11652
Bubbles   7305
Bubo, the Great Horned Owl
   6751
Buccaneer   2676
Buccaneers   6807
Buccaneers and Pirates of Our
   Coasts   16330
Buck Schiwetz's Texas   15060
Buck, Wild   991
Bucketful of Moon, A   16625
Buckeye Boy   12002
Buckskin Scout and Other Ohio
   Stories   14248
Bucky's Friends   14213
Bud Harrelson, Super Shortstop
   10760
Buddha   3755
Buddhism   5255
Buddy and the Old Pro   17048
Buffalo Bill (d'Aulaire)   4547
Buffalo Bill (Stevenson)   16272
Buffalo Book, The   4514
Buffalo Box, The   14104
Buffalo Chief   557
Buffalo Gold   18333
Buffalo Harvest   14695
Buffalo King, the Story of Scotty
   Philip   17268
Buffalo Knife, The   16166
Buffalo Man and Golden Eagle
   8129
Buffalo Soldiers in the Indian Wars
   5050
Buffy-Porson, The   16296
Bug Clan, The   8846
Bug Club Book, The   3943
Bugaboo Bill   4221
Bugs in Your Ears   1172
Bugs: Poems   8306
Builders on the Desert   17200
Building Goes Up, A   9458
Building Tables on Tables   17018
Building with Balsa Wood   10778
Building with Cardboard   10779
Buildings of Ancient Egypt, The

10453
Buildings of Ancient Greece, The
   10454
Bulbs, Corms, and Such   15276
Bull Beneath the Walnut Tree, The
   8135
Bull of the Kraal and the Heavenly
   Maidens, The   9781
Bull Pen Hero   5571
Bulletin Boards About Careers
   4601
Bullfrog Builds a House   4526
Bullfrog Grows Up   4527
Bullwhip Griffin   see   By the Great
   Horn Spoon
Bully of Barkham Street, The
   16343
Bumblebee, The   15522
Bun, The   2372
Bunch on McKellahan Street, The
   5682
Bundle Book, The   10074
Bungling Pedro and Other Majorcan
   Tales   12016
Bunk Beds   18129
Bunnicula   8682
Bunting and Baserunning   4777
Bunya the Witch   10055
Bunyip of Berkeley's Creek, The
   17385
Burbujas   17202
Burglar Bill   174
Burglar Next Door, The   18008
Buried Cities   7596
Buried Moon, The   9043
Buried Moon and Other Stories, The
   1045
Burma Boy   10855
Burma Rifles, The   1887
Burnie's Hill   1767
Burning Lamp, The   12580
Burning Mountain, The   16509
Burning Rice Fields, The   2464
Burning Star   3604
Burning Thorn, The   7229
Burnish Me Bright   4368
Burro Benedicto ...   9384
Burro That Had a Name, The   1343
Burt Dow, Deep-Water Man   11235
Burton and Dudley   15459
Burundi   3045
Bus Station Mystery   17525
Bus Trip, The   10326
Buscabichos   4432
Bush Walkabout   13767
Bushbabies, The   16300
Bushman Speaks, The   13630

Bushman's Dream, The   15226
Bushmen and Their Stories, The
    8025
Bushmen of South Africa, The
    8977
Busy, Busy World   14987
Busy Day, Busy People   6765
Busy Honeybee, The   9967
Busy Office, Busy People   1106
Busy Seeds   1697
Busybody Nora   8823
But I Am Sara   11997
But I'm Ready to Go   217
But Names Will Never Hurt Me
    17358
But Ostriches ...   5907
But What About Me?   11094
But Where Is the Green Parrot?
    18479
Butter at the Old Price   4631
Butter on Both Sides   5386
Butterflies Come, The   13777
Butterflies of the World   9922
Butterfly, The   15523
Butterfly Ball and the Grass-
    hopper's Feast, The   243
Butterfly Cycle, The   13225
Butterfly Swimming   14816
Butterfly Time   7089
Button Boat, The   16548
Button in Her Ear, A   10929
By Compass Alone   6166
By Crumbs, It's Mine!   1270
By George, Bloomers!   16110
By Loch and By Lin   12817
By Secret Railway   11987
By Sheer Pluck   8088
By Space Ship to Saturn   14546
By the Great Horn Spoon   6003
By the Highway Home   16344
By the Sea   415
By the Shores of Silver Lake
    17900
By These Words   542
By Wagon and Flatboat   11988
Bystander, The   7250
Byzantines, The   3438
Buzo loco y otras aventuras, El
    2891
Buzz, Buzz, Buzz   1148
Buzzy Bear's Winter Party   11681
Bzzz--A Beekeeper's Primer   5715

- C -

CDB!   16190
C Is for Circus   3275
"C" Is for Cupcake   7949
C. N. Tower Guidebook, The   2802
c/o Arnold's Corners   12808
C. W. Anderson's Complete Book of
    Horses and Horsemanship   464
C. W. Anderson's Favorite Horse
    Stories   465
Caballito que queria volar, El
    13198
Cabana Botoncito de Oro, La   8039
Cabeza de Vaca   9728
Cabin Faced West, The   6383
Cabin for Ducks   17522
Cabin in the Sky   4130
Cabinet, The   9267
Cable Car and the Dragon   2805
Caboose Who Got Loose, The   13469
Caddie Woodlawn (Brink)   2264
Caddie Woodlawn (Russell)   14791
Cadmus Henry   5267
Cajun Alphabet   14311
Cajun Columbus   5166
Cajun Night Before Christmas
    17019
Cake Story, The   18183
Cakes and Custard   238
Calculator Puzzles, Tricks, and
    Games   13249
Caldicott Place   see   Family at
    Caldicott Place, The
Caleb and Kate   16191
Calendar, The   111
Calendar Moon   1375
Calendario de mis recuerdos, El
    12868
Calf, Goodnight   9214
Calf Is Born, A   3795
Calico Bush   5850
Calico Captive   16049
California Gold Rush, The   11470
California Indian Days   1188
Call Drum, The   5475
Call It Courage   16071
Call Me Bandicoot   5081
Call Me Charley   9000
Call Me Clown   23
Call Me Danica   11526
Call of a Loon, The   7637
Call of the Wild   11041
Call Car 24 Frank   1250
Cambridge Book of Poetry for Chil-
    dren, The   7152

Came Liberty Beyond Our Hope
3758
Camel Caravan   3157
Camel Express   2705
Camel for a Throne, A   11123
Camel for Saida, A   5227
Camel in the Sea, A   6971
Camel in the Tent, A   5588
Camel Who Took a Walk, The
17087
Camello Cojito, El   6427
Camels   17555
Camels West   9282
Camera on Africa   5455
Camera on Ghana   5456
Camera on the Sahara   5457
Cameroon   2997
Camino de Tio Conejo, El   378
Camioneros: Que Hacen?, Los
see Truck Drivers: What
Do They Do?
Camp Keewee's Secret Weapon
15118
Campanillitas Folkloricas   13350
Campfire Frontier   7553
Camping Out   433
Campo, El   9227
Can Do, Missy Charlie   17455
Can I Have a Cookie?   9585
Can I Help How I Feel?   12465
Can I Keep Him?   9652
Can Invertebrates Learn?   6104
Can You Find the Animal?   14663
Can You Talk with Someone Else?
18288
Canada Geese   15196
Canalboat to Freedom   5648
Canals   1824
Cancer   15679
Cancer Lab   1511
Cancion verde, La   13740
Cancioncitas para Chiquitines
9222
Cancionero del duende verde
6479
Cancionero Infantil Universal
6804
Canciones de España y America
14293
Canciones y Juegos de Nuevo
Mexico   7029
Candies, Cookies, Cakes   13393
Candilejas infantiles   18503
Candita's Choice   10730
Candle at Dusk   373
Candle in Her Room, A   687
Candle in the Mist   11998

Candle in the Night   8668
Candles for Beginners to Make
6818
Candles in the Dark   2268
Canguro bizco, El   13542
Canoe Country   9148
Canoeing   2029
Canoeing with the Cree   15387
Can't You Make Them Behave, King
George?   6384
Canta Pirulero   14754
Canthook Country   402
Canto al amanecer   6512
Canyon Treasure   2706
Canyon Winter   12424
Cap for Jack, a Coat for Jill, A
12709
Cap for Mul Chand, A   1167
Cap o' Rushes   5879
Cape May Packet, The   11982
Cappy and the River   813
Caps for Sale   15849
Captain Butcher's Body   4101
Captain: Canada's Flying Pony
7598
Captain Cook and the South Pacific
8612
Captain Cook Explores the South
Seas   16072
Captain Cook, Pacific Explorer
16578
Captain Cortes Conquers Mexico
9302
Captain Jiri and Rabbi Jacob   8231
Captain Kidd's Cat   10420
Captain of the Planter   16236
Captains of Industry   17674
Captains of the City Streets   803
Captive Indian Boy   7554
Captive Island   4844
Captive Thunder   2742
Captured by the Abnakis   13621
Captured by the Mohawks   12921
Capyboppy   13470
Car Called Camellia, A   13003
Car Racing Against the Clock
14642
Caramelos de menta   17262
Caras   2188; see also Faces
Caravan, The   7842
Caravan from Timbuktu   10678
Carbonel   15832
Cardinal Bird, The   2349
Care of Uncommon Pets   17639
Careers in a Bank   4596
Careers in a Department Store
4765

Careers in a Medical Center 4597
Careers in a Supermarket 10610
Careers in Agriculture 1474
Careers in Animal Care 1475
Careers in Auto Sales and Service
 1476
Careers in Aviation in the Sky
 and on the Ground 11343
Careers in Baseball 4598
Careers in Computers 14157
Careers in Conservation 1477
Careers in Construction 14099
Careers in Education 1478
Careers in Football 14158
Careers in Hockey 14159
Careers in Office Work 8630
Careers in Printing 4599
Careers in Soccer 13246
Careers in Sports 11344
Careers in the Army 13247
Careers in the Navy 13248
Careers in the Theater 850
Careers with a Fire Department
 13552
Careers with a Newspaper 10611
Careers with a Police Department
 14160
Careers with a Railroad 11978
Careers with a Telephone Com-
 pany 4600
Careers with a Television Station
 14161
Careers with an Airline 4766
Careers with the Circus 9666
Careers with the City 1479
Careers with the Postal Service
 13553
Careful Carlos 14855
Cargo for a King 521
Cargo Ships 18567
Cargoes in the Great Lakes 11500
Caribbean--The English-Speaking
 Island--in Pictures, The
 5591
Caribou Crossing 5376
Caring for Trees on City Streets
 5279
Carl Akers' Colorado 207
Carl Sandburg 6197
Carl Sandburg, Young Singing
 Poet 12030
Carl Schurz, Patriot 17079
Carla-Too-Little 16767
Carlitos 12268
Carlito's World 12649
Carlo the Curious Crocodile 7223
Carlos and the Brave Owl 2865

Carlos Goes to School 478
Carlos of Mexico 3192
Carlota 13011
Carlotta and the Scientist 10599
Carly Simon 12483
Carmen 1652
Carnival in Paris 2956
Carnival of Speed 12887
Carol see Carol from the Country
Carol Barker's Birds and Beasts
 1074
Carol Burnett 3442
Carol from the Country 6354
Carolina's Courage 18377
Caroline and Her Kettle Named Maud
 11785
Caroline and the Seven Little Words
 11786
Carol's Side of the Street 1341
Carp in the Bathtub, The 3739
Carpet of Solomon, The 8944
Carrie Hepple's Garden 4233
Carrie's War 1215
Carrot and Other Root Vegetables,
 The 15277
Carrot Cake 8408
Carrot for a Nose, A 6876
Carrot Seed, The 10075
Carrousel 10102
Carry On, Mr. Bowditch 10313
Cars Against the Clock 9009
Cart and Cwidder 9339
Carta para Mi Amigo, La 4340
Cartier 16579
Cartier Discovers the St. Lawrence
 16963
Cartier Sails the St. Lawrence 804
Cartoonist, The 2782
Caruso 9027
Carver and the Leopard, The 12076
Carver's George 11999
Carving on the Tree, The 2872
Casa Means Home 2886
Casa que crecio, La 13230
Cascanueces y los Ratones 8370
Case Against the Wind ..., The
 13505
Case of the Cat's Meow, The 1903
Case of the Condemned Cat, The
 8173
Case of the Dumb Bells, The 1904
Case of the Elevator Duck, The
 1488
Case of the Gone Goose, The 4102
Case of the Hungry Stranger, The
 1905
Case of the Invisible Dog 8174

Case of the Marble Monster and Other Stories, The 5256
Case of the Missing Link, The 3641
Case of the Nervous Newsboy, The 8175
Case of the Scaredy Cats, The 1906
Case of the Semi-Human Beans, The 17568
Case of the Silver Egg, The 15808
Case of the Silver Skull, The 4103
Case of the Stolen Bagels, The 3861
Casey at the Bat 16777
Casey Jones 14696
Casey, the Utterly Impossible Horse 5735
Casimir Gzowski 15525
Casserole Cooking Fun 11296
Castaways in Lilliput 18123
Castaways on Long Ago 13174
Castillito de papel 5876
Castillo en el camino, Un 14876
Castle 11201
Castle, Abbey and Town 1698
Castle Book, The 1489
Castle in My City 18510
Castle Merlin 18045
Castle of Bone, A 5694
Castle of Ladies, The 8156
Castle of Lyr, The 264
Castle on the Border 1392
Castles 1825
Castles of the Two Brothers, The 6352
Castors Away 2723
Cat Across the Way, The 8827
Cat and Mouse Who Shared a House, The 7388
Cat and Mrs. Cary, The 6659
Cat and the Captain, The 3673
Cat at Bat 16126
Cat Ate My Gymsuit, The 4489
Cat Book, The 1612
Cat Called Camouflage, A 9338
Cat Came Back, The 8913
Cat Club, The 805
Cat Hotel 9295
Cat in the Hat, The 15367
Cat in the Hat in English and French, The 15368
Cat in the Mirror, The 16345
Cat on the Dovrefell, The 4515
Cat Sitter Mystery, The 138

Cat Who Went to Heaven, The 3674
Cat Who Went to School, The 10216
Cat Who Wished to Be a Man, The 265
Catastrophe Cat at the Zoo 13268
Catbird 6513
Catch a Cricket 16259
Catch a Dancing Star 1331
Catch a Little Fox 4734
Catch a Sunbeam 52
Catch a Whale by the Tail 14297
Catch as Catch Can 13819
Catch That Pass! 3415
Catch the Wind 4829
Catch Your Breath 12405
Catchers, The 17081
Catching the Cattle Thief and Another Story 675
Catching the Football 4778
Caterpillars 16237
Caterpillars and How They Live 11246
Catfish Hunter 16132
Cathedral 11202
Cathie Runs Wild 11184
Cathy at the Crossroads 5633
Cathy Rigby 9057
Cathy Uncovers a Secret 18260
Cathy's First School 9528
Cathy's Little Sister 18261
Cathy's Secret Kingdom 5634
Catrin in Wales 319
Cats (Bronson) 2297
Cats (Holman) 8513
Cats, The (Phipson) 13634
Cats and Bats and Things with Wings 178
Cats and Kittens 14537
Cats for Kansas 10512
Cats of Sea-Cliff Castle, The 9089
Cats of the World 17531
Cat's Quizzer, The 15369
Catseye 12932
Cattle Drive 3252
Cattle of Kumalo, The 14716
Cattle People of Nigeria, The 9858
Causa, La 6443
Cavalcade of Goblins, A 6612
Cavalcade of Magicians, A 7246
Cavalcade of Sea Legends, A 2411
Cavalcade of Witches, A 8572
Cavalcade of Young Americans, A 2981
Cave, The (Bronin) 2293
Cave, The (Coatsworth) 3675
Cave of Danger 17505

Cave of Riches 8537

Cave of Shouting Silence, The 2707

Caverns of the World 13814

Caves (Gans) 6536

Caves (Laycock) 10430

Caves of Chinoyi, The 683

Caves of the Great Hunters, The 1204

Caxton's Challenge 7737

Cay, The 16712

Cayuse Courage 10221

Cecilia's Older Brother 18489

Cecily G. and the Nine Monkeys 14261

Celebrate the Morning 5369

Celebrate the Sun 12829

Celebrating Nature 8026

Celebrations 127

Celestino Piatti's Animal ABC 13649

Celia en el Colegio 6131

Cendrillon/Cinderella 10373

Cenicienta, La 3218

Centerburg Tales 11236

Centerman from Quebec 8892

Central Africa 9871

Central African Republic (Carpenter) 2998

Central and East Africa 3549

Central City/Spread City 15138

Central Heating and How It Works 17168

Ceramics from Clay to Kiln 17686

Cereal Box, The 11494

Ceremony of Innocence 6113

Certain Magic, A 13160

Certain Small Shepherd, A 3165

Certainly, Carrie, Cut the Cake 12406

Cesar Chavez (Franchere) 6198

Cesar Chavez (White) 17798

Chad 2999

Chad and the Elephant Engine 16395

Chains, Webs, and Pyramids 13948

Chaka, King of the Zulus 9588

Chalk Box Story, The 6257

Chalk Cross, The 416

Challenge for a Rookie 1863

Challenge of the Prairie 1885

Challenge to Become a Doctor 8142

Challenging Careers in Urban Affairs 11450

Chama's Choice 1936

Chameleon Was a Spy 11803

Chameleon Who Couldn't Stop Changing His Mind, The 12980

Chameleons and Other Quick-Change Artists 15715

Champ 10344

Champion Dog Prince Tom 6396

Champion of Merrimack County, The 5075

Champions at Bat 5880

Champions Don't Cry 6812

Champions of the Tennis Court 8159

Championship Teams of the NFL 1533

Championship Trail 9010

Champlain of the St. Lawrence 16580

Chance Child, A 17477

Chancy and the Grand Rascal 6004

Change and Time 13754

Changeling, The 15964

Changes 14048

Changes, Changes 8831

Changing City, The 12550

Changing of the Guard 5100

Changing Roles of Men and Women 15163

Changing World of Birds, The 480

Channel Chuckles 9586

Chanticleer and the Fox 3307

Chanukah Fable for Christmas, A 4090

Chaplin, the Movies and Charlie 9034

Charco 7647

Charge of the Light Brigade, The 16741

Chariot in the Sky 1915

Charles 15810

Charles Addams Mother Goose, The 73

Charles de Gaulle 5489

Charles Drew 1608

Charles F. Kettering, Inventor and Idealist 18506

Charles New 6102

Charles Richard Drew 7720

Charley 14472

Charley Pride 1070

Charley Yee's New Year 482

Charley's Clan 15267

Charlie and the Chocolate Factory 4440

Charlie and the Great Glass Elevator 4441

Charlie Brown's All-Stars 15132
Charlie Brown's Super Book of
 Questions and Answers 15133
Charlie Dick 5938
Charlie Needs a Cloak 4716
Charlie the Tramp 8278
Charlie's Dream 5707
Charlotte Forten 5037
Charlotte Sometimes 5695
Charlotte's Web 17792
Charm for Paco's Mother, A
 16322
Charmed Life, A 9340
Chasing the Goblins Away 16896
Chasing Trouble 11160
Cheaper by the Dozen 6822
Checker Players, The 17276
Checkered Flag, The 6680
Checking and Defensive Play
 6808
Cheer the Lonesome Traveler
 10177
Cheerful Heart, The 7203
Cheetahs, the Swift Hunters 3944
Chemicals We Eat and Drink, The
 15680
Chemistry in the Kitchen 15737
Chemistry of a Lemon, The
 16363
Chendru 16439
Cher 9058
Cherokee Animal Tales 15026
Cherokee Bill, Oklahoma Pacer
 909
Cherokee Boy 9769
Cherokee Chief 3510
Cherokee Indians of the Moun-
 tains, The 1747
Cherokee Removal, 1838, The
 6021
Cherokees 8951
Cherry Ann and the Dragon Horse
 3676
Chesapeake Bay in Maryland, The
 10899
Chesapeake Circle 2650
Chess Book, The 14916
Chess for You 5814
Chess for Young Beginners 11451
Chester 8348
Chi Po and the Sorcerer 11591
Chi-Wee 12377
Chicago Burns 6189
Chicago Fire-1871, The 12625
Chicano, Amigo 6705
Chicano Girl 3862
Chicano Roots Go Deep 4228

Chicanos (De Garza) 4655
Chicanos (Martin) 11744
Chichi Hoohoo Bogeyman, The
 15947
Chick and the Duckling, The 6844
Chick and the Egg, The 11674
Chick Hatches, A 3796
Chicken and the Egg, The 13226
Chicken Book 17998
Chicken Forgets 12180
Chicken Licken see Henny Penny
Chicken Little, Count-to-Ten 6370
Chicken Soup with Rice 15329
Chicken's Child, The 7803
Chicos en la Cocina / Kids in the
 Kitchen 4913
Chie and the Sports Day 11824
Chief 1888
Chief Joseph (Davis) 4611
Chief Joseph (Montgomery) 12360
Chief Joseph of the Nez Percé
 7168
Chief of the Night, The 2350
Chief Seattle 12361
Chief's Bride, The 13644
Chief's Counsellors ..., The 11570
Chike and the River 37
Chikka 12846
Child in Prison Camp, A 16614
Child Jesus, The 5966
Child of Fire 13012
Child of the Arctic 18249
Child of the Hogan 11087
Child of the Navajos 14232
Child of the Owl 18395
Child of the Silent Night 8771
Children in Czechoslovakia 531
Children in Hiding see Tomas
 Takes Charge
Children in the Wind 7441
Children of Africa (Baird) 914
Children of Africa, The (Marston)
 11719
Children of Ananse, The 590
Children of Appalachia 15617
Children of Central Africa 17520
Children of Green Knowe, The
 1969
Children of Hong Kong 15410
Children of Morrow 8562
Children of Night 17795
Children of Noisy Village, The
 10832
Children of Odin 3876
Children of Rhodesia 968
Children of South Africa 16323
Children of South Africa in the Time

of the Great War   10727
Children of the Covered Wagon
    3064
Children of the Dragon   3363
Children of the Great Smoky
    Mountains   9438
Children of the Incas   11598
Children of the Kalahari   12118
Children of the Northlights   4548
Children of the North Pole   8109
Children of the Red King   13795
Children of the Resistance   4215
Children of the Seed Gatherers
    18283
Children of the Sun   14477
Children of the Wind, The   7478
Children of Vietnam   3364
Children of Vietnam (Lifton)
    10793
Children of West Africa   41
Children of Zambia   4446
Children on the Top Floor, The
    16407
Children Sing in the Far West,
    The   799
Children Who Returned, The
    13858
Children's Bells, The   5675
Children's Book of American Land-
    marks, The   2463
Children's Book on How to Use
    Books and Libraries, The
    12518
Children's Dream Book, The   8034
Children's Games in Street and
    Playground   13146
Children's Homage to Picasso
    1183
Children's Rhymes   17250
Children's Songs from Japan
    17802
Children's War, The   16713
Child's Bestiary, A   6581
Child's Book of Animals, A   4464
Child's Book of Dreams, A   4735
Child's Book of Flowers, A   4465
Child's Book of Seasons, A   8880
Child's Calendar, A   17162
Child's Christmas in Wales, A
    16808
Child's Garden of Verses, A
    16297
Child's Gifts, The   see   Aguinaldos
    del Infante, Los
Child's Good Night Book, A
    2383
Child's History of America, A

11370
Child's History of Indianapolis, A
    11573
Child's Life of Mary Baker Eddy
    7907
Child's World of Stamps, A   4732
Childtimes   7313
Chili Pepper Children, The   663
Chili Peppers   16494
Chimney Corner Stories   8858
Chimpanzee Roams the Forest   3945
Chimpanzees   12642
China (Clayton)   3550
China (Scott)   15204
China and the Chinese   7755
China Boat Boy   14228
Chinatown Sunday   1008
Chinchilla maravilla, La   17265
Chincoteague for Children   1552
Chinese and Oriental Art   1182
Chinese Children Next Door, The
    2483
Chinese Daughter, The   10327
Chinese Eyes   17612
Chinese Helped Build America, The
    5039
Chinese in America, The (Jones)
    9336
Chinese in America, The (Sung)
    16504
Chinese Knew, The   13680
Chinese Myths and Fantasies   1657
Chinese Mother Goose Rhymes
    18351
Chinese New Year, The   3325
Chinese Story Teller, The   2484
Chinese Writing   18207
Chinese Year, A   8700
Chingo Smith of the Erie Canal   60
Chip   988
Chipmunk in the Forest   3642
Chipmunks on the Doorstep   17037
Chippewa Dawn   16047
Chippewa Indians, The   1748
Chippewa Music   4837
Chitina y su gato   409
Chito   2628
Chitty-Chitty-Bang-Bang   6038
Chloris and the Creeps   13737
Chloris and the Freaks   13738
Chocolate Moose for Dinner, A
    7534
Chocolate Mouse and Sugar Pie
    7918
Chocolate War, The   4158
Choctaw Boy   3963
Chogorrom   6482

Choice of Magic, A   11638
Choice of Stars, A   17180
Chongo   8923
Choogoowarra   9782
Chosen Baby, The   17552
Chou En-Lai   609
Chouteau and the Founding of
  St. Louis   18257
Chris   8340
Chris Evert (Jacobs)   9059
Chris Evert (May)   11862
Chris Evert (Smith)   15905
Chris Evert, the Young Champion
  7692
Christ Child, as Told by Matthew
  and Luke   13556
Christina Katerina and the Box
  6671
Christmas (Bruna)   2449
Christmas (Cooney)   4059
Christmas (Haugan)   3402
Christmas All Around the House
  13589
Christmas Anna Angel, The   14967
Christmas at the Tomten's Farm
  17854
Christmas Bells Are Ringing
  2215
Christmas Book, The   14203
Christmas Bunny   17947
Christmas Card, A   16791
Christmas Card Magic   13539
Christmas Carol, A   4881
Christmas Cat, The   8518
Christmas Churchmouse, The   see
  Christmas Mouse, The
Christmas Comes Once More   11154
Christmas Cookbook   13996
Christmas Cookie Tree, The   8926
Christmas Crafts   12124
Christmas Crafts for Everyone
  4181
Christmas Donkey, The   16695
Christmas Eve   8798
Christmas Everywhere   15217
Christmas Fantasy, A   7950
Christmas Feast, A   1133
Christmas Feasts and Festivals
  13379
Christmas Folk   1376
Christmas Gif'   14580
Christmas Grump, The   11113
Christmas Hut, The   412
Christmas in Britain and Scan-
  dinavia   13380
Christmas in Georgia   15648
Christmas in Noisy Village   10833

Christmas in the Barn   2384
Christmas in the Stable   10834
Christmas in the Woods   6410
Christmas Kitten, The   3106
Christmas Mouse, The   17741
Christmas on the Mayflower   7931
Christmas Party, A   903
Christmas Piñata, The   9703
Christmas Sky, The   2122
Christmas Stories Round the World
  9290
Christmas Story, The   12929
Christmas Strangers, The   16790
Christmas Tales for Reading Aloud
  11034
Christmas the World Over   6088
Christmas Through the Years   3095
Christmas Tree, The   2314
Christmas Tree Crafts   16865
Christmas Tree Forest   229
Christmas Tree House, The   17463
Christmas Tree Mystery, The
  16114
Christmas Window, The   11600
Christopher Columbus (Heimann)
  8018
Christopher Columbus (Kaufman)
  9533
Christopher Columbus (McGovern)
  11348
Christopher Columbus (Ventura)
  17279
Christopher Goes to the Castle
  8470
Christy and the Cat Jail   18457
Chucaro   9474
Chucho, the Boy with the Good
  Name   13625
Chuck   5354
Church Cat Abroad, The   12983
Church Mice and the Moon, The
  12984
Church Mice at Bay, The   12985
Church Mice Spread Their Wings,
  The   12986
Church Mouse, The   12987
Cid, El   6714
Cien nuevos cuentos   10194
Cigarette Sellers of Three Crosses
  Square, The   18534
Cigarra fantastica, La   682
Cimarron Kid   3964
Cincinnati Reds, The   3833
Cinco Sentidos, Los   3469
Cinderella (Brown)   2373
Cinderella (Evans)   5579
Cinderella (Fowles)   6163

Cinderella (Montresor) 12373
Cinders 6789
Cindy Nelson 9060
Cindy's Sad and Happy Trees
  13161
Cindy's Snowdrops 13162
Cine, v.1, El 6558
Cine, v.2, El 6559
Cine, v.3, El 6560
Cinnabar, the One O'Clock Fox
  8068
Cinnamon and Nutmeg 4751
Cinnamon Cane 13801
Circle of Life 8046
Circle Sarah Drew, The 1116
Circle of Seasons 3482
Circles 15798
Circles, Triangles, and Squares
  8297
Circo, El 9228
Circo, v.1, El 6561
Circo, v.2, El 6562
Circo, v.3, El 6563
Circus, The (Phelan) 13612
Circus (Prelutsky) 13884
Circus Baby, The 13557
Circus Book, The 4918
Circus Cannonball 17244
Circus Day in Japan 8154
Circus Heroes and Heroines 9850
Circus in the Mist, The 12556
Circus Numbers 13498
Cissy's Texas Pride 11565
City 11203
City ABC's 4770
City and Its People, The 15139
City and Suburb 13949
City Beneath the Sea 1035
City Book 4147
City Cop 3988
City-Country ABC, The 17503
City High Champions 8131
City High Five 8132
City Horse 4825
City in All Directions 128
City in the Summer 15043
City in the Winter 15044
City Leaves, City Trees 6525
City Neighbor 9420
City Noisy Book, The 2385
City of Birds and Beasts 15197
City of Gold 6324
City of Gold and Lead, The 3404
City of the Dagger ..., The
  9614
City Poems 10562
City Rhythms 7363

City Rocks, City Blocks, and the
  Moon 6526
City Rose, The 12238
City Spreads Its Wings 8588
City Street Games 399
City Traffic 16646
City Under the Back Steps, The
  10222
City Under the Ground, The 11722
City Witch and the Country Witch,
  The 18009
Ciudad, La 9229
Ciudad de arena, La 248
Ciudad perdida, La 6553
Civil Rights 7004
Civil War Nurse 4697
Claim to Freedom 16062
Claire Lee Chennault see Com-
  mander of the Flying Tigers
Clan Texas 4353
Clancy's Witch 11448
Clara Barton (Boylston) 2053
Clara Barton (Grant) 7169
Clara Barton (Mann) 11606
Clara Barton (Rose) 14607
Clara Barton (Stevenson) 16273
Clarinet and Saxophone Book, The
  1512
Clarion the Killdeer 14786
Clashing Rocks 15347
Classmates by Request 3863
Claude the Dog 6451
Claudia 17456
Clay-Dough Play-Dough 3327
Clay Play 13836
Clay Pot Boy, The 9126
Clay Projects 2281
Clay, Wood and Wire 17687
Clean Air 16647
Clean Air--Clean Water for Tomor-
  row's World 12209
Clean Air--Sparkling Water 15632
Clean Brook, The 1143
Clean Streets, Clean Water, Clean
  Air 3265
Clearing in the Forest, A 3080
Clearing Weather 12020
Clemente (United Press International)
  17141
Clemente! (Wagenheim) 17382
Clementine 14022
Cleopatra (Crayder) 4263
Cleopatra (Leighton) 10521
Cleopatra's Egypt 4587
Clever Cooks 7291
Clever Hare and the Terrible Lion,
  The 2351

Clever Kate 7389
Clever Princess, The 16929
Clever Turtle, The 14493
Click 361
Clickety Cricket 15896
Cliff, The 3274
Cliff Dwellers 6095
Cliff Dwellers of Walnut Canyon
 5806
Cliff Dwellings 3777
Clifford Gets a Job 2225
Clifford the Big Red Dog 2226
Clifford's Good Deeds 2227
Clifford's Halloween 2228
Climb a Lonely Hill 12903
Climbing to the Sun 3097
Clinic, The 9562
Clint Lane in Korea 14190
Clock Museum, The 15990
Clock We Live On, The 738
Clocks and More Clocks 8832
Clocks for the Ages 15666
Clorinda of Cherry Lane Farm
 16372
Close to the Rising Sun 17341
Closed Circle, The 6769
Closer Look, A 6960
Closer Look at Apes, A 3987
Cloth 9949
Cloth from Fiber to Fabric 2515
Clothes Tell a Story ... 11131
Clothing 17467
Cloud Book, The (De Paola)
 4717
Cloud Book, The (May) 11863
Cloud Forest, The 12918
Cloud with the Silver Lining, The
 13254
Clouds 12842
Clovis Crawfish and His Friends
 6097
Clovis Crawfish and the Singing
 Cigales 6098
Clown, The 4131
Club Against Keats, A 8328
Clue of the Black Cat 1556
Clues in the Woods 13286
Clumpets Go Sailing, The 17394
Clumsy Cowboy, The 1621
Clyde Beatty 17932
Clyde Monster 4330
Clyde of Africa 11784
Clyde's Clam Farm 7730
C'mon Ducks! 4075
Coach Nobody Liked, The 3118
Coal (Adler) 112
Coal (Kraft) 10015

Coal Camp Boy 5315
Coal Camp Girl 10563
Coal, Energy and Crises 3236
Coarse Gold Gulch 6643
Coat Hanger Christmas Tree, The
 5547
Coats and Covers 14793
Cochise (Carlson) 2973
Cochise (Johnson) 9260
Cochise (Wyatt) 18331
Cock-a-Doodle-Doo! Cock-a-Doodle-
 Dandy! 9495
Cock and Lion 10167
Cock and the Ghost Cat, The 10794
Cock Robin 4060
Cockle Stew and Other Rhymes
 11804
Cockleburr Quarters 937
Cockroaches (Cole) 3797
Cockroaches (Pringle) 13950
Coconut Girl, The 9443
Coconut Thieves, The 6159
Code and Cipher Book, The 14921
Code of Life, The 15681
Code: Polonaise 18326
Codes and Ciphers 10185
Codes and Secret Writing 18538
Codes, Ciphers and Secret Writing
 6585
Coins Have Tales to Tell 2328
Coins You Can Collect 8312
Cola Magica, La 6528
Cold Against Disease 9555
Cold Wind Blowing, A 17952
Coleen the Question Girl 8315
Colette and Baba at Timbuctoo
 15211
Colibri con cola de pavo real, El
 8971
Coll and His White Pig 266
Collage 11688
Collage and Construction 17688
Collared Peccary 8248
Collect, Print and Paint from Nature
 7896
Collected Verse of Lewis Carroll,
 The see Humorous Verse of
 Lewis Carroll, The
Collecting Cocoons 8824
Collecting for the City Naturalist
 8825
Collecting Small Fossils 8826
Collection of Folklore for Children
 in Elementary School and at
 Home, A 11093
Collector's Guide to American Indian
 Artifacts, The 7740

Collision Course 8215

Colonel Sheperton's Clock 17072

Colonial Conquest of Africa, The 11434

Colonial Cookbook, The 13490

Colonial Crafts for You to Make 4472

Colonial Craftsmen ... 17038

Colonial Delaware 3395

Colonial Farm 1330

Colonial Georgia 2906

Colonial Life in America 5702

Colonial Living 17039

Colonial Maryland 5881

Colonial New Jersey 4367

Colonial New York 3396

Colonial North Carolina 2672

Colonial South Carolina 2673

Colonists for Sale 232

Colonists from Scotland 7128

Colony Leader, A (Faber) 5623

Colony Leader, A (Graves) 7189

Colony of Maryland, The 7510

Colony of New Jersey, The 12626

Colony of North Carolina, The 10175

Colony of Pennsylvania, The 10553

Colony of Rhode Island, The 17633

Colony of Virginia, The 10176

Color in Your Life 101

Color of Life, The 4759

Color of Man, The 3770

Colorado, The (Buff) 2538

Colorado (Carpenter) 3000

Colorado (Crosby) 4308

Colorado (Downey) 5052

Colorado on Glass 11595

Colorado Sketchbook 2736

Colorado Wild Flowers 14429

Colorado Without Mountains 7644

Colorado's Hall of Fame 11737

Colors (Pienkowski) 13658

Colors (Reiss) 14225

Colors Around Me 3447

Colour of Ontario, The 2307

Colt Named Mischief, A 14051

Columbia and Beyond 2123

Columbus 4549

Columbus Day 15593

Columbus, Finder of the New World 16581

Columbus Sails 8317

Columbus Story, The 4456

Columbus, the Buckeye Capital 11724

Columpio-tobogan-noria gigante 14354

Comanche of the Seventh 10522

Comanches and Other Indians of Texas 13718

Come Again in the Spring 9691

Come Along! 3166

Come Along to Ethiopia 15772

Come Along to Japan 13883

Come Along to Portugal 7556

Come Along to Romania 14256

Come Along to South Africa 14487

Come Along to Tanganyika 7592

Come Along to the Congo 17763

Come and Have Fun 8799

Come Away 10967

Come Away from the Water, Shirley 2679

Come Back, Amelia Bedelia 13287

Come Back, Lucy see Mirror of Danger

Come Back, Peter 18244

Come by Here 4017

Come for to Sing 17353

Come Here, Cat 12864

Come Hither 4686

Come On Out, Daddy! 14880

Come On Seabiscuit 12375

Come Play with Corally Crothers see Coralito

Come Play with Me 8200

Come to Me Nice Butterfly 1549

Come to Our Salmon Feast 11424

Come to Power 11088

Come to the Circus 6164

Come to the City 16743

Come to the Edge 4369

Come to the Fair 4920

Come to the Pet Shop 16744

Come to the Zoo 16745

Come Visit a Prairie Dog Town 382

Come with Me to Nursery School 8800

Come with Me to the Edge of the Sea 16227

Come with Us 3896

Comeback Guy, The 6349

Comets 18539

Comick Book of Sports, A 14674

Coming Back 8527

Coming Home to a Place You've Never Been Before 3595

Coming of the Civil War, The 7019

Coming of the Mormons, The 9877

Commander of the Flying Tigers 618

Commandos of World War II, The 3126

Commercial Fishing 18565

Commodore Perry and the Opening of Japan 10128

Common Frog 13227

Common Illinois Insects and Why They Are Interesting 18305

Commune on the Frontier 16317

Communication (Adler) 113

Communication (Neal) 12694

Communications Satellites 9968

Communism: An American's View 9268

Competing in Karate 10012

Complete Beginner's Guide to Bicycling, The 11195

Complete Beginner's Guide to Bowling, The 4973

Complete Beginner's Guide to Motorcycling, The 14679

Complete Beginner's Guide to Photography, The 10431

Complete Beginner's Guide to Skin Diving 6348

Complete Beginner's Guide to Soaring and Hang Gliding, The 14335

Complete Book of Autograph Collecting, The 16461

Complete Book of Baseball Cards, The 3523

Complete Book of Bicycling, The 15834

Complete Book of Children's Theater, The 8681

Complete Book of Dragons, The 12730

Complete Book of Hanukkah, The 3351

Complete Book of Horses and Ponies 15263

Complete Book of Indian Crafts and Lore, The 8765

Complete Book of Nascar Stock Car Racing 5445

Complete Book of Outdoor Lore 13171

Complete Book of Practical Camping, The 9237

Complete Book of Puppetry, The 4386

Complete Book of Swimming, The 4194

Complete Christmas Book, The 17608

Complete Fairy Tales and Stories, The 434

Complete Guide to Fishing 5578

Complete Guide to Softball, The 16462

Complete How-to Book of Indiancraft, The 8766

Complete Nonsense Book 10463

Complete Peterkin Papers, The 7577; see also Peterkin Papers, The

Complete Poems of Paul Laurence Dunbar 5116

Complete Works: Lewis Carroll 3099

Compost Heap, The 14531

Computer: The Mind Stretcher 9368

Computers (Berger) 1513

Computers (De Rossi) 4752

Computers (Srivastava) 16107

Con vosotros esta, v.1 3904

Con vosotros esta, v.2 3905

Con vosotros esta, v.3 3906

Con vosotros esta, v.4 3907

Conchita and Juan 15076

Concise History of Early Texas, A 6806

Concrete Is Not Always Hard 13673

Conejita blanca y el viaje a la luna 2854

Conejitos con hijitos 12082

Confessions of a Toe-Hanger 7760

Confessions of an Only Child 9905

Confetti for Cortorelli 6049

Confrontation 5016

Congo (Archer) 610

Congo (Carpenter) 3001

Congo, The (Lauber) 10345

Congo Boy 3534

Congo Explorer 2915

Congo Fireside Tales 14959

Congo, River of Mystery, The 11435

Congress, The 9269

Congressman from India 14941

Conjure Tales 3334

Connecticut Yankee at the Court of King Arthur, A see Connecticut Yankee in King Arthur's Court, A

Connecticut Yankee in King Arthur's Court, A 17084

Connie's New Eyes 18195
Conoce los Habitantes del Mar 3969
Conrad: The Hilarious Adventures of a Factory-made Child see Konrad
Conrad's Castle 15513
Conscience Pudding, The 12731
Consejos de un padre a su hija 3974
Conservation of Michigan's Natural Resources 13550
Constance 3473
Constantinople 9037
Consul's Daughter, The 15061
Consumer Protection Labs 1514
Contemporary American Folk Artists 8637
Contemporary American Indian Leaders 7348
Contemporary Black Leaders 5733
Contemporary Children's Theater 10795
Contender, The 10901
Contest, The 8409
Contests at Cowlick, The 9692
Continent in the Sky 1557
Continental Shelves, The 17556
Contrary Jenkins 3176
Contrary Orphans, The 16428
Contributions of Women: Aviation 6728
Contributions of Women: Education 2648
Contributions of Women: Sports 14822
Controversial Coyote, The 13951
Coo-My-Dove, My Dear 9044
Cookbook for Boys and Girls see Betty Crocker's Cookbook for Boys and Girls
Cookbook for Girls and Boys, A 14590
Cookie Book, The 12386
Cookie Tree, The 18010
Cool Ride in the Sky, The 18210
Coping with Cliques 18289
Coplas 16626
Copper Country Adventure 2247
Copper Sunrise 2466
Copper-Toed Boots 4632
Cop's Kid 4104
Coral Reef, The 1507
Coralito 6701
Corals 14593
Corduroy 6258

Corduroy Road, The 3660
Corduroy Trail, The 11342
Coretta King 16697
Corn Farm Boy 10564
Corn Grows Ripe, The 14285
Corn Is Maize 298
Cornelia, Story of the Civil-War Nurse 11261
Cornhusk Doll, The 17890
Corrie and the Yankee 10679
Costa Rica 3002
Costumes for You to Make 13997
Costumes to Make 13288
Cottage at Bantry Bay, The 17227
Cotton: From Farm to Market 7669
Cotton in My Sack 10565
Cottontail Rabbit 15152
Cougar (McDearmon) 11282
Cougar, The (Quimby) 14037
Could Anything Be Worse? 8232
"Could Be Worse!" 16286
Couldn't We Have a Turtle Instead 17303
Count and See 8298
Count Me Gone 9241
Count on Calico Cat 3277
Countdown 3778
Countdown to Christmas 13471
Counting Carnival 18583
Counting on an Elephant 11309
Counting Rhyme 8969
Counting Systems 11139
Country Bunny and the Little Gold Shoes, The 8143
Country Fireman 1336
Country in the Boy, The 16827
Country Noisy Book, The 2386
Country of Strangers, A 14346
Country of the Hawk, The 4845
Courage 15399
Courage of Bethea, The 8669
Courage of Kazan, The 17428
Courage of Sarah Noble, The 4457
Courage to Adventure 3356
Courage Wins 9272
Court of the Stone Children 2856
Courtship of Animals 15278
Cousins and Circuses 16602
Cousins at Camm Corners 15766
Covered Bridge, The 16510
Covered Bridge House ..., The 16149
Covered Bridges on the Byways of Ohio 9754
Cow Called Boy, A 13255
Cow for Jaya, A 7167
Cow Says Moo, The 12230

Cow-tail Switch, and Other West African Stories, The   4206
Cow Who Fell in the Canal, The   10034
Cowardly Clyde   13472
Cowboy and His Friend   545
Cowboy-Artist   6631
Cowboy Boots   6632
Cowboy Capital of the World   3127
Cowboy in Art, The   195
Cowboy in the Making   9123
Cowboy Jamboree   5774
Cowboy Joe of the Circle S   14772
Cowboy on Ice   11847
Cowboy on the Ranch, The   6054
Cowboy Songs ...   11039
Cowboy Surprise, The   18138
Cowboy Trade, The   14697
Cowboys (Greene)   7264
Cowboys (Silcott)   15661
Cowboys and Cattle Country   17513
Cowboys and Cattle Drives   11221
Cowboys and the Songs They Sang   14848
Cowboy's Christmas, The   546
Cowslip   7926
Coyote Cry   1235
Coyote Goes Hunting for Fire   1575
Coyote in Manhattan   6734
Coyote Stories of the Navajo People   14553
Coyote Tales (Jones)   9354
Coyote Tales (Morgan)   12446
Coyote the Trickster   14465
Coyote Winter   18036
Coyotes, Last Animals on Earth?   16811
Crabapple Night   17395
Crabs   18564
Crack in the Pavement, A   8685
Crack of the Bat   5790
Crackajack Pony, The   2654
Craft of Sail, The   87
Crafts and Toys from Around the World   12802
Crafts for Christmas   4428
Cranberry Thanksgiving   4869
Crane, The   18581
Crane Maiden, The   11828
Cranes in My Corral   8866
Crash! Bang! Boom!   16085
Crazy Cantilever ..., The   9444
Crazy Flight   10968
Crazy Horse (Dines)   4908

Crazy Horse (Garst)   6633
Crazy Horse (Grant)   7170
Crazy Horse (Meadowcroft)   11989
Crazy to Be Alive in Such a Strange World   10272
Crazy to Race   2757
Crazylegs Merrill   2987
Creating Mosaics   15250
Creating Things That Move   8030
Creating with Clay   15251
Creating with Paint   15252
Creating with Paper   15253
Creation, The (Lemke)   10544
Creation, The (Spier)   16083
Creation of the Sun and the Moon, The   16969
Creative Paper Crafts in Color   316
Creative Plays and Programs for Holidays   1471
Creative Shell Craft   4427
Creatures' Choir, The   4656
Creatures of Darkness   17557
Creatures of the Cosmos   4651
Crece y camina   13199
Creepies, Creepies, Creepies   8417
Creepy Castle   7037
Creoles of Color of New Orleans, The   7820
Cricket and the Emperor's Son   3677
Cricket Boy   18584
Cricket in a Thicket   5908
Cricket in Times Square, The   15258
Cricket Songs   1315
Cricket Winter, The   8502
Crickets and Frogs   12278
Cricket's Jokes, Riddles and Other Stuff   10600
Crickety-Cricket!   16881
Crictor   17132
Crinkleroot's Book of Animal Tracks and Wildlife Signs   670
Crises Youth Face Today   15164
Crispus Attucks   12211
Crissy at the Wheel   10403
Cristobal and the Witch   17396
Crocodile, The   see   Crocodile, Crocodile
Crocodile and Hen   10736
Crocodile, Crocodile   12830
Crocodile Has Me by the Leg, A   5012
Crocodile in the Tree, The   5176
Crocodile Man, The   15418
Crocodile Medicine   17611

Crocodile Who Liked Stories,
The 14286
Crocodile's Eggs for Supper
1487
Crocodile's Tale, A 699
Crocus 5177
Crocuses Were Over, Hitler Was
Dead 16598
Crooked Colt, The 466
Cross and the Sword of Cortes,
The 3823
Cross-Country Cat 2830
Cross-Country Courage 9792
Cross Country Runner 11233
Cross-Country Skiing 12310
Cross-Fire 7127
Cross Your Fingers, Spit in Your
Hat 15140
Crossroads for Chela 18171
Crow Boy 18365
Crow Indians, The 1749
Crown for Thomas Peters, A
8052
Crown Snatchers, The 17381
Cruise of the Aardvark, The
12646
Cruise of the Happy-Go-Gay,
The 18046
Cruisin for a Bruisin 14615
Cruising 16869
Crumb, The 5026
Crusaders, The 2516
Crusty Ones 14794
Cry, Baby! 7620
Cry from the Earth, A 1637
Cry in the Wind, A 3058
Cry Jungle Children 11128
Cry of the Wolf 16068
Cry Sorrow, Cry Joy! 12391
Crystal Apple, The 11286
Crystal Cabinet, The 7333
Crystal Cornerstone 1311
Crystal Gryphon, The 12933
Crystal Is My Friend 7073
Crystal Is the New Girl 7074
Crystal Magic 4560
Crystal Mountain 14755
Crystal Nights, The 12582
Crystal Tree 10852
Csonka 7517
Cuatro Sombreros de Benny,
Los 9165; see also Benny's
Four Hats
Cuckoo Clock, The 12325
Cuckoo Tree, The 181
Cuckoo's Reward, The 10010
Cuddly Dolls 12491

Cuento de Ferdinando, El/Story of
Ferdinand, The 10456
Cuento de las Dos Lunas, El 15032
Cuento para sonar 6551
Cuentos 435
Cuentos a Beatriz 4170
Cuentos casi reales 16006
Cuentos de Colorin, Los 3227
Cuentos de Gulubu 17488
Cuentos de la selva 16731
Cuentos de mis hijos, Los 14042
Cuentos de siempre 8253
Cuentos del Norte 10242
Cuentos del perdido camino 3133
Cuentos del Viejo Reloj, Los 12548
Cuentos del zodiaco 14851
Cuentos Folkloricos de Puerto Rico
249
Cuentos indigenas 7032
Cuentos mexicanos 12275
Cuentos para chicos de hoy en el
mundo de ayer 4380
Cuentos para chicos y grandes
13503
Cuentos para grandes y chicos
13488
Cuentos para Marisol 2455
Cuentos para mis nietos 13813
Cuentos para ti 8107
Cuentos populares de Asia 2165
Cuentos y leyendas infantiles
16002
Cuentos y risas 1457
Cumberland Gap and Trails West
11222
Cunningham's Rooster 2189
Cup and Saucer Chemistry 15406
Cupola House 8757
Curious Clubhouse, The 7107
Curious Cow, The 12009
Curious George 14262
Curious George Flies a Kite 14270
Curious George Gets a Medal 14263
Curious George Goes to the Hospital
14264
Curious George Learns the Alphabet
14265
Curious George Rides a Bike 14266
Curious George Takes a Job 14267
Curious Missie 16024
Curious Raccoons, The 8117
Curious World of Crystals, The
14891
Curl Up Small 17511
Curly, the Piglet 13210
Curse of the Moonraker, The 3605
Curse of the Viking Grave, The

12522
Curse of the White Panther 7297
Curses, Hexes and Spells 3745
Curtain Rises, The 6442
Custard the Dragon 12647
Custer's Last Stand 14280
Customs Across the Border
    12659
Customs and Holidays Around the
    World 4938
Cycle of Verse, A 6618
Cycling 2030
Cyclone 7165
Cyrus Holt and the Civil War
    7583
Czech Family Sunday Dinner 8262
Czechoslovak Fairy Tales 5867
Czechs and Slovaks in America,
    The 14691

- D -

D Is for Rover 9898
D. J.'s Worst Enemy 2596
Daba's Travels from Ouadda to
    Bangui 1034
Daddy 2810
Daddy Book, The 16311
Daddy Was a Number Runner
    12089
Daedalus and Icarus 5696
Dagda's Harp 12796
Dagger and the Bird, The 7230
Dahomey 6133
Dailan Kifki 17489
Daisy 3678
Dakota and Ojibwe People in
    Minnesota 4838
Dakota Indian Lore 18256
Dakota Sons 4921
Dakotas 8952
Dallas Cowboys, The 11864
Damp and Daffy Doings of a Dar-
    ing Pirate Ship, The 12418
Dan and the Miranda 6470
Dan Beard 11787
Dan Frontier 8819
Dan Frontier Goes to Congress
    8820
Dan Henry in the Wild West 5526
Dan Yaro--Double Agent 18097
Dance 1636
Dance Around the Fire 3917

Dance, Dance, Amy-Chan! 7901
Dance for Three, A 15176
Dance of Africa, The 17536
Dance of the Animals, The 1367
Dance of the Planets 17269
Dance on the Dusty Earth 13911
Dance to a Happy Song 17569
Dance to Still Music, A 4132
Dancers, The 12607
Dancers of the Ballet 781
Dancing Bear, The 4891
Dancing Camel, The 2783
Dancing Cloud, the Navajo Boy
    2539
Dancing Gods 5824
Dancing Granny, The 2458
Dancing Horses of Acoma ..., The
    14776
Dancing in the Moon 5297
Dancing Kachinas 876
Dancing Kettle and Other Japanese
    Folk Tales, The 17091
Dancing Masks of Africa 13912
Dancing Palm Tree ..., The 17429
Dancing Plates and Spoons, The
    6444
Dancing Star 11584
Dancing Stars, The 14507
Dandelion (Freeman) 6259
Dandelion (Svatos) 16543
Dandelion Cottage 14111
Dandelions Don't Bite 84
Dandy's Mountain 5649
Dandy's Summer 5650
Danger at Sneaker Hill 10932
Danger Below 3824
Danger Downriver 17757
Danger from Below 15738
Danger on the Ski Trails 18316
Danger! White Water 13495
Dangerous Air 9556
Dangerous Journey 7677
Daniel 1857
Daniel Boone (Brown) 2363
Daniel Boone (Daugherty) 4532
Daniel Boone's Echo 16167
Daniel Hale Williams 5786
Daniel in the Cub Scout Den 9961
Daniel Inouye 7055
Danielito y el Dinosauro 8349; see
    also Danny and the Dinosaur
Daniel's Duck 2551
Danish Fairy Tales 7463
Dannie, a Tale of the Galveston
    Hurricane of 1900 8617
Danny and His Thumb 5530
Danny and the Anaconda 7063

Danny and the Dinosaur   8350
Danny Dunn and the Homework
    Machine   18030
Danny Dunn and the Smallifying
    Machine   18031
Danny Dunn and the Swamp Mon-
    ster   18032
Danny Dunn, Invisible Boy
    18033
Danny Dunn on the Ocean Floor
    18034
Danny Goes to the Hospital
    3837
Danny Kaye's Around the World
    Story Book   9575
Danny on the Lookout   15583
Danny Rowley   11514
Danny, the Champion of the
    World   4442
Danny's Heart Operation   3365
Dar Tellum   1591
Daredevils Do Amazing Things
    10046
Dark Circle of Branches   636
Dark Didn't Catch Me, The
    16853
Dark Dove   16302
Dark Dreams   14379
Dark Horse of Woodfield   8167
Dark Eagle, The   233
Dark House of the Sea Witch,
    The   14473
Dark Is Rising, The   4082
Dark of the Cave, The   14825
Dark Princess, The   9693
Dark Sunshine   11186
Dark Venture   1626
Darkness of Giants, A   1979
Darl   3617
Darwin and the Enchanted Isles
    15420
Dash for Khartoum, A   8089
Dateline: Talladega   2758
Daughter of Delaware   14946
Daughter of the Church, A   4916
Daughter of the Mountains   14112
Daughter of the Sun and Other
    Stories   5704
Daughter of the Tejas   14161
D'Aulaire's Trolls   4550
Dave and His Dog, Mulligan   9878
Dave's Song   11405
Davey   7614
Davey Come Home   16730
David (Bollinger)   1858
David (Petersham)   13558
David and Goliath   4736

David and the Gangsters   4899
David He No Fear   7130
David in Silence   14486
David Livingstone   7184
David Livingstone in East Africa
    10312
David the Giantkiller   17782
David y los tulipanes   1453
David: Young Chief of the Qui-
    leutes   9851
David's Pockets   6982
David's Windows   11109
Davy Crockett (Ford)   6103
Davy Crockett (Holbrook)   8434
Davy Crockett, Frontier Hero   1712
Davy Crockett's Earthquake   16168
Dawn   15611
Dawn and Dusk   3180
Dawn of Fear   4083
Dawn over Saratoga   3989
Dawn Wind   16519
Day After Christmas, The   853
Day and Night in the Arctic, A
    141
Day at the Farm, A   1696
Day at the LBJ Ranch, A   14949
Day Daddy Stayed Home, The
    9744
Day I Had to Play with My Sister,
    The   1907
Day in Oraibi, A   9115
Day in the Country, A   1095
Day Luis Was Lost, The   1134
Day of Autumn, A   12169
Day of Pleasure, A   15776
Day of the Bomb, The   2446
Day of the Drones, The   10809
Day Off, A   16897
Day the Circus Came to Lone Tree,
    The   14698
Day the Gang Got Rich, The
    10006
Day the Hurricane Happened, The
    495
Day the Rooster Didn't Crow, The
    10117
Day the Spaceship Landed, The
    11065
Day the Sun Danced, The   8801
Day the Tide Went Out ... and
    Out ... and Out ..., The   11408
Day They Gave Babies Away, The
    5577
Day We Saw the Sun Come Up, The
    7090
Day with Honau, A   9116
Day with Tupi, A   8701

Dayapala of Ceylon   16078
Daybreakers, The   4396
Days I Like   7902
Days of Courage   9204
Days to Remember   10890
Days When the Animals Talked,
   The   5729
Days with Frog and Toad   10991
Daytona Five Hundred, The
   (Krishef)   10098
Daytona 500 (May)   11865
Dazzle   11805
De oir y contar   9221
De quien es el bosque?   2892
Dead as the Dodo   5282
Dead Before Docking   4105
Dead Bird, The   2387
Dead End Bluff   18158
Dead End School   3828
Dead Tree, The   16997
Deadly Ants   15739
Dealing with Fairies   see   Light
   Princess, The
Dear Dolphin   9701
Dear Garbage Man   18587
Dear Little Mumps Child   10604
Dear Lovey Hart, I Am Desperate
   3932
Dear Prosper   6178
Dear Rat   4370
Dear Readers and Riders   8069
Dear Uncle Carlos   14233
Death   10235
Death in Early America   3733
Death Is Natural   13952
Death of a Wombat, The   15902
Death of "Evening Star," The
   5942
Deathwatch   17810
Debbie and Her Pets   10566
Deborah Sampson Gannett   11349
Decathlon Men   5882
December Dog, The   14468
December Tale, A   14839
Decoupage for Young Crafters
   10871
Dee and Curtis on a Dairy Farm
   10792
Dee Dee's Heart Test   3366
Deenie   1816
Deep Dives of Stanley Whale,
   The   1397
Deep in the Forest   17057
Deep-Sea World   4035
Deep Silence, The   14198
Deep Trouble   12425
Deepwater Family   5119

Deer in the Pasture, The   3084
Deer, Moose, Elk and Their Family
   9190
Deer Valley Girl   10567
Defend Yourself with Kung Fu
   7751
Defender, The   9462
Defensive Football   476
Deirdre (Guard)   7464
Deirdre (Polland)   13796
Delano   5151
Delaware Colony, The   14184
Delaware Indians, The   1750
Delawares   4961
Delikon, The   8563
Delilah   7801
Delpha Green and Company   3574
Delta Mystery   17519
Demasiados Perros   5156
Demeter and Persephone   13973
Demo of 70th Street   6731
Demons and Beasts in Art   17988
Deneki, an Alaskan Moose   1595
Denetsosie   9247
Denver: A Pictorial History   9371
Department Store Model   14478
Depend on Katie John   2831
Depths of the Earth   7623
Descubrimiento, conquista y coloni-
   zacion de Puerto Rico   250
Desert, The   10602
Desert Boy   7640
Desert Caravans   9404
Desert Dog   9879
Desert Is Theirs, The   1236
Desert Life   9852
Desert People, The   3483
Desert Road Racer   13033
Deserter, The   7220
Deserts   6964
Desmond the Dog Detective   1614
Desperate Dragons, The   10982
Desventuras de Andrajo, Las   4171
Desventuras del Sol, Las   12007
Detective Book, The   4919
Detective Mole   14023
Detective Poufy's First Case   13806
Detectives in Togas   18124
Detectives of the Sky   5017
Devil by the Sea   1216
Devil Did It, The   9209
Devil Hole, The   16059
Devil-in-the-Fog   6601
Devil's Children, The   4892
Devils, Devils, Devils   8418
Devil's Hill   3310
Devil's Horse, The   1968

Devil's Piper, The 13929
Devil's Storybook, The 840
Devil's Tramping Ground and Other North Carolina Mystery Stories, The 7713
Devin and Goliath 3397
Dexter 2552
Dia en la vida de Juan Trebol, Un 5555
Diablo ingles, El 17490
Diamond in the Window, The 10261
Diamond Ring, The 13006
Diamonds 18540
Diana and Her Rhinoceros 621
Diario Secreto de Papelucho y el marciano 13409
Diary of a Frantic Kid Sister 3864
Diary of a Monarch Butterfly 16837
Diary of a Young Girl, The 6220
Diary of the Strawbridge Place, The 9028
Diary of Trilby Frost, The 6880
Dias sin colegio 9230
Dick Bass Story, The 10761
Dick Foote and the Shark 841
Dick Gregory's Bible Tales with Commentary 7331
Dick Whittington and His Cat 2374
Dictionary of Mythical Places, A 13263
Did the Sun Shine Before You Were Born? 7075
Did You Carry the Flag Today, Charley? 3167
Did You Feed My Cow? 2696
Did You Ever? 7016
Did You Say Dogs? 13244
Did You See What I Said? 5356
Diddakoi, The 6949
Diddie, Dumps and Tot 14020
Difference of Ari Stein, The 8101
Different Ball Game, A 12318
Different Kind of Sister, A 14276
Different Ones, The 11120
Dig, Drill, Dump, Fill 8299
Digger Wasp 12064
Digging for Dinosaurs 16568
Digging into Yesterday 6353
Digging Up the Bible Lands 7722
Digging-est Dog, The 13508
Diggings and Doings in Park City 13928
Digs and Diggers 4190
Diller, a Dollar, A 12468
Dimakatsho and Ntogeleng 6308
Din Dan Don 4994
Dinky Hocker Shoots Smack! 9733
Dinner at Alberta's 8279
Dinner's Ready 12710
Dinosaur Hunt 17775
Dinosaur Story 3798
Dinosaur Time 13289
Dinosaurs (Shapiro) 15430
Dinosaurs (Zim) 18541
Dinosaurs and All That Rubbish 6110
Dinosaurs and Beasts of Yore 3811
Dinosaurs and Their World 13953
Dinosaur's Housewarming Party 9906
Diogenes, the Story of the Greek Philosopher 299
Dipper of Copper Creek 6752
Directions and Angles 114
Dirt Bike Racer 3416
Dirt Road, The 3081
Dirt Track Daredevils 14981
Dirt Track Speedsters 5761
Dirt Track Summer 6681
Dirty Dinky and Other Creatures 14554
Disappearing Energy 15646
Disappointed Lion, The 17025
Disarmament 7300
Discontented Ghost, The 4106
Discover Your Neighborhood Heritage 15194
Discoveries of Esteban the Black, The 15534
Discovering Design 5045
Discovering Dinosaurs 1797
Discovering Insects 1798
Discovering Plants 1799
Discovering the American Stork 15198
Discovering the World of the Three-toed Sloth 8424
Discovering Tut-Ankh-Amen's Tomb 6936
Discovering What Earthworms Do 15740
Discovering What Frogs Do 15741
Discovering What Garter Snakes Do 15742
Discovering What Puppies Do 15743
Disguises You Can Make 1156
Disney's America on Parade 9035

Disobedient Eels and Other Italian Tales, The 3468
Diverting Adventures of Tom Thumb, The 17944
Diving for Treasure 1726
Diving the Great Barrier Reef 5836
Djugurba 800
Do a ZOOMdo 3333
Do Baby Bears Sit in Chairs? 9745
Do Bears Have Mothers, Too? 5909
Do I Know the "Me" Others See? 15165
Do-It-Yourself Dinosaurs 12492
Do Not Annoy the Indians 923
Do Tigers Ever Bite Kings? 17750
Do Toads Give You Warts? 14298
Do You Have the Time, Lydia? 12742
Do You Know What? 9166
Do You Know What I Know? 1962
Do You Know What I'll Do? 18600
Do You Know What Time It Is? 26
Do You Love Me? 6452
Do You Want to Be My Friend? 2921
Do You Want to See Something? 12096
Dobry 15409
Doctor Dolittle and the Secret Lake 11021
Doctor Dolittle's Post Office 11022
Doctor Dolittle's Zoo 11023
Doctor Kalulu 18111
Doctor Livingstone 14005
Doctor Paracelsus 14613
Doctor Proctor and Mrs. Meriwether 1699
Doctor Rabbit 17397
Doctor Shawn 2173
Doctor to the Galaxy 10810
Doctors and Nurses 7265
Doctor's Boy 427
Doctors' Tools 10605
Dodo Every Day 17332
Dodos and Dinosaurs Are Extinct 11866
Doers and Dreamers 4858
Does Anybody Care About Emma Miller? 3976

Dog and a Half, A 17953
Dog by Your Side, A 8118
Dog Days of Arthur Cane 1618
Dog for David, A 1664
Dog on Barkham Street, A 16346
Dog So Small, A 13426
Dog Soldiers 4912
Dog Team for Ongluk, A 15411
Dog That Flew ..., The 13027
Dog Who Came to Dinner, The 16706
Dog Who Could Swim Under Water, The see Oscar Lobster's Fair Exchange
Dog Who Insisted He Wasn't, The 15791
Dog Who Thought He Was a Boy, The 552
Dog Who Wouldn't Be, The 12523
Dogs 2298
Dogs and More Dogs 2059
Dogs and the Bones, The 6445
Dogs at Work 11242
Dog's Book of Birds, A 13338
Dog's Book of Bugs, A 7366
Dogs: Heroes, Adventures, Friends 13568
Dogs of Fear 12631
Dogsbody 9341
Doing Something About the Weather 1849
Doll Who Came Alive, The 16990
Dollar Man, The 11967
Dolley Madison (Grant) 7171
Dolley Madison (Martin) 11745
Dolley Madison (Nolan) 12875
Dolley Madison, First Lady 12028
Dollhouse Caper, The 12999
Dollhouse Magic 14494
Dolls 1395
Dolls, Dolls, Dolls 6937
Dolls' Day for Yoshiko 8940
Dolls' House, The 6950
Dolls the World Over 861
Dolly Madison (Davidson) 4576
Dolly Madison (Monsell) 12356
Dolor de Muelas de Alberto, El 17973
Dolphin 12462
Dolphin Crossing, The 17478
Dolphin Island 3525
Dolphins 12305
Dolphins in the City 2994
Dom and Va 3405
Dome People, The 8686
Dominic 16192
Dominique and the Dragon 16643

Don and Donna Go to Bat   13509
Don Coyote   13444
Don Sturdy in Lion Land ...
   598
Don Sturdy in the Tombs of
   Gold ...   599
Dona Felisa   12917
Donald and the Fish That Walked
   14299
Donde duerme el agua   8910
Donkey for Abou, A   5589
Donkey for the King, A   1265
Donkey Prince, The (Carter)
   3122
Donkey Prince, The (Grimm
   Bros.)   7390
Donkey Ysabel   17236
Don't Come Back a Stranger
   16500
Don't Count Your Chicks   4551
Don't Cry for Me   9159
Don't Feel Sorry for Paul   18196
Don't Forget the Bacon!   8833
Don't Forget Michael   16833
Don't Hurt Laurie!   14436
Don't Look and It Won't Hurt
   13446
Don't Mention Moon to Me   15870
Don't Ride the Bus on Monday
   12090
Don't Sit Under the Apple Tree
   2093
Don't Slam the Door When You Go
   4133
Don't Spill It Again, James   17729
Don't Take Teddy   6366
Don't Tell the Scarecrow ...   8955
Don't Throw Another One, Dover!
   9637
Don't Worry, Dear   5710
Don't You Remember?   3622
Don't You Turn Back   8716
Doodle and the Go-Cart   2597
Doodlebug   2080
Door, The   13048
Door in the Tree, The   2092
Door in the Wall, The   4633
Dope Book, The   10781
Dorothea Dix, Girl Reformer
   12031
Dorothea L. Dix   11579
Dorothy and Lillian Gish   6872
Dorothy Hamill   17223
Dorp Dead   4371
Dorrie and the Amazing Elixir
   4044
Dorrie and the Birthday Eggs
   4045
Dorrie and the Blue Witch   4046
Dorrie and the Dreamyard Monsters
   4047
Dorrie and the Fortune Teller   4048
Dorrie and the Goblin   4049
Dorrie and the Halloween Plot   4050
Dorrie and the Haunted House   4051
Dorrie and the Weather Box   4052
Dorrie and the Witch Doctor   4053
Dorrie and the Witch's Imp   4054
Dorrie's Book   14840
Dos Amigos, Los   6523
Double-Dog-Dare   13875
Double Fun   7989
Double Helix, The   17567
Double Heritage   18082
Double Spell   11172; see also Twin
   Spell
Doug Meets the Nutcracker   8551
Dougal Looks for Birds   16313
Dove and the Jackal and Other
   Stories, The   6314
Doves and Pomegranates   14666
Down a Dark Hall   5122
Down, Down the Mountain   4268
Down from the Lonely Mountain
   4397
Down in the Boondocks   6471
Down the Colorado with Major Powell
   17123
Down the Mississippi   2553
Down the River Without a Paddle
   17884
Down to Earth   18317
Down to Earth Cookbook, The
   1949
Down to the Beach   6595
Down to the Sea in Subs   11015
Downright Dencey   15945
Downtown Fairy Godmother, The
   13807
Downtown Is   16804
Dr. Anno's Magical Midnight Circus
   572
Dr. Beaumont and the Man with the
   Hole in His Stomach   5490
Dr. Elizabeth   3474
Dr. George Washington Carver,
   Scientist   7151
Dr. Merlin's Magic Shop   4107
Dr. Seuss' ABC   15370
Drac, The   8510
Dracula, Go Home   13739
Drag Racing (Coombs)   4036
Drag Racing (Morgan)   12444
Drag Racing (Nentl)   12729

Drag Racing (Puleo) 13988
Drag Racing for Beginners 5257
Drag Strip 6682
Dragging, Driving and Basic
  Customizing 11507
Dragon and the Doctor, The 4484
Dragon Circle, The 10091
Dragon, Dragon and Other Tales
  6582
Dragon Franz 9996
Dragon Hoard, The 10495
Dragon in the Clock Box, A
  4236
Dragon in the Garden, The 11515
Dragon in the Ghetto Caper,
  The 9987
Dragon Kite, The 10728
Dragon Magic 12934
Dragon of an Ordinary Family,
  The 11552
Dragon of Santa Lalia, The 3071
Dragon on Parade 5053
Dragon Slayer 16520
Dragon Takes a Wife, The 12608
Dragonfall 5 and the Empty Planet
  5215
Dragonfall 5 and the Space Cow-
  boys 5216
Dragonflies 15716
Dragons of the Queen, The 16347
Dragons, Ogres, and Scary Things
  676
Dragonsinger 11212
Dragonsong 11213
Dragonwings 18396
Draw, Draw, Draw 400
Draw Fifty Airplanes, Aircraft
  and Spacecraft 401
Draw Me an Elephant 14873
Drawings to Live With 8515
Dream for Addie, A 14497
Dream of the Blue Heron 1094
Dream Runner, The 4922
Dream Time, The 16984
Dream Tree, The 4361
Dream Watcher, The 17751
Dreamland Lake 13447
Dreams 9593
Dreams of Victory 3933
Dribbling, Shooting, and Scor-
  ing--Sometimes 13400
Drifting Continents, The 452
Driftway, The 10954
Drink for Little Red Diker, A
  16780
Drinking Gourd, A 12336
Driven to Win 10137

Drop of Blood, A 15594
Drop-Out 5612
Drowning Boy, The 16753
Drug Use and Drug Abuse 18248
Drugs (Houser) 8653
Drugs (Modell) 12300
Drugs and Man 12667
Drugs and You 11520
Drujienna's Harp 11422
Drum, The 8192
Drum Beats 8888
Drumbeats in Williamsburg 10398
Drummer Boy, The 5316
Drummer Hoff 5404
Drummer of Vincennes 15339
Drums Along the Mohawk 5268
Drums at Buntale 379 8692
Drums, Rattles and Bells 9756
Drums Speak, The 1566
Drusilla 2275
Dry Victories 9377
Duchess Bakes a Cake, The 9453
Duck in the Gun, The 4219
Ducks Don't Get Wet 6996
Duee, a Boy of Liberia 15077
Dueling Machine, The 2002
Duet 10169
Duey's Tale 913
Duffy 219
Duffy and the Devil 18513
Duffy's Rocks 5811
Duke Ellington (Barclay) 1071
Duke Ellington (Montgomery)
  12362
Dumb Joey 6718
Dumb Like Me, Olivia Potts 13517
Dumb Old Casey Is a Fat Tree
  1990
Dunderhead War, The 924
Dune Boy 16723
Dune Buggies 6875
Dune Fox 14417
Dupper 925
Durango Street 1889
Dust 102
Dust Bowl 10346
Dust of the Earth 3575
Dusty 10243
Dusty Desert Tales 11413
Dutch in America, The 16738
Dvora's Journey 1709
Dwarf Long-Nose 7843
Dwarf Pine Tree, The 10796
Dwellers of the Tundra 9194
Dwight D. Eisenhower 12451
Dynamite 8528

- E -

ESP   829
Each Peach Pear Plum   175
Eagle Feather   2554
Eagle Feather Prize, The   8366
Eagle Hunt, The   16617
Eagle Mask   8656
Eagle of the Ninth, The   16521
Eagle Pine, The   7415
Eagle's Gift, The   14137
Earl Mar's Daughter see Coo-
   My-Dove, My Dear
Earl the Pearl   9011
Earliest Americans, The   15023
Earl's Falconer, The   18047
Early America, 1492-1812   9522
Early Britain   13715
Early Days in Kansas   8939
Early Days in Ohio   5604
Early Indians, The   11849
Early Loggers in Minnesota
   14818, 14819
Early Moon   14885
Early Rising   3528
Early Thunder   6385
Early Years of Some Great Men
   and Women   11736
Ears and Tails and Common Sense
   15547
Ears of Louis, The   7283
Earth, Air, Fire and Water
   11281
Earth and Space, The   10210
Earth for Sam, The   14187
Earth Is Near, The   13543
Earth Is on a Fish's Back, The
   1377
Earth Is the Lord's, The   13744
Earth Namer   1576
Earth, the Great Recycler   14787
Earth Times Two   14277
Earth, Water, Wind, and Sun
   7571
Earthfasts   11953
Earth's Crust, The   11832
Earth's Story, The   397
Earthwatch   15157
Earthworms   10347
Easing the Scene   15166
East Africa (Fellows)   5768
East Africa (Kirby)   9846
East Africa (Perl)   13518
East African How Stories   13042
East African When Stories   13043
East African Why Stories   13044

East Africans at Work   13047
East Indians and the Pakistanis in
   America, The   873
East of the Sun and West of the
   Moon   715
Easter (Benoit)   1473
Easter (Fisher)   5910
Easter (Patterson)   13381
Easter Book of Legends and Stories,
   The   7959
Easter Buds Are Springing   8589
Easter Bunny That Overslept, The
   6360
Easter Cat, The   4673
Easter Chimes   7745
Easter Egg Artists, The   46
Easter Eggs for Everyone   4182
Easter Fires   7932
Easter Story for Children   15992
Eastern Religions   15234
Eastern Superstar: Olga Korbut
   5585
Eastward to India   14893
Easy Book of Numbers and Numerals
   17823
Easy Book of Sets   17824
Easy Costumes You Don't Have to
   Sew   3328
Easy Crafts Book   16247
Easy Does It   17863
Easy Embroidery   13267
Easy Enameling on Metal   5324
Easy Experiments with Water Pollu-
   tion   16021
Easy Gourmet Cooking for Young
   People and Beginners   9969
Easy Physics Projects   5817
Easy Quilling   406
Easy to Grow Vegetables   6529
Eat!   13364
Eating and Cooking Around the
   World   1582
Eating Places   18568
Ebbie   14303
Ebony Book of Black Achievement
   13549
Ebony Tree and the Spirit of
   Christmas, The   7245
Echoes of the Sea   13310
Ecidujerp, Prejudice   6772
Eclipse   2124
Ecology (Bendick)   1415
Ecology (Pringle)   13954
Ed Emberley's ABC   5408
Ed Emberley's Big Green Drawing
   Book   5409
Ed Emberley's Drawing Book   5410

Ed Emberley's Drawing Book of
   Animals 5411
Ed Emberley's Drawing Book of
   Faces 5412
Eddie and Gardenia 7951
Eddie No-Name 5651
Eddie Rickenbacker 3600
Eddie's Bear 12181
Eddie's Happenings 7952
Eddie's Valuable Property 7953
Edgar Allan 12754
Edge of Manhood 5652
Edge of Next Year, The 16348
Edge of Nowhere, The 16603
Edge of the Forest, An 15868
Edge of the Sea, The 3120
Edge of Two Worlds 9369
Edie Changes Her Mind 9306
Edith Cavell (DeLeeuw) 4698
Edith Cavell (Elkon) 5355
Education of a Baseball Player,
   The 11648
Edward Rose 5775
Edwardian Summer, An 7038
Ee Ar Ee Ar Ee Ar 2352
Eels' Strange Journey, The 6359
Egerton Ryerson 4469
Egg Book, The 9704
Egg Craft 12803
Egg-Speriment 13608
Egg Thoughts and Other Frances
   Songs 8280
Egg to Chick 15279
Egg Tree, The 12205
Egg-Ventures 12202
Eggchild, The 1228
Eggs, The 300
Eggs--And What Happens Inside
   Them 4175
Eggs Beautiful 11153
Ego Tripping & Other Poems for
   Young People 6861
Egypt 3003
Egypt and the Sudan 8042
Egypt, Child of the Nile 17570
Egypt Game, The 15965
Egypt in Pictures 12269
Egyptian Hieroglyphs for Every-
   one 15192
Egyptian Necklace, The 13262
Egyptians, The (Asimov) 739
Egyptians, The (Van Duyn) 17201
Egyptians in the Middle Kingdom,
   The 12997
Egyptians Knew, The 13681
Eight Black American Inventors
   7911

Eight Cousins 222
Eight Delightful Folk Tales 13191
Eight Tales of Mr. Pengachoosa
   14767
8,000 Stones 18211
1812: The War and the World
   2517
18th Emergency, The 2784
El Salvador 3004
Elbert, the Mind Reader 14384
Eleanor Roosevelt (Blassingame)
   1727
Eleanor Roosevelt (Goodsell) 7056
Eleanor Roosevelt (Graves) 7190
Eleanor Roosevelt (Richards)
   14331
Eleanor Roosevelt (Weil) 17653
Election Day 13613
Electric Radish and Other Jokes,
   The 16843
Electricity (Epstein) 5491
Electricity (Wade) 17377
Electronic Olympics, The 8160
Electronics for Young People 1446
Elefish 1299
Elephant 1149
Elephant Adventure 13931
Elephant and His Secret, The
   12279
Elephant and the Bad Baby, The
   17325
Elephant Bridge 13853
Elephant Buttons 17119
Elephant Girl 4425
Elephant in a Well 5560
Elephant in Trouble 4259
Elephant Outlaw 16324
Elephant Road 7479
Elephant Seals 2367
Elephant's Bathtub, The 3051
Elephant's Child, The 9842
Elephant's Heart ..., The 14065
Elephants Live Here 5238
Elephants of Africa 3946
Elephants of Sargabal, The 7480;
   see also Three Hundred Ninety-
   Seventh White Elephant, The
Elephant's Wish, The 12557
Elephi, the Cat with the High I.Q.
   16128
Eleven Folk Plays 4485
Eleven Steps, The 6290
Eleven! Time to Think of Marriage,
   Farhut 9472
Elf Owl 2540
Eli 13473
Elidor 6613

Elijah the Slave 15777
Elin's Amerika 4634
Elisabeth and the Marsh Mystery
  8503
Elizabeth (Harris) 7785
Elizabeth (Molnar) 12331
Elizabeth (Skorpen) 15811
Elizabeth Blackwell (Grant) 7172
Elizabeth Blackwell (Henry) 8059
Elizabeth Blackwell (Latham)
  10314
Elizabeth Catches a Fish 16819
Elizabeth, Elizabeth 5135
Elizabeth for Lincoln 11486
Elizabeth Gets Well 17638
Elizabeth's Tower 16303
Eliza's Daddy 16814
Ella of All-of-a-Kind Family
  16707
Ellen 374
Ellen and the Gang 6355
Ellen and the Queen 809
Ellen Elliott 519
Ellen Grae 3576
Ellen Tebbits 3555
Ellen the Expert 9061
Ellie to the Rescue 18193
Ellipse 3289
Elmo Doolan and the Search for
  the Golden Mouse 12574
Eloquent Crusader 16445
Elsa 67
Elsa and Her Cubs 66
Elton John 12787
Elusive Zebra, The 8921
Elves and the Shoemaker, The
  10948
Elvira Everything 717
Elvis and His Secret 7428
Ely S. Parker 5776
Emancipation of Joe Tepper, The
  4873
Emeka-Driver's Guard 12970
Emergency! 1251
Emergency Book, The 1416
Emergency Room (Feagles) 5736
Emergency Room, The (Kay)
  9563
Emergency Room (Steedman)
  16157
Emergent Continent, The 7616
Emil and Piggy Beast 10835
Emil and the Detectives 9508
Emilio's Summer Day 1996
Emily 15885
Emily and the Klunky Baby and
  the Next-door Dog 10737

Emily Dickinson 11050
Emily Dunning 5142
Emily Murphy 9110
Emily-San 14272
Emily Upham's Revenge 814
Emily's Runaway Imagination 3556
Emir's Son, The 1031
Emma Edmonds 16637
Emma in Winter 5697
Emma Tupper's Diary 4893
Emma's Afternoon see Betsy's Af-
  ternoon
Emma's Dilemma 10615
Emma's Search for Something 505
Emmeline and Her Daughters 12855
Emmet Otter's Jug-Band Christmas
  8281
Emmet's Pig 16349
Emotan and the Kings of Benin
  13121
Emperor and the Drummer Boy, The
  14423
Emperor and the Kite, The 18406
Emperor of Space see Boy Beyond
  the Moon
Emperor Penguin 4801
Emperor Penguins, The 12291
Emperor's New Clothes, The 436
Emperor's Oblong Pancake, The
  8726
Emperor's Winding Sheet, The
  17479
Empire of Fur 4846
Empty Chair, The 9492
Empty Moat, The 15530
Empty Schoolhouse, The 2957
En el cielo las estrellas 6841
Enchanted Castle, The 12732
Enchanted Forest, The 4737
Enchanted Hill, The 14056
Enchanted Orchard and Other Folk-
  tales of Central America 3124
Enchanted Savannah, The 3472
Enchanted Schoolhouse, The 14968
Enchantress from the Stars 5436
Encounter Near Venus 17845
Encounters with the Invisible World
  14418
Encyclopedia Brown 15977
Encyclopedia Brown and the Case
  of the Dead Eagles 15976
Encyclopedia Brown Gets His Man
  15978
Encyclopedia Brown Lends a Hand
  15979
Encyclopedia Brown Saves the Day
  15980

Encyclopedia Brown Takes the
   Case 15981
Encyclopedia Brown Tracks Them
   Down 15982
End of Exile 2003
End of the Beginning 11567
End of the Game 3865
End of the World, The 2125
Endangered Plants 8402
Endangered Predators 7776
Endless Dark, The 5791
Endless Pavement, The 8998
Endless Steppe, The 7853
Endless Treasure 7679
Enduring Beast, The 1309
Enduring Navajo, The 6837
Enemy at Green Knowe, An 1970
Energy (Adler) 103
Energy (Gutnik) 7529
Energy (Pringle) 13955
Energy All Around 13682
Energy and Power 8930
Energy and the Environment
   15924
Energy and the Future 14690
Energy for the 21st Century
   2126
Energy from the Sun 1515
Energy Workers, The 12711
English Boy's Life and Adventures
   in Uganda, An 7840
English Fables and Fairy Stories
   14204
English Fairy Tales 9045
English Folk Tales and Fairy
   Tales 9046
English in America, The 3153
English Mummers and Their Plays,
   The 2286
Enjoying Birds in Michigan 12145
Enjoying Gymnastics 4875
Enjoying the World of Art 1386
Enormous Egg, The 2754
Enrico Fermi 5492
Enrique 5863
Enterprising Women 1658
Entertaining with Number Tricks
   1101
Entre juego y juego ... un libro!
   4879
Enuk, Eskimo Boy 5767
Environmental Careers 7560
Environments Out There 740
Enzymes in Action 1516
Epaminondas 12097
Ephemeral Folk Figures 12693
Epilepsy 15682

Episcopalians 5331
Equatorial Africa 9872
Erase una vez un pueblo 4341
Eres Tu Mi Mama? 5224; see also
   Are You My Mother?
Eric and Enid 15055
Eric Carle's Storybook 2922
Eric in Alaska 15584
Eric Plants a Garden 8708
Erie Canal, The (Adams) 61
Erie Canal, The (Andrist) 529
Erie Canal, The (Spier) 16086
Ernie Banks 11867
Ernie Banks: Mr. Cub 10762
Ernie Pyle 18075
Escape (Bova) 2004
Escape (Fryer) 6424
Escape! (White) 17803
Escape from Nowhere 5613
Escape from Splatterbang 5960
Escape from the Crater 1635
Escape from the Evil Prophecy
   9825
Escape from the Shawnees 18168
Escape into Daylight 8652
Escape into the Zoo 9261
Escape King 5529
Escape of the Giant Hogstalk, The
   8504
Escape the River 2426
Escape to Freedom 9366
Escape to King Alfred 16981
Escape to Witch Mountain 9770
Escuela encantada, La 6554
Eskimo, The 1751
Eskimo Birthday, An 14485
Eskimo Boy 6345
Eskimo Boy Today 5900
Eskimo Crafts 3902
Eskimo of Little Diomede 11922
Eskimo Songs and Stories 5846
Eskimo Twins, The 13513
Eskimos (Bringle) 2259
Eskimos (Martin) 11746
Eskimos (Wally) 17473
Eskimos Knew, The 13683
Eskimos of the World 5366
Especially Humphrey 10731
Esta era una Vez Bajo las Palmeras
   13351
Estebanico 13280
Estimation 10869
Estuaries 13956
Ethan's Favorite Teacher 3866
Ethel Barrymore (Fox) 6190
Ethel Barrymore (Newman) 12797
Ethiopia (Blanchard) 1720

Ethiopia (Edmonds) 5258
Ethiopia (Nolen) 12890
Ethiopia (Perl) 13519
Ethiopia in Pictures 42
Ethiopia, Mountain Kingdom 17571
Etiquette 8419
Eugene the Brave 3934
Euphonia and the Flood 2832
Europe for Young Travelers 16564
European Folk Festivals 5493
Evangeline and the Acadians 16631
Evan's Corner 8181
Evel Knievel 14982
Even the Devil Is Afraid of a Shrew 16131
Evening Gray, Morning Red 18206
Ever-After Island 8182
Ever Ride a Dinosaur? 4108
Everett Anderson's Christmas Coming 3623
Everett Anderson's Friend 3624
Everett Anderson's 1-2-3 3625
Everett Anderson's Year 3626
Everglades, The 1728
Every Boy's Judo 7752
Every Child's Nursery Song Book 12281
Every Day a Dragon 10738
Every Day Is Earth Day 13755
Every Girl's Judo 7753
Every Man Heart Lay Down 7131
Everybody In! 14718
Everybody Needs a Rock 1237
Everybody's a Winner 15099
Everyday Animals 335
Everyday Insects 336
Everyday Inventions 8555
Everyday Life in Ancient Egypt 17804
Everyday Life in Prehistoric Times 14033
Everyday Life in the Roman Empire 10966
Everyday Life of the Aztecs 2166
Everyday Life on the American Frontier 18309
Everyday Machines and How They Work 15089
Everyday Weather and How It Works 15090
Everyday Things in Ancient Greece 14034
Everyday Train, The 5292

Everyday Trees 337
Everyday Turtles, Toads and Their Kin 338
Everyday Wildflowers 339
Everyman's United Nations 5605
Everyone Knows What a Dragon Looks Like 18011
Everything 7998
Everything About Easter Rabbits 14637
Everything Happens to Stuey 12396
Everything Has a Shape and Everything Has a Size 9970
Everything Moves 15744
Every Time I Climb a Tree 11265
Evonne Goolagong (Jacobs) 9062
Evonne Goolagong (Morse) 12484
Ex, The 11081
Exactly Alike 12743
Exactly Like Me 13629
Excretory System, The 15683
Executive Order 9066 3973
Exhibition Gymnastics 9415
Exiles of the Stars 12935
Exit from Home 8141
Exotic Fish as Pets 17307
Experiments in Art 16125
Experiments in Optical Illusion 1307
Experiments with a Microscope 1308
Experiments with Water 16022
Exploits in Africa 1232
Exploration of Africa 16248
Explorations in Chemistry 12605
Explorations of Pere Marquette, The 9880
Explorers of the Atom 6515
Exploring a Coral Reef 2649
Exploring an Ocean Tide Pool 1417
Exploring and Understanding Fish 2091
Exploring as You Walk in the City 2737
Exploring as You Walk in the Meadow 2738
Exploring Black America 16854
Exploring Canada from Sea to Sea 12657
Exploring Chemistry 6516
Exploring Earth and Space 8869
Exploring for Mushrooms 5300
Exploring Illinois 14011
Exploring Michigan 12776
Exploring the Brain 15684
Exploring the Planets 6517

Exploring the Universe 6518
Exploring the Weather 6519
Exploring the World of Leaves 18173
Exploring the World of Social Insects 15717
Exploring Toronto 15824
Exploring Triangles 13626
Exploring Wisconsin 14589
Exploring with Metrics 1688
Exploring with Pocket Calculators 1689
Explosives 7567
Extraordinaria vida de Pablo Casals, La 215
Extraordinary Adventures of Chee-Chee McNerney, The 12768
Extraordinary North Dakotans 14576
Extraordinary Tug-of-War, The 15014
Eye in the Forest, The 16163
Eye of Conscience, The 12040
Eye Teasers 13279
Eye Winker, Tom Tinker, Chin Chopper 6889
Eyes and Ears of the Civil War, The 6138
Eyes in the Fishbowl 15966
Eyes of the Amaryllis, The 842

- F -

FDR and the Supreme Court Fight, 1937 10309
FDR Story, The 13432
FDR's New Deal 10411
F* T* C* Superstar 506
Faber Book of Nursery Verse, The see Barnes Book of Nursery Verse, The
Fabian 12839
Fable of the Fig Tree, The 7447
Fables from Aesop (Rees) 14199
Fables from Aesop (Reeves) 14205
Fables of India, The 6461
Fables of Indian Dances 3538
Fables of Northern Ghana 16121
Fabula del bosque 3219
Fabulas 14872

Fabulas de La Fontaine 10188
Fabulas en accion para la escena y para el aula 1484
Fabulous Earthworm Deal, The 16147
Fabulous Firework Family, The 6059
Fabulous Fox, The 9307
Fabulous Voyage of the Pegasus, The 13826
Face of Abraham Candle, The 3589
Face of Louisiana, The 5218
Face of Maryland, The 1838
Face-Off at Center Ice 14358
Faces 2190
Faces of the Frontier 1691
Faces of the Great Lakes, The 5323
Fact and Fancy in American Wildlife 12165
Fact, Fiction and Folklore of Southern Indiana 16554
Facts About Our Fifty States 2107
Facts About Sex for Today's Youth 7076
Facts and Fantasies About Alcohol 18290
Facts and Fantasies About Drugs 18291
Facts and Fantasies About Smoking 18292
Fair American, The 3679
Fairies and Chimneys 6448
Fairy Caravan, The 13839
Fairy Elves 13264
Fairy Ring 17887
Fairy Rings and Other Mushrooms 3947
Fairy Shoemaker and Other Fairy Poems, The 360
Fairy Tale Treasury, The 7869
Fairy Tales (Anderson) 437
Fairy Tales (Cummings) 4357
Fairy Tales (Grimm Bros.) 7391
Fairy Tales for Today's Children 6591
Fairy Tales from South Africa 1995
Fairy Tales from Viet Nam 14438
Fairy Tales of the Orient 2485
Faithful Fish, The 12757
Faithless Lollybird, The 182
Falcons Return 9545
Fall Down, Break a Bone, Skin Your Knee, Book, The 5332
Fall from the Sky, A 15348
False Flamingoes, The 4456

False Start 14049

Falter Tom and the Water Boy 5112

Familia, La 9231

Families Are Like That! 3357

Families Live Together 12012

Family (Donovan) 5008

Family (Simmons) 15708

Family at Caldicott Place, The 16408

Family at Ditlabeng, The 12285

Family Book of Nursery Rhymes, A 13147

Family Conspiracy, The 13635

Family Failing, A 702

Family from One End Street, The 6619

Family Grows in Different Ways, A 13342

Family Minus, The 10017

Family Treasury of Children's Stories, The 5595

Family Tree, The 16381

Family Under the Bridge, The 2958

Famous American Artists 10525

Famous American Athletes 10526

Famous American Doctors 10527

Famous American Engineers 10528

Famous American Explorers 9589

Famous American Fiction Writers 10529

Famous American Indians (Heuman) 8133

Famous American Indians (Leipold) 10530

Famous American Indians of the Plains 8220

Famous American Musicians 10531

Famous American Negro Poets 14581

Famous American Negroes 10532

Famous American Poets (Benet) 1458

Famous American Poets (Leipold) 10533

Famous American Revolutionary War Heroes 8221

Famous American Teachers 10534

Famous American Trails 7166

Famous American Women (Leipold) 10535

Famous American Women (Stoddard) 16333

Famous Artists of the Past 3293

Famous Battle of Bravery Creek, The 7599

Famous Black Entertainers of Today 19

Famous Conductors 5608

Famous Curses 3746

Famous Custom and Show Cars 1122

Famous Firsts in Baseball 3991

Famous Firsts in Sports 9108

Famous Fossil Finds 8440

Famous Frontiersmen 12526

Famous Hockey Players 6235

Famous Indians 17171

Famous Mathematicians 16362

Famous Merchants 10378

Famous Mexican-Americans 12784

Famous Modern American Women Athletes 9041

Famous Negro Athletes 1916

Famous Negro Entertainers of Stage, Screen and TV 14582

Famous Negro Music Makers 8717

Famous Paintings 3294

Famous Pirates of the New World 17773

Famous Poets for Young People 1459

Famous Puerto Ricans 12785

Famous Railroad Stations of the World 12653

Famous Spies 16513

Famous Stanley Kidnapping Case, The 15967

Famous U.S. Air Force Bombers 4003

Famous U.S. Navy Fighter Planes 4004

Fancy Free 3193

Fannie Farmer Junior Cookbook, The 13515

Fannie Lou Hamer 9378

Fanny Kemble's America 15206

Fantastic Brothers, The 7481

Fantastic Mr. Fox 4443

Fantastic Toys 1346

Far and Few 11266

Far Distant Oxus 8737

Far East Stories 4988

Far Frontier, The 16169

Far in the Day 4372

Far into the Night 11085

Far Journey, The 5511

Far-Off Land, The 3168

Far Out the Long Canal 4674

Far Side of Evil, The 5437

Far Voice Calling 45

Far Voyager 10315

Far Wilderness 18435
Faraway Dream 6069
Faraway Island, The 4134
Faraway Lurs, The 1316
Faraway Princess 13081
Farewell, the Little People
 13766
Farewell to Shady Glade 13474
Farm, The 14795
Farm Boy 7083
Farm Numbers 15879
Farm Town 8017
Farmer and the Witch, The 4804
Farmer Boy 17901
Farmer Giles of Ham 16912
Farmer Palmer's Wagon Ride
 16193
Farmers of the East 3665
Farming Around the World 6055
Farming in Early Minnesota
 10639
Farms for Today and Tomorrow
 15645
Farthest-Away Mountain, The
 1051
Farthest Shore, The 10513
Fast and Easy Needlepoint 8338
Fast and Slow 3459
Fast and Smart 2759
Fast Break 1681
Fast Break Forward 5572
Fast Friends 16287
Fast Green Car 2760
Fast Is Not a Ladybug 15065
Fast Man on a Pivot 4771
Fast Sam, Cool Clyde and Stuff
 12609
Fast-Slow, High-Low 16087
Fast Sooner Hound, The 1926
Fastest Quitter in Town, The
 7241
Fat and Skinny 1011
Fat Cat, The 9705
Fat Elliot & the Gorilla 13698
Fat Ernest 17656
Fat Free 6815
Fat Men from Space 13699
Fat Polka-Dot Cat and Other
 Haiku 11532
Fat Woman, The 77
Fate of the Griffon, The 11444
Fate of the Lakes, The 1126
Father Christmas 2233
Father Christmas Letters, The
 16913
Father Every Few Years, A
 854

Father Flanagan 7191
Father Fox's Penny Rhymes 17564
Father Is Big 14080
Father Like That, A 18601
Father Reads to His Children, A
 13893
Father's Arcane Daughter 9988
Fathers of Industry 5657
Faun and the Woodcutter's Daughter,
 The 13651
Favorite Children's Stories from
 China and Tibet 8740
Favorite Christmas Carols 1897
Favorite Fairy Tales Told in
 Czechoslovakia 7870
Favorite Fairy Tales Told in
 Denmark 7871
Favorite Fairy Tales Told in Eng-
 land 7872
Favorite Fairy Tales Told in Ger-
 many 7873
Favorite Fairy Tales Told in
 Greece 7874
Favorite Fairy Tales Told in India
 7875
Favorite Fairy Tales Told in Ire-
 land 7876
Favorite Fairy Tales Told in Japan
 7877
Favorite Fairy Tales Told in Judea
 7878
Favorite Fairy Tales Told in Russia
 7879
Favorite Fairy Tales Told in Scot-
 land 7880
Favorite Fairy Tales Told in Sweden
 7881
Favorite Plays for Classroom Read-
 ing 5170
Favorite Poems, Old and New 5839
Favorite Stories for the Children's
 Hour 908
Favorite Tales from Shakespeare
 12166
Favorite Uncle Remus, The 7774
Fawn 13454
Fawn in the Woods 5242
Fay Gow, a Boy of Hong Kong
 15078
Fear in the Forest 4709
Fearsome Inn, The 15778
Feast Day, The 5635
Feast of Lanterns, The 14976
Feast of Light, A 12907
Feast of Thanksgiving 1323
Feast on Sullivan Street 12170
Feasts and Frolics 5792

Feather in the Wind 2743
Feather Mountain 13072
Feather Star, The 18318
Feathered Ones and Furry 5911
Feathered Serpent 9500
Feathers and Floods 12718
Febechi and Group in Cave Adventure 13058
Febechi down the Niger 13059
February Dragon 16794
Federal Case, A 14913
Fee Fi Fo Fum 2234
Feeding the City 16648
Feeling Free 16493
Feelings (Dunn) 5139
Feelings (Polland) 13793
Feelings Between Brothers and Sisters 3982
Feelings Between Friends 3983
Feelings Between Kids and Grownups 3984
Feelings Between Kids and Parents 3985
Feldman Fieldmouse 1398
Felice 2375
Felicia Cartright and the Pink Poodle 13251
Felicia the Critic 3935
Felipe the Bullfighter 17258
Felipe y sus gatos 17186
Felisa Rincon de Gautier 7461
Felita 12315
Felix in the Attic 1851
Fellowship of the Ring, The 16914
Felt Craft 16733
Femi and the Old Grandaddie 14453
Fence, The 1014
Ferdinand and Isabella 8613
Ferdinand Magellan, Master Mariner 13815
Fern Is Born, A 7468
Ferris Wheel 16350
Festivals 11639
Festivals for You to Celebrate 13998
Festivals of Japan 2533
Fetish Hide-Out, The 4661
Few Fair Days, A 6573
Few Flies and I, A 8954
Fiddle-I-Fee, a Traditional American Chant 16145
Fiddlefoot Jones of the North Woods 9385
Fiddler of High Lonesome 17058
Fiddlestrings 4635

Fidelia 59
Field Book of Common Rocks and Minerals 11052
Field of Buttercups, The 1834
Fields of Peace 2095
Fierce John 5812
Fiesta, La 9397
Fiesta Time in Mexico 11661
Fifer of San Jacinto, The 11328
15 Fables of Krylov 10122
Fifth Base, The 620
Fifth Inning Fade-Out 8980
Fifty Common Trees of Indiana 15506
Fifty-first Dragon, The 2325
57 Stories of Saints for Boys and Girls 4536
Fifty-Six Who Signed, The 5873
Fifty Strange Stories of the Supernatural 2897
50,000 Names for Jeff 15954
Figgie Hobbin 3181
Figgs and Phantoms 14120
Fight Against Albatross Two 16795
Fight for Union, The 3775
Fighting Indians of America 4005
Fighting Indians of the West 4006
Fighting Shirley Chisholm 7821
Figure in the Shadows, The 1360
Figure of Speech, A 11970
Filippo's Dome 14508
Filled Up Full 5102
Filming Works Like This 1443
Filmmaking for Beginners 8635
Final Mystery, The 9914
Finches' Fabulous Furnace, The 5076
Find Debbie! 2427
Find the Cat 10961
Find the Constellations 14268
Find the Hidden Insect 3805
Finders Keepers (Shulman) 15618
Finders Keepers (Will and Nicolas) 17948
Finders Keepers, Losers Weepers 10739
Finding a Poem 12098
Finding 1 to 10 64
Finding Out About Jobs: TV Reporting 1444
Finding Out About Shapes 6292
Finding Out About the Past 6293
Finding Out with Your Senses 15745
Finest Kind O'day 11457
Finger Puppets 14650
Finist the Falcon Prince 14211

Finn Family Moomintroll   9141
Fiona's Bee   9638
Fiorello La Guardia   9534
Fir Tree, The   438
Fire   7568
Fire Bringer, The   8329
Fire Canoe   5644
Fire Cat   806
Fire Dragon, The   15893
Fire Fighters the World Over
    16940
Fire in the Stone   16796
Fire in the Wind   943
Fire on the Mountain, and Other
    Ethiopian Stories, The   4207
Fire Plume, The   1638
Fire Plume Legends of the Amer-
    ican Indian, The   15103
Fire Trail, The   17506
Firearms by Winchester   3779
Fireball Mystery, The   142
Fireballers, The   12778
Firefighter, The   13548
Fireflies   14829
Firefly Named Torchy, A   17359
Firegirl   14316
Firelight Fables   4487
Firerose   9210
Fireside Book of Children's Songs,
    The   18114
Fireside Book of Favorite Amer-
    ican Songs, The   1898
Fireside Book of Folk Songs, The
    1899
Fireside Book of Fun and Game
    Songs, The   18115
Fireside Tales from the North
    14960
Fireside Tales of the Hare and
    His Friends   14961
Firestorm   6706
Fireweed   17480
First ABC   10273
First American Revolution, The
    11038
First Americans, The (Claiborne)
    3470
First Americans, The (James)
    9117
First Artists, The   14870
First Book Edition of Casey at
    the Bat, The   16778
First Book of Africa, The   8718
First Book of Airplanes, The
    1418
First Book of Alaska, The   16429
First Book of American History,

The   3909
First Book of American Negroes,
    The   18453
First Book of Ancient Araby, The
    12530
First Book of Ancient Egypt, The
    14459
First Book of Ancient Mesopotamia
    and Persia, The   14460
First Book of Ancient Rome, The
    14461
First Book of Archaeology, The
    10125
First Book of Australia, The   9548
First Book of Automobiles, The
    1419
First Book of Baseball, The   2208
First Book of Basketball, The
    15053
First Book of Birds, The   18054
First Book of Black Africa on the
    Move, The   10178
First Book of Brazil, The   15539
First Book of Camping, The   9132
First Book of Central America and
    Panama, The   11691
First Book of Chess, The   10502
First Book of Communist China
    9834
First Book of Congress, The   4229
First Book of Copper, The   2708
First Book of East Africa, The
    11009
First Book of Ecology, A   8425
First Book of Elections, The   10847
First Book of Energy, The   7798
First Book of Eskimos, The   2209
First Book of Ethics, The   1693
First Book of Facts and How to
    Find Them, The   17825
First Book of First Ladies   1812
First Book of Gases, The   3706
First Book of Ghana, The   11010
First Book of Hiking, The   7795
First Book of Holidays, The   2666
First Book of Hospitals, The   4230
First Book of How to Make a
    Speech, The   13866
First Book of How to Write a Re-
    port, The   2108
First Book of India, The   1982
First Book of Indians, The   2210
First Book of Islam, The   5259
First Book of Japan, The   12001
First Book of Jazz, The   8719
First Book of Judaism, The   14665
First Book of Local Government,

The 5299
First Book of Lumbering, The 14317
First Book of Magic, The 16332
First Book of Mammals, The 18055
First Book of Maps and Globes, The 5494
First Book of Mars, The 9927
First Book of Mexico, The 5495
First Book of Microbes, The 10707
First Book of Mining, The 11692
First Book of Modern Greece, The 17543
First Book of Negroes, The 8720
First Book of New World Explorers, The 14318
First Book of New Zealand, The 9549
First Book of Norse Legends, The 5333
First Book of Nurses, The 9564
First Book of Paintings, The 12395
First Book of Physical Fitness, The 17483
First Book of Pioneers, The 7861
First Book of Politics, A 11693
First Book of Presidents, The 4231
First Book of Printing, The 5496
First Book of Puerto Rico, The 3872
First Book of Rhythms, The 8721
First Book of Safety, The 1855
First Book of Salt, The 2709
First Book of Science Experiments, The 18337
First Book of Sharks, A 1813
First Book of Skydiving, The 9565
First Book of Smoking 16020
First Book of Soccer 16962
First Book of Sound, The 9928
First Book of South America, The 3130
First Book of Space Travel, The 1420
First Book of Stone Age Man, The 4889
First Book of Stones, The 4156
First Book of Swamps and Marshes 15892
First Book of Swimming, The 15054
First Book of Tales of Ancient Egypt, The 12531

First Book of the Arctic, The 10964
First Book of the Civil War, The 10643
First Book of the Cliff Dwellers, The 11662
First Book of the Clinic, The 9566
First Book of the Congo, The 11312
First Book of the Constitution, The 12460
First Book of the Early Settlers, The 14319
First Book of the Fur Trade, The 14320
First Book of the Human Senses, The 10776
First Book of the Indian Wars, The 12461
First Book of the Netherlands, The 3772
First Book of the Nile River, The 12627
First Book of the Olympic Games, The 17484
First Book of the Red Cross, The 14684
First Book of the Rise of American Political Parties, The 3990
First Book of the Vikings, The 14321
First Book of Time, The 1421
First Book of Turtles and Their Care, The 8426
First Book of Vegetables, The 1287
First Book of Vice-Presidents of the United States, The 5755
First Book of Wool, The 3208
First Book of World War I, The 15959
First Book of World War II, The 15960
First Book of Zoos, A 13538
First Bow and Arrow 3780
First Camping Trip 3781
First Christmas Gifts, The 13397
First Counting 15396
First Crop 1349
First Crowing of the Cocks ..., The 11138
First Day in School 1653
First Days of the World 398
First Electrical Book for Boys, A 12436
First Farmers in the New Stone Age, The 17677
First Fish 3782

First Five Fathoms, The 18089
First Four Years, The 17902
First Graces 17030
First in Their Hearts 6041
First Ladies 13946
First Lady of America 13628
First Lady of India 17894
First Lady of the Renaissance
 12129
First Living Things 11868
First Look at Animals Without
 Backbones 15316
First Look at Birds, A 15317
First Look at Fish 15318
First Look at Flowers, A 15319
First Look at Insects, A 15320
First Look at Leaves, A 15321
First Look at Mammals 15322
First Look at Sharks, A 15323
First Look at the World of Plants,
 A 15324
First Man and Fire, The 2353
First Man to Cross America 16582
First Men, The 11869
First Morning, The 1577
First Night Away from Home 2416
First of the Penguins, The 16159
First on the Land 17765
First on the Moon 644
First Pink Light 7306
First Plays for Children 12226
First Prayers 17031
First Serve 16947
First Ships Around the World,
 The 2441
First Snow 4213
First Step 15955
First Steps in Ballet 11656
First Thanksgiving, The 1083
First Transatlantic Cable, The
 12651
First Two Lives of Lukas-Kasha,
 The 267
First Up Everest 16435
First Wheel, The 13190
First Woman Ambulance Surgeon
 12856
First Woman Doctor 984
First Woman Editor 2710
Fish, The 2450
Fish and How They Reproduce
 13353
Fish Do the Strangest Things
 8622
Fish for Supper 6973
Fish Hawk's Nest, The 11983
Fish Head 6386

Fish in the Air 17870
Fish Is Fish 10875
Fish Out of School 15496
Fisherman and His Wife, The 7392
Fisherman and the Goblet, The
 16686
Fisherman Who Needed a Knife, The
 18116
Fisherman's Bride, The 16559
Fisherman's Son, The (Ginsburg)
 6845
Fisherman's Son, The (Lattimore)
 10328
Fishes and Their Young 6044
Fishes Dangerous to Man 6045
Fishing 2031
Fishing All Waters 3806
Fishing River, The 17523
Fishing with Dad 6060
Fisk of Fenway Park 9012
5A and 7B 15045
Five Against the Odds 6350
Five Boys in a Cave 3445
Five Bushel Farm 3680
Five Cent, Five Cent 3253
Five Children and It 12733
Five Chinese Brothers 1672
Five-Color Buick and a Blue-Eyed
 Cat, A 18239
Five Friends in School 2502
500 [Five Hundred] 1036
500 Hats of Bartholomew Cubbins,
 The 15371
500 Miles to Go 1788
Five Kidnapped Indians 12328
Five Knucklebones 5639
Five Little Foxes and the Snow
 9326
Five Little Peppers 15655
Five Lives of Great Ghanaian
 Pioneers 75
5 Men Under 1 Umbrella 11114
Five O'Clock Charlie 8070
Five Pennies, The 2191
Five Points for Hockey 14240
Five Were Missing see Ransom
Five Women 8928
Fixing Up Motorcycles 15917
Flag at the Pole, A 4608
Flags of All Nations ... 5395
Flags of American History 4326
Flags of Louisiana 2222
Flags of the World 5587
Flame Tree and Other Folk-lore
 Stories from Uganda 1158
Flaming Arrows 16170
Flash, Crash, Rumble and Roll

2127

Flash the Dash 6260

Flashback 362

Flashes and Flags 3735

Flashlight 16860

Flat on My Face 5895

Flat Stanley 2361

Flatboat Days on Frontier Rivers
11214

Flattered Flying Fish, The 14376

Flea Story, A 10876

Fleas 3799

Flicka, Dicka and the Big Red
Hen 10844

Flickertail 904

Flight of Exiles 2005

Flight of the Doves, The 11419

Flight of the Fox 12575

Flight of the Lone Eagle, The
6152

Flight of the White Wolf 5377

Flight to Freedom 2504

Flight to the Promised Land
7678

Flight to the South Pole 1037

Flight Today and Tomorrow 8870

Flim and Flam and the Big
Cheese 6624

Flint's Island 17846

Flip 4831

Flip and the Cows 4832

Flip and the Morning 4833

Floating and Sinking 2128

Floating Clouds, Floating Dreams
9434

Flood Friday 10568

Flood of Creatures, A 8914

Flor de Leyendas 3146

Florence Nightingale (Colver)
3887

Florence Nightingale (Hume) 8741

Florence Nightingale (Nolan)
12876

Florence the Blue Flamingo 12592

Flower Moon Snow 12292

Flower Pot Is Not a Hat, A
12306

Flower with Love, A 12558

Flowerpot Gardens 2555

Flowers and Flowering Plants
242

Flowers of Anger 7600

Flowers That Bloom in the Spring
5301

Flutes, Whistles, and Reeds
9757

Fly Away Home 12954

Fly Away Paul 4583

Fly Away Peter 4884

Fly by Night (Jarrell) 9158

Fly-by-Night (Peyton) 13596

Fly High, Fly Low 6261

Fly Homer Fly 13475

Fly into Danger 13636

Fly, Jimmy, Fly 12610

Fly Went By, A 11231

Fly, Wheels, Fly! 14953

Flying Aces of World War I 7507

Flying Carpet, The 2376

Flying Cow, The 3855

Flying Hand-Launched Gliders 9540

Flying High 14315

Flying Lesson of Gerald Pelican,
The 1399

Flying Machine, The 11018

Flying Paper Airplane Models
14643

Flying Reptiles in the Age of Dinosaurs 9541

Flying Saucer Full of Spaghetti, A
10018

Flying Ship ... 16575

Flying Shoes, The 9127

Flying Skis 18325

Flying to the Moon and Other
Strange Places 3853

Flying Today and Tomorrow 12668

Foal Creek 3767

Focus the Bright Land 6361

Fodai and the Leopard-Men 7482

Fofana 7483

Fog Comes on Little Pig Feet, The
17730

Fog in the Meadow 14830

Fog Island 5645

Fog Magic 14937

Foilcraft 4430

Foley's Poems 6089

Folk Crafts for World Friendship
16734

Folk Instruments 6836

Folk Music in America 17195

Folk Songs of China, Japan, and
Korea 4903

Folk Stories of the South 9095

Folk Tales and Stories from Around
the World 12139

Folk Tales of a Savage, The
11008

Folk Tales of Liberia 4273

Folk Toys Around the World and
How to Make Them 9389

Folklore and Early Customs of
Southeast Missouri 12957

Folklore in America 3734

Folktales and Fairy Tales of Africa 7237
Folktales from Asia for Children Everywhere 730
Folktales of France 11807
Folktales of the Irish Countryside 4478
Folkways Omnibus of Children's Games, The 17314
Follow a Fisher 13957
Follow Me Cried Bee 17398
Follow My Leader 6599
Follow That Bus! 8834
Follow the Fall 10130
Follow the Golden Goose 17270
Follow the Honey Bird 7625
Follow the Leader 14344
Follow Your Nose 15595
Fonabio and the Lion 7484
Food 104
Food as a Crutch 15167
Food from Farm to Home 2518
Foods and Festivals of the Danube Lands 13520
Foods the Indians Gave Us 7945
Fool of the World and the Flying Ship, The 14114
Fooling Around with Words 16992
Fooling of King Alexander, The 15807
Foolish Filly 14076
Foolish Frog, The 15236
Fools of Chelm and Their History, The 15779
Foot Book, The 15372
Foot-Fighting Manual for Self-Defense and Sport Karate 12706
Foot in Two Worlds, A 11764
Football (Miers) 12156
Football (Sullivan) 16463
Football Boys 14241
Football for Young Champions 583
Football Fugitive 3417
Football Players Do Amazing Things 3215
Football Replay 17615
Football Running Backs 3846
Football Talk for Beginnners 10912
Football Techniques Illustrated 12393
Football's Clever Quarterbacks 14093
Football's Greatest Coach 15106

Football's Greatest Passer 2161
Football's Rugged Running Backs 14094
Footprints and Fingerprints 6315
Footprints in the Trail 12266
Footsy 14826
For All That Lives 789
For Ma and Pa 7933
For Me to Say 11267
For One--Or for All 9063
For the Love of Ann 4094
For the Ohio Country 971
Forbidden Bridge, The 14572
Forbidden Forest, The 5082
Forces of Superstition, The 5557
Forecast 7609
Forespoken, The 10648
Forest Christmas, A 8499
Forest Is Our Playground, The 12572
Forest Princess, The 8103
Forest Rose 1466
Forests Are for People 18226
Forever Christmas Tree, The 17092
Forever Free (Adamson) 68
Forever Free (Sterling) 16238
Forge and the Forest, The 17125
Forgetful Fred 18012
Forgetful Robot, The 5640
Forging of Our Continent, The 13037
Forgotten Beasts of Eld, The 11427
Forgotten Door, The 9771
Fork in the Trail, The 403
Fort in the Forest, The 10984
Fort Snelling, Anchor Post of the Northwest 18530
Fort York 17554
Forten the Sailmaker 5038
Forts in America 13570
Forts in the Wilderness 11223
Fortunately 3280
Fortune Cake, The 9375
Forty Million School Books Can't Be Wrong 5374
Forty-Ninth Magician, The 849
Forty-Six Days of Christmas 16076
Forward March to Freedom 7314
Fossil Snake, The 1971
Fossils 14288
Fossils Tell of Long Ago 301
Foster Child 1192
Foster Mary 16403
Founding Mothers 4730

Foundling, The 3072
Foundling and Other Tales of Prydain, The 268
Four and Twenty Blackbirds 5902
Four Clever Brothers, The 7393
Four Corners of the Sky 3658
Four Days in Philadelphia, 1776 13614
Four Donkeys, The 269
Four Fur Feet 2388
Four Leaf Clover 17949
Four Miles to Pinecone 7833
Four Plays for Schools 9868
Four Seasons, Five Senses 13311
Four Stories About the Tortoise 78
Four Stories for Four Seasons 4718
Four-Story Mistake, The 5463
Four Took Freedom 16246
4-Way Stop 10969
Four Women in a Violent Time 4253
Four Women of Courage 17616
Fourscore ... and More 8222
Fourteen Hundred Cowries and Other African Tales 6430
Fourteenth Dragon, The 15254
Fourth of July (Graves) 7192
Fourth of July, The (Phelan) 13615
Fourth of July Story, The 4458
Fourth World of the Hopis, The 4195
Fox and the Fire 12182
Fox at Drummer's Darkness, The 16404
Fox Farm 5136
Fox Hole, The 16038
Fox Mykyta 6226
Fox Running 9953
Fox That Wanted Nine Golden Tails, The 9941
Fox Went Out on a Chilly Night, The 16088
Foxes and Wolves 14404
Foxes Three 2657
Foxtails, Ferns and Fish Scales 7118
Fractions Are Parts of Things 4828
Fran Tarkenton (Burchard) 2607
Fran Tarkenton (Libby) 10763
Fran Tarkenton (May) 11870
Fran Tarkenton (Smith) 15906

France 2285
France and the French 5278
Frances Face-maker 3812
Frances Willard 11788
Francie on the Run 17228
Francis Lee Jaques 9149
Francisco Coronado 9202
Francisco Coronado and the Seven Cities of Gold 16583
François and the Langouste 14852
Frank Luke, Balloon Buster 4037
Frankie and the Fawn 13772
Franklin Delano Roosevelt 16498
Franklin Stein 14121
Franklin Watts Concise Guide to Good Grooming for Boys 14944
Franklin's Tale, The 3308
Franz Kafka 4254
Freaky Friday 14548
Freckle Juice 1817
Freckles 13828
Fred, Fred, Use Your Head 9917
Freddie found a Frog 12643
Freddy the Detective 2319
Freddy's Book 12755
Frederic Remington 13545
Frederick 10877
Frederick Banting 15500
Frederick Douglass (Bontemps) 1917
Frederick Douglass (Graves) 7193
Frederick Douglass (Patterson) 13382
Frederick Douglass Fights for Freedom 4569
Frederick's Alligator 13567
Frederik med Bilen/Frederik and the Bus 11814
Free 16334
Free as a Frog 8323
Free at Last 1918
Free but Not Equal 15390
Free Nation, A 2342
Free Spirit 8098
Free Throw 12713
Free to Be You and Me 9884
Free Woman 11979
Freedom Bound 2505
Freedom Crossing 3512
Freedom for a Cheetah 3158
Freedom from Bondage 639
Freedom Now! 9885
Freedom Ship of Robert Smalls, The 12091
Freedom Star, The 11813
Freedom Trail 18037
Freelon Starbird 15953

Freeman 3237
Freestyle Swimming 14817
Freewheeling of Joshua Cobb,
  The 8330
Freezing Point 9557
French Detection, The 17423
French Explorers of America,
  The 2519
French Explorers of North Amer-
  ica 31
French Founders of North Amer-
  ica and Their Heritage, The
  8431
French in America, The 10134
French Legends, Tales and Fairy
  Stories 13652
French Lieutenant, The 3446
Frenchmen, Desire, Good Children
  3298
Frere Jacques 7964
Fresh as a Daisy, Neat as a Pin
  18139
Fresh, Canned and Frozen 18140
Fresh Cider and Pie 2099
Fresh Fish and Chips 524
Friction All Around 13684
Friday Night Is Papa Night
  16015
Friday Nights and Robert 9619
Friday's Tunnel 17288
Fridtjof Nansen 1583
Friedrich 14348
Friend 18407
Friend Can Help, A 1540
Friend in the Park, A 997
Friend Is "Amie," A 16213
Friend Is Someone Who Likes You,
  A 547
Friend Monkey 16970
Friend of Miguel 11747
Friend of the Singing One, The
  6137
Friend Within the Gates 7343
Friendly Beasts, The 972
Friendly Dolphins, The 10348
Friendly Wolf, The 6945
Friendly Woods, The 8650
Friends (Dunn) 5140
Friends, The (Guy) 7532
Friends and Enemies 12286
Friends Are Like That! 3360
Friends! Friends! Friends!
  9167
Friends of the Loony Lake Mon-
  ster, The 1890
Friends of the Road 16025
Friendship Hedge, The 12908

Fright in the Forest, A 13120
Frightened Forest, The 17064
Fritzi's Winter 3247
Frog and Toad All Year 10992
Frog and Toad Are Friends 10993
Frog and Toad Together 10994
Frog Band and the Mystery of Lion
  Castle, The 15912
Frog Band and the Onion Seller,
  The 15913
Frog Goes to Dinner 11927
Frog in the Coconut Shell 15556
Frog in the Well, The 16998
Frog Prince, The (Canfield) 2895
Frog Prince, The (Tarcov) 16654
Frog Went A-Courtin' 10246
Frog, Where Are You? 11928
Frogmen, The 17811
Frogs and Toads of the World
  15718
Frogs, Toads, Salamanders and
  How they Reproduce 13354
From A to Z 3832
From Afar It Is an Island 12559
From Anna 10935
From Apple Seed to Applesauce
  9275
From Bush to City 1567
From Casablanca to Berlin 1777
From Early American Paintbrushes
  226
From Famine to Fame 8475
From Fins to Hands 14148
From Footpaths to Freeways 14796
From Ghetto to Glory 6788
From Ice Set Free 3590
From Idea into House 12616
From Inside Scotland Yard 15191
From King Boggen's Hall to
  Nothing-at-All 10595
From Lew Alcindor to Kareem Abdul
  Jabbar 7822
From Lupita's Hill 6127
From Many Lands 5306
From Morn to Midnight 12509
From One Ancestor 18496
From One Cell to Many Cells 18497
From One Drop of Water 12721
From Pearl Harbor to Okinawa
  1778
From Pigeons to People 7586
From Pond to Prairie 13958
From Poverty to Prosperity 155
From Slave to Abolitionist 17529
From Slovenia--to America 13972
From Stones to Skyscrapers 1545
From the Ashes 16557

From the Basque Kitchen 14253
From the Mixed-Up Files of Mrs. Basil E. Frankweiler 9989
From the Progressive Era to the Great Depression 9523
From the Roots 9109
From Trails to Superhighways 13275
From Whole Log to No Log 10640
Front Court Hex 3418
Frontier Leaders and Pioneers 8010
Frontier Living 17040
Frontiers of Dance 16762
Frowning Prince, The 9249
Frozen Fire 8657
Fruit Is Born, A 7469
Fruits We Eat 5808
Fuel for Today and Tomorrow 10509
Fuerza de la gacela, La 17263
Fulani Boy 18003
Full Moons 2509
Fullback Fury 2988
Fumio and the Dolphins 12636
Fun and Experiments with Light 6300
Fun and Festival from Africa 18314
Fun Food Factory, The 12788
Fun for One or Two 2945
Fun in American Folk Rhymes 18243
Fun with Chemistry 6301
Fun with Clay 10503
Fun with Cooking 6294
Fun with Crewel Embroidery 18076
Fun with French 4078
Fun with Growing Things 5250
Fun with Lines and Curves 5385
Fun with Naturecraft 12632
Fun with Pencil and Paper 10504
Fun with Photography 10375
Fun with Puppets 2287
Fun with Science 6302
Fun with Spanish 4076
Fun with the New Math 12134
Fun with Your Fingers 8031
Funniest Story Book Ever, The 14988
Funny Bags 13609
Funny Bananas 11389
Funny-bone Dramatics 2946
Funny Friend from Heaven, A 10019
Funny Little Woman, The 12498

Funny Magic 18341
Funny Number Tricks 18342
Funny Old Bag, The 17657
Funny Questions and Funny Answers 17875
Funny Side of Science, The 1532
Funny Stories to Read or Tell 11155
Fur Magic 12936
Fur Trader of the North 16584
Furious Flycycle, The 17399
Furl of Fairy Wind, A 8779
Further Tales of Mr. Pengachoosa 14768
Fury on Ice 8893
Future Kin 5401
Future of Hooper Toote, The 8508

- G -

GT Challenge 16054
G. Washington 6311
Gabon 3005
Gabriel 5027
Gabrielle and Selena 4857
Gadget Book, The 17689
Galaxies 741
Gale Sayers 11871
Galileo and the Magic Numbers 14614
Gallant Women 15921
Gallery-Wonders 7231
Gallimaufry 7232
Gallinita Costurera y Otros Cuentos, La 13064
Galong, River Boy of Thailand 16079
Galumph 10265
Gambia 3006
Game, The 5066
Game of Baseball, The 5497
Game of Basketball 17218
Game of Catch, A 4282
Game of Dark, A 11954
Game of Football, The 12779
Game of Functions, A 6401
Game on Thatcher Island, The 4799
Game Time 7705
Gamebreakers of the NFL 7518
Games 1042
Games (and How to Play Them) 14509
Games and Puzzles You Can Make

Yourself 17690
Games and Sports the World
Around 8763
Games and Stunts for Schools,
Camps and Playgrounds
12546
Games for a Rainy Day 13707
Games for Boys and Girls 7711
Games of the American Indian
1003
Games the Indians Played, The
10379
Gammage Cup, The 9679
Gandhi 5230
Gang Girl 6002
Gao of the Ivory Coast 15212
Garabatos 14565
Garage de los Animales, El 6546
Garbage Can Cat, The 15481
Garden Is Doing Fine, The 5683
Garden of Abdul Gasazi, The
17188
Garden of Broken Glass 12764
Gardener of the Dark Forest,
The 11679
Gardening Book, A 17476
Gardening ... Naturally 5798
Gargantua the Mighty Gorilla
6897
Garland for Gandhi, A 9029
Garram the Hunter 1615
Garranane 8902
Garth Pig and the Ice Cream
Lady 14164
Gasoline Buggy of the Duryea
Brothers, The 9013
Gasoline Cowboy 6683
Gassire's Lute 8973
Gaston, the Green-Nosed Alligator
14312
Gaston's Ghastly Green Thumb
10931
Gata como hay pocas, Una 15130
Gateway States, The 6242
Gatherers, The 9086
Gathering of Days, A 1793
Gatitos Mellizos, Los 15355
Gaudenzia, Pride of the Palio
8071
Gay-Neck 12543
Gazan the Warthog 11730
Gee Whillikins 15483
Geese Are Back 11621
Geese Fly High, The 9150
Geeta and the Village School
16774
General Billy Mitchell 12380

General Billy Mitchell, Champion of
Air Defense 2660
General Billycock's Pigs 13407
General's Lady 6028
Generations of Denial 16683
Genesis Two 4581
Genghis Khan and the Mongol Horde
10209
Genie of Sutton Place, The 15259
Gennet Lives in Ethiopia 6124
Gente y las cosas en el Uruguay
de 1830, La 12060
Gentle Ben 12426
Gentle Desert, The 13959
(George) 9990
George and Martha 11709
George and Martha Encore 11710
George and the Ferocious Ferblund-
get 1785
George and the Goblins 8233
George Carver 16274
George Morrison 10005
George Pullman 12598
George Rogers Clark (De Leeuw)
4699
George Rogers Clark (Lee) 10493
George Rogers Clark (Lockridge)
11014
George Rogers Clark (Miller)
12227
George Rogers Clark (Nolan)
12877
George Rogers Clark (Wilkie)
17933
George, the Babysitter 8728
George, the Drummer Boy 1400
George Washington (d'Aulaire)
4552
George Washington (Foster) 6142
George Washington (Graff) 7115
George Washington (Judson) 9421
George Washington (Lee) 10494
George Washington (Steiner)
16217
George Washington and the First
Balloon Flight 10848
George Washington and the Making
of a Nation 4365
George Washington Carver (Epstein)
5498
George Washington Carver (Thomas)
16812
George Washington Carver (Towne)
16950
George Washington Carver (White)
17783
George Washington's Breakfast

6387

George Washington's World 6143

Georgia Colony, The 2359

Georgia from Plum Orchard to Plum Nelly 15209

Georgie 2237

Georgie and the Noisy Ghost 2238

Georgie and the Robbers 2239

Georgie Goes West 2240

Georgie to the Rescue 2241

Georgie's Capital 4058

Georgie's Christmas Carol 2242

Georgie's Halloween 2243

Georgina and the Dragon 9826

Gerald Ford 12083

Gerald R. Ford 14

Geraldine the Music Mouse 10878

Gerbil for a Friend, A 13274

Gerbils 15685

German Hero-Sagas and Folktales 13653

German Immigrants in America 8476

Germans Helped Build America 6699

Germans in America, The (Kunz) 10135

Germans in America (Wittke) 18169

Germs Make Me Sick 5004

Geronimo (Grant) 7173

Geronimo (Syme) 16585

Geronimo (Wilson) 18070

Geronimo (Wyatt) 18332

Gertie and Gus 17658

Gertie the Duck 6756

Gertrude Kloppenberg, Private 8548

Gertrude Kloppenberg II 8549

Gertrude Stein 2665

Gertrude the Goose Who Forgot 6495

Gertrude's Pocket 12183

Getting Along in Your Family 12678

Getting It All Together 4887

Getting Nowhere 7284

Getting Rid of Roger 11831

Getting Smarter 5896

Getting Something on Maggie Marmelstein 15460

Getting Started in Treasure Hunting 15869

Getting to Know Africa's French Community 13068

Getting to Know Alaska 2170

Getting to Know Algeria 4823

Getting to Know American Indians Today 16832

Getting to Know Australia 13305

Getting to Know Brazil 2171

Getting to Know Canada 14584

Getting to Know Egypt, U.A.R. 17465

Getting to Know Hong Kong 9405

Getting to Know India 10293

Getting to Know Indonesia 16675

Getting to Know Iran and Iraq 875

Getting to Know Israel 9406

Getting to Know Japan 9107

Getting to Know Kenya 8897

Getting to Know Lebanon 2172

Getting to Know Liberia 4264

Getting to Know Mexico 7027

Getting to Know New York State 5874

Getting to Know Nigeria 13069

Getting to Know Ourselves 3663

Getting to Know Pakistan 10294

Getting to Know Puerto Rico 14585

Getting to Know Saudi Arabia 13631

Getting to Know South Africa 8898

Getting to Know Southern Rhodesia, Zambia and Malawi 3594

Getting to Know Tanganyika see Getting to Know Tanzania

Getting to Know Tanzania 9407

Getting to Know Thailand 826

Getting to Know the Central Himalayas 14177

Getting to Know the Congo River 14451

Getting to Know the Hudson River 5875

Getting to Know the Mississippi River 4265

Getting to Know the Missouri River 17271

Getting to Know the Ohio River 12878

Getting to Know the Philippines 16939

Getting to Know the River Ganges 16014

Getting to Know the Sahara 9408

Getting to Know the Suez Canal 2643

Getting to Know the Virgin Islands, U.S.A. 8432

Getting to Know the World Health

Organization   15928
Getting to Know Virginia   16535
Getting to Know You   14948
Gettysburg (Kantor)   9484
Gettysburg (Monjo)   12337
Ghana   3007
Ghana and Ivory Coast   13521
Ghana Folk Tales   76
Ghana in Pictures   18528
Ghost and the Magic Saber, The   16549
Ghost Around the House, A   11415
Ghost Belonged to Me, The   13448
Ghost Dance Messiah   912
Ghost Dance on Coyote Butte   14773
Ghost Diviners, The   11316
Ghost Dog of Killicut   5378
Ghost Garden, The   5759
Ghost in a Four-Room Apartment   14122
Ghost in the Capitol   1835
Ghost in the Far Garden ...,   The   11602
Ghost in the Noonday Sun, The   6005
Ghost Lane   4398
Ghost Named Fred, A   1401
Ghost Next Door, The   16115
Ghost of Bally-hooly, The   3194
Ghost of Black Hawk Island   4847
Ghost of Five Owl Farm, The   6472
Ghost of Follonsbee's Folly, The   8168
Ghost of Opalina ..., The   869
Ghost of Padre Island   15705
Ghost of Peg-leg Peter and Other Stories of Old New York, The   9096
Ghost of the Gravestone Hearth, The   7927
Ghost of Thomas Kempe, The   10955
Ghost of Windy Hill, The   2556
Ghost on Saturday Night, The   6006
Ghost on the Steppe   8464
Ghost Paddle   8658
Ghost Ships of the Great Lakes   2042
Ghost Story (Gray)   7206
Ghost Story, A (Martin)   11726
Ghost Town for Sale   17538
Ghost Town Mystery, The   143

Ghost Towns of the West   2711
Ghost Towns of Wyoming   12217
Ghost with the Halloween Hiccups, The   12414
Ghostly Folktales   9097
Ghosts, The (Barber)   1066
Ghosts (Simon)   15746
Ghosts and Goblins   7746
Ghosts I Have Been   13449
Ghosts of Glencoe, The   8780
Ghosts of the Carolinas   14430
Ghosts the Indians Feared, The   10380
Ghosts Who Went to School, The   16051
Gianni and the Ogre   11640
Giant, The   5083
Giant Book, The   4738
Giant Book of Sport   4589
Giant Book of Strange but True Sport Stories, The   10913
Giant Devil-Dingo, The   14692
Giant Golden Book of Mathematics, The   105
Giant Jam Sandwich, The   11075
Giant John   10995
Giant Leap, The   4321
Giant Nursery Book of Things That Go, The   18481
Giant Panda at Home, The   14143
Giant Sandwich, The   167
Giant Snakes and Other Amazing Reptiles   18141
Giant Under the Snow, The   7069
Giant Walked Among Them, A   6868
Giants!   14917
Giants' Feast, The   1859
Giant's Farm, The   18408
Giants Go Camping, The   18409
Giants of Space   16775
Giants on the Earth   13544
Gift, The (Balet)   1015
Gift, The (Dickinson)   4893
Gift, A (Fregosi)   6309
Gift-Bear for the King, A   12057
Gift for the Children, A   2486
Gift from the Bride, A   4290
Gift from the Mikado, A   6036
Gift of Gold   2744
Gift of Hawaii, The   1057
Gift of Magic, A   5123
Gift of the Deer, The   8568
Gift of the Forest   15795
Gift of the Mmoatia   591
Gift of the River   11990
Gifts from the Greeks   2049

Gifts of the Child Christ, The
  11300
Gigantic Balloon, The 13303
Gila Monster, The 8249
Gilberto and the Wind 5561
Gilberto y el Viento 5562; see
  also Gilberto and the Wind
Gildaen 2472
Gilgamesh 2465
Gillespie and the Guards 5345
Gilly Gilhooley 4945
Ginger Horse, The 4466
Ginger Pye 5548
Gingerbread 14890
Gingerbread Boy, The 6498
Gingerbread Man, The 656
Ginnie and Geneva 18262
Ginnie and Geneva Cookbook
  18263
Ginnie and Her Juniors 18264
Ginnie and the Mystery Cat
  18265
Ginnie and the Mystery Light
  18266
Ginnie Joins In 18267
Ginny Harris on Stage 5890
Giraffe, the Silent Giant 15066
Giraffes at Home 3998
Girasol de la Mañana 5829
Girl and the Goatherd ..., The
  12744
Girl Called Al, A 7285
Girl from Nowhere, The 17350
Girl from Puerto Rico, The 3867
Girl from Two Miles High, The
  12329
Girl Grows Up, A 5745
Girl in the Opposite Bed, The
  703
Girl Inside, The 5614
Girl Like Me, A 5615
Girl Like Tracy, A 4246
Girl Missing 12955
Girl of the Limberlost, A 13829
Girl of the North Country, A
  8670
Girl on the Yellow Giraffe, The
  8209
Girl Scout Cookbook 6870
Girl Scout Story, The 4700
Girl Soldier and Spy 8339
Girl Who Cried Flowers ..., The
  18410
Girl Who Had No Name, The
  14044
Girl Who Loved the Wind, The
  18411

Girl Who Slipped Through Time,
  The 8048
Girl Who Was a Cowboy, The 10035
Girl Who Would Rather Climb Trees,
  The 15067
Girl Who Wouldn't Talk, The 6992
Girl with a Donkey Tail, The 14510
Girl with a Pen 10170
Girl with Spunk, The 16111
Girls Are Equal Too 2950
Girls Are Girls and Boys Are Boys
  7077
Girls' Basketball 1089
Girls Can Be Anything 9907
Girls Can Too 8590
Girls' Gymnastics 17373
Girls in Africa 1584
Girls in the Velvet Frame, The
  6764
Give a Guess 12233
Give Dad My Best 3838
Give Me Freedom 11471
Give Me Your Hand 4710
Giving Tree, The 15701
Glacier Tracks 16633
Glaciers 11011
Glad Man, The 7031
Gladiola Garden 12804
Gladys Told Me to Meet Her Here
  15461
Glass Ball, The 11955
Glass House at Jamestown 4939
Glass Man and the Golden Bird,
  The 11641
Glass Mountain ..., The 10289
Glass Phoenix, The 3531
Glass Room, The 16948
Glass Slipper, The 5676
Glass, Stones and Crown 14511
Glassblower's Children, The 7429
Glassmakers, The 5943
Glenda 17110
Gliders 9758
Glimpse of Eden, A 396
Global Food Shortage, The 13522
Global Jigsaw Puzzle 9784
Globe for the Space Age, The 8223
Globo de Papel, El 17329
Gloomy Gus 12427
Glooskap's Country ... 11458
Glorious Age in Africa, A 3437
Glorious Christmas Soup Party, The
  7576
Glorious Hour of Lt. Monroe, The
  7703
Glory Horse, The 11546
Glory in the Flower 9321

Glowing in the Dark 16417
Glue Fingers 3419
Go and Catch a Flying Fish 16351
Go and Hush the Baby 2785
Go Away, Dog 12865
Go, Dog, Go! 5225
Go Find Hanka! 4309
Go for Six 9064
Go, Indians! 7612
Go Saddle the Sea 183
Go, Team, Go 17049
Go Tell Aunt Rhody (Aliki) 302
Go Tell Aunt Rhody (Quackenbush) 14024
Go to Bed! 8591
Go to It, You Dutchman! 16978
Go Up the Road 10223
Goal! A Soccer Handbook for Young Players 7788
Goalkeepers Are Different 6877
Goat in the Rug, The 1789
Goats of Agadez, The 5458
Goats Who Killed the Leopard, The 7885
Gobble, Growl, Grunt 16089
Goblin, a Wild Chimpanzee 16732
Goblin Market 14667
Goblin Under the Stairs, The 2833
Goblins Giggle ..., The 1046
God Wash the World and Start Again 7132
Gods in Winter, The 12194
God's Trombones 9286
Goggles 9594
Gogo Gets There 13372
Going Back 10956
Going Barefoot 5912
Going for a Walk with a Line 11198
Going, Going, Gone? 11711
Going into Hospital 386
Going on Sixteen 3195
Going Out in the Car and Other Stories 6081
Going the Distance 8529
Going to a Moonlight Play 8967
Going to Moscow 4946
Going to School in 1776 11019
Going to the Sun 6735
Going to the Westward, A 10569
Going to the Zoo with Roger Caras 2909
Going to Waste 11712
Gold and Gods of Peru 1205
Gold City Girl 18186
Gold Cup Rookies 16053

Gold Disc of Coosa, The 2434
Gold Dust and Petticoats 1463
Gold Rush 13870
Golda 11607
Golda Meir Story, The 4570
Golden Age of Railroads, The 8435
Golden Animal A.B.C., The see Big Golden Animal ABC
Golden Book of Astronomy, The see New Golden Book of Astronomy, The
Golden Book of Crafts and Hobbies 8767
Golden Book of Fun and Nonsense, The 17156
Golden Book of Indian Crafts and Lore 8768
Golden Book of the Civil War, The 5999
Golden Book of the Mysterious, The 17581
Golden Circle, The 1951
Golden Coyote, The 16829
Golden Crane, The 18360
Golden Days of Greece, The 4018
Golden Fleece and the Heroes Who Lived Before Achilles 3877
Golden Footprints, The 18370
Golden Future, The 16185
Golden Gate 539
Golden Goblet, The 11371
Golden Happy Book of ABC, The 5748
Golden Hive, The 1317
Golden Horseshoe, The 3681
Golden Impala, The 14597
Golden Journey, The 1850
Golden Key, The 11301
Golden Mare, The 4126
Golden Name Day, The 10853
Golden Picture Dictionary, The 13039
Golden Slippers (Bontemps) 1919
Golden Slippers, The (Shermaun) 15553
Golden Song Book, The 17756
Golden Swans, The 10111
Golden Touch, A 9242
Golden Treasury of Poetry, The 17157
Golden Vanity, The 10247
Golden Venture, The 6070
Goldenrod 16949
Goldfish 18542
Goldie the Dollmaker 6974
Goldwater Kachina Doll Collection, The 7025

Golem, The 11287
Golf Techniques 15926
Golfing Greats 17219
Golito y un emisario de la cuarta dimension 169
Gollywhopper Egg, The 14512
Gondolier of Venice, The 10056
Gone and Back 1402
Gone-Away Lake 5464
Gone Is Gone 6464
Gone to Texas 18274
Gongong Man and Other Verses for the Very Young, The 5462
Good and Bad Feelings 16199
Good Bird, The 17768
Good Bugs and Bad Bugs in Your Garden 8403
Good-by to Stony Crick 1957
Good-bye, Chicken Little 2786
Good-bye, Funny Dumpy-Lumpy 17360
Good-bye, Kitchen 9486
Good-Bye, My Lady 16414
Good-Bye to the Jungle 16953
Good-Byes of Magnus Marmalade, The 13163
Good Drug and the Bad Drug, The 11696
Good Ethan 6179
Good for Nothing Prince, The 18013
Good Friends Come in Many Shapes 8521
Good Greenwood, The 14291
Good Guys and the Bad Guys, The 12319
Good Hunting, Little Indian 13290
Good Land, The 5512
Good Lemonade 718
Good Luck, Arizona Man 1451
Good-Luck Feather, The 7913
Good Luck Spider and Other Bad Luck Stories, The 12065
Good Luck to the Rider 13637
Good Master 15341
Good Morning to You, Valentine 8592
Good Morning, Whale 2290
Good Morrow, The 12909
Good News 4437
Good Night 3682
Good Night Little ABC 10057
Good Night Little One 10058
Good-Night, Owl! 8835
Good Night Richard Rabbit 10059

Good, Says Jerome 3627
Good Stones 5479
Good Wife, Good Wife 4888
Good Work, Amelia Bedelia 13291
Goodbye, Arnold 14495
Goodbye, Dove Square 11481
Goodbye, Hello 17712
Goodbye, Mr. Chips 8204
Goodbye River, Goodbye 12066
Goodbye to the Purple Sage 1452
Goodliest Land, The 14431
Goodnight, Andrew: Goodnight, Craig 15462
Goodnight Moon 2389
Goodnight, Orange Monster 10797
Goody Hall 843
Goof That Won the Pennant, The 9464
Goose That Was a Watchdog, The 7934
Goose That Went to Hollywood 1571
Goosehill Gang and a Stitch-in-Time Solution, The 3398
Gopher in the Garden and Other Animal Poems, A 13885
Gopher Reader 13752
Gopher Reader II 13753
Gopher Tails for Papa 14577
Gordie Howe (Batson) 1176
Gordie Howe (Fischler) 5898
Gordon Goes Camping 2252
Gordon Parks (Harman) 7733
Gordon Parks (Turk) 17055
Gordon's House 2253
Gorgon's Head, The 15349
Gorilla Did It, The 7965
Gorilla Gorilla 5789
Gorillas 11283
Governors of Ohio, The 7110
Gozo's Wonderful Kite 9300
Gracie 14434
Graciela 12332
Grains of Pepper 7813
Gran at Coalgate 3212
Gran Cesar, El 14761
Gran dragon, El 16941
Grand Papa and Ellen Aroon 12338
Grand Prix 11872
Grand Prix at the Glen 9014
Grand Prix Driver 2761
Grand Prix Monaco 727
Grand Slam 2587
Grandfather and I 2495
Grandfather Rock 12489
Grandfather Stories of the Navahos 9248

Grandfather Stories of the Navajos 2851
Grandfather Tales 3301
Grandma Didn't Wave Back 1805
Grandma Is Somebody Special 7005
Grandma Moses 7194
Grandma's Beach Surprise 10924
Grandmother and I 2496
Grandmother Came from Dworitz 17311
Grandmother Lucy Goes on a Picnic 18234
Grandmother Lucy in Her Garden 18235
Grandmother Oma 9888
Grandmother Told Me 17400
Grandmother's Pictures 4163
Grandpa 1942
Grandpa and Me 6672
Grandpa Had a Windmill, Grandma Had a Churn 9005
Grandpa, Me and Our House in the Tree 9849
Grandparents Around the World 14166
Grandpa's Farm 6061
Grandpa's Ghost Stories 6062
Grandpa's Long Red Underwear 15101
Grandpa's Maria 8033
Granite Harbor 1659
Granja saltimbanqui, La 13231
Granny and the Desperadoes 13292
Granny and the Indians 13293
Granny's Fish Story 10183
Granny's Wonderful Chair 2437
Graph Games 6241
Graphology 830
Graphs 11121
Grass Pipe, The 3829
Grass Rope, A 11956
Grass Tower, The 12576
Grasshopper to the Rescue 2919
Grasshopper Year 10238
Grasslands 6965
Gravity 1517
Gravity at Work and Play 5449
Gravity Is a Mystery 2129
Gray Duck Catches a Friend 694
Graywings 7091
Greased Lightning 12922
Great Accidents in Science That Changed the World 12133
Great American Authors 7988

Great American Book of Sidewalk, Stoop, Dirt, Curb and Alley Games, The 5835
Great American Fighter Pilots of World War II 11053
Great American Naturalists 3664
Great American Negroes 14339
Great American Negroes in Verse 4350
Great American Nurses 3847
Great Animal Land, The 11129
Great Aquarium Book, A 14922
Great Auto Racing Champions 13089
Great Balloon Race, The 16874
Great Baseball Pitchers 2321
Great Big Box Book, The 12952
Great Big Dummy, The 15119
Great Big Elephant and the Very Small Elephant, The 15363
Great Big Enormous Turnip, The 16920
Great Big Ugly Man Came Up and Tied His Horse to Me, A 17015
Great Bow, The 11516
Great Brain, The 5970
Great Brain at the Academy, The 5971
Great Brain Does It Again, The 5972
Great Brain Reforms, The 5973
Great Cat Chase, The 11929
Great Catchers of the Major Leagues 18493
Great Christmas Kidnapping Caper, The 17210
Great Civilizations of Ancient Africa 2315
Great Constitution, The 3910
Great Custard Pie Panic, The 4109
Great Dane Thor, The 5691
Great Day for Up 15373
Great Day in China 11163
Great Day in Ghana 9576
Great Day in Israel 15407
Great Declaration, The 3911
Great Energy Search, The 8949
Great Fire, The 4885
Great Fish, The 13339
Great Geppy, The 5084
Great Ghost Rescue, The 8876
Great Gilly Hopkins, The 13368
Great Goalies of Pro Hockey 13181
Great-Grandfather in the Honey Tree 16552
Great Grandmother Goose 4071
Great-Great Uncle Henry's Cats

1665
Great Green Apple War, The
9918
Great Green Turkey Creek Monster, The   6063
Great Hamster Hunt, The   1771
Great Hitters of the Major Leagues
7124
Great Houdini, The   17985
Great House, The   7738
Great Ideas of Science   742
Great Indian Chiefs   14571
Great Indian Tribes   9087
Great Jewish Women   10656
Great Lakes, The (Allen)   352
Great Lakes, The (Barry)   1127
Great Lakes, The (Outdoor World)
13208
Great Lakes Frontier, The
3139
Great Lakes Indians   10124
Great Lakes Nature Guide   8096
Great Lakes Sailor   14373
Great Lakes Shipwrecks and Survivals   14140
Great Lakes Steam Vessels   477
Great Lakes Story, The   3116
Great Latin Sports Figures   8970
Great McGoniggle Rides Shotgun,
The   4110
Great Minu, The   18065
Great Miracle, A   12477
Great Moments in Auto Racing
13182
Great Moments in Pro Football
8486
Great Moments in Stock Car
Racing   16133
Great Monsters of the Movies
5254
Great Negroes, Past and Present
58
Great Olympic Champions   4863
Great Parade, The   7416
Great Pass Receivers of the NFL
475
Great Pennant Races of the Major
Leagues   7125
Great Pete Penney, The   16919
Great Pro Quarterbacks   5167
Great Pro Running Backs   5168
Great Quarterbacks, The   7519
Great Quillow, The   16855
Great Rain Robbery, The   12503
Great Rat Island Adventure, The
16620
Great Rebellion, The   16352

Great River Hunt, The   16229
Great Rookies of the Major Leagues
2322
Great Rulers of the African Past
4943
Great Ship Vasa, The   6227
Great Sports Humor   4590
Great Stories of the Great Lakes
2043
Great Swedish Fairy Tales   13077
Great Thirst, The   15227
Great upon the Mountain   2431
Great Upsets of the NFL   9493
Great Whales, The   18543
Great Wheel, The   10421
Great White, The   558
Great Women of Medicine   8742
Great Women Teachers   6029
Greatest, The   295
Greatest American Leaguers, The
8241
Greatest Cattle Drive, The   17723
Greatest Giants of Them All, The
7699
Greatest World Series Thrillers
14480
Greatest Yankees of Them All
14481
Greece   5816
Greedy Mariani, and Other Folktales
of the Antilles   3125
Greedy One, The   11748
Greek Myths   4019
Greeks in America   9358
Green and Something Else   12910
Green Blades Rising   4318
Green Christmas, A   10103
Green Eggs and Ham   15374
Green Eyes   1661
Green Flash and Other Tales, The
184
Green Gate, The   2900
Green Ginger Jar, The   9422
Green Grass and White Milk   303
Green Harpy at the Corner Store,
The   368
Green Hero, The   5606
Green Hills of Nendrum   522
Green Is for Growing   11133
Green Is Like a Meadow of Grass
10274
Green Roads, The   16809
Green Says Go   5413
Green Song, The   13741
Green Tree of Democracy, The   3451
Green Turtle Mysteries   17558
Greenbay Packers, The   11873

Greenhead 4510
Greenhorn on the Frontier 5883
Greensleeves 11372
Greentail Mouse, The 10879
Greenwitch, The 4184
Gregory Gray and the Brave
  Beast 5152
Gregory's Stitches 17304
Greg's Microscope 15280
Greta the Strong 15983
Grettir the Strong 12790
Grey Cloud 7114
Grey King, The 4085
Greyhound, The 7373
Greyling 18412
Griffin and the Minor Canon, The
  16331
Griffon's Nest, A 10649
Grillos y Ranas; una Fabula see
  Crickets and Frogs: A Fable
Grimbold's Other World 7218
Grinny 5960a
Griselda's New Year 15463
Grishka and the Bear 7485
Grizzly, The 9243
Grizzly Bear 6331
Grizzwold 8351
Grocery Store Botany 14083
Grouchy Ladybug, The 2923
Ground Afire 973
Groundhog's Horse 14543
Grover 3577
Grow a Plant Pet 5325
Growin' 7385
Growing Anyway Up 8002
Growing Story, The 10076
Growing Time 17512
Growing Up 4753
Growing Up Black 4562
Growing Up in Israel 8448
Growing Up in Old New England
  1568
Growing Up in the White House
  14234
Growing Up in 13th Century
  England 5110
Growing Up of Mary Elizabeth,
  The 11208
Growing Up Slim 1854
Growing Up Yanqui 4216
Grownups Cry, Too 7970
Grub the Bush Baby 7034
Guadalcanal Diary 16991
Guard Mouse, The 6262
Guardians, The 3406
Guardians of the House, The
  1972

Guardians of Tomorrow 8224
Guards for Matt 11066
Guarneri 17847
Gudgekin the Thistle Girl and Other
  Tales 6583
Guess What Grasses Do 14385
Guess What Rocks Do 14386
Guess Who My Favorite Person Is
  1238
Guest, The 11713
Guests in the Promised Land 8776
Guide Dog 3602
Guide to African History, A 4565
Guide to Nature Projects, A 13592
Guide to Ohio Outdoor Education
  Areas, A 12054
Guideposts to the Stars 13487
Guilty or Not? 14132
Guinea 3008
Guinea Pigs That Went to School,
  The 5766
Guitar, The 8193
Gulf Stream, The 2256
Gull 737 6736
Gulliver's Travels 16563
Gulls of Smuttynose Island, The
  15199
Gull's Way, The 4511
Gumdrop 1662
Gun Is Not a Toy, A 2204
Gunhilde and the Halloween Spell
  9454
Gunhilde's Christmas Booke 9455
Gunniwolf, The 7747
Guns of Darkness, The 15062
Gunshot Grand Prix, The 14809
Gus and Buster Work Things Out
  2294
Gus and the Baby Ghost 16781
Gus Was a Christmas Ghost 16782
Gussuk Boy 9195
Guy Can Be Wrong, A 14387
Guy Lenny 11968
Gwot! Horribly Funny Hairticklers
  12067
Gymnastics for Girls and Women
  14730
Gymnastics School 14074
Gyo Fujikawa's A to Z Picture Book
  6431
Gypsies, The 9971
Gypsy Laddie, The 14301

- H -

Habia una vez ... 14450
Habitantes del planeta inhabitable, Los 6555
Hada acaramelada, El 6428
Hadassah 648
Hah-Nee of the Cliff Dwellers 2541
Haiku: The Mood of Earth 784
Haiku: Vision in Poetry and Photography 785
Hail Columbia 1271
Hailstones and Halibut Bones 13131
Haji of the Elephants 10856
Hakon of Rogen's Saga 7845
Half a Kingdom 11350
Half-Breed 10224
Half-Brothers, The 10395
Half Magic 5198
Half Sisters, The 2959
Hallelujah 5370
Halloween (Borten) 1963
Halloween (Patterson) 13383
Halloween Kangaroo, The 10709
Halloween Party, The 496
Halloween Tree, The 2069
Halloween with Morris and Boris 18153
Halls of Lincoln's Greatness, The 12224
Hallucinogenic Plants 15123
Hamburger Book, The 13523
Hamburgers--And Ice Cream for Dessert 3643
Hamdaani 1632
Hamid and the Palm Sunday Donkey 5068
Hamilton Duck 6779
Hamilton Duck's Springtime Story 6780
Hamisi's Hardest Safari 4344
Hammerhead Light, The 16797
Hammet and the Highlanders 11367
Hamsters 15686
Han raptado a "Ney" 14877
Hand-Fighting Manual for Self-Defense and Sport Karate 12707
Hand-Me-Down House 12897
Hand of Apollo, The 3683
Hand Puppets 14651
Handbook for Emergencies, A 7255

Handbook of Adolescence, The 6768
Handmade Secret Hiding Place 8410
Handtalk 3281
Hang Gliding 13496
Hang Tough, Paul Mather 15851
Hangin' Out 17383
Hangin' Out with Cici 13348
Hanging On 6247
Hank 2282
Hank Aaron (Deegan) 4779
Hank Aaron (Gutman) 7520
Hank Aaron (Sullivan) 16464
Hank Aaron Clinches the Pennant 11874
Hank Aaron 715 5057
Hannah Courageous 11043
Hannah Herself 6199
Hannah's House 18258
Hannibal 9079
Hannibal and His 37 Elephants 8234
Hans and Peter 13584
Hans Brinker 4966
Hans Clodhopper 439
Hans in Luck 7394
Hansel and Gretel (Grimm Bros.) 7395
Hansel and Gretel (Wiesner) 17876
Hanukkah 15726
Hanukkah Book, The 14500
Hanukkah Story (Bial) 1627
Hanukkah Story, The (Hirsh) 8235
Happenings at North End School, The 3868
Happiness for Kimi 10329
Happiness Is a Warm Puppy 15134
Happy Apple Told Me 18511
Happy Birthday, Mole and Troll 9327
Happy Birthday Present, The 8015
Happy Birthdays Round the World 9291
Happy Christmas! (Bishop) 1673
Happy Christmas (Seymour) 15400
Happy Days, The (Ik) 8887
Happy Days (Nava) 12660
Happy Days (Price) 13913
Happy Days with Lonee and Nonee 18202
Happy Dolphins, The 3128
Happy Dromedary, The 6332
Happy Ever-After Book 9706
Happy Easter 17871
Happy Families 17954
Happy-Go-Lucky 17877

Happy Hanukkah Everybody 3262
Happy Horse, The 6310
Happy Hospital Surprises 16630
Happy Jack 3086
Happy Lion, The 5716
Happy Lion in Africa, The 5717
Happy Lion's Treasure, The 5718
Happy Lion's Vacation, The 5719
Happy Little Family 3169
Happy New Year 10756
Happy New Year Round the World
  9292
Happy Orpheline, The 2960
Happy Owls, The 13650
Happy Prince, The 17897
Happy Ranch 14214
Happy Sound, The 7146
Happy Valley, The 16610
Haran's Journey 16392
Hard Luck Horse 2344
Hard Scrabble Harvest 8915
Hardlucky 3241
Hare and Hyena 9822
Hare and the Bear ..., The
  11562
Hare and the Termites, The
  2354
Hare and the Tortoise, The
  (Galdone) 6499
Hare and the Tortoise, The (La
  Fontaine) 10189
Hare, Baboon and Their Friends
  7731
Hare's Race, The 1206
Hari the Jungle Lad 12544
Hark! Hark! The Dogs Do Bark
  1769
Harlem (Halliburton) 7622
Harlem (Young) 18442
Harlem Summer 17356
Harlequin and the Gift of Many
  Colors 3284
Harlequin Moth, The 15281
Harmony Ahead 9962
Harnessing the Sun 9929
Harold and the Purple Crayon
  9250
Harp of Fishbones and Other
  Stories, A 185
Harriet and the Promised Land
  10399
Harriet and the Runaway Book
  9308
Harriet Beecher Stowe (Rouverol)
  14715
Harriet Beecher Stowe (Widdener)
  17857

Harriet Beecher Stowe (Wise) 18147
Harriet Goes to the Circus 11533
Harriet the Spy 5979
Harriet Tubman (Grant) 7174
Harriet Tubman (Humphreville)
  8743
Harriet Tubman (Winders) 18104
Harriet Tubman, Guide to Freedom
  5499
Harrow and Harvest 17955
Harry and Shellburt 17237
Harry and the Lady Next Door
  18588
Harry by the Sea 18589
Harry Cat's Pet Puppy 15260
Harry Helps Out 9122
Harry Houdini 10047
Harry Is a Scaredy-Cat 1150
Harry S Truman 3848
Harry, the Dirty Dog 18590
Harry, the Fat Bear Spy 18078
Harry Truman 5624
Harry's Bee 2879
Hart Massey 3854
Harvest Feast, The 7748
Harvest of Russian Children's Lit-
  erature, A 12494
Harvesting the Sea 5799
Harvey S. Firestone 13276
Harvey's Hideout 8282
Hassan and the Spirits 18099
Hassan, Boy of the Desert 4492
Hassan in Egypt 11298
Hat-Shaking Dance and Other
  Ashanti Tales from Ghana, The
  4208
Hatching of Joshua Cobb, The
  8331
Hating Book, The 18602
Hattie Be Quiet, Hattie Be Good
  6453
Hattie Rabbit 6454
Hattie, the Backstage Bat 6263
Haunt Fox 9881
Haunt of High Island 17767
Haunted Boma, The 9823
Haunted Churchbell, The 2797
Haunted Ghost, The 2798
Haunted Houses 9759
Haunted Houses on Halloween 13384
Haunted Kitchen, The 17539
Haunted Mountain, The 8781
Haunted Summer 9376
Haunted Tower, The 2799
Haunting Air, A 6251
Haunting of America, The 479
Haunting of Ellen, The 15241

Haunting of Julie Unger, The 11175

Haunting Tales 8925

Have a Happy Measle, a Merry Mumps and a Cheery Chickenpox 1422

Have Space Suit--Will Travel 8020

Have You Seen a Comet? 13485

Have You Seen Boats? 13151

Have You Seen My Brother? 7471

Have You Seen My Cat? 2924

Have You Seen Roads? 13152

Have You Seen Trees? 13153

Have You Seen Wilhelmina Krumpf? 3306

Haven-Screamers, The 15557

Having a Friend 12171

Hawaii Nei 16609

Hawaiian Birdlife 1506

Hawaiian Myths of Earth, Sea and Sky 16839

Hawaiian Tales of Heroes and Champions 16840

Hawaiian Treasure 12981

Hawaiians, The 13882

Hawaii's Queen 16370

Hawk, I'm Your Brother 1239

Hawkstone, The 18014

Hayburners, The 15897

Hayes Story Reader of Young Black Americans 7920

Hayes-Tilden Election of 1876, The 17254

Haym Salomon 12196

Hazy Mountain 1687

He and She 8225

He Bear, She Bear 1496

He Is Your Brother 13317

He Looks This Way 4410

He Sailed with Captain Cook 1944

He Went with Magellan 9716

He Went with Marco Polo 9717

He Went with Vasco da Gama 9718

He Who Runs Far 6240

He Who Saw Everything 5737

Head to the West 8341

Headed for Trouble 14388

Headless Cupid, The 15968

Headlines 7610

Heads Up--Heels Down 467

Headsparks 3830

Hear Ye of Boston 4387

Hear Ye of Philadelphia 4388

Hear Your Heart 15596

Heart Disease 15687

Heart for Business, A 4701

Heart Man, The 12092

Heart of Ice 4652

Heart-of-Snowbird 11079

Heart of the Wood, The 15482

Heart to the Hawks, A 12501

Hearthstone in the Wilderness 1585

Heartland, The (Havighurst) 7862

Heartland, The (Havighurst--rev. ed.) 7863

Heartland, The (McLaughlin) 11442

Hearts Courageous 8105

Hearts, Cupids and Red Roses 1135

Heartsease 4894

Heat 17299

Heat and Fire 15207

Heat and Its Uses 115

Heat and Temperature 1423

Heather, Oak and Olive 16522

Heaven to Betsy 11106

Heavenly Host, The 743

Heavenly Tenants, The 11848

Heavyweight Champions, The 5159

Hebrew Alphabet Book, The 11665

Hector and Christina 5720

Hector Penguin 5721

Hector Protector and As I Went over the Water 15330

Heidi 16102

Heirs of the Ancient Maya 13914

Helen Keller (Bigland) 1646

Helen Keller (Davidson) 4571

Helen Keller (Graff) 7116

Helen Keller (Richards) 14336

Helen Keller (Tibble) 16864

Helen Keller (Wilkie) 17934

Helen Keller Story, The 13433

Helen Keller's Teacher 4572

Helen Oxenbury's ABC of Things 13222

Helena 7786

Helga's Dowry 4719

Helga's Magic 9729

Helicopter Pilot 2762

Helicopters 10681

Helicopters and Airplanes of the U.S. Army 4811

Hello, Aurora 17296

Hello, George Washington 8471

Hello, Henry 17333

Hello, Mexico 17646

Hello, Puerto Rico 17647

Hello, Small Sparrow 9276

Hello, the Boat 4257

Hell's Edge 16954

Help! Emergencies That Could Happen to You and How to Handle Them 17193
Help, Help, the Globolinks! 12080
Helter-Skelter 12527
Hemi: A Mule 2192
Henchmans at Home, The 2724
Henner's Lydia 4636
Henny Penny (Galdone) 6500
Henny Penny (Hutchinson) 8859
Henny-Penny (Stobbs) 16328
Henri Goes to the Mardi Gras 18310
Henrietta Goes to the Fair 8352
Henrietta Goes West 2941
Henrietta, the Wild Woman of Borneo 14616
Henry Aaron (Epstein) 5500
Henry Aaron (Hirshberg) 8242
Henry Aaron, Quiet Superstar see Up-to-Date Biography of Henry Aaron: Quiet Superstar, The
Henry and Beezus 3557
Henry and Ribsy 3558
Henry and the Clubhouse 3559
Henry and the Paper Route 3560
Henry Bear's Park 11495
Henry Explores the Mountains 16687
Henry-Fisherman 2377
Henry Ford (Caldwell) 2816
Henry Ford (Kelly) 9670
Henry Ford (Montgomery) 12363
Henry Ford (Paradis) 13277
Henry Ford and Mass Production 1128
Henry Ford, Boy with Ideas 198
Henry Ford, Engineer 12812
Henry Hudson (Carmer) 2982
Henry Hudson (Joseph) 9390
Henry Huggins 3561
Henry M. Stanley, the Man from Africa 383
Henry Possum 1599
Henry Reed, Inc. 14439
Henry Reed's Baby-Sitting Service 14440
Henry Reed's Big Show 14441
Henry Reed's Journey 14442
Henry the Castaway 16688
Henry the Explorer 16689
Henry 3 10114
Henry Woodward of Carolina see Surgeon Trader, Indian Chief
Henry's Dog Henry 2320

Henry's Lincoln 12813
Henry's Pennies 11462
Her Own Way 12357
Heracles the Strong 15350
Herbert Hoover 3897
Herbert's Treasure 11110
Herbie Capleenies 1941
Hercules 7156
Herdman's Daughter, The 3240
Here and Now Story Book 12283
Here Come the Dolphins! 7092
Here Come the Elephants! 7093
Here Comes Bobby Orr 9015
Here Comes Herb's Hurricane! 16288
Here Comes the Bus! 7954
Here Comes the Strikeout 9748
Here I Am! 1097
Here Is Alaska 16184
Here Is Mexico 4754
Here Is Your Career: Veterinarian 16320
Here Is Your Hobby: Archery 14680
Here Is Your Hobby: Fishing 12411
Here Is Your Hobby: Indian Dancing and Costumes 13868
Here Is Your Hobby: Skiing 6132
Here Is Your Hobby: Stamp Collecting 3228
Here Lies the Body 4111
Hereafterthis 9047
Here's Howie 11580
Here's Pippa Again! 1841
Here's Your Hobby 18499
Heritage of Music 5311
Heritage Sampler, The 8560
Herman the Helper 10060
Herman the Loser 8283
Hermes, Lord of the Robbers 13974
Hermit Boy, The 3383
Hermit Crab Lives in a Shell 16228
Hernando Cortes 9080
Hero Ain't Nothin' but a Sandwich, A 3373
Hero by Mistake, A 2180
Hero from Otherwhere, The 18015
Hero of Vincennes, The 16821
Hero Tales from the Age of Chivalry 17108
Heroes and Hero Tales of Michigan 6106
Heroes and Heroines of Liberia 8055
Heroes and Leaders of West Point

14191
Heroes in American Folklore 15421
Heroes of a Different Kind 10536
Heroes of American Jewish History 9504
Heroes of Greece and Troy 7247
Heroes of Polar Exploration 8614
Heroes of Pro Basketball 1534
Heroes of Puerto Rico 17024
Heroes of Stock Car Racing 10764
Heroes of Texas 331
Heroes of the Kalevala 4860
Heroes of the Major Leagues 13546
Heroes of the Olympics 8161
Heroic Nurses 11436
Heroin Was My Best Friend 1590
Heroine of Long Point, The 1464
Heroines of '76 580
Heroines of the Early West 14654
Heroines of the Sky 55
He's My Brother 10296
Hester 1151
Hester and Timothy 8427
Hester the Jester 15514
Hew Against the Grain 4356
Hex House 10650
Hey, Bug! And Other Poems About Little Things 8957
Hey Diddle Diddle Picture Book, The 2811
Hey, Ey, Ey, Lock! 6195
Hey Hey Man, The 6007
Hey-How for Halloween 8593
Hey, Look at Me! 7186
Hey Riddle Diddle! 13499
Hey, That's My Soul You're Stomping On 4135
Hey, What's Wrong with This One? 18176
Hezekiah Horton 16655
Hi, Cat! 9595
Hi Diddle Diddle 12514
Hi Fly 14656
Hi! Ho! The Rattlin' Bog 10248
Hi Jolly! 9882
Hi, Mister Robin 16999
Hi, Mrs. Mallory! 16815
Hi Neighbor Book No. 4 17174
Hi, New Baby 533
Hi There, High School 7971
Hibernian Nights 11455
Hickory 2420
Hidden Animals 15282
Hidden Forest, The 13114

Hidden Heroines 10236
Hidden Messages 17238
Hidden Treasure of Glaston, The 9217
Hidden World, The 13960
Hide-and-Seek 12135
Hide and Seek Fog 17000
Hideaway House 4708
Hiding Game, The 15515
Hiding Out 14538
Hiding the Bell 12408
Hieroglyphs for Fun 15193
Higgins and the Great Big Scare 3170
Higglety Pigglety Pop! 15331
High Arctic 16541
High Country 2974
High Country Canvas 2975
High Deeds of Finn MacCool, The 16523
High Elk's Treasure 15948
High Fly to Center 2989
High Heels for Jennifer 15888
High House, The 704
High in the Rockies 6218
High King, The 270
High Pasture, The 7734
High Ridge Gobbler 16221
High Sounds, Low Sounds 2130
High Water at Catfish Bend 2661
High Water Cargo 5013
High, Wide and Handsome and Their Three Tall Tales 12109
High Wind for Kansas 2834
Highdays and Holidays 54
Higher Than the Arrow 17197
Highest Balloon on the Common, The 3073
Highland Rebel 17595
Highlights of Puebloland 9362
Highlights of the Hill see Songs of the Sage
Highlights of the World Series 5160
Highpockets 17050
Hiking 2032
Hildilid's Night 14813
Hilili and Kilili, a Turkish Silly Tale 17430
Hill of Fire 10729
Hill of Little Miracles 540
Hill Road, The 11957
Hill That Grew, The 12010
Hill's End 16039
Hindu Boyhood, A 15561
Hinduism 5260
Hip, High-Prote, Low-Cal, Easy-

Does-It Cookbook, The 7910
Hippity Hopper, The 17469
Hippo Who Couldn't Stop Crying,
  The 12593
Hippopotamus Book, The 3145
His Enemy, His Friend 17051
His Indian Brother 18079
Hisako's Mysteries 17093
Hispano American Contributors
  to American Life 6210
Historia de Azulita y Rompeta-
  cones 14488
Historia de Nuestros Indios 251
Historia en cuentos, La 2803
Historia Verdadera de una Botella
  de Leche, La 6483
Historia Verdadera de una Gota
  de Miel 6484
Historic American Landmarks
  3783
Historic Fires of the West 526
Historic Kansas 17843
Historical Catastrophes: Earth-
  quakes 2331
Historical Catastrophes: Fires
  2435
Historical Catastrophes: Floods
  2332
Historical Sketches of Ontario
  13137
History of Colorado for Children
  5509
History of Ethiopia in Pictures,
  A 10306
History of Firearms, A 13571
History of Negro Humor in
  America, A 15022
History of Ohio, A 14610
History of the Indians of Puerto
  Rico 252
History of the Toronto Islands
  8254
Hit Hard! 15929
Hit the Bike Trail 14908
Hitching Post, The 4274
Hitters, The 2162
Hitting, Pitching, and Running--
  Maybe 13401
Hitting the Baseball 4780
Hitty 5851
Ho Fills the Rice Barrel 15541
Hoagie's Rifle Gun 12184
Hobberdy Dick 2230
Hobbies 15141
Hobbit, The 16915
Hobby Collections A-Z 14863
Hobnailed Boots 12879

Hobo Toad and the Motorcycle Gang
  18413
Hoboken Chicken Emergency, The
  13700
Hockey 5541
Hockey: Checking and Defensive
  Play 4781
Hockey for Beginners 17486
Hockey Girls, The 4112
Hockey Heroes 16465
Hockey--It's Your Game 13135
Hockey: Shooting 4782
Hockey: Skates and Skating 4783
Hockey: Stickhandling and Passing
  4784
Hockey Talk for Beginners 10914
Hockey Trick, The 4113
Hockey's Hall of Fame 12449
Hockey's Masked Men 5573
Hoddy Doddy 9707
Hodge-Podge Book, The 5432
Hog Butcher 5638
Hogan for the Bluebird, A 4331
Hogboon of Hell and Other Strange
  Orkney Tales, The 4348
Hoists, Cranes and Derricks 18569
Hokahey! 5014
Hokusai 14400
Hola Jesus 15353
Hold Fast to Dreams 1920
Hold Fast to Your Dreams 1724
Hold My Hand 18603
Hold Zero! 6737
Holdfast 1283
Holdup on Bootjack Hill 6644
Hole in the Dike, The 7239
Hole in the Tree, The 6738
Hole Is to Dig, A 10077
Holiday Cards for You to Make
  13999
Holiday Cook, The 10245
Holiday Gifts, Favors, and Decora-
  tions 14935
Holiday Hobbycraft 17504
Holiday Programs for Boys and
  Girls 5913
Holiday Puppets and Plays 14652
Holiday Round Up 3189
Holiday Song Book, The 14025
Holiday Story Book 3358
Holiday Tales of Sholom Aleichem
  14053
Holidays Around the World 6462
Hollering Sun 18236
Holly, Reindeer and Colored Lights
  1136
Holy Night, The 9414
Hombre de paja, El 3225

Hombres y oficios 2901
Home (Hearne) 7983
Home, A (Rudstrom) 14751
Home and Child Life in Colonial Days 5202
Home Before Dark 2221
Home Book of Animal Care 7515
Home Free 12567
Home from Far 10936
Home from the Hill 977
Home Is over the Mountain 16415
Home Is the North 12428
Home Is Where Your Feet Are Standing 18108
Home on the Range 7543
Home Run! 16466
Home Run Trick, The 4114
Home to My Valley 7240
Home with Aunt Florry, A 16621
Homecoming 4438
Homer Price 11237
Homer the Hunter 11670
Homerhenry 553
Homestead of the Free 5914
Homesteaders and Indians 10644
Hometown Stock Car Racing 7551
Homework Caper, The 10740
Homing Pigeons 18544
Hominy and His Blunt-Nosed Arrow 11789
Honest Thief, The 1663
Honestly, Katie John! 2835
Honey Hunters, The 575
Honey in the Rock 9859
Honeybees, The 14784
Hongry Catch the Foolish Boy 7133
Honk, The Moose 16379
Honor Bound 5054
Honor Sands 10484
Honorable Shirley Chisholm, The 8155
Honorable Sword, The 10711
Honschi 6882
Hoofprint on the Wind 3484
Hook a Fish, Catch a Mountain 6739
Hooks and Loops 10807
Hoop to the Barrel, A 14894
Hooray for Jasper 8632
Hooray for Me 3283
Hooray for Pig! 16260
Hoosier Boy 12284
Hoosier City 12880
Hoosier School-Boy, The 5288
Hop-high the Goat 1058

Hop on Pop 15375
Hop, Skim and Fly 8847
Hopi Bride at the Home Dance 16618
Hopi Indian Butterfly Dance, The 9118
Hopi Kachinas 9687
Hopi Way, The 5391
Horace Higby, Coxswain of the Crew 8134
Horas del Dia, Las 9232
Horatio 3644
Horatio's Birthday 3645
Horgle and the King's Soup 4149
Hormiguita cantora y el duende melodia, La 12419
Hormones 14365
Hornbill and the Tortoise and Another Story, The 3353
Horns of Plenty 559
Horombo, the Chief Who United His People 10542
Horrible Hepzibah 13897
Horse and His Boy, The 10688
Horse Called Dragon, A 7601
Horse Called Mystery, A 14275
Horse Came Running, A 4675
Horse Comes First, The 2836
Horse Family, The 8404
Horse for the Island, A 5294
Horse Fox X, Y, Z, A 12302
Horse Grows Up, A 14330
Horse Hunters, The 11329
Horse in Harry's Room, The 8353
Horse in the Camel Suit, The 5085
Horse Like Mr. Ragman, A 14413
Horse of Two Colors 992
Horse Talker 18004
Horse with Eight Hands 13638
Horse with the Easter Bonnet, The 16783
Horse Without a Head, The 1558
Horseback Riding 4867
Horseback Riding for Beginners 12034
Horsecatcher, The 14901
Horseman's Etiquette Book, The 4079
Horsemanship for Beginners 15826
Horsemen of the Western Plateaus 1752
Horses (Ferguson) 5823
Horses (May) 11875
Horses (Reddick) 14176
Horses and Foals 14050
Horses in Battle 390
Horses of America 16536

Horses of Anger 6114
Horses the Indians Rode, The 10381
Horseshoe Harry and the Whale 4702
Horton Hatches the Egg 15376
Horton Hears a Who! 15377
Hosannah the Home Run! 6030
Hosea Globe and the Fantastical Peg-Legged Chu 1306
Hosie's Alphabet 1160
Hosie's Aviary 1161
Hospital, A 4785
Hospital Book, The 5327
Hospital Is Where ..., The 15900
Hospital Story, A 16204
Hostage to Alexander 525
Hot Air Ballooning 12311
Hot Air Balloons 14075
Hot and Cold 15747
Hot as an Ice Cube 1012
Hot Day, The 7318
Hot Dog Man, The 11182
Hot Rod 5769
Hot Rod Rodeo 2019
Hot Rodding for Beginners 5261
Hot Shots of Pro Hockey 11492
Hotel for Dogs 5124
Hotheads 10616
Hotshot, The 15852
Houdini 9682
Hound and Bear 6455
Hound-Dog Man 6863
Hound of Ulster, The 16524
House at Pooh Corner, The 12246
House Cat 5884
House for Everyone, A 12172
House for Little Red, A 8201
House for Ten, A 11790
House Full of Mice, A 10868
House in Norham Gardens, The 10957
House in the Tree, The 3918
House Mouse, The 7770
House Next Door, The 16026
House of Arden, The 12734
House of Dies Drear, The 7659
House of Four Seasons 5178
House of Secrets, The 1217
House of Sixty Fathers, The 4675
House of Stairs 15831
House of the Four Winds, The 17330
House of Wings, The 2787
House on Charlton Street, The 4668

House on East 88th Street, The 17361
House on Liberty Street, A 17650
House on Mayferry Street, The 5137
House on Parchment Street, The 11428
House on Pendleton Block, The 17424
House on Stink Alley, The 12339
House on the Mountain, The 3646
House on the Roof, The 94
House That Jack Built, The 6228
House That Sailed Away, The 8836
House upon a Rock 13464
House with a Clock in Its Walls, The 1361
House with 100 Lights, The 11318
House Without a Christmas Tree, The 14498
Houseboat Girl 10570
Houseboat Summer 3684
Housebuilding for Children 17447
Household Stories 7396
Housenapper, The see Mindy's Mysterious Miniature
Houses Around the World 6056
Houses from the Sea 7094
Houses Keep the Weather Out 15975
Houses the Indians Built, The 10382
How a Law Is Made 16267
How a Little Girl Went to Africa 1633
How a Piglet Crashed the Christmas Party 18486
How a Rock Came to Be in a Fence on a Road Near a Town 14740
How a Seed Grows 9373
How and Why Wonder Book of North American Indians, The 16537
How and Why Wonder Book of Oceanography, The 15010
How Animals Behave 1424
How Animals Hide 11247
How Animals Learn 6250
How Animals Live Together 15283
How Animals Sleep 15284
How Animals Survive 8848
How Animals Tell Time 15285
How Animals Work for Us 17895
How Art and Music Speak to Us 16063
How Automobiles Are Made 4007
How Babies Are Made 534

How Big Is a Foot? 12617
How Big Is a Stick? 13756
How Big Is Big? 15091
How Birds Fly 6248
How Canada Got Its Capital 4154
How Democracy Failed 16569
How Did Numbers Begin? 15799
How Did We Find Out About Antarctica? 744
How Did We Find Out About Atoms? 745
How Did We Find Out About Black Holes? 746
How Did We Find Out About Comets? 747
How Did We Find Out About Electricity? 748
How Did We Find Out About Germs? 749
How Did We Find Out About Numbers? 750
How Did We Find Out the Earth Is Round? 751
How Djadja-em-ankh Saved the Day 11623
How Do I Feel? 15727
How Do I Put It On? 17553
How Do They Build It? 16467
How Do They Find It? 16468
How Do They Get Rid of It? 8206
How Do They Grow It? 16469
How Do They Make It? 16470
How Do They Package It? 16471
How Does a Czar Eat Potatoes? 14601
How Does It Feel to Be Old? 5664
How Does It Feel When Your Parents Get Divorced? 1541
How Does It Get There? 16472
How Far Is Berkeley? 3337
How Far Is Far? 17001
How Heredity Works 1425
How, Hippo! 2378
How I Came to Be a Writer 12679
How I Feel 1324
How I Hunted the Little Fellows 18529
How I Went Shopping and What I Got 3647
How Immigrants Contributed to Our Culture 16140
How Insects Communicate 13355
How Insects Grow 3948
How Juan Got Home 11608
How Kittens Grow 15286

How Lazy Can You Get? 12680
How Life Begins 13865
How Little and How Much 2131
How Man Began 7266
How Man Discovered His Body 14366
How Many Kids Are Hiding on My Block? 12116
How Many Miles to Babylon? 6180
How Many Miles to Sundown? 1272
How Money Works 13278
How Mrs. Santa Claus Saved Christmas 11335
How New Life Begins 12013
How Our Alphabet Grew 5108
How People Live in Africa 7336
How People Live in Australia 11740
How Plants Are Pollinated 14084
How Plants Travel 14085
How Puppies Grow 15287
How Santa Had a Long and Difficult Journey Delivering His Presents 10020
How Silly Can You Be? 17878
How Spider Saved Christmas 10061
How Spider Saved Halloween 10062
How Tevye Became a Milkman 10908
How the Animals Came to North America 11876
How the Children Stopped the Wars 17401
How the Chipmunk Got Its Stripes 3573
How the Devil Gets His Due 1600
How the Doctor Knows You're Fine 3707
How the Donkeys Came to Haiti 9273
How the Earth Was Satisfied 1787
How the Grinch Stole Christmas 15378
How the Indians Really Lived 1004
How the Left-Behind Beasts Built Ararat 5665
How the Leopard Got His Claws 38
How the Moolah Was Taught a Lesson ... 16884
How the People Sang the Mountains Up 10446
How the Pilgrims Came to Plymouth 7628
How the Rabbit Stole the Moon 12303
How the Rooster Saved the Day 10996
How the Sun Made a Promise and Kept It 1578

How the Sun Was Brought Back to the Sky   6846

How the True Facts Started in Simpsonville and Other Tales of the West   7921

How the Witch Got Alf   554

How the Withered Trees Blossomed   11829

How the World Got Its Color   8236

How They Grow   2475

How They Started   7653

How to Be a Nature Detective   15288

How to Be a Puppeteer   2050

How to Be a Successful Teenager   12078

How to Become King   16749

How to Bring Up Your Pet Dog   17143

How to Build a Better Mousetrap Car ...   14249

How to Care for Your Monster   2229

How to Count Like a Martian   16112

How to Count Sheep Without Falling Asleep   10523

How to Dig a Hole to the Other Side of the World   11487

How to Draw the Wild West   18484

How to Draw with Pen and Brush   18485

How to Eat a Poem and Other Morsels   168

How to Eat Fried Worms   14539

How to Eat Your ABC's   9355

How to Form a Rock Group   10780

How to Get in Shape for Sports   5451

How to Get It Together When Your Parents Are Coming Apart   14328

How to Give a Party   6196

How to Go About Laying an Egg   17362

How to Grow a Jelly Glass Farm   11592

How to Grow House Plants   15289

How to Have Fun Making Puppets   4266

How to Lose Your Lunch Money   17799

How to Make a Cloud   1426

How to Make a Dinosaur   9468

How to Make a Hit Record   9106

How to Make and Use a Microlab   14250

How to Make and Use Electric Motors   14251

How to Make Elephant Bread   11593

How to Make Flibbers, Etc.   11059

How to Make 19 Kinds of American Folk Art from Masks to TV Commercials   9835

How to Make Snop Snappers and Other Fine Things   11060

How to Make Things Grow   17855

How to Make Whirligigs and Whimmy Diddles and Other American Folkcraft Objects   13590

How to Make Your Own Books   17691

How to Make Your Own Movies   17692

How to Make Your Science Project Scientific   12413

How to Photograph Your World   8480

How to Play Baseball   8884

How to Play Baseball Better Than You Did Last Season   9465

How to Play Better Baseball (Harrelson)   7750

How to Play Better Baseball (Jackson)   8981

How to Play Better Basketball   8982

How to Play Better Football   8983

How to Play Drums   14687

How to Play Little League Baseball   11263

How to Play Soccer   9480

How to Play the Outfield   156

How to Play the Piano Despite Years of Lessons   2896

How to Raise a Puppy   16205

How to Raise Mice, Rats, Hamsters, and Gerbils   16206

How to Read a Highway Map   6284

How to Read and Write Poetry   4183

How to Run a Railroad   17693

How to Sharpen Your Study Skills   9469

How to Star in Basketball   11776

How to Star in Football   11777

How to Star in Track and Field   13005

How to Teach an Old Dog New Tricks   17144

How to Turn Lemons into Money

642
How to Turn Up into Down into
Up 643
How to Watch Wildlife 2664
How to Win: Bicycle Motocross
16776
How to Write a Story 13729
How to Write Codes and Send
Secret Messages 13579
How Tom Beat Captain Najork
and His Hired Sportsmen
8284
How Was I Born? 12844
How We Are Born 11877
How We Are Born, How We Grow,
How Our Bodies Work ...
and How We Learn 9531
How We Choose a President 7216
How We work 7744
How Wild Animals Fight 15633
How Wilka Went to Sea ... 6847
How You Talk 15597
Howdy! 17670
Howie Helps Himself 5711
How's Inky? 2880
Hrafkel's Saga 15056
Hubba-Hubba 3856
Hubert the Traveling Hippopota-
mus 10849
Huckleberry Finn see Adven-
tures of Huckleberry Finn
Hudson, River of History, The
11472
Hudson River Valley, The 14185
Huerta de Donana, La 13421
Huffler, The 17481
Hugo 7430
Huit Enfants et un Bebe 9899;
see also Eight Children and
One Baby
Hullabaloo! 17956
Hullo Sun 8337
Human Apes, The 2951
Human Body, The (Elgin) 5334
Human Body (Rutland) 14811
Human Mandolin, The 8677
Human Rights Day 5931
Human Story, The 8395
Humans of Ziax II, The 12454
Humbug Mountain 6008
Humbug Rabbit 1019
Humbug Witch, The 1020
Hummingbirds in the Garden
6537
Humorous Verse of Lewis Carroll,
The 3100
Hundred and One Dalmatians,

The (Disney) 4917
Hundred and One Dalmatians, The
(Smith) 15875
Hundred Dresses, The 5549
Hundred in the Hands, The see
Brave Eagle's Account of the
Fetterman Fight: 21 December,
1866
Hundred Penny Box, The 11815
Hundred Thousand Dollar Farm,
The 17441
Hungarians in America 7113
Hungry Cloud, The see Garranane
Hungry Fox and the Foxy Duck,
The 10647
Hungry Leprechaun, The 2837
Hungry Moon, The 14659
Hungry Snowbird, The 5706
Hunt for Rabbit's Galosh, The
15177
Hunt for the Mastodon, The 5473
Hunted in Their Own Land 3311
Hunted Like a Wolf 12041
Hunter and His Dog 17923
Hunter and the Hen, The 16612
Hunter, the Tick and the Gumberoo,
The 12068
Hunters, The 9088
Hunters and Collectors 9790
Hunter's Cave, The 5359
Hunters of the Black Swamp 7741
Hunters of the Whale 9856
Hunter's Stew and Hangtown Fry
13524
Hunting 11460
Hunting Dog, The 16547
Hunting for Boys see Hunting
Hunting of the Snark, The 3101
Hunting Trip, The 2598
Hur Gick det Sen? 9142; see also
Book About Moomin, Mymble
and Little My, The
Hurrah for Alexander! 11705
Hurrah for Captain Jane! 14175
Hurricane 1025
Hurry Henrietta 3919
Hurry Home 8530
Hurry Home, Candy 4676
Hurry Hurry 8802
Hurry, Hurry, Mary Dear! 1829
Hurry, Skurry, and Flurry 2542
Hurry the Crossing 17277
Hurry-Up Harry Hanson 5379
Hush, Jon! 6826
Hush Little Baby (Aliki) 304
Hush Little Baby (Zemach) 18523
Hut School and the Wartime Home-

Front Heroes 2599
Huts, Hovels and Houses 5958

- I -

I, Adam 6388
I Am 10904
I Am a Giant 15550
I Am a Man 12099
I Am a Pueblo Indian Girl 21
I Am a Stranger on the Earth
  4947
I Am Adopted 10271
I Am Better Than You 11061
I Am from Puerto Rico 2500
I Am Going Nowhere 2326
I Am Here/Yo Estoy Aqui 1806
I Am Kofi 710
I Am Maria 16627
I Am Not a Short Adult! 2688
I Am One of These 10002
I Am the Darker Brother 129
i am the running girl 130
I Became Alone 16861
I Breathe a New Song 10713
I Can Be Anything You Can Be
  14688
I Can Count the Petals of a
  Flower 17415
I Can Dress Myself 2451
I Can Help Too! 17888
I Can Read About Dinosaurs 8676
I Can See What God Does 18181
I Can't Draw Book, The 17545
"I Can't," Said the Ant 2864
I Caught a Lizard 3949
I, Charlotte Forten, Black and
  Free 11051
I Climb Mountains 16674
I Cry When the Sun Goes Down
  1501
I Did It 14532
I Didn't Know That 8140
I Discover Columbus 10422
I Do Not Like It When My Friend
  Comes to Visit 15551
I Don't Care 15464
I Drove Mules on the C & O
  Canal 18201
I, Dwayne Kleber 3968
I, Elizabeth 14108
I Feel 431
I Feel the Same Way 12397

I Go by Sea, I Go by Land 16971
I Had a Little ... 10642
I Hate Mathematics! Book, The
  2689
I Hate to Go to Bed 1111
I Hate to Take a Bath 1112
I Have a Dream (Kinnick) 9838
I Have a Dream (Sterne) 16253
I Have a Sister 13578
I Have a Tree 3238
I Have Feelings 1542
I Have Four Names for My Grand-
  father 10301
I Have Spoken 646
I Hear 13040
I Hear You Smiling ... 8506
I Heard a Scream in the Street
  10275
I Heard of a River 15797
I Heard the Owl Call My Name
  4250
I, Juan de Pareja 4755
I Keep Changing 6824
I Know! 14918
I Know a Baseball Player 2610
I Know a Dentist 1092
I Know a Farm 3836
I Know a Football Player 2295
I Know a Garageman 17974
I Know a Librarian 17342
I Know a Lot of Things 14100
I Know a Mayor 17975
I Know a Nurse 15059
I Know a Plumber 4389
I Know a Policeman 17976
I Know an Electrician 4390
I Know an Old Lady 1900
I Know What I Like 15728
I Know What You Did Last Summer
  5125
I Know You, Al 7286
I Like Beetles 3950
I Like Old Clothes 8307
I Like the Library 14513
I Like Trains 18268
I Like Winter 10571
I Like You ... 18362
I Live in East Africa 17248
I Love Gram 16016
I Love My Anteater with an A
  8916
I Love My Mother 18582
I Love to Sew 4165
I Love You, Mouse 7129
I Loved Rose Ann 8594
I Marched with Hannibal 1207
I Met a Penguin 719

I Met a Man 3460
I Met a Traveller 8268
I, Momolu 7134
I Need a Friend 9447
I Need All the Friends I Can Get
  15135
I Never Saw Another Butterfly
  10714
I Paint the Joy of a Flower
  11727
I Read Signs 6441
I Sailed on the Mayflower 13672
I Saw a Ship A-Sailing (Domanska)
  4995
I Saw a Ship A-Sailing (Montresor)
  12374
I Saw You from Afar 13511
I See the Winds 12293
I Should Have Stayed in Bed
  10741
I Should Worry, I Should Care
  3242
I Sing of Michigan 12277
I Speak for My Slave Sister
  863
I Spy 13041
I Sure Am Glad to See You,
  Blackboard Bear 281
I Tell a Lie Every So Often
  3591
I Think I Saw a Snail 8595
I Think I Will Go to the Hospital
  16642
I, Trissy 11971
I Used To 10905
I Used to Be an Artichoke 11341
I, Varina 14109
I Wanna Go Home! 9755
I Want Mama 15465
I Want My Sunday, Stranger
  1273
I Want to Be a Bank Teller 946
I Want to Be a Baseball Player
  7267
I Want to Be a Basketball Player
  947
I Want to Be a Computer Operator
  948
I Want to Be a Dentist 7268
I Want to Be a Fireman 7269
I Want to Be a Football Player
  949
I Want to Be a Forester 950
I Want to Be a Gymnast 951
I Want to Be a Hockey Player
  952
I Want to Be a Jeweler 953

I Want to Be a Librarian 939
I Want to Be a Musician 7270
I Want to Be a Nurse 7271
I Want to Be a Postal Clerk 954
I Want to Be a Printer 955
I Want to Be a Secretary 956
I Want to Be a Service Station At-
  tendant 957
I Want to Be a Soccer Player 958
I Want to Be a Space Pilot 7272
I Want to Be a Storekeeper 7273
I Want to Be a Swimmer 959
I Want to Be a Taxi Driver 960
I Want to Be a Teacher 7274
I Want to Be a Telephone Operator
  961
I Want to Be a Tennis Player 962
I Want to Be a Travel Agent 963
I Want to Be a Waitress 964
I Want to Be a Weatherman 965
I Want to Be a Zoo-Keeper 7275
I Want to Be an Architect 966
I Want to Be an Auto Mechanic
  967
I Want to Be Big 8958
I Want to Know About Pebbles,
  Shells, Honeybees and Little
  Eskimos 4091
I Want to Know About the United
  States Senate 13502
I Was a 98-Pound Duckling 17211
I Was a Savage see Royal African,
  A
I Was All Thumbs 17363
I Was So Mad! 15729
I Was There 14349
I Watch Flies 3951
I Went to the Animal Fair 3813
I Went to the Hospital 15709
I Will Adventure 7204
I Will Be Heard 5625
I Will Catch the Sun 4712
I Will Try 9584
I Wish I Had an Afro 15510
I Wish I Was Sick Too! 2100
I Wish Laura's Mommy Was My Mom-
  my 13864
I Wonder About the Sky 5848
I Wonder as I Wander 8722
I Wonder If Herbie's Home Yet
  9487
I Wonder What's Under 11167
I Won't Go Without a Father 16141
I Would Rather Be a Turnip 3578
I Write It 10078
I Wrote My Name on the Wall 15997
Ibo of Biafra, The 1753

Ibrahim the Teacher ... 16850
Ice-Cream Cone Coot ..., The 10997
Ice Cream Next Summer 7109
Ice Ghosts Mystery, The 4399
Ice Hockey 17814
Ice Is Coming, The 18319
Ice Pilot 14923
Ice River 7242
Iceberg Alley 501
Iceberg Hermit, The 14676
Icebergs 6538
Icebergs and Their Voyages 15125
Ick's ABC 7535
I'd Rather Do It Myself, If You Don't Mind 15168
I'd Rather Stay Home 1080
I'd Rather Stay with You 16214
Ida Makes a Movie 3388
Ida Tarbell 6031
Ida Tarbell, Muckraker 3966
Ida, the Bareback Rider 8354
Ideas About Choosing 11543
Ideas About Measuring and Accounting 11542
Idy the Fox-Chasing Cow and Other Stories 11668
If All the Seas Were One Sea 4996
If He's My Brother 17977
If I Built a Village 12294
If I Could Be My Grandmother 10106
If I Drove a Car 18458
If I Drove a Truck 18459
If I Ever Marry 13597
If I Flew a Plane 18460
If I Had a Hammer 10305
If I Had My Way 9908
If I Ran the Circus 15379
If I Ran the Zoo 15380
If I Were a Bird 3952
If I Were a Cricket 12295
If I Were a Mother 12296
If It Weren't for You 18604
If the Earth Falls In 3517
If Wishes Were Horses ... (Jeffers) 9181
If Wishes Were Horses (Robertson) 14443
If You Grew Up with Abraham Lincoln 11351
If You Had a Pony 8675
If You Listen 12911
... If You Lived in Colonial Times 11352

If You Lived in the Days of the Wild Mammoth Hunters 5396
If You Lived with the Circus 11353
If You Lived with the Sioux Indians 11354
If You Sailed on the Mayflower 11355
Ifrit and the Magic Gifts 17431
Iggie's House 1818
Iguana's Tail, The 15544
Ijapa the Tortoise and Other Tales from Nigeria see Olode the Hunter and Other Tales from Nigeria
Ikwa of the Temple Mounds 15213
Iliad, The 8524
I'll Always Love You, Paul Newman see Lisa, Bright and Dark
I'll Be the Horse If You'll Play with Me 282
I'll Be You--You Be Me 10079
I'll Build My Friend a Mountain 9514
I'll Draw a Meadow 1959
I'll Fix Anthony 17319
I'll Get There, It Better Be Worth the Trip 5009
I'll Protect You from the Jungle Beasts 283
I'll Tell on You 10742
Illinois 3009
Illinois at War 8891
Illinois, Crossroads of a Nation 12119
Illinois Grows Up 1741
Illinois in Words and Pictures 6192
Illinois Story, The 13881
Illinois Women 3850
Illustrated Baseball Dictionary for Young People 17445
Illustrated Book About Africa, The 16538
Illustrated Chess for Children 9783
Illustrated Football Dictionary for Young People 13079
Illustrated Hassle-Free Make Your Own Clothes Book, The 14622
Illustrated Hockey Dictionary for Young People, The 17446
I'm Bored, Ma! 1601
I'm Deborah Sampson 3475
I'm Glad I'm a Boy! I'm Glad I'm a Girl! 10063
I'm Glad I'm Me 16374

I'm Going on a Bear Hunt 15803

I'm Going to Have a Baby! 8313

I'm Going to Run Away! 16834

I'm Like Me 17860

I'm Moving 8148

I'm Nobody! Who Are You? (Anderson) 507

I'm Nobody! Who Are You? (Barth) 1137

I'm Not Oscar's Friend Anymore 15466

I'm Really Dragged, but Nothing Gets Me Down 8084

I'm Terrific 15467

Important Book, The 2390

Impossible Charlie 12447

Impossible Dogs and Troublesome Cats 7505

Impossible Major Rogers, The 6673

Impossible People, The 11390

Impossible Possum 3936

Improbable Book of Records, The 1716

Impunity Jane 6951

In a Certain Kingdom 17839

In a Pumpkin Shell 548

In a Pygmy Camp 15535

In a Sacred Manner We Live 4411

In a Spring Garden 10715

In a Window on Greenwater Street 3230

In Africa 1569

In-Between Miya 17094

In Chains to Louisiana 12930

In Face of Danger 9574

In Front of the Table and Behind It 18293

In Her Father's Footsteps 2060

In Mexico They Say 14660

In My Mother's House 3485

In Navajo Land 637

In Orbit 8744

In Prehistoric Seas 5804

In School: Learning in Four Languages 7854

In Search of a Sandhill Crane 14444

In Search of Coffee Mountains 7087

In Search of the Abominable Snowman 8110

In Search of Their Parents 14759

In Spite of All Terror 2725

In Tennis Love Means Nothing 9065

In the Beginning 10391

In the Center 16771

In the Circle of Time 502

In the Company of Clowns 866

In the Eye of Teddy 720

In the Flaky Frosty Morning 10157

In the Forest 5563

In the Keep of Time 503

In the Land of Small Dragon 9776

In the Land of Ur 1208

In the Middle of the Night 5915

In the Morning of Time 9815

In the Night Kitchen 15332

In the Park 7855

In the Public Service 1088

In the Rabbitgarden 10880

In the Shadow of a Rainbow 10627

In the Shadow of Man 10393

In the Time of the Bells 7431

In the Trail of the Wind 1639

In the Troll Wood 1190

In the Wilds of Africa 7633

In the Woods, in the Meadow, in the Sky 5916

In Their Own Words 12042

In This Proud Land 18197

In Time of Trial see Time of Trial

In Woods and Fields 2476

In Yards and Gardens 2477

Inatuk's Friend 12480

Incas, Indians of the Andes, The 1754

Incas Knew, The 13685

Inch by Inch 10881

Incident at Hawk's Hill 5246

Incorruptible Judge, The 13062

Incredible A. J. Foyt, The 5444

Incredible Deborah, The 3320

Incredible Detectives, The 3177

Incredible Journey, The 2674

Increible mundo de Llanca, El 12420

Independent Voices 12100

India 6492

India, Old Land, New Nation 17572

Indian America 7502

Indian and Eskimo Children 17172

Indian and Free 2246

Indian and His Horse, The 8380

Indian and His Pueblo, The 6057

Indian Art of the Americas 4963

Indian Arts 8381

Indian Arts and Crafts see Arizona Highways Indian Arts and Crafts

Indian Beadwork 8382

Indian Boyhood 5219

Indian Bunny 1960
Indian Canoe-Maker 1274
Indian Captive 10572
Indian Chiefs 4859
Indian Chiefs of the West 16539
Indian Children of America 5703
Indian Corn and Other Gifts 10383
Indian Costumes 8383
Indian Crafts 4473
Indian Crafts for Campers 12894
Indian Cultures of the Southwest 9363
Indian Drums Beat Again 11386
Indian Fairy Book, The 15104
Indian Fairy Tales 9048
Indian Festivals 15598
Indian Fishing and Camping 8384
Indian Friends and Foes 8011
Indian Gallery 7858
Indian Games and Crafts 8385
Indian Harvests 7411
Indian Heart of Carrie Hodges, The 13422
Indian Hill 2557
Indian Hunting 8386
Indian Legends of American Scenes 7349
Indian Legends of Eastern America 11177
Indian Legends of the Great West 11178
Indian Lore 10205
Indian Medicine Man, The 8387
Indian Mound Farm 3685
Indian Mummy Mystery 6092
Indian Music Makers 8388
Indian Nations 7350
Indian Paint 993
Indian Paintbrush 3254
Indian Picture Writing 8389
Indian Pony 4909
Indian Patriots of the Eastern Woodlands 17617
Indian Portraits of the Pacific Northwest 3719
Indian Rock Painting of the Great Lakes 4872
Indian Saddle-up 994
Indian Sign Language (Hofsinde) 8390
Indian Sign Language (Tomkins) 16927
Indian Sign Talk in Pictures 3723
Indian Softball Summer 1776
Indian Summer 12340

Indian Tales (DeAngulo) 4644
Indian Tales (Raskin) 14133
Indian Tales of the Desert People 7922
Indian Tales of the Northern Plains 16909
Indian Tales of the Northern Rockies 16910
Indian Talk 3724
Indian Tribes of America 7351
Indian Twins, The 13514
Indian Two Feet and His Eagle Feather 6371
Indian Two Feet and His Horse 6372
Indian Two Feet and the Grizzly Bear 6373
Indian Two Feet and the Wolf Cubs 6374
Indian Warriors and Their Weapons 8391
Indian Wars and Warriors East 17724
Indian Wars of the Pacific Northwest 6888
Indian Women 17508
Indiana (Carpenter) 3010
Indiana (Nolan) 12881
Indiana Artists (Active) 1940 10371
Indiana Birds see Permanent Resident Birds of Indiana
Indiana Festivals 11625
Indiana Through the Years 5982
Indianapolis 500, The (Devaney) 4865
Indianapolis "500," The (Engel) 5446
Indianapolis 500, The (Krishef) 10099
Indianapolis 500, The (May) 11878
Indianapolis 500, The (Yates) 18374
Indians (Chisholm) 3380
Indians (Ernst) 5531
Indians (Martin) 11749
Indians (Scherer) 15035
Indians (Tunis) 17041
Indians and the Strangers, The 9309
Indians at Home 8392
Indians' Book, The 4413
Indians, Indians, Indians 5793
Indians, Jacks, and Pines 7453
Indians Knew, The 13677
Indians of Early Maryland 11587
Indians of Early Southern California 18531
Indians of Kansas, The 17194

Indians of Michigan, The 7316
Indians of New Jersey, The 7758
Indians of Northeastern America, The 1690
Indians of Pennsylvania 17470
Indians of the Eastern Woodlands 15540
Indians of the Great Basin and Plateaus 7566
Indians of the Longhouse 1755
Indians of the Ohio Country 9944
Indians of the Plains 14054
Indians of the Southwest (Atkinson) 780
Indians of the Southwest (Baldwin) 1005
Indians of the Southwest, The (Dutton) 5173
Indians of the Woodland 15656
Indians of Today 7352
Indians of Yesterday 7353
Indians on Horseback 11699
Indians on the Bonnet, The 10179
Indians on the Warpath 4008
Indians on the Move 8393
Indians' Secret World, The 8394
Indians Who Lived in Texas 17532
India's Tales and Legends 7215
Indoor and Outdoor Gardening for Young People 9958
Indoor and Outdoor Grow-It Book, The 987
Indoor Games and Activities 3149
Indoor Gardening 5800
Indoor Noisy Book, The 2391
Infielders, The 15907
Infinite Variety of Music, The 1574
Infinity 11148
Inga of Porcupine Mine 16373
Inheritance of Poetry, An 149
Ini Abasi and the Sacred Ram 212
Ink, Ark., and All That 13716
Inki see Inky: Seeing Eye Dog
Inky: Seeing Eye Dog 8093
Innkeeper's Daughter, The 3740
Innocent Wayfaring, The 3452
Insect-Eating Plants 13822
Insect Masquerades 15719
Insect Zoo 5607
Insects and the Homes They Build 16239
Insects and Their Young 8849

Insects as Pets 17308
Insects Build Their Homes 3953
Insects Do the Strangest Things 8623
Insects in Armor 8850
Insects in Their World 16545
Inside 88
Inside Animals 4069
Inside Baseball 1620
Inside Corner 3756
Inside Gymnastics 6478
Inside Jazz 3839
Inside Mom 3209
Inside, Outside, Upside Down 1497
Inside Tennis 15932
Inside the Synagogue 6285
Inspector Peckit 6264
Instruments of Music, The 11176
Integration of Mary-Larkin Thornhill, The 17425
Internal Combustion Engine and How It Works, The 17169
International Book of Christmas Carols, The 5291
International Cookie Jar Cookbook, The 1950
International Flag Book in Color, The 13463
Interview with Alan Page, An 1177
Interview with Rod Carew, An 1178
Into Space 3526
Into the Forest 5543
Into the Painted Bear Lair 16155
Into the Road 14326
Into the Unknown 5194
Into the Woods 13961
Introducing Archaeology 11540
Introducing Shirley Braverman 18208
Introducing the Earth 11833
Introduction to Archaeology 7080
Introduction to Backpacking 3895
Introduction to Birds, An 9785
Introduction to Shakespeare, An 3453
Intruder, The 16955
Inuk 7187
Invaders, The 16985
Invention of the Negro 3971
Inventions That Made History 4009
Inventors in Industry 14057
Investigating Psychics 9760
Investigating Science in the Swimming Pool and Ocean 510
Investigating Science Using Your Whole Body 511

Investigating Science with Nails 17805

Invincible Louisa   12021

Invitation to Birds   5302

Invitation to Music   15659

Invitation to Sailing   2329

Invitation to the Butterfly Ball, An   18414

Iowa   3011

Iowa Hannah   7987

Iowa Inside Out   7570

Ira Sleeps Over   17364

Iran (Lengyel)   10555

Iran (Taylor)   16672

Iran, Crossroads of Caravans 17746

Ireland   4948

Irish   4949

Irish Helped Build America, The 11313

Irish in America, The   9280

Irish Sagas and Folk-Tales   13026

Irish Stories   4978

Iroko Man and the Wood Carver, The   13063

Iron Giant, The   8730

Iron Lily, The   17957

Iron Lion, The   4895

Iron Man, The   see   Iron Giant, The

Iroquoians of the Eastern Woodlands   14557

Iroquois   5544

Irrigation   116

Irving and Me   8355

Is It Bigger Than a Sparrow? 2193

Is Milton Missing?   10107

Is Somewhere Always Far Away? 9054

Is That Mother in the Bottle? 4567

Is That You, Miss Blue?   9734

Is That Your Sister?   2586

Is the Grass Greener?   17774

Is There a Bermuda Triangle? 4419

Is There Life in Outer Space? 10048

Is There Life on a Plastic Planet? 404

Is This a Baby Dinosaur?   15290

Is This You?   10082

Isaac and Snow   5284

Isabelle the Itch   7287

Isamu Noguchi, the Life of a Sculptor   16898

Isfendiar and the Bears of Mazandaran   13848

Isfendiar and the Wild Donkeys 13849

Ishi, Last of His Tribe   10104

Island City   4588

Island Ghost   14105

Island in a Green Sea, An   320

Island in the Crossroads   2160

Island Mackenzie   18048

Island of Fish in the Trees, The 18327

Island of Puerto Rico, The   2016

Island of the Blue Dolphins   13013

Island of the Grass King, The 17965

Island of the Great Yellow Ox 11420

Island of the Skog, The   9653

Island of Yo   12692

Island Through the Gate, The 16544

Isle Royale Calling   3636

Israel's Golda Meir   12857

Issun Boshi, the Inchling   8941

It   11958

It All Began with a Drip, Drip, Drip ...   10743

It All Depends   18415

It Can't Hurt Forever   15792

It Could Always Be Worse   18524

It Does Not Say Meow   4739

It Doesn't Always Have to Rhyme 12101

It Happened Here   8043

It Happened in Chichipica   9475

It Happened in Illinois   18199

It Happened on Thursday   4815

It Is I, Sea Gull   15488

It Is the Poem Singing into Your Eyes   131

It Is Time for Stories   79

It Looked Like Spilt Milk   14493

It Looks Alive to Me!   1201

It, Us and the Others   3448

It Was a Pretty Good Year   6071

It Works Like This   831

Italians in America, The   7458

Itch, Sniffle and Sneeze   15688

It's a Baby!   432

It's a Mile from Here to Glory 10489

It's About Time   15068

It's All Done with Numbers   18343

It's Fun to Know Why   15158

It's Fun to Make Pictures   4761

It's Getting Beautiful Now   2838

It's Halloween 13886
It's Like This, Cat 12765
It's Magic? 11062
It's Mine! (Bonsall) 1908
It's Mine (McKean) 11407
It's Nesting Time 6539
It's Nice to Be Little 16146
It's Not the End of the World
  1819
It's Raining Said John Twaining
  1830
It's So Nice to Have a Wolf
  Around the House 324
It's the Final Score That Counts
  8484
It's Time for Brotherhood 15220
It's Time for Christmas 15221
It's Time for Easter 15222
It's Time for Thanksgiving 15218
It's Time Now! 17002
It's Time to Go to Bed 15242
It's Wings That Make Birds Fly
  17665
Ittki Pittki 3243
Ivan the Fool ... 16921
Ivan the Great 4418
Ivanko and the Dragon 14743
Ivanov Seven 9133
I've Missed a Sunset or Three
  18240
Ivory, Apes and Jimibel 12991
Ivory Coast 3012
Iyabo of Nigeria 9325
Izzard 497
Izzie 13441

- J -

J. C. Penney 8711
J. D. 5592
J. T. 17384
Jabbar 9016
Jabberwocky 3102
Jabberwocky and Other Poems
  see Humorous Verse of
  Lewis Carroll, The
Jack and the Beanstalk 9049
Jack and the Three Sillies 3302
Jack and the Wonder Beans 16315
Jack Holborn 6602
Jack Jouett's Ride 7580
Jack Kent's Book of Nursery
  Tales 9708

Jack Kent's Fables of Aesop 9709
Jack Kent's Twelve Days of Christ-
  mas 9710
Jack Nicklaus 4786
Jack-o-Lantern 1138
Jack Tales, The 3303
Jack the Bum and the Halloween
  Handout 15120
Jack the Bum and the Haunted
  House 15121
Jackal and the Camel, The 2355
Jackie 10708
Jackie Robinson (Epstein) 5501
Jackie Robinson (Olsen) 13105
Jackie Robinson (Rudeen) 14745
Jackie Robinson of the Brooklyn
  Dodgers 15432
Jackie Robinson's Little League
  Baseball Book 14466
Jackson Five 12485
Jacko 7039
Jacob Two-Two Meets the Hooded
  Fang 14343
Jacqueline Cochran 5955
Jacqueline Kennedy Onassis 11750
Jacques Cousteau 8959
Jade 17596
Jaguar, My Twin 10798
Jake 15853
Jake Gaither 1729
Jamba the Elephant 17418
Jambo Means Hello 5751
Jambo Sungura 7973
James and the Giant Peach 4444
James and the Rain 10158
James Bowie and His Famous Knife
  6634
James Buchanan Eads 18358
James Edward Oglethorpe 1702
James J. Hill 3898
James Marshall's Mother Goose
  12515
James the Jaguar 11190
James Weldon Johnson (Egypt)
  5290
James Weldon Johnson (Felton)
  5777
Jamestown (Campbell) 2873
Jamestown (Fishwick) 5959
Jamestown Adventure 7629
Jamie's Tiger 17402
Jane Addams (Gilbert) 6810
Jane Addams (Grant) 7175
Jane Addams (Keller) 9644
Jane Addams (Mooney) 12381
Jane Addams (Peterson) 13573
Jane Addams (Wagoner) 17387

Jane and the Mandarin's Secret 10706
Jane-Emily 3476
Jane, Wishing 16899
Jane's Adventures on the Island of Peeg see Operation Peeg
Janet Lynn (Jacobs) 9066
Janet Lynn (May) 11879
Janet Reachfar and the Kelpie 5121
Janey 18605
Janitor's Girl, The 6356
Janko's Wish 17245
January Fog Will Freeze a Hog ... 4561
Japan 16251
Japan in Story and Pictures 5253
Japan, Islands of the Rising Sun 17573
Japanese Americans 9147
Japanese Children's Favorite Stories 14858
Japanese Children's Stories 14859
Japanese Fairy Tales 13667
Japanese Helped Build America, The 5040
Japanese in America, The 10472
Japanese Tales and Legends 11199
Jareb 13862
Jared's Island 4637
Jardin de las siete puertas, El 3156
Jasmine 5179
Jason and the Money Tree 10659
Jason's Quest 10368
Jasper and the Cakes 16973
Jasper Makes Music 8633
Jasper the Drummin' Boy 2697
Jataka Tales 4750
Jay-Jay and the Peking Monster 5597
Jayhawker Book, The 8739
Jayhawker Johnny 2712
Jazz Ambassador 14896
Jazz Country 8085
Jazz Man, The 17651
Jean Baptiste Pointe De Sable 7148
Jean-Claude's Island 2961
Jeanne d'Arc 5917
Jeanne-Marie Counts Her Sheep 6212
Jed 2629
Jed Smith 10310
Jedediah Smith 2713
Jedediah Smith on the Far Frontier 12228

Jeep Trails to Colorado Ghost Towns 2424
Jeffers Petroglyphs 11084
Jeff's Hospital Book 15987
Jellybeans for Breakfast 18461
Jellyfish Is Not a Fish, A 17559
Jellyfishes 15536
Jemimalee 14448
Jennie Jenkins 16690
Jennie's Hat 9596
Jennie's Mandan Bowl 8367
Jennifer and Josephine 13476
Jennifer Gift, The 15889
Jennifer, Hecate, Macbeth, William McKinley, and Me, Elizabeth 9991
Jennifer Jean, the Cross-Eyed Queen 12681
Jennifer Prize, The 15890
Jennifer Takes Over P.S. 94 11191
Jennifer Wish, The 15891
Jennifer's Rabbit 13403
Jennifer's Walk 3090
Jenny and the Cat Club 807
Jenny Kimura 3196
Jenny Lind 12599
Jenny Lind and Her Listening Cat 3185
Jenny's Cat 12185
Jenny's Corner 1348
Jenny's Revenge 998
Jeremiah Knucklebones 17403
Jerry at the Academy 5837
Jerry of Seven Mile Creek 5838
Jerry West 4787
Jersey Shore, The 11959
Jesse Owens 9535
Jesse Owens Story, The 13216
Jesse Tree, The 514
Jessie Fremont 17388
Jessika in Trouble 8693
Jet Journey 18090
Jethro and the Jumbie 4086
Jets 17293
Jewelry Making 17309
Jewish Holiday Cookbook 14000
Jewish Holiday Crafts 1291
Jewish Holidays 12478
Jewish Holidays, Facts, Activities, and Crafts 14001
Jewish New Year, The 3920
Jewish Sabbath, The 3921
Jews Helped Build America, The 10145
Jews in America, The 2776
Jezebel Wolf, The 12341
Jill the Pill 3154

Jillions of Gerbils 4950
Jim Along, Josie 10258
Jim and the Beanstalk 2235
Jim Beckwourth (Blassingame) 1730
Jim Beckwourth (Felton) 5778
Jim Bowie's Lost Mine 6207
Jim Bridger (Garst) 6635
Jim Bridger (Luce) 11149
Jim Bridger (Winders) 18105
Jim Bridger, American Frontiersman 16943
Jim Bridger's Alarm Clock ... 6009
Jim Brown 9897
Jim Can Swim 13073
Jim Grey of Moonbah 13205
Jim Long-Knife 16677
Jim Plunkett 7521
Jim Ryun Story, The 12722
Jim Thorpe (Fall) 5653
Jim Thorpe (Reising) 14222
Jim Thorpe Story, The 15107
Jimmy and Joe Catch an Elephant 6899
Jimmy and Joe Have a Real Thanksgiving 6900
Jimmy Has Lost His Cap 12560
Jimmy Murphy and the White Dusenberg 3123
Jimmy Yellow Hawk 15949
Jingo Django 6010
Jinx Glove 3420
Jo, Flo, and Yolanda 4731
Joan Moore Rice 9067
Joan of Arc (Churchill) 3450
Joan of Arc (Ross) 14655
Joan of Arc (Williams) 18035
Joanjo 1016
Joanna Runs Away 10184
Joanna's Miracle 649
Jobs Book, The 15008
Jobs in Agribusiness 8648
Jobs in Business and Office 7823
Jobs in Construction 10782
Jobs in Fine Arts and Humanities 1518
Jobs in Health Care 5452
Jobs in Manufacturing 8649
Jobs in Marine Science 14644
Jobs in Marketing and Distribution 7589
Jobs in Personal Services 4297
Jobs in Transportation 7207
Jobs That Save Our Environment 1519
Jock of the Bushveld 5983

Jockey--Or Else! 2345
Joe and Andy Want a Boat 9296
Joe Bean 158
Joe Jacoby 17588
Joe Namath (May) 11880
Joe Namath (Olsen) 13106
Joe Namath, Maverick Quarterback 1535
Joe Namath, Superstar 9017
Joel Is the Youngest 8942
Joey and the Fawn 10710
Joey's Cat 2600
John Adams 1703
John Billington 2558
John Boyd's Adventures 9952
John Brown (Iger) 8883
John Brown (Nolan) 12882
John Burningham's ABC 2680
John Charles Fremont (Burt) 2714
John Charles Fremont (Carlson) 2976
John Come Down the Backstay 16653
John Deere 1072
John Denver 9068
John F. Kennedy 7195
John Fitzgerald Kennedy 11751
John Glenn 205
John H. Glenn, Astronaut 13663
John Havlicek 2163
John Henry (De Leeuw) 4703
John Henry (Keats) 9597
John Henry and His Hammer 5779
John Henry and the Double Jointed Steam-Drill 15422
John Henry McCoy 3239
John J. Pershing 6153
John J. Plenty and Fiddler Dan 3461
John L. Lewis 10000
John Muir (Clark) 3513
John Muir (Dines) 4910
John Muir (Graves) 7196
John Muir (Norman) 12898
John Muir, Prophet Among the Glaciers 15666a
John Muir, Young Naturalist 5132
John Rattling-Gourd of Big Cove 1347
John Smith of Virginia 16586
John Tabor's Ride 10596
John Treegate's Musket 17848
John Wesley Powell 13719
John Wesley Powell, Conquest of the Canyon 2977
Johnnie Tigerskin see Tiger Nanny

Johnny and His Mule 4269
Johnny Appleseed (Moore) 12387
Johnny Appleseed (Norman)
  12899
Johnny Appleseed and Other
  Poems 10858
Johnny Bench (Heaslip) 7985
Johnny Bench (Jackson) 9018
Johnny Bench (Libby) 10765
Johnny-Cake 9050
Johnny Cash 16698
Johnny Crow's Garden 2303
Johnny Goes to the Hospital
  15388
Johnny Hong of Chinatown 2559
Johnny Lee 8531
Johnny Lion's Rubber Boots
  8803
Johnny Long Legs 3421
Johnny Lost/Juanito Perdido
  13938
Johnny Maple-Leaf 17003
Johnny May 2154
Johnny Texas 8342
Johnny Texas on the San An-
  tonio Road 8343
Johnny Tremain 6101
Johnny Unitas and the Long Jump
  11881
Johnny Unitas Story, The 7295
Joi Bangla! The Children of
  Bangladesh 10366
Joji and the Amanojaku 10799
Jokes and Jests from American
  Folklore 15142
Jokes for Children 9960
Jokes, Puns, and Riddles 3509
Jolly Christmas at the Patter-
  prints, A 12974
Jon the Unlucky 3686
Jonah and the Great Fish 2560
Jonah and the Lord 11207
Jonathan 11108
Jonathan Livingston Seagull 859
Jonathan's Friends 13304
Joneses, The 14095
Jonica's Island 11585
Jordan 13816
Jordan, River of the Promised
  Land 17668
Jorge el Curioso 14269; see
  also Curious George
Jorinda and Joringel 7397
Jory and the Buckskin Jumper
  18060
Jose and the Mexican Jumping
  Bean 16908

Josefina February 12745
Joseph and His Brothers 13559
Joseph and Koza 15780
Joseph and the Wonderful Tree
  10244
Joseph Brant 234
Joseph Had a Little Overcoat
  16607
Joseph Pulitzer (Myers) 12604
Joseph Pulitzer (Noble) 12858
Joseph, the Border Guard 1213
Joseph the Dreamer 2561
Josephine 7432
Josephine's 'Magination 4951
Joseph's Yard 9616
Jose's Christmas Secret 10744
Josfa, su mundo y la oscuridad
  14355
Josh 16040
Joshua's Day 16516
Josie and the Snow 2497
Josie's Handful of Quietness 15923
Journals and Indian Paintings of
  George Winter, 1837-39, The
  1023
Journey Back, The 14223
Journey Between Worlds 5438
Journey Cake, Ho! 14969
Journey for Three 8468
Journey for Tobiyah 12441
Journey from Peppermint Street
  4677
Journey into Danger 8094
Journey into Jazz 8086
Journey of Ching Lai 10330
Journey of the Grey Whales 3954
Journey Outside 16160
Journey to America 10660
Journey to the Moon 6425
Journey to the People 3486
Journey to Topaz 17095
Journey to Washington 8906
Journey Toward Freedom 1562
Journeys 10716
Journeys of Sebastian, The 10021
Joy to the World 14970
Joyful Poems for Children 14378
Joyride 3197
Juan 16353
Juan Bobo and the Pig 3276
Juan Bobo and the Queen's Neck-
  lace 1368
Juan Diego and the Lady 17404
Juan of Paricutin 17828
Juan Patricio 16905
Juanita 13778
Juanito Makes a Drum 3255

Juanito's Railroad in the Sky 8104
Juarez 36
Juarez, Man of Law 4756
Juarez, the Founder of Modern Mexico 16587
Juba This and Juba That 16659
Jud 14163
Judge, The 18514
Judge Not 5727
Judith Lankester 327
Judo 2444
Judy George 16378
Judy's Journey 10573
Juegos, v. 1, Los 6564
Juegos, v. 2, Los 6565
Juegos, v. 3, Los 6566
Juegos Meniques 9223
Juegos y otros poemas 170
Juglar del Cid, El 172
Julia and the Hand of God 2857
Julia and the Third Bad Thing 17457
Julia Ward Howe 17389
Julia's House 7433
Julie of the Wolves 6740
Julie's Decision 10951
Juliette Low (Higgins) 8165
Juliette Low (Radford) 14058
Julius 8356
Julius Erving 2164
Julius K. Nyerere 7149
Juma the Little African 11646
Jumblies, The 10464
Jumbo Giant Circus Elephant 4840
Jumbo the Boy and Arnold the Elephant 7260
Jump at the Sun 12581
Jump the Rope Jingles 18277
Jumping Mouse, The 6333
Jumping-Off Place, The 11465
June the Tiger 6129
Jungle, The 1964
Jungle Books, The 9843
Jungle Lore ... 16556
Jungle Picnic 17629
Junichi, a Boy of Japan 15079
Junior Book of Insects, The 16724
Junior Football Playbook, The 4713
Junior Girl Scout Handbook 6871
Junior History of the American Negro 7051
Junior Science Book of Flying 5818
Junior Science Book of Heat 5819
Junior Science Book of Icebergs and Glaciers 10349
Junior Science Book of Magnets 5820
Junior Science Book of Pond Life 4310
Junior Science Book of Rain, Hail, Sleet and Snow 10276
Junior Science Book of Rock Collecting 4313
Junior Skipper 13438
Junior Tennis 10520
Juniper Tree and Other Tales from Grimm, The 7398
Junk Day on Juniper Street ... 12398
Junket 17777
Just a Box? 3329
Just a Dog 7374
Just a Minute 9900
Just Awful 17821
Just Dial a Number 11846
Just for Fun 5162
Just for Manuel 7680
Just Like Everyone Else 10159
Just Like Nancy 4354
Just Me 5564
Just Momma and Me 5235
Just Morgan 13603
Just One Apple 9139
Just One Indian Boy 18159
Just Only John 9711
Just Say Hic 17432
Just So Stories 9844
Just Suppose 6596
Just the Beginning 12173
Just the Mat for Father Cat 4898
Just the Thing for Geraldine 3937
Just the Two of Them 508
Just Think! 1794
Justice Denied 4317

- K -

K Mouse and Bo Bixby 159
Kaha Bird, The 6848
Kahtahah 13396
Kai Ming, Boy of Hong Kong 4493
Kaibah 1468
Kain & Augustyn 4503
Kaleku 13768
Kalena 1937

Kalena and Sana 1938
Kalu and the Wild Boar 7618
Kalulu the Hare 18280
Kamanda 6667
Kamara Family, The 816
Kamiti, a Forester's Dream 986
Kangaroos and Other Animals with
   Pockets 4512
Kangaroos, Opossums and Other
   Marsupials 9191
Kano and His Dog 8114
Kansas (Carpenter) 3013
Kansas (Miller) 12237
Kansas (Writers' Program) 18324
Kansas City Chiefs, The 11882
Kansas Folklore 14849
Kansas Impressions 11179
Kansas--The 34th Star 12236
Kantchil's Lime Pit and Other
   Stories from Indonesia 4196
Kappa's Tug-of-War with Big
   Brown Horse 1155
Karankawa Boy 49
Karate for Young People 10013
Karate Power 10014
Kareem 7700
Kareem Abdul Jabbar 11883
Kari the Elephant 12545
Karlsson-on-the-Roof 10836
Karting 14067
Kassim's Shoes 1602
Kate 10937
Kate Can Skate 13074
Kate Douglas Wiggin 11791
Kate Ryder 2726
Kateri Tekakwitha 2343
Kate's Story 10445
Katey 9179
Katharine Lee Bates 12600
Kathy Whitworth 5328
Katia 375
Katie and the Sad Noise 6531
Katie Goes to Camp 15046
Katie John 2839
Katie's Chickens 17590
Katie's Magic Glasses 7057
Katsi and His Cattle 9442
Katy and the Big Snow 2729
Katy, Be Good 15326
Katy No-Pocket 13405
Katzimo, Mysterious Mesa 7466
Kaunda of Zambia 16737
Kavik the Wolf Dog 12429
Kawin: A Book of Indian Crafts
   1285
Keep Running see Ask Me No
   Questions

Keep Running, Allen 2562
Keep Stompin' till the Music Stops
   13594
Keeping Days, The 9322
Keeping in Shape 10712
Keeping the Plants You Pick 6157
Keeping Time 2471
Kee's Home 7593
Keiko's Bubble 10705
Kellyburn Braes 12818
Kelly's Creek 15880
Kelpie's Pearls, The 8782
Kemba 1086
Kemi 2543
Ken of Centennial Farm 16729
Kenny 9254
Kentucky Time 18231
Kenya (Carpenter & Delany) 3043
Kenya (Foster) 6134
Kenya in Pictures 14259
Kenya's Nomads 14672
Keoni, My Brother 12835
Kep 1027
Ketse and the Chief 12287
Kettle of Hawks and Other Wildlife
   Groups, A 671
Ketut, Boy Woodcarver of Bali
   16080
Kevin Cloud 1009
Kevin's Grandma 17978
Key, The 8003
Key of Gold 3321
Key to Chicago, The 9820
Key to Dallas, The 16879
Key to New York, The 6032
Key to St. Louis, The 15255
Key to the Treasure 13294
Keys and the Candle, The 18270
Khama of Botswana 4433
Kick a Stone Home 15881
Kick, Pass, and Run 9749
Kickle Snifters and Other Fearsome
   Critters ... 15143
Kid Camping from Aaaaiii! to ZIP
   11454
Kid from Cuba 16763
Kid Power 13604
Kid Who Only Hit Homers, The
   3422
Kid Who Owned Manhattan Island,
   The 11416
Kidnapers Upstairs, The 14618
Kidnapped Circus, The 18275
Kidnappers, The 18098
Kidnapping of the Coffee Pot, The
   14833
Kids and Alcohol, the Deadliest

Drug 5453
Kids and Dog Shows 7602
Kids Are Natural Cooks 795
Kids Camping 13390
Kids Can Count 18224
Kid's Cat Book, The 4720
Kids Cooking 13394
Kids Cooking Complete Meals 13391
Kids' Gardening 13392
Kid's Lib 8219
Kids' Money-Making Book 18450
Kids of Colombia 14914
Kids' Own XYZ of Love and Sex, The 17861
Kigo in England 9499
Kijanaj's Lucky Escape 11842
Kikuyu Live Off the Land, The 14673
Kilango 1947
Kildee House 12369
Killer Insects 3179
Killer-of-Death 926
Killing Tree, The 1467
Kilroy and the Gull 1403
Kim of Korea 12906
Kim Walk-in-My-Shoes 13924
Kim's Place 8596
Kind of Secret Weapon, A 660
Kindle of Kittens, A 6952
King and the Mangoes, The 6717
King and the Pauper ..., The 16613
King Arthur 726
King at the Door, The 3794
King Boy of Brass 214
King Dogho of Warri 8889
King for One Day 2201
King George's Head Was Made of Lead 12342
King Grisly-Beard 7399
King Krakus and the Dragon 4997
King Laurence the Alarm Clock 11609
King Midas Has a Gilt Complex 5030
King Mombo 5096
King of Haiti, A 7990
King of Ireland's Son, The 3878
King of Kazoo 13455
King of Men, The 4020
King of Squaw Mountain 1952
King of the Copper Mountains, The 1634
King of the Dollhouse 3477
King of the Golden River 14778

King of the Grizzlies see Biography of a Grizzly
King of the Mountain 17864
King of the Mountains, The 9098
King of the Snakes and Other Folklore Stories from Uganda 1159
King of the Wind 8072
King Orville and the Bullfrogs 22
King Pancho and the First Clock 11057
King Philip 5276
King Phillip: The Indian Chief 808
King Rooster, Queen Hen 10987
King Solomon's Horses 10126
King Stork 14012
King Who Caught Ghosts ..., The 16335
King Who Could Not Sleep, The 5346
King Who Rained, The 7536
King Who Rides a Tiger, The 8258
King Who Saved Himself from Being Saved, The 3462
King with 6 Friends, The 18016
Kingdom and the Cave, The 186
Kingdom Lost for a Drop of Honey and Other Burmese Folktales, A 796
Kingdom of Carbonel, The 15833
Kingdom of the Sun 9501
Kingdom of Wolves, The 1131
Kings and Queens 2311
King's Beard, The 16966
King's Birthday Cake, The 4364
King's Choice 15574
King's Contest, The 8443
King's Daughter ..., The 9448
King's Drum and Other African Stories, The 4197
King's Falcon, The 6181
King's Fifth, The 13014
King's Flower, The 573
King's Fountain, The 271
Kings of Motor Speed 13090
Kings of the Surf 13094
King's Pardon 4333
King's Procession, The 11278
King's Road, The 8465
King's Tea, The 12863
Kintu 5465
Kip on the Farm 13007
Kipchoge of Kenya 12905
Kirsti 12229
Kirt's New House 2898
Kisalu and His Fruit Garden 11561
Kiss for a Warthog, A 4870

Kiss for Little Bear, A   12259
Kiss Is Round, A   2514
Kit Carson (Bell)   1352
Kit Carson (Campion)   2887
Kit Carson (Garst)   6636
Kit Carson (Grant)   7176
Kit Carson (Stevenson)   16275
Kitchen Madonna, The   6953
Kitchen Window Squirrel, The
   11048
Kitchener   9956
Kite   14573
Kite for Bennie, A   7208
Kite That Won the Revolution, The
   752
Kites (Downer)   5046
Kites (Fowler)   6162
Kitten for a Day   9598
Kitten in the Pumpkin Patch, The
   15503
Kittens' ABC, The   12772
Kivi Speaks   4349
Kiviok's Magic Journey   8659
Klippity Klop   5414
Knee-baby, The   9154
Knee-Deep in Thunder   12379
Knee-High Man ..., The   10630
Knee-Knock Rise   844
Knight and Chivalry, The   1067
Knight of the Lion, The   11291
Knight Prisoner   8332
Knight's Castle   5199
Knights in Armor   6938
Knights of the Crusades   18017
Knitted Cat, The   1862
Knock Knocks   3814
Knots on a Counting Rope   11728
Know About Alcohol   8871
Know Your Declaration of Inde-
   pendence and the 56 Signers
   14646
Know Your Feelings   8873
Know Your Presidents and Their
   Wives   14647
Know Your U.S.A.   9947
Knowing Your Trees   3845
Knute Rockne (Daley)   4451
Knute Rockne (Sullivan)   16473
Knute Rockne (Van Riper)   17220
Knutty Knitting for Kids   3915
Koalas   9972
Kodi's Mare   8166
Kofi and the Eagle   9577
Kofi Mensah   422
Kofi the Good Farmer   17164
Koku Baboni   13122
Kon-Tiki   8139

Kon-Tiki and I   8128
Kongo and Kumba   15036
Kono Diamond, The   4483
Konrad   12956
Konyu's Dreams Come True   6873
Koos the Hottentot   11657
Korean Boy   13241
Korean Folk Tales   8896
Korolu, the Singing Bandit   17433
Koto and the Lagoon   9578
Kpo the Leopard   7486
Kristli's Trees   5134
Kristy's Courage   6367
K'Tonton in Israel   17662
Kulumu the Brave   15228
Kumar   3250
Kung of the Kalahari   1170
Kwabena   1861
Kwaku, a Boy of Ghana   15080
Kwame Nkrumah of the New Africa
   13857
Kwasi and the Parrot ...   9579
Kwi-Na the Eagle and Other Indian
   Tales   9099
Kyle Rote, Jr.   4975

- L -

L. C. Is the Greatest   10036
Labor Day   11694
Labor on the March   6584
Labor's Defiant Lady   17753
Lace Snail, The   2788
Lacy Makes a Match   1275
Lad   16748
Ladder Company 108   1252
Ladies of Fantasy   11603
Ladies of Seneca Falls, The   7503
Ladies of the Gothic   11604
Ladis, un gran pequeño   14878
Lady Bird, Quickly   9724
Lady Ellen Grae   3579
Lady for the Defense   6170
Lady Who Saw the Good Side of
   Everything, The   16652
Lady with the Lamp, The   18348
Ladybug, Ladybug, Fly Away Home
   7886
Lafayette, French-American Hero
   1674
Laika and the Elephant   15537
Lakeland Vet   16405
Lakes   6966

Lakes, Hills and Prairies 18228
Lakshmi, the Water Buffalo Who Wouldn't 6941
Lambs 17627
Lamb's Warrior 864
Lament of the Deer, The 13056
Lance of Kanana, The 6325
Land and People of Algeria, The 16066
Land and People of Australia, The 1823
Land and People of Austria, The 18174
Land and People of Brazil, The 2425
Land and People of Canada, The 14641
Land and People of Cuba, The 13186
Land and People of Egypt, The 11549
Land and People of Ethiopia, The 9550
Land and People of Finland, The 1586
Land and People of Germany, The 18175
Land and People of Ghana, The 14860
Land and People of Japan, The 17256
Land and People of Liberia, The 3613
Land and People of Libya, The 4095
Land and People of Morocco, The 16067
Land and People of New Zealand, The 9551
Land and People of Nigeria, The 6112
Land and People of Poland, The 9662
Land and People of Rhodesia, The 9552
Land and People of Russia, The 12690
Land and People of Sierra Leone, The 3614
Land and People of South Africa, The 13374
Land and People of Spain, The 11016
Land and People of Tanganyika, The see Land and People of Tanzania, The
Land and People of Tanzania, The 9553
Land and People of the Arabian Peninsula, The 3615
Land and People of the Congo, The 4247
Land and People of the Guianas, The 6046
Land and People of the West Indies, The 15545
Land and People of Uruguay, The 4940
Land and People of Zambia, The 5067
Land Beneath the Sea, The 11884
Land Beyond, The 7434
Land Beyond the Rivers 2280
Land Divided, the World United, The 14383
Land in the Sun 4612
Land Lies Pretty, The 7298
Land of Heroes 16601
Land of Lincoln 1775
Land of Lost Things, The 17450
Land of Silence 18299
Land of the Crocodile's Teeth, The 18099
Land of the Free, The 11991
Land of the Hibernating Rivers 3324
Land of the Inland Seas 5384
Land of the Pharaohs 4191
Land of the Sky-Blue Waters 4848
Land of the Taffeta Dawn, The 1378
Land, Wildlife and People of the Bible, The 5661
Landing of the Pilgrims, The 2072
Landmark History of the American People, The 1935
Lands Adrift 17703
Lands and Peoples of West Africa, The 12847
Lands End! 16354
Landslide! 4627
Langston Hughes (Dunham) 5133
Langston Hughes (Meltzer) 12043
Langston Hughes (Myers) 12601
Langston Hughes, American Poet 17427
Language and Man 109
Language of Animals, The 15291
Lantern Bearers, The 16525
Lantern in the Window, A 5918
Lanterns for Fiesta 6437
Lanterns over the Prairies 14578
Larbi and Leila 1603
Lark and the Laurel, The 17958

Lark in the Morn, The 17326
Lark's Castle 18434
Larry 2510
LaSalle and the Discovery of the
Great West 13332
LaSalle of the Mississippi 16588
LaSalle, River Explorer 7121
Lasers 7799
Lassie Come Home 9937
Last Battle, The (Lewis) 10689
Last Battle, The (Wibberly)
17849
Last Buffalo, The 14633
Last Camel, The 7049
Last Eagle, The 5217
Last Elizabethan, The 5742
Last Forest, The 6902
Last Free Bird, The 16364
Last Guru, The 13701
Last Lap, The 6684
Last Little Cat, The 4678
Last Night I Saw Andromeda 550
Last of the Great Picnics, The
11324
Last of the Mohicans, The 4072
Last of the Peterkins, The see
Complete Peterkin Papers,
The
Last of the Really Great Whang-
doodles, The 5280
Last One Home Is a Green Pig
8804
Last One In Is a Rotten Egg
9750
Last Plane from Uli 9587
Last Queen of Hawaii 18080
Last Stronghold, The 11161
Last Summer, The 7375
Last Sunday 13456
Last Trip of the Juno, The 5534
Last Trumpeters, The 8851
Last Two Elves in Denmark, The
2840
Latin American Crafts and Their
Cultural Backgrounds 3903
Latin American Game Songs 4653
Latin American Tales 1084
Latin Americans of the Southwest
10364
Laugh and Cry 1337
Laugh with Lucy 3757
Laughable Limericks 2216
Laughing Time 15937
Laughter Is a Wonderful Thing
2362
Launching of Sputnik, October 4,
1957, The 7511

Laura Baugh (Jacobs) 9069
Laura Baugh (O'Shea) 13193
Laura Ingalls Wilder Songbook,
The 6628
Laura Secord: A Canadian Heroine
1165
Laura's Luck 14841
Laura's Story 4740
Laurie 2061
Laurie's New Brother 15069
Lavender-Green Magic 12937
Lavender's Blue 10861
L'Aventura de Yolanda see Yo-
landa's Hike
Lawrence of Arabia 11443
Laws and Trials That Created His-
tory 837
Lawyers for the People 10670
Lays of the New Land 15710
Lazies, The 6849
Lazy Bear, The 17924
Lazy Dog, The 7638
Lazy Little Zulu, The 8444
Lazy Stories 18212
Lazy Tommy Pumpkinhead 5086
Lazy Young Duke of Dundee, The
18142
Lazyjack 17754
Leader by Destiny 5231
Leaders of the New Africa 9554
Leafs, The 12989
Lean Out of the Window 7697
Leap Before You Look 16355
Leap into Danger 7681
Learn to Count 14989
Learning About Michigan's Govern-
ment 10699
Learning to Ride, Hunt and Show
18306
Learning to Say Good-By 10618
Learning to Swim Is Fun 14821
Leashed Lightning 16571
Leatherman, The 6456
Leave Herbert Alone 17822
Leave Horatio Alone 3648
Leave Well Enough Alone 17731
Leaves 3178
Leccion de poesia 13197
Lechera/Las Habichuelas Magicas,
La 10475
Lechuza, La 13501
Lecturas Clasicas para Niños 6655
Lee and Grant at Appomattox 9485
Lee de Forest 4941
Lee Lan Flies the Dragon Kite 8111
Lee Natoni 39
Lee Wong, Boy Detective 1043

Leela and the Watermelon 8239
Left-Hander's World, The 15689
Left, Right, Left, Right 16142
Lefty 10606
Legacy of the Desert 611
Legend of Africania, The 14464
Legend of Befana, The 3232
Legend of New Amsterdam, The 16090
Legend of the Cid, The 7020
Legend of the Orange Princess, The 6942
Legend of the Willow Plate, The 17012
Legends for Everyone 5400
Legends of Green Sky Hill 17448
Legends of Hawaii 3879
Legends of Northern Ghana 16122
Legends of the Great Chiefs 11822
Legends of the Mighty Sioux 5747
Legends of the North 4021
Legends of the Saints 13586
Legends of the United Nations 6411
Leif Ericson 7177
Leif Erikson the Lucky 9203
Leif Eriksson, First Voyager to America 15565
Leif the Lucky 4553
Lemming Condition, The 632
Lemon and a Star, A 16101
Lemonade Trick, The 4115
Lengthy 8357
Lens and Shutter 17694
Lentil 11238
Lentil Soup 10297
Leo Possessed 13213
Leo the Late Bloomer 10064
Leo the Lioness 7288
Leonard Bernstein 3922
Leopard, The 1839
Leopard Dagger, The 5743
Leopards, The 12239
Leopard's Daughter, The 11801
Leopard's Tooth, The 10007
Leprechaun of Bayou Luce, The 13408
Leroy Oops 6886
Lesotho 3014
Less Than Nothing Is Really Something 6402
Lester's Overnight 3389
Let Joybells Ring 8257
Let Me Be a Free Man 9519
Let Me Fall Before I Fly 17752
Let the Balloon Go 16041

Let Us Be Men 9839
Let X Be Excitement 7761
Let's Bake Bread 9277
Let's Be Early Settlers with Daniel Boone 13295
Let's Be Enemies 17111
Let's Be Indians 13296
Let's Catch a Fish! 16338
Let's Catch a Monster 15185
Let's Celebrate 13297
Let's Celebrate Christmas 6579
Let's Color Michigan 7417
Let's Count 8450
Let's Count and Count Out! 7227
Let's Do Fingerplays 7228
Let's Explore the Great Lakes 5389
Let's Face It 608
Let's Find Out 15092
Let's Find Out About a Book 12828
Let's Find Out About Abraham Lincoln 15437
Let's Find Out About Birds 15438
Let's Find Out About Cavemen 15439
Let's Find Out About Christopher Columbus 15440
Let's Find Out About Color 2867
Let's Find Out About Daniel Boone 15441
Let's Find Out About Earth 9930
Let's Find Out About Eskimos 17873
Let's Find Out About Frogs 12628
Let's Find Out About Halloween 4081
Let's Find Out About Indians 15442
Let's Find Out About Insects 9931
Let's Find Out About Jewish Holidays 15446
Let's Find Out About Rivers 17874
Let's Find Out About Safety 15447
Let's Find Out About Snakes 15443
Let's Find Out About Space Travel 15444
Let's Find Out About Subtraction 17826
Let's Find Out About the City 13713
Let's Find Out About the Clinic 6403
Let's Find Out About the Family 13714
Let's Find Out About the Hospital 9567
Let's Find Out About the Moon 15448
Let's Find Out About the Ocean

9932

Let's Find Out About the Sun 15449

Let's Find Out About the Weather 9933

Let's Find Out About Thomas Alva Edison 15445

Let's Find Out About Water 15450

Let's Find Out About Words 5969

Let's Find Out What Electricity Does 15451

Let's Find Out What's Big and What's Small 15452

Let's Find Out What's Light and What's Heavy 15453

Let's Get Turtles 15292

Let's Go Boating 18500

Let's Go Camping 18501

Let's Go Down the Mississippi with LaSalle 2470

Let's Go Sailing 13091

Let's Go to a Basketball Game 8544

Let's Go to a Horse Show 14639

Let's Go to a Hospital 14723

Let's Go to a Stock Exchange 821

Let's Go to a Supermarket 3270

Let's Go to Africa 12084

Let's Go to an Indian Cliff Dwelling 17979

Let's Go to Stop Water Pollution 3336

Let's Go to the Brook 8792

Let's Hear It for America 17618

Let's Hear It for the Queen 3374

Let's Knot 10808

Let's Learn About Lighthouses 7276

Let's Learn About Silk 13560

Let's Learn About the Orchestra 7277

Let's Learn Ski Touring 16877

Let's Learn to Snorkel 16878

Let's Look at Costume 4064

Let's Look at Insects 8793

Let's Look at Reptiles 8794

Let's Look at Tracks 9863

Let's Look Under the City 15093

Let's Make a Deal 6904

Let's Make a Play 11506

Let's Make More Presents 7856

Let's Make Soup 9278

Let's Marry Said the Cherry 1831

Let's Meet the Chemist 7278

Let's Play Desert 14881

Let's Re-Discover Indiana, Vol. I: Northwest Indiana 2693

Let's Re-Discover Indiana, Vol. II: Southeast Quadrant 2694

Let's Steal the Moon 15357

Let's Talk About the Jewish Holidays 10097

Let's Talk About the Metric System 10214

Let's Think About Time 7802

Let's Travel in Nigeria and Ghana 9873

Let's Travel in the Congo 9874

Let's Visit Afghanistan 2817

Let's Visit Australia 2818

Let's Visit Formosa 2819

Let's Visit Indonesia 2820

Let's Visit Mexico 2820a

Let's Visit Middle Africa 2821

Let's Visit New Zealand 2822

Let's Visit Nigeria 6346

Let's Visit North Africa 17940

Let's Visit Rhodesia 18103

Let's Visit South Africa 12786

Let's Visit Southeast Asia 2823

Let's Visit Thailand 2824

Let's Visit the Middle East 2825

Let's Visit the Philippines 2826

Let's Visit West Africa 2827

Letter for Amy, A 9599

Letter on the Tree, The 2962

Letter Perfect 4252

Letter, the Witch, and the Ring, The 1362

Letters and Words 10095

Letters from the Calico Cat 3278

Letters to Children 13840

Letters to Horseface 12343

Letters to Pauline 10118

Level Land, The 4669

Lever and the Pulley, The 8036

Lew Wallace 14999

Lewanika, Paramount Chief of the Barotse and Allied Tribes, 1875-1916 11433

Lewis and Clark Expedition, The 12753

Lexington and Concord in Color 1245

Lexington and Concord, 1775 3790

Lexington, Concord, and Bunker Hill 14783

Leyendas amazonicas 9386

Leyendas de España 9233

Leyendas de los Andes 12415

Leyendas del Caribe 12416

Leyendas Mexicanas 12417
Li Lun, Lad of Courage 16989
Liam's Catch 13308
Libby's Step-Family 15767
Liberation of Clementine Tipton,
  The 6072
Liberia 3015
Liberia in Pictures 12270
Liberian Folklore 8056
Liberty Book 5944
Libro de los Alimentos, El 13561
Libro de los animales, El 9234
Libro para Mis Nietos, Un 4584
Libya 3016
Life and Death 18563
Life and Death in Nature 15748
Life and Death of Nazi Germany,
  The 7021
Life and Death of Yellow Bird,
  The 6115
Life and Legend of George Mc-
  Junkin 6093
Life and Times of Frederick Doug-
  lass, The (Douglass) 5036
Life and Times of Frederick Doug-
  lass (Gray) 7209
Life Battles Cold 9558
Life for Israel, A 4952
Life in a Bucket of Soil 14284
Life in a Drop of Water 15155
Life in a Log 15156
Life in America: Alaska 16932
Life in America: The Midwest
  7864
Life in Lincoln's America 4315
Life in New York 11620
Life in the Ancient World 18110
Life in the Dark 15749
Life in the Desert 10292
Life in the Middle Ages 18018
Life in the Pit 10766
Life in the Zoo 3378
Life of Benjamin Banneker, The
  1298
Life of Keshav, The 12018
Life of Numbers, The 10027
Life of Pocahontas, The 5626
Life of Saint Patrick, The 14281
Life of the African Plains, The
  2365
Life of the Loyalists 12703
Life of Their Own, A 9196
Life on a Lost Continent 4621
Life on the Line 12859
Life on the Texas Range 15887
Life Story 2730
Life with Working Parents 7857

Lift Every Voice 16243
Lift Every Voice and Sing 9288
Lift Line 5794
Lift-Off 4038
Light 8706
Light a Single Candle 2745
Light and Darkness 2132
Light and Radiation 6288
Light and Shadow 15137
Light at Tern Rock, The 14938
Light in the Dark, A 12044
Light in the Dark Forest 9409
Light in the Forest, The 14347
Light in the Grotto 4537
Light Motorcycle Repair and Main-
  tenance 13092
Light Princess, The 11302
Lighthouse Mystery, The 17526
Lightning and Thunder 18545
Lightning Slinger 6774
Lightning Time 11541
Like a Lady 4499
Like and Unlike 14797
Like You, Like Me 4496
Likely Lad, A 810
Likely Place, A 6182
Lilies, Rabbits and Painted Eggs
  1139
Liliuokalani 11581
Liliuokalani, Young Hawaiian Queen
  12798
Lillan 12912
Lillian Wald 17986
Lillie of Watts 17501
Lillie of Watts Takes a Giant Step
  17502
Lily at the Table 8035
Limericks by Lear 10465
Limpieza en el bosque 13232
Lincoln 11412
Lincoln a Big Man 9571
Lincoln and Douglass 7671
Lincoln Country in Pictures, The
  6237
Lincoln Lived Here 12240
Lincoln Treasury, The 7743
Lincoln's Animal Friends 14110
Lincoln's Birthday 2563
Linda Goes to the Hospital 5101
Linda Richards 3849; see also
  America's First Trained Nurse
Linda's Indian Home 11425
Linda's Raintree 7648
Lindbergh the Lone Flier 5961
Linebacker! 16474
Linebackers 7809
Lines and Shapes 14798

Lines, Segments, Polygons 15800
Linnet 17597
Linnets and Valerians 7096
Lion (DuBois) 5087
Lion, The (Kessel) 9738
Lion Adventure 13932
Lion and Blue 17259
Lion and the Bird's Nest, The 9870
Lion and the Rat, The 10190
Lion Boy 16256
Lion Boy's White Brother 16257
Lion Family, The 3955
Lion Gate and Labyrinth 1209
Lion in the Box, The 4638
Lion in the Gateway, The 14238
Lion in the Meadow, A 11553
Lion, Jackal and Hare 6308
Lion of the Kalahari, The 8314
Lion on the Mountain 4926
Lion on the Path ..., The 16967
Lion on the Run 14763
Lion Outwitted by Hare ... 14962
Lion Sneezed, The 10447
Lion, the Witch, and the Wardrobe, The 10690
Lion Yellow 4914
Lionhearted, The 14954
Lion's Cub, The 8564
Lions in the Way 14549
Lions of Africa, The 9299
Lions on the Hunt 17419
Lion's Whiskers, The 4613
Lisa and Her Soundless World 10653
Lisa and Lottie 9509
Lisa and the Grompet 4055
Lisa, Bright and Dark 12756
Lisa Cannot Sleep 1295
Lise Meitner 4255
Lisette 8451
Lissamor's Child 355
Listen, Children, Listen 10970
Listen for the Singing 10938
Listen Rabbit 5919
Listen to Me! 1091
Listen to the Crows 13962
Listening Point 13115
Listening Walk, The 15599
Literature of the Supernatural 1289
Lithuanian Folk Tales 18597
Lito and the Clown 13779
Lito the Shoeshine Boy 11599
Litter, the Ugly Enemy 15644
Little Apes 3956
Little Appaloosa 7544

Little at a Time, A 95
Little Auto, The 10574
Little Bear 12260
Little Bear Learns to Read the Cookbook 9134
Little Bear's Christmas 9135
Little Bear's Friend 12261
Little Bear's New Year's Party 9136
Little Bear's Thanksgiving 9137
Little Bear's Visit 12262
Little Big Man 1544
Little Black, a Pony 5692
Little Black Bear Goes for a Walk 6334
Little Black Puppy, The 18606
Little Black Stories for Little White Children 3217
Little Blue and Little Yellow 10882
Little Boat Boy 1983
Little Book of Anagrams, The 1123
Little Book of Little Beasts, A 8308
Little Book of Soccer, The 7789
Little Bookroom, The 5677
Little Boy Who Lives Up High 7900
Little Boy with Three Names 3487
Little Britches 12376
Little Broomstick, The 16309
Little Brother of the Wilderness 10635
Little Brown Gazelle 1069
Little Brown Hen 11752
Little Brute Family, The 8285
Little Calf 15029
Little Carousel, The 2379
Little Chalk Man, The 4339
Little Chief 8358
Little Circle, The 786
Little Destiny, A 3580
Little Dickens, Jaguar Cub 1303
Little Dinosaurs and Early Birds 9542
Little Dog Lost 7487
Little Dogs of the Prairie 15200
Little Drawing Book of Weirdos 5415
Little Drummer Boy, The 9600
Little Duster, The 3287
Little Eddie 7955
Little Ego 6838
Little Elk Hunts Buffalo 11326
Little Engine That Could, The 13708
Little Fir Tree, The 2392
Little Fire Engine, The (Greene) 7293

Little Fire Engine, The (Lenski) 10575

Little Fisherman, The 2393

Little Fishes, The 7846

Little Flute Player, The 1984

Little Fox Goes to the End of the World 16930

Little Fox in the Middle, The 2487

Little Fu 4279

Little Game Hunter, The 13020

Little Giant, The 12883

Little Giant Girl and the Elf Boy, The 12263

Little Girl with Seven Names 8758

Little Gorilla 1961

Little Hatchy Hen 6064

Little Hellion, a Story of "Egypt," The 14147

Little Hill, The 1318

Little Hippo 334

Little House, The (Burton) 2731

Little House, The (Thayer) 16784

Little House Cookbook, The 17439

Little House in the Big Woods 17903

Little House of Your Own, A 4741

Little House on the Prairie 17904

Little Igloo, The 1344

Little Indian 13298

Little Indian Basket Maker, The 3488

Little Indian Pottery Maker, The 3489

Little Indians' ABC 11152

Little Island, The 11307

Little John 16383

Little Jonathan 11792

Little Juggler, The 4061

Little Kid's Americana Craft Book, The 17284

Little Kid's Craft Book, The 17285

Little Kingdom, The 2848

Little Koala 12869

Little Lame Prince, The 12552

Little Laughter, A 11092

Little League Heroes 1682

Little League Leader 10490

Little League Victory 1683

Little Leftover Witch, The 10362

Little Leo 13780

Little Lion, A 17761

Little Locomotive 13098

Little Lone Coyote 7935

Little Long-Nose and His Animal Friends 12762

Little Lost Bee, The 9496

Little Man, The 9510

Little Man and the Big Thief, The 9511

Little Man in the Family 15511

Little Match Girl 440

Little Men 223

Little Men of the NFL 14734

Little Mohee 17022

Little Mops at the Seashore 5402

Little Mossback Amelia 6167

Little Naturalist, The 6412

Little Navajo Bluebird 3490

Little O 17147

Little Old Man Who Cooked and Cleaned, The 1700

Little Old Man Who Could Not Read, The 1701

Little Old Mrs. Pepperpot ... 13983

Little Old Woman Who Used Her Head, The 12782

Little One Inch 2194

Little Owl Indian 1261

Little Owl, Keeper of the Trees 8211

Little Park, The 5856

Little Pear 10331

Little Pear and His Friends 10332

Little Pear and the Rabbits 10333

Little Pieces of the West Wind 6625

Little Pig and the Big Bad Wolf 17896

Little Plum 6954

Little Prince, The 14857

Little Princess, A 2669

Little Queen of Sheba 6988

Little Rabbit Who Wanted Red Wings 905

Little Rabbit's Loose Tooth 1168

Little Raccoon and No Trouble at All 12399

Little Raccoon and the Thing in the Pool 12400

Little Rascal 12923

Little Red Hen (Domanska) 4998

Little Red Hen (Galdone) 6501

Little Red Lighthouse and the Great Gray Bridge, The 16560

Little Red Riding Hood 6502

Little Rhody 6237

Little Riders 15531

Little Runner of the Longhouse 927

Little Sail Boat, The 10576

Little Sasabonsam, The 4662

Little School at Cottonwood Corners, The 15047

Little Schubert, A 6975

Little Silver House 10854

Little Sioux Girl 10577

Little Sister and the Month Brothers 4742

Little Spotted Fish, The 18416

Little Stripe 706

Little Swineherd and Other Tales, The 6183

Little Thunder 3216

Little Tim and the Brave Sea Captain 622

Little Time, A 999

Little Tiny Rooster, The 17950

Little Tiny Woman, The 18525

Little Toot 7157

Little Toot on the Mississippi 7158

Little Toot on the Thames 7159

Little Toot Through the Golden Gate 7160

Little Town on the Prairie 17905

Little Train, The (Greene) 7294

Little Train (Lenski) 10578

Little Tumbler, The 10334

Little Turtle 3057

Little Two and the Peach Tree 11753

Little Vic 6660

Little Viking, The 8452

Little Wee Tyke, The 15393

Little Whale 11356

Little Whistler, The 6413

Little White Hen 9786

Little White Hen and the Emperor of France 16875

Little White Horse, The 7097

Little Wild Elephant 12141

Little Wind 2753

Little Wise One, The 18281

Little Witch 1465

Little Witch's Black Magic Book of Games, The 6905

Little Witch's Book of Yoga, The 6906

Little Witch's Christmas Book, The 6907

Little Witch's Halloween Book 6908

Little Wolf, the Rain Dancer 15412

Little Woman Wanted Noise, The 16722

Little Women 224

Little Wonders of Nature 7555

Little Wood Duck, The 17925

Little Wooden Doll, The 1630

Little Wooden Farmer, The 4459

Little Wu and the Watermelons 10950

Little Yellow Fur 7936

Littlest Angel, The 16719

Littlest Witch, The 11802

Lives of My Cat Alfred, The 18577

Living Amphibians of the World 3718

Living Architecture 14113

Living Community, The 8226

Living Free 69

Living in a Castle 17149

Living in a Crusader Land 17150

Living in a Medieval City 17151

Living in a Medieval Village 17152

Living in Indiana 10173

Living in Indiana History 3611

Living in Navajoland 8539

Living Lanterns 15720

Living Past, A 5575

Living Things (Allred) 370

Living Things (Bendick) 1427

Living Things and Their Young 11885

Living Things That Poison, Itch, and Sting 2739

Living with a Parent Who Drinks Too Much 15257

Living with Differences 15169

Living with Loneliness 18294

Living with Mommy 15657

Living World of the Sea, The 4304

Liza Lou and the Yeller Belly Swamp 11930

Lizard Lying in the Sun 6335

Lizard Music 13702

Lizard Tails and Cactus Spines 2195

Lizards as Pets 7972

Lizzie Lies a Lot 10671

Llamas of South America 3957

Llega un hermanito 10981

Lloron hijo de dragon 14356

Lo Chau of Hong Kong 3198

Lo que sabia mi loro 12422

Load of Unicorn, The see Caxton's Challenge

Lobster, The 16682

Lock Her Through ... 1587

Lock, Stock and Barrel 15984

Lodge Stories 4979
Log Cabin Family 8618
Lokoshi Learns to Hunt Seals
    4272
Lollipop 17605
Lollipop Party, The 16017
London and Port Stanley Railway,
    The 517
London Bridge Is Falling Down
    (Emberley) 5416
London Bridge Is Falling Down
    (Spier) 16091
Lone Bull's Horse Raid 6946
Lone Hunt, The 16171
Lone Hunter and the Cheyennes
    18271
Lone Journey 5232
Lonely Black Pig ..., The 11819
Lonely Doll, The 18301
Lonely Maria 3687
Lonely Veronica 5180
Lonely Village, The 11808
Loner, The (Bradbury) 2062
Loner, The (Kwolek) 10166
Loner, The (Wier) 17865
Loners, The 6576
Lonesome Boy 1921
Lonesome Egg, The 8651
Lonesome Little Colt 468
Lonesome Traveler 8194
Long Ago 16606
Long Ago Lake, The 17942
Long Black Schooner, The 16254
Long, Broad & Quickeye 12746
Long Day in November, A 6481
Long Grass Whispers, The 5360
Long Green, The 6685
Long Hungry Night, The 6137
Long Journey, The 4136
Long Journey Home 10631
Long Live the Delta Queen 7296
Long-Lost Coelacanth and Other
    Living Fossils, The 305
Long Man's Song 14544
Long Pony Race, The 10551
Long Secret, The 5980
Long-Shadowed Forest, The 8569
Long Ships Passing, The 7865
Long, Short, High, Low, Thin,
    Wide 5843
Long Shot for Paul 3423
Long Tailed Bear, The 1379
Long Time Growing, A 12027
Long Trail for Francisco 17198
Long View into Space, The 15750
Long Voyage, The 15690
Long Way from Verona, A 6574

Long Way Home, The 1393
Long Way to Whiskey Creek, A
    1276
Long Winter, The 17906
Long Winter Sleep, The 6983
Long Year, The 17866
Longhouse Legends 11823
Longhouse to Blast Furnace 6123
Longhouse Winter 9356
Longleaf 2278
Look Again 8300
Look at a Calf 18302
Look at a Flower 5042
Look at a Kitten 18303
Look at Annette 17499
Look at Cars 11067
Look at Divorce, A 14003
Look at Me! 3362
Look at Your Eyes 15600
Look for the Stars 8185
Look for Words 17643
Look How Many People Wear Glasses
    2257
Look-It-Up Book of Mammals 10350
Look-It-Up Book of Stars and
    Planets, The 10351
Look of Cars, The 10597
Look Out for the Ostriches 9441
Look, There Is a Turtle Flying
    4999
Look Through My Window 10939
Look to the Night Sky 15751
Look to the River 13217
Look to This Day! 2889
Look What I Can Do 696
Look What I Found! 3141
Lookalikes 5477
Looking at Ancient History 17153
Looking at Architecture 13239
Looking at Art 3295
Looking at China 7221
Looking at France 3444
Looking at Germany 9847
Looking at Holland 11037
Looking at Israel 14812
Looking at Nigeria 10308
Looking at Norway 725
Looking at Paintings 9700
Looking at Sculpture 13240
Looking at You 15862
Looking Book, A 8309
Looking Down Game, The 4767
Looking for a Place 11671
Looking for Orlando 2327
Looking Forward to a Career:
    Dentistry 9481
Looking Forward to a Career:

Veterinary Medicine   6832
Looking Glass Book of Verse,
  The   15904
Loon, The   341
Loon's Necklace, The   16964
Loosen Your Ears   5684
Lorax, The   15381
Lord Is My Shepard, The (Barn-
  hart)   1093
Lord Is My Shepherd, The (Kraus)
  10052
Lord of the Dance, The   344
Lord of the Sky   6661
Lords Baltimore, The   164
Lords of the Earth   11033
Lordy, Aunt Hattie   16816
Lore of the Great Turtle   7418
Lore of the Lakes   2013
Lorenzo and Angelina   5826
Lose Four Trying for Eight
  11030
Loss and How to Cope with It
  1572
Lost   10906
Lost and Found   10962
Lost Bear, Found Bear   11945
Lost Boy, The   10519
Lost Ear-ring, The   592
Lost Farm, The   4400
Lost Half-Hour, The   14640
Lost in the Barrens   12524
Lost in the Desert   14764
Lost in the Forest   15179
Lost in the Jungle   5097
Lost in the Museum   3760
Lost in the Storm   3074
Lost in the Zoo   7545
Lost John   13654
Lost Kingdom, The   2462
Lost Kingdom of Karnica, The
  9694
Lost Lakes, The   13434
Lost Princess, The   11303
Lost Queen of Egypt, The   12473
Lost Sister Among the Miamis,
  The   18112
Lost Treasures of America   11521
Lost Violin, The   9423
Lost Waters, The   14756
Lost World, The   5058
Lost Worlds   17784
Lost Zoo, The   4345
Lotor the Raccoon   14785
Lotta Crabtree   13720
Lottery Rose, The   8749
Lotte's Locket   16027
Lottie Moon of China   16501

Lotus and the Grail, The   see
  Sea Magic and Other Stories of
  Enchantment
Lotus Caves, The   3407
Lou Gehrig   11150
Loudest Noise in the World, The
  5347
Louie   9601
Louie's Snowstorm   8176
Louis Armstrong (Cornell)   4160
Louis Armstrong (Richards)   14332
Louis Braille   10127
Louis D. Brandeis Story, The
  13435
Louisa May Alcott (Colver)   3888
Louisa May Alcott (Papashvily)
  13273
Louisa May Alcott (Wagoner)   17390
Louisiana   3017
Louisiana Man   9737
Louly   2265
Lovable Lyle   17365
Love and Sex in Plain Language
  9262
Love, Bid Me Welcome   11124
Love Comes to Eunice K. O'Herlihy
  7655
Love from Uncle Clyde   13315
Love Is a Special Way of Feeling
  549
Lower East Side, The   3183
Lucille   10998
Lucinda   6253
Lucinda, a Little Girl of 1860   8759
Luck of Brin's Five, The   17899
Luck of Harry Weaver, The   17964
Luck of Pokey Bloom, The   3938
Luck of the La Verendryes, The
  7756
Luckie Star, The   17426
Lucky Book of Riddles   12388
Lucky Ghost Shirt, The   11768
Lucky Ladybugs   3958
Lucky, Lucky, White Horse   5481
Lucky Mtende ...   9449
Lucky Sew-It-Yourself Book, The
  15995
Lucky Stone, The   3628
Lucky Wilma   9812
Lucky Year   240
Lucretia Mott (Burnett)   2668
Lucretia Mott (Faber)   5627
Lucretia Mott (Sterling)   16240
Lucy   16384
Lucy Brown and Mr. Grimes   623
Lucy Learns to Weave   8374
Lucy Runs Away   16385

Ludell   17945
Ludell and Willie   17946
Ludo and the Star Horse   16310
Luis   6777
Luis Muñoz Marin   11610
Luke and the Indians   8428
Luke Baldwin's Vow   2849
Luke Was There   3649
Lullabies and Night Songs   5461
Lum Fu and the Golden Mountain
    9808
Lumber Camp Life in Michigan
    5195
Lumberjack   10139
Lumberjacks of the North Woods
    13385
Lumps, Bumps and Rashes   12960
Lurk of Leopards, A   4915
Luther Burbank, Nature's Helper
    2089
Luther from Inner City   2105
Luther Raps   2106
Luther Tarbox   89
Luvvy and the Girls   2963
Lyle and Humus   18490
Lyle and the Birthday Party
    17366
Lyle Finds His Mother   17367
Lyle, Lyle, Crocodile   17368
Lyncoya   5602
Lyndon Baines Johnson   13075
Lyrico   6136
Lysbet and the Fire Kittens
    12504

- M -

MBD   6592
M. C. Higgins, the Great   7660
M for Mischief   13318
M Is for Moving   8895
Ma nDa la   132
Maasai, The   14907
Mabel the Whale   9821
Macaroon   4373
McBroom and the Beanstalk   6011
McBroom Tells a Lie   6012
McBroom Tells the Truth   6013
McBroom the Rainmaker   6014
McBroom's Ear   6015
McBroom's Wonderful One Acre
    Farm   see   McBroom Tells the
    Truth

McBroom's Zoo   6016
McElligot's Pool   15382
Machine Gunners, The   17752
Machine Tools   18570
Machines   14514
Machines for You   14942
Mackinac Island   13551
Mackinac Island and Sault Ste.
    Marie   12806
MacLeod Place, The   650
McWhinney's Jaunt   10423
Mad Martin   18109
Mad Wet Hen ..., A   11115
Madagascar   880
Madame Curie (Bigland)   1647
Madame Curie (Henriod)   8058
Made in Ancient Egypt   13915
Made in Ancient Greece   13916
Made in Japan   16064
Made in Mexico   14661
Made in the Renaissance   13917
Made in West Africa   13918
Madeleine   1387
Madeleine Takes Command   2248
Madeleine's Rescue   1388
Mademoiselle Louise   4991
Magdalena   15589
Magellan, First Around the World
    16589
Maggie and the Pirates   9602
Maggie B, The   7539
Maggie Marmelstein for President
    15468
Maggie of Barnaby Bay   18083
Maggie Rose   14971
Magic at Wychwood   17598
Magic Bedknob, The   see   Bedknob
    and Broomstick
Magic Bridle and Other Folk Tales
    from Great Britain and Ireland,
    The   see   Witch's Bridle, The
Magic Calabash and Other Stories
    12026
Magic Cave and Other Stories, The
    13859
Magic Christmas Tree, The   9827
Magic Cooking Pot, The   16946
Magic Drum, The (Burton)   2734
Magic Drum, The (Kirkup)   9861
Magic Egg ..., The   14749
Magic Eye for Ida, A   3390
Magic Finger, The   4445
Magic Fingers   12547
Magic Fishbone, The   4882
Magic Flute, The   4336
Magic for Mary M   938
Magic Grandfather, The   18019

Magic Hat, The   3269
Magic Horns, The   16421
Magic House of Numbers   106
Magic in My Pocket   17176
Magic in the Mist   9811
Magic in Your Pockets   15391
Magic Jacket, The   4687
Magic Land of the Shadows, The
   13123
Magic Lantern, The   16862
Magic Listening Cap, The   17096
Magic Little Ones, The   1297
Magic Lollipop, The   10003
Magic Made Easy   9761
Magic Maker, The   17249
Magic Meadow, The   9772
Magic Michael   15839
Magic Mirrors, The   7369
Magic Money   3491
Magic Moth, The   10498
Magic Number   7060
Magic of Black Poetry, The   20
Magic of Paper, The   2520
Magic of the Glits, The   91
Magic of the Little People, The
   3747
Magic or Not?   5200
Magic People   15993
Magic Porridge Pot, The   6503
Magic Pot, The   4056
Magic Pumpkin, The   15819
Magic Rug, The   4542
Magic Secrets   18344
Magic Shop   4976
Magic Sled, The   1404
Magic Sledge, The   see   Magic
   Sled, The
Magic Stick, The   14380
Magic Stone, The   9997
Magic Summer, The   16409
Magic Three of Solatia, The   18417
Magic Tortoise, The   16387
Magic Touch, The   870
Magic Tree, The   11292
Magic Umbrella and Other Stories
   for Telling, The   3893
Magic Wall   17246
Magic Well, The   17280
Magic World, The   12735; see also
   Awkward Magic
Magical Cupboard, The   4401
Magical Melons   2266
Magical Story Book   18020
Magician, The   15612
Magician of Cracow, The   17076
Magicians Do Amazing Things
   10049

Magician's Nephew, The   10691
Magna Carta   8318
Magnets (Adler)   117
Magnets (Podendorf)   13757
Magnets (Sacks)   14850
Magnificent House of Man Alone,
   The   14774
Maha and Her Donkey   18102
Mahalia, Gospel Singer   11284
Mahalia Jackson (Cornell)   4161
Mahalia Jackson (Dunham)   5134
Mai Asigiri   2041
Mai-Ling and the Mirror   27
Maid of Artemis, The   4022
Maildun the Voyager   14206
Majesty of Grace, The   10262
Majola, a Zulu Boy   16200
Major and His Camels, The   11793
Make a Bigger Puddle, Make a
   Smaller Worm   17500
Make a Circle, Keep Us In   133
Make a Joyful Noise unto the Lord!
   9001
Make a Witch, Make a Goblin   4953
Make It and Use It!   2947
Make No Sound   4137
Make the Team in Baseball   473
Make the Team in Basketball   1300
Make the Team in Football   474
Make-Up, Costumes and Masks for
   the Stage   2456
Make-up Monsters   4220
Make Way for Ducklings   11239
Make Your Own Animated Movies
   450
Make Your Own Chess Set   3094
Make Your Own Hot Rod   15918
Make Your Own Model Forts and
   Castles   4360
Makers of a Better America   10537
Making a Native Plant Terrarium
   8099
Making Babies   16207
Making Costumes for Parties, Plays,
   and Holidays   6819
Making Easy Puppets   10724
Making Fishing Tackle   14004
Making Friends   15048
Making It Happen   12682
Making Music for Money   3840
Making Musical Things   18149
Making of a Detective, The   12245
Making of a Police Officer, The
   5801
Making of a Rookie, The   10915
Making of Joshua Cobb, The
   8333

Making Our Way   9527
Making Teen Parties Click   14421
Making Things   18150
Making Things Book 2   18151
Making Your Own Movies   8032
Makoto, the Smallest Boy   17097
Maku   11035
Malagasy Republic (Carpenter & Maginnis)   3046
Malagasy Republic, The (Marshall)   11708
Malawi   3018
Malawi in Pictures   881
Malcolm X (Adoff)   134
Malcolm X (White)   17800
Malcolm Yucca Seed   6775
Maldonado Miracle, The   16714
Mali   3019
Malibu ..., The   10971
Mama   8597
Mama Hattie's Girl   10579
Mamakuu's Family   16792
Mama's Ghosts   11080
Mammals of Algonquin Provincial Park   13141
Mammals of Ontario   4435
Mammals of the World   2494
Man and Mastiff   9572
Man and Materials: Coal   14362
Man and Materials: Gas   14363
Man and Materials: Oil   14364
Man and Woman   11886
Man Changes the Weather   2006
Man Comes to America   4232
Man from the Sea, The   523
Man in Flight   13479
Man in Space to the Moon   2133
Man in the Box, The   5143
Man in the Moon, The   8974
Man in the Moon as He Sails the Sky ..., The   15178
Man Is, A   13482
Man Must Speak   6520
Man Named Columbus, A   12900
Man Named Lincoln, A   12901
Man Named Washington, A   12902
Man of the Family, A   2658
Man of the House, The   5712
Man on the Iron Horse, The   17893
Man the Measurer   6521
Man Who Changed China, The   2488
Man Who Didn't Wash His Dishes, The   10037
Man Who Had No Dream, The   8453

Man Who Lost His Head, The   1675
Man Who Made Everyone Late, The   16446
Man Who Made Fine Tops, The   18117
Man Who Said No, The   5285
Man Who Sang the Sillies, The   3463
Man Who Took the Indoors Out, The   10999
Man Who Tried to Save Time, The   10038
Man Who Was Going to Mind the House, The   11409
Man with a Mission   123
Man with the Silver Eyes, The   16172
Man Without a Face, The   8469
Managers, The   15908
Mañana de parque   5883
Mañana Is Now   5307
Manchita   2056
Mandy   5281
Mandy's Grandmother   15812
Mango Tooth, The   13808
Mango's Grass House and Other Stories   9450; see also Stories of Konga, The
Manhattan Is Missing   8177
Manifesto and Me--Meg, The   9515
Manners Made Easy   1312
Manners to Grow On   10497
Man's Mark on the Land   7328
Man's Marvelous Computer   14766
Man's Reach for the Stars   6522
Man's Useful Plants   17664
Mansa Helps at Home   711
Manso vidrio del aire   14599
Manual of Throws for Sport Judo and Self-Defense   12708
Manuel, Young Mexican-American   7279
Manuela's Birthday   1059
Manuelito, el Niño Navajo   14098
Many Faces of Slavery, The   10654
Many Hands Cooking   4089
Man Is How Many?   13758
Many Lives of Benjamin Franklin, The   306
Many Lives of Chio and Goro, The   10800
Many Moons   16856
Many Names of Lee Lu, The   3637
Many Paths to God   14059
Many Ways of Seeing, The   12392
Many Winters   18237
Many Worlds of Benjamin Franklin,

The 5007
Manzana Es Roja, La 4407
Mao Tse-Tung 612
Maoris of New Zealand, The 11385
Map Making 2366
Maple Harvest 6726
Maple Street 160
Maple Tree 15293
Mapmakers of America 8227
Maps, Tracks, and the Bridges
of Konigsberg 8522
Maquina escarbadora, La 6556
Mara, Daughter of the Nile
11373
Marassa and Midnight 16426
Marathon Miranda 18130
Marc and Pixie and the Walls in
Mrs. Jones' Garden 5723
Marcel Marceau Alphabet Book,
The 12069
Marcel Marceau Counting Book,
The 12070
Marcelo casi-casi 11664
March of the Lemmings, The
12805
March Toward Freedom 1050
Marchers for the Dream 2964
Marching Toward Freedom 11504
Marco and Michela 14254
Marco and the Tiger 6154
Marco Polo 13898
Marco Polo's Adventures in China
14758
Marconi 3725
Marcus and Narcissa Whitman,
Oregon Pioneers 13721
Margaret Mead (Church) 3443
Margaret Mead (Morse) 12481
Margaret Sanger 10180
Margaret's Birthday 17405
Margaret's Heart Operation 3367
Marguerite de Angeli's Book of
Nursery and Mother Goose
Rhymes 4639
Maria 10745
Maria and Ramon 15081
Maria Cristina's World 13483
Maria Luisa 11527
Maria Lupin 5673
Maria Making Pottery 8867
Maria Martinez 12724
Maria Mitchell 17935; see also
America's First Woman Astron-
omer
Maria Mitchell, Girl Astronomer
12032
Maria Sanford 7804

Maria Tallchief (De Leeuw) 4704
Maria Tallchief (Gridley) 7354
Maria Tallchief (Tobias) 16900
Mariah Delany Lending Library
Disaster, The 7319
Marian Anderson (Newman) 12799
Marian Anderson (Tobias) 16901
Maria's Cave 8552
Maria's House 12110
Marie Curie (De Leeuw) 4705
Marie Curie (Henry) 8060
Marie Curie (Ivimey) 8960
Marie Curie (McKown) 11437
Marie Louise and Christophe 2965
Marie Louise's Heyday 2966
Marigold Garden 7252
Marijuana 16434
Marinka, Katinka and Me (Susie)
11528
Marion Hilliard 18088
Mario's Mystery Machine 7687
Mariposa, La 11683
Mark of Conte, The 10661
Mark Spitz 13107
Mark Twain 13436
Marko the Rich and Vasily the
Unlucky 150
Marks of Lincoln on Our Land
14178
Marly the Kid 13605
Marooned in Orbit 1032
Marquette and Joliet 16590
Marra's World 3688
Marrow of the World, The 12821
Marshes and Marsh Life 4954
Marshmallow 12773
Marsuf, el vagabundo del espacio
14868
Martha Ann and the Mother Store
3288
Martha Berry (Blackburn) 1704
Martha Berry (Phelan) 13616
Martha, Daughter of Virginia 17189
Martha the Millipede 9793
Martha Washington (Anderson) 488
Martha Washington (Wagoner) 17391
Martha's Mad Day 7710
Martin and Abraham Lincoln 3714
Martin de Porres, Hero 1676
Martin Luther King (Boone-Jones)
1933
Martin Luther King (Clayton) 3547
Martin Luther King, Jr. (McKee)
11411
Martin Luther King, Jr. (Millender)
12212
Martin Luther King, Jr. (Patterson)

13386
Martin Luther King, Jr. (Wilson)
18066
Martin Pippin in the Apple Orchard
5678
Martin Pippin in the Daisy Field
5679
Martin Rides the Moor 15934
Martin's Father 5298
Marty and the Micro-Midgets
2763
Marv 14842
Marvel of Glass, The 2551
Marvelous Catch of Old Hannibal,
The 417
Marvelous Light, The 13745
Marvelous Misadventures of Se-
bastian, The 272
Marvelous Mud Washing Machine,
The 18184
Mary Alice, Operator No. 9
342
Mary Cassatt 12602
Mary, Come Running 12111
Mary Decker 9070
Mary Jane 16241
Mary Jemison, Seneca Captive
6580
Mary Jo's Grandmother 17112
Mary Lou and Johnny 7721
Mary Lyon of Putnam's Hill 1056
Mary McLeod Bethune (Anderson)
489
Mary McLeod Bethune (Burt)
2715
Mary McLeod Bethune (Greenfield)
7307
Mary McLeod Bethune (Radford)
14060
Mary McLeod Bethune (Sterne)
16255
Mary Mapes Dodge 11794
Mary of Mile 18 1708
Mary Poppins 16972
Mary, Queen of Apostles 4538
Mary Todd Lincoln (Anderson)
490
Mary Todd Lincoln (Wilkie) 17936
Marya 1782
Maryland Colony, The 11780
Maryland Personality Parade
14586
Mary's Monster 1711
Mary's Star 7937
Mas paginas para imaginar 2814
Mas Poemas Parvulos 6485
Masai, The 1756

Masai of East Africa, The 17422
Mask-Making with Pantomime and
Stories from American History
14653
Mask of Akhnaten, The 15667
Mask, the Door County Coon 15559
Masks 317
Masks and Mask Makers 8754
Master Builders of the Middle Ages
9036
Master Cornhill 11374
Master Entrick 12519
Master Key, The 1199
Master Magicians, The 6791
Master of All Masters 9051
Master of Miracle, The 8945
Master of the Winds, The 6850
Master Puppeteer, The 13369
Master Rosalind 1284
Master Simon's Garden 12022
Master Spy 7572
Masters of Magic 9683
Mat Pit and the Tunnel Tenants
7320
Matabele Fireside Tales 14963
Matabele Folk Tales 10220
Match Point 8984
Matchlock Gun, The 5269
Math Menagerie 9445
Mathematical Games and Puzzles
14314
Mathematical Games for One or Two
3290
Mathematical Princess ..., The
12976
Mathematical Puzzles 6586
Matilda Investigates 509
Matilda, Who Told Lies and Was
Burned to Death 1363
Matilda's Buttons 8760
Matt Gargan's Boy 15854
Matter of Life and Death, A 3059
Matter of Miracles, A 5813
Matter with Lucy, The 7364
Matthew Henson 14403
Matthew Looney's Voyage to the
Earth 1262
Matthew, Mark, Luke and John
2489
Mattie Fritts and the Flying Mush-
room 9200
Mattie, the Story of a Hedgehog
7372
Matt's Grandfather 11170
Matt's Mitt 14843
Maud Reed Tale, The 11028
Maurice Maeterlinck's Blue Bird

17926
Maurice's Room   6184
Mauritania   3020
Mausito, El   14357
Mavericks   15002
Max   8936
Maxie   9488
Maximilian's World   16356
Maximus   16402
Max's Wonderful Delicatessen
   11529
May Day   10634
May I Bring a Friend?   4743
May I Cross Your Golden River?
   4927
May I Visit?   18607
Maya, The   1757
Mayans Knew, The   13686
Maybe, a Mole   4374
Maybelle the Cable Car   2732
Mayo Brothers, The   7058
Maypoles and Wood Demons   8027
Mazel and Shlimazel   15781
Mazes   14762
Mbuku the Hare   13860
Me! A Book of Poems   8598
Me and Arch and the Pest   5163
Me and Caleb   12132
Me and Fat Glenda   13525
Me and Mr. Stenner   8773
Me and My Captain   6976
Me and My Little Brain   5974
Me and My Million   9814
Me and Neesie   7308
Me and the Eggman   3650
Me and the Man on the Moon-
   Eyed Horse   6017
Me and the Terrible Two   3939
Me and Willie and Pa   12344
Me and You and a Dog Named
   Blue   4138
Me, California Perkins   1277
Me, Cassie   5738
Me, Cholay & Co.   15034
Me Day   10746
Me, Myself and I   4291
Me Nobody Knows, The   9392
Me Too   3581
Meal One   4426
Mean Mouse and Other Mean
   Stories, The   17113
Meanest Squirrel I Ever Met, The
   18591
Meaning and Wonder of Art, The
   6778
Meaning of Music, The   15266
Meaning Well   3807

Measure with Metric   2134
Measurement   11140
Measurements and How We Use Them
   13687
Measuring   1428
Measuring Things   7337
Meat in the Sandwich, The   855
Meat Pies & Sausages   17239
Mechido, Aziza and Ahmed   10755
Medallones de luna   379
Medallones de sol   380
Medias de los flamencos, Las   14043
Medical Center Lab   1520
Medical Mystery, A   18100
Medical Talk for Beginners   4415
Medicine   18546
Medicine Maid   8561
Medicine Makers, The   17451
Medicine Man's Daughter   3492
Medicine Men of Hooper Bay   6829
Medicine Show   2841
Medicines from the Sea   1592
Meeker Massacre, The   13211
Meet Abraham Lincoln   3140
Meet Benjamin Franklin   14983
Meet Guguze   17206
Meet Martin Luther King   4683
Meet Me at Tamerlane's Tomb   4139
Meet Miki Takino   4093
Meet Miss Liberty   13387
Meet Mr. Lincoln   7704
Meet My Psychiatrist   1706
Meet the Austins   10546
Meet the Defensive Linemen   16845
Meet the Monkeys   348
Meet the North American Indians
   13404
Meet the Presidents   3188
Meet the Quarterbacks   16846
Meet the Real Pilgrims   11017
Meet the Running Backs   16847
Meet the Vampire   11391
Meet Thomas Jefferson   1115
Meeting Post, The   9828
Meeting with a Stranger   2074
Meg's Eggs   12833
Mei Li   7689
Mejores versos para niños, Los
   14592
Melinda's Christmas Stocking   9168
Melindy's Happy Summer   5725
Melindy's Medal   5726
Melting Girl and Other Stories, The
   12077
Melville in the South Pacific   8646
Member of the Gang   14389
Memorable Days in Music   4346

Memorial Book and Recipes   852
Memories of the Lakes   2014
Men at Work in the Great Lakes
   States   10598
Men, Beasts, and Gods   3117
Men from the Village Deep in the
   Mountains ...   1047
Men in the Sea   2231
Men of Iron   14013
Men of Masaba   7724
Men of the Mirage   6414
Men on Iron Horses   11224
Men Under the Sea   4763
Men Who Dig Up History   13823
Mendelssohn   8817
Menelik of Ethiopia   4502
Mennonite Martha   16398
Mental Magic Tricks   10206
Mentiras de algodon   11388
Merlin's Mistake   12791
Mermaid and the Whale, The
   11392
Mermaid's Daughter, The   6570
Mermaid's Three Wisdoms, The
   18418
Merrie's Miracle   12587
Merry Adventures of Robin Hood,
   The   14014; see also Some
   Merry Adventures of Robin
   Hood
Merry Christmas from Betsy   7956
Merry Christmas, Harry   3245
Merry Christmas to You   7749
Merry Ever After   10298
Merry-Go-Round Family   1868
Merry-Making   17374
Merry, Merry FiBruary   13164
Merry Tales for Children   906
Merrymaker, The   16447
Mesopotamia   5641
Messages and Voices   4176
Messenger for Parliament, A
   7847
Messy   1991
Messy Rabbit, The   12848
Messy Sally   4292
Metamorphosis   15691
Meteorites   6085
Meter Means Measure   8228
Metric Can Be Fun   10457
Metric Measure   18571
Metric Power   4824
Metric System, The (Hahn)   7561
Metric System, The (Rahn)   14086
Metric, the Modern Way to Meas-
   ure   15070
Mets from Mobile, The   18439

Mexacali   16055
Mexicali Soup   8261
Mexican American, The   11763
Mexican American Profiles   12666
Mexican Folk Tales   2890
Mexican Folktales   13668
Mexican Story, The   11473
Mexicans in America, The   13675
Mexico   14662
Mexico A-Z   12138
Mexico for Kids   16565
Mfums, The   7460
Mi gorrion   13084
Mi musica   12840
Mi Paraguas Rojo   2244; see also
   My Red Umbrella
Mi Primer Gran Libro para Leer
   14990
Mia, Grandma and the Genie   9211
Miami Indian Stories   6961
Mice Came in Early This Year, The
   10270
Mice, Moose and Men   11248
Mice on My Mind   17369
Michael   15813
Michael Bird-Boy   4721
Michael Gets the Measles   10607
Michael Is Brave   2498
Michael Naranjo   12725
Michael's Heart Test   3368
Michael's Victory   9424
Michigan (Carpenter)   3021
Michigan (Dunbar)   5118
Michigan (Nye)   12979
Michigan (Osolinski)   13196
Michigan (Praeger)   13871
Michigan Cooking ...   5243
Michigan Fur Trade, The   9279
Michigan Historical Markers   12151
Michigan Historical Sights   6759
Michigan in Four Centuries   995
Michigan in the War of 1812   7643
Michigan Men   6760
Michigan Soldiers in the Civil War
   17994
Michigan Trees Worth Knowing
   12148
Michigan Undiscovered   16419
Michigan Whitetails   12146
Michigan Wildlife Sketches   12147
Michigan Women   6761
Michigan Yesterday and Today
   10700
Michigan's First Settlers--The In-
   dians   6762
Michigan's Fossil Vertebrates   8511
Michigan's Indians   7419

Michigan's White Pine Era, 1840–1900 11921
Mickey Mantle 15673
Mickey Mantle Slugs It Out 11887
Mickey Mouse Make-It Book, The 17497
Mickey Mouse's Riddle Book 17498
Mickey's Magnet 2153
Mico and Piccolino 9819
Microbes at Work 15294
Middle Five, The 10187
Middle Moffat, The 5550
Middle Sister 11795
Middl'un 2659
Midnight Adventures of Kelly, Dot and Esmeralda 7040
Midnight and Jeremiah 12924
Midnight, Champion Bucking Horse 14950
Midnight Fox, The 2789
Midnight Ghost, The 18430
Midnight Is a Place 187
Midsummer Magic 7292
Midsummer Night's Death, A 13598
Midway 1108
Midwest and Great Plains 7866
Mieko 13781
Mightiest of Mortals 6662
Mighty Atom, The 10682
Mighty Hard Road 16765
Mighty Hunter, The 7546
Mighty Mac 14737
Mighty Macs, The 17221
Mighty Mekong, The 10916
Mighty Midgets, The 14068
Mighty Minicycle 2764
Mighty Mississippi, The 9590
Mighty Mississippi and New Orleans, The 1993
Mighty Mo 707
Mighty Ones, The 4679
Mighty Prince, The 16615
Mighty Soo 9425
Migrant Girl 10197
Migrant Workers and Cesar Chavez, The 18447
Miguel en invierno 1454
Miguel's Mountain 1654
Mik and the Prowler 17098
Mika's Apple Tree 2564
Mike Fink 2020
Mike Fink, Best of the Keelboatmen 5780
Mike Mulligan and His Steam Shovel 2733

Mike's House 14939
Mike's Toads 6473
Mildred Murphy, How Does Your Garden Grow? 7243
Milenka's Happy Summer 1076
Milestones in African History 15358
Military Uniforms, 1686–1918 12919
Milk, Butter and Cheese 12125
Milkmaid, The 2812
Milkweed 15295
Milkweed and Its World of Animals, The 7119
Milkweed Days 18419
Milky Way and Other Chinese Folk Tales, The 10821
Mill Creek Irregulars, The 4849
Miller's Boy, The 17959
Millicent Maybe 17685
Millicent the Monster 11192
Millicent's Ghost 10747
Millions and Millions and Millions! 15840
Millions and Millions of Crystals 6540
Millions of Cars 2749
Millions of Cats 6465
Millions of Years Ago 3776
Millions of Years of Eggs 11888
Milton Hershey, Chocolate King 11582
Milton the Early Riser 10065
Mime Alphabet Book, The 6650
Mimi Goes to New Orleans 11012
Mimosa Tree, The 3582
Min-Min, The 3518
Mind Benders, The 18295
Mind-Boggling Brain Benders 4568
Mind Your Manners 330
Mind Your Own Business 14612
Mindscapes 13450
Mindy (Hamilton) 7649
Mindy (Shiefman) 15562
Mindy's Mysterious Miniature 4402
Mine! 11931
Mine for Keeps 10940
Mine of the Lost Days, The 2098
Mineralogy of Michigan 8024
Mine's the Best 1909
Miney and the Blessing 11796
Minibikes and Minicycles for Beginners 5262
Minn of the Mississippi 8491
Minna and Pippin 13676
Minneapolis 5996
Minnesota (Carpenter) 3022
Minnesota (Van Zee) 17242
Minnesota Heritage 2260

Minnesota in Focus 12502
Minnesota Lumberjack 14862
Minnesota Panorama 9274
Minnesota Vikings, The 11889
Minnesota Walk Book, Vol. I
    2467
Minnesota Walk Book, Vol. II
    2468
Minnesota Walk Book, Vol. III
    2469
Minnesota's Major Historic Sites
    8519
Minnesota's Vikings 14735
Minnetonka Story 18069
Minnikin, Midgie and Moppet 8454
Minnipins, The see Gammage
    Cup, The
Minnow Family, The 13963
Minnow Leads to Treasure, The
    13427
Minoo's Family 4258
Minou 6213
Mio and Other Plays for Young
    People 13541
Mira! Mira! 16805
Miracle Bridge at Mackinac 16220
Miracle Chip 5454
Miracle Dish, The 17769
Miracle Hill 12282
Miracle in the Wilderness 6524
Miracle of Purun Bhagat, The
    see Miracle of the Mountain
Miracle of the Mountain, The
    9845
Miracles 10717
Miracles on Maple Hill 16028
Mireya en otono 1455
Miriam Lives in a Kibbutz 5287
Mirror of Danger 16573
Mishmash 3923
Misplaced Animals, Plants, and
    Other Creatures 8582
Miss Betty of Bonnet Rock
    School, 1864-1865 16100
Miss Bianca 15485
Miss Bianca in the Salt Mines
    15486
Miss Charity Comes to Stay 3977
Miss Clayfoot and the Demon
    16951
Miss Flora McFlimsey's Christmas
    Eve 11676
Miss Flora McFlimsey's Halloween
    11677
Miss Flora McFlimsey's Valentine
    11678
Miss Happiness and Miss Flower
    6955

Miss Hickory 907
Miss Jaster's Garden 1832
Miss Jefferson in Paris 9672
Miss Jellytot's Visit 8761
Miss Nelson Is Missing! 325
Miss Osborne-the-Mop 6474
Miss Pickerell and the Earthquake
    Rescue 11381
Miss Pickerell and the Geiger Coun-
    ter 11378
Miss Pickerell Goes to Mars 11379
Miss Pickerell Harvests the Sea
    11382
Miss Pickerell Meets Mr. H.U.M.
    11383
Miss Rivers and Miss Bridges
    16599
Miss Suzy's Birthday 18462
Miss Suzy's Easter Surprise 18463
Missing Melinda 8995
Missing Piece, The 15702
Missing Violin, The 1985
Mission Indians of California 1758
Mission to Cathay 13797
Mission to Metlakatla 17742
Mississippi, The (Foster) 6155
Mississippi, The (Lauber) 10352
Mississippi, The (Naden) 12629
Mississippi, The (Solomon) 16004
Mississippi Possum 12186
Mississippi Steamboat Days 11215
Missouri 3023
Mist on the Mountain 6073
Mister Biddle and the Birds 498
Mister Corbett's Ghost 6603
Mister Mole 12585
Mister O'Brien 518
Mister Peale's Mammoth 5502
Mister Penny 5565
Mister Penny's Race Horse 5566
Mister Rogers' Songbook 14559
Mister Wolf and Me 15622
Misty of Chincoteague 8073
Misunderstood Animals 8583
Mitch and Amy 3562
Mitchells, The 17229
Mitten, The 17004
Mittens for Kittens and Other Rhymes
    About Cats 1770
Mitty on Mr. Syrup's Farm 8429
Mixed-Marriage Daughter 3869
Mixed-Up Chameleon, The 2925
Mixed-Up Mystery Smell, The
    3730
M'Kuti's Adventures in the Bushveld
    16751
Mobiles You Can Make 8523

Moccasin Tracks 7420
Moccasin Trail 11375
Mochica, The 1480
Mochito 2893
Mock Revolt, The 3583
Mockingbird Trio 16802
Model Airplanes and How to Fly
  Them 17695
Model Cars and Trucks and How
  to Build Them 17696
Model Planes for Beginners 6834
Model Rockets for Beginners
  6835
Model Satellites and Spacecraft
  14645
Modeling Careers 17443
Modeling in Clay, Plaster and
  Papier-Mache 15823
Models of America's Past and How
  to Make Them 11539
Modern America 10850
Modern American Career Women
  3657
Modern Art in America 12622
Modern Ballads and Story Poems
  3182
Modern Baseball Superstars 7522
Modern Basketball Superstars
  7523
Modern China 15033
Modern Egypt 10556
Modern Hockey Superstars 7524
Modern Olympic Superstars
  16475
Modern Poetry 16956
Modern Russian Poetry 2940
Modoc 16994
Moe Q. McGlutch, He Smoked Too
  Much 14123
Moffats, The 5551
Mog the Mound Builder 4338
Mogo's Flute 17230
Mohammed 13669
Mohawk, The 8251
Moja Means One 5752
Mojo and the Russians 12611
Moke and Poki in the Rain Forest
  6440
Moki 13491
Mokokambo, the Lost Land 7488
Mole and Troll Trim the Tree
  9328
Mole Family's Christmas, The
  8286
Mole, Rat and the Mountain
  14760
Mollie Garfield in the White

House 5765
Mollie Make-Believe 856
Molly and the Giant 17755
Molly Mullett 4057
Molly Patch and Her Animal Friends
  15516
Molly Pitcher 16276
Molly's Moe 3391
Mom and Me 8666
Mom! I Broke My Arm! 18204
Mom! I Need Glasses 18205
Mom, the Wolfman and Me 9909
Moment of Silence, A 9140
Moment of Wonder, The 10718
Mommies at Work 12102
Mommy, Buy Me a China Doll 18515
Momoko and the Pretty Bird 8962
Momo's Kitten 18364
Momotaro 3535
Monarch Butterfly 11660
Money 14940
Money Machine, The 14445
Money, Money, Money 7450
Mongo Homecoming, A 5398
Mongoose, the Buffalo and the
  Crocodile, The 2356
Monkey and the Crocodile, The
  6504
Monkey Day 10080
Monkey Face 721
Monkey in the Family, A 9320
Monkeys 18547
Monkeys and the Pedlar, The 16436
Monkeys Have Tails 17204; see
  also Tricky Questions to Fool
  Your Friends
Monkey's Uncle, A 7844
Monkey's Whiskers, The 14515
Monnie Hates Lydia 13442
Monopoly Book, The 2086
Monsieur Jolicoeur's Umbrella 16511
Monster Bubbles 12870
Monster Goes to the Hospital 1719
Monster Poems 17461
Monster Riddle Book, The 14919
Monster Too Many, A 11482
Monsters from Outer Space? 18143
Monsters from the Movies 832
Monster's Nose Was Cold 7706
Monsters of the Deep 18144
Monster's Visit, A 11068
Montgomery Bus Boycott, December,
  1955, The 16291
Month of Christmases, A 9297
Month of Sundays, A 1807
Monty 16289
Mooch the Messy 15469

Moominvalley in November   9143
Moon, The (Branley)   2135
Moon (Shuttlesworth)   15634
Moon and a Star ..., The   10972
Moon Blossom and the Golden
   Penny   15841
Moon Cannot Fight, The   1332
Moon Explorers   15768
Moon Eyes   13820
Moon, for What Do You Wait?
   16611
Moon Guitar, The   12837
Moon in Fact and Fancy, The
   15855
Moon in the Cloud, The   7792
Moon Is Like a Silver Sickle, The
   12495
Moon Jumpers, The   17114
Moon Man   17133
Moon Moth   8830
Moon Mouse   8455
Moon of Gomrath, The   6614
Moon of the Alligators, The   6741
Moon of the Bears, The   6742
Moon of the Moles, The   6743
Moon of the Mountain Lions, The
   6744
Moon of the Wild Pigs, The   6745
Moon of the Winter Bird, The
   6746
Moon of Three Rings   12938
Moon on the One Hand, The   4299
Moon Painters, The   11196
Moon Seems to Change, The   2136
Moon Story, The   13861
Moon Tenders, The   4850
Moon-Uncle, Moon-Uncle   3148
Moon Walker, The   15601
Moon-Watch Summer   1772
Moon-Whales and Other Moon
   Poems   8731
Moonball, The   18049
Moonbeam   17548
Moonbeam and Sunny   17549
Moonbeam and the Rocket Ride
   17550
Moonbeam at the Rocket Port
   17551
Mooncoin Castle   17059
Mooncusser, The see Mystery
   at Boulder Point, The
Mooncusser's Daughter, The   188
Mooneyed Hound, The   3506
Moose Baby   6336
Moose, Goose and Little Nobody
   14124
Moose in Ontario, The   4352

Moose Is Not a Mouse, A   1604
Mop Top   6265
Mopsa the Fairy   8899
Moral Alphabet, A   1364
More About Heroes and Heroines of
   Liberia   8057
More About Little Pear   10335
More About What Plants Do   14087
More Adventures of Spider   631
More Adventures of the Great Brain
   5975
More All-of-a-Kind Family   16708
More Ballpoint Bananas   9640
More Beasts for Worse Children
   1365
More Beginning Crafts for Begin-
   ning Readers   6820
More Brain Boosters   17641
More Championship Teams of the
   NFL   1536
More Chucklebait   15182
More Cricket Songs   1319
More Fables of Aesop   9713
More from Hound and Bear   6457
More Glooscap Stories   8184
More Hand Shadows to Be Thrown
   upon the Wall   2698
More Indian Friends and Foes   8012
More Maple Hill Stories   17066
More New Ways in Math   9330
More Potatoes!   15296
More Riddles   3224
More Science Experiments You Can
   Eat   3708
More Small Poems   18278
More Sports Titans of the Twentieth
   Century   15674
More Stories of Favorite Operas
   2565
More Stories of Life   8904
More Strange but True Baseball
   Stories   10917
More Strange but True Football
   Stories   8487
More Tales from the Story Hat   2
More Tales from the Welsh Hills
   13986
More Tales of Faraway Folk   4861
More Tales Told Near a Crocodile
   7725
More Than a Queen   12511
More Than a Summer Love   5616
More Than Halfway There   5535
More Tongue Tanglers and a Rig-
   marole   13850
More Welsh Fairy and Folk Tales
   16826

More West African Folk Tales 17289

More Words of Science   753

Morena   3768

Morning Arrow   4967

Moroccan Roundabout   4467

Morocco (Carpenter)   3024

Morocco (Cavanna)   3199

Morocco in Pictures   15542

Morris and Boris   18154

Morris and His Brave Lion   14561

Morris Brookside, a Dog   15470

Morris Brookside Is Missing 15471

Morris Goes to School   18155

Morris Tells Boris   18156

Morris's Disappearing Bag   17732

Mortal Instruments, The   1619

Moses (Kimenye)   9794

Moses (Petersham)   13562

Moses and Mildred   9795

Moses and the Ghost   9796

Moses and the Kidnapper   9797

Moses and the Penpal   9798

Moses' Band of Chimpanzees   9284

Moses in a Muddle   9799

Moses in Trouble   9800

Moses on the Move   9801

Moses the Camper   9802

Moshweshwe   14895

Most Amazing Hide-and-Seek Alphabet Book, The   4335

Most Dangerous Animal in the World, The   14681

Most Delicious Camping Trip Ever 857

Most Important Thing in the World, The   5685

Most Terrible Turk, The   10115

Most Wonderful Doll in the World, The   11336

Moth Manor   867

Mother, Aunt Susan and Me   9081

Mother Beaver, The   8805

Mother Deer, The   8806

Mother Goose (Fujikawa)   6432

Mother Goose (Tudor)   12512

Mother Goose (Volland)   12513

Mother Goose Abroad   17026

Mother Goose and Nursery Rhymes 12516

Mother Goose Book, The   13977

Mother Goose in French   4062

Mother Goose in Hawaii   16608

Mother Goose Lost   17027

Mother Goose Nursery Rhymes 14055

Mother Goose on the Rio Grande 259

Mother Goose, or the Old Nursery Rhymes   7253

Mother Goose Riddle Rhymes   11116

Mother Goose Treasury, The   12517

Mother Holly   7400

Mother Is a Pitcher   9460

Mother Kangaroo, The   8807

Mother, Mother, I Feel Sick   3285

Mother Nature's Michigan   12149

Mother Owl, The   8808

Mother Tree, The   17816

Mother Whale, The   8809

Motherly Smith and Brother Bimbo 14799

Mothers Can Do Anything   10299

Mother's Day   13618

Mother's Pots   5070

Moths and Butterflies and How They Live   11249

Motion and Gravity   1429

Motocross   5762

Motor Racing Story   6622

Motorcycle Moto Cross School   14071

Motorcycle Racing   13989

Motorcycles   18399

Motorcycles on the Move   7368

Motorcycling   4039

Motorcycling and the New Enthusiast   14861

Motoring Millers, The   3978

Motors and Engines and How They Work   17697

Mound Builders, The (Le Sueur) 10636

Mound Builders, The (Scheele) 15024

Mound Builders, The (Silverberg) 15668

Mounds, Towns, and Totems   12623

Mountain, The   13340

Mountain Conquest   15567

Mountain Doves ..., The   18596

Mountain Goats of Temlaham, The 16965

Mountain Lion, The   8250

Mountain Magic for Rosy   13177

Mountain Man (Place)   13722

Mountain Man, Indian Chief   1296

Mountain of Truth, The   2952

Mountain People, Mountain Crafts 8638

Mountain Top Mystery   17527

Mountain Troopers   3143

Mountains   6967

Mouse and Company   8119

Mouse and His Child, The 8287
Mouse and the Elephant, The
  8137
Mouse and the Motorcycle, The
  3563
Mouse and the Song, The 14419
Mouse Book, The 15504
Mouse God, The 9695
Mouse House 6956
Mouse in the House, A 14179
Mouse Named Mus, A 2081
Mouse Soup 11000
Mouse Tales 11001
Mouse to Be Free, A 17535
Mouse Trouble 18392
Mouse Woman and the Mischief-
  Makers 7762
Mouse Woman and the Vanished
  Princesses 7763
Mousekin De Viaje 12219
Mousekin Finds a Friend 12220
Mousekin's Christmas Eve 12221
Mousekin's Family 12222
Musekin's Golden House 12223
Mousewife, The 6957
Mouth of the Night, The 11323
Movie Horses 388
Moving 17606
Moving Day 16902
Moving Hills of Sand 11890
Moving into Manhood 1194
Moving Molly 8729
Moving to Win 3305
Moy Moy 13782
Moya and the Flamingoes 7624
Mozart 9984
Mpala 8115
Mpengo of the Congo 11325
Mr. and Mrs. Pig's Evening Out
  14165
Mr. Bear and the Robbers 10138
Mr. Bell Invents the Telephone
  15566
Mr. Blue 5421
Mr. Brimble's Hobby 14304
Mr. Brown and Mr. Gray 18217
Mr. Charley's Chopsticks 5580
Mr. Chu 9591
Mr. Drackle and His Dragon 6398
Mr. Fong's Toy Shop 13783
Mr. Gumpy's Motor Car 2681
Mr. Gumpy's Outing 2682
Mr. Hamilton and Mr. Jefferson
  3349
Mr. Kelso's Lion 1922
Mr. Lincoln's Inaugural Journey
  13617

Mr. Lion Thatches His Roof ...
  9780
Mr. McFadden's Halloween 6958
Mr. Mead and His Garden 11076
Mr. Meebles 9712
Mr. Moonlight and Omar 8445
Mr. Moon's Last Case 13376
Mr. Mysterious & Company 6018
Mr. Mysterious's Secrets of Magic
  6019
Mr. Noah and the Second Flood
  2675
Mr. Pig and Sonny Too 8269
Mr. Popper's Penguins 783
Mr. Rabbit and the Lovely Present
  18608
Mr. Revere and I 10424
Mr. Smith and Other Nonsense
  15938
Mr. Tall and Mr. Small 2196
Mr. Tamarin's Trees 5532
Mr. Toast and the Secret of Gold
  Hill 2202
Mr. Toast and the Woolly Mammoth
  2203
Mr. Twigg's Mistake 10425
Mr. Whittier 17312
Mr. Wiggle's Book 4245
Mr. Wizard's Experiments for Young
  Scientists 8095
Mr. Wolf Gets Ready for Supper
  9128
Mr. Yowder and the Lion Roar Cap-
  sules 14699
Mr. Yowder and the Steamboat
  14700
Mrs. Beggs and the Wizard 11932
Mrs. Frisby and the Rats of NIMH
  12992
Mrs. Gaddy and the Ghost 6475
Mrs. Mike 6243
Mrs. Moon and the Dark Stairs
  7807
Mrs. Moon's Story Hour 7808
Mrs. Perley's People 9256
Mrs. Piggery Snout 4528
Mrs. Piggle-Wiggle 11297
Mrs. Switch 8359
Mrs. Vinegar 16250
Mrs. Wappinger's Secret 8169
Mrs. Wiggs of the Cabbage Patch
  7999
Ms. Africa 4248
M'Toto 5744
Much Bigger Than Martin 9654
Muchacho sefardi, Un 13506
Muchas veces cuatro patas 11572

Mud Ponies, The 9684
Mud Snail Son, The 10801
Muffel and Plums 6407
Muffletump Storybook, The 17406
Muffletumps' Christmas Party,
The 17407
Muffy Mouse and the Bush Birth-
day 12851
Muhammad Ali (May) 11891
Muhammad Ali (Olsen) 13108
Muhammad Ali (Rudeen) 14746
Muhammad Ali (Wilson) 18067
Mukasa 12630
Mukhtar's Children 17599
Mulberry Music, The 13165
Mule in the Mail 11594
Mule on the Expressway, The
1559
Mule Who Refused to Budge,
The 18087
Mulga Bill's Bicycle 13360
Mumbet--The Story of Elizabeth
Freeman 5781
Mumbi's Brideprice 11974
Mummies 11393
Mummies Made in Egypt 307
Mummy Market, The 2177
Mumo and the Lost Cow 8244
Mumo and the Safari 8245
Mumo at the Coast 8246
Mumo Goes to Town 8247
Munachar and Manachar 9052
Muncus Agruncus 17591
Mundo de Tio Conejo, El 14412
Mundo poetico de Trikis Trikis,
El 11766
Muneco de Aserrin y otros cuen-
tos, El 5289
Mungo 6421
Mungo Park in Africa, 1795-1797
17167
Munita Goes Hunting 551
Mural Master, The 9333
Musa, Son of Egypt 5476
Musa the Shoemaker 16325
Muse of the Round Sky 10719
Museum Mystery, The 2882
Mushroom Center Disaster, The
1833
Mushroom in the Rain 16531
Mushy Eggs 53
Music Across Our Country
18203
Music and Instruments for Chil-
dren to Make 7898
Music and Song of Ukraine
13145

Music: Invent Your Own 5724
Music of Africa, The 17534
Musica Folklorica de Puerto Rico,
La 11056
Musica y canciones para los mas
pequeños 13238
Musical Instruments of Africa 4902
Musical Palm Tree, The 1129
Muskego Boy 8526
Muskie Hook, The 3769
Mustang Roundup 10365
Mustang, Wild Spirit of the West
8074
Mwangi and the Cattle Thieves
4409
My American Heritage 8081
My Animals 651
My Animals and Me 161
My Backyard History Book 17711
My Best Friend 5103
My Black Me 135
My Bondage and My Freedom see
Life and Times of Frederick
Douglass, The
My Brother Angel 1292
My Brother Bernard 5357
My Brother Fine with Me 3629
My Brother Never Feeds the Cat
14753
My Brother Plays the Clarinet
254
My Brother Sam Is Dead 3844
My Brother Steven Is Retarded
15988
My Brother Stevie 3651
My Castle 8004
My Cat Has Eyes of Sapphire Blue
5920
My Childhood in Siberia 16720
My Counting Book 4366
My Cousin Abe 5921
My Cousin, the Arab 12967
My Crazy Sister 6977
My Dad Lives in a Downtown Hotel
11611
My Daddy Is a Cool Dude 6429
My Daddy Longlegs 7887
My Dad's a Park Ranger 8186
My Dad's a Smokejumper 8187
My Daughter, Nicola 688
My Day on the Farm 12637
My Dentist 14533
My Doctor 14534
My Dog Is Lost! 9609
My Dog Rinty 16656
My Dog Your Dog 11117
My Enemy, My Brother 6116

My Family 12661
My Father and I 8456
My Father, the Coach 15856
My Father's Dragon 6532
My First Counting Book 12401
My First Love & Other Disasters 13349
My Five Senses 308
My Friend Charlie 6065
My Friend Fish 8000
My Friend Flicka 13049
My Friend in Africa 6208
My Friend Is Mrs. Jones see Señora Jones Es Mi Amiga, La
My Friend John 18609
My Friend Little John and Me 16442
My Friend Mac 11474
My Friend, the Babysitter 17582
My Friend, the Dentist 17583
My Friend, the Doctor 17584
My Friend William Moved Away 8149
My Friend Yakub 9463
My Friends 12662
My Goldfish 18219
My Grandpa Died Today 5713
My Grandson Lew 18610
My Great-Grandfather and I 10119
My Great-Grandfather, the Heroes, and I 10120
My Happy Days 15401
My Home in South Africa 4302
My House 15071
My House Is Your House 16628
My Island Grandma 10302
My Japan, 1930-1951 12635
My Journals and Sketchbooks by Robinson Crusoe 13791
My Journey see Anno's Journey
My Kind of Verse 15914
My Ladybug 18220
My Learn to Fish Book 4826
My Life as an Indian 15126
My Little Cabbage 14002
My Little Hen 13978
My Mama Says There Aren't Any Zombies ... 17320
My Mane Catches the Wind 8599
My Maryland 11586
My Measure It Book 1472
My Michigan 6107
My Mom Got a Job 15919
My Mom Hates Me in January 4816
My Mother and I 5922

My Mother Is Lost 12596
My Mother Is the Most Beautiful Woman in the World 14271
My Mother the Mail Carrier 11843
My Name Is ... 12536
My Name Is Davy, I'm an Alcoholic 15956
My Name Is Emily 7657
My Name Is Jose 1254
My Name Is Lion 5422
My Name Is Not Odessa Yarker 5448
My Name Is Pablo 16010
My Nebraska Childhood 3522
My Number Two Wife 14313
My Nursery School 14535
My Pardner 5594
My People of the Kikuyu and the Life of Chief Wangombe 9723
My Pretty Girl 2063
My Puppy Is Born 3800
My Red Umbrella 2245
My Robot Buddy 15857
My Secrets of Playing Baseball 11966
My Several Worlds 2490
My Shalom, My Peace 18576
My Side of the Mountain 6747
My Sister 8218
My Special Best Words 16232
My State and Its Story 10701
My Street's a Morning Cool Street 16817
My Sunday Best 6000
My Sword My Life 10165
My Tang's Tungled and Other Ridiculous Situations 2219
My Teddy Bear 12638
My Tricycle and I 9169
My Turn, Your Turn 17594
My Turtle Died Today 16430
My Twin Sister Erika 17334
My Very First Book of Numbers 2926
My Very First Book of Shapes 2927
My Very Special Friend 8019
My Village in Brazil 6795
My Village in England 6796
My Village in Ghana 6797
My Village in India 6798
My Village in Japan 6799
My Village in Korea 6800
My Village in Morocco 6801
My Village in Portugal 6794
My Village in Thailand 6802
My Village, Sturbridge 2017
My Visit to the Dinosaurs 309

Myeko's Gift 7851

Myself (Ashton-Warner) 728

Myself (Nava) 12663

Mysteries from the Past 833

Mysterious Appearance of Agnes,
The 7376

Mysterious Caitlin McIver, The
11530

Mysterious Disappearance of Leon
(I Mean Noel) 14125

Mysterious Gold and Purple Box,
The 17574

Mysterious Grain, The 5399

Mysterious Schoolmaster, The
428

Mysterious Tadpole, The 9655

Mysterious Zetabet, The 4116

Mystery at Boulder Point 9218

Mystery at Indian Island 6980

Mystery at Laughing Water 1660

Mystery at Skull Castle 7421

Mystery Began in Madeira, The
321

Mystery Coach 3424

Mystery Cottage in Loft Field,
The 2992

Mystery Cup, The 1986

Mystery Gatepost, The 1987

Mystery Guest at Left End 11069

Mystery Hotel 9319

Mystery in Little Tokyo 1891

Mystery in Manhattan 322

Mystery in Marrakech 3200

Mystery in the Square Tower
8534

Mystery Mammals of the Ice Age
8512

Mystery Next Door, The 14596

Mystery of Emily Dickinson, The
1460

Mystery of Ghost Valley, The
3061

Mystery of Green Hill 10152

Mystery of Hurricane Castle
12852

Mystery of Lincoln Detweiler and
the Dog Who Barked Spanish,
The 14469

Mystery of Masks, The 13919

Mystery of Morgan Castle, The
14097

Mystery of Old Mobeetie 2883

Mystery of Saint-Salgue, The
1560

Mystery of Stonehenge, The 2137

Mystery of the Aztec Idol, The
3062

Mystery of the Bewitched Bookmobile
8008

Mystery of the Eagle's Claw 18285

Mystery of the Farmer's Three
Fives, The 6375

Mystery of the Fat Cat 1892

Mystery of the Fog Man 5686

Mystery of the Giant Giraffe, The
3857

Mystery of the Giant's Footprints,
The 10022

Mystery of the Gingerbread House
16116

Mystery of the Golden Horn 17829

Mystery of the Golden Ram 11583

Mystery of the Great Swamp, The
18494

Mystery of the Green Cat 17830

Mystery of the Gulls 17831

Mystery of the Haunted Pool 17832

Mystery of the Hidden Hand 17833

Mystery of the Inside Room, The
6105

Mystery of the Loch Ness Monster,
The 1430

Mystery of the Maya Jade 8535

Mystery of the Minoan Civilization,
The 4192

Mystery of the Missing Red Mitten,
The 9656

Mystery of the Pharaoh's Treasure
12699

Mystery of the Pirate's Treasure,
The 1836

Mystery of the Red Tide, The
1893

Mystery of the Roman Ransom
18125

Mystery of the Schoolhouse Dog,
The 7603

Mystery of the Secret Message
8536

Mystery of the Stolen Painting,
The 10153

Mystery of the Third Twin, The
18389

Mystery of the Woods, The 16357

Mystery of Time, The 12695

Mystery on Nine-Mile Marsh 9130

Mystery on Safari 3201

Mystery Player at Left End see
Mystery Guest at Left End

Mystery Plays a Golden Flute 17075

Mystery Waters of Tonbridge Wells,
The 11769

Mystical Beast, The 5708

- N -

N. B. A. Playoffs 11892
Na-ni 4866
Na of Wa, The 3
Nabby Adams' Diary 1997
Naboth Pulls the Wheeled Elephant 8691
Nacar, the White Deer 4757
Nadia Comaneci 12161
Naftali the Storyteller and His Horse, Sus ... 15782
Naha, Boy of the Seminoles 18315
Nail Soup 18516
Nailheads and Potato Eyes 1157
Nails to Nickels 2874
Naim, a Boy of Turkey 15082
Naimbana of Sierra Leone 8885
Naja the Snake and Mangus the Mongoose 9860
Name: Johnny Pierce 14390
Names and Places 12664
Names, Sets and Numbers 1431
Namesake, The 8319
Namesake for Nathan, A 12345
Naming Living Things 14369
Namu 5956
Nana of the Niger Delta 8890
Nana Upstairs and Nana Downstairs 4722
Nancy Hanks 16277
Nancy Hanks of Wilderness Road 10637
Nancy Kimball, Nurse's Aide 10198
Nancy Ward, Cherokee 5782
Nancy's Back Yard 9621
Nannabah's Friend 13534
Nanny Goat and the Fierce Dog, The 9617
Nantucket Summer 7244
Naomi 14045
Naomi in the Middle 9910
Nappy Has a New Friend 8396
Narc, The 2765
Narcissa Whitman 17521
Narcotics and Drug Abuse 17990
Nargun and the Stars, The 18320
Narni of the Desert 17764
Narrow Passage, The 2755
Nashdoi Yaazh 12892
Nashville Sound, The 8040
Nat Love, Negro Cowboy 5783
Nat Turner 7370
Nate the Great 15472
Nate the Great Goes Undercover 15473
National Anthems of the World 15501
National Holidays Around the World 4942
National Road, The 2716
National Velvet 874
Native Fairy Tales of South Africa 11502
Natural Cook's First Book, The 6782
Natural Fire 13964
Natural History of Marine Mammals, A 15030
Natural Partnerships 15635
Naturalist's Guide to Ontario, A 9416
Nature at Its Strangest 4159
Nature Detective see How to Be a Nature Detective
Nature Sleuths 11274
Nature's Flying Janitor 4222
Nature's Gliders 2779
Nature's Merry-Go-Round 12825
Nature's Nursery: Baby Birds 8709
Nature's Nursery: Baby Mammals 8710
Nature's Pretenders 8584
Nature's Water Clowns 2780
Nature's Wonderful Family 12606
Nature's World Records 14039
Naughty Nancy 7041
Navaho Indians Today 14463
Navaho Land 14800
Navaho Stories in Basic Vocabulary 4980
Navajo, The 1759
Navajo Biographies 8375
Navajo Bird Tales 3315
Navajo Design Book, The 7315
Navajo Heritage 2038
Navajo History, Vol. 1 18384
Navajo of the Painted Desert 1171
Navajo Pet 11754
Navajo Rugs 4773
Navajo Sister 10225
Navajo Slave 6776
Navajo Weaving Today 5174
Navidad del niño venezolano 16876
Navigation 16870
Near East, The 754
Near the Window Tree 10160
Near Thing for Captain Najork, A 8288
Nearsighted Knight, The 15623
Nebraska 12832

Nebraska Centennial Literary Map and Guide to Nebraska Authors 9529

Nebraska Pioneer Cookbook 7111

Nebraska Place-Names 5984

Nebraska Women Through the Years, 1867-1967 12700

Necklace of Fallen Stars, A 8180

Needlework Book of Bible Stories, The 12126

Needs of Man, The 13891

Negatu in the Garden 9813

Negro Folk Tales for Pupils in the Primary Grades 17817

Negro in America, The 16046

Negro in Maryland, The 14587

Negro in the Civil War, The 14032

Negroes in the Early West 2717

Negroes of Achievement in Modern America 6084

Nehru's Story 11773

Neighbor to the World 1786

Neighborhood, The 14899

Neighborhood Knight 15049

Neighborhood Puddle 17560

Nellie Bly (Dunnahoo) 5148

Nellie Bly (Graves) 7197

Nellie Bly (Noble) 12860

Nellie Bly, Reporter 979

Nellie Cameron 12583

Nelly Custis' Diary 1998

Nemo Meets the Emperor 1060

Nessie the Mannerless Monster see Nessie the Monster

Nessie the Monster 8732

Nest, The 6763

Nest of Wood Ducks, A 15497

Net to Catch the Wind, A 7233

Nettlewood 12055

Neva's Patchwork Pillow 7650

Never-Empty 15015

Never Is a Long, Long Time 3152

Never Jam Today 1866

Never Run from a Lion ... 14360

Never Say Ugh to a Bug 5666

Never to Forget 12045

Never Trust a Cowbird 10432

Never Younger, Jeannie 18160

New Adventures in Origami 7712

New American Continent, The 2937

New Amsterdam 5425

New Amsterdam Days and Ways 8738

New at the Zoo (Lippman) 10898

New at the Zoo (Shannon) 15416

New Baby, A 1543

New Baby Comes, A 11893

New Baby Is Coming to My House, A 8963

New Blue Shoes 14305

New Book for Tobias, A 16974

New Boots for Salvador 6656

New Boy in School 9439

New Boy on the Sidewalk, The 4237

New Breed Heroes in Pro Baseball 7525

New Breed of Athlete, The 6722

New Day, A 1864

New England Bean Pot 9100

New Feminism, The 9982

New Friend, The 18611

New Golden Book of Astronomy, The 18345

New Guinea 941

New Home, The 8619

New Home for Billy, A 9440

New Home for Theresa, A 1197

New House, New Town 12712

New Ideas in Card and Paper Crafts 199

New Kid in Town 14462

New Kind of Joy, A 7824

New Life, The 4955

New Life: New Room 9379

New Look at the Pilgrims, A 15658

New Magic 1939

New Medicine 18038

New Moon Cove 787

New Nations of Africa, The 17607

New Neighbors 13876

New Nutcracker Suite ..., The 12648

New Orleans 9673

New Patches for Old 17438

New Tall Tales of Pecos Bill 5784

New Teacher, The 3761

New Testament in Art, The 15572

New Trail Blazers of Technology 11590

New Vestments, The 10466

New Water Book, The 1521

New Ways in Math 9331

New Women in Media 2024

New Women in Medicine 2025

New World Held Promise, The 7185

New World Journey of Anne Mac-Vicar 1826

New World of Computers, The 10686

New World of Construction Engineering 16476

New World of Helicopters, The 4812

New World of the Atom, The 18245

New Year's Day 7438

New York Jets, The 11894

New York to Nome 13723

New Zealand 942

Newcomer and Other Stories, The 9779

Newcomers 14134

News or Not? 17682

Next Door 7735

Next Door to Xanadu 13166

Next 50 Years on the Moon, The 1504

Nez Percé Buffalo Horse 14897

Nezbah's Lamb 166

Ngoma the Drum Beater 12243

Nhoti, Son of India 10392

Ni tuyo ni mio 2905

Nibble, Nibble 2394

Nice Fire and Some Moonpennies, A 7993

Nice Little Girls 10672

Nice New Neighbors 2101

Nicest Gift, The 13784

Nicest Time of the Year, The 6702

Nicholas (Cowles) 4218

Nicholas (Kempner) 9678

Nicholas and the Fast Moving Diesel 624

Nicholas and the Wool-Pack 7739

Nicholas Knock and Other People 10481

Nickel-Plated Beauty, The 1278

Nicky's Bugle 14374

Nicky's Football Team 14242

Nicky's Sister 2197

Nicola Bayley's Book of Nursery Rhymes 1230

Nieve y el Sol, La 6229; see also Snow and the Sun, The

Niger (Carpenter) 3025

Niger, The (Finley) 5888

Niger, The (Watson) 17575

Nigeria (Dunbar) 5115

Nigeria (Hanson) 7709

Nigeria (Schultz) 15128

Nigeria (Watson) 17576

Nigerian Fables and Stories for Beginners 5619

Nigerian Pioneer 16591

Night Animals 3748

Night Before Christmas, The 12384

Night Daddy, The 7435

Night Journeys 815

Night People 3784

Night Rider, The 8903

Night Sky Book, The 9236

Night Spell 12792

Night Watchmen, The 4283

Nightbirds on Nantucket 189

Nightingale, The 441

Nightmares 13887

Nightmares of Geranium Street, The 15608

Nights of Danger 5375

Nihal 12566

Nii Ayi Bontey 18133

Nii-Ofrang and His Garden ... 9580

Nika Illahee (My Homeland) 18284

Nikki 108 1808

Nikoline's Choice 11845

Nilda 12316

Nile, Lifeline of Egypt, The 17669

Nils 4554

Nimbo the Driver 12081

Niña de mi cuento, La 8106

Niña que Celebra el Cumpleaños, La 9170; see also What Is a Birthday Child?

Nine Days to Christmas 5569

Nine in a Line 9864

Nine Lives see Time Cat

Nine Lives of Moses on the Oregon Trail 613

Nine Planets, The 2138

Nine Tales of Coyote 11731

Nine Tales of the Raven see Raven-Who-Sets-Things-Right

Nine True Dolphin Stories 4573

Nineteenth State--Indiana, The 10471

Ninji's Magic 11400

Nino 541

Nino and His Fish 8810

Niño Bach, El 3545

Niño Llamado Manuel, Un 18505

Niño que enloquecio de amor, El 1121

Niño y el bosque, El 12093

Niños de Viet Nam 13710

Niobrara Breezes see Songs of the Sage

Nipper, The (Cookson) 4016

Nipper (Turner) 17070

Nisei Daughter 16013

Nisse from Timsgaard, The 1548

Nitty Gritty, The 1894

Nkwala 15484
No Applause, Please 15793
No Arm in Left Field 3425
No-Bark Dog, The 18058
No Boys Allowed 16754
No Children, No Pets 8474
No Dogs Allowed, Jonathan! 3399
No Ducks in Our Bathtub 284
No Easy Circle 12683
No Fighting, No Biting! 12264
No Flying in the House 2273
No Golden Cities 12650
No Kiss for Mother 17134
No Man's Land 17603
No Moccasins Today 11013
No More Lies 7332
No More the Round Mud Hut 14683
No More Work 14516
No Mules 13272
No-Name Man of the Mountain, The 16173
No! No! 12615
No, No, Natalie 12421
No One Noticed Ralph 1670
No Pigs, No Possums, No Pandas 3610
No Place for Mitty 18464
No Promises in the Wind 8750
No Pushing, No Ducking 14391
No Room 4935
No Roses for Harry 18592
No School Today 2102
No-Talent Letterman 8988
No Time for School 2806
No Trespassing 13877
No Turning Back 14021
No Way of Telling 15886
No Word for Goodbye 4242
Noah and the Great Flood 8863
Noah and the Rainbow 1860
Noah Riddle? 1668
Noah's Ark (Haley) 7581
Noah's Ark (Spier) 16092
Noah's Castle 16957
Noble Doll, The 3689
Noble Lady 4539
Nobody Asked Me If I Wanted a Baby Sister 285
Nobody Has to Be a Kid Forever 3870
Nobody Is Perfick 17370
Nobody Likes Trina 17834
Nobody Listens to Andrew 7472
Nobody Said It's Easy 15931
Nobody's Cat 12187
Nobody's Child 12195

Nobody's Family 15957
Nobody's Family Is Going to Change 5981
Noche de los sprunkos, La 17266
Nocturnal World of the Lobster, The 3992
Noel for Jeanne-Marie 6214
Noel the Coward 10066
Noise in the Night 256
Noisy Hornbill, The 173
Noisy Nancy and Nick 6459
Noisy Nancy Norris 6460
Noisy Nora 17733
Nok Noy and the Charcoal Man 13624
Noko 7938
Noko of Japan 3202
Nolle Smith 7467
Nomi and the Magic Fish 13648
Nomusa and the New Magic 12271
Nonna 1146
Nono 8116
Nonsense Book of Riddles, Rhymes, Tongue Twisters, Puzzles and Jokes from American Folklore, The 5433
Noodle 10458
Noodlehead Stories from Around the World 9101
Noodles, Nitwits and Numskulls 10448
Noonan 5945
Noonday Friends, The 16358
Nora Kramer's Storybook 10030
Norman the Doorman 6266
Norse Gods and Giants 4555
North Africa 14670
North American Bighorn Sheep, The 144
North American Indians, The 1551
North American Legends 7882
North American Wolf, The 145
North and South Korea 7508
North Carolina Colony, The 13863
North Carolina Parade 17475
North Country 5954
North Dakota (Carpenter) 3026
North Dakota (Wills) 18061
North Dakota Decision Makers 2097
North, South, East, West 2139
North Star 15112
North Star Shining 16561
North to Freedom 8498
North to Liberty 17785
North Town 7135
North Wind and the Sun, The

10191
North Winds Blow Free 8671
North Woods, The 9923
Northern Nativity, A 10140
Northern Ontario 16926
Northern Ontario Anthology I
  11647
Northern Phantom, The 17913
Northland Wild Flowers 12528
Northwest Coast Indians ABC
  Book, The 2972
Norwegian Folk Tales 713
Norwegians in America, The
  8195
Nose Knows, The 8178
Noses and Toes 7994
Not All Girls Have Million Dollar
  Smiles ... 13031
Not Bad for a Girl 16669
"Not Charity, but Justice" 12130
Not Just Sugar and Spice 15526
Not Only for Ducks 1800
Not over Ten Inches High 10677
Notes and Comments from Nigeria
  4808
Notes on the Hauter Experiment
  7442
Nothing at All 6466
Nothing but a Dog 9516
Nothing but Cats and All About
  Dogs 15804
Nothing Ever Happens Here 18431
Nothing Ever Happens on My
  Block 14126
Nothing Is Impossible 241
Nothing Much Happened Today
  3400
Nothing Place, The 16060
Nothing Rhymes with April 9505
Nothing Said 1973
Nothing Special, The 16924
Nothing to Do 8289
November's Wheel 12256
Now and Then see Crocuses
  Were over, Hitler Was Dead
Now It's Fall 10580
Now or Never 7573
Now We Are Six 12247
Now You See It 2288
Nthee the Mongoose 13860
Nu Dang and His Kite 823
Nubber Bear 10891
Nubia 5073
Nuclear Power 13965
Nuestro Mundo Es Sonoro/Sound
  All Around 13688
Nuestros muchachos 18477

Nueva poesia infantil 3067
Nuevas aventuras de Marsuf 14869
Number Four 3924
Number Ideas Through Pictures
  3291
Number Men 17023
Number Stories of Long Ago 15873
Numbers (Allen) 351
Numbers (Pienkowski) 13659
Numbers (Reiss) 14226
Numbers of Things 13223
Numbers Old and New 118
Numerals 119
Nungu and the Hippopotamus 3793
Nuns Go to Africa, The 14714
Nunurs en el Mar 10437
Nurit and Guri 603
Nurse in Training 10199
Nurse of the Keys 6205
Nurses and What They Do 9568
Nursing as a Career 3249
Nutcracker, The 8371
Nuts 5213
Nuts to You and Nuts to Me 8310
Nyanga's Two Villages 1940

- O -

O Children of the Wind and Pines
  974
O Frabjous Day! 10973
O. J. (Gutman) 7526
O. J. (Libby) 10767
O. J. Simpson (Deegan) 4788
O. J. Simpson (Hill) 8189
O. J. Simpson (May) 11895
O the Red Rose Tree 1279
O Zebron Falls 5840
Oars, Sails and Steam 17042
Oasis of the Stars 5251
Oba of Benin, An 1075
Obadai and the Tomatoes ... 9581
Obadiah the Bold 17060
Obadzeng Goes to Town 43
Obaseki of Benin 8882
Obioma and the Wonderful Ring
  11650
Observation 1432
Obstinate Land, The 9625
Oceania 11850
Oceanography 18041
Oceanography Lab 1522
Oceans 1085

Oceans in Tomorrow's World, The 12144

Ocracoke 6962

Octagon Magic 12939

Octavia Told Me a Secret 15474

Octopus 15498

Octopus and Other Cephalopods, The 3959

Odale's Choice 2159

Odd Jobs 9329

Odd One Out 13500

Odds and Evens 12995

O'Donnells 16497

Odyssey, The 8525

Odyssey from River Bend 11368

Odyssey of Ben O'Neal, The 16715

Of Courage Undaunted 4533

Of Course Polly Can Ride a Bike 10837

Of Course You Can Sew! 4166

Of Dikes and Windmills 16093

Of Man and Mouse 10353

Of Nightingales That Weep 13370

Of Quarks, Quasars and Other Quirks 2220

Of This World 10720

Of Time and Seasons 9323

Off We Go! 18145

Offshore 16871

Ogre and His Bride, The 9869

Ogre Downstairs, The 9342

Oh, a-Hunting We Will Go 10249

Oh, How Silly! 3815

Oh, Lizzie! The Life of Elizabeth Cady Stanton 5628

Oh, Lord, I Wish I Was a Buzzard 7259

Oh, No, Go (a play) 11496

Oh, Say Can You Say? 15383

Oh, That's Ridiculous! 3816

Oh, What a Noise 15613

Oh, What Nonsense! 3817

Ohia and the Animals 17255

Ohio (Campen) 2885

Ohio (Carpenter) 3027

Ohio (Perry) 13536

Ohio (Renick) 14243

Ohio Canals, The 17891

Ohio Farm 11459

Ohio in Words and Pictures 6193

Ohio Indian Trails 17892

Ohio Portrait, An 9924

Ohio Quiz Book 18287

Ohio Scenes and Citizens 7105

Ohio Story, The 15248

Ohio Town Names 13212

Ohio's Prehistoric People 13855

Oil (Gans) 6541

Oil (Wade) 17378

Oil and Gas 12849

Oil, Today's Black Magic 2522

Oji the Hen and Other Stories 3352

Ojibwa Indian Legends 17392

Ojibway 8953

Ojo de Dios 216; see also Eye of God

Ojuk Angwec Kwan/Ojuk the Runaway 13046

Okelo and Akelo 13053

Oklahoma 3028

Okolo of Nigeria 2501

Ol' Paul, the Mighty Logger 14701

Ola 4556

Ola and the Ball 6446

Olaf Is Late 10748

Olaf Reads 10749

Old Abe 18471

"Old Abe," American Eagle 15560

Old America Comes Alive 2718

Old and New in Sierra Leone 7084

Old Arthur 15814

Old Barn, The 3082

Old Bill, the Whooping Crane 10894

Old Black Witch 4871

Old Bullfrog, The 6337

Old China Trade, The 3052

Old Cities and New Towns 15144

Old Con and Patrick 14972

Old Dog, The 18

Old Father 17274

Old Forts and Real Folks 4615

Old Greek Fairy Tales 7248

Old Hasdrubal and the Pirates 418

Old Jo, the Talking Drum 6447

Old Liberty Bell 14558

Old Macdonald Had a Farm 7112

Old MacDonald Had an Apartment House 1113

Old Man Coelacanth 1354

Old Man Riddle 12058

Old Man Whickutt's Donkey 2842

Old Monkey and the Young Monkey, The 14490

Old Mother Hubbard and Her Dog 12747

Old Mother West Wind 2651

Old Mother Witch 3075

Old Names and New Places 381

Old New Orleans, the Creole City 7630

Old Niagara on the Lake 16341

Old One-Toe 1187

Old Peter's Russian Tales 14115
Old Possum's Book of Practical
  Cats 5340
Old Powder Line, The 13319
Old Rail Fence Corners 12459
Old Ramon 15003
Old Sam, Thoroughbred Trotter
  16676
Old Songs and Singing Games
  3304
Old Tale Carved out of Stone,
  An 10862
Old Witch and the Dragon, The
  4805
Old Witch and the Wizard, The
  4806
Old Woman and Her Pig, The
  (Galdone) 6505
Old Woman and Her Pig ...,
  The (Rockwell) 14517
Old Woman and the Mushroom ...,
  The 13055
Old Woman and the Red Pump-
  kin, The 1044
Old Woman Who Lived in a Vine-
  gar Bottle, The 6959
Old Yeller 6864
Older Kind of Magic, An 18321
Oldest Man in America, The 9853
Olga 1305
Olga Carries On 1874
Olga Korbut (Jacobs) 9071
Olga Korbut (Smith) 15909
Olga Korbut (Suponev) 16505
Olga Meets Her Match 1875
Oliver 8360
Oliver Hazard Perry 11044
Oliver Hyde's Dishcloth Concert
  9696
Oliver Wendell Holmes 13574
Olivia Newton-John 9072
Ollie Ollie Oxen-Free 17517
Ollie's Go-Kart 8828
Ollie's Team and the Basketball
  Computer 13622
Olly's Polliwogs 14518
Olode the Hunter, and Other
  Tales from Nigeria 4205
Oluronbi's Promise and Other
  Stories 85
Olympic Games, The (May) 11896
Olympic Games, The (Paul)
  13395
Olympic Games in Ancient Greece
  6939
Oma 7552
Omar at Christmas 17796

Omar Nelson Bradley 14192
Omoteji's Baby Brother 6770
On a Picnic 4817
On and Off the Street 81
On Beyond Zebra 15384
On Christmas Day 8611
On Christmas Day in the Morning
  10250
On City Streets 10277
On Mother's Lap 15186
On Our Way 8600
On Reading Palms 16842
On Safari 17420
On Safari with Roger Caras 2910
On Stage (Bowman) 2026
On Stage (Lake) 10196
On Stage, Please 16740
On the Banks of Plum Creek 17907
On the Beat 14458
On the Day Peter Stuyvesant Sailed
  into Town 11002
On the Drag Strip 14077
On the Farm (Duncan) 5128
On the Farm (Scarry) 14991
On the Frontier with Mr. Audubon
  2198
On the Move 14955
On the Other Side of the Gate
  16448
On the Other Side of the River
  13154
On the Track of Bigfoot 13724
On the Track of the Child
  Stealers ... 16269
On the Wasteland 689
On the Water 14078
On the Way Home 17908
On the Way Up 9892
On the Wing 8894
On Your Mark, Get Set, Go! 9751
Once a Mouse ... 2380
Once-a-Year Day, The 2591
Once-a-Year Witch 17247
Once in a Lifetime 9507
Once in a Wood 14306
Once in Puerto Rico 1369
Once More upon a Totem 7764
Once the Hodja 9674
Once the Mullah 9675
Once There Was a Passenger Pigeon
  7065
Once There Was and Twice There
  Wasn't 17434
Once There Was and Was Not 16660
Once Under the Cherry Blossom
  Tree 14977
Once upon a Dinkelsbuhl 6674

Once upon a Lake 9367
Once upon a Mountain 1865
Once upon a Thermal 18216
Once upon a Time 4936
Once upon a Time in Delaware
  14019
Once upon a Time 150 Years Ago
  13466
Once upon a Totem 7765
Once upon the Little Big Horn
  10226
Once We Had a Horse 14702
Once We Went on a Picnic 5923
One and One 5953
One at a Time 11268
One Bad Thing About Father,
  The 12346
One Bright Monday Morning 1196
One Day at a Time 18254
One Day Everything Went Wrong
  17355
One Day for Peace 4311
One Dragon's Dream 13402
One Earth, Many People 13966
One-Eyed Jake 8837
One Fat Summer 10902
One Fine Day 8411
One Fish, Two Fish, Red Fish,
  Blue Fish 15385
One for the Price of Two 9129
One Frog Too Many 11933
One God 5967
One Good Deed Deserves Another
  5590
One Hundred and Eight Bells
  6074
101 Costumes for All Ages, All
  Occasions 4358
101 Masks 4359
101 Words 16156
102 Questions and Answers About
  the Sea 10820
One Hundred Armenian Tales
  and Their Folkloristic Rele-
  vance 8546
100 Butterflies 5658
100 Greatest Baseball Heroes
  4591
100 Greatest Football Heroes
  4592
One Hundred Greatest Sports
  Feats 4593
One Hundred Greatest Sports
  Heroes 4594
100 Greatest Women in Sports
  8483
One Hundred Hamburgers 16005

100 Keys 6048
One Hundred One Things the In-
  dians Made 17745
100 Outstanding Puerto Ricans
  14294
100 Pounds of Popcorn 10032
100 Story Poems 13312
One Hundred White Horses 10404
One I Love, Two I Love 8412
One Is God 13920
One Is Good, Two Are Better
  15842
One Is No Fun but Twenty Is
  Plenty 17335
One Is One (Picard) 13655
1 Is One (Tudor) 17032
One Is the Engine 12011
One Is Unique 11141
One-Legged Ghost, The 10802
One Little Girl 5714
One Little Goat 8237
One Little Indian 12378
One Little Indian Boy 2276
One Little Kitten 8301
One Little Room, an Everywhere
  10974
One Luminaria for Antonio 8540
One Man's Wilderness 9630
One Misty Moisty Morning 12235
One Mitten Lewis 9573
One Monday Morning 15614
One More and One Less 11536
One More Flight 2592
One Morning in Maine 11240
One Old Oxford Ox 1231
1, One Dancing Drum 10084
1 Pinch of Sunshine, 1/2 Cup of
  Rain 3210
One Sad Day 9973
One Small Blue Bead 15175
One Small Candle 6042
One Small Dog 17036
One Snail and Me 11449
One Summer in Between 11812
One Summer Night 15050
One to Eleven 16443
One to Fifty Book, The 18353
One to Grow On 10941
One to Teeter-Totter 1185
One to Ten, Count Again 10963
One Trick Too Many 6851
One, Two and Three with Ant and
  Bee 1054
One Two Three 2368
One, Two, Three and Many 14801
One, Two, Three for Fun 16143
1 2 3 for the Library 10946

One, Two, Three, Four 7345
1 2 3 4 5 6 7 8 9 Benn 11410
1, 2, 3 to the Zoo 2928
One, Two, Where's My Shoe?
   17135
One Was Johnny 15333
One Way 15585
One Week One Trouble 13060
One Wide River to Cross 5405
One Winter Night in August 9698
Oneida People 14329
Ong, the Wild Gander 8082
Onion John 10116
Onion Journey 4375
Only Birds Have Feathers 12500
Only Earth We Have, The 13967
Only One Ant 9901
Only Silly People Waste 15863
Only the Names Remain 1248
Ontario (Harrington) 7757
Ontario (Ontario Ministry of Cul-
   ture & Rec.) 13136
Ontario/Canada 13139
Ontario Historic Sites, Museums,
   Galleries and Plaques 13138
Ontario of Yesterday 12159
Ontario Turtles 6409
Ontario's Conservation Authorities
   13142
Ooka the Wise see Case of the
   Marble Monster and Other
   Stories, The
Oo-oo'nah Art 177
Oops 11934
Ootah's Lucky Day 13299
Op-Tricks 11689
Open Door to the Great Lakes
   7422
Open Gate 7939
Open the Door and See All the
   People 2566
Opening of the Suez Canal, The
   14685
Operacion alegria 9153
Operacion "Pata de Oso" 13992
Operating Room, The 9569
Operation Arctic 7682
Operation Blue Bear 12430
Operation Peeg 6665
Operation That Happened to
   Rupert Piper, The 13329
Opossum 12297
Opposites 17889
Optical Illusion Book, The 15752
Optimists of Nine Elms, The
   15707
Orange Is a Color 10612

Orange October 8907
Orange-robed Boy 6610
Orbit 14741
Orchard Cat, The 9657
Ordeal by Mountains 16148
Ordeal of the Young Hunter, The
   10370
Ordinary Jack 4284
Oregon at Last! 14808
Oregon Trail, The 13333
Organic Living Book, The 9974
Oriental Immigrants in America
   8477
Orienteering 2033
Origami in the Classroom 604
Origins of Language, The 11158
Origins of Man, The 12641
Orisha 6892
Orlando the Brave Vulture 17136
Oros Viejos 377
Orphan for Nebraska, An 16622
Orphan Jim 3826
Orphans of Simitra, The 1927
Orphans of the Wind 7848
Orphelines in the Enchanted Castle,
   The 2967
Orr on Ice 13180
Oscar en Africa 10147
Oscar espeleologo 10148
Oscar espia atomico 10149
Oscar Lobster's Fair Exchange
   15261
Oscar Otter 1405
Oscar y corazon de purpura 10150
Oscar y los hombres rana 10151
Osceola (Blassingame) 1731
Osceola (Gridley) 7355
Osceola (Hall) 7595
Osceola (Syme) 16592
Osceola and the Seminole War 7178
Osceola and the Seminole Wars 235
Osceola, Young Seminole Indian
   3511
Osmonds, The 5145
Osprey Island 5844
Ossian House 16304
Ostrich Chase, The 8678
Ote 1370
Other Americans 18307
Other City, The 17336
Other Face, The 6252
Other Girl, The 7611
Other People, The 11483
Other Sandals 17600
Other Side of a Poem, The 24
Other Side of the Fence, The 3925
Other Side of the Street, The 2423

Other Way Round, The 9730
Other World, The 8334
Otherwise Known as Sheila the
    Great 1820
Otis Spofford 3564
Ottawa 15903
Otter, The 15524
Otter in the Cove 12188
Otter's Story, An 10790
Ottie and the Star 346
Otto and the Magic Potatoes 5088
Otto in Africa 5089
Otto in Texas 5090
Otto Is a Rhino 9857
Otto of the Silver Hand 14015
Otwe 4
Ounce, Dice, Trice 14215
Our African Heritage 1260
Our Alphabet 13126
Our Animal Friends at Maple Hill
    Farm 13979
Our Blood and Tears 18093
Our Captive Animals 11275
Our Common Insects 18437
Our Dirty Air 5367
Our Dirty Land 5368
Our Eddie 8946
Our Family 14370
Our Fathers Had Powerful Songs
    1380
Our Fifty States 12157
Our First Ladies 11262
Our Foreign-Born Citizens 1256
Our Fragile Earth 8028
Our Friends in Africa 8213
Our Human Ancestors 3264
Our Hungry Earth 13968
Our Indian Heritage 16650
Our Lady of Guadalupe 13281
Our Names 10212
Our Neighbors in Africa 2828
Our New Motor Car 12594
Our Noisy World 12669
Our People of the Sierra Leone
    Protectorate 7085
Our Poets Speak 16123
Our Senses and How They Work
    18548
Our Sister 2341
Our Snowman Has Olive Eyes
    8102
Our State Birds 4412
Our Street Feels Good 9943
Our Terrariums 18221
Our Theatres 15591
Our Tiny Servants 9975
Our Tooth Story 9746

Our Utah Pioneers 7727
Our Veronica Goes to Petunia's
    Farm 5181
Our Vital Need 2523
Our Wonderful Hands 10100
Our World (Rau) 14144
Our World (Werner) 17747
Out from Under 782
Out Jumped Abraham 2433
Out Loud 12103
Out of Love 18209
Out of the Ark 14182
Out of the Cauldron 9976
Out of the Earth I Sing 10721
Out of the Midwest 15249
Out of the Sun 2007
Out, Out, Out! 286
Out There 16393
Outcast 16526
Outcasts, The 11645
Outdoor Art for Kids 9840
Outdoor Cookbook, The 1721
Outnumbered, The 2308
Outpost Stories of the Police of
    Rhodesia 13209
Outrageous Kasimir 2291
Outside 12940
Outside My Window 15815
Outsiders, The 8216
Ovada 9119
Over in the Meadow (Keats) 9603
Over in the Meadow (Langstaff)
    10251
Over Sea, Under Stone 4087
Over the Hills and Far Away
    14781
Over the Hills to Fabylon 7219
Over the Mormon Trail 9352
Over the River and Through the
    Wood 3354
Over, Under and Through ...
    8302
Overhead the Sun 17819
Overland Launch, The 8320
Overpraised Season, An 18612
Owen of the Bluebird 16678
Owl and the Woodpecker, The
    17927
Owl at Home 11003
Owl in the Cedar Tree 12334
Owl Service, The 6615
Owlet 2082
Owliver 10067
Owls 8422
Owls in the Family 12525
Owl's Kiss, The 16161
Owl's Nest 16077

Owl's New Cards 5533
Ownself 2843
Ox 12810
Ox-Cart Man 7584
Ox Goes North 12811
Ox of the Wonderful Horns ...,
The 2459
Oxford Book of Poetry for Chil-
dren, The 1774
Oxford Nursery Rhyme Book,
The 13148
Oxygen Keeps You Alive 2140
Ozarks, The 14290

- P -

P. G. A. Championship Tourna-
ment, The 11897
Pa Demba's Heir 817
Pablita Velarde 12726
Pablito's New Feet 16806
Pablo Paints a Picture 12241
Pablo Picasso 7302
Pablo the Potter 16375
Pacific Northwest Indian Wars
see Indian Wars of the
Pacific Northwest
Pack of Riddles, A 6766
Pack Rat's Day and Other Poems,
The 13888
Package, The 483
Packet Alley 12015
Paco's Miracle 3493
Paddington Abroad 1876
Paddington Bear 1877
Paddington Goes to Town 1878
Paddington Helps Out 1879
Paddington on Stage 2073
Paddington on Top 1880
Paddington's Garden 1881
Paddle-to-the-Sea 8492
Paddy Pork's Holiday 7042
Paddy's Christmas 12358
Paddy's Evening Out 7043
Paddy's Preposterous Promises
1666
Padre Porko 4609
Pagan the Black 1450
Pagoo 8493
Pai-Pai Pig, The 481
Paint a Rainbow 7897
Paint All Kinds of Pictures
16097

Paint-Box Sea, The 11168
Paint, Brush and Palette 17698
Paintbrush and Peacepipe 14519
Painted Pig, The 12479
Painted Pony Runs Away 11327
Painter and the Bird, The 17275
Painter's Trick, The 17282
Painting and Sculpture in Minnesota,
1820-1914 3728
Painting Free 11690
Painting the Moon 18161
Paintings 2868
Pair of Red Clogs, A 11825
Pair of Shoes, The 6883
Pais de la geometria, El 17491
Pais de las cien palabras, El 11810
Pais de los ojos transparentes, El
4381
Pajarita sabia, La 13507
Pajaro de Nieve, El 16000
Pajaro pinto y otras cosas, El
16001
Paji 9833
Palace in Bagdad 10290
Palace Wagon Family 16542
Paleface Redskins, The 8996
Palmer Patch 17458
Pamela the Probation Officer 8769
Pampalche of the Silver Teeth 6852
Pan-African Short Stories 4835
Pancakes, Pancakes! 2929
Pancakes--Paris 1677
Pancita del gato, La 6842
Panda 1901
Pandas Live Here 5239
Pandilla de los diez, La 2914
Panga Raiders, The 12972
Panki y el guerrero 247
Pantaloni 1622
Pantheon Story of American Art for
Young People, The 1181
Pantheon Story of Art, The 14777
Pantheon Story of Art for Young
People 1180
Panther 7564
Panther Lick Creek 7928
Panuck 11397
Papa and the Animals 4663
Papa, como nace un niño? 1852
Papa Es Grande 14081; see also
Father Is Big
Papa Ewusi and the Magic Marble
4664
Papa Like Everyone Else, A 16709
Papa Ojo and His Family 80
Papa Pequeño 10581
Papa Small 10582

Papacito and His Family 17533
Papalote para Carlos, Un 13939
Papa's Lemonade ..., The 14307
Papa's Panda 17966
Papa's Secret Chocolate Dessert 15455
Papa's Wife 1692
Papeek 17215
Papelucho 13410
Papelucho casi huerfano 13411
Papelucho detective 13412
Papelucho en vacaciones 13413
Papelucho historiador 13414
Papelucho: Mi hermana, Ji 13415
Papelucho: Mi hermano Hippie 13416
Papelucho misionero 13417
Papelucho perdido 13418
Papelucho: ¿Soy dix leso? 13419
Paper 16735
Paper Airplane Book, The 15753
Paper Bead Box, The 4900
Paper Cutting 16736
Paper Dragon, A 12505
Paper-Flower Tree, The 824
Paper Hornets 8852
Paper, Ink and Roller 17699
Paper of Pins, A 7070
Paper Zoo, A 17710
Papier-Mache 9289
Pappa Pellerin's Daughter 7436
Para Chiquitines 9224
Parade, The 8457
Parakeets and Peach Pies 15915
Paramedic Emergency! 12162
Parents Can Be a Problem 15170
Parents' Magazine's Christmas Holiday Book 8047
Park Ranger 3785
Parnelli, a Story of Auto Racing 10768
Parque de leyendas 4877
Parrak, the White Reindeer 1948
Parrakeets 18549
Parsley 1389
Parsley, Sage, Rosemary and Time 4403
Part for Addie, A 13009
Partisan, The 17604
Partners, The 17867
Partridge in a Pear Tree, A 2167
Party at the Old Farm, The 13316
Party That Lasted All Summer, The 11531

Pasakon 17267
Pascal and the Lioness 7489
Pass to Win 16477
Passage to Texas 17315
Passage to the Golden Gate 3436
Passengers Must Not Ride on Fenders 5864
Passing the Football 4789
Passover 15730
Passover Story, The 1628
Passport of Mallam Ilia, The 5317
Pat the Bunny 10133
Patchwork, Applique, and Quilting Primer, A 16009
Path Above the Pines, The 14757
Path of Hunters 13457
Path of the Orange Peels 7528
Path to Snowbird Mountain, The 16968
Paths of Poetry, The 17158
Pathways to Independence 12197
Pato correntino que se fue a la luna 14096
Patricia Crosses Town 1198
Patrick Comes to Puttyville and Other Stories 7917
Patrick des Jarlait 4856
Patrick Henry 2888
Patriotism, Patriotism, Patriotism 8420
Patriots' Days 13335
Patriot's Gold 17343
Patriots in Petticoats 3661
Patrol Car 9187
Patsy-O and His Wonderful Pets 11453
Pattern of Roses, A 13599
Pattern of Things, The 13021
Patterns 15563
Patty Reed's Doll 10369
Paul and Etta 13320
Paul Bunyan (Kumin) 10131
Paul Bunyan (Shephard) 15533
Paul Bunyan (Stevens) 16266
Paul Bunyan and His Great Blue Ox 17380
Paul Bunyan and Other Tales 15423
Paul Bunyan Fights the Monster Plants 1732
Paul Bunyan Finds a Wife 4706
Paul Bunyan Swings His Ax 11271
Paul Bunyan, the Work Giant 17074
Paul Bunyan Tricks a Dragon 15424
Paul Cuffee 9310

Paul Laurence Dunbar 15129
Paul Revere 7198
Paul Robeson (Greenfield) 7309
Paul Robeson (Hamilton) 7661
Paulina 11838
Paulo's Strange Adventure 9803
Paulossie 16566
Pavo and the Princess 12748
Paws, Hoofs, and Flippers 5206
Pea Patch Island 4391
Pea Soup and Sea Serpents 15115
Peace Is an Adventure 9631
Peachblossom 10336
Peaches 11227
Peachtree Island 10405
Peacock and the Crow, The
    9865
Peacock and the Snake, The
    15994
Peacock Pie 4688
Peacocks 11734
Peanut 15297
Peanut Craft 5006
Peanuts for Billy Ben 10583
Peanuts, Popcorn, Ice Cream,
    Candy, Soda Pop, and How
    They Began 14802
Pearl Buck 12603
Pearl Harbor! December 7, 1941
    7022
Peas in a Pod 18465
Peasant and the Donkey, The
    12633
Peasants Pea Patch, The 4480
Pebbles and Pods 3330
Pebbles from a Broken Jar 260
Pecos Bill and the Mustang 5785
Pecos Bill Rides a Tornado 1733
Pecos Bill, the Greatest Cowboy
    of All Time 2021
Pecosos, Los 13420
Peculiar Magic, A 9244
Peddler's Cart, The 3690
Peddler's Girl 8672
Peddler's Summer 6075
Pedlar of Swaffham, The 4319
Pedrin, el Conejo Travieso
    13841
Pedro, El Angel de la Calle Olvera
    13785
Pedro, the Angel of Olvera
    Street 13786
Pedruquito y sus amigos 4878
Peeper, First Voice of Spring
    11250
Peetie the Pack Rat 3524
Peg-Leg Willy 5423

Peg-Legged Pirate of Sulu, The
    3322
Pegasus 17077
Pegeen 17231
Peggy 5126
Peggy Fleming 12486
Peggy's New Brother 15051
Pegleg Mystery, The 5598
Pele (Gault) 6677
Pele (Gutman) 7527
Pele (Haskins) 7825
Pele (May) 11898
Pele (Taylor) 16699
Pelican Chorus, The 10467
Pelican Mystery, The 8550
Pelle's New Suit 1610
Pelly and Peak 18170
Pelo Lacio, Pelo Rizo 6997
Pelusa rumbo al sol 12006
Pencil and Paper Tricks 10207
Pencil Families, The 16755
Pencil, Pen and Brush 17700
Pencil to Press 16052
Penelope and the Earth 1827
Penelope and the Mussels 1828
Penengro 17232
Penguin, The 16828
Penguins Are Coming! 13493
Penguins, of All People 6267
Penguin's Way 9311
Penn 7205
Pennington's Last Term 13600
Pennington's Seventeenth Summer
    see Pennington's Last Term
Pennsylvania 3029
Pennsylvania Colony, The (Neal)
    12696
Pennsylvania Colony (Stevens)
    16270
Penny 1953
Penny a Look, A 18517
Penny Crossword Puzzles 17644
Penny Fiddle, The 7201
Penny Puppets, Penny Theatre and
    Penny Plays 9102
Penny Tunes and Princesses 10668
Penny Whistles see Child's Garden
    of Verses, A
Penny-wise, Fun-foolish 4818
Penny's Worth of Character, A
    16425
People and Places 11977
People Are Important 5582
People Downstairs and Other City
    Stories 862
People from the Sky 3053
People of the Ax, The 18021

People of the Dream 6117
People of the Ice Age 7048
People of the Short Blue Corn
  4198
People Who Make Things 12127
People Words 15392
People's Hero, A 14220
People's Republic of China, The
  17577
Pepe's Private Christmas 4151
Pepi's Bell 18057
Pepito's Story 5827
Pepper 14273
Pepper and All the Legs 6458
Pepperfoot of Thursday's Market
  4610
Peppermint Pig, The 1218
Peppersalt Land, The 7783
Peppino 18533
Pequeño mundo infantil 12561
Peregrine Falcons, The 15037
Perez and Martina 1371
Perez y Martina 1372
Perez Arson Mystery, The 16944
Perfect Life, The 5629
Perico 12452
Perihan's Promise, Turkish Rela-
  tives, and the Dirty Old
  Imam 3338
Perilous Gard, The 13824
Perilous Road, The 16174
Perils of Putney, The 10092
Periwinkle 5182
Permanent Resident Birds of In-
  diana 7550
Perplexing Puzzles and Tanta-
  lizing Teasers 6587
Perrault's Classic French Fairy
  Tales 13532
Perronique 12142
Perry and the Open Door to
  Japan, July, 1853 8878
Persephone 16922
Persephone and the Springtime
  8335
Persia see Iran
Persian Folk and Fairy Tales
  12017
Pet Birds 9391
Pet of the Met 6291
Pet Parrot 4277
Pet Show! 9604
Petar's Treasure 9426
Pete 12438
Pete Cass 16764
Pete Pack Rat 14026
Pete Rose (Libby) 10769

Pete Rose (Rose) 14608
Peter and Butch 13639
Peter and Mr. Brandon 15052
Peter and Nancy in Africa 3899
Peter and the Piskies 11642
Peter and the Rocket Ship 4169
Peter and the Wolf 13975
Peter and Veronica 14844
Peter Bull 13024
Peter Gets the Chickenpox 10608
Peter Graves 5091
Peter Holt, P.K. 1988
Peter Jumping Horse at the Stampede
  7594
Peter Learns to Crochet 10657
Peter Pan 1117
Peter Pan in Kensington Gardens
  1118
Peter Penny's Dance 14038
Peter Piper's Alphabet 2381
Peter Rabbit see Tale of Peter
  Rabbit
Peter Rabbit's Natural Foods Cook-
  book 4956
Peter, Sani and the Smugglers
  16801
Peter Stuyvesant 17858
Peter Stuyvesant of Old New York
  4323
Peter the Wanderer 625
Peter Treegate's War 17850
Peter Zenger 6527
Peterkin Papers, The 7578; see
  also Complete Peterkin Papers,
  The
Peter's Adventures in Blueberry
  Land 1611
Peter's Angel 2876
Peter's Chair 9605
Peter's Long Walk 9829
Peter's Pinto 2544
Pete's Home Run 14244
Pete's House 15989
Petey 16903
Petit Chaperon Rouge (Little Red
  Riding Hood), Le 10374
Petits contes Negres pour les en-
  fants des blancs, see
  Little Black Stories for Little
  White Children
Petrol Thieves and Happy Anna, The
  16975
Petronella 18022
Petros' War 18507
Pets 3435
Pets and People 15636
Pets from the Pond 2478

Pets in a Jar 15754
Petticoat Politics 5630
Petticoat Rebel 3532
Petunia 5183
Petunia, Beware 5184
Petunia, I Love You 5185
Petunia Takes a Trip 5186
Petunia's Christmas 5187
Petunia's Treasure 5188
Pezzettino 10883
Phaedra Complex, The 5617
Phantom Carousel and Other
   Ghostly Tales, The 197
Phantom Deer, The 10895
Phantom Roundabout and Other
   Ghostly Tales, The see
   Phantom Carousel and Other
   Ghostly Tales, The
Phantom Tollbooth, The 9437
Philip and the Pooka and Other
   Irish Fairy Tales 7236
Philip Hall Likes Me, I Reckon
   Maybe 7261
Phillis Wheatley (Borland) 1958
Phillis Wheatley (Fuller) 6438
Philosopher's Stone, The 10933
Phoebe and the Prince 13167
Phoebe's Family 16574
Phoebe's Revolt 845
Phoenix and the Carpet, The
   12736
Phoenix Feathers 15664
Photographs and Poems by Sioux
   Children ... 10777
Photography (Kohn) 9980
Photography (Noren) 12896
Photography for Young People
   9284
Physical Fitness for Young
   Champions 584
Physics Lab of Your Own, A
   11687
Piankhy the Great 9255
Pia's Journey to the Holy Land
   6831
Pia's Safari 6830
Picaro, a Pet Otter 18135
Pick a Peck of Puzzles 14675
Pick It Up 5503
Picken's Exciting Summer 4604
Picken's Great Adventure 4605
Picken's Treasure Hunt 4606
Pickle 16756
Pickle in the Middle and Other
   Easy Snacks 18631
Picnics and Parades 9902
Pico, el Patito Presumido 14089

Pictorial History of Algonquin Pro-
   vincial Park, A 13143
Pictorial History of Immigration
   7691
Pictorial History of the American
   Indian, A 10181
Pictorial History of the Great Lakes,
   A 7838
Pictorial History of the Negro in
   America, A 8725
Pictorial History of the Western Re-
   serve, 1796 to 1860 2752
Pictorial History of Women in Amer-
   ica, A 17544
Picture Book Farm 7903
Picture Book of Arizona 882
Picture Book of Arkansas 883
Picture Book of Colorado 884
Picture Book of Florida 885
Picture Book of Illinois 886
Picture Book of Indiana 887
Picture Book of Iowa 888
Picture Book of Kansas 889
Picture Book of Michigan 890
Picture Book of Minnesota 891
Picture Book of Missouri 892
Picture Book of Musical Instruments
   10174
Picture Book of Nebraska 893
Picture Book of North Dakota 894
Picture Book of Ohio 895
Picture Book of Oklahoma 896
Picture Book of Pennsylvania 897
Picture Book of Salt, The 2306
Picture Book of South Dakota 898
Picture Book of Texas 899
Picture Book of Wisconsin 900
Picture for Harold's Room, A 9251
Picture Gallery of Canadian History,
   The 9185
Picture Has a Special Look, A 1965
Picture Life of Bobby Orr, The
   5273
Picture Life of Elizabeth 2nd, The
   10965
Picture Life of Herman Badillo, The
   372
Picture Life of Jesse Jackson, The
   7621
Picture Life of Malcolm X, The
   7826
Picture Life of Martin Luther King,
   Jr. 18454
Picture Life of Muhammad Ali, The
   5274
Picture Life of Ralph J. Bunche,
   The 18455

Picture Life of Stevie Wonder,
The 5275
Picture Life of Thurgood Marshall,
The 18456
Picture Map Geography of Africa
14040
Picture Map Geography of the
USSR 12691
Picture Poetry Book 11209
Picture Signs and Symbols 11134
Picture-Skin Story 1249
Picture Story and Biography of
Admiral Christopher Columbus,
The 9427
Picture Story and Biography of
Red Cloud, The 6637
Picture Story of Frank Robinson,
The 18443
Picture Story of Hank Aaron,
The 18444
Picture Story of Japan, The
3066
Picture Story of Walt Frazier,
The 10918
Picture Tales from Mexico 16382
Pictures to Live With 8516
Piece of Fire and Other Haitian
Tales, The 4199
Pieces of Another World 2141
Pied Piper of Hamelin, The 2438
Piemakers, The 4285
Piero Ventura's Book of Cities
17281
Pierre 15334
Pierre the Muskrat 13082
Pieter Brueghel's The Fair 4234
Pig 791
Pig and the Blue Flag 16261
Pig Tale, The (Carroll) 3103
Pig Tale (Oxenbury) 13224
Pig War, The 928
Pigeon Flight 16359
Pigeon, Fly Home 10805
Pigeon Man, The 33
Pigeon Pair, The 13038
Pigeon with the Tennis Elbow,
The 3426
Piggle 1910
Piggy in the Puddle, The 13809
Pigs Wild and Tame 8585
Pilgrim Courage 15884
Pilgrim Thanksgiving 7940
Pilgrimage, The 10864
Pilgrims, The 7439
Pilgrims of Plymouth 1288
Pilgrim's Progress 2595
Pilyo the Piranha 697

Pima Indian Legends 15491
Pima Past, A 15492
Pima Remembers, A 17630
Pimm's Cup for Everybody 4928
Piñatas 2279
Pinballs, The 2790
Pinch 2872
Pinchpenny Mouse 10068
Pineapple Child and Other Tales
from Ashanti, The 593
Piney Woods 4189
Piney's Summer 1195
Pink Like the Geranium 839
Pink Pig 8644
Pink Puppy 8541
Pinkerton, Behave! 9658
Pinkertons Ride Again, The 4851
Pinocchio see Adventures of
Pinocchio, The
Pins, Picks, and Popsicle Sticks
17983
Pint-Size Fun 13610
Pintadita la vikuna 1120
Pintas de las mariquitas y otros
cuentos, Las 13065
Pinto's Journey 2299
Piojo y la Liendre, El 14411
Pioneer Astronomers 16496
Pioneer Gardens 10240
Pioneer of Alaska Skies 3258
Pioneers and Patriots 4944
Pioneers in Freedom 16292
Pioneers in Petticoats 2054
Pioneers in Print 6033
Pip Moves Away 2417
Piper, Pipe That Song Again!
10278
Pipes and Plumbing Systems 18572
Piping Down the Valleys Wild
10279
Pipkin 6128
Pipo 4585
Pippa 70
Pippa Mouse 1842
Pippa Pops Out! 1843
Pippi Longstocking 10838
Pirata malapata, El 14255
Pirate Lafitte and the Battle of New
Orleans 16632
Pirate of Puerto Rico, The 4077
Pirates' Adventure on Spooky Is-
land, The 9752
Pirates in Panama 12347
Pirates in the Park 14435
Pirate's Island 16958
Pirates of Samarkand 14408
Pishtosh, Bullwash and Wimple 6066

Pistol 14327
Pistol in Greenyards, A 8783
Pitch Dark and No Moon 10413
Pitchers, The 15910
Pitchers and Pitching 16478
Pitching the Baseball 4790
Pitching with Tom Seaver 15215
Pitschi 5897
Pittsburgh Steelers, The 11899
Pizorro 17260
Place, The 3691
Place in the Sun, A 4506
Place in the Woods, A 8570
Place to Live, A 1433
Placekicking and Punting 4791
Plague of Frogs 16757
Plain Girl 16029
Plain Princess, The 11337
Plain Princess and the Lazy
    Prince, The 15113
Plains Indian Mythology 11703
Planes the Axis Flew in World
    War II, The 4010
Planet-Girded Suns 5439
Planet of Death 15669
Planet of Junior Brown, The
    7662
Plant Communities 18222
Plant Fun 16034
Plant Sitter, The 18593
Plants 18550
Plants and Insects Together
    13356
Plants Are Like That 16367
Plants for Kids to Grow Indoors
    12208
Plants for Pots 5802
Plants in Time 4177
Plants in Winter 3801
Plants on the Go 7974
Plants That Move 15298
Plastics 7562
Play a Part 2948
Play Ball, Amelia Bedelia 13300
Play for Yejide and Other Plays,
    The 2302
Play It in Spanish 13940
Play the Bach, Dear! 7437
Play the Man 13302
Play with Leaves and Flowers
    see Plants That Move
Play with Me 5567
Play with Vines see Plants That
    Move
Playing and Composing on the
    Recorder 5556
Playing with a Football 15571

Playing with Numbers 7338
Playing with Shapes and Sizes
    7339
Plays About Our Nation's Songs
    5924
Plays from African Folktales 10001
Plays from Folktales of Africa and
    Asia 18127
Plays to Enjoy 13657
Playtime 12280
Playtime in Africa 16532
Pleasant Fieldmouse 17408
Please Don't Go 18246
Please Don't Say Hello 6984
Pleasures and Palaces 12496
Plenty for Three 15816
Plenty of Fish 15299
Plenty of Riddles 17879
Plenty to Watch 18371
Plimoth Plantation 3791
Plink, Plink, Plink 1240
Plum Pudding for Christmas 9456
Plush 4855
Plymouth Thanksgiving, The 17678
Poachers in the Serengeti 11089
Pocahontas (d'Aulaire) 4557
Pocahontas (Martin) 11755
Pocahontas (Seymour) 15397
Pocahontas (Wilkie) 17937
Pocahontas and Captain John Smith
    10416
Pocahontas and the Strangers
    2567
Pocahontas in London 17409
Pocket Calculator Game Book, The
    15085
Pocket Full of Seeds, A 14845
Pocketful of Cricket, A 3171
Poco de Mexico, Un 6486
Poem for Putting to Sea 12071
Poemas Parvulos 6487
Poemas Pe-que Pe-que Pe-que-ñitos
    6488
Poemas y Colores 12841
Poems (Browning) 2439
Poems (Coatsworth) 3692
Poems (Coleridge) 3827
Poems (Dickinson) 4890
Poems (Field) 5852
Poems (Herrick) 8108
Poems (Keats) 9610
Poems (Longfellow) 11045
Poems (Shakespeare) 15404
Poems (Tennyson) 16742
Poems by Kali 7459
Poems Children Will Sit Still For
    4744

Poems for Red Letter Days 15219
Poems for Seasons and Celebra-
    tions 3818
Poems from Africa 354
Poems from France 15939
Poems from the German 13746
Poems Here and Now 9778
Poems of Childhood 5849
Poems of Magic and Spells 3819
Poems of Percy Bysshe Shelley
    15529
Poems of Robert Burns 2691
Poems, Selected for Young People
    12210
Poems to Hear and See 5878
Poems to Read to the Very Young
    6221
Poems to Solve 16558
Poesia menuda 13066
Poesias de la Madre Oca 14217;
    see also Mother Goose in Span-
    ish
Poesias de Mari Pepa, Las 3467
Poetry 13577
Poetry for Chuckles and Grins
    9055
Poetry for Holidays 10280
Poetry for Spring 13388
Poetry Is 8733
Poetry of Earth 47
Poetry of the Negro, 1746-1970,
    The 8724
Poetry Sampler, A 7585
Poet's Tales, The 3820
Pointed Brush, The 11756
Points, Lines, and Planes 11142
Poison Factory, The 2109
Poison Tree and Other Poems, A
    11935
Poisonous Plants 10814
Poisonous Snakes of Alabama
    18096
Poko and the Golden Demon 8446
Poland 5341
Polar Bear 11285
Polar Bear Called Pingo, A 9981
Polar Deserts 8097
Poles in America, The 18356
Police Dog 9188
Police Lab 1523
Policeman in Your Community,
    The 13547
Polish Christmas Traditions and
    Legends 16923
Polizon del Ulises, El 11839
Pollito de fuego, El 14416
Pollution 2176

Pollution Lab 1524
Pollution: The Noise We Hear
    9337
Polly Harris, The 16977
Polly Kent Rides West 11280
Polly's Tiger 13640
Poltergeist of Jason Morey, The
    15820
Poltergeists 9934
Polyhedrons 11143
Polynesians Knew, The 13689
Pomo Indians of California and Their
    Neighbors, The 2432
Pond, The (Carrick) 3083
Pond, The (Samson) 14875
Pond and Marsh Plants 5207
Pond Life (Reid) 14219
Pond Life (Wong) 18223
Pontiac (Grant) 7179
Pontiac (Gridley) 7356
Pontiac (Hays) 7941
Pontiac (Hollman) 8497
Pontiac (Voight) 17344
Pontiac, Young Ottawa Leader
    13461
Pontiac's War, 1763-1766 7053
Pony Care 15827
Pony Express 62
Pony for Linda, A 469
Pony for Three 470
Pony of the Sioux 13440
Pony Soldier 11330
Pony to Jump 17989
Pony to Love, A 8120
Pooh Cook Book, The 5387
Pooh Party Book, The 5388
Pooh's Alphabet Book 12248
Pool of Fire, The 3408
Pool of Swallows 3704
Poor Felicity 17601
Poor Goose 14520
Poor Jenny, Bright as a Penny
    12577
Poor Pumpkin see Mathematical
    Princess and Other Stories, The
Poor Richard 4534
Poor Richard in France 12348
Poor Stainless 12950
Poor Tom's Ghost 4404
Pop Corn and Ma Goodness 13899
Pop! Goes the Weasel 14027
Pop-Up Going to the Hospital 3505
Popcorn 15300
Popcorn Book, The 4723
Popcorn Dragon 16785
Poppy Seed Cakes, The 3515
Poppy Seeds, The 2568

Popular Girls Club, The 10039
Porcelain Man, The 9697
Porko von Popbutton 5092
Pornada 15624
Portmanteau Book, The 14540
Portrait of Deborah 3754
Portrait of Ivan 6185
Portrait of Margarita 690
Portugee Phillips and the Fighting Sioux 453
Portuguese Explorers, The 2524
Posadas, Las 6233
Posse of Two 1350
Possible Impossibles of Ikkyu the Wise, The 5263
Possum 11251
Posts and Rugs 9114
Pot Bank, The 10757
Pot of Honey 11130
Potato Talk 14200
Potatoes 15692
Potatoes, Potatoes 10988
Potawatomi Indian Summer 13072
Potlatch Family, The 10227
Potterymaking 5326
Pouce par Pouce 10884
Power at Niagara 3096
Power of Three, The 9343
Powhatan 12701
Practical Macrame 516
Practical Princess, The 18023
Prairie Boy's Summer, A 10141
Prairie Boy's Winter, A 10142
Prairie Dog Summer 11488
Prairie Dogs in Prairie Dog Town 5240
Prairie School 10584
Prairie Schooners, The 14703
Prairie-Town Boy 14886
Prairie Winter 5847
Prancing Pony, The 4654
Prapan, a Boy of Thailand 15083
Prayer for a Child 5853
Prayers from the Ark 4657
Praying Mantis (Earle) 5208
Praying Mantis, The (Hess) 8121
Preacher's Kid, The 1809
Prefabulous Animiles 14207
Preguntas y Respuestas Sobre Ciencia Elemental 16018
Preguntas y Respuestas Sobre el Cuerpo Humano 11357
Preguntas y Respuestas Sobre la Naturaleza 14943
Prehistoric America 17786
Prehistoric Animals 15025

Prehistoric Life 11949
Prehistoric Man (Bailey) 910
Prehistoric Man (Simak) 15706
Prehistoric Monsters Did the Strangest Things 8624
Prepare for a Career in Radio and Television Announcing 11345
Prepare to Dive! 3736
Preposterous Adventures of Swimmer, The 9773
Present for Mother, A 6316
Present for Yanya, A 11619
Presidency, The 9270
President from Texas, The 11181
Presidents of the United States 10552
Presto 14420
Pretty-Shield 10828
Pretzel Hero, The 14392
Price of Free Land, The 16401
Price of the Phoenix, The 11706
Priest on Horseback 1624
Primer Libro de Oro de los Numeros 5749
Primes Are Builders 11144
Primrose Day 7956
Prince and the Pauper, The 17085
Prince Bertram the Bad 11004
Prince Caspian 10692
Prince Henry the Navigator 9082
Prince in Waiting, The 3409
Prince of the Akans, A 601
Prince of the Bay, The 15229
Prince Who Gave Up a Throne, The 15340
Princess and Curdie, The 11304
Princess and Froggie, The 18521
Princess and the Admiral, The 13810
Princess and the Clown, The 11554
Princess and the Giants, The 15969
Princess and the Goblin, The 11305
Princess and the Lion, The 3693
Princess and the Woodcutter's Daughter, The 2292
Princess Book, The 3384
Princess Hynchatti and Some Other Surprises 10496
Princess Mary of Maryland 162
Princess of the Full Moon 7497
Princess of the Rice Fields, The 9809
Princess September 11840
Princesses, The 9294

Princesses & Peasant Boys 5795
Principito, El 14856
Print a Book 10144
Print Making 11509
Printcrafts 6024
Printing 4764
Printing from a Stone 8229
Printmaking 14536
Prison Window, Jerusalem Blue 3592
Prisoner in the Park, The 11484
Prisoner of the Iroquois 16925
Prisoner of the Mound Builders 7742
Prisoners in the Snow 3159
Private Eye 5976
Private Matter, A 5610
Private Zoo 11394
Pro Football Heroes of Today 16130
Pro Football's Greatest Upsets 16479
Pro Football's Kicking Game 16480
Pro Football's Passing Game 16481
Pro Football's Unforgettable Games 16482
Pro Quarterbacks, The 15433
Pro Sports Trivia 13904
Probability 10870
Probing the Unknown 13619
Procession, The 11555
Prodigal Brothers 8416
Professor Coconut and the Thief 6719
Professor Diggins' Dragons 8507
Professor Egghead's Best Riddles 18338
Professor Q's Secret 18101
Professor Wormbog in Search for the Zipperump-a-Zoo 11936
Profile of American History 11475
Profile of Kenya 9721
Profile of Nigeria 9722
Profiles in Black and White 3381
Profiles in Black Power 7827
Profiles in Courage 9688
Progress of the Afro-American, The 13375
Project Cat 2639
Project: Genius 7923
Project 1-2-3 12104
Project: Scoop 7924
Projects with Air 15755
Promise Is a Promise, A 3926
Promised Year, The 17099
Promises in the Attic 6362
Promises to Keep 4929

Proper Place, A 10865
Protest 2 2778
Proud Lady 4334
Proud Maiden, Tungak, and the Sun, The 6853
Proud Prisoner 7867
Proud Taste for Scarlet and Miniver, A 9992
Proud to Be Amish 9383
Proud Warrior 10417
Prove It! 18346
Provensen Book of Fairy Tales, The 13980
Proverbs of Many Nations 9632
Proving Years, The 4711
Prudence Crandall, Woman of Courage 18378
Psst! Doggie 9606
Psychiatry 9886
Pua Pua Lena Lena and the Magic Kihapu 2546
Puckered Moccasins 901
Puddles and Ponds 2740
Pueblo Indian Cookbook 8727
Pueblo Indians, The (Bleeker) 1760
Pueblo Indians, The (Erdoes) 5516
Pueblo Stories 4981
Puerto Rican Patriot 14274
Puerto Ricans 10146
Puerto Ricans in America, The 10288
Puerto Rico (Elisofon) 5342
Puerto Rico (Rivera) 14410
Puerto Rico en Mi Corazon 14295
Puffin Book of Lettering, The 7106
Puffin Book of Nursery Rhymes, The 13149; see also Family Book of Nursery Rhymes, A
Puffin Quartet of Poets, A 7123
Pugwash in the Pacific 14823
Pulanito 11165
Puleng of Lesotho 16201
Pulga 17207
Pulgarcita 13990
Pulgarcito 13991
Puma, The 5869
Pumpernick and Pimpernell 6408
Pumpers, Boilers, Hooks and Ladders 5946
Pumpkin Giant, The 17943
Pumpkin in a Pear Tree, A 3792
Pumpkin Smasher, The 1564
Pumpkinseeds 18400
Punch & Judy 5417
Punda the Tiger Horse 18095

Punia and the King of the Sharks 12307
Punkin Summer 2692
Puppet Party 3331
Puppets for Beginners 9103
Puppy Lost in Lapland 7619
Puppy Named Gih, A 11398
Puppy Who Wanted a Boy, The 16786
Puptents and Pebbles 15940
Pure Magic 3694
Purim 3927
Puritan Adventure 10585
Purple Cow and Other Nonsense ..., The 2646
Purple Mouse, The 11401
Push-Pull, Empty-Full 8303
Push, Pull, Stop, Go 10510
Pushcart War, The 12112
Puss in Boots (Galdone) 6506
Puss in Boots (Perrault) 13533
Pussy Merry's Birthday Party 818
Put Her to Port, Johnny 13345
Put Me in the Zoo 11063
Put on Your Thinking Cap 6050
Puttering with Paper 16368
Putting the Sun to Work 1434
Puzzle Patterns 9762
Puzzles and Brain Twisters 17472
Pygmies, The 1761
Pygmy's Arrow 6043
Pyramid 11204
Python's Party 17928

- Q -

Quack? 14350
Quakers, The 5335
Quanah, Leader of the Comanches 11900
Quanah Parker 491
Quarreling Book, The 18613
Quarter Boy 13321
Quarter-Mile Combat 9019
Quarterback Gamble 6686
Quarterbacks, The (Hasegawa) 7810
Quarterbacks, The (Smith) 15877
Quarterback's Aim 11070
Quasars, Pulsars, and Black Holes in Space 1525

Que Dices? 4337
Que pasa en mi pueblo? 13085
Que Se Dice, Niño? 9398
Queen Always Wanted to Dance, The 11937
Queen Amina 18134
Queen Elizabeth I 1648
Queen Elizabeth Story, The 16527
Queen Nzinga 16555
Queen of England 7694
Queen of Hearts 3584
Queen of Populists 16318
Queen of Spells 8917
Queen Victoria (Glendinning) 6901
Queen Victoria (Haycraft) 7909
Queen Victoria (Streatfeild) 16410
Queen Who Couldn't Bake Gingerbread, The 17240
Queenie Peavy 2601
Queen's Gold, The 18474
Queens of the Court 16483
Queen's Tears and Elephant's Ears 10029
Quest, The 16222
Quest for the Dead Sea Scrolls 13259
Quest of Captain Cook, The 15301
Quest of the Otter 17628
Questing Heart, The 10406
Question Box, The 18024
Question of Courage, A 4501
Question of Harmony, A 16099
Question of Time, A 423
Questions and Answers About Alcoholism 4416
Questions and Answers About Ants 15302
Questions and Answers About Horses 15303
Questions and Answers About Seashore Life 10925
Questions and Answers About the Weather 4238
Questions of Lifu, The 10337
Quetico Wolf 13025
Qui qui ri qui 17264
Quicksand Book, The 4724
Quiet Legend, The 12257
Quiet Noisy Book, The 2395
Quiet on Account of Dinosaur 16787
Quiet Place, A 1810
Quiet Rebels, The 16245
Quilts in the Attic 6023
Quips and Quirks 17565
Quitting Deal, The 16904
Quiz Book on Black America 1714

- R -

Rabbi and the Twenty-nine
  Witches, The 8238
Rabbit and Pork Rhyming Talk
  10402
Rabbit Finds a Way 4819
Rabbit for Easter, A 3076
Rabbit Garden 12189
Rabbit Hill 10426
Rabbits 15693
Rabbits and Hares 17815
Rabbits and Redcoats 13458
Rabbits in the Meadow 8122
Rabbits' Wedding, The 17999
Rabbit's World, The 15072
Raccoons Are for Loving 1999
Raccoons Are the Brightest
  People 12925
Race Against Time 1006
Race Car Drivers School 14072
Race Car Team 2766
Race to the Golden Spike 17725
Racecourse for Andy, A 18322
Racers and Drivers 18375
Raceway Charger 13034
Rachel 5659
Rachel and Herman 10732
Rachel Carson 10316
Rachel Jackson 7108
Racing 16872
Racing Cars That Made History
  4011
Racing on the Water 5763
Racing on the Wind 14079
Racing to Win 7335
Racketty-Packetty House 2670
Radigan Cares 5618
Rafael and the Raiders 1293
Railroad Engineers and Airplane
  Pilots 7280
Railroad to Freedom, The 16562
Railroad Yard 4923
Raimundo, the Unwilling Warrior
  13941
Rain and Hail 2142
Rain and the Valley 8811
Rain Comes to Yamboorah 13206
Rain Dance People, The 5517
Rain Drop Splash 17005
Rain Forest, The 16073
Rain in the Winds 11086
Rain Makes Applesauce 15027
Rain Puddle, The 8458
Rain Rain Rivers 15615
Rain, Rivers and Reservoirs
  616
Rainbow Book of American Folk
  Tales and Legends 10449
Rainbow for Robin, A 17190
Rainbow in the Sky 17159
Rainbow of My Own, A 6268
Rainbow of Sound, A 10136
Rainbow Origami Book for Children
  18373
Rainbow Rider 18420
Rainbow-Tinted Scarf ..., The
  5318
Rainbow Writing 12105
Rainbows & Fireworks 13606
Rainbows, Halos and Other Wonders
  8130
Rainmaker ..., The 5319
Rains of Eridan, The 8565
Rainy Day Book, The 15145
Rainy Day Together 13344
Rakoto and the Drongo Bird 11438
Rally to the Death 14810
Ralph & the Queen's Bathtub 3392
Ralph Bunche (Cornell) 4162
Ralph Bunche (Haskins) 7828
Ralph Nader 13109
Ralph Proves the Pudding 14617
Rama the Gypsy Cat 2791
Ramayana, The 15235
Ramon and the Pirate Gull 1130
Ramon Makes a Trade 14407
Ramona 8994
Ramona and Her Father 3565
Ramona and Her Mother 3566
Ramona the Brave 3567
Ramona the Pest 3568
Ramshackle Roost 6076
Ramu 12019
Ramu and Chennai 6171
Rancho de Muchachos, El 11055
Ranger in Skirts 14915
Ransom 5127
Ransom of Red Chief, The 8080
Raphael Semmes 15951
Rare and Rugged Sports 13157
Rare One, The 14562
Rascal 12926
Rascals from Haskell's Gym, The
  1895
Rasmus and the Vagabond 10839
Rass 14046
Rassin 18330
Rat-Catcher's Daughter, The 8654
Rat Hell 2630
Rat, the Ox, and the Zodiac 17241
Rats and Mice 15694
Rats Who Lived in the Delicatessen,

The 1605
Ratsmagic 11032
Rattlesnake Cave 10228
Rattlesnake Run 10439
Raucous Auk, The 8311
Raven 12056
Raven-Who-Sets-Things-Right
11732
Raven's Cry 7766
Ray Charles 11816
Raymond and Me That Summer
13537
Razorbacks Are Really Hogs!
15712
Razzberry Jamboree 9963
Reach Out, Ricardo 5153
Read About the Policeman 15843
Reading, Writing, Chattering
Chimps 413
Real Book of First Stories, The
7015
Real Ghosts 3749
Real Hole, The 3569
Real Life Monsters 349
Real Magnet Book, The 6295
Real Me, The 12174
Real Mother Goose, The 18300
Real Science Riddles 18339
Real Thief, The 16194
Really Rosie 15335
Really Weird Summer, A 11376
Realm of Measure, The 755
Realm of Numbers 756
Reaper Man 9428
Reason for the Pelican, The 3464
Reasons for Seasons, The 365
Rebecca Hatpin 10069
Rebecca of Sunnybrook Farm
17886
Rebecca's War 5885
Rebecka 722
Rebel, The 2727
Rebel in the Night 9364
Rebel Witch, The 11096
Rebellion at Christiana 865
Rebellion Town 16716
Rebels and Reformers 5308
Receivers, The 15911
Recollection Creek 6865
Recollections of Life in Ohio
from 1813 to 1840 8689
Reconstruction 10645
Reconstruction and National
Growth 9524
Record Breakers of the NFL
10919
Recycling 7563

Recyclopedia 15771
Red Balloon 10217
Red Bantam 5722
Red Baron, The 18312
Red Carpet 13328
Red Carpet for Lafayette, A 6158
Red Cloud 17345
Red Drum's Warning, The 10857
Red Eagle 6638
Red Flannel Hash and Shoo-Fly
Pie 13526
Red Fox 14427
Red Fox and His Canoe 1406
Red Hart Magic 12941
Red Hawk's Account of Custer's
Last Battle 6947
Red Horse and the Bluebird, The
14052
Red Indian Folk and Fairy Tales
11643
Red Jaguar, The 13945
Red Letter Days 15223
Red Light, Green Light 11308
Red Light Says Stop! 14393
Red Lion, The 18213
Red Man in Art, The 3729
Red Man, White Man, African Chief
10609
Red Mittens 1061
Red Moon and Black Mountain 3263
Red Mouse 17993
Red Pawns 17851
Red Planet 8021
Red Power on the Rio Grande 6094
Red Riding Hood 4745
Red Rock over the River 1280
Red Room Riddle, The 4117
Red Sails to Capri 17654
Red Sea Rescue 3160
Red Shadows 6730
Red Sky at Night 2064
Red Son Rising 657
Red Tag Comes Back 13646
Red Towers of Granada, The
16982
Redbird 11252
Redbirds Are Flying, The 12728
Redcoat in Boston 5886
Redline 7100 2767
Redwoods Are the Tallest Trees in
the World 96
Reflections on a Gift of Watermelon
Pickle ... 5154
Reggie and Nilma 16651
Reggie's No-Good Bird 2640
Reindeer Trail 7547
Reino del reves, El 17492

Relato de un niño indigena 13236
Religions 7829
Religions Around the World 18182
Religions, East and West 9763
Reluctant Dragon, The 7153
Remarkable Chameleon, The 8123
Remarkable Egg, The 8459
Remarkable Ride of Israel Bis-
   sell ..., The 15040
Remarkable Ride of the Abernethy
   Boys, The 9020
Remember Me When This You See
   12469
Remember the Alamo 17541
Remember the Days 12046
Remove Protective Coating a
   Little at a Time 5010
Renacaujo en la Escuela, Un
   13086
Renanco y los ultimos huemules
   12565
Renfroe's Christmas 2602
Renowned History of Little Red
   Riding Hood 8413
Repair of Uncle Toe 3393
Report from a Chinese Village
   12619
Report from Engine Co. 82
   15874
Report on Planet Three and Oth-
   er Speculations 3527
Reportaje sensacional, El 13233
Reportajes supersonicos 13773
Reporters at War 6034
Representing Super Doll 13451
Reproductive System, The 15695
Reptiles, The 3060
Reptiles and Amphibians 18575
Reptiles and Amphibians of Al-
   gonquin Provincial Park
   13144
Reptiles and Amphibians of
   Minnesota 2169
Reptiles and How They Reproduce
   13357
Reptiles and Their World 5809
Reptiles as Pets 17310
Reptiles Do the Strangest Things
   8625
Republic of Zaire, The 11439
Requiem for a Princess 691
Rescue of Charlie Kalu, The
   3633
Rescue of the Sun ..., The 12781
Rescuers, The 15487
Research Adventures for Young
   Scientists 1102

Research Ideas for Young Scientists
   1103
Resettling, The 10866
Resident Witch, The 13725
Respiratory System, The 15696
Restless Feet 5510
Restless Ghost, The 6604
Restless Robin, The 5990
Restless Spirit 7504
Retreat to Glory 10317
Retreat to the Bear Paw 13726
Return of Shettima, The 13124
Return of the Buffalo 15201
Return of the Gray Man, and
   Georgetown Ghosts, The 1856
Return of the Great Brain, The
   5977
Return of the King, The 16916
Return of the Twelves, The 3536
Return to Daytona 2768
Return to Gone-Away 5466
Return to Hiroshima 10803
Return to Racing 2769
Return to Rainbow Country 4579
Return to Ramos 2916
Return to South Town 7136
Return to the Level Land 4670
Revolt Along the Rio Grande 14820
Revolt of the Darumas, The 18148
Revolutionary China 15654
Rex 15475
Rey: aventuras de un condor neu-
   quino, El 12450
Rhodesia (Carpenter) 3030
Rhodesia (Fawcett) 5732
Rhodesia in Pictures 902
Rhymes and Verses 4689
Rhythms, Music, and Instruments
   to Make 7899
Rice Bowl Pet, The 11757
Rice Cakes and Paper Dragons
   14235
Rice, Spice and Bitter Oranges
   13527
Rich and Famous 3841
Rich Cat, Poor Cat 17371
Rich Man and the Singer, The
   11675
Richard Scarry Huckle's Book
   14992
Richard Scarry's ABC Word Book
   14993
Richard Scarry's Best Counting
   Book Ever 14994
Richard Scarry's Best Word Book
   Ever 14995
Richard Scarry's Nicky Goes to the

Doctor 14996
Richard Scarry's Storybook Dictionary 14997
Richleighs of Tantamount, The 17960
Rick Barry 6987
Rico's Cat 2305
Riddle-Master of Hed, The 11429
Riddle Me, Riddle Me, Ree 10450
Riddle of Seeds, The 7670
Riddle of Teeth 7671
Riddle of the Caid's Jewels, The 6415
Riddle of the Drum, The 5
Riddle of the Shy Stegosaurus, The 8922
Riddle of Time, The 1358
Riddle Pot, The 17880
Riddler 1038
Riddles of Mermaid House, The 4260
Ride a Northbound Horse 18276
Ride a Wild Horse 2942
Ride a Wild Pony see Sporting Proposition, A
Ride 'Em Cowgirl! 7693
Ride for Texas 11331
Ride on High, A 13257
Ride on the Wind 4460
Ride the Cold Wind 16512
Ride the Crooked Wind 5857
Ride the Pale Stallion 16670
Ride the White Tiger 3521
Ride with the Sun 4200
Riders of the Wind 7490
Riding Free 3831
Riding the Pony Express 2569
Riding to Canonbie 15872
Riff, Remember 7604
Rifka Bangs the Teakettle 2699
Rifka Grows Up 2700
Rifleman of the Ohio 387
Rifles and War Bonnets 13727
Rifles for Watie 9626
Right Angles 13627
Right on Dellums! 5963
Right On, Shane 15818
Right Thumb, Left Thumb 12320
Right to Be Let Alone, The 15958
Rikka and Rindji, Children of Bali 4494
Rikki-Tikki 11684
Rima and Zeppo 9212
Rimas Tontas 6489
Rimes de la Mere Oie 4684; see also Mother Goose Rhymes
Ring, The 17163

Ring Around the Moon 6160
Ring in the Jubilee 1853
Ring in the Prairie, The 15105
Ring o' Roses 2304
Ring-Out 18421
Ring the Judas Bell 6118
Ringling Brothers, The (Burt) 2719
Ringling Brothers, The (Cone) 3928
Ringling Brothers, The (Glendenning) 6898
Rio Grande, The 4312
Riot of Quiet, A 15650
Rip Van Winkle 8931
Rip Van Winkle and the Legend of Sleepy Hollow 8932
Ripley's Believe It or Not! 14401
Ripley's Believe It or Not! Book of the Military 14402
Riptide 5371
Rise and Fall of Adolf Hitler, The 15568
Rise and Fall of Toledo, Michigan ..., The 6755
Rise of the Robots 16484
Rita en la Cocina de Su Abuela 4343
Rita, the Weekend Rat 10662
River, The see Escape the River
River at Green Knowe, The 1974
River Bank, The 7154
River Book, The 1264
River Boy of Kashmir, The 1989
River of the Hot Waters 11090
River Song 12439
River Spirit and the Mountain Demons, The 12769
Rivers of Canada 11446
Road Down in the Sea, A 7137
Road Race of Champions 16056
Road-Race Rookie 6687
Road Race Round the World 9021
Road Racer 2770
Road Racing in America 5447
Road Racing, U.S.A. 9022
Road to Agra, The 16011
Road to Fort Sumter, The 7925
Road to Freedom, The 11216
Road to Miklagard, The 16986
Roadbuilders, The 9665
Roadmakers 16533
Roads 4971
Roadside Flowers of Texas 18062
Roam the Wild Country 5372
Roan Colt, The 13207
Roanoke 10663

Roar and More 10162
Roaring Road, The 13111
Robber! A Robber!, A 2103
Robber Ghost, The 429
Robbers, The 1219
Robert and Jane Catch a Thief 1645
Robert and the Magic String 15552
Robert Bennett 12727
Robert Cavalier de la Salle 9083
Robert E. 12588
Robert E. Lee 4481
Robert Fulton 14061
Robert Fulton and the Steamboat 8188
Robert Goddard (Moore) 12385
Robert Goddard (Verral) 17294
Robert Levy's Magic Book 10680
Robert Todd Lincoln 492
Roberta Flack (Jacobs) 9073
Roberta Flack (Morse) 12487
Roberto Clemente (Mercer) 12085
Roberto Clemente (Olsen) 13110
Roberto Clemente (Rudeen) 14747
Roberto Clemente and the World Series Upset 11901
Robins Fly North, Robins Fly South 9543
Robins on the Window Sill 5241
Robinsheugh see Elizabeth, Elizabeth
Robinson Crusoe 4798
Rock and the Willow, The 10485
Rock-Hound's Book, The 15756
Rock Music 17196
Rock River Ranger 18441
Rock Taylor 6648
Rocket in My Pocket, A 18162
Rocket Pioneer 4040
Rocket Ship Galileo 8022
Rocking-Chair Ghost, The 9131
Rocks and Gems 7991
Rocks and How We Use Them 13690
Rocks and Minerals of Michigan 12150
Rocks and Minerals of Ontario 8136
Rocks and Rills 16366
Rocks and Their Stories 5805
Rocks, Rivers 15094
Rocky 10770
Rocky Point Campers 14375
Rod and Reel Trouble 9517
Rod Carew 10771

Rodeo (Rounds) 14704
Rodeo! (Thorne) 16848
Rodeo Roundup 6222
Rodeo School 14069
Rodrigo and Rosalita 2547
Roger Staubach 16485
Roger Williams 9084
Rogers' Rangers and the French and Indian War 15871
Rogue Elephant 3261
Rokubei and the Thousand Rice Bowls 17100
Roland the Minstrel Pig 16195
Roll of Thunder, Hear My Cry 16693
Roller Skates 14973
Roller Skating 8100
Rolling Rice Ball, The 18403
Roman Numerals 97
Roman Republic, The 757
Romanian Cook Book, The 16139
Romans, The 5111
Romansgrove 323
Rome and the Barbarians 4363
Rome Under the Emperors 4906
Rompetacones y 100 cuentos mas 14489
Ron Santo 2323
Ronne Expedition to Antarctica, The 14594
Ronnie 14619
Ronnie and Rosie 536
Ronnie and the Chief's Son 3695
Ronnie's Wish 2360
Roofs of Gold 3880
Roofs over America 5047
Rooftop Mystery, The 10750
Rooftops and Alleys 9537
Rookie of the Year 17052
Room, The 8478
Room for Me and a Mountain Lion 10281
Room Made of Windows, A 2858
Room 10 11228
Room to Grow 5513
Rooms for Rent 11556
Roosevelt Grady 15590
Rooster Brother 8414
Rooster Crows, The 13563
Rooster Who Set Out to See the World, The 2930
Rooster Who Understood Japanese, The 17101
Roots Are Good Finders 2143
Roots of Time 9184
Rope in the Jungle, The 9198
Roque, el Trapero 17187

Rory Story, The 1655
Rosa 13787
Rosa Bonheur 13925
Rosa de Navidad 6552
Rosa Parks 7310
Rosa-Too-Little 5771
Rosachok 18487
Rosanna the Goat 3722
Rosaria 16773
Rose and the Ring, The 16772
Rose Bowl, The 11902
Rose Bowl All-American 8985
Rose-Colored Glasses 14062
Rose Greenhow 5631
Rose Kennedy (Eldred) 5329
Rose Kennedy (Hawkes) 7892
Rose on My Cake, The 10163
Rosemary Casals 9074
Roses Are Red 13981
Rosh Hashana and Yom Kipper
  7303
Rosie and Michael 17321
Rosie's Walk 8838
Rossini 7719
Rotten Kidphabets 16634
Rotten Ralph 6543
Rough Ice 11071
Rough Road to Glory 6688
Round About and Long Ago 3894
Round About Eight 13260
Round About the City 3359
Round and Round and Square
  15454
Round of Carols, A 12862
Round Sultan and the Straight
  Answer 17435
Round Things Everywhere 14236
Roundabout Road 1351
Roundabout Turn 3279
Rover, Jr.'s Baseball Career
  16768
Row of Tigers, A 4140
Rowboat War on the Great Lakes,
  1812-1814, The 16553
Rowing 2034
Roy Campanella 15108
Roy Campanella Story, The 15434
Royal African, A 12301
Royal Book of Ballet, The 7103
Royal Giraffe 7101
Royal Harry 11960
Royal Persia 227
Rozy Dozy 14803
Rrra-ah 9622
Rubber Bands, Baseballs, and
  Doughnuts 6404
Ruby's Revenge 13481

Rudi and the Distelfink 12349
Ruffles and Drums 3203
Rufus M. 5552
Rum, Slaves and Molasses 236
Rumpelstiltskin 7401
Rumptydoolers, The 17868
Run Away, Habeeb 4293
Run Away Home 15625
Run, Jump, Bump Book, The 2317
Run, Little Monkeys! Run, Run,
  Run 9725
Run of the Sea Witch 6206
Run, Reddy, Run 1641
Run, Westy, Run 220
Run, Zebra, Run 3317
Runaway, The 13322
Runaway Boy 3539
Runaway Bunny, The 2396
Runaway Cattle, The 4617
Runaway Flying Horse, The 1928
Runaway Hat, The 8460
Runaway Jonah ... 17410
Runaway Ralph 3570
Runaway Slave 11358
Runaway Stallion 12431
Runaway Summer, The 1220
Runaways, The 9804
Runaway's Diary, The 7784
Runner, The 560
Runner-Up 12714
Running Backs, The 12488
Running Elk 8368
Running Fox 15413
Running Harder 8532
Running, Jumping, Throwing, Slid-
  ing, Racing, Climbing Book,
  The 17648
Running Owl the Hunter 1407
Running Scared 12493
Running Wild 7377
Running with Rachel 724
Runt of Rodgers School, The 9627
Rupert Hatton's Story 11029
Rupert Piper and the Boy Who
  Could Knit 13330
Rushton Inheritance, The 11317
Russian Ballet and Three of Its
  Masterpieces, The 14871
Russian Ballet School, The 7780
Russian Blue 7378
Russian Composers 13832
Russian Fairy Tales (Afanasyev)
  151
Russian Fairy Tales (Budberg)
  2508
Russians in America 5576
Rutgers and the Watersnouts 4477

Ruth 13564
Ruth Crane 12440
Rutherford T. Finds 21B 14394
Rwanda 3047

- S -

Saber-Toothed Tiger and Other
    Ice Age Mammals 3802
Sabes Que? 9171; see also Do
    You Know What?
Sabrina 287
Sacajawea (Blassingame) 1734
Sacajawea (Seibert) 15247
Sacajawea (Seymour) 15398
Sacajawea (Voight) 17346
Sacajawea of the Shoshones 5430
Sacred Drum, The 1792
Sacrifice, The 2418
Sad Day, Glad Day 16841
Sad-Faced Boy 1923
Sad Song of the Coyote 5380
Sad Story of the Little Bluebird
    and the Hungry Cat, The
    13900
Sadako and the Thousand Paper
    Cranes 3731
Saddle the Storm 7423
Saddle Up 1024
Saddles & Sabers 493
Sade and Her Friends 211
Safari Adventure 13933
Safe Motorboating for Kids 12670
Safety on Wheels 2047
Safiri the Singer 7975
Sage Smoke 7976
Sahara Trail 6416
Sail, Calypso! 9334
Sailing (Gibbs) 6785
Sailing (Mohn) 12312
Sailing (Somerville) 16007
Sailing Small Boats 17701
Sailing to Cythera ... 17967
Sailor Dog, The 2397
Sailor's Choice 2968
Saint Agnes 1483
Saint Francis and the Animals
    13788
Saint George and the Dragon
    10252
Sainte Marie Among the Hurons
    7893
Salah of Sierra Leone 3616

Salami and Musa 5197
Salima Lives in Kashmir 6125
Sallinka and the Golden Bird 15102
Sally Go Round the Sun 6161
Salt (Goldin) 6998
Salt (Zemach) 18518
Salt and Pepper 3111
Salt Boy 13535
Salute 471
Salvage Diver 1028
Sam (Corcoran) 4141
Sam (Scott) 15187
Sam Adams 14340
Sam and Emma 12720
Sam and Me 16666
Sam, Bangs and Moonshine 12749
Sam Bottleby 2943
Sam Henderson, Texas Ranger
    11333
Sam Houston (Johnson) 9303
Sam Houston (Latham) 10318
Sam McLaughlin 13585
Sam Savitt's True Horse Stories
    14951
Sam the Minuteman 1408
Sam Who Never Forgets 14308
Sama 7491
Samankwe and the Highway Robbers
    5320
Samankwe in the Strange Forest
    5321
Samori Toure 9789
Sam's First Fish 15586
Samson 11253
Samuel Adjai Crowther 12255
Samuel Clemens 4529
Samurai of Gold Hill 17102
San Domingo 8075
San Francisco 6389
San Francisco Boy 10586
San Jacinto 3093
Sancho the Homesick Steer 14775
Sand 3135
Sand Bird, The 978
Sand in Her Shoes 10407
Sand in the Bag ... 9104
Sand Ponies, The 12578
Sand, the Sea, and Me, The 4239
Sand Tiger Shark 3077
Sandile, the Fall of the Xhosa Na-
    tion 12025
Sandpipers 8812
Sandwich, The 17464
Sandy MacDonald's Man 6108
Sandy Shoes Mystery, The 12382
Sangamon Country, The 1723
Santa Fe Trail, The 63

Santa Makes a Change 3259
Santa Mouse 2412
Santa's Crash-Bang Christmas 10108
Santiago (Belpre) 1373
Santiago (Clark) 3494
Santiago's Silver Mine 3652
Sara and the Apartment Building 15794
Sara and the Door 9205
Sara and the Winter Gift 11797
Sara Somebody 15836
Sarah and After 1052
Sarah and Katie 17791
Sarah and the Boy 9805
Sarah Janes 614
Sarah's Unicorn 4214
Sarang 2911
Saranga the Pygmy 6668
Sara's Granny and the Groodle 6827
Sargasso Sea, The 9038
Sasha, My Friend 4142
Sasquatch 8770
Satanic Mill, The 13906
Satchel Paige 14738
Satchkin Patchkin 12443
Satellites 2938
Satellites in Outer Space 758
Sati the Rastifarian 17797
Saturday, the Twelfth of October 11972
Saturdays, The 5467
Saturday's Child 15233
Saturn and Beyond 759
Saucepan Journey, The 17148
Savage Gold 6439
Savage Island 16098
Savage Sam 6866
Savage Son 666
Savage Survivor 4097
Save Alice! 18328
Save Sirrushany! 929
Save the Earth! 12175
Save the Mustangs! 17683
Saving Electricity 5504
Saving Lake Superior 71
Saving of P.S., The 2155
Say Hello, Vanessa 15476
Saynday's People 11700
Scaly Wings 8853
Scandinavian Legends and Folk-tales 9349
Scandinavian Stories 16074
Scapegoat, The 6450
Scarab for Luck 11992
Scarabee, the Witch's Cat 3401

Scarecrow Clock, The 12072
Scaredy Cat 10040
Scarlet Badge, The 7942
Scarlet Monster Lives Here 15477
Scat! 4957
Scat Cat Finds a Friend 3458
Scavengers 5209
Scenes from South African Life 13347
Scent Talk Among the Animals 18122
Scholastic "Scratch and Sniff" Book, A 17655
School, The 2683
School Bell in the Valley 2969
School Bell Rings, The 15649
School Daze 9641
School for Julio 14724
School for Sillies 18025
School Newspaper 11180
School Segregation Cases, The 16293
Schooldays of Shango Solomon, The 16770
Schoolhouse in the Woods 3172
Schooling for Young Riders 18451
Science at the Ball Game 834
Science at Work: Projects in Oceanography 15757
Science at Work: Projects in Space Science 15758
Science Experiments for the Space Age 14631
Science Experiments with Water 14632
Science Experiments You Can Eat 3709
Science Fiction Trilogy One 3410
Science Fun for You in a Minute or Two 15095
Science Fun with a Flashlight 15096
Science Games 17806
Science-Hobby Book of Fishing 15576
Science in a Vacant Lot 15759
Science in Your Own Backyard 4065
Science of Chemistry, The 6289
Science of Ourselves, The 11206
Science on the Shores and Banks 4066
Science Projects That Make Sense 16365
Science Puzzlers 6588
Science Puzzles 17807
Science Ship 2232

Science Toys 17808
Science Tricks 17809
Scoring the Shots 6809
Scots and Scotch-Irish in America, The 9281
Scots Helped Build America, The 8045
Scott Joplin and the Ragtime Years 5593
Scottish Folk-Tales and Legends 18064
Scram, Kid! 11359
Screeching Door 17411
Screwball 635
Scroobius Pip, The 10468
Scrub Dog of Alaska 12432
Se Quien Soy/I Know Who I Am 4813
Sea and Cedar 11260
Sea and Earth 16244
Sea Around Us, The 3121
Sea Beach Express 13269
Sea Beggar's Son, The 12350
Sea Broke Through, The 5995
Sea Cart, The 9995
Sea Challenge 5450
Sea Egg, The 1975
Sea Glass 18397
Sea Hunters, The 1762
Sea Magic and Other Stories of Enchantment 7793
Sea Monkey, The 9582
Sea Monsters of Long Ago 15304
Sea of Gold ..., The 17103
Sea of Troubles, A 11276
Sea Otter (Annixter) 561
Sea Otter (May) 11903
Sea Otters and Seaweed 10354
Sea Pair, The 1281
Sea Pup 1650
Sea Robbers, The 10050
Sea Serpent of Horse, The 17021
Sea Shells of the World 17
Sea So Big, Ship So Small 1435
Sea Star (Henry) 8076
Sea Star (McClung) 11254
Sea Stranger, The 4320
Sea-Thing Child, The 8290
Seabird 8494
Seabury Cookbook for Boys and Girls 12389
Seahorse 12463
Seal and the Slick, The 6269
Seamanship 16873
Seamstress of Salzburg, The 10989
Search, The 16321

Search for a Lost City 5353
Search for Big Foot, The 2801
Search for Charlie, The 4930
Search for Delicious, The 846
Search for King Arthur, The 8144
Search for Life, The 835
Search for Planet X, The 15769
Search for the Crescent Moon 3606
Search of Mary Katherine Mulloy, The 1867
Sea's Harvest, The 2364
Seashore 10211
Seashore Story 18366
Season for Singing, The 10253
Season In-Between, A 7258
Season of Discovery 7006
Season of Ponies, A 15970
Season of Silence, The 15626
Season Songs 8734
Seasons 2684
Seasons of the Eskimo 2447
Seasons of Time, The 1098
Seatmates 14197
Sebastian & the Mushroom 10023
Second-Hand Family 13323
Second Mrs. Giaconda, The 9993
Second Sight for Tommy 18255
Second Springtime, A 4070
Second Stone, The 2408
Second Witch, The 15327
Second Year Nurse 10200
Secret at the Old Coach Inn, The 5600
Secret Birthday Message, The 2931
Secret Box, The 3803
Secret Box Mystery, The 12853
Secret Castle 3889
Secret Clocks, The 15760
Secret Codes and Ciphers 9977
Secret Country of C. S. Lewis, The 672
Secret Cowboy, The 14638
Secret Dog of Little Luis, The 11612
Secret Elephants, The 11704
Secret Emily 15180
Secret Friends, The 3312
Secret Garden, The 2671
Secret Hiding Place, The 1470
Secret in Miranda's Closet, The 7321
Secret in the Congo 15713
Secret Island 12409
Secret Language, The 12897
Secret Life of T. K. Dearing, The

14470
Secret Lives   419
Secret Lover of Elmtree, The
   14677
Secret Museum, The   7322
Secret Name, The   17980
Secret Neighbors   146
Secret of Opokuwa, The   4665
Secret of Stonehouse Farm, The
   18466
Secret of Telfair Inn, The   1837
Secret of the Andes   3495
Secret of the Disappearing Sultan,
   The   17530
Secret of the Emerald Star   17835
Secret of the Hawk   17852
Secret of the Old Brownstone,
   The   9945
Secret of the Rosewood Box
   13189
Secret of the Sabbath Fish, The
   679
Secret of the Sachem's Tree, The
   12351
Secret of the Samurai Sword
   17836
Secret of the Seven Crows, The
   ?6117
Secret of the Stone Face   17837
Secret of the Stone Frog, The
   15952
Secret of the Strawbridge Place,
   The   9030
Secret of the Tiger's Eye   17838
Secret of Van Rink's Cellar,
   The   10479
Secret of Willow Castle, The
   3994
Secret Places   655
Secret River, The   14153
Secret Seller, The   10804
Secret Soldier, The   11360
Secret Story of Pueblo Bonito,
   The   5397
Secret Summer of L.E.B., The
   17459
Secret Three, The   12621
Secret Under the Sea   4897
Secret World of the Baby, The
   4622
Secret Writing Tricks   10208
Secrets in Stones   18347
Secrets of a Cypress Swamp
   13802
Secrets of Base Running and In-
   field Play   4314
Secrets of Hidden Creek, The

16118
Secrets of Shaolin Temple Boxing
   15930
Secrets of the Pirate Inn, The
   16119
Security Is a Thumb and a Blanket
   15131
Sedna   11288
See Along the Shore   15305
See and Say   6230
See for Yourself   10282
See Inside a Castle   17154
See My Lovely Poison Ivy   12402
See No Evil, Hear No Evil, Smell
   No Evil   7929
See Through the Forest   15306
See Through the Sea   15307
Seed, The   2855
Seed Is Blown, The   18298
Seed the Squirrel Dropped, The
   13583
Seeds and More Seeds   15308
Seeds by Wind and Water   9374
Seeds, Embryos, and Sex   4178
Seeds of Time   15405
Seeing Eye, The   15031
Seeing Fingers   4659
Seeing Is Believing   15610
Seeing Itasca   13934
Seeing Stars   12407
Seeing Stick, The   18422
Seeing Through the Dark   17704
Seeing What Plants Do   14088
Seen Any Cats?   12299
Seesaws to Cosmic Rays   18091
Selchie's Seed, The   13155
Selected Writings of Joaquin Miller
   14636
Self-Made Snowman, The   10024
Self-Portrait: Erik Blegvad   1768
Self Portrait in Art, The   10613
Selfish Giant, The   17898
Seminole Indians, The   1763
Seminole Wars, The   2506
Seminoles   5545
Senator from Maine, The   6035
Send Wendell   7210
Sending Messages   16312
Senegal   3031
Senegal in Pictures   7068
Señora Jones Es Mi Amiga, La   4408
Sense of Discovery   14432
Senses, The   15208
Sensible Kate   6663
Separate Peace, A   9948
Septimus and the Danedyke Mystery
   3248

Sequoya 14063
Sequoyah (Campbell) 2870
Sequoyah (Coblentz) 3715
Sequoyah (Marriott) 11701
Sequoyah (Patterson) 13389
Serendipity Tales 8324
Serengeti Cats 15038
Sergeant Finney's Family 5687
Serie de Rimas Ilustradas 5539
Serilda's Star 3996
Serpent and the Sun, The 14726
Serpent Prince, The 10112
Serving in the Peace Corps 10201
Sesame Street Book of Letters,
    The 3369
Sesame Street Book of Numbers,
    The 3370
Sesame Street Book of Shapes,
    The 3371
Sesame Street 1, 2, 3 Storybook,
    The 3372
Seth Eastman's Mississippi 11295
Sets 120
Sets and Numbers for the Very
    Young 121
Sets, What Are They? 11145
Settlers and Strangers 930
Seven African Tales 6317
Seven at One Blow 18026
Seven Black American Scientists
    7912
Seven-Day Magic 5201
Seven Diving Ducks 6376
Seven for the Sea 4429
Seven Founders of American
    Literature 7683
Seven Grandmothers 12272
700 Science Experiments for
    Everyone 17129
Seven in a Bed 16019
Seven Little Monsters 15336
Seven Little Rabbits 1290
Seven Magic Orders 12541
Seven Plays and How to Produce
    Them 15922
Seven Queens of England 16983
Seven Ravens, The 7402
Seven Seas, The 3596
Seven Short Stories 13218
Seven Simeons 695
Seven Tales 442
Seven True Horse Stories 4574
Seven Voyages of Sinbad the
    Sailor, The 14186
Seven Wishes of Joanna Peabody,
    The 7211
Seven Women 12719

Seven-Year-Old Wonder-Book
    18334
17 Gerbils of Class 4A, The 8553
Seventeenth-Street Gang, The
    12766
Seventh Cousin, The 10363
Seventh Mandarin, The 18423
Several Tricks of Edgar Dolphin
    1409
Sex: Telling It Straight 9263
Seymour, a Gibbon 1945
Seymour the Prince 291
Seymourina 10367
Shad of the Circle "C" Ranch 7513
Shades, The 2274
Shades of Difference 1154
Shadi 5424
Shadow Army, The 14827
Shadow Book, The 4749
Shadow Cage ..., The 13428
Shadow Geometry 17017
Shadow in the Pines 11984
Shadow of a Bull 18177
Shadow of the Crooked Tree, The
    5828
Shadow of the Gloom World, The
    5330
Shadow of the Hawk (Myron)
    12624
Shadow of the Hawk ..., The
    (Reeves) 14208
Shadow of the Lighthouse 4448
Shadow on the Pueblo 4332
Shadow on the Sun, The 7794
Shadow on the Water 1096
Shadow Puppets in Color 3720
Shadow Science 6593
Shadows 7605
Shadrach 4680
Shag, Last of the Plains Buffalo
    11255
Shaka, King of the Zulu 18269
Shaka, King of the Zulus 3750
Shaka Zulu 12549
Shakes, Quakes, and Shifts 2144
Shakespeare's England 8615
Shakespeare's Theatre 8321
Shalakos Are Coming, The 7028
Shall We Meet the Lion 6318
Shalom, Golda 12464
Shaman's Last Raid, The 931
Shamrocks, Harps and Shillelaghs
    1140
Shane 15004
Shane Gould 9075
Shan's Lucky Knife 12113
Shantyman of Cache Lake 6254

Shape of Me and Other Stuff, The 15386
Shape of Three, The 12904
Shape of Water, The 6999
Shape Shifters 18425
Shape Up, Burke 15505
Shapers of Africa 13769
Shapes (Bendick) 1436
Shapes (Pienkowski) 13660
Shapes (Reiss) 14227
Shapes and People 7382
Shapes and Stories 7383
Shapes and Things 8304
Shapes, Sides, Curves, and Corners 13759
Shaping of England, The 760
Shaping Room, The 2076
Shark in the Window, The 10440
Shark Lady 11361
Sharks 11362
Sharo, The 17970
Sharpur the Carpet Snake 13489
Shattered Skull, The 13512
Shattered Stone, The 12793
Shawl of Waiting, The 10268
Shawn Goes to School 2174
Shawnee Lance 347
Shawn's Red Bike 2175
Shaw's Fortune 17043
She and the Dubious Three 4261
She Come Bringing Me That Little Baby Girl 7311
She, the Adventuress 4262
She Wanted to Read 3115
She Was Nice to Mice 15521
Sheep Book, The 7064
Sheep of the Lal Bagh, The 11685
She'll Be Comin' Round the Mountain 14028
Shells Are Where You Find Them 3597
Shelter from the Wind 1193
Shen of the Sea 3394
Shepherd, The 176
Shepherdess of France 11774
Shepherd's Nosegay, The 5868
Sheridan 14193
Sheriff Stonehead and the Teenage Termites 1263
Sherman 12333
Sherwood Ring, The 13825
Sherwood Walks Home 6067
Shetland Ponies 8124
Shimmy Shimmy Coke-Ca-Pop! 10257
Shinty Boys, The 11505
Ship in a Storm on the Way to

Tarshish, A 5667
Ship That Flew, The 10704
Shipbuilders, The 7574
Ships 9938
Ships and Men of the Great Lakes 2044
Ships at Work 5392
Ships of the Great Lakes 2525
Shipwreck 4351
Shipwrecks of the Lakes 2015
Shirley Chisholm 2442
Shirleybird 11653
Shiver, Gobble and Snore 18118
Shoe Full of Shamrock 15627
Shoemaker and the Elves, The 7403
Shoemakers, The 5947
Shoes for Matt 5646
Shoeshine Boys 13270
Shoeshine Girl 2570
Shoestrings 7086
Shoo-Fly Girl 10587
Shooting Stars 18551
Shortstop from Tokyo 3427
Shot-Put Challenge 11072
Shoto-Kan Karate 17278
Show Me! 6001
Show Ring Rogue 7224
Show Time for Young Scientists 1104
Showboat in the Backcourt 6689
Showboat Summer 5099
Showdown at Daytona 8162
Shrewbettina's Birthday 7044
Shrieks at Midnight 2217
Shrimps 7888
Shrimp's Soccer Goal 11073
Shrinking of Treehorn, The 8005
Shrinking Outdoors, The 9199
Shumway 12120
Shutterbug 15620
Shy Girl 6811
Shy Little Girl, The 10041
Shy One, The 12654
Shy Stegosaurus of Cricket Creek, The 10229
Shy Stegosaurus of Indian Springs, The 10230
Si Yo Hiciese un Parque 17184
Sia Lives on Kilimanjaro 10840
Siamang Gibbons, The 15039
Siblings, The see Find Debbie!
Sicilian Mystery 3161
Sick Day, The 11441
Sideline Pass 1684
Sidewalk Indian 5381
Sidewalk Racer ..., The 12470

Sidewalk Story 11817
Sidney 9213
Siege of Silent Henry, The 7606
Siege of Trapp's Mill, The 5674
Siege! The Story of St. Augustine in 1702 7943
Siempre paginas para imaginar 2815
Sierra Club Summer Book, The 366
Sierra Leone 3032
Sigemi 9854
Sigh of Relief, A 7238
Sign at Six Corners, The 3997
Sign of the Chrysanthemum, The 13371
Sign of the Ivory Horn, The 14634
Signs and Symbols Around the World 8029
Sigurd F. Olson's Wilderness Days 13116
Sikkim: The Hidden Kingdom 9479
Silas and Con 16305
Silbo del aire--Antologia lirica infantil, Vol. I, El 12004
Silbo del aire--Antologia lirica infantil, Vol. II, El 12005
Silence over Dunkerque 17053
Silencio en el bosque 12591
Silent Concert, The 10541
Silent Message, The 8712
Silent Night 13398
Silent Storm, The 2410
Silk and Satin Lane 18227
Silk Spinners, The 10291
Silkworm Is Born, A 16230
Silly Story, A 11938
Silver Arrow and Other Indian Romances of the Dune Country, The 14180
Silver Branch, The 16528
Silver Chair, The 10693
Silver Christmas Tree, The 8839
Silver Coach, The 92
Silver Crest, The 3439
Silver Crown, The 12993
Silver Curlew, The 5680
Silver for General Washington 11993
Silver from the Sea 16937
Silver Hills, The 12370
Silver Mace, The 13565
Silver Nutmeg, The 2421
Silver on the Tree 4088
Silver Pencil, The 4461

Silver Pony, The 17515
Silver Sword, The 15351
Silver Whistle, The 18027
Silver Wolf 4931
Silver Woven in My Hair 12579
Silverhorn 3965
Silversmiths, The 5948
Silvia y Miguel en verano 1456
Simba of the White Mane 708
Simon and the Game of Chance 2603
Simon Boom Gives a Wedding 16449
Simon Kenton 17938
Simon's Song 5406
Simple Facts of Simple Machines, The 9111
Simple Gifts 18424
Simple Machines and How We Use Them 13691
Simple Pictures Are Best 17969
Simple Printing Methods 4316
Simple Printmaking 17708
Simple Shelters 8795
Sinbad the Sailor 12867
Sinbad the Seaman and the Ebony Horse 17787
Sing a Song of Seasons 2218
Sing a Song of Sixpence 2813
Sing, Children, Sing 12216
Sing Down the Moon 13015
Sing for Christmas 17770
Sing Hey for Christmas Day 8601
Sing Mother Goose 17771
Sing-Song 14668
Sing Song Scuppernong 7715
Sing to the Dawn 8263
Sing Together Children 520
Singers of the Blues 16514
Singing Chameleon, The 5361
Singing Grass, The 10823
Singing Hill, The 4681
Singing Leaf, The 14725
Singing Minister of Nigeria, The 4809
Singing Sioux Cowboy 3496
Singing Strings 9764
Singing Tales of Africa 14454
Singing Tree, The 15342
Singing Turtle ..., The 16798
Singing Way, The 17663
Singing Wilderness, The 13117
Single Light, A 18178
Single Speckled Egg, A 10664
Single Standard, A 7771
Single to Center 2990
Single Trail, A 14605
Sink It, Rusty 3428

Sinking of the Bismarck, The 15569

Sioux Are Coming, The 13118

Sioux Buffalo Hunters 14782

Sioux Indians, The 1764

Sioux Today, The 10269

Sir Gawain and the Green Knight 8157

Sir Kevin of Devon 8461

Sir Ribbeck of Ribbeck of Havelland 6096

Sir Toby Jingle's Beastly Journey 17016

Sirena y el capitan, La 17493

Sirga 7492

Siri the Conquistador 16360

Sister 7312

Sister of the Bride 3571

Sisters Impossible, The 10237

Siti's Summer 9473

Sitting Bull (Anderson) 494

Sitting Bull (Garst) 6639

Sitting Bull (O'Connor) 13004

Sitting Bull (Stevenson) 16278

Sitting Bull, Chief of the Sioux 11904

Six and Silver 13641

Six Black Masters of American Art 1257

Six Chinese Brothers 3326

Six Days from Sunday 1642

Six Days to Saturday 12780

Six Foolish Fishermen 5348

666 Jellybeans! All That? 17705

Six Impossible Things Before Breakfast 5668

Six Little Ducks 3970

Six-Million-Dollar Cucumber, The 3449

Six Seconds to Glory 8163

Six Silver Spoons 11125

Sixes and Sevens 18393

Sixth Sense 9765

Sixty and Three on the Flying C 6219

Sixty Million Years of Horses 4507

Size, Distance, Weight 14804

Sizes 13661

Sizes and Shapes in Nature--What They Mean 13358

Skateboard Book, The 4566

Skateboard Mania 14073

Skateboarding 14221

Skateboards 2594

Skates and Skating 4792

Skating 2035

Skating for Beginners 15188

Skating Rink, The 10486

Skeezer 18379

Skeletal System, The 15697

Skeleton Book, The 10952

Skeleton Inside You, The 1013

Ski Run 12715

Ski Touring 13192

Skid 7914

Skier's Handbook, The 3144

Skies of Crete, The 6119

Skiing 2036

Skiing for Beginners 6696

Skin, The 15698

Skin Divers in Action 1505

Skin-Diving Adventures 6058

Skin Spinners, The 190

Skinny 2604

Skip to My Lou 14029

Skippack School 4640

Skunk and Possum 16942

Skunk Baby 6338

Skunk for a Day 2912

Skunny Wundy 13306

Sky Dog 17061

Sky-Eater and Other South Sea Tales, The 8447

Sky Full of Dragons, A 18311

Sky-God Stories, The 6

Sky Hooks 4041

Sky Is Free, The 3519

Sky Man on the Totem Pole 7767

Sky Rocket 15264

Sky Was Blue, The 18614

Skylab (Coombs) 4042

Skylab (Cromie) 4305

Skyscraper Goes Up, A 7723

Slab, Coil and Pinch 6821

Slake's Limbo 8508

Slapdash Alterations 1079

Slapdash Cooking 1081

Slave Dancer, The 6186

Slave Raid That Failed ..., The 7122

Slave Who Bought His Own Freedom, The 9699

Slavery in America 10926

Slavery in the United States 8901

Slavery One 12047

Slavery Past and Present 13706

Slavery to Civil War, 1812-1865 9525

Slave's Tale, A 7849

Sleep 9512

Sleep and Dreams 15699

Sleep Is for Everyone 15602

Sleep Out 3078

Sleepers, The 4405
Sleeping Beauty, The (Chappell)
    3272
Sleeping Beauty, The (Hutton)
    8864
Sleepless Day, A 7639
Sleepy Book, The 18615
Slim Goodbody 2701
Slim Green 7782
Slip! Slop! Gobble! 7716
Sliver of Liver ..., A 10975
Sloan and Philamina or How to
    Make Friends with Your
    Lunch 16249
Slovenly Peter 8378
Slugger Sal's Slump 8361
Slumps, Grunts, and Snicker-
    doodles 13528
Sly Old Cat, The 13842
Small Bear Solves a Mystery
    8462
Small-Boy Chuku 17718
Small Child's Bible, A 4934
Small Clown 5728
Small Deer's Magic Tricks 1844
Small Hands, Big Hands 17666
Small Lot, A 9623
Small Mammals Are Where You
    Find Them 16728
Small One 6703
Small Pig 11005
Small Plays for You and a Friend
    292
Small Poems 18279
Small Rabbit 12190
Small Rain 9359
Small Sheep in a Pear Tree, A
    10985
Small Wolf 1410
Small Wonders 5669
Small Worlds 14788
Smallest Boy in the Class, The
    1338
Smart Kid Like You, A 13595
Smart Shopping and Consumerism
    14945
Smartest Bear and His Brother
    Oliver 858
Smartest Man in Ireland, The
    8784
Smashup 1039
Smile for Auntie 13365
Smiley Sherman, Substitute
    12716
Smiling Hill Farm 11798
Smith 6605
Smith of Wootton Major 16917

Smoke (Corbin) 4127
Smoke (Olsen) 13099
Smoke from Cromwell's Time and
    Other Stories 191
Smoke Hole, The 12775
Smoke over Golan 13028
Smokey Bear's Camping Book 15425
Smoking and You 11522
Smoky-House 7098
Smoky, the Cowhorse 9124
Smugglers of Buenaventura, The
    17208
Smuggler's Road 5599
Snail and Caterpillar 13665
Snail in the Woods 14831
Snail, Where Are You? 17137
Snails 18566
Snail's a Failure Socially ..., A
    16150
Snails of Land and Sea 15721
Snail's Pace, A 8125
Snake Among the Sunflowers 10867
Snake Dance of the Hopi Indians,
    The 6122
Snake Fights, Rabbit Fights and
    More 15073
Snake Horn, The 7455
Snake-Lover's Diary, A 2199
Snake Secrets 14555
Snake That Couldn't Slither, The
    2068
Snake That Sneezed!, The 10753
Snake That Went to School, The
    12403
Snakes (Simon) 15722
Snakes (Young) 18440
Snakes (Zim) 18552
Snakes of Ontario, The 11031
Sneaker Hill see Danger at Sneak-
    er Hill
Sneakers 15532
Sneaky Machine, The 14750
Snipp, Snapp, Snurr and the Red
    Shoes 10845
Snopp on the Sidewalk ..., The
    13889
Snorkel 6053
Snorri and the Strangers 1411
Snow (Bell) 1355
Snow (Eastman) 5226
Snow (McKie) 11426
Snow and the Sun, The 6231
Snow Is Falling 2145
Snow Monkey at Home, The 14145
Snow Parlor and Other Bedtime
    Stories, The 3696
Snow Party, The 4746

Snow Queen, The   443
Snow Shoe Trek   2512
Snow Storm Before Christmas
   13258
Snow Treasure   11510
Snow-White and the Seven Dwarfs
   7404
Snowbound   11969
Snowbound in Hidden Valley
   18084
Snowbound with Betsy   7957
Snowed Up   6422
Snowfoot   4841
Snowmobiles   12445
Snowshoe Country   9151
Snowshoe Trek to Otter River
   2513
Snowy Day, The   9607
Snuff   1715
Snuggle Bunny, The   9215
So Dear to My Heart   12927
So Far from Home   7066
So Much to Live For   6787
So They Say   13045
So What About History?   12442
So What If It's Raining?   18467
So You Shouldn't Waste a Rhinoceros
   18578
Soap-Box Derby   17672
Soap Box Racing   14070
Soaring   7575
Soccer   9848
Soccer for the American Boy
   15941
Social Welfare   12612
Socks   3572
Sod House, The   3697
Sod-House Winter   9429
Sod Walls   17735
Softball Rules in Pictures   11279
Soil (Cromer)   4303
Soil (Russell)   14789
Soil That Feeds Us   7977
Sojourner Truth (Ortiz)   13187
Sojourner Truth (Peterson)
   13575
Sokar and the Crocodile   8665
Sol, la Luna y las Estrellas, El
   11512
Solar Energy   2146
Solar System, The   761
Soldier and Me   10860
Soldier and Tsar in the Forest
   152
Soldier Doctor   9430
Soldier of Africa   8053
Soldier of Israel   16664

Solecito Andres, El   10903
Solid Gold Kid, The   11973
Solids, Liquids and Gases   1437
Solitaire Games   1385
Solomon Grundy, Born on Oneday
   17706
Solomon Juneau, Voyageur   10418
Solve It!   5985
Some Common and Uncommon Birds
   of Ontario and Quebec   7684
Some Common Crutches   18296
Some Crops We Use   246
Some Folk Tales of Sierra Leone
   3541
Some Gold, a Little Ivory   7814
Some Haystacks Don't Even Have
   Any Needle   5155
Some Merry Adventures of Robin
   Hood   14016; see also Merry
   Adventures of Robin Hood, The
Some of the Days of Everett Ander-
   son   3630
Some Popular Ananse Stories   4486
Some Short Fireside Stories   13019
Some Swell Pup   15338
Some Things Weird and Wicked
   9459
Somebody Else's Child   15663
Somebody Go and Bang a Drum
   3173
Somebody Stole Second   6090
Somebody Will Miss Me   4256
Somebody's Angel Child   12383
Somebody's Dog   12191
Someday, Said Mitchell   17981
Someone Could Win a Polar Bear
   3465
Someone for Maria   14287
Someone New   18616
Someone Small   1943
Someplace Else   15517
Something, The   847
Something About a Mermaid   13771
Something for Christmas   2422
Something for the Medicine Man
   8542
Something from Nothing Crafts
   5478
Something Left to Lose   2094
Something Queer at the Ball Park
   10673
Something Queer at the Library
   10674
Something Queer Is Going On
   10675
Something Special   4747
Something to Shout About   1282

Sometimes I Dance Mountains 1241

Sometimes I Get Angry 17585

Sometimes I Hate School 1082

Sometimes I'm Afraid (Tester) 16769

Sometimes I'm Afraid (Watson) 17586

Sometimes I'm Jealous 17587

Sometimes Island, The 1000

Sometimes It's Turkey, Sometimes It's Feathers 1021

Son of Fortune 5049

Son of Raven, Son of Deer 3639

Son of Someone Famous, The 9735

Son of the Lakes 16371

Son of the Leopard, The 4201

Son of the Sahara 6417

Son of the Whiteman 1616

Son of This Land 15773

Song for Gilgamesh, A 8325

Song of Deborah 9192

Song of Hiawatha 11046

Song of Robin Hood 11568

Song of St. Francis 2571

Song of the Boat 7138

Song of the Earth Spirit 515

Song of the Empty Bottles 12321

Song of the Maples, The 3299

Song of the Pines 7868

Song of the Quail 9502

Song of the Shaggy Canary 18241

Song of the Smoggy Stars 12322

Song of the Sour Plum 8217

Song of the Swallows 13789

Song of the Trees 16694

Song, Speech and Ventriloquism 9766

Song That Sings Itself, The 15998

Songs and Stories from Uganda 15356

Songs and Stories of Afro-Americans 6884

Songs and Stories of the North American Indians 6885

Songs Children Like 771

Songs from Alice 3104

Songs of Innocence 1717

Songs of Sango 9983

Songs of the Chippewa 1640

Songs of the Dream People 8660

Songs of the Fog Maiden 4725

Songs of the Sage 17165

Songs of the Yokuts and Paiutes 13666

Songs the Sandman Sings 14183

Sonia Delaunay's Alphabet 4810

Sonrisa del gato o una manera de pasar el rato, La 4362

Sons of Liberty 16540

Sons of Mercury 6649

Sons of the African Veld 8609

Sons of the Desert 6803

Sons of the Steppe 1210

Soo Ling Finds a Way 1325

Soon After September 1801

Soot Devil 6707

Sophia Scarlatti and Ceecee 5739

Sophia Scrooby Preserved 868

Sophie and Gussie 15478

Sorcerer's Apprentice, The 6467

Sore Loser 7212

Sorely Trying Day, The 8291

Sorrow's Song 2853

Soul Brothers and Sister Lou, The 8777

Soul of Christmas, The 9817

Soulscript: Afro-American Poetry 9380

Sound All Around 13093

Sound of Axes, The 15894

Sound of Boomerangs, The 13510

Sound of Chariots, A 8785

Sound of Flutes and Other Indian Legends, The 5518

Sound of Sunshine, Sound of Rain 8006

Sound of the Dragon's Feet, The 18508

Sound of Trumpets, The 5426

Sound Science 294

Sound to Remember, A 10665

Sounder 652

Sounds All About 13760

Sounds in the Sea 9039

Sounds of Animals at Night 14300

Sounds of Time, The 8126

Soup 13459

Soup and Me 13460

Soupbone 13032

Sour Land 653

Sourwood Tales 3507

South Africa (Hopkinson) 8607

South Africa (Taylor) 16673

South Africa in Pictures 5460

South by Southwest 16727

South Central States 7062

South Dakota for Young People 13228

South Star 7984

South Town 7139

Southeast Asia 13817
Southern Africa (Clayton) 3551
Southern Africa (Stein) 16197
Southern Frontiersman 6156
Southern Indiana 359
Southpaw Speed 619
Southwest Desert Wonderland 17417
Southwest Indian Country 16044
Southwestern Arts and Crafts Projects 10094
Southwestern Indian Ceremonials 877
Southwestern Indian Recipe Book 8127
Southwestern Indian Tribes 878
Soviet Dissent 819
Space Age Fire Fighters 3786
Space Age Spinoffs 3787
Space Alphabet 18480
Space and Time 1438
Space Base 6296
Space Cat 16906
Space Hostages 5962
Space Ship Returns to the Apple Tree, The 15844
Space Ship Under the Apple Tree, The 15845
Space Stations '80 9078
Space Witch 6270
Spacecraft at Work 5393
Spacetrack 4043
Spain 7023
Spanish Conquistadores in North America 2526
Spanish for Children see Berlitz Spanish for Children
Spanish Letters, The 8786
Spanish Nuggets 8514
Spanish-Speaking Heroes 820
Spare Parts for the Human Body 12891
Spark of Opal 3520
Sparkle and Spin 14101
Sparky 7161
Sparrow Bush, The 3698
Sparrow Hawk 10638
Sparrow's Magic, A 12160
Speak Roughly to Your Little Boy 10976
Speak to the Winds 13150
Speak Up, Edie! 9312
Speaking of Mrs. McCluskie 11559
Speaking Out 4797
Special Bravery, A 9313
Special Gift, A 15723

Special Kind of Sister, A 15920
Special Trick, A 11939
Special World of the Artisan, The 13878
Speckled Hen, The 18519
Spectacles 14127
Speed King, The 10893
Speed Kings of the Base Paths 14482
Speedway Challenge 6690
Spell Is Cast, A 2859
Spell of the Northern Lights, The 16604
Spell of the White Sturgeon, The 9883
Spell Seven 13324
Spice Island Mystery 3204
Spider of Brooklyn Heights, The 17272
Spider Plant, The 16057
Spider Silk 7000
Spider, the Cave and the Pottery Bowl, The 3653
Spider Web, The 2254
Spiderweb for Two 5468
Spies and Traitors 14135
Spike 11256
Spill 13
Spin a Soft Black Song 6862
Spirals (Kettelkamp) 9767
Spirals (Sitomer) 15801
Spirit Is Willing, The 932
Spirit of Cochise, The 661
Spirit of Jem, The 12774
Spirit of the Wild, The 11369
Spirit Rocks and Silver Magic 11626
Spirits of Chocamata, The 17209
Splash and Flow 8687
Splasher 6514
Splendor That Was Africa, The 14635
Splish Splash 9747
Splodges 3087
Spokesman for Freedom 16294
Spook 10934
Sport Magazine's All-Time All Stars 12584
Sporting Proposition, A 244
Sports and Games 9628
Sports and Games in Art 15573
Sports and Games in Verse and Rhyme 9032
Sports Cards 11452
Sports Cars 9023
Sports Hero: Billie Jean King 2611
Sports Hero: Bobby Orr 2612

Sports Hero: Brooks Robinson 2613

Sports Hero: Fred Lynn 2608

Sports Hero: Henry Aaron 2614

Sports Hero: Joe Namath 2615

Sports Hero: Johnny Bench 2616

Sports Hero: Kareem Abdul Jab- bar 2617

Sports Hero: Larry Csonka 2618

Sports Hero: Muhammad Ali 2619

Sports Hero: O. J. Simpson 2620

Sports Hero: Pete Rose 2621

Sports Hero: Phil Esposito 2622

Sports Hero: Reggie Jackson 2623

Sports Hero: Roger Staubach 2624

Sports Heroes Who Wouldn't Quit 2750

Sports Illustrated Ice Hockey 12553

Sports Star: Bob Griese 2632

Sports Star: Brad Park 2633

Sports Star: Chris Evert 2634

Sports Star: Franco Harris 2635

Sports Star: Mean Joe Greene 2636

Sports Star: Pele 2637

Sports Star: Tom Seaver 2625

Sports Star: Walt Frazier 2638

Sports Titans of the Twentieth Century 15675

Spots Are Special! 6494

Spotted Flower and the Ponokomita 3314

Spotted Salamander 11257

Sprig of Broom, The 17961

Spring Begins in March 10942

Spring Comes First to the Wil- lows 13993

Spring Comes to the Ocean 6748

Spring Holidays 5505

Spring Is 5000

Spring Is Here 10588

Spring on the Mountain, The 345

Spring Peepers 7889

Spring Rider, The 10414

Springfield Home see Contrary Orphans, The

Springing of the Rice, The 1588

Springtime for Jeanne-Marie 6215

Springtime in Noisy Village 10841

Sprints and Distances 12471

Sprout and the Magician 17622

Spunkwater, Spunkwater! 18232

Spy and General Washington, The 18146

Spy in Old Detroit, A 5427

Spy in Old Philadelphia, A 5428

Spy in Williamsburg, A 10397

Spy, the Lady, the Captain and the Colonel, The 16319

Squad Car 55 3266

Squanto (Graff) 7117

Squanto (Grant) 7180

Squanto, Friend of the Pilgrims 2572

Squanto, Friend of the White Men 2573; see also Squanto, Friend of the Pilgrims

Squash Pie 6476

Squaw Man's Son 10231

Squawk to the Moon, Little Goose 13901

Squeals and Squiggles and Ghostly Giggles 11363

Squib 1221

Squire's Bride, The 714

Squirrel and His Mother ..., The 12998

Squirrel Wife, The 13429

Squirrels (Laycock) 10433

Squirrels (Wildsmith) 17929

St. Bernadette 4540

St. Lawrence Seaway 9431

St. Lawrence Seaway of North America 17788

St. Nicholas Anthology, A 6423

St. Patrick's Day 2899

St. Valentine's Day 2574

Stagecoach Days and Stagecoach Kings 17347

Stained Glass Crafting 18238

Stainless Steel Rat Saves the World, The 7800

Stalwart Men of Early Texas 11225

Stamp Collector's Guide 18502

Stamp Collector's History of the United States, A 16945

Stamp Pad Printing Book, The 13591

Stampede North 6200

Stampede to Timberline 18215

Stamps Tell the Story of Space Travel 9633

Stamps Tell the Story of the United

Nations 9634
Stan Musial 14483
"Stand Back," Said the Elephant, "I'm Going to Sneeze!!" 16823
Stand in the Wind 10943
Stand Up, Lucy 7587
Standing in the Magic 12913
Stanley 8362
Stanley, African Explorer 15895
Stanley, Henry Bear's Friend 11497
Star 8547
Star Born 12942
Star Bright 7225
Star Circus 10811
Star Girl (Winterfeld) 18126
Star Girl (Wyss) 18355
Star in the Pail, The 11269
Star in the Sea 15700
Star Island Boy 14322
Star Lost 7226
Star Maiden 14452
Star Mother's Youngest Child 12304
Star Mountain and Other Legends of Mexico 2871
Star of Morning, The 12244
Star of Wild Horse Canyon 2575
Star Pitchers of the Major Leagues 10772
Star Quarterbacks of the NFL 10773
Star Running Backs of the NFL 10774
Star-Spangled Banana ..., The 9643
Star-Spangled Banner, The 9775
Star-Spangled Fun! 14170
Star to the North, A 4146
Starfish 8813
Stargazer to the Sultan 17437
Starman's Son 12943
Stars and Planets 17856
Stars and Serendipity, The 14342
Stars and Stripes 6297
Stars for Sam, The 14188
Stars in Her Eyes 3205
Stars in Our Heavens, The 11164
Stars of Pro Basketball 14835
Stars of the Major Leagues 9893
Stars of the Modern Olympics 5887
Stars over Texas 50
Stars, Spells, Secrets and Sorcery 7569
Stars To-Night (Teasdale) 16725

Stars to Steer By 17160
Stars Tonight, The (Polgreen) 13774
Start to Draw 2869
Starting Out 10028
Starting Soccer 4974
State and Local Government in Michigan 10702
State Birds and Flowers 5210
State Capital Cities 6968
State Champs 2653
State Trees 5211
States of the Nation: North Carolina 1359
Statesmanship of Abraham Lincoln 4023
Statistics 16108
Staying Alive! 911
Staying Home Alone on a Rainy Day 8964
Steadfast Tin Soldier, The 444
Steady, Freddie! 4118
Steal Away Home 10101
Steam Cars of the Stanley Twins, The 9024
Steamboats 17518
Steamboats on the Mississippi 530
Steamroller, The 2398
Steel 5936
Steel Magic 12944
Stefanii doo Ma'ii 4328
Steffie and Me 8372
Steinmetz 7531
Step It Down 9335
Stephannie and the Coyote 4329
Stephen Comes to Town 4015
Stepsister Sally 4500
Steve Bellamy 2771
Steve Marches with the General 14245
Steven Caney's Play Book 2894
Stevie 16233
Stevie and His Seven Orphans 11799
Stevie Wonder (Hasegawa) 7811
Stevie Wonder (Wilson) 18068
Stevie's Other Eyes 11310
Stewed Goose 6068
Stick-in-the-Mud Turtle 8270
Sticks Across the Chimney 2652
Sticks, Stones 169a
Stiff Ears 17820
Still Another Alphabet Book 3456
Still Another Number Book 3457
Stitch in Time, A 10958
Stock-Car Racer 2772
Stock Car Racing 9025

Stocking Child, The 15518
Stolen by the Indians 8013
Stolen Fire, The 1211
Stolen Images, The 1333
Stolen Mirror, The 13837
Stolen Pony 14705
Stolen Ruler, The 9264
Stolen Seasons, The 4925
Stolen Telesm, The 1225
Stomach and His Friends, The
    4347
Stone Angel, The 14563
Stone Book, The 6616
Stone-Faced Boy, The 6187
Stone Flight 11395
Stone Man, Stone House 5480
Stone of Peace, The 5750
Stone of Terror 7234
Stone of Victory, The 3881
Stone Soup 2382
Stonecutter, The 11293
Stones, The 8145
Stones, Bones, and Arrowheads
    15414
Stones of Green Knowe, The
    1976
Stonewall 6390
Stonewall Jackson 4482
Stop, The 18218
Stop Stop 8814
Stopping Place, The 4449
Stores 15146
Stories and Plays from Africa
    6319
Stories at Sundown 210
Stories California Indians Told
    5934
Stories for All Seasons 13343
Stories for Christmas 17177
Stories for Fun and Adventure
    5797
Stories for Little Children 2491
Stories from a Snowy Meadow
    16262
Stories from Africa (Dolch) 4990
Stories from Africa (Goulden)
    7104
Stories from an African Village
    202
Stories from Canada 4982
Stories from Hawaii 4983
Stories from India 4984
Stories from Masailand 6792
Stories from Mexico 4985
Stories from Nabdam 18387
Stories from Shakespeare 3454
Stories from the Bible 17006

Stories from the Sands of Africa
    16671
Stories in String 16867
Stories My Grandfather Should Have
    Told Me 2284
Stories of Dixie 12824
Stories of Famous Explorers by
    Land 9939
Stories of Favorite Operas 2576
Stories of Gilbert and Sullivan
    Operas 2577
Stories of Indiana 16836
Stories of Konga, The 9451; see
    also Mango's Grass House and
    Other Stories
Stories of Life 8905
Stories of Ohio 8690
Stories of Our American Patriotic
    Songs 11189
Stories of the Benin Empire 15651
Stories of the Gods and Heroes
    1481
Stories of the Gorilla Country
    5098
Stories the Iroquois Tell Their
    Children 13867
Stories to Tell Boys and Girls 2461
Stories Told in an African Forest
    by Grown-Up Children of Africa
    9206
Storm at Sand Points 7079
Storm Book, The 18617
Storm from the West 17962
Storm over Innish 3603
Storm Warning 2527
Storms 1526
Stormy, Misty's Foal 8077
Story, a Story, A 7582
Story About Ping, The 5991
Story Ananse Told, The 13220
Story Behind Modern Books, The
    12364
Story Catcher, The 14902
Story Grandmother Told, The 288
Story Lives of Great Composers
    918
Story Number 4 8908
Story of a Simple Man and Other
    Stories, The 7325
Story of Aida, The 16284
Story of Akimakoo 12551
Story of Albert Schweitzer, The
    (Daniel) 4479
Story of Albert Schweitzer, The
    (Manton) 11649
Story of Amelia Earhart, The 4707
Story of an English Village, The

7045
Story of Ancient Egypt, The 15395
Story of Annie Oakley, The   3834
Story of Ants, The   15637
Story of Atomic Energy, The 5825
Story of Babar, the Little Elephant, The   4646
Story of Baseball, The   14629
Story of Baseball in Words and Pictures, The   5161
Story of Ben Franklin, The 12106
Story of Bip, The   11658
Story of Cake, The   15864
Story of Cattle Ranching, The 664
Story of Christmas, The   8377
Story of Clara Barton of the Red Cross, The   12884
Story of Cole Porter, The   5609
Story of Comock the Eskimo, The 3049
Story of Corn, The   10815
Story of Crazy Horse, The   11994
Story of D-Day, The   1779
Story of Dams, The   5662
Story of Design, The   5048
Story of Doctor Dolittle, The 11024
Story of Dogs, The   10355
Story of Edith Cavell, The   17316
Story of Edward, The   5114
Story of Eleanor Roosevelt, The 4575
Story of Electricity, The   6303
Story of Eli Whitney, The   10319
Story of Ellis Island   7980
Story of Esther, The   2251
Story of Fanny Burney, The 9478
Story of Ferdinand, The   10459
Story of Fire Fighting, The 16225
Story of Flight, The   15361
Story of Folk Music, The   1527
Story of Football, The   10477
Story of Fort Snelling, The 13465
Story of Geology, The   18336
Story of George Washington Carver, The   12390
Story of Helen Keller, The   8150
Story of Hiawatha   3234
Story of Hockey, The   13183
Story of Illinois, The   7702

Story of Johnny Appleseed, The 310
Story of King Arthur and His Knights, The   14017
Story of Little Black Sambo, The 1055
Story of Lyndon B. Johnson, The 12800
Story of Madame Curie, The   16844
Story of Man Against Winter, The 665
Story of Mankind, The   17216
Story of Marco Polo, The   13926
Story of Masada, The   18357
Story of Mrs. Tubbs, The   11025
Story of My Life, The   9645
Story of New England, The   16154
Story of Numbers, The   10356
Story of Oakville Harbour, The 2249
Story of Oceanography, The   2048
Story of Offshore Oil, The   12697
Story of Old Ghana, Melle and Songhai, The   18113
Story of Old Ironsides, The   14337
Story of Our National Ballads, The 2436
Story of Painting, The   329
Story of Pancho and the Bull with the Crooked Tail, The   7548
Story of Paul Bunyan, The   5407
Story of Persephone, The   5698
Story of Phillis Wheatley, The 7150
Story of Prince Ivan, the Firebird, and the Gray Wolf, The   17840
Story of Pueblo Pottery, The 18272
Story of Ricky the Royal Dwarf, The   15609
Story of Rocks, The   15638
Story of Rodents, The   15639
Story of Roland, The   1007
Story of Saul the King, The   17376
Story of Sault Ste. Marie and Chippewa County, The   12807
Story of Sea Otters, The   9304
Story of Spanish Moss and the Wax Tree, The   11765
Story of Spiders, The   15640
Story of Stevie Wonder, The   7830
Story of the Alamo, The   14338
Story of the Amulet, The   12737
Story of the Boy Scouts   1735
Story of the Capitol, The   13976
Story of the Conestoga Wagon, The 14333

Story of the Dictionary, The 10051

Story of the Four Little Children Who Went Around the World, The 10469

Story of the Grateful Crane, The 1147

Story of the Great Chicago Fire, The 13620

Story of the Great Lakes 6823

Story of the Haida, The 7357

Story of the International Red Cross, The 5482

Story of the Iroquois, The see Indian Nations: The Story of the Iroquois

Story of the Jewish Calendar, The 5309

Story of the Little Round Man, The 296

Story of the Mexican-Americans, The 44

Story of the Mexican War, The 14194

Story of the Mississippi Choctaws, The 1994

Story of the Navajo, The 7358

Story of the Negro, The 1924

Story of the Presidents of the United States of America 13566

Story of the Secret Service, The 12698

Story of the Seminole, The 7359

Story of the Sioux, The 7360

Story of the Southern Highlands, The 11476

Story of the Southwest, The 11477

Story of the Totem Pole, The 2258

Story of the Treasure Seekers, The 12738

Story of the Ukrainian Congress Committee of America (1945-1951) 16389

Story of the United Nations, The 14947

Story of the United States Flag, The 1736

Story of Things, The 9436

Story of Thomas Alva Edison, The 4211

Story of Uganda, The 16810

Story of Valentine, The 7944

Story of Volcanoes and Earthquakes, The 11834

Story of William Penn, The 311

Story of World War II, The 10478

Story of Yogi Berra, The 15109

Story of Your Brain and Nerves, The 17625

Story of Your Heart, The 10816

Story of Zambia, The 14744

Story on the Willow Plate, The 16820

Story Poems 3821

Story Snail, The 14521

Story Time with the Animals 9613

Storybook, A 17138

Storybook Cookbook, The 11377

Stout-Hearted Seven 6238

Stout Rider 1685

Straight Hair, Curly Hair 7001

Straight Lines, Parallel Lines, Perpendicular Lines 3292

Straight Mark 7651

Straight on Till Morning 8183

Stranded 3429

Strange Adventures of the Great Lakes 2045

Strange Affair of Adelaide Harris, The 6606

Strange and Incredible Sports Happenings 4595

Strange but True Baseball Stories 1667

Strange but True Football Stories 8488

Strange but True Hockey Stories (Fischler) 5899

Strange but True Hockey Stories (Liss) 10920

Strange but Wonderful Cosmic Awareness of Duffy Moon, The 14471

Strange Companions in Nature 5212

Strange Disappearance of Arthur Cluck, The 1412

Strange Dreams of Rover Jones, The 640

Strange Hockett Family, The 14415

Strange Island 7859

Strange Monsters of the Sea 641

Strange New World Across the Street, The 6813

Strange Plants and Their Ways 8854

Strange Servant, A 6507

Strange Story of the Frog Who Became a Prince 8639

Strange Street 13856

Strange Voyage of Neptune's Car,

The 10300
Strange World of Dinosaurs, The 13201
Stranger and Afraid, A 933
Stranger at Green Knowe, A 1977
Stranger Came Ashore, A 8787
Stranger in Singamon 18085
Stranger in the Hills 13798
Stranger in the Pines 11478
Stranger in the Storm 11851
Stranger on the Ball Club 15858
Stranger's Bread 17968
Strangers in Africa 4614
Stratford, Around and About 16127
Strawberry Book of Colors, The 7995
Strawberry Dress Escape 5059
Strawberry Girl 10589
Strawberry Roan, The 14706
Strawberry Thumb, The 9919
Strawberry Word Book, The 7996
Stray 7607
Strays, The 11157
Stream Runner 15224
Streamlined 9544
Street Gangs 7831
Street Kids, The 4488
Street Markets Around the World 11135
Street of the Flower Boxes, The 11613
Street Poems 6405
Street Smart 7615
Strega Nona 4726
Striding Slippers 6854
String Art 15490
String in the Harp, A 1883
String, Straightedge, and Shadow 4904
Stripe 11258
Striped Ice Cream 10751
Strong Land and a Sturdy, A 1068
Strong Wings 14476
Stronger Than Hate 944
Strongest One of All, The 6855
Stronghold, The 8788
Struggle for North America 17984
Stuart Little 17793
Stubborn Bear 1644
Stubborn Sam 6691
Student Who Became King in Spite of Himself, The 3873
Students' Guide to Localized History, A 17675

Study of Coal, The 1226
Stuff and Nonsense (Dugan) 5106
Stuff and Nonsense (Parker) 13309
Stuff It 12520
Stupid Marco 18028
Su An 9252
Su-Mei's Golden Year 2272
Such Is the Way of the World 5349
Sudan 3033
Sudan in Pictures, The 8948
Suddenly--A Witch 2018
Sue Ellen 8772
Sueños del astronauta, Los 10202
Sue's Secondhand Horse 17301
Sugar Bee 12152
Sugar from Farm to Market 7672
Sugar Girl 13125
Sugar Mouse Cake, The 18594
Sugar on Snow 17592
Sugar Pear Tree, The 2578
Sugar Petite 11511
Sugar Snow Spring, The 8271
Sugarcane Island 13235
Suho and the White Horse 13202
Suicide and Young People 11523
Suimi 10885
Suki and the Magic Sand Dollar 1705
Sulizo Achieves Greatness 7533
Sultan's Bath, The 391
Sultan's Fool ..., The 6839
Sumatra Alley 3981
Sumi and the Goat and the Tokyo Express 17104
Sumi's Prize 17105
Sumi's Special Happening 17106
Summer Adventure, A 10722
Summer After the Funeral, The 6575
Summer at High Kingdom 14323
Summer Birds 5699
Summer Book, The 9144
Summer Ends Too Soon, The 7457
Summer Growing Time 9648
Summer I Was Lost, The 17302
Summer in the South, A 11714
Summer Is ... 18618
Summer Is for Growing 3497
Summer Maker, The 1579
Summer Night, The 18619
Summer Noisy Book, The 2399
Summer of My German Soldier 7262
Summer of the Burning 5129
Summer of the Falcon, The 6749
Summer of the Stallion 7707
Summer of the Swans, The 2792

Summer of the White Goat 4932
Summer Olympics, The 17485
Summer on the Salt Fork 17348
Summer Pony 5028
Summer Secret, A 15519
Summer Secrets 6881
Summer Snowman 18595
Summer Storm 15579
Summer to Die, A 11127
Summer Under Sail 8673
Summer's Coming In 1381
Sun, The (Asimov) 762
Sun, The (Branley) 2147
Sun, The (Zim) 18553
Sun and Moon 12288
Sun and Saddle Leather 3504
Sun and the Cloud, The 14381
Sun and Wind, The 11820
Sun Chief, The 11738
Sun Dance People, The 5519
Sun Dust 18630
Sun Is a Golden Earring, The
    1382
Sun Journey 3498
Sun Men and Other Plays, The
    11821
Sun Power 15925
Sun Salutes You, The 13256
Sun, Sand and Steel 4911
Sun, the Moon, and the Stars,
    The 6304
Sun Train, The 14212
Sun Up 17007
Sundae with Judy, A 6357
Sundance Coyote 6172
Sunday for Sona 4294
Sunday Saves the Village ...
    9689
Sundiata 1609
Sunflower Garden 17115
Sunflowers for Tina 1001
Sung Under the Silver Umbrella
    772
Sungura Njanja 4924
Sunlight 3136
Sunlight and Shadows 13775
Sunlit Sea, The 7002
Sunnyside Up 3286
Sunnyvale Fair 7095
Sunrise Island 228
Sunset in a Spider Web 1099
Sunshine Family and the Pony,
    The 11077
Sunshine Makes the Seasons 2148
Super Animals and Their Unusual
    Careers 3588
Super Bowl 4864

Super Sam and the Salad Garden
    18185
Super Showmen, The 17619
Supercars 12671
Superfight II 13061
Superior (Litteljohn) 10930
Superior (Steinhacker) 16219
Superlative Horse, The 12114
Supermachines 7685
Supermex 9026
Superplanes 12672
Superpuppy 13693
Supersuits 3710
Supertrains 12673
Supposing 14216
Supposings 9314
Supreme Court, The 9271
Supreme Court and How It Works
    10687
Supreme, Superb, Exalted and
    Delightful, One and Only Magic
    Building 10008
Surangini Tales, The 15456
Surfing, the Big Wave 15878
Surf's Up! 9895
Surgeon, Trader, Indian Chief,
    Henry Woodward of Carolina
    16175
Surprise for Carlotta, A 2641
Surprise for Mrs. Burns 17068
Surprise Party, The (Hutchins)
    8840
Surprise Party, The (Praeger)
    13872
Surprise Picnic, The 7046
Survivors, The 15202
Survivors of the Stone Age 11663
Susan 15943
Susan B. Anthony (Grant) 7181
Susan B. Anthony (Monsell) 12359
Susan B. Anthony (Noble) 12861
Susan B. Anthony (Peterson)
    13576
Susan, Beware! 8762
Susan Comes Through the Fire
    11311
Susan in the Driver's Seat 6786
Susan Sometimes 10042
Susanna and Tristram 328
Susannah, the Pioneer Cow 11800
Susan's Magic 163
Susan's Secret 18323
Susie and Sophie ... 9583
Susie King Taylor, Civil War Nurse
    1931
Suspicion Is My Name 17088
Susy's Scoundrel 9629

Suzette La Flesche 4249
Suzu and the Bride Doll 11758
Suzuki Beane 15183
Swallows 14405; see also Pool of
  Swallows
Swallows and Amazons 14116
Swamp Boy 4157
Swamp Fox, The 2409
Swamp Spring 3079
Swampfire 7540
Swapping Boy 10254
Swarm in May, A 11961
Swaziland 3034
Sweden 12107
Swedes in America, The 8196
Sweeny's Ghost 5949
Sweet and Sour 9681
Sweet Betsy from Pike 29
Sweet Land of Michigan 4852
Sweet Pea 10085
Sweet Promised Land 10428
Sweet Touch, The 1022
Sweetly Sings the Donkey 10255
Sweets and Sugar Cane 13008
Sweetwater 18398
Swift Deer--The Navajo 1594
Swiftly Tilting Planet, A 10547
Swiftwater 568
Swim Little Duck 12192
Swimming 10031
Swimming Hole 1339
Swimming the Shane Gould Way
  7102
Swimmy 10886
Swineherd, The 445
Swing in the Summerhouse, The
  10263
Swinging and Swinging 11654
Swiss Family Robinson, The
  18354
Switch on the Night 2070
Sword and the Grail, The 8158
Sword in the Stone, The 17813
Sword in the Tree 2579
Sword of Aradel, The 9774
Sword of Culann, The 10651
Sword of the Hausas 8054
Sycamore Tree, The 7860
Sycamore Tree and Other African
  Tales, The 10488
Sycamore Year 10487
Syd Hoff's Joke Book 8363
Sylvester and the Magic Pebble
  16196
Symbioses--A Book of Unusual
  Friendship 698

- T -

Taash and the Jesters 11423
Tabibu Kalulu see Doctor Kalulu
Tabkin Kwatto see Battle of Tab-
  kin Kwatto, The
Table Games 11697
Table Top Science 5957
Tabletop Theatres and Plays 3721
Tacho, Boy of Mexico 4495
Tad Lincoln and the Green Umbrella
  6377
Tadpole Taylor 10441
Tailypo, The 6496
Taiwa Goes to Sea 712
Taiwan 5264
Taiwo and Her Twin 15016
Takao and Grandfather's Sword
  17107
Take a Balloon 16369
Take a Horse to the Wilderness
  16164
Take a Long Jump 14246
Take a Number (Bendick) 1447
Take a Number (O'Neill) 13132
Take All to Nebraska 18128
Take It or Leave It 12323
Take Joy 17033
Take Me Home 6793
Take Me Out to the Airfield 14030
Take Me to the Moon 12563
Take My Waking Slow 12914
Take Shapes, Lines, and Letters
  1448
Take Sky 11270
Take Three Witches 12140
Take Wing 10944
Taken Girl, The 17313
Takers and Returners 18432
Taki 6948
Taking Pictures 10507
Taking Root 12048
Taking Sides 9911
Takula Tree, The 6037
Tal 4080
Tal of Four Tribes 1617
Talargain 6571
Tale of a Black Cat, The 18163
Tale of a Crocodile 9866
Tale of a Meadow, The 9482
Tale of Jemima Puddle-Duck, The
  13843
Tale of Lazy Lizard Canyon, The
  2663
Tale of Peter Rabbit, The 13844
Tale of Squirrel Nutkin, The 13845

Tale of Tawny and Dingo   654
Tale of the Czar Saltan, The
  14006
Tale of the Faithful Dove, The
  13846
Tale of the Golden Cockerel, The
  14007
Tale of the Magic Bread, The
  15005
Tale of Three Wishes, A   15783
Tale of Tsar Saltan, The   see
  Tale of the Czar Saltan, The
Tale of Two Bicycles, A   9753
Tales and Legends of Morocco
  3377
Tales and Stories for Black Folks
  1033
Tales by M'Passou, the Hyena's
  Tail   12534
Tales for Boys and Girls   1743
Tales for the Third Ear ...   7
Tales for Tobias   16976
Tales from a Finnish Tupa   2023
Tales from Africa (Kelsey)   9676
Tales from Africa (Savory)
  14964
Tales from an African Drum   3339
Tales from an Ashanti Father
  594
Tales from Atop a Russian Stove
  8171
Tales from Central Russia   14396
Tales from Czechoslovakia   2644
Tales from Grimm   6468
Tales from Moominvalley   9145
Tales from Old China   3260
Tales from Shakespeare   10203
Tales from Sierra Leone   18372
Tales from Tartary   14397
Tales from the Heart of Africa
  17185
Tales from the Igloo   12121
Tales from the Mohaves   7344
Tales from the South Pacific
  6874
Tales from the Story Hat   8
Tales from the Welsh Hills   13987
Tales of a Chinese Grandmother
  3054
Tales of a Fourth Grade Nothing
  1821
Tales of a Korean Grandmother
  3055
Tales of Ancient Egypt   7249
Tales of Ancient Persia   13656
Tales of Arabel's Raven   see
  Arabel's Raven

Tales of Brave African Boys   9207
Tales of Brave Girls   9208
Tales of Christophilos   12640
Tales of Faraway Folk   4862
Tales of Grimm and Andersen   7410
Tales of Land of Death   13054
Tales of Mogho   7498
Tales of Myrtle the Turtle   14446
Tales of Nanabozho   14218
Tales of Nso   10266
Tales of Olga Da Polga   1882
Tales of Oliver Pig   17212
Tales of Peter Parley About Africa
  7054
Tales of Temba   677
Tales of the African Wilds   11739
Tales of the Blue Mountains   10812
Tales of the Cheyennes   13492
Tales of the Elders   1010
Tales of the Forest   4772
Tales of the Hodja   5056
Tales of the Nimipoo   7978
Tales of the Yoruba Gods and
  Heroes   4202
Tales of Thunder and Lightning
  4868
Tales of Wamugumo, The   17510
Tales the People Tell in China
  18352
Tales the People Tell in Mexico
  11188
Tales the People Tell in Russia
  1849
Tales Tiv Tell   1546
Tales Told Near a Crocodile   7726
Tales Told to Kabbarli   1174
Taliesin   12977
Taliesin and King Arthur   14424
Talking About Death   7444
Talking About Divorce   7445
Talking Animals   7641
Talking Cat, The   2970
Talking Clowns, The   11588
Talking Drums of Africa   13921
Talking Hands   414
Talking Leaf, The   9370
Talking Leaves   9978
Talking of Horses   4886
Talking Parcel, The   5171
Talking Stone, The   4760
Talking Table Mystery, The   11396
Talking Totem Pole, The   11965
Talking Totem Poles   8438
Talking Tree and Other Stories,
  The   919
Talking with the Animals   3751
Talking Without Words   5568

Tall and Proud 15935
Tall as Standing Rock 356
Tall Book of Mother Goose, The 14569
Tall Book of Nursery Tales, The 14570
Tall Grass Zoo, The 11136
Tall Like a Pine 17645
Tall Man from Boston, The 16151
Tall One, The 13112
Tall Ships 10304
Tall Tale America 1713
Tall Tales from the High Hills 4270
Tall Tales of America 15426
Tall Timber Tales 11272
Taller Than Bandai Mountain 4474
Talpa 12033
Tamarack Tree, The 17126
Tame the Wild Stallion 18005
Taming of Tiger, The 10338
Tan, a Wild Dog 8214
Tana and the Useless Monkey 16314
Tanaina Tales from Alaska 17253
Tangle of Roots, A 6869
Tangles 17468
Tani 11686
Tanners, The 5950
Tan's Fish 16907
Tansy for Short 8430
Tanzania 3035
Tanzania in Pictures 14260
Taos Indians and Their Sacred Blue Lake, The 9612
Tapestries in Sand 17306
Tar Beach 6781
Taran Wanderer 273
Tarantula 3960
Tarantulas 17300
Tarea de vacaciones 12074
Taro and the Bamboo Shoot 11826
Taro and the Tofu 11827
Taro and the Turtles 4958
Tarzan of the Apes 2695
Taste of Blackberries, A 15882
Taste of Chaucer, A 3309
Taste of Spruce Gum, The 8997
Tatsinda 5469
Tattooed Potato and Other Clues, The 14128
Tatu and the Honey Bird 17719
Tavern at the Ferry, The 17044
Tavern Lamps Are Burning, The 2983

Tawny 2986
Taxis and Toadstools 5854
Taylor's Bible Story Book 16684
Teacher 729
Teacher for Tibby, A 13936
Teacup Full of Roses 11818
Team, The 13601
Team Racer 2773
Team That Couldn't Lose, The 3430
Team That Stopped Moving 3431
Teapot, Switcheroo and Other Silly Games 16993
Tear Down the Walls! 16242
Tears of the Dragon, The 7636
Teatro comico para los niños 1485
Teatro escolar 16437
Teatro para niños 13250
Teatro, v. 1, El 6567
Teatro, v. 2, El 6568
Teatro, v. 3, El 6569
Tecumseh (Cooke) 4012
Tecumseh (Creighton) 4275
Tecumseh! (Eckert) 5247
Tecumseh (Stevenson) 16279
Tecumseh and the Indian Confederation, 1811-1813 8879
Tecumseh, Shawnee Warrior-Statesman 11217
Tecwyn 4619
Ted and Bobby Look for Something Special 14035
Teddy and the Moon 11775
Teddy Bear Habit, The 3842
Teddy Bears 1 to 10 7342
Teddy Roosevelt and the Rough Riders 3151
Teddy Roosevelt in Africa 8696
Teen-Age Guide to Healthy Skin and Hair, A 11137
Teen-Ager's Guide to Collecting Practically Anything, The 15867
Teen-Ager's Menu Cookbook, The 51
Teenage Hall of Fame 14289
Teenage Jobs 10543
Teeny, Tiny Witches, The 17412
Teeny Tiny Woman, The 15364
Teetoncey 16717
Teetoncey and Ben O'Neal 16718
Tejanos 6135
Tekla's Easter 2511
Telephone, The (Chukovsky) 3440
Telephone, The (O'Connor) 13001
Telephone Systems 18573
Television Magic 9347
Television Works Like This 1445

Tell a Tale of Iowa   2340
Tell It--Make It Book, The   10725
Tell Me a Mitzi   15244
Tell Me a Trudy   15245
Tell Me About Death   4155
Tell Me, Mister Rogers   14560
Tell Me, Please! What's That?
   9172
Tell Me Some More   1911
Telltale Line, The   11614
Telltale Summer of Tina C   13529
Temba Dawn   10443
Temper Tantrum Book, The
   13902
Temples of Dendur, The   9635
Ten   11146
Ten American Cities, Then and
   Now   980
Ten Apples Up on Top   10620
10 Bears in My Bed   11403
Ten Big Farms   8918
Ten Brave Men   4535
Ten Brothers with Camels   4295
Ten Cousins   2884
Ten in a Family   16215
Ten Little Elephants   10754
Ten Saints   5681
Ten Tales from Shakespeare
   10204
Ten Tall Texans (Kubiak)   10123
Ten Tall Texans (McGiffin)   11332
Ten Texas Tales Retold   6840
Ten What?   8292
Tenase Brave   5142
Tenggren Mother Goose, The
   16739
Tenggren's Cowboys and Indians
   9004
Tennis (Lawrence)   10394
Tennis (McCormick)   11273
Tennis (Riessen)   14371
Tennis (Seewagen)   15240
Tennis Bum   13035
Tennis for Anyone!   13245
Tennis for Beginners   5169
Tennis Machine, The   9042
Tennis: Serving and Returning
   Service   4793
Tennis: The Basic Strokes   4794
Tennis: Volleying and Lobs
   4795
Tenth Good Thing About Barney,
   The   17322
Tenth Life of Osiris Oaks, The
   4223
Teo en avion   2902
Teo en barco   2903

Teo en tren   2904
Tepee and Moccasin   218
Tepee Stories   4986
Tepee Tales of the American Indian
   2338
Teresita y las Orugas   15309
Terrapin's Pot of Sense   4203
Terrible Churnadryne, The   2860
Terrible Temptation, The   705
Terrible Thing That Happened at
   Our House   1710
Terrible Trick or Treat, The   1186
Terrible Troll Bird, The   4558
Terrible Wave, The   4450
Terror on the Ice   12717
Terror on the Mountain see Sum-
   mer I Was Lost, The
Terry and the Caterpillars   15310
Tessie   9002
Testing of Charlie Hammelman, The
   2312
Testing of Tertius, The   12794
Texas   3036
Texas and the War with Mexico
   5051
Texas in Color   13156
Texas News, The   16183
Texas Ranch Boy   11844
Texas Rangers, The (Henry)   8083
Texas Rangers, The (Webb)   17634
Texas Tomboy   10590
Texas Traildrive   6641
Texas Treasure   14010
Textiles   15538
Thailand   13818
Thailand, Rice Bowl of Asia   17578
Thank-You Book, The   6216
Thank You, Jackie Robinson   3741
Thank You--You're Welcome   15846
Thanksgiving   18350
Thanksgiving Day   1144
Thanksgiving, Feast and Festival
   11156
Thanksgiving Story, The   4462
Thanksgiving Treasure, The   14499
That Bad Carlos   10733
That Cat! 1-2-3   11759
That Crazy April   13550
That Dunbar Boy   7100
That Jud!   2087
That Lincoln Boy   12158
That Lively Man, Ben Franklin
   5233
That Makes Me Mad   10109
That New Baby (Mann)   11615
That New Baby (Stein)   16208
That New Boy   11193

That New River Train 7904
That Quail, Robert 16144
That Ruby 2406
That Summer with Ora 10219
That Useless Hound 17827
That Wonderful Pelican 15203
That's Enough for One Day 13443
That's Mine 18131
That's the Way It Is, Amigo 3871
That's the Way, Joshuway 18259
That's What It Is! 9173
Theater of Africa, The 17537
Thee, Hannah! 4641
Their Eyes on the Stars 3514
Their Search for God 5968
Their Shining Hour 11547
Then Again, Maybe I Won't 1822
Then and Now in Michigan 10703
Then Came Adventure 2277
Then There Were Five 5470
Theodore 13175
Theodore and the Talking Mush-
room 10887
Theodore Roosevelt 394
Theodore Roosevelt, the Strenuous
Life 6620
Theodore Turtle 11380
There and Back Again 9351
There Are Two Kinds of Terrible
11616
There Goes Feathertop! 5670
There Is a Bull on My Balcony
9399
There Is a Happy Land 615
There Is a Season 14606
There Is a Tide 2088
There Ought to Be a Law! 16570
There Was an Old Lady 13588
There Was an Old Woman 9659
There'll Be a Hot Time in the Old
Town Tonight 14031
There's a Nightmare in My
Closet 11940
There's a Sound in the Sea 7381
There's No Such Thing as a
Dragon 9714
There's Only One You 12475
These Are the Great Lakes 794
These Happy Golden Years
17909
These Islands Are Alive 11905
These Were the Sioux 14903
They Call Me Jack 17667
They Came from Germany 4378
They Came from Italy 11680
They Came from Poland 13670
They Came from Sweden 9432;

see also Sod-house Winter
They Came to Pennsylvania 17471
They Came to Stay 11667
They Changed the Game 10921
They Changed the World 6608
They Dared the Deep 11771
They Dared to Lead 8485
They Like You Better 6600
They Lived in the Ice Age 11906
They Lived Like This in Ancient
Africa 12758
They Lived Like This in Ancient
China 12759
They Lived Like This in Ancient
Palestine 12760
They Lived Like This in Old Japan
12761
They Put on Masks 1242
They Put Out to Sea 5189
They Say Stories 3273
They Showed the Way 14583
They Turned to Stone 11907
They Walk in the Night 3699
They Were Made of Rawhide 13445
They Were Strong and Good 10427
They Wouldn't Quit 6716
They've Discovered a Head in the
Box for the Bread ... 2212
Thief, The 14541
Thief-Catcher, The 18119
Thief Catcher and Other Stories
from Ethiopia, The 7384
Thief Who Hugged a Moonbeam, The
1606
Thimble Summer 5471
Thing at the Foot of the Bed ...,
The 10451
Things 5141
Things Are Made to Move 13761
Things I Hate! 18167
Things in Dolores' Piano, The
16636
Things That Go Bump in the Night
9361
Things That Measure 2991
Things to Make and Do for Valen-
tine's Day 4727
Things to See 11837
Things You've Wondered About
12137
Think About It, You Might Learn
Something 16506
Think Metric! 2149
Third and Goal 4225
Third Eye, The 11399
Third Gift, The 2917
Third World Voices for Children

11315

Thirteen 3282

13 Alabama Ghosts and Jeffrey
18107

Thirteen Clocks 16857

13 Danish Tales 7837

Thirteen Georgia Ghosts and
Jeffrey 18106

13th Member, The 8789

Thirty Days in May 8164

Thirty-One Brothers and Sisters
12273

Thirty-Second State, The 8014

Thirty Seconds over Tokyo 3975

32 Feet of Insides 15999

Thirty-two Moons, The 9935

This and That and Thus and So
see Girl and the Goatherd,
The

This Can Lick a Lollipop 14689

This Can't Be Happening at Macdonald Hall 9999

This Crowded World 6223

This Dear-Bought Land 10320

This for That 3499

This Hawk Belongs to Me 13803

This Is a Leaf 8855

This Is a Recording 4143

This Is a River 13969

This Is a Tree 8856

This Is Advertising 18233

This Is an Orchestra 13833

This Is Antarctica 5113

This Is Australia 14924

This Is Cape Kennedy 14925

This Is Espie Sanchez 5149

This Is Historic Britain 14926

This Is Hong Kong 14927

This Is Illinois 12335

This Is Israel 14928

This Is My Father and Me 14167

This Is New York 14929

This Is Ohio 8968

This Is Our Michigan 915

This Is Paris 14930

This Is Pro Basketball 16486

This Is Pro Football 16487

This Is Rome 14931

This Is San Francisco 14932

This Is Texas 14933

This Is the Ambulance Leaving
the Zoo 5671

This Is the Forest 8815

This Is the House Where Jack
Lives 8016

This Is the United Nations 14934

This Land Is Mine 8212

This Man Jesus 12037

This Nation 18225

This Noble Harvest 5043

This Restless Earth 10357

This School Is Driving Me Crazy
8087

This Star Shall Abide 5440

This Stranger, My Son 945

This Street's for Me! 8602

This Time, Tempe Wick? 6675

This Way, Delight 14172

This World of Wonder 1954

Thistle and Thyme 12819

Thomas Alva Edison (Garbedian)
6547

Thomas Alva Edison (Martin) 11760

Thomas and the Warlock 8790

Thomas Book, The 14609

Thomas Jefferson 9433

Thomas Jefferson and His World
12497

Thor 11259

Thor and the Giants 5740

Thor Heyerdahl 1258

Thor Heyerdahl, Viking Scientist
1737

Thornbush Jungle 12371

Those Amazing Computers! 1528

Those Foolish Molboes! 1162

Those Miller Girls! 3979

Those Mysterious UFO's 9936

Those Traver Kids 2065

Thread One to a Star 8604

Threading Beads 14491

Threat to the Barkers 13642

Three Aesop Fox Fables 6508

Three African Tales 14455

Three and the Shape of Three
14168

Three Apples Fell from Heaven
16661

Three Baby Chicks 9174

Three Bears, The 6509

Three Beggar Kings, The 7613

Three Big Hogs, The 13703

Three Billy Goats Gruff, The
(Asbjornsen) 716

Three Billy Goats Gruff, The (Galdone) 6510

Three Boy Scouts in Africa 5035

Three Boys and a Lighthouse 165

Three Brothers of Ur, The 6449

Three Buckets of Daylight 2156

Three by Mistake 13325

Three by Three 10121

3 D, 2 D, 1 D 98

Three Drops of Water 9470

Three Ducks Went Wandering 14729

Three Firecrackers, The 10339

Three Foolish Tales 16931

Three Fools and a Horse 934

Three Funny Friends, The 18620

Three Gay Tales from Grimm 7405

Three Guardsmen and Other Stories from the Apocrypha, The 12131

Three Hundred Ninety-seventh White Elephant 7493

Three-in-One-Car 14909

Three Jovial Huntsmen 9182

Three Kinds of Stubborn 2844

Three Kings of Saba, The 5603

Three Little Chinese Girls, The 10340

Three Little Indians 16423

Three Little Pigs, The (du Bois) 5093

Three Little Pigs, The (Galdone) 6511

Three of a Kind 14324

Three on the Run 1222

Three Policemen, The 5094

Three Poor Tailors 392

Three Princes of Serendip, The 8326

Three Red Herrings, The 17673

Three Rivers South 5303

Three Robbers, The 17139

Three Rolls and One Doughnut 6856

Three Royal Monkeys, The 4690

Three Sides and the Round One 6378

Three Sillies, The 18526

Three Sneezes and Other Swiss Tales, The 5190

Three Sons, The 9561

Three Sorrowful Tales of Erin, The 13671

Three Sparrows and Other Nursery Poems 12448

Three Stalks of Corn 13790

Three Stone Woman 3662

Three Strong Women 16137

Three Tales of Monkey 16938

Three to Get Ready 1845

Three Toymakers, The 18050

Three Trees of the Samurai, The 3717

Three Visitors, The 8606

Three Wars of Billy Joe Treat, The 2157

Three Who Dared 3771

Three Wishes, The (Alegria) 253

Three Wishes (Clifton) 3631

Three Wishes, The (Craig) 4240

Three Wishes, The (Jacobs) 9053

Throme of the Erril of Sherrill, The 11430

Through a Brief Darkness 13452

Through an Opera Glass 6653

Through Black Eyes 5734

Through Eyes of Wonder 2008

Through Five Hundred Years 15011

Through the Line 6692

Through the Locks 2528

Through the Looking Glass and What Alice Found There 3105

Through the Magnifying Glass 15159

Through the Window 9618

Through These Arches 12206

Throwing Shadows 9994

Thruway 14529

Thumbelina 446

Thunder at Gettysburg 6676

Thunder of the Gods 8641

Thunder Road 6693

Thunderbird, The 16849

Thunderbird and Other Stories 3233

Thunderhoof 8364

Thurgood Marshall 5787

Thursday 16386

Thursday's Child 16411

Thy Friend, Obadiah 17062

Ti Jacques 5312

Tia Maria's Garden 3500

Tico and the Golden Wings 10888

Ticonderoga 6704

Tide, The 3137

Tide Treasure Camper 12365

Tides of Danger 7961

Tie-Dyed Paper 11560

Tie Dyeing and Batik 4874

Tienes Tiempo, Lidia? 12750

Tiger, The 15007

Tiger and the Rabbit and Other Tales, The 1374

Tiger Burning Bright 5077

Tiger Called Thomas, A 18621

Tiger!/El Tigre!, The 18042

Tiger Flower 17261

Tiger in the Bush 3313

Tiger in the Teapot, The 18478

Tiger-Lily Years, The 14579

Tiger Nanny 18051

Tiger of Bitter Valley 18475

Tiger Skin Rug, The 14603
Tiger Stripes and Zebra Stripes
11908
Tiger Up a Tree 17145
Tiger Who Wore White Gloves,
The 2310
Tigers and Other Lilies 12510
Tiger's Bones and Other Plays
for Children, The 8735
Tigers in the Woods 2000
Tiger's Tail, The 17273
Tiger's Whisker and Other Tales
and Legends from Asia and
the Pacific, The 4204
Tiguas, The 16218
Tikki Tikki Tembo 12499
Tikta' Liktak 8661
Tilingo! 3091
Tillo 15009
Tilted Sombrero, The 10232
Tim All Alone 626
Tim Mouse and the Major 2300
Tim Mouse Goes Down the Stream
2301
Tim Tadpole and the Great Bull-
frog 5992
Tim, the Peacemaker 6365
Tim to the Rescue 627
Timber! Logging in Michigan
5925
Timber Trade in the Ottawa Val-
ley, The 2178
Time After Time 1529
Time-Ago Lost 7663
Time-Ago Tales of Jahdu, The
7664
Time and Again 5889
Time and Mr. Bass 2861
Time at the Top 13176
Time Cat 274
Time for Courage, A 18304
Time for Flowers, A 16691
Time for Jody 9740
Time for Tenderness, A 3206
Time for Watching, A 12915
Time in Your Life 107
Time Is Day 14727
Time of Anger, The 12968
Time of Fearful Night 17720
Time of Hunting, A 4964
Time of Rosie, The 9201
Time of Terror, A 5248
Time of the Wolves, The 4618
Time of Trial 2728
Time of Trial, Time of Hope 12053
Time of Wonder 11241
Time Piper 8707

Time Sweep 17717
Time to Choose, A (Parker) 13326
Time to Choose, The (Rivkin)
14414
Time to Get Out of the Bath, Shir-
ley 2685
Time to Go House 5270
Time to Keep, A 17035
Time to Laugh 5796
Time to Take Sides 6986
Times They Used to Be, The 3632
Timid Ghost, The 2181
Timid Timothy 18002
Timmy and the Golden Spike 11151
Timmy and the Tin-Can Telephone
2150
Timothy and Madam Mouse 16788
Timothy Eaton 1163
Timothy the Terror 3211
Timothy Turtle 7120
Timothy's Flower 17213
Timothy's Horse 11920
Tim's Last Voyage 628
Tim's Place 5583
Tin Cans 14542
Tin Lizzie 16094
Tina and David 16667
Tinker and the Medicine Men
18198
Tinker Tales 4620
Tino and the Typhoon 9677
Tiny Little House, The 3654
Tiny Seed, The 2932
Tiny Tim Pine 14141
Tip Off 11171
Tippecanoe and Tyler, Too! 18473
Tirra Lirra 14334
Tistou of the Green Fingers see
Tistou of the Green Thumbs
Tistou of the Green Thumbs 5074
Tit for Tat and Other Latvian Folk
Tales 5164
Titania's Lodestone 7656
Titans of the American Stage 15494
Titch 8841
Titeres con Cachiporra 6654
Tituba of Salem Village 13587
Tizz at the Fiesta 1629
To America 17014
To Be a Pioneer 2690
To Be a Slave 10632
To Build a Land 17602
To California by Covered Wagon
16307
To Fight in Silence 18329
To Find a Dinosaur 15641
To Hang a Rebel 17067

To Hilda for Helping 18527
To Katmandu 4959
To Like and Be Liked 15171
To Live a Lie 257
To Look at Any Thing 8603
To Make a Wee Moon 12684
To Market, to Market 16095
To My Son, the Teen-age Driver 5770
To Nowhere and Back 504
To Peril Strait 1353
To Play Man Number One 7696
To Save a Tree 14106
To See or to Walk 2357
To See the World Afresh 12404
To Smoke or Not to Smoke 16760
To Spoil the Sun 14545
To Sunset and Beyond 10444
To Tame a Sister 811
To Tell My People 13799
To the Barricades 15619
To the Bright and Shining Sun 2655
To the Ends of the Universe 763
To the Green Mountains 2862
To the Top of the World 537
To Touch the Sky 5872
To Walk on Two Feet 3995
To Walk the Sky Path 12685
To Yellowstone 11432
Toad 14530
Toad for Tuesday, A 5522
Toad Hunt, The 3318
Toad Is the Emperor's Uncle, The 17331
Toadstools and Such 14805
Tobe 15489
Tobie and the Christmas Bell 18436
Tobogan, El 12996
Toby 17454
Toby, Granny, and George 2158
Today I Am a Ham 13331
Today in Old New York 7590
Today in Old Philadelphia 7591
Today Is Shrew's Day 3088
Todo Mundo Lee 6490
Todos tenemos hermanos pequeños 5542
Together 1326
Together in America 9315
Togo 3037
Tohi 5647
Told in the Twilight 7754
Told Under Spacious Skies 773
Told Under the Blue Umbrella 774
Told Under the Christmas Tree 775
Told Under the City Umbrella 776
Told Under the Green Umbrella 777
Told Under the Magic Umbrella 778
Told Under the Stars and Stripes 779
Toliver's Secret 2077
Tom and Sam 8842
Tom and the Two Handles 8293
Tom Ass or the Second Gift 10396
Tom B. and the Joyful Noise 4420
Tom Edison 7514
Tom Fox and the Apple Pie 17566
Tom in the Middle 420
Tom Sawyer see Adventures of Tom Sawyer
Tom Sawyer, Detective 17086
Tom Seaver 4796
Tom Seaver of the Mets 16488
Tom Sullivan's Adventures in Darkness 6825
Tom Swift and His Electric Rifle 600
Tom Thumb 7406
Tom Thumb's Alphabet 8934
Tom Tichenor's Puppets 16866
Tom Tiddler's Ground 4691
Tom Tit Tot 12751
Tom-Toms in Kotokro 7494
Tom y Jim 10171
Tomahawk Border 16176
Tomahawk Family, The 2971
Tomas Takes Charge 16623
Tomato and Other Fruit Vegetables, The 15311
Tomato Boy 13942
Tombi's Song 15230
Tombs of Atuan, The 10514
Tomfoolery--Trickery and Foolery with Words 15147
Tommy and Dee-Dee 10758
Tommy and Sarah Dress Up 18191
Tommy Goes to the Doctor 18192
Tommy Learns to Fly 10683
Tommy--Soap Box Derby Champion 8986
Tommy's Mommy's Fish 17593
Tomorrow You Can 4152
Tomorrow's Children 764
Tom's Big Fish and Other Stories 6082
Tom's Midnight Garden 13430
Tomten, The 10842
Tomten and the Fox, The 10843
Tongue of Flame 12049

Tongue Tanglers 13851
Tonweya and the Eagles 18386
Tony and Me 15859
Tony's Birds 15312
Tony's First Dive 15587
Tony's Hardwork Day 633
Too Funny for Words 9642
Too Hot for Ice Cream 17214
Too Many Babas 4301
Too Many Rabbits 13301
Too Much Dog 6126
Too Much Garbage 10358
Too Much Noise 11364
Too Much Nose 18520
Too Much Salt and Pepper 2881
Toolbox, The 14522
Toolchest 90
Toolmaker 17482
Tools in Your Life 108
Tools of Modern Biology 1530
Toontoony Pie ... 15653
Toothpaste Millionaire, The 12115
Top Cat of Tam 15628
Top-Flight Fully-Automated Junior
   High School Girl Detective,
   The 8179
Top o' the Tom 3892
Top of the World 16959
Top Secret: Alligators! 7061
Top Step, The 12916
Tops 17881
Tops and Bottoms 3942
Topsy-Turvies, The 574
Topsy-Turvy Emperor of China,
   The 15784
Tor, Wyoming Bighorn 2800
Torn Veil ..., The 8956
Tornado! (Adoff) 136
Tornado (Laffoon) 10186
Tornado Jones 4880
Tornadoes, Killer Storms 10434
Toro Pinto ..., El 14523
Torre, La 410
Torres de celofan 3092
Torrie 9245
Torten's Christmas Secret 4977
Tortoise and the Sword, The
   16644
Tortoise Dreams, The 16388
Tortoise in the Stream and Other
   Stories, The 6083
Tortoise of Koka and Other
   Stories, The 6320
Tortoise Tales 11644
Tortoise's Tug of War, The 11537
Total Turtle, The 14210
Toto 12506

Toto and the Aardvark 10824
Toucans Two and Other Poems
   13890
Touch-and-Go Year, The 13854
Touch of Magic, A (Cavanna) 3207
Touch of Magic (Hickok) 8151
Touchmark, The 10408
Touchstone, The 16298
Tough Chauncey 15883
Tough Enough 3112
Tough Enough's Indians 3113
Tough Jim 3762
Tough to Tackle 3432
Tour on the Prairies, A 8933
Tourney Team 6351
Toussaint, the Black Liberator
   16593
Towappu 16226
Toward Infinity 9925
Toward Peace 13399
Towards a High Attic 17327
Tower of Babel, The 17882
Tower of Baboons, The 2358
Town Cats and Other Tales, The
   275
Town of Hercules, The 4802
Town Rat and Country Rat 6321
Town That Launders Its Water
   16268
Toy Trumpet, The 7365
Toyanuki's Rabbit 7806
Toymaker's Daughter, The 18052
Trabajos del domingo, Los 6557
Trace Through the Forest 14457
Track and Field for Young Champi-
   ons 585
Track Comes to Lonesome Point
   822
Track Watching 17642
Trademark Scandinavia 871
Tradition 5429
Traditional Voice in the Barrio, A
   12665
Trail Blazer of the Seas 10321
Trail Boss in Pigtails 16396
Trail Drive 14707
Trail-Driving Rooster, The 6867
Trail of Apple Blossoms 8751
Trail to the Marked Tree 16546
Trailblazer 13711
Trailblazers in American Arts
   15865
Trails of Tears 18039
Train, The (McPhail) 11498
Train, The (Welber) 17713
Train for Jane, A 9912
Train Ride 16234

Trainful of Strangers, A 8736
Training a Companion Dog 2283
Trains at Work 5394
Traitors, The 6120
Transcontinental Railroad, 1862-69,
The 10311
Transfigured Hart, The 18426
Transport 7-41-R 4800
Transportation in the World of the
Future 8037
Trapp Family Book of Christmas
Songs, The 17547
Trapped 9189
Trappers, Trains, and Mining
Claims 15770
Traveler in Time, A 17178
Travelers All 17636
Traveling Musicians, The 7407
Traveling with Oma 9889
Travelling Magic 1499
Travels in West Africa 9832
Travels of a Raindrop 12814
Travels of Atunga, The 3659
Travels of Colin O'Dae, The 6201
Travels of Monarch X, The 8857
Travels of Ms. Beaver, The 369
Treasure, The 15616
Treasure in Devil's Bay 2330
Treasure Is the Rose, The 4376
Treasure Island 16299
Treasure of Diogenes Sampuez,
The 12562
Treasure of Green Knowe, The
1978
Treasure of Lebna Dengel, The
15555
Treasure of Li-Po, The 14406
Treasure of the Muleteer ...,
The 9235
Treasure of the Sangre de
Cristos 2866
Treasure of Tolmec, The 16326
Treasure of Topo-el-Bampo, The
13016
Treasure on the Johnny Smoker
3900
Treasure Trap, The 11809
Treasure Trove of the Sun, The
13971
Treasured Tales 3163
Treasurer of Darkness, A 15499
Treasures Beyond the Snows 7099
Treasures in the Sea 12658
Treasures of Lin Li-Ti 3323
Treasures of Morrow 8566
Treasures to See 17679
Treasury of Christmas Plays, A

9477
Treasury of Delaware Poetry, A
7688
Treasury of Irish Saints, A 8929
Treasury of Jewish Folklore, A
802
Treasury of Mexican Folkways
16936
Tree, The (Carrick) 3085
Tree, The (Tate) see Tina and
David
Tree for Peter, A 15343
Tree for Tompkins Park, A 16807
Tree House Island 4119
Tree Hurts Too, A 17175
Tree in the Trail 8495
Tree Is a Plant, A 2580
Tree Is Born, A 7470
Tree Is Nice, A 17116
Tree Is Something Wonderful, A
4068
Tree of Freedom, The 3174
Tree of Language, The 10195
Tree on Your Street, A 15761
Tree That Conquered the World,
The 10500
Tree That Stayed Up Until Next
Christmas, The 10070
Tree This Tall, A 14310
Treeful of Pigs 11006
Treeless Plains, The 14708
Trees 18554
Trees and Their World 5810
Trees of Indiana 4762
Trees of Minnesota 12265
Trees Stand Shining, The 9357
Tren que Perdio una Rueda, El
14492
Trenton Pickle Ordinance and Other
Bonehead Legislation, The 8875
Tres Caballeros Altos, Los 4342
Tres niños, dos hombres y un
perro 12453
Tressa 860
Trial Valley 3585
Trick of Light, A 4144
Trick or Treat 15847
Tricks Animals Play 3543
Tricky Peik and Other Picture Tales
7717
Tricky Questions to Fool Your
Friends 17205
Trigger John's Son 14484
Trillium and Toronto Island 5865
Trilogy of Christmas Plays for Chil-
dren, A 13895
Trina's Boxcar 11761

Trip Through a School, A   14720
Triple-Crown Winners (Liss)
   10922
Triple Crown Winners, The
   (Wilding)   17911
Trips   363
Tristan and Iseult   16529
Triumph Clear   1342
Triumph of the Seeing Eye, The
   14008
Triumphs of Fuzzy Fogtop, The
   14602
Trixie and the Tiger   2804
Trojan Horse, The   14209
Troll Music   10990
Trolley Car Family, The   3655
Tropical Africa   4193
Tropical Africa Today   9791
Tropical Fish   18250
Tropical Forest, The   1179
Tropical Rain Forests   6969
Troubadour   4300
Trouble After School   1340
Trouble at Second Base   4226
Trouble for Lucy   16263
Trouble in Form Six   5322
Trouble in the Ark   14604
Trouble in the Jungle   16960
Trouble in the Village   8877
Trouble on Shake-Rag Creek
   8704
Trouble on Treat Street   258
Trouble River   2794
Trouble with Alaric, The   18053
Trouble with Dragons, The
   15265
Trouble with Explosives   9649
Trouble with Francis, The
   11074
Trouble with Jenny's Ear, The
   2756
Trouble with Magic, The   3341
Trouble with Terry, The   10752
Trouble with Thirteen, The
   12176
Trouble with Toby, The   3929
Troubled Summer, The   7537
Troublemaker (Hall)   7608
Troublemaker, The (McKay)   11406
Troubles of Kings, The   15017
Trovato   1623
Truck Drivers   7281
Trucks   18574
Trudel's Siege   225
Trudie and the Milch Cow   8041
True and Untrue ...   17128
True Book of African Animals,

The   13994
True Book of Airports and Air-
   planes, The   10684
True Book of Dinosaurs, The   3516
True Book of Elephants, The   13834
True Book of Indians, The   11770
True Book of Little Eskimos, The
   4092
True Book of Magnets and Electrici-
   ty, The   13762
True Book of Metric Measurement,
   The   1327
True Book of Money, The   5350
True Book of Pets, The   13763
True Book of Pioneers, The   7728
True Book of Rivers, The   2939
True Book of Rodeos, The   5741
True Book of the Mars Landing,
   The   6723
True Book of Time, The   18585
True Book of Toys at Work, The
   10685
True Book of Weather Experiments,
   The   13764
True Grit   13830
True Men, The   16162
True or False?   14732
True Sea Adventures   15985
True Story of Albert Schweitzer,
   Humanitarian, The   12094
True Story of David Livingstone,
   Explorer, The   669
True Story of Gandhi, Man of
   Peace, The   14283
True Tales of the Great Lakes
   2046
Truffle Pig, The   1678
Trumpet of the Swan, The   17794
Trumpeter   562
Trumpeter of Krakow, The   9661
Trumpeter's Tale   5234
Trust a City Kid   8829
Trust Reba   11118
Truth About Drugs, The   801
Truth About Mary Rose, The
   14846
Truth About Stone Hollow, The
   15971
Truth About the Man Behind the
   Book That Sparked the War
   Between the States, The   3186
Truth and Consequences   18468
Truth on Trial   3711
Truthful Harp, The   276
Try and Catch Me   9216
Try It Again, Sam   17323
Tryouts, The   10676

Tsuru no Ongaeshi see Crane Maiden, The
Tuareg, The 1765
Tuck Everlasting 848
Tucker's Countryside 15262
Tuesday Elephant, The 6607
Tugboat 13748
Tugboats 14627
Tugboats Never Sleep 10303
Tuhurahura and the Whale 14524
Tula, la tortuga 13087
Tulip Time 7424
Tumble 4834
Tunde in Trouble 16934
Tunde's Drum 15018
Tune Beyond Us, A 10977
Tune for the Towpath, A 6077
Tunisia 3042
Tunisia in Pictures 11036
Tunnel Builders, The 9663
Tunnel in the Sky 8023
Tunnel of Hugsy Goode, The 5553
Turkey 7003
Turkey Brother and Other Tales 2445
Turkeys, Pilgrims and Indian Corn 1141
Turkish Fairy Tales 5313
Turn the Next Corner 221
Turnabout 17883
Turnabout Year, The 16605
Turning Off 12163
Turning Place, The 9503
Turning Point, The 9506
Turning the World Upside Down 18059
Turnip, The 5001
Turquois 13765
Turquoise Horse, The 8543
Turquoise Treasures 8975
Turtle Pond 6339
Turtles (Darling) 4508
Turtles (Waters) 17561
Turtles and Tortoises 9265
Turtles, Tortoises and Terrapins 7047
Tuscaroras, The 18166
Tusya and the Pot of Gold 18363
Tuttle's Shell 12564
Tutu Maramba 17494
TV and Radio Careers 5803
TV Kid, The 2793
'Twas in the Moon of Wintertime 28
Twelve and the Genii, The see Return of the Twelves, The

Twelve at War 8545
Twelve Bells for Santa 1912
Twelve Clever Brothers and Other Fools, The 6857
Twelve Dancing Princesses 7408
Twelve Days of Christmas, The 9498
Twelve Great Black Cats ... 12820
Twelve Labors of Hercules, The 12795
Twenty and Ten 1679
Twenty-eight Days 5337
Twenty-Elephant Restaurant, The 8294
Twenty Gallant Horses 472
20 Mentires de verdad 15
Twenty Modern Americans 4063
Twenty-One Balloons, The 5095
Twenty-One Children Plus Ten 13178
21 Kinds of American Folk Art and How to Make Each One 9836
27th Annual African Hippopotamus Race, The 11174
Twenty-six Ways to Be Somebody Else 2027
Twenty Thousand Leagues Under the Sea 17287
23 Varieties of Ethnic Art and How to Make Each One 9837
Twenty-Two, Twenty-Three 14129
Twice upon a Time 15427
Twig 9346
Twilight of Magic, The 11026
Twilight Province see Watch Fires to the North
Twin Spell 11173; see also Double Spell
Twins (Cole) 3804
Twins (Williams) 18001
Twins at the Matopo Hills, The 12529
Twins in South Africa 14595
Twins of the Rain Forest, The 17121
Twist, Wiggle and Squirm 13970
Twister of Twists, a Tangler of Tongues, A 15148
'Twixt Twelve and Twenty 1932
Two African Tales 12831
Two Against the Tide 3593
Two and Me Makes Three 7299
Two Blocks Apart 11946
Two Boys and a Soap Box Derby 8987
Two Boys of Baghdad 11095
Two Brothers 15161

Two by Two 16629
Two Centuries of Weapons: 1776–
  1976 3788
Two Children of Troy 9719
Two Faces of Silenus, The 3537
Two Fools and a Faker 15821
Two for Survival 14678
Two Friends, The 11622
Two Giants, The 6111
Two Good Friends 4820
Two Greedy Bears 6858
Two Hundred Rabbits 499
Two If by Sea 5951
Two Is a Line 11519
Two Is a Team 1345
Two Is Company 4821
Two Is Company, Three's a Crowd
  7549
Two Little Bears 18401
Two Little Confederates 13237
Two Logs Crossing 5271
Two Lonely Ducks 5191
Two Magicians, The 10256
Two More Moral Tales 11941
290, The 13017
Two of Them, The 312
Two on an Island 2066
Two Pesos for Catalina 9867
Two Piano Tuners 6978
Two Places to Sleep 15116
Two P's in a Pod 16758
2-Rabbit, 7 Wind 4658
Two Reds 17951
Two Roman Mice 8610
Two Sides of the River 4298
Two Sieges of the Alamo 384
Two Special Cards 10907
Two Stonecutters, The 16893
Two Stories from Africa 213
Two That Were Tough 2605
Two Tickets to Freedom 6244
Two Towers, The 16918
Two Uncles of Pablo, The 1320
Two-Wheel Wonder 10410
Two Worlds of Beatrix Potter,
  The 11923
Two Worlds of Damyan, The
  1783
Two Worlds of Davy Blount 1356
Twyla 17452
Tyger Voyage 56
Tyler, Wilkin and Skee 2606
Tyrannosaurus Game, The 10110
Tyto 6347

- U -

U. S. Grant (Reeder) 14195
U. S. Grant (Stevenson) 16280
U. S. Open Tennis Championship,
  The 11909
USSR, The 3552
UFO's and IFO's 16035
Uganda 3044
Ugly Bird 8295
Ugly Duckling, The 447
Uhu 11200
Ukrainian Folk Tales 1784
Ukrainians in America, The 10143
Ultra Violet Catastrophe! 11557
Ulysses S. Grant (Grant) 7182
Ulysses S. Grant (Olgin) 13080
Ulysses S. Grant (Thomas) 16813
Umbrella, The (Khanganya) 9777
Umbrella (Yashima) 18367
Unbeatable Five, The 4227
Unchosen, The 6814
Uncle Harry 15088
Uncle Mike's Boy 2313
Uncle Misha's Partisans 16450
Uncle Remus 7775
Uncle Robert's Secret 16120
Uncle Tom's Cabin 16397
Under Christopher's Hat 2850
Under the City 10376
Under the Green Willow 3700
Under the Haystack 5442
Under the Shade of the Mulberry
  Tree 4822
Under the Tent of the Sky 2211
Under the Tree 14428
Under the Window 7254
Under This Roof 4439
Under Three Flags 18382
Under 21 5018
Undercover Cat Prowls Again 7071
Underground 11205
Underground Man 12050
Underground Riches 2529
Underground Skipper, The 6694
Underground to Canada 15944
Undergrounders, The 2067
Undersea Base 6298
Underside of the Leaf, The 6979
Understanding Africa 12569
Understanding Animals as Pets
  17199
Understanding Architecture 16489
Understanding Ecology 1649
Understanding Egypt 6645
Understanding Ethiopia 6646

Understanding Liberia 6647
Understanding Photography 16490
Understanding Science 4324
Understanding Sex 7530
Understanding the Law of Our
  Land 15172
Understanding Weather 12203
Understood Betsy 5935
Underwater Dig, The 11772
Underwater Zoos 15313
Undine 10218
Unfinished March, The 5069
Unfortunately Harriet 17734
Unfriendly Book, The 18622
UNICEF and the World 16058
UNICEF's Festival Book 16081
Unicycle Book, The 17930
Unitarians, The 5336
United Nations 5484
United Nations at Work Through-
  out the World, The 10285
United Nations Day 14047
United Nations in War and Peace,
  The 5758
United States Book, The 15581
Universal Sign Language of the
  Plains Indians of North Amer-
  ica 16928
Universe Ahead 5441
Universe Between, The 12961
Unmaking of Rabbit, The 7289
Unstill Life 1449
Unsung Black American Heroes
  and Heroines 16431
Unsung Heroes of Pro Basketball
  8190
Unsung Heroes of the Major
  Leagues 1550
Until the Celebration 15972
Untold Tale, The 7850
Untune the Sky 13747
Unusual Aquarium Fishes 6047
Unusual Automobiles of Today and
  Tomorrow 16134
Up a Road Slowly 8752
Up Above and Down Below 17637
Up and Down the River 10696
Up from El Paso 4876
Up from Never 16030
Up from Slavery 17546
Up from the Ghetto 5072
Up on a Hilltop 16645
Up Periscope 17812
Up the Alley with Jack and Joe
  10009
Up the Big Mountain 9955
Up the Hill 4642

Up the Pier 4286
Up the Trail from Texas 4937
Up-to-Date Biography of Henry
  Aaron, The 8243
Upper Volta 3038
Uproar, The 13168
Ups and Downs 17912
Ups and Downs of Drugs, The
  5338
Ups and Downs of Jorie Jenkins
  1173
Ups and Downs of Marvin, The
  7966
Upside Down and Inside Out 9518
Upside Down Day 15028
Upstairs Room, The 14224
Upstate, Downstate 9105
Uptown 16235
Urban Blues 9620
Us Maltbys 12000
Use Your Brain 15603
Usha, the Mouse Maiden 6943
Ut y las estrellas 12327
Utah Indian Stories 8778
Utah Lion 9285
Uttam, a Boy of India 15084

- V -

VD: The Silent Epidemic 8872
V.I.P. 7324
Vaccination and You 3752
Valentine Box, The 11107
Valentine Cat, The 2581
Valentine Fantasy, A 7958
Valentine for Cindy 4355
Valentine Party, The 1631
Valentine's Day 7473
Valerie Harper 9076
Valiant Chattee-Maker, The 13922
Valiant Companions 17416
Valiant Few, The 16880
Valley Grows Up, A 13194
Valley of the Crooked Rocks 11091
Valley of the Dead ..., The 11601
Valley of the Hawk 11054
Valley of the Shadow, The 8146
Valley of the Smallest 5926
Valleys 6970
Vampires and Other Ghosts 836
Vanishing Giants 15670
Vaquero Pequeño 10591
Varenka 1561

Varnell Roberts, Super Pigeon 7213

Vasco da Gama, Sailor Toward the Sunrise 16594

Vasilisa the Beautiful 17841

Vatican, The 4774

Veckor over Tiden, The see Mia Alone

Vegetables in Patches and Pots 12267

Velvet Room, The 15973

Velveteen Rabbit, The 18043

Vem Ska Trosta Knyttet? 9146; see also Who Will Comfort Toffle?

Vendetta 4768

Vengeance of the Zulu King 15231

Venn Diagrams 6406

Ventriloquism 8862

Venture for Freedom 18483

Vermilion Clay 16679

Veronica 5192

Veronica Ganz 14847

Verrazano 16595

Verses for Children 17251

Verses on Nigerian State Capitals 17252

Versitos para chiquitines 9225

Versos tradicionales para los cebollitas 17495

Very Far Away from Anywhere Else 10515

Very First Story Ever Told, The 17659

Very Hungry Caterpillar, The 2933

Very Important People Behind the Scene in Medical Work 6272

Very Important People in Food Services 6273

Very Important People in Maintenance Services 6274

Very Important People in Personal and Protective Services 6275

Very Important People on the Backup Team in Medical Work 6276

Very Important People on the Scene in Medical Work 6277

Very Important People Who Carry Messages 6278

Very Important People Who Print and Publish 6279

Very Important People Who Work with Cars, Buses, and Trucks 6280

Very Important People Who Work with Farm and Earth-moving Machines 6281

Very Important People Who Work with Recreation Vehicles 6282

Very Important People Who Work with Sight and Sound 6283

Very Little Boy, The 10043

Very Little Girl, The 10044

Very Long Tail, A 2934

Very Long Way from Anywhere Else see Very Far Away from Anywhere Else

Very Special Badgers, The 16138

Very Special House, A 10081

Very Tall Little Girl, The 421

Very Worst Thing, The 10045

Very Young Circus Flyer, A 10086

Very Young Dancer, A 10087

Very Young Rider, A 10088

Very Young Skater, A 10089

Very Young Verses 6715

Veterinarian 16418

Viaduct, The 2428

Viaje a la luna y otros cuentos, Un 14865

Viaje de Babar, El 4647

Viaje de nunca acabar, El 13234

Vicki 12136

Vicksburg Veteran, The 12352

Vicky Barnes, Junior Hospital Volunteer 3882

Victor 6493

Victoria 17460

Victoria-Bess and Others see Victorian Doll Stories

Victorian Doll Stories 812

Victorian Parlor Games 1286

Victory at Le Mans 3546

Victory Drum, The 12885

Victory Volley 8861

Vida Blue 10011

Vida de perros 7030

Viento y Daniel, El 14853

Viet Nam 3534

Vietnamese Revolution, The 7024

View from the Cherry Tree, The 14437

View from the Oak, The 9959

Vigilantism in America 11524

Viking Adventure 2582

Viking Dawn 16987

Vikings Bold 3129

Vikings of the West 8479

Viking's Sunset 16988

Village That Allah Forgot, The

10983

Village That Learned to Read, The 16658

Village Tree, The 18368

Vim the Rag Mouse 4468

Vince Lombardi (Etter) 5574

Vince Lombardi (Zalewski) 18492

Viola Hates Music 15041

Violet Tree, The 13742

Violin, The (Allen) 353

Violin, The (Ballantine) 1029

Violin and Its Masters, The 3267

Violin Book, The 1531

Violins and Shovels 12051

Viollet 4377

Virgil I. Grissom 3271

Virginia Dare 16281

Viruses 12962

Visionary Girls, The 16152

Visit from St. Nicholas, A see Night Before Christmas, The

Visit to a Chief's Son, A 7635

Visit to the Dentist, A 6611

Visit to the Doctor, A 1508

Visit to the Hospital, A 3297

Visit to Zululand, A 8978

Visit with Rosalind, A 15479

Visiting American Caves 15835

Visitor, The 13821

Visitors, The 16961

VISTA 17844

Vitamin Puzzle, The 17707

Vitamins 12963

Viva Chicano 1896

Viva Morelia 17305

Vixie 6173

Vodnik 18504

Voice of the Children, The 9382

Voice of the Great Elephant, The 15232

Voices from the Southwest 1563

Voices in the Fog 17507

Voices of Joy, Voices of Free-dom 4960

Voices of the Rainbow 14611

Voici Henri 9457

Volcano 2530

Voyage of Osiris, The 11294

Voyage of the Dawn Treader, The 10694

Voyage of the Floating Bed-stead, The 3246

Voyages of Doctor Dolittle, The 11027

Voyageurs, The 389

Voyaging to Cathay 16640

Vuelta al camino, La 6550

Vulpes, the Red Fox 6753

Vulture! Vulture! 16534

- W -

W. E. B. DuBois 7665

Wa O'Ka 10322

Wabash Knows the Secret, The 6363

Wacheera, Child of Africa 3376

Wacky Wednesday 10621

Wagon Wheels to Denver 11314

Wagonmen, The 8679

Wahoo Bobcat, The 10896

Wait for William 5993

Wait Till the Moon Is Full 2400

Waiting for Cherries 8208

Waiting for Mama 12507

Wakaima and the Clay Man ... 9467

Wake Up and Good Night 18623

Wake Up and Open Your Eyes 12539

Wake Up, City! 17008

Wake Up, Farm! 17009

Wake Up, Jeremiah 8210

Wake Up, Rodney! 7371

Walk a Mile and Get Nowhere 16042

Walk a Narrow Bridge 5858

Walk a Rocky Road 10409

Walk Home Tired, Billy Jenkins 16818

Walk in Beauty 1840

Walk in My Moccasins 17540

Walk in Space 7509

Walk in the Forest, A 10923

Walk in the Neighborhood, A 1328

Walk in the Sky 8947

Walk in the Snow 2741

Walk On! 18056

Walk Out of the World, A 12822

Walk the World's Rim 935

Walk Together 8044

Walk Together Children 2460

Walkabout 11715

Walking Away 18132

Walking Calabash ..., The 13221

Walking Catfish and Other Aliens 14682

Walking Stones, The 8791

Walking Through the Dark 12686

Wallpaper 364

Walls Are to Be Walked 18579

Walls of Windy Troy, The 2168
Walt and Pepper 17660
Walt Disney (Hammontree) 7674
Walt Disney (Montgomery)
 12366
Walt Disney's Bambi Gets Lost
 12214
Walter 12965
Walter Cronkite 16700
Walter in Love 17776
Walter Reed 7440
Walter the Baker 2935
Walter the Lazy Mouse 5994
Walter the Wolf 15480
Walter Was a Frog 11806
Waltzing Matilda 13361
Wampum 12338
Wanderers, The 3701
Wandering Knight, The 15057
Wapiti, The 4168
Wapootin 563
War and Weapons 12656
War Chief of the Seminoles 11479
War Eagle 10851
War for the Lot 10264
War of 1812 11852
War on the Darnel 17073
War Paint and Wagon Wheels
 14621
War with the Seminoles 9360
War Work 13128
Warlock of Westfall, The 5952
Warlord of the Gengi 2953
Warm Up for Little League Base-
 ball 15570
Warm Up for Soccer 10215
Warmint, The 4692
Warrior for a Lost Nation 9253
Warrior Goddess 6664
Warrior with Wings 8972
Warriors and Worthies 12827
Wart Snake in a Fig Tree, A
 12073
Warton and Morton 5523
Warton and the Traders 5524
Warton's Christmas Eve Adven-
 ture 5525
Was It a Good Trade? 4748
Washday 12117
Washington, D.C. 15901
Washington's Birthday 2583
Watch Fires to the North 5877
Watch Me Indoors 9175
Watch Me Outdoors 9176
Watch Out for the Chicken Feet
 in Your Soup 4728
Watch Out, It's Poison Ivy!

10817
Watch Those Red Wheels Roll 14247
Watcher in the Woods, A 14103
Watcher on the Heights, The 4853
Watchers, The (Curry) 4406
Watchers, The (Rinkoff) 14395
Watching the New Baby 14874
Watching the Wild Apes 9768
Watching Them Grow 8138
Water Babies 9831
Water Buffalo Children and the
 Dragon Fish, The 2492
Water for Dinosaurs and You 6542
Water on Your Street 15762
Water Plants 8405
Water Pollution 10435
Water Rat 13036
Water: Riches or Ruin 1189
Water Sprite of the Golden Town,
 The 14041
Water We Drink!, The 1791
Water Wheels and Millstones 6548
Waterless Mountain 638
Watermelons, Walnuts, and the Wis-
 dom of Allah ... 17436
Watership Down 57
Waterskiing 2037
Watersnake, The 6340
Wave, The 8336
Waves 18555
Waves, Tides and Currents 3598
Way Down Yonder on Troublesome
 Creek 16316
Way Home, The 13643
Way It All Began, The 17649
Way It Was: 1876, The 8207
Way Mothers Are, The 15074
Way of Danger, The 15352
Way of Knowing, A 11306
Way of Our People, The 7362
Way Our People Lived, The 18252
Way Things Are ..., The 10978
Way to Go, Teddy! 8533
Way We Lived, The 14900
Way with Boys, A 14721
Wayah of the Real People 16177
Wayfarer's Tree, The 3891
Ways of Nesting Birds, The 8441
Waza Winds at Windy Gulch 3732
We Alcotts 5932
We All Come from Puerto Rico, Too
 15789
We All Come from Someplace 15790
We Are Chicano 1811
We Are Having a Baby 8481
We Came Rejoicing 9040
We Can Teach You to Play Soccer

12586

We Dickinsons 5933

We Have Not Vanished 16638

We Hide, You Seek 700

We Interrupt This Semester for an Important Bulletin 3940

We Like Bugs 3961

We Live in the City 10592

We Live in the North 10593

We Live in the South 10594

We Lived in the Almont 3656

We Made It Through the Winter 13119

We Never Get to Do Anything 289

We Reach the Moon 17931

We Read: A to Z 4296

We Rode the Wind 9520

We Shall Live in Peace 7797

We Three Kings 11485

We Too Belong 17069

We Walk in Sandy Places 1243

We Want Sunshine in Our Houses 2949

We Went Looking 5927

We Were There at the Alamo 4212

We Were There at the Battle for Bataan 587

We Were There at the Opening of the Erie Canal 11995

We Were There on the Chisholm Trail 16701

We Were There on the Santa Fe Trail 16702

We Were Tired of Living in a House 15817

We Will Be Heard 17684

Weasels, Otters, Skunks, and Their Family 13359

Weather (May) 11910

Weather (Ryan) 14824

Weather All Around 13692

Weather and Climate 15763

Weather Changes Man, The 2009

Weather Instruments 16135

Weather or Not 4962

Weathermaker, The 2010

Weathermonger, The 4896

Weaver of Dreams 17328

Weaving 9667

Web in the Grass, The 6341

Wedding Procession of the Rag Doll ..., The 14887

Wednesday Witch, The 3342

Wee Gillis 10460

Wee Joseph 11417

Weed Is a Flower, A 313

Week in Amy's World, A 11210

Week in Aya's World, A 1570

Week in Bico's World, A 14237

Week in Henry's World, A 11211

Week in Lateef's World 18624

Week in Robert's World, A 14433

Week in Windley's World, A 11185

Weekend, The 14564

Weighing and Balancing 16109

Weight and Weightlessness 2151

Weird and Wacky Inventions 12571

Weirdstone of Brisingamen, The 6617

Welcome Child 2493

Welcome Christmas 5229

Welcome Roberto! /Bienvenido, Roberto! 15345

Welcome to England 6379

Well Done 12476

We'll Have a Friend for Lunch 6078

Well Met by Witchlight 1246

Welsh Legends and Folk Tales 9350

Wembi, the Singer of Stories 3712

Wendy Well and Billy Better and the Hospital See-Through Machine 17740

Wendy Well and Billy Better Ask a "Mill-Yun" Hospital Questions 17737

Wendy Well and Billy Better Meet the Hospital Sandman 17738

Wendy Well and Billy Better Say "Hello Hospital!" 17739

We're Very Good Friends, My Brother and I 7626

Were-Wolves and Will-o-the-Wisps 7425

Werefox, The see Pure Magic

Werewolves 6577

Wes Powell 17853

Wesley Paul, Marathon Runner 6087

West African Folk-Tales 1077

West African Folk Tales Book I 17290

West African Folk Tales Book II 17291

West African Folktales 4434

West from Home 17910

West Indian Folk-Tales 15546

West Indies, The 3131

West Point 3789

West with the White Chiefs 7768

Western Africa 3553

Western Outlaws (Rennert) 14252

Western Outlaws (Surge) 16515

Westward Adventure 16178

Westward by Canal 6202
Westward with American Explorers 2531
Wet and Sandy Day, A 14832
Wet Monday, A 5277
Wetlands 2473
Whale People, The 7565
Whaleboat Raid 2631
Whales (Hoke) 8423
Whales (McNulty) 11489
Whales (Pluckrose) 13751
Whales (Watson) 17579
Whales Go By, The 13647
Whales to See The 16550
Whaling Boy 6344
Whang Doodle, The 4186
Wharf Rat 12193
What a Baseball Manager Does 8559
What a Funny Thing to Say 9979
What-a-Mess the Good 12542
What? A Riddle Book 14920
What a State Governor Does 8556
What a United States Senator Does 8557
What a Wonderful Bird the Frog Are 10979
What About Me? (Evenhuis) 5601
What About Me? (Rodowsky) 14550
What About the Wankel Engine? 4120
What About Tomorrow? 16043
What Are We Going to Do, Michael? 2642
What Are You Up to, William Thomas? 12809
What Boys Want to Know About Girls 8636
What Can I Do Today? 9916
What Can Money Do? 1107
What Can She Be? A Farmer 7007
What Can She Be? A Geologist 7008
What Can She Be? A Lawyer 7009
What Can She Be? A Musician 7010
What Can She Be? A News-caster 7011
What Can She Be? A Police Officer 7012
What Can She Be? A Veterinarian 7013

What Can She Be? An Architect 7014
What Can You Do Without a Place to Play? 8260
What Can You Make of It? 2104
What Did the Dinosaurs Eat? 14664
What Did the Rock Say? 14648
What Did You Bring Me? 10164
What Did You Do When You Were a Kid? 16432
What Do Animals Eat? 7451
What Do I Do? 15731
What Do I Say? 15732
What Do I Say? / ¿Que Digo? 15733
What Do People Do All Day? 14998
What Do the Animals Say? 15805
What Do You Do with a Kangaroo? 11942
What Do You Mean by Average? 9112
What Do You Say? see Que Dices?
What Do You Say, Dear? 9400
What Do You See? 5002
What Do You Think I Saw? 14978
What Do You Want to Know? 8667
What Do You Want to Know About Guppies? 15764
What Does a Barometer Do? 4209
What Does a Coast Guardsman Do? 3913
What Does a Congressman Do? 10377
What Does a Geologist Do? 6086
What Does a Librarian Do? 2735
What Does a Paramedic Do? 13486
What Does a Photographer Do? 12088
What Does a Test Pilot Do? 17726
What Does a Witch Need? 4807
What Does an Airline Crew Do? 14156
What Does an Oceanographer Do? 17562
What Ever Happened to the Baxter Place? 14657
What Ever You Want 11020
What Every Kid Should Know 9466
What Floats? 2206
What Folk Music Is All About 1930
What Good Is a Weed? 18313
What Happened in Hamelin 15822
What Happened in Marston 6578
What Happens at a Television Station 15507
What Happens If? 18340
What Happens to a Hamburger 15604

What Happens to Garbage? 1253
What Happens When You Build
a House 15508
What Happens When You Go to
the Hospital 15509
What Harry Found When He Lost
Archie 1502
What Have I Got? 11232
What Holds It Together 17702
What I Like About Toads 7890
What I Want to Be When I Grow
Up 2667
What If ...? 11119
What If a Lion Eats Me and I
Fall into a Hippopotamus' Mud
Hole? 7695
What Indian Is It? 13709
What Is a Birthday Child? 9177
What Is a Fruit? 4625
What Is a Man? 10025
What Is a Masterpiece? 17963
What Is a Migrant? 16680
What Is a Shadow? 14361
What Is an Inch? 9903
What Is an Insect? 4626
What Is Black? 936
What Is Bowling? 14149
What Is Electronic Communication?
13835
What Is Fear? 14620
What Is Golf? 14150
What Is It? 11083
What Is It For? 8745
What Is New? 14733
What Is Papa Up to Now? 2001
What Is Pink? 14669
What Is Symmetry? 15802
What Is That Alligator Saying?
7452
What Is That Sound? 13133
What It's All About (Frolov)
6397
What It's All About (Klein) 9913
What Jazz Is All About 5528
What Kind of Bird Is That? 6859
What Little Anna Saved 14882
What Made Me? 7652
What Made You You? 1439
What Makes a Boat Float? 4121
What Makes a Car Go? 4122
What Makes a Light Go On? 4123
What Makes a Plane Fly? 4124
What Makes a Telephone Work?
4513
What Makes an Orchestra? 1017
What Makes Day and Night 2152
What Makes It Go? 9532

What Makes Me Feel This Way?
10619
What Makes the Sun Shine? 765
What Makes TV Work? 4125
What Mary Jo Shared 17117
What Mary Jo Wanted 17118
What Really Happened to the Dino-
saurs? 3753
What Sadie Sang 14309
What Shall We Do and Allee Galloo!
18120
What the Moon Astronauts Do 8191
What the Moon Astronauts Will Do
All Day see What the Moon
Astronauts Do
What the Neighbors Did ... 13431
What the President of the United
States Does 8558
What the Wind Told 1846
What the Witch Left 3343
What Then, Ramon? 681
What Time Is It, Jeanne-Marie?
6217
What to Do When There's No One
but You 7078
What Was It Like? 3986
What We Eat 9293
What We Find When We Look at Maps
13083
What Whiskers Did 3107
What Would We See? 9324
What Would You Do? 2808
What You Should Know About
Drugs 7082
What You Should Know About Drugs
and Drug Abuse 7257
What's a Ghost Going to Do? 16789
What's Fun Without a Friend? 8965
What's Going on in Space 8050
What's Going to Happen to Me?
1596
What's Good for a Three-Year-Old?
3822
What's Happening to Me? 10617
What's Hatching out of That Egg?
10359
What's in a Map? 3138
What's in a Word? 6626
What's in the Dark? 12059
What's in the Names of Birds 10818
What's in the Names of Wild Animals
10819
What's Inside? 8746
What's Inside of Animals? 18556
What's Inside of Engines? 18557
What's Inside of Me? 18558
What's Inside the Earth? 18559

What's New, Lincoln? 5859
What's the Big Idea, Ben Frank-
lin? 6391
What's the Matter with Car-
ruthers? 11716
What's the Matter with Wakefield?
15580
What's the Prize, Lincoln? 5860
What's This About Pete? 16495
What's Wrong with Being a Skunk?
15075
What's Wrong with Julio? 13179
Wheat Won't Wait 12652
Wheel of a Fast Car 2774
Wheel on the Chimney 2401
Wheel on the School, The 4682
Wheels (Miller) 12232
Wheels (Tunis) 17045
Wheels for Ginny's Chariot 11162
Wheels for Kids 12674
Wheels of the Bus Go Round and
Round 10283
When a Boy Wakes Up in the
Morning 11490
When Air Moves 6299
When Americans Came to New Or-
leans 3187
When an Animal Grows 15314
When Animals Are Babies 15153
When Buffalo Run 7427
When Carlos Closed the Street
11617
When Chicago Was Young 11218
When Clay Sings 1244
When Cowboys Rode the Chisholm
Trail 11219
When Coyote Walked the Earth
14765
When Everyone Was Fast Asleep
4729
When Grandfather Journeys into
Winter 16416
When Grandpa Wore Knickers
2346
When Hitler Stole Pink Rabbit
9731
When I First Came to This Land
2096
When I Go to the Moon 10697
When I Have a Little Girl 18625
When I Have a Son 18626
When Insects Are Babies 3962
When It Flooded the Elementary
School 18383
When Jays Fly to Barbmo 996
When Light Turns into Night 5060
When Lightning Strikes 5382

When Lucy Went Away 14649
When Marnie Was There 14474
When Mountain Men Trapped Beaver
6896
When Nantucket Men Went Whaling
11996
When Our Country Was Young
10538
When People Die 1573
When Pictures Began to Move 11589
When Rebels Rode 8713
When Shlemiel Went to Warsaw ...
15785
When Shoes Eat Socks 9920
When Sparks Fly Upward 4504
When the Corn Is Red 15578
When the Dinosaurs Disappeared
4578
When the Drum Sang 14525
When the Land Lay Waste see
Days of Courage
When the Legends Die 1955
When the Monkeys Wore Sombreros
13943
When the Moon Is New 1062
When the Pines Grew Tall 11538
When the Porcupine Moved In 555
When the Railroad Was King 5364
When the Rattlesnake Sounds 3375
When the Sad One Comes to Stay
8007
When the Sirens Wailed 16412
When the Sky Is Like Lace 8640
When the Stones Were Soft 7979
When the Tide Goes Far Out 12254
When the Whale Came to My Town
18449
When the Wild Ducks Come 3382
When the Wind Blew 2402
When the Wind Stops 18627
When the World Was Rome 2316
When the World's on Fire 5286
When Thunders Spoke 15950
When Violet Died 9489
When Wagon Trains Rolled to Santa
Fe 1589
When Walls Are High 7654
When Water Animals Are Babies
15154
When We Go to Market 14359
When We Were Very Young 12249
When Will I Read? 3763
When Willy Went to the Wedding
9732
When Windwagon Smith Came to
Westport 11548
When Winter Comes 6165

When You Find a Rock   9887
When You Go to the Zoo   1803
Where Animals Live   11659
Where Are the Mothers?   11682
Where Are You Going with That Coal?   5031
Where Are You Going with That Energy?   5032
Where Are You Going with That Oil?   5033
Where Can an Elephant Hide?   11499
Where Continents Meet   10213
Where Did I Come From?   11947
Where Did My Mother Go?   13903
Where Did You Come From?   9957
Where Do Babies Come From?   15527
Where Do Bears Sleep?   7967
Where Do I Belong?   4241
Where Do Insects Go in Winter?   12276
Where Does All That Smoke Come From?   14883
Where Does Everyone Go?   5928
Where Does the Butterfly Go When It Rains?   6597
Where Does the Day Go?   12614
Where Does the Garbage Go?   15605
Where Does the Summer Go?   7067
Where Does the Teacher Live?   5746
Where Freedom Grew   16427
Where Have You Been?   2403
Where Is Daddy?   6972
Where Is It?   8305
Where Is My Friend?   11535
Where Is Whiffen?   9178
Where the Good Luck Was   12324
Where the Leopard Passes   5362
Where the Lilies Bloom   3586
Where the Ohio Flows   4325
Where the People Are   6700
Where the Red Fern Grows   14155
Where the Road Ends   5373
Where the Saints Have Trod   16113
Where the Sidewalk Ends   15703
Where the Trees Never End   16336
Where the Turnpike Starts   3063
Where the Wild Things Are   15337
Where the Wind Blows Free   9348
Where They Go in Winter   2479
Where Time Stood Still   14426

Where to Go and What to Do with the Kids in Detroit   9646
Where Was Patrick Henry on the 29th of May?   6392
Where Were You That Year?   16399
Where's Aggie?   5537
Where's Al?   1152
Where's Florrie?   3742
Where's Gomer?   5672
Where's the Bunny?   3108
Where's Wallace?   9940
Which Is the Best Place?   6860
Which Is the Witch?   17580
Which Is Which?   14806
Which Was Witch?   9219
Whichaway   16551
While Mrs. Coverlet Was Away   12644
While Shepherds Watched   17191
While Susie Sleeps   15098
While the Horses Galloped to London   17610
Whim-Wham Book, The   5434
Whingdingdilly, The   13477
Whirling Rainbows   16759
Whirlwind Is a Ghost Dancing   1383
Whiskers of HoHo, The   10949
Whisper of Glocken, The   9680
Whispering House, The   7557
Whispering in the Reeds   10813
Whispering Knights, The   10959
Whispering Mountain, The   192
Whispering Trees   9727
Whispering Wind, The   357
Whispers and Other Poems   10980
Whistle for Willie   9608
Whistle in the Graveyard   10452
Whistle Up the Bay   16376
Whistling Boy, The   692
Whistling Whirligig, The   15520
White Archer   8662
White Bird   2584
White Boy   11655
White Bungalow, The   16012
White Calf, The   5730
White Cap for Rechinda   17353
White Captives   10233
White Cat, The   10474
White Deer, The   16858
White Fang   11042
White Harvest   17509
White Heron, A   9220
White Horse, The (Coatsworth)   3702
White Horse, The (Hurd)   8816
White Horse (U.S. Bureau of Indian Affairs)   17173

White Horse Gang, The 1223
White Horse of Morocco, The see
  White Horse, The (Coatsworth)
White House, The 10540
White Indian Boy, The 18072
White Land, The 2236
White Lark, The 17063
White Marble, The 18628
White Monkey King 18297
White Mountains, The 3411
White Palace, The 13134
White Rat's Tale, The 15058
White Shadow, The 7495
White Shell Horse 564
White Snow, Bright Snow 17010
White Sparrow, The 2429
White Stag, The 15344
White Stallion of Lipizza 8078
White Stone, The 10826
White Twilight, The 13800
White Water, Still Water 1980
White Wave 18214
White Witch Doctor 16327
White Witch of Kynance 2845
Whitepaws 6174
Whitewater Challenge 12313
Whitey and the Colt-Killer 14709
Whitey and the Wild Horse 14710
Whitey Ropes and Rides 14711
Whitney Young, Jr., Crusader
  for Equality 11618
Whizz! Six Limericks 10470
Who Am I? 1329
Who Built the Bridge? 1169
Who Cares About Espie Sanchez?
  5150
Who Comes to King's Mountain?
  1266
Who Discovered America? 10360
Who Found America? 9316
Who Goes Next? 385
Who Goes There? 10323
Who Goes There, Lincoln? 5861
Who Has Poisoned the Sea? 4096
Who I Am 10633
Who Is Victoria? 5538
Who Keeps America Clean? 16209
Who Knows? 8573
Who Likes It Hot? 6598
Who Lives in This House? 1802
Who Look at Me? 9381
Who Needs Alligators? 10361
Who Owns a River? 72
Who Owns the Moon? 10666
Who Puts the Plane in the Air?
  424
Who Really Invented the Sub-

marine? 18335
Who Really Killed Cock Robin?
  6750
Who Rides in the Dark? 11985
Who, Said Sue, Said Whoo? 14130
Who Says So? 8049
Who Says You Can't 5483
Who Shall Pay? 10927
Who Speaks for the Negro? 17542
Who Took the Farmer's Hat? 12866
Who Walks the Attic? 1063
Who Wants a Cheap Rhinoceros?
  15704
Who Wants to Be a Prairie Dog?
  3501
Who Wants to Be Alone? 4243
Who Will Be My Friends? 8365
Who Will Clean the Air? 13504
Who Will Wash the River? 13170
Whole World of Cooking, A 15436
Whoppers 15149
Who's a Pest? 1913
Who's Afraid? Not You 5104
Who's Calling 17375
Who's in Charge of Lincoln? 5862
Who's in Rabbit's House? 9
Who's Seen the Scissors? 10026
Who's That Stepping on Plymouth
  Rock? 6393
Whose Eye Am I? 1914
Whose Mouse Are You? 10071
Whose Nose Is This? 17203
Whose Town? 7140
Whose Tree House? 3155
Wht's Yr Nm? 16685
Why a Donkey Was Chosen 7330
Why Am I Different? 15734
Why Are There More Questions
  Than Answers, Grandad? 11550
Why Birds Migrate 11911
Why Can't I? 1440
Why Can't I Be William? 3941
Why Couldn't I Be an Only Kid Like
  You, Wigger? 7968
Why Did He Die? 7759
Why Did They Name It? 2875
Why Don't You Get a Horse, Sam
  Adams? 6394
Why Frogs Are Wet 7891
Why Glasses? 14905
Why I Built the Boogle House 13261
Why Me? 2110
Why Mosquitoes Buzz in People's
  Ears 10
Why Noah Chose the Dove 15786
Why Not Join the Giraffes? 2877
Why People Are Different Colors

11912

Why So Much Noise? 5003

Why So Stories 13052

Why the Chimes Rang and Other Stories 230

Why the Chinese Are the Way They Are 588

Why the Earth Quakes 11913

Why the Jackal Won't Speak to the Hedgehog 1607

Why the North Star Stands Still 13266

Why the Pig Scratches the Ground 13050

Why the Sky Is Far Away 6771

Why the Spider Lives in Corners 16340

Why the Sun and the Moon Live in the Sky 4628

Why the Sun Was Late 5351

Why the Tides Ebb and Flow 2012

Why the Wind God Wept 16894

Why There Are So Many Roads 595

Why Things Work 1441

Why We Do What We Do 7588

Why We Live Where We Live 5584

Why Worry? 9810

Why You Feel Hot, Why You Feel Cold 1593

Why You Look Like You, Whereas I Tend to Look Like Me 13811

Why You Say It 6627

Whys and Wherefores of Littabelle Lee, The 3587

Wicked City, The 15787

Wicked Enchantment, The 1394

Wicked Wizard and the Wicked Witch, The 10518

Widdecombe Fair 13923

Wide-Awake Jake 18446

Wide Horizon 5514

Wide World Weather 12675

Wiggle to the Laundromat 10482

Wigwam Evening 5220

Wigwam in the City see Susan

Wigwam Stories 4987

Wiki of Walpi 15933

Wilbur and Orville Wright 16282

Wild and Woolly Mammoths 314

Wild Animal Rescue! 13022

Wild Animals and Their Babies 13607

Wild Animals of the Southwest 6225

Wild Babies 2083

Wild Bill Hickok (Anderson) 451

Wild Bill Hickok (Garst) 6640

Wild Bill Hickok Tames the West 8436

Wild Bill Hicup's Riddle Book 1669

Wild Boy (Fall) 5654

Wild Boy (Tate) 16668

Wild Burro Rescue 10628

Wild Cats 1934

Wild Cats of Rome, The 4067

Wild Colt 14828

Wild Cousins of the Horse 8586

Wild Dogs Three 6175

Wild Donahues, The 6364

Wild Flowers 5845

Wild Flowers of Ohio and Adjacent States 9896

Wild Geese Calling 12573

Wild Goose Tale, A 6477

Wild Green Things in the City 5044

Wild Heart, The 7379

Wild Horse Killers, The 5383

Wild Horse of Santander, The 7380

Wild Horse Running 14952

Wild Horse Trap, The 17790

Wild Horses of the Red Desert 14712

Wild Hunt of the Ghost Hounds, The 10960

Wild Hunter 14107

Wild in the World 5011

Wild Inside, The 367

Wild Jack 3412

Wild Mouse 2084

Wild Oats of Han, The 13935

Wild One, The 3607

Wild Orphan Babies 17640

Wild Robin 9183

Wild Season 5249

Wild Swans, The 448

Wild Turkeys 11914

Wild Washerwomen, The 18394

Wild Wheels 11404

Wild Willie, Wide Receiver 6695

Wild Wing 4842

Wild Young Desert, The 788

Wildcat Furs to China 2984

Wildcat Under Glass 18509

Wilderness Adventure 13731

Wilderness Bride 9246

Wilderness Champion 10897

Wilderness Has Ears, The 17721

Wilderness Journey 16179

Wilderness Mission 7919

Wilderness Pioneer 8344

Wilderness Tattoo, The 16180

Wilderness Venture 8674
Wilderness Way, The 350
Wilderness Wife 4660
Wilderness Writers 13792
Wildest Horse Race in the World,
    The 8079
Wildfire 17182
Wildflowers of Louisiana and Ad-
    joining States 2337
Wildlife 7796
Wildlife and Plants of the South-
    ern Rocky Mountains 18402
Wildlife at Your Doorstep 14713
Wildlife in the City 11915
Wildlife Mysteries 8442
Wildlife of Africa, The 709
Wildlife of South America, The
    15642
Wildlife of the Southern Rocky
    Mountains see Wildlife and
    Plants of the Southern Rocky
    Mountains
Wildwing 5521
Wiley and the Hairy Man 1048
Wilfred the Rat 16290
Wilkin's Tooth see Witch's Busi-
    ness
Will and Charlie Mayo 7675
Will I Go to Heaven? 11948
Will I Have a Friend? 3764
Will It Be Okay? 5061
Will Rogers 4623
Will Rogers: The Boy Roper 4624
Will the Real Monday Please Stand
    Up 14278
Will the Real Tommy Wilson Please
    Stand Up? 8634
Will There Never Be a Prince?
    14624
Will to Be Free, The 17991
Will You Be My Friend? 8966
Will You Carry Me? 3256
Will You Sign Here, John Han-
    cock? 6395
Willa 6203
Willa Cather (Bonham) 1886
Willa Cather (Slote) 15860
Willaby 8937
William 8753
William and Mary 5700
William, Andy, and Ramon 2503
William Barret Travis 11220
William Beebe 1738
William Beltz 18200
William Berczy 2686
William Blake 1718
William Bradford of Plymouth

Colony 9085
William C. Handy 12367
William Crawford Gorgas 17987
William H. McGuffey 17982
William Hamilton Merritt 1166
William Henry Harrison 13462
William Henry Jackson's Colorado
    9372
William Penn (Dolson) 4992
William Penn (Haviland) 7883
William Penn (Syme) 16596
William Penn (Wilkie) 17939
William Tecumseh Sherman 1739
William Tell 6434
William Tell and His Son 8822
William Warren 577
William's Doll 18629
Willie and the Wildcat Well 3980
Willie Bryant and the Flying Otis
    7323
Willie Horton Story, The 2751
Willie Jasper's Golden Eagle 12353
Willie Mays (Einstein) 5305
Willie Mays (Epstein) 5506
Willie Mays (Hano) 7701
Willie Mays (Sullivan) 16491
Willie Mays, Modest Champion
    15110
Willie Mays, Most Valuable Player
    11916
Willie Stargell, Baseball Slugger
    10775
Willie's Adventures 2404
Willie's Whizmobile 15428
Willing Workers ... 13307
Willis 11717
Willow Tree Village 10341
Willow Whistle, The 12023
Will's Quill 6271
Willy (King) 9818
Willy! (Shoberg) 15575
Willy and His Wheel Wagon 6783
Willy Bear 9490
Willy Runs Away 14526
Willy Wong, American 12982
Wilma Rudolph 9077
Wilson at Work 8694
Wilt Chamberlain (Heaslip) 7986
Wilt Chamberlain (Rudeen) 14748
Wily Wizard and the Wicked Witch,
    The 1869
Wim of the Wind 4758
Winabojo 2022
Winabozho, Hero-God of the Indians
    of the Old Northwest 2336
Wind, The 1442
Wind and Shadows 4541

Wind and the Rain, The 10723
Wind Before the Dawn 2720
Wind Blew, The 8843
... Wind Blows Free, The 5515
Wind Dies at Sunrise, The 14910
Wind Eye, The 17760
Wind Has Wings, The 5055
Wind in My Hand 6435
Wind in the Chimney 12024
Wind in the Door, A 10548
Wind in the Willows, The 7155
Wind Is Air, The 2207
Wind Is Round, The 7698
Wind of Chance, The 7496
Wind of Change, A 1087
Wind Rose 5062
Wind, Sand and Sky 3175
Wind Song 14888
Wind Thief, The 1114
Windigo 565
Windmill Summer 5760
Window into a Nest 5998
Window into an Egg 5997
Window on Williamsburg, A 17453
Windows for Rosemary 17192
Windows in the Sea 15417
Windows on the World 17789
Winds and Lights 12971
Wind's Child, The 16692
Winds in the Woods 16308
Winds of Time, The 4145
Windwagon Smith 15419
Windy Morning 1321
Wing on a Flea, The 5418
Winged Adventure, The 9806
Winged Colt of Casa Mia, The 2795
Winged Moccasins 5701
Winged Watchman, The 17233
Wingfin and Topple 17183
Wingman 13704
Wingman on Ice 3433
Wings of Adventure 16885
Wings of the Morning 13265
Wings over Alaska 8112
Wingspread 10436
Winifred 35
Winnebago Boy 14979
Winner, The 14382
Winner at the Dub-Dub Club 11666
Winners, The 17869
Winnie Puh en el Cumpleaños de Igor 12250
Winnie-the-Pooh 12251
Winning Kicker 5196
Winning Plays in Pro Football 16492
Winston Churchill 5507
Winter 14790
Winter at Valley Forge, The 11781
Winter Bear, The 4235
Winter Cat, The 9946
Winter Cottage 2267
Winter Danger 16181
Winter in Wartime 16750
Winter Noisy Book, The 2405
Winter of the Birds, The 4287
Winter Olympics, The 11917
Winter Patriot 15087
Winter Picnic, The 17714
Winter Pony 5029
Winter Rabbit Hunt 16619
Winter-Sleeping Wildlife 1078
Winter Sports 5764
Winter-Telling Stories 11702
Winter Thunder 14904
Winter Wedding 17715
Winter Wheat 18040
Winter Wife, The 4306
Winter's Coming 2593
Winter's Eve 1384
Winterthing 193
Wintertime for Animals 4179
Wisconsin (Carpenter) 3039
Wisconsin (Dearn) 4769
Wisconsin (Derleth) 4854
Wisconsin Historical Sights 6757
Wisconsin in Words and Pictures 6194
Wisconsin Lore 6572
Wisconsin Lore for Boys and Girls 4616
Wisconsin's First Settlers--The Indians 6758
Wisdom of Mallam Faruku 18098
Wise Little Dini 13861
Wise Men of Gotham, The 3089
Wise Monkey Tale, A 11534
Wise Rooster, The 13944
Wise Woman, The see Lost Princess: A Double Story, The
Wisest Man in the World, The 5352
Wish Again, Big Bear 11672
Wish Around the World 5214
Wish at the Top, The 2585
Wish for a Little Sister, A 825
Wish for Lutie 7905
Wish You Were Here 5866
Wishing Gold 12978
Wishing Pear, The 3703
Wit and Wisdom of Fat Albert, The 4173
Witch Family, The 5554

Witch Fear see Mysterious Appearance of Agnes, The
Witch, Goblin & Sometimes Ghost 293
Witch in the Cherry Tree, The 11558
Witch in the House, A 3344
Witch Kitten, The 3109
Witch Lady Mystery, The 18433
Witch Mobile, The 18469
Witch of Blackbird Pond, The 16050
Witch of Fourth Street ..., The 10669
Witch of Glen Gowrie, The 11418
Witch of the Cumberlands 16223
Witch of the Woods 12973
Witch Poems 17462
Witch Water 12687
Witch Who Forgot, The 2936
Witch Who Lost Her Shadow, The 2846
Witch Who Saved Halloween, The 13728
Witch Who Wasn't, The 18427
Witchcraft in America 237
Witchcraft, Mysticism and Magic in the Black World 7832
Witches of Worm, The 15974
Witches, Pumpkins and Grinning Ghosts 1142
Witches' Sabbath 4148
Witches, Wit and a Werewolf 7718
Witches, Witches, Witches 8421
Witch's Brat, The 16530
Witch's Bridle, The 16422
Witch's Broom 3345
Witch's Business 9344
Witch's Buttons 3346
Witch's Daughter 1224
Witch's Egg, The 5272
Witch's Garden, A 18470
Witch's Magic Cloth, The 11830
Witch's Sister 12688
Witchcracks 15150
With a Deep Sea Smile 16662
With a Motor Truck in Africa 7642
With an Open Hand 12508
With Bells On 12207
With Books on Her Head 3257
With Buller in Natal, or a Born Leader 8090
With George Washington at Valley Forge 16082
With Robert to Pretoria 8091
With Stanley in Africa 7631

With the Indians in the Rockies 15127
With These Hands They Built a Nation 10442
Without Burnt Offerings 1694
Without Hats, Who Can Tell the Good Guys? 405
Witness, The 17120
Wives of the Presidents 12029
Wizard in the Tree, The 277
Wizard in the Well, The 1322
Wizard Islands, The 18428
Wizard McBean and His Flying Machine 12871
Wizard of Earthsea, A 10516
Wizard of Op, The 5419
Wizard of Oz, The 1200
Wizard of Wallaby Wallow, The 9715
Wizard of Walnut Street, The 15181
Wizards and Wampum 16103
Wizards and Witches 17941
Wizard's Tears, The 10132
Wobble, the Witch Cat 2847
Woggle of Witches, A 48
Wolf, The 6176
Wolf and the Seven Kids, The 7409
Wolf Country 3542
Wolf in Olga's Kitchen 13531
Wolf King, The 17065
Wolf of Badenoch 3379
Wolf of My Own, A 17413
Wolf Run 8663
Wolf Who Had a Wonderful Dream, The 14527
Wolfie 3319
Wolves of Willoughby Chase, The 194
Woman and Her Son and Other Stories, The 6322
Woman Chief 15991
Woman Is, A 13484
Woman of the Wood, The 1695
Woman Who Lived in Holland, The 8688
Woman with the Eggs, The 449
Wombles in Danger 1500
Women at Their Work 5459
Women at Work 12008
Women in Policing 6099
Women in Sports (Stambler) 16136
Women in Sports (Van Steenwyk) 17224
Women in Sports: Scuba Diving 7852
Women in Sports: Swimming 6890
Women in Sports: Tennis 11980
Women in Sports: Track and Field

6891

Women in Television 9915
Women in Zambia 4447
Women of America 5144
Women of Courage 12655
Women of Nebraska Hall of Fame
    9647
Women of the West 10646
Women on the March 7512
Women Themselves 9317
Women Today 17444
Women Who Changed History
    4602
Women Who Dared to Be Different
    17620
Women Who Made America Great
    6767
Women Who Shaped History 2507
Women Who Win 14834
Women with a Cause 17621
Womenfolk and Fairy Tales 12258
Women's Rights (Coolidge) 4024
Women's Rights (Stevenson) 16295
Wonder-Book for Girls and Boys
    7906
Wonder Book of Counting Rhymes
    13662
Wonder Clock, The 14018
Wonder of Animals, The 4466
Wonder of Hands, The 872
Wonder Tales of Dogs and Cats
    3056
Wonder Tales of South Africa
    11503
Wonder Why 7736
Wonderful Adventures of Nils,
    The 10192
Wonderful Cassava Plant, The
    576
Wonderful Chirrionera and Other
    Tales from Mexican Folklore,
    The 10859
Wonderful Egg, The 8919
Wonderful Farm, The 838
Wonderful Flight to the Mushroom
    Planet 2863
Wonderful Garden, The 12739
Wonderful Kite, The 17414
Wonderful Little Boy, The 2499
Wonderful O, The 16859
Wonderful Pumpkin, The 8038
Wonderful Story of How You
    Were Born, The 7462
Wonderful, Terrible Time, A
    16361
Wonderful Time 11338
Wonderful White Horse ..., The

4580

Wonderful Winter, The 3455
Wonderful Wizard of Oz, The see
    Wizard of Oz, The
Wonderful World of Dance, The
    7812
Wonderful World of Energy 8398
Wonderful World of J. Wesley Smith,
    The 15403
Wonderful World of Mathematics
    8399
Wonderful World of Music, The
    2270
Wonderful World of Paper, The
    3773
Wonderful Year 1090
Wonders in Words 12969
Wonders, Inc. 9787
Wonders of Algae, The 9559
Wonders of Ancient Chinese Science
    15671
Wonders of Caribou 14174
Wonders of Corals and Coral Reefs
    9092
Wonders of Crows 1740
Wonders of Fossils 11835
Wonders of Fungi, The 9560
Wonders of Geese and Swans 5756
Wonders of Herbs 10384
Wonders of Marsupials 10385
Wonders of Mathematics 5821
Wonders of Prairie Dogs 3229
Wonders of Rocks and Minerals
    13437
Wonders of Sea Gulls 15114
Wonders of Seeds 16186
Wonders of Sponges 9093
Wonders of Starfish 9090
Wonders of the Bat World 10386
Wonders of the Cactus World
    10387
Wonders of the Eagle World 10388
Wonders of the Hawk World 10389
Wonders of the Human Body 14151
Wonders of the World of Horses
    10390
Wonders of the World of Shells
    9091
Wonders of the World of the Alba-
    tross 5937
Wonders of Wild Ducks 5757
Wonky Donkey 8645
Won't Somebody Play with Me?
    9660
Wood 17379
Wood Is Sweet, The 3478
Woodchuck 11491

Woodcutter's Duck, The 17078
Wooden Cat Man, The 6020
Wooden Horse, The 17992
Wooden Horse of Troy, The
   12532
Wooden River, The 16377
Woodland Crossings 10093
Woodland Indians of the Western
   Great Lakes, The 14409
Woodstock Craftsman's Manual
   18448
Woody and Me 12767
Wool Gathering 6727
Wool-Pack, The see Nicholas
   and the Wool-Pack
Words by Heart 15216
Words from History 766
Words from the Exodus 767
Words from the Myths 768
Words in Genesis 769
Words of Science and the History
   Behind Them 770
Workhouse Child 16600
Working with Wool 1469
Workshop Book of Knitting, The
   17352
Workshops in Space 2011
World Beneath Our Feet, The
   9615
World Beneath the Oceans 6651
World Beneath the Sea 5105
World Conductors 18472
World Faiths 975
World Friends 8369
World Full of Horses 8920
World Heavyweight Championship
   Fights 11918
World in the Candy Egg, The
   17011
World Is Round, The 14152
World of African Song, The
   11564
World of Albert Schweitzer, The
   5611
World of Ben Lighthart, The
   16747
World of Big Game, The 11197
World of Candle and Color, The
   17089
World of Captain John Smith,
   1580-1631, The 6144
World of Chocolate, The 15866
World of Christopher Robin, The
   12252
World of Columbus and Sons,
   The 6145
World of Living Things, The

   12014
World of Manabozho, The 10501
World of Marco Polo, The 2532
World of Mary Cassatt, The 11440
World of Nonsense, A 18164
World of Our Fathers 12052
World of Rice, The 1848
World of Samuel Adams, The 3350
World of the Giant Panda, The
   13540
World of the Pharaohs, The 1212
World of the Prairie Dog, The
   4185
World of the White-Tailed Deer,
   The 14752
World of the Wolf, The 13674
World of William Penn, The 6146
World of Wonderful Difference, The
   7465
World on a String 18429
World on Wheels 12289
World Series, The 11919
World War II 16499
World War II Resistance Stories
   13873
World We Live In, The 10791
World, World, What Can I Do?
   7969
World's Fair, 1992 15672
World's Great Race Drivers 13184
World's Great Stories, The 17161
World's Greatest Freak Show, The
   14131
Worlds of Ernest Thompson Seton,
   The 15360
Wormburners, The 4244
Worms (Darling) 4509
Worms (Nespojohn) 12740
Worst Hound Around 5064
Worth Fighting For 11229
Would-Be Witch, The 3347
Would You Put Your Money in a
   Sand Bank? 11049
Would You Rather Be a Tiger?
   16507
Wounded Knee 2339
Wrapped for Eternity 13229
Wrath of Moto, The 6669
Wreath of Christmas Legends, A
   11339
Wren 9788
Wrestle the Mountain 12689
Wrestling 13467
Wright Brothers, The (Franchere)
   6204
Wright Brothers, The (Glines)
   6903

Wright Brothers, The (Graves) 7199

Wright Brothers, The (Kaufman) 9536

Wright Brothers, The (Reynolds) 14282

Wright Brothers at Kitty Hawk, The 15986

Wright Brothers, First to Fly, The 12455

Wrinkle in Time, A 10549

Writing with Light 4431

Written on Film 14854

Wrong Side of the Bed 629

Wufu 6342

Wuggly Ump, The 7081

Wump World, The 13478

Wyatt Earp, U.S. Marshal 8437

Wyoming Winds _see_ Songs of the Sage

- X -

Xhosa Fireside Tales 14965

- Y -

Yael and the Queen of Goats 1040

Yagua Days 11721

Yak/Le Yak, The 368a

Yak, the Python and the Frog, The 1366

Yaller-Eye 1357

Yangtze, China's River Highway 16065

Yangtze River, The 14146

Yankee Doodle (Bangs) 1049

Yankee Doodle (Schackburg) 15000

Yankee Doodle Boy 11733

Yankee Doodle Painter 3890

Yankee Doodle's Cousins 11569

Yankee Driver 2775

Yankee in German America, A 5986

Yankee Spy 12886

Yankee Thunder 15429

Yankel the Fool 5358

Yao and the Python 596

Yarn--The Things It Makes and How to Make Them 12128

Yasu and the Strangers 15848

Yea, Coach! Three Great Football Coaches 17222

Yea! Wildcats! 17054

Year, The 10241

Year After Year 1656

Year and a Day, A 11962

Year Around, The 7960

Year at Maple Hill Farm, The 13982

Year for Growing, A 2071

Year in the Life of Rosie Bernard, A 2200

Year Mom Won the Pennant, The 3434

Year of Columbus, 1492 6147

Year of Independence, 1776 6148

Year of Lincoln, 1861 6149

Year of Mr. Nobody, The 9816

Year of Small Shadow, The 10234

Year of the Badger, The 2656

Year of the Black Pony 12433

Year of the Bloody Sevens, The 16182

Year of the Cafeteria 17449

Year of the Christmas Dragon, The 14974

Year of the Horse, The 17442

Year of the Horseless Carriage, The 6150

Year of the Jeep, The 14447

Year of the Pilgrims, 1620 6151

Year of the Raccoon, The 9830

Year of the She-Grizzly, The 566

Year of the Three-Legged Deer, The 3608

Year on Muskrat Marsh 6343

Year on the Desert, A 7050

Year They Won the Most Valuable Player Award, The 15435

Year to Grow, A 8509

Year Walk 3502

Year Without a Santa Claus, The 11340

Yearling, The 14154

Years Between, The 18081

Years of Strife: 1929-1956 9526

Years of the Forest, The 8571

Yeck Eck 12752

Yellow Airplane, The 11963

Yellow Bone Ring, The 7214

Yellow Canary whose Eye Is So Black, The 5158

Yellow House Mystery, The 17528

Yellow Leaf 2907
Yellow Silk for May Lee 12801
Yellow, Yellow 723
Yellowstone 9855
Yes and No 7997
Yes and No Book!, The 658
Yes-No; Stop-Go 6773
Yeshua, Called Jesus 1680
Yesterday's People 11762
Yesterday's Snowman 11402
Yiddish Stories, Old and New
  8683
Yippy 14302
Yo quiero ser capitan 7235
Yo Quisiera Vivir en un Parque
  de Juegos 12845
Yo soy el amarillo 9401
Yo soy el azul 9402
Yo soy el rojo 9403
Yo y Honerin 10172
Yobgorgle, Mystery Monster of
  Lake Ontario 13705
Yoga for Children 3316
Yolanda's Hike 6652
Yomi in Paris 200
Yomi's Adventures 201
Yong Kee of Korea 513
Yonie Wondernose 4643
Yosuf bin Hasan 4421
You 11387
You Always Communicate Some-
  thing 15173
You Among the Stars 15097
You and the Metric System 16394
You and Your Alcoholic Parent
  8628
You and Your Body 9891
You and Your Child: Playing
  with Numbers see Playing
  with Numbers
You and Your Child: Playing
  with Shapes and Sizes see
  Playing with Shapes and Sizes
You Be the Judge 3114
You Better Come Home with Me
  10415
You Can 13611
You Can Be a Carpenter 10783
You Can be a Machinist 10784
You Can Be a Mechanic 10785
You Can Be a Plumber 10786
You Can Be a Professional Driver
  10787
You Can Be an Electrician 10788
You Can Be a Taller 8616
You Can Catch Fish 16337
You Can Cook 15160

You Can Put on a Show 13078
You Can Work in the Health Serv-
  ices 4901
You Can Write Chinese 17872
You Can't Eat Peanuts in Church
  15365
You Can't Make Me If I Don't Want
  To 3930
You Can't Put Braces on Spaces
  14345
You Come Too 6418
You Don't Look Like Your Mother
  5930
You Go Away 4153
You Have to Draw the Line Some-
  where 7769
You Look Ridiculous, Said the
  Rhinoceros to the Hippopotamus
  17372
You Never Can Tell 8472
You Ought to See Herbert's House
  11169
You Read to Me, I'll Read to You
  3466
You Should Have Been Here an
  Hour Ago 5283
You Will Go to the Moon 6305
You Will Remember Me and Other
  African Stories 6323
Young and Black in Africa 13051
Young and Black in America 290
Young and Female 14658
Young Baseball Champions 6720
Young Booker 1925
Young Changing Earth 14742
Young Colonists, The 8092
Young Cowboy 9125
Young Eagles 1625
Young Fifty-Niners, The 5358
Young Fu of the Upper Yangtze
  10698
Young Grizzly, The 4933
Young Henry Ford 13113
Young Hockey Champions 12990
Young Hunter of Picuris 3503
Young Ike 7835
Young Land Lords, The 12613
Young Mac of Fort Vancouver 3065
Young Marie Curie 32
Young Mark 376
Young Mary Queen of Scots 13730
Young Mr. Big 14142
Young Olympic Champions 6721
Young Paul Revere's Boston 5508
Young People and Crime 2807
Young People of East and South
  Africa 9410

Young People of South Asia 9411
Young People of the Pacific Islands 9412
Young People of West Africa 9413
Young Person's Guide to Ballet, A 16413
Young Puerto Rico 11624
Young Readers' Book of Christian Symbolism 4559
Young Scientist and Sports 1105
Young Sports Photographer with the Green Bay Packers 1643
Young Sportsman's Guide to Motor Boating 13439
Young Sportsman's Guide to Water Safety 18092
Young Squire Morgan 17722
Young Teens Away from Home 1313
Young Thomas Edison 12928
Young Traveller in Tropical Africa, The 14449
Young Unicorns, The 10550
Young United States, 1783 to 1830, The 17046
Young Voices 15001
Young Voyageur, The 7426
Younger's Race 332
Youngest Camel, The 2052
Youngest Captain, The 18029
Youngest General, The 7088
Youngest One 18369
Your Book of Badminton 18308
Your Book on Trampolining 8626
Your Brain and How It Works 18560
Your Busy Brain 11463
Your Capital and Mine 7839
Your Career in Civil Service 10928
Your Career in Hotels and Motels 18172
Your Career in Parks and Recreation 11226
Your Children's Hospital Book 11159
Your Ears 122
Your Face Is a Picture 3609
Your Family Goes Camping 13377
Your First Pet and How to Take Care of It 16264
Your Friend, the Tree 17801
Your Friends from Sesame Street 15942
Your Growing Cells 11464

Your Hand in Mine 4164
Your Heart and How It Works 18561
Your Hospital 4180
Your Legal Rights 12953
Your Maryland 14588
Your Neighbor Celebrates 6805
Your Nerves and Their Messages 9471
Your Old Pal, Al 7290
Your Own Book of Campcraft 7668
Your Own Little Elf 11767
Your Prayers and Mine 18380
Your Science Fair Project 12412
Your Skin and Mine 15606
Your Stomach and Digestive Tract 18562
Your Wonderful World of Science 6306
You're a Good Dog, Joe 17146
You're a Good Sport, Charlie Brown 15136
You're the Scaredy-Cat 11943
You're Too Sweet 3967
Yours Till Niagara Falls 12472
Yours Till Niagara Falls, Abby 13000
Yucatan Monkey 1304
Yugoslav Folk-Tales 4382
Yukiyu (El Espiritu de Borinquen) 13158
Yummers! 11718
Yusuf, Boy of Cyprus 14138

- Z -

Z for Zachariah 12994
Zach see Who Wants to Be Alone?
Zack and the Magic Factory 15122
Zaire (Carpenter) 3040
Zaire (Elisofon) 5343
Zamani Goes to Market 5753
Zambezi, The 17842
Zambia 3048
Zambia's President 13770
Zanballer 9954
Zapata, Mexican Rebel 16597
Zarga's Shadow 11040
Zeb 500
Zeb Pike (Aronson) 680
Zeb Pike (Stevenson) 16283
Zebra Came to drink, A 3162
Zeee 5472

SUBJECT/CONCEPT INDEX

NOTE: Numbers after each subject refer to entry numbers, not page numbers.

ABC see ALPHABET
AARDVARKS 10824
AARON, HENRY "HANK" (1934-) 2614, 4779, 5057, 5500, 7520, 7819, 8242, 8243, 11874, 12257, 14736, 16464, 18444
ABACUS 4907
ABDUL-JABBAR, KAREEM (1947-) 2617, 7700, 7822, 9016, 11883, 16771
ABERNATHY, LOUIE (1900-) 9020
ABERNATHY, TEMPLE (1904-) 9020
ABNAKI INDIANS 5479
  legends 8184, 17341
ABOLITIONISTS 863, 1917, 3381, 4569, 5036, 5625, 5627, 5648, 9885, 13187, 15206, 17125, 17313, 18059
ABORIGINES 11715
ABZUG, BELLA S. (1920-) 5622
ACADIANS 16631
ACCIDENTS 1416, 1855, 3695, 5332, 5736, 7238, 7255, 7632, 8694, 11934, 14391, 16551, 17304, 17734, 17323
  prevention 501, 11664, 15447, 17193
    education 11664, 17193
    handbooks, manuals, etc. 7238
ACCOUNTING 11542
ACOMA INDIANS 7466, 9113
  legends 14776
ACOMA (NEW MEXICO) 9113
ACTING 506, 2948, 13078, 16406
ACTORS AND ACTRESSES 5890, 6201, 15494
ADAM (BIBLICAL CHARACTER) 14181
ADAMS, ABIGAIL (SMITH), (1744-1818) 9668, 13572, 17386
ADAMS, JOHN (1735-1826) 1703
ADAMS, SAMUEL (1722-1803) 3350, 6394, 14340
ADAPTATION (BIOLOGY) 1413, 4179, 13703, 15631
ADDAMS, JANE, (1860-1935) 6810, 7175, 9420, 9644, 12381, 13573, 17387
ADIRONDACK MOUNTAINS 5649
ADJUSTMENT (PSYCHOLOGY) 7999, 8285
ADMIRALS 12350
ADOLESCENCE see YOUTH
ADOLESCENT PSYCHOLOGY 8636, 14328
ADOPTION 691, 1172, 2061, 2493, 2586, 2809, 3601, 5049, 5235, 5615, 5651, 10271, 10445, 12087, 12177, 12368, 12754, 14190, 14677, 15663, 17540, 17552, 18130
  personal narratives 11667

ADVENT--prayer books and devotions 514
ADVENTURE AND ADVENTURERS 154, 186, 188, 189, 326, 343, 600, 624,
625, 675, 683, 814, 868, 1035, 1037, 1051, 1232, 1558, 1560, 1585, 1616,
1743, 1885, 1923, 1927, 1980, 2019, 3159, 3226, 3445, 3633, 3655, 3666,
3671, 4036, 4061, 4271, 4579, 4846, 5315, 5317, 5320, 5321, 5358a, 5850,
6606, 6665, 7476, 7815, 8252, 8355, 8786, 9189, 9476, 9801, 10046,
10050, 10147, 10150, 10151, 10550, 10857, 10860, 11371, 11386, 11650,
11655, 12409, 12522, 12551, 12981, 13235, 13372, 13848, 14066, 14112,
14457, 14678, 14759, 14906, 15399, 15985, 16038, 16073, 16101, 16192,
16299, 16326, 16544, 17065, 17186, 17749, 17810, 18003, 18098, 18099,
18101, 18123
ADVERTISING 506, 718, 1760, 13812, 14617, 18233
    vocational guidance 2760
AERIAL COMBAT 8972
AERIALISTS 10086
AERODYNAMICS 4124, 6299, 9544
AERONAUTICS 424, 1418, 4040, 5390, 5818, 8870, 10683, 12455, 12668,
13645
    accidents 5017, 11715
    biography 6204, 7199, 9536, 14030
    commercial 13479, 18090
    flights 6152, 13723, 16885
    history 15361
    piloting 4025, 4321, 4460
    sports 14079
    vocational guidance 11343, 14156, 17726
AESTHETICS 14131
AFGHANISTAN 2817
AFRICA 358, 712, 914, 1068, 1087, 1260, 1569, 1615, 1743, 1870, 1872,
1936, 1937, 1981, 2315, 2821, 2827, 2828, 2910, 2917, 2999, 3001, 3003,
3005, 3006, 3007, 3008, 3012, 3014, 3015, 3016, 3018, 3019, 3020, 3024,
3025, 3030, 3031, 3032, 3033, 3034, 3035, 3037, 3038, 3040, 3041, 3042,
3043, 3044, 3045, 3046, 3047, 3048, 3201, 3231, 3339, 3471, 3695, 3699,
3702, 3793, 3899, 4201, 4410, 4483, 5020, 5021, 5022, 5023, 5024, 5025,
5314, 5753, 6037, 6607, 6719, 7138, 7304, 7482, 7491, 7617, 7624, 7635,
8213, 8369, 8692, 8718, 9581, 9676, 9807, 10178, 10840, 12506, 12569,
12631, 12836, 13766, 13932, 14464, 14683, 14714, 15189, 15231, 15774,
15796, 16061, 16327, 16340, 16830, 17607, 17718, 17720, 17744
    art 153
    authors 5012
    biography 208, 209, 4248, 7149, 9554
    Central 1034, 2998, 3549, 9483, 9871, 9872, 13930
        description and travel 9206, 9409, 9950, 9951
        discovery and exploration 7631
    civilization 1030, 12758, 13678
    colonization 11434
    description and travel 5096, 7054, 7640, 8202, 10492, 12084, 14040,
    16538, 17420
    discovery and exploration 16248, 17167
    East 204, 396, 3549, 4344, 4775, 9476, 9846, 12770, 13518, 14066, 16062,
    17422
        description and travel 5734, 11009
        history 5768, 14634
        social life and customs 5751, 5752
    French Equatorial--discovery and exploration 2915
    French West--social life and customs 12301
    history 4565, 7836, 9184, 10557, 11384, 11434, 12777, 15358, 16933

19th century   74, 3437, 7616, 9388, 15457
kings and rulers   4943
literary collections   7340
North   14670, 17940, 18102
poetry   354
politics and government   6657, 8496
social life and customs   7336, 7367, 12589, 13051, 13921, 17536, 18286, 18314
songs and music   14566
Southwest--history   15227
Sub-Saharan   1567, 4193, 9791, 10178
  biography   13769
  civilization   12888
  politics and government   12535
West   1087, 1566, 1616, 2827, 3553, 7479, 9577, 9952, 11035, 13521, 14453, 15012, 15016, 17719
  description and travel   4612, 5097, 9832, 12847, 15098
  Free Colony   1030, 1075
  history   14635, 18113
  religion   9832
  social life and customs   12847, 13912, 14313
see also specific countries, e.g., NIGERIA
AFRICA, SOUTH see SOUTH AFRICA
AFRICAN LITERATURE   12231, 12889, 16339
AFRICAN POETRY   10624, 14064, 16123
AFRICAN PROSE   8888
AFRICANS   10178, 12888
AFRO-AMERICANS see BLACK AMERICANS
AGADEZ (NIGER)--social life and customs   5458
AGEE, TOMMIE (1942-)   18439
AGGREY (EDUCATOR)   12590
AGNES, SAINT (A.D. 291-304)   1483
AGRIBUSINESS--vocational guidance   8648
AGRICULTURAL IMPLEMENTS--Minnesota   10639
AGRICULTURAL LABORERS   6437
AGRICULTURE   213, 3665, 6055, 8028, 15645, 16469
  Africa   132, 246
  careers   1474, 2518
  Great Plains   10346
  machinery   3854
   operators--vocational guidance   6281
  Minnesota--history   10639
  primitive   17677
AGRICULTURISTS   5498, 7151, 11999
AIKIDO   18359
AIR   99, 2112, 2207, 6299
  experiments   15755
  pollution   1790, 2006, 4341, 5367, 9556, 10429, 12322, 13099, 13504, 14878, 16647
  law and legislation   16267
AIR LINES
  flight attendants   14315
  vocational guidance   4766
AIR PILOTS   4586, 7280, 7507, 7681, 8112, 15246, 16885, 18465
  Germany   18312
  military   5955
  United States   7963, 13334

AIR TRAFFIC CONTROL   13088
AIRPLANES   1418, 2902, 4004, 4460, 4766, 10684, 12668, 12672, 18090
   in art   401
   maintenance and repair--vocational guidance   10785
   military   4811
   models   6834, 11058, 17695
   testing   17726
AIRPORTS   9664, 10684, 18090
AJAYI, BISHOP   208
AKANS (AFRICAN PEOPLE)--history   601
ALABAMA   5386, 6881, 17722
   history   206
ALAMO MISSION   384, 4212
   siege (1836)   6135, 11547, 14338, 16880, 17541
ALASKA   486, 1353, 2170, 2591, 2746, 5900, 7362, 9194, 9195, 11041, 11398,
   12425, 12426, 12427, 12428, 12432, 12480, 12768, 13464, 16429, 16713,
   16932, 17631, 18186
   biography   8112
   description and travel   16184
   Eskimos   6829
   politics and government (1867-1959)   18200
ALBATROSSES   5937, 8345
ALCHEMY   827, 2796
ALCINDOR, LEW   see   ABDUL-JABBAR, KAREEM
ALCOHOL AND ALCOHOLISM   4416, 5453, 5596, 5613, 6025, 8628, 8871,
   12000, 12683, 15162, 15256, 15257, 15956, 18254, 18290
   physiological effect   8871, 10483, 15676
   treatment   10483, 15676
ALCOHOL AND YOUTH   8871, 15162
ALCOHOLICS--family relationships   15257
ALCOTT, LOUISA MAY (1832-1888)   3888, 12021, 13273, 17390
ALCOTT FAMILY   5932
ALDRIDGE, IRA FREDERICK (d. 1867)   11576
ALEXANDER, KATHERINE (HUSTON) (b. 1830 or 1831)   2720
ALEXANDER THE GREAT (356-323 B.C.)   525, 7499, 12086, 16440
ALEXANDRIA (EGYPT)   12288
ALFRED THE GREAT (KING OF ENGLAND), (849-901)   8319, 16981
ALGAE--economic aspects   9559
ALGEBRA   17705
ALGERIA   14670, 16066
   description and travel   4823
ALGIERS, BATTLE OF (1816)   15061
ALGONQUIAN INDIANS   14556, 15540, 17115
ALI, HADJI   see   JOLLY, HI
ALI, MUHAMMAD (1942-)   295, 2619, 5274, 11891, 13061, 13108, 14746,
   18067
ALIENATION (SOCIAL PSYCHOLOGY)   1470, 1537, 1959, 2487, 2566, 3393,
   3630, 3687, 4164, 5011, 5479, 5583, 5697, 6184, 6576, 6600, 6971, 8194,
   8964, 9146, 9440, 9488, 9813, 10650, 11753, 12023, 12329, 12505, 12654,
   13480, 13800, 14287, 18261, 18289, 18294, 18400
ALIENS--Mexican--California   17666
ALIMENTARY CANAL   18562
ALL-TERRAIN VEHICLES   15876
ALLEGORIES   2595, 5543, 10689, 10691, 11303, 16265
ALLEN, ETHAN (1738-1789)   8433
ALLERGY   15688
ALLIED HEALTH PERSONNEL   4597, 4901, 5452, 6272, 6276, 12162

ALLIGATORS 139, 1482, 4417, 4666, 6741, 7061, 7803, 7915, 8927, 10361,
    11245, 12264, 13567, 14296, 15495, 16289, 18535
    poetry 14312
ALLOWANCES 5467
ALPHABET 255, 543, 548, 569, 731, 732, 733, 734, 1160, 1364, 1870, 2027,
    2369, 2381, 2448, 2647, 2677, 2680, 2920, 2972, 3275, 3278, 3335, 3369,
    3456, 3620, 3832, 4116, 4296, 4335, 4770, 4810, 5175, 5221, 5296, 5408,
    5655, 5671, 5748, 5751, 5855, 5940, 6079, 6255, 6426, 6431, 6463, 6642,
    7186, 7251, 7454, 7535, 7998, 8001, 8310, 8520, 8774, 8916, 8934, 9226,
    9370, 9898, 10057, 10083, 10095, 10273, 10873, 10945, 11152, 11334,
    11341, 11456, 11596, 11836, 12061, 12069, 12179, 12199, 12213, 12215,
    12248, 12372, 12406, 12536, 12554, 12772, 12843, 13126, 13222, 13284,
    13497, 13649, 13908, 14265, 14311, 14490, 14501, 14567, 14598, 14731,
    14993, 15086, 15328, 15370, 15384, 15629, 15872, 15940, 16634, 16635,
    16788, 16859, 16952, 17028, 17503, 17914, 18480
    Hebrew 11665
    history 5108
ALSATIAN AMERICANS 5858
ALTAMIRA CAVE (SPAIN) 8552
AMAIN, KING OF BRASS (1790-ca. 1846) 214
AMATEUR MOTION PICTURES 450, 8032, 17692
AMATEUR RADIO STATIONS 13331
AMBASSADORS 7818
AMERICA
    antiquities 10360
    discovery and exploration 917, 1411, 4453, 7177, 8227, 9316, 9427, 9589,
        10360
        French 31, 2519, 8431, 16595, 16963
        Irish 6382
        Norse 9203, 15565
        pre-Columbian 14892
        Spanish 2434, 2526, 13280, 14892, 15534, 17279
    see also specific countries, e.g., UNITED STATES
AMERICAN LITERATURE 1289
    Black American authors 9109, 14580
    collections 8081
    history and criticism 10529
    Indian authors 10777
    Indiana--bibliography 13466
AMERICAN LOYALISTS 5054, 6424
    England 12951
AMERICAN NATIONAL RED CROSS 5482, 7169, 14607, 14684
AMERICAN POETRY 24, 133, 178, 1309, 3460, 3462, 3465, 3630, 3698,
    5666, 5668, 5669, 5848, 5911, 6089, 6188, 6410, 6413, 6418, 6429, 6448,
    7231, 7553, 7585, 7688, 7736, 8200, 8280, 8311, 8500, 8506, 8543, 8591,
    8596, 10078, 10154, 10160, 10562, 10633, 10696, 10858, 10968, 10969,
    10971, 10972, 10975, 10978, 10980, 11045, 11264, 11266, 11267, 11268,
    11269, 11270, 11306, 11544, 11604, 11671, 12035, 12062, 12071, 12098,
    12103, 12105, 12210, 12280, 12384, 12394, 12397, 12406, 12470, 12510,
    12647, 12648, 12767, 12804, 13311, 13563, 13747, 13885, 14377, 14378,
    14428, 14762, 14885, 14888, 15936, 15937, 15999, 16126, 16149, 16150,
    16558, 16777, 16778, 16860, 16881, 17157, 17462, 17819, 17889, 18278,
    18279, 18623
    Black American authors 127, 129, 135, 5116, 6861, 6862, 7459, 8600,
        8716, 8724, 9380, 9381
    collections 4686, 6027, 6160, 6221, 7333, 7696, 7698, 8588, 8595, 8598,
        8604, 8957, 9382, 9778, 9884, 10274, 10277, 10278, 10279, 10973, 10976,

11935, 13450, 13453, 14183, 15001
concrete 13673
history and criticism 15710
Indian authors 11089, 14611
patriotic 8212, 8420
20th century 131, 5154, 5155, 13673, 14611, 15001, 16956
collections 10272
AMERICAN REVOLUTION see UNITED STATES--HISTORY--REVOLUTION
(1775-1783)
AMERICAN WIT AND HUMOR--pictorial works 15403
AMISH 4636, 4643, 10587, 12677, 15326, 16029
in Pennsylvania 8629
social life and customs 8629
AMISTAD (SCHOONER) 9965
AMNESIA 2942
AMPHIBIANS 338, 3718, 12434, 13144, 13354, 15754, 18498, 18575
Illinois 13336
Kansas 3852
Minnesota 2169
AMULETS 1360
AMUNDSON, ROALD (1872-1928) 4608
AMUSEMENT PARKS 13447
AMUSEMENTS 4519, 13707, 14675, 17314
England 1286
ANATOMY 12320
comparative 4174
human 2187, 2702, 6895, 9891, 14151, 14689, 14811, 17203, 18558
ANDERSEN, HANS CHRISTIAN (1805-1875) 7653
ANDERSON, MARIAN (1902-) 12799, 16901
ANDERSON, SWEET PEA (1958-) 10085
ANDREWS RAID (1862) 5487
ANGELS 16719, 17487, 18436
ANGLO-SAXONS see ENGLAND--HISTORY--ANGLO-SAXON PERIOD
ANGOLA 7642, 17721
ANIMAL DEALERS 9256
ANIMAL PAINTING AND ILLUSTRATION 5411
ANIMALS 9, 10, 243, 342, 349, 555, 567, 651, 671, 682, 707, 721, 904,
1074, 1109, 1148, 1206, 1367, 1802, 1803, 1914, 2368, 2388, 2403, 2651,
2661, 2854, 2908, 2920, 3219, 3229, 3235, 3335, 3588, 3700, 4069, 4377,
4424, 4432, 4464, 4466, 4477, 4526, 4527, 4544, 4651, 4672, 4678, 4718,
4733, 4743, 4751, 4814, 4817, 4818, 4819, 4820, 4821, 4884, 4989, 5002,
5019, 5035, 5093, 5176, 5177, 5179, 5180, 5181, 5182, 5183, 5184, 5185,
5186, 5187, 5188, 5192, 5212, 5228, 5244, 5349, 5351, 5354, 5360, 5380,
5477, 5522, 5523, 5524, 5525, 5533, 5558, 5560, 5563, 5564, 5565, 5566,
5567, 5590, 5620, 5663, 5665, 5707, 5718, 5719, 5720, 5721, 5722, 5723,
5760, 5891, 5892, 5893, 5904, 6226, 6255, 6312, 6317, 6491, 6532, 6546,
6597, 6598, 6642, 6860, 7060, 7129, 7154, 7155, 7407, 7475, 7500, 7542,
7581, 7609, 7637, 7716, 7773, 8407, 8458, 8466, 8567, 8620, 8798, 8835,
8840, 8914, 9136, 9157, 9214, 9234, 9259, 9451, 9452, 9496, 9546, 9738,
9749, 9810, 9829, 9841, 9843, 9844, 9862, 9865, 9870, 9906, 10083,
10093, 10162, 10251, 10264, 10426, 10458, 10541, 10620, 10722, 10736,
10819, 10898, 10903, 11008, 11023, 11024, 11025, 11057, 11063, 11231,
11394, 11408, 11449, 11499, 11562, 11609, 11644, 11646, 11714, 11739,
11805, 11915, 11942, 12093, 12163, 12259, 12296, 12303, 12369, 12371,
12399, 12555, 12557, 12565, 12606, 12639, 12720, 12998, 13055, 13064,
13065, 13231, 13243, 13531, 13665, 13839, 13885, 13930, 13933, 13960,
14026, 14042, 14052, 14119, 14124, 14129, 14130, 14230, 14284, 14350,

14357, 14412, 14604, 14806, 14830, 14961, 14984, 14988, 15026, 15214,
15242, 15260, 15359, 15476, 15480, 15487, 15547, 15786, 15805, 15912,
15913, 16089, 16287, 16289, 16290, 16360, 16382, 16387, 16388, 16531,
16556, 16629, 16695, 16731, 16751, 16788, 16823, 16931, 16967, 17063,
17199, 17203, 17237, 17261, 17393, 17398, 17458, 17792, 17820, 17896,
17928, 17947, 17997, 18217, 18281, 18390, 18391, 18487
Africa 13021, 13352
anatomy 15683
in art 14368, 14369
classification 17922
communication 413, 3717, 4176, 6520, 6533, 7452, 13355, 13962, 15291,
  17238
courtship 8225, 15278
defense 3543, 8584, 8848
desert 6745, 9852
diseases 17640
folklore 16421, 17331
food habits 8574
forest 8211, 8499
habitations 3134
habits and behavior 204, 700, 1078, 1175, 1191, 1424, 1795, 1802, 2479,
  3132, 3748, 4179, 5206, 5249, 5344, 5904, 6044, 6165, 6245, 6246,
  6249, 7017, 7451, 7494, 7555, 8225, 8583, 8650, 9298, 10393, 10432,
  10622, 11659, 12165, 13457, 13994, 14298, 14713, 15028, 15153, 15202,
  15278, 15283, 15284, 15631, 15715, 15749, 17557, 18122, 18223
hibernation 1041, 1078, 6983
in the city 146
infancy 2083, 5930, 6246, 6247, 6336, 6338, 6725, 8710, 8809, 10359,
  12013, 12141, 12892, 13210, 15153, 15154, 15269, 15286, 15314, 15416,
  17640
  pictorial works 6247, 13607
intelligence 6104, 6250
legends 567, 651, 1379, 1841, 2674, 2880, 3056, 4470, 5987, 6098, 6225,
  7641, 7775, 9546
in literature 2059, 2211
locomotion 6247
migration 6368, 11876, 14682
miscellanea 9959, 15735
mythical 1203, 1801, 4214, 14356, 15143, 15664, 16331, 17385, 17581,
  18426
  in art 17988
nocturnal 3748, 14300
North America 11782
parental behavior 2083, 6245, 6247, 8807, 8809, 15270, 15416
pictorial works 2934, 3610, 4544, 5296, 8296, 10726, 12298, 14568, 17914
poetry 178, 1362, 1365, 1366, 2440, 3317, 3809, 3810, 3813, 4656, 4739,
  5405, 5905, 5912, 5927, 6412, 6581, 8308, 8311, 8774, 8957, 12295,
  13888, 13890, 14182, 14554, 16126, 16663, 17710
poisonous 2185, 2739
populations 11248
predatory 7776
prehistoric 1234, 4578, 10230
rare 8442, 10505, 15665, 18230
  North America 7776
societies 671
sounds 9039, 14300
tracks 670, 1243, 9863

treatment 3117, 17640
see also DOMESTIC ANIMALS; MARINE ANIMALS; and individual animal
  names, e.g., SKUNKS
ANIMATION 450
ANKHSENAMEN (QUEEN OF EGYPT), (1362-ca. 1351 B.C.) 12473
ANNING, MARY (1799-1847) 1711
ANTARCTIC REGIONS 744, 5113, 14594, 15415, 16068
ANTEATERS 17357
ANTELOPES 16780
ANTHONY, SISTER, (1814-1897) 3847
ANTHONY, SUSAN B. (1820-1906) 7181, 9081, 12359, 12861, 13576
ANTHROPOGEOGRAPHY 5584
ANTHROPOLOGISTS 12481, 12581
ANTHROPOLOGY 11976, 11977
ANTIQUES 15867
ANTI-SEMITISM 12763
APACHE INDIANS 659, 661, 920, 926, 934, 1451, 1744, 2973, 8950, 14477,
  15034, 18070
  biography 657, 7173, 16585
  wars (1833-1886) 18332
APARTMENT HOUSES 3399, 6460, 6781, 8823, 9163, 15794
APES 3956, 3987, 5008, 10689
  habits and behavior 9768
APODOCAS 5423
APOLLO, PROJECT 644, 2133, 6425, 7506, 8191, 15768, 17931
APOSTLES 1184
APPALACHIA 2655, 3165, 3167, 3237, 3239, 3303, 7650
APPALACHIAN MOUNTAINS 9438, 10409, 11476, 12183, 12184
APPALACHIAN REGION 15617
  economic conditions 16935
  social conditions 14426
  social life and customs 14426
APPLE 8747, 9139, 9275, 12387, 15272
APPLESEED, JOHNNY see CHAPMAN, JOHN
APPRENTICESHIP 3875, 7737, 7739
APRIL FOOL'S DAY 10016
AQUANAUTS 17811
AQUARIUM FISHES 17307
AQUARIUMS 2478, 6047, 12434, 14922, 15313, 17307, 18250
AQUATIC RESOURCES
  Chesapeake Bay--maps 10899
  Maryland--maps 10899
  safety measures 18092
ARAB COUNTRIES--politics and government 611, 10947
ARABIA 3615, 6325
ARABS 611, 5750, 6416, 13679, 17599, 18282
ARAKI, DAISUKE 16251
ARAPAHO INDIANS 5521
ARBLAY, FRANCES (BURNEY) D' (1752-1840) 9478
ARBOR DAY 5905
ARCHEOLOGISTS 3193, 13823
ARCHEOLOGY 833, 1208, 1613, 4014, 4190, 4392, 4802, 5353, 6227, 6293,
  6353, 6909, 7722, 9121, 10125, 10360, 11540, 11772, 13823, 14010, 14325,
  15667, 17779, 18357
  history 17784
  methodology 7080
ARCHERY 2028, 3780, 14680, 16452

ARCHITECTURE   2898, 7014, 9458, 11277, 13239, 16489
  domestic
    designs and plans   12616
    history   8164
  Egypt   10453
  Gothic   11202
  Greece   10454
  history   1545
  United States   5047
    Ohio   2885
  vocational guidance   966
ARCTIC REGIONS   3324, 6963, 7682, 8657, 10964, 14676, 16069, 16653
  ecology   141
ARDENNES, BATTLE OF THE (1944-1945)   16911
ARGENTINA   5372, 7379, 9474
  music   13238
ARICKARA INDIANS (also called ARICKAREE INDIANS)   8368, 12023
ARIK-BUKA (d. 1263)   1210
ARITHMETIC   169, 756, 1100, 1431, 1553, 6402, 9330, 10455, 11536, 17018,
  17706, 17826
  poetry   9031, 13132
ARIZONA   882, 2995, 3251, 5806, 11186, 16551
ARKANSAS   343, 883, 2154, 2155, 2156, 2157, 2158, 2996, 7062
  description and travel   16546
ARMADILLOS   8579
ARMENIA   4290
ARMENIAN AMERICANS   4294
ARMIES   8780
ARMS AND ARMOR   6938, 12474
  Africa   12826
  history   12656, 12827
  Spanish--Southwest, New   4911
ARMSTRONG, LOUIS (1900-1971)   4160, 5234, 14332, 14896
ARNOLD, BENEDICT (1741-1801)   233, 12874
ARNOLD, MARGARET (SHIPPEN) (1760-1804)   5126
ART   1180, 1181, 1386, 1580, 1691, 1965, 2664, 3294, 3295, 6778, 7382,
  7383, 9840, 15573, 16063, 17963, 18353
  African   153, 4470, 6910, 11707, 16339
    West   12676, 13918
  ancient   6909, 6914, 6915, 6916, 6917, 6918, 6919, 6923
  appreciation   4234, 9700, 17988
  Asian   1182
  Chinese   1182, 6919
  collections   13485
  Dutch   4905
  East Indian   6921
  Egyptian   6914, 13915
  Etruscan   6927
  Greek   6915, 13916
  history   1180, 14777
  industry and trade
    Colonial Period (ca. 1600-1775)   17038
    Mexico   14661
    Renaissance   13917
  Iranian   227
  Japanese   228, 785, 6922
  Mexican--history   5830

modern 3728
  19th century 6911
  20th century 6920, 11198, 12051, 12622
Near Eastern 6923
objects--collectors and collecting 15867
Peruvian 6917
Prehistoric 1234, 14870
primitive 6910
  Africa--West 12676
Roman 6918
study and teaching 2867, 10094, 10096, 11043, 12392, 15572
technique 4761, 11509, 11560, 11689, 16125
thefts--Cameroon 5834
United States 226, 1181, 3726, 3728, 12622
  Black 3727
  history 6911, 6928
  Colonial Period (ca. 1600-1775) 6920
  Indiana 10371
  Southwest 16650
  Spanish American 6934
  19th century 6912
  20th century 6913
vocational guidance 1518
see also CAVE DRAWINGS
ARTHUR, KING see KING ARTHUR
ARTIFICIAL ISLANDS 12697
ARTIFICIAL ORGANS 12891
ARTIFICIAL SATELLITES 758, 2119, 2938, 4042, 4305, 9968
  models 14645
  Russian 7511
ARTISTS 541, 1181, 2198, 2547, 2550, 3293, 3299, 4755, 4947, 5734, 6074,
  7769, 9149, 9730, 9833, 10525, 10613, 12110, 12127, 12724, 12726, 13321,
  13545, 13655, 13925, 14506, 14508, 15409, 15624, 15865, 17282, 18073,
  18259
  dissent--Russia 819
  English 11923
  United States 8063, 10371
ASHANTI WAR (1873-1874) 8088
ASHANTIS 1745, 7222, 10165, 10168
ASHE, ARTHUR (1943-) 11855, 12482, 14475
ASIA
  art 1182
  description and travel 9411
  East 13810
  religion 5968, 15234
  Southeast 2823, 13817
  West 875
    antiquities 14460
ASIAN AMERICANS 8477
ASSATEAGUE ISLAND 1552
ASSINIBOIN INDIANS--legends 9354
ASSISI, SAINT FRANCIS OF see FRANCIS OF ASSISI, SAINT
ASSYRIA--history 12441
ASTHMA 18130
ASTROLOGY 828, 2111, 13738, 14851, 16310
ASTRONAUTICS 732, 3526, 5993, 6522, 7059, 8050, 10697, 12984, 15444,
  15758, 15768, 16775

civilization 3527
experiments 14631
Russia 15488
ASTRONAUTS 3271, 3853, 7272, 10202, 15488, 16775
ASTRONOMERS 985, 12032, 14614, 16496, 17269
ASTRONOMY 741, 747, 763, 2114, 2117, 2120, 2121, 2124, 2125, 6304,
    6517, 6518, 10210, 10351, 11512, 12958, 14188, 14268, 15097, 15769,
    16321, 17856, 18354, 18539, 18551
  charts, diagrams, etc. 12407
  history 14342
  Italian 3711
  observers' manuals 9236, 12959, 13487, 13774, 15751
  spherical and practical 15157
ASWAN 3190
ATHAPASCAN INDIANS 7361
ATHLETES 1554, 2750, 4594, 4667, 4776, 5653, 5882, 5887, 6721, 8161,
    8482, 8483, 12716, 14222, 16136, 16475, 17485
  Latin America 8970
  miscellanea 13904
  United States 4863, 8970, 10526, 11082
    biography 6722
ATHLETICS 4033, 9628
ATLANTIC CITY (NEW JERSEY) 17411
ATOMIC ENERGY 100, 110, 745, 5825, 8868, 10682, 12142, 13965, 18245
  bombs 2446
    physiological effects 3731
  power-plants 13965
  submarines 14198
  theory 6515, 14630, 15315
ATTICS 1851
ATTITUDE (PSYCHOLOGY) 5081, 7083, 11006, 11483, 11490, 11786, 11812,
    12022, 12716, 12728, 12750, 16026, 16040, 16233, 16356, 16652, 16951,
    18445, 18474, 18527
ATTUCKS, CRISPUS (d. 1770) 12211
AUDUBON, JOHN JAMES (1785-1851) 2198
AUSTIN, STEPHEN FULLER (1793-1836) 8344
AUSTRALIA 244, 1823, 2818, 3517, 3518, 3519, 4751, 5836, 8252, 9876,
    11740, 12903, 12904, 13203, 13204, 13205, 13206, 13207, 13303, 13632,
    13634, 13637, 13638, 13639, 13935, 14572, 16036, 16039, 16040, 16043,
    16059, 16060, 16794, 16795, 16796, 16797, 18063, 18244, 18318
  aborigines 8698
    legends 1174
  description and travel 9548, 13305, 14924
  social life and customs 9782
AUSTRALIAN POETRY 13360, 13361
  collections 5106
AUSTRIA 3159, 18174
  history--1938-1945 12954
AUSTRIAN AMERICANS 5583
AUTHORS 728, 4461, 8722, 11794, 12603, 15865
  Canadian 13792
  English 672, 11923, 17327
    Middle English (1100-1500) 8332
  United States 5290, 6033, 7988, 10529, 14715, 17142
    Nebraska--directories 9529
    19th century 7683, 9308
    20th century 12679

Yiddish 15776
AUTHORSHIP 16185
AUTISM 5294, 6984, 13317, 16059
   England--biography 4094
AUTOBIOGRAPHIES 662, 8722, 8906, 10172, 10822, 11796, 13160, 16415,
   17066, 17546, 18135, 18216, 18534
AUTOGRAPHS--collectors and collecting 16461
AUTOMATA 16484
AUTOMOBILES 1122, 1419, 1662, 2749, 3123, 4007, 4122, 6022, 6038, 10403,
   10574, 11067, 11507, 12594, 12671, 13476, 14447, 14909, 16094, 16134,
   16655, 17974, 18458
   design and construction 2749, 3119, 4128, 7777, 10597
   drivers 2681, 5642, 5769, 5770, 8215, 11404, 11507
   history 9006, 17045
   industry and trade--biography 9670
   models 16296, 17696
   racing 332, 727, 1036, 1038, 1039, 1788, 2757, 2758, 2759, 2760, 2761,
      2766, 2767, 2768, 2769, 2770, 2772, 2773, 2774, 2775, 3546, 4011,
      4026, 4036, 4685, 5257, 5261, 5445, 5446, 5447, 5761, 6622, 6680, 6681,
      6682, 6684, 6687, 6688, 6690, 6693, 7335, 7551, 8162, 8164, 8245, 9009,
      9010, 9014, 9019, 9021, 10098, 10099, 10137, 10764, 11404, 11865,
      11872, 11878, 12444, 12729, 12823, 12887, 13002, 13033, 13034, 13090,
      13111, 13184, 13988, 14072, 16924, 17629, 18374
      drivers 5444, 8162, 8163, 9007, 10137, 10764, 10768, 11853, 13089,
         13090, 13100, 13184, 14642, 14981, 18375
      history 13182, 16133
      motors 14918
      speed records 14642
      United States 9022, 9025
   service stations 957
      vocational guidance 957, 8316
   steam 9024
   touring 7642
   United States
      history 2609
      Utah--Great Salt Lake Desert 7335
   vocational guidance 967, 1476, 1510, 2075, 6280, 6282
AUTUMN 10130, 10270, 12169, 16995
   poetry 9741, 10580
AZTEC POETRY 4658
AZTECS 1746, 2166, 3604
   history 9500

- B -

BABIES see INFANTS
BABOONS 5403, 6589
BABY SITTERS 2966, 7256, 7433, 7435, 8728, 10326, 12680, 14440, 16949,
   17296, 17582, 17731
BACA, ELFEGO (1865-1945) 1563
BACH, JOHANN SEBASTIAN (1685-1750) 3545
BACKPACKING 2467, 2468, 2469, 3895, 6784
BACTERIOLOGY 15294
BADGERS 2656, 5246, 8272, 8273, 8274, 8275, 8276, 8277, 16138

BADILLO, HERMAN (1929-) 372
BADMINTON 18308
BAGHDAD (IRAQ) 11095
BAJA CALIFORNIA 5599, 13010, 15876
BAJUN (AFRICAN PEOPLE) 14671
BAKERS AND BAKERIES 1742, 2588, 2935
BAKING 1950, 9277, 9453, 14392, 15864, 16003, 18183, 18594; see also
  COOKERY
BALAKLAVA, BATTLE OF (1854)--poetry 16741
BALANCE 16109
BALEARIC ISLANDS 18327
BALI (ISLAND) 10307
  description and travel 11085
  social life and customs 16080
BALL, LUCILLE (1911-) 3757
BALL PLAYERS 6446; see also under specific sport with subheading "play-
  ers," e.g., BASEBALL--PLAYERS
BALLADS 11568
  Australian 13361
  English 10256, 13743
  Scottish 14301
  United States 2979, 8703, 13743
    Ohio 5252
    The West 11039
BALLET 318, 1331, 1724, 1990, 4503, 5065, 8551, 10087, 10237, 11656,
  12607, 14871, 15723, 16407, 16413, 16740, 16761, 16895, 17166
  Russian 7780
  stories, plots, etc. 7103, 11951
  study and teaching--Russia 7780
BALLOONS AND BALLOONING 2626, 3073, 4037, 5095, 5267, 7946, 10217,
  10848, 12311, 13303, 14075, 16874, 17329, 17749
BALSA WOOD 10778
BALTIMORE (MARYLAND)--history 14899
BANDS (MUSIC) 14344, 16494
BANGALORE (INDIA) 12846
BANGLADESH--social conditions 10366
BANK TELLERS 946
BANKERS 4596
BANKS, ERNIE (1931-) 10762, 11867
BANKS AND BANKING 16657
  vocational guidance 4596
BANNEKER, BENJAMIN (1731-1806) 1298, 10695, 18093
BANNOCK INDIANS--legends 7976, 18355
BANTING, SIR FREDERICK GRANT (1891-1941) 15500
BANTUS 9547, 12568
BARBADOS (ISLAND) 16803
BARBAROSSA, KHAYR AL-DIN (d. 1546) 7183
BARBOSA, JOSE CELSO (1857-1921) 16245
BARCELONA (SPAIN) 16032
BARNS 2590, 15100
BAROMETER 4209
BARONS' WAR (1263-1267) 16979
BAROTSES 11433
BARRINGER, EMILY (DUNNING) (1876-1961) 5147, 12856
BARRY, RICK (1944-) 6987
BARRYMORE, ETHEL (1879-1959) 6190
BARTHOLDI, FREDERIC AUGUSTE (1834-1904) 13387

BARTLETT, ROBERT ABRAM (1875-1946) 14923
BARTON, CLARA (HARLOWE) (1821-1912) 2053, 7169, 11606, 12884, 14607, 16273
BASEBALL 156, 473, 581, 619, 620, 1620, 1682, 1683, 1863, 2208, 2322, 2608, 3756, 4138, 4598, 4771, 4779, 4780, 4790, 5160, 5161, 5172, 5571, 5790, 5895, 5945, 6090, 6307, 6691, 6694, 6788, 7125, 7267, 7700, 7729, 7750, 7819, 7914, 8243, 8361, 8530, 8531, 8533, 8884, 8936, 8980, 8981, 9012, 9460, 9464, 9465, 9748, 9893, 9985, 10011, 10490, 10673, 10742, 10759, 10760, 10771, 10772, 10892, 11064, 11263, 11359, 11648, 11919, 11966, 12154, 13032, 13215, 13300, 13401, 13456, 13509, 13546, 13877, 14239, 14244, 14466, 14628, 14736, 14843, 15215, 15570, 15577, 15850, 15851, 15853, 15854, 15856, 15858, 15859, 15908, 15916, 15929, 16451, 16466, 16478, 16669, 16768, 16919, 17048, 17050, 17052, 17070, 18247
  addresses, essays, lectures 2587
  anecdotes, facetiae, satire, etc. 10917
  batting 2162
  cards 3523
  dictionaries 617, 17445
  history 5497, 6940, 14480, 14629
  managers 8559, 14479, 15908, 17221
  pitches 2321, 2748
  players 1178, 1550, 2162, 2323, 2608, 2610, 2613, 2614, 2616, 2621, 2623, 2625, 2747, 2748, 3213, 4591, 4779, 4796, 5305, 5488, 5500, 5501, 5506, 5880, 6720, 6940, 7124, 7516, 7520, 7522, 7525, 7819, 7985, 8241, 8243, 9012, 9018, 9892, 9893, 10011, 10759, 10760, 10762, 10765, 10769, 10771, 10772, 10775, 10892, 11867, 11874, 11887, 11901, 11916, 12085, 12257, 12584, 12778, 13105, 13110, 14090, 14467, 14481, 14482, 14483, 14608, 14738, 14745, 14747, 15108, 15109, 15110, 15431, 15432, 15434, 15435, 15577, 15907, 15910, 16132, 16464, 16488, 16491, 16771, 17081, 17141, 17217, 17292, 17613, 18439, 18443, 18444, 18493
  poetry 16777, 16778
  stories 1667, 2989, 2990, 3213, 3413, 3420, 3422, 3424, 3425, 3427, 3431, 3434, 3741, 3833, 3991, 4000, 4098, 4099, 4114, 4224, 4226, 4314
  teams 3833, 7699
  vocational guidance 4598
  World Series 14480
BASHFULNESS 6187, 9146, 10734, 15476, 15881, 16667, 17117, 18002, 18265, 18369
BASKETBALL 333, 582, 1292, 1300, 1681, 2163, 3118, 3214, 3414, 3418, 3421, 3423, 3428, 4027, 4227, 5572, 6350, 6351, 6689, 8131, 8132, 8544, 8979, 8982, 9016, 9491, 10676, 10918, 11066, 11171, 11513, 11776, 11892, 12155, 12355, 12457, 12520, 12713, 13400, 13622, 14826, 15053, 16486, 16766, 17049, 17050, 17054, 17421, 17758
  caricatures and cartoons 8489
  dictionaries 8489, 10909
  history 17218
  players 947, 1534, 2163, 2164, 2617, 3214, 4776, 4787, 5570, 7523, 7822, 7986, 8190, 8240, 9016, 10918, 11883, 14091, 14748, 14835, 17080
  for women 1089
BASKETS AND BASKETMAKING 3488, 17609
BASQUES 8938
BASS, DICK (1937-) 10761
BATES, KATHARINE LEE (1859-1929) 12600
BATHS 1112, 2685, 13362, 18184
BATHURST ISLAND (NORTHWEST TERRITORIES, CANADA) 2535
  description and travel 16541
BATIK 4874

BATRACHIA 2169, 2478
BATS (ANIMALS) 6263, 6342, 9157, 9538, 10343, 10386, 10506, 13712
  poetry 9156
BATTLES 2040; see also specific battles, e.g., LEXINGTON, BATTLE OF
BATTLESHIPS 15569
BAUGH, LAURA (1955-) 9069, 13193
BAYOUS 10558
BEACHES 8246, 8965, 9966, 10129, 13349, 15261
BEADWORK 4582, 4900
BEARD, DANIEL CARTER (1850-1941) 11787
BEARS 278, 281, 545, 566, 857, 858, 1490, 1491, 1492, 1493, 1494, 1495,
  1496, 1497, 1644, 1873, 1876, 1877, 1878, 1879, 1880, 1881, 2333, 2954,
  3235, 4241, 4455, 4855, 4891, 4933, 5079, 5080, 5236, 6068, 6129, 6331,
  6334, 6455, 6457, 6509, 6742, 7916, 7917, 8351, 8462, 9122, 9134, 9135,
  9137, 9981, 10138, 10626, 10789, 10891, 11118, 11253, 11285, 11493,
  11495, 11563, 11571, 11672, 12181, 12260, 12261, 12262, 12358, 12426,
  12427, 12430, 12507, 13468, 13695, 13749, 14258, 15359, 15558, 15815,
  16216, 17057, 17514, 17553, 17658, 18121, 18156, 18310, 18580
  pictorial works 18401
  polar 558
BEAR'S HEART (INDIAN ARTIST), (1851-1882) 16508
BEASTS 1362, 1366
BEATRICE (CONSORT OF LUDOVICO SFORZA, IL MORO, DUKE OF MILAN),
  (1475-1497) 9993
BEATTY, CLYDE (1903-1965) 17932
BEAUMONT, WILLIAM (1785-1853) 5490
BEAUREGARD, PIERRE GUSTAVE TOUTANT (1818-1893) 8554
BEAUTY, PERSONAL 608, 10412, 12234
BEAUTY CONTESTS 13451, 13602
BEAVERS 369, 556, 2079, 5237, 5265, 8278, 8805, 12964, 14693, 16996
BECKWOURTH, JAMES PIERSON (1798-1866) 1730, 5778, 13722
BEDOUINS 6803
BEEBE, CHARLES WILLIAMS (1877-1962) 1738
BEEKEEPERS 16329
BEETHOVEN, LUDWIG VAN (1770-1827) 9033
BELL, ALEXANDER GRAHAM (1847-1922) 15566
BELL FOUNDERS 7443
BELLO, EMIR MOHAMMEDU 2041
BELLS 9680, 18421
BELTZ, WILLIAM (1912-1960) 18200
BEN BAZALEEL, JUDAH LOW (d.1609) 11287
BENCH, JOHNNY (1947-) 2616, 7985, 9018, 10765
BENEDICTINE ABBEY (SAINT-DENIS, FRANCE) 14511
BENIN (NIGERIA) 1075, 6133
  history 5365
  social life and customs 10286
BENIN (PROVINCE, NIGERIA) 15651
BENNETT, ROBERT LaFOLLETTE (1912-) 12727
BENT, WILLIAM (1808-1869) 1725
BENT'S FORT (COLORADO) 1725
BERBERS 4610
BERCHTOLD ZU SONNENBURG, MARIA ANNA (MOZART) REICHSFRIIN VON
  (1751-1829) 12343
BERCZY, WILLIAM (1748-1813) 2686
BEREAVEMENT see DEATH
BERMUDA TRIANGLE 4419
BERNADETTE, SAINT (1844-1879) 4537, 4540

BERNSTEIN, LEONARD (1918-) 3922
BERRA, YOGI (1925-) 15109
BERRY, MARTHA (McCHESNEY), (1866-1942) 1704, 12597, 13616
BETHLEHEM, STAR OF 2122
BETHUNE, MARY JANE (McLEOD), (1875-1955) 489, 2715, 3115, 7307, 14060, 16255
BHUTAN 14177
BIBLE 648, 1052, 1093, 2251, 2560, 2561, 2803, 4657, 4679, 4736, 4934, 5352, 5656, 5667, 7331, 12126, 13423, 13558, 16684, 17071
    antiquities 7722
    commentaries 7331
    natural history 5661, 5901
    plays 5339
    selections 13265
BIBLE. N.T. 7131, 7133
    gospels--pictorial works 13556
    pictorial works 15572
BIBLE. O.T. 535, 1860, 4736, 5175, 5665, 5672, 7130, 7132, 7137, 7792, 8863, 10544, 13559, 13562, 13564, 15777, 15786, 15787, 16083, 16092, 17006, 17376, 17410, 17782, 17882
    Apocrypha 12131
    biography 14911
    Genesis 17659
      language style 769
    Pentateuch--language style 767
    pictorial works 6923
    poetry 4657, 5405
    Psalm XXIII 10052
BIBLIOTHERAPY 3365, 3366, 3367, 3368
BICKERDYKE, MARY ANN (BALL), (1817-1901) 4697
BICYCLES AND BICYCLING 2030, 2047, 2175, 2764, 3416, 4034, 4422, 4423, 5262, 6224, 6224a, 8051, 8330, 9169, 9890, 10423, 11195, 11320, 11447, 11501, 12309, 14266, 14908, 15834, 16453, 16645, 16776, 16799, 16803, 17930
    addresses, essays, lectures 10508
    maintenance and repair 4422
    poetry 13360
    racing 9008, 14980
    safety measures 9753
    touring 12309
BIGFOOT see SASQUATCH
BILLINGTON, JOHN (d. 1773) 2558
BINARY SYSTEM (MATHEMATICS) 17563
BINI (AFRICAN PEOPLE) 13121
BIOETHICS 835
BIOGRAPHY 8105, 11469, 11736, 13358
    collections 578, 1256, 4504, 4858, 5586, 6608
    see also individual subjects and characters
BIOLOGICAL RHYTHMS 1529
BIOLOGISTS 10316
BIOLOGY 370, 1427, 6894, 15290
    classification 14367, 14797
    fieldwork 14790
    freshwater 4066
    periodicity, 15760
    social aspects 8976

technique 1530
BIOLUMINESCENCE 14829, 15720
BIONICS 11720, 15678
BIRDS 179, 341, 480, 498, 797, 1074, 1161, 1506, 1720, 1796, 2182, 2186,
2584, 2592, 2640, 2829, 3851, 3952, 4377, 4412, 4511, 4801, 5109, 5203,
5204, 5205, 5210, 5222, 5223, 5224, 5241, 5282, 5705, 5706, 5720, 5721,
5937, 5990, 6248, 6261, 6264, 6513, 6534, 6535, 6537, 6746, 6752, 6763,
6882, 7091, 8064, 8459, 8621, 8709, 8962, 9391, 9624, 10818, 11252,
11438, 12439, 12500, 12610, 13084, 13475, 13750, 13789, 13900, 14405,
14769, 14786, 15151, 15312, 15317, 15725, 15809, 16000, 16802, 16999,
17059, 17340, 17709, 17762, 17768, 17927, 18054
banding 17736
Canada
   Northwest Territories--Bathurst Island 16541
   Ontario 7684, 13140
   Quebec 7684
eggs and nests 1967, 5204, 5997, 5998, 6539, 8441, 8708
flight 9539
folklore 1147, 3315
fossil 9542
habits and behavior 2193, 13580, 15714
migration 9543, 11911
nomenclature 10818
North America 5756, 9785, 10436, 15196, 15198
pictorial works 13338, 15438, 17915
poetry 15502
of prey 8401, 10389
protection of 3851, 11243
rare 11243
songs 6533
state 4412
United States 5757
   Illinois 5302, 5304
   Indiana 7550
   Maine--Smuttynose Island 15199
   Michigan 2145
watching 2193, 15312, 16313
BIRTH 3152, 16430
BIRTH CONTROL 10180
BIRTHDAYS 818, 1059, 1110, 2931, 3110, 3230, 3622, 3822, 3834, 4364,
5988, 6549, 7044, 8015, 8276, 8810, 8961, 9170, 9177, 9291, 9599, 9660,
10745, 10746, 10751, 10837, 12851, 13378, 13442, 13872, 13913, 14485,
16231, 17090, 17106, 17405, 17413, 17501, 17589, 17593, 18462
poetry 2214
BISON 557, 4514, 11255, 11326, 14695, 14782, 15201
BLACK AMERICANS 19, 58, 124, 134, 158, 652, 690, 1050, 1070, 1071,
1501, 1714, 1730, 1916, 1917, 1924, 1925, 2250, 2309, 2360, 2453, 2703,
3115, 3425, 3618, 3620, 3628, 3771, 5536, 5725, 5726, 6788, 7135, 7136,
7139, 7241, 7259, 7305, 7306, 7307, 7308, 7537, 7664, 7666, 7705, 7981,
8085, 9439, 9513, 9593, 9957, 10325, 10579, 10594, 10679, 10709, 11051,
11514, 11735, 11818, 12089, 12218, 13112, 13214, 13875, 16361, 16655,
16693, 16816, 17356, 17449, 17795, 17945, 17946, 18438, 18439, 18440,
18443, 18444, 18453, 18454, 18455
actors and actresses 14582
art 3727
artists 1257, 5754
athletes 1916, 8485, 13105, 13185, 14475

authors   3514, 5290, 5777, 6429, 6438, 6442, 17427
biography   290, 313, 489, 493, 2717, 3381, 3508, 4562, 4563, 4569, 4944,
   5036, 5037, 5038, 5072, 5100, 5133, 5134, 5274, 5275, 5498, 5499, 5500,
   5501, 5775, 5777, 5778, 5783, 5787, 6084, 6093, 6209, 6244, 7151, 7174,
   7309, 7313, 7314, 7467, 7621, 7661, 7665, 7733, 7811, 7816, 7817, 7818,
   7821, 7826, 7827, 7828, 7830, 7920, 8155, 8189, 8520, 8818, 9073, 9305,
   9313, 9378, 9535, 9699, 10532, 11618, 11816, 11856, 11999, 12090,
   12091, 12485, 12487, 12930, 13187, 13549, 13575, 14060, 14339, 14467,
   14583, 15111, 15129, 16198, 16246, 16252, 16253, 16255, 16319, 16415,
   16431, 16697, 16895, 17546, 17614, 17800, 18066, 18067, 18068, 18093,
   18452
children   4562
   Huntersville (North Carolina)   14433
   Southern states   10085
civil rights   2778, 2985, 3771, 7004, 7310, 7537, 7772, 9003, 9377, 12090,
   16291, 16697, 17542
   history   16242
   pictorial works   14719
composers   5593
cowhands   5165
folklore   5729
history   1050, 3971, 4830, 5071, 5100, 6436, 7051, 7772, 8725, 8818, 9003,
   9315, 11216, 11229, 13375, 16046, 16854
   miscellanea   7787
   sources   6239, 12042
   to 1863   8989, 8993
   1863-1877   2505, 8990
   1877-1964   5069, 8991, 8992, 12053
inventors   7541, 7911
lawyers   5787, 18456
literature   969, 1033
Maryland--history   14587
Michigan--history   10284
Montgomery (Alabama)   16291
music--history and criticism   9620, 14739
musicians   4161, 4960, 6884, 8717, 14896, 16514
in New York (City)   7622, 15510, 17665
nurses   13711
physicians   5786
poetry   20, 1919, 1920, 4350, 5116, 6861, 6862, 16561
poets   14581
policemen   6358
politics and suffrage   2985
psychology   15022
race identity   3663, 3971, 8720
religion   7832
scientists   7541, 7912
sermons   9286
social conditions   1197, 1889, 2430, 3373, 6481, 8776, 8777, 11817, 12583,
   15022, 17502, 18056
social life and customs   15401
sociologists   10177
soldiers   3529, 7214, 13727
songs   7775, 9287, 9288, 9335
Southern states   6887
wit and humor   8715
   history and criticism   15022

women 2715
   health and hygiene 12234
   musicians 9353
BLACK CREEK PIONEER VILLAGE (TORONTO, CANADA) 10240
BLACK ENGLISH 3211
BLACK HAWK (SAUK CHIEF), (1767-1838) 487, 1294, 3599, 7502, 10417, 10638
BLACK HAWK WAR (1832) 1294, 7502
BLACK HOLES (ASTRONOMY) 746
BLACK POWER--United States 2778, 7827
BLACK SPIRITUALS 2460
BLACKSMITHING
   biography 1072, 5941
   history 5941
BLACKWELL, ELIZABETH (1821-1910) 984, 3474, 7172, 8059, 8142, 10314
BLANE, MARION 11314
BLESSING AND CURSING 3745, 3746
BLIND see PHYSICALLY HANDICAPPED
BLIZZARDS 6422, 11851, 17906, 18084, 18405
BLONDIN, JEAN FRANÇOIS GRAVELET, known as, (1824-1897) 10046
BLOOD 15594, 16252, 18536
   bank 7720
   circulation 3366
BLUE, VIDA (1949-) 10011
BLUE JACKET (SHAWNEE CHIEF), (b.ca. 1752) 5245
BLUE RIDGE MOUNTAINS (NORTH CAROLINA) 1357, 4268
BLUES (SONGS, ETC.)
   United States 9353
    history and criticism 9620
BLY, NELLIE see COCHRANE, ELIZABETH
BOATS AND BOATING 89, 1435, 2034, 2064, 2377, 2682, 2968, 3246, 4257,
   4271, 5099, 5763, 5865, 5989, 6201, 6206, 7143, 8134, 9296, 9334, 10576,
   11214, 12061, 12113, 12521, 14175, 14373, 14700, 16301, 16512, 16868,
   16869, 17766, 18029, 18500
   poetry 10696, 12071, 13151
   racing 16871, 16872
BOBCATS 10896
BOBSLEDDING 7334
BODY TEMPERATURE--regulation 1593
BOGARDUS, ANNETJE JANS (1600?-1663) 16091
BOHEMIAN AMERICANS 9423
BOK, EDWARD WILLIAMS (1863-1930) 16978
BOLIVAR, SIMON (1783-1830) 16577
BOMBERS 4003, 4010
BONDI, AUGUST (1833-1907) 263
BONES 1013, 5332, 5334, 7449, 18537
BONHEUR, ROSA (1822-1899) 13925
BONPLAND, AIME JACQUES ALEXANDRE GOUJAUD, called (1773-1858) 16822
BOOKMOBILES 8008, 16024
BOOKS 5183, 5201, 5282, 7301, 10082, 10120, 10144, 12828, 13995, 14990,
   16052, 16974, 17691
   binding 13995
   care 4245
   history 1145
   industry and trade 7301
   Polyglot 6804, 18223

and reading 6490
BOONE, DANIEL (1734-1820) 2363, 4532, 15441, 16167
BOONE, REBECCA (BRYAN), (1739-1813) 4660
BORDER GUARDS 1213
BOREDOM 1601, 8289
BORNEO--history 18474
BOSTON (MASSACHUSETTS) 11210, 11239
  Colonial Period (ca. 1600-1775) 10677
  history 4387
  social life and customs, Colonial period (ca. 1600-1775) 5508
BOTANISTS 1224, 1391
BOTANY 2143, 5043, 5044, 17636, 17637, 18222, 18313, 18550
  classification 15319, 15324
  ecology 5212, 8402, 12253
  economic 5043, 9559, 17664
  experiments 14083, 14087, 14088, 16367, 17855
  miscellanea 14039
  pictorial works 7469, 7470
  Rocky Mountains 18402
BOTSWANA 3041, 7708, 12285, 12287
BOURCLAY, JULES 6456
BOWDITCH, NATHANIEL (1773-1838) 10313
BOWIE, JAMES "JIM" (1805-1836) 6207, 6634
BOWLING 4001, 4973, 14149
  dictionaries 10911
BOXCARS 11761
BOXERS (SPORTS) 5274, 11891, 13108, 14092, 14746, 18067
BOXES 3329, 12952, 13555
BOXING 2619, 10901, 11891, 11918, 14092, 14746, 15662, 15930, 16454, 18067
  biography 295
  history 5159, 5161
  pictorial works 13061
BOY SCOUTS OF AMERICA 1735, 5035, 6705, 8996, 9961, 9962, 11787
BOYD, BELLE (1844-1900) 12873
BOYS 710, 5009, 9207, 10043, 11938, 15064
BRADFORD, WILLIAM (1588-1657) 7189, 9085
BRADLEY, OMAR NELSON (1893-1981) 14192
BRADSHAW, TERRY (1948-) 7519
BRADSTREET, ANNE (1612?-1672) 5131
BRAILLE, LOUIS (1809-1852) 4659, 10127
BRAIN 15603, 15684, 17625, 18560
BRANDEIS, LOUIS DEMBITZ (1856-1941) 5308, 13435
BRANT, JOSEPH (1742-1807) 234
BRAZIL 2171, 2425, 15539
  social life and customs 6121, 6795, 14237
BREAD 86, 4869, 9277
BRECKINRIDGE, SALLY (1881-1965) 3847
BRENDAN, SAINT (484?-577?) 6382
BRENT, MARY (KITTAMAQUUND), (1630?-?) 162
BRIDGER, JAMES, (1804-1881) 6009, 6635, 11149, 16943, 18105
BRIDGES 1169, 7026
  Ohio 9754
BRIDGMAN, LAURA (DEWEY), (1829-1889) 8771
BRITISH COLUMBIA 1708, 12703
BROADCASTING
  vocational guidance 5803, 6283

see also RADIO--BROADCASTING and TELEVISION--BROADCASTING
BRONTE, CHARLOTTE (1816-1855) 10170, 17328
BRONZE AGE 523, 1316, 14033
BROOKLYN (NEW YORK CITY) 8101
BROOKLYN BRIDGE (NEW YORK CITY) 17272
  social conditions 17336
BROTHERS AND SISTERS 282, 285, 420, 678, 811, 825, 1538, 1543, 1547,
  1821, 1907, 1913, 1927, 1943, 2066, 2197, 2294, 2413, 2510, 2562, 2586,
  2678, 2785, 2990, 3154, 3160, 3340, 3355, 3423, 3554, 3571, 3585, 3586,
  3627, 3629, 3651, 3864, 3935, 3939, 3982, 4146, 4439, 4498, 4500, 4517,
  4731, 4799, 5137, 5357, 5448, 5464, 5466, 5470, 5520, 5523, 5602, 6023,
  6290, 6352, 6366, 6449, 6624, 6718, 6826, 6977, 7282, 7311, 7471, 7626,
  7657, 7760, 8218, 8267, 8275, 8282, 8291, 8469, 8481, 8841, 8963, 9241,
  9379, 9637, 9654, 9729, 9830, 9905, 9910, 9913, 9988, 10053, 10237,
  10324, 10326, 10499, 10519, 10616, 10739, 10831, 10938, 10943, 10956,
  11126, 11127, 11190, 11652, 11824, 11831, 12480, 12578, 12678, 12767,
  12835, 12941, 13159, 13304, 13317, 13412, 13415, 13416, 13442, 13517,
  13578, 13837, 13874, 14171, 14473, 14495, 14753, 14839, 15051, 15161,
  15920, 16101, 16173, 16208, 16548, 16754, 16755, 16766, 16819, 17303,
  17319, 17524, 17587, 17729, 17862, 17977, 18129, 18189, 18261, 18489,
  18527, 18599, 18600, 18608
BROWN, JAMES NATHANIEL (1936-) 9897
BROWN, JOE E. (1892-1973) 2362
BROWN, JOHN (1800-1859) 8883, 12882
BROWN, WILLIAM WELLS (1815-1884) 17529
BRUCE, BLANCHE KELSO (1841-1898) 16246
BRUNELLESCHI, FILIPPO (1377-1446) 14508
BUCCANEERS 4077
BUCK, PEARL (SYDENSTRICKER), (1892-1973) 12603
BUDDHA 3755, 15340
BUDDHISM 5255
  education 6610
BUENOS AIRES (ARGENTINA) 18477
BUFFALO, AMERICAN see BISON
BUILDING 633, 5958, 7723, 8410, 8686, 9458, 12616, 12712, 13584, 15508,
  15989, 17447
  inspectors 4876
  industry and trade--vocational guidance 10782, 14099
  maintenance and repair--vocational guidance 6274
  Rome (Italy) 11203
BULBS (BOTANY) 15276
BULGARIA 15409
BULLETIN BOARDS 4601
BULLFIGHTS 13373, 18177
  in art 1183
BULLS 4384, 7548, 10456, 10459
BUNCHE, RALPH JOHNSON (1904-1971) 4162, 7828, 18455
BURBANK, LUTHER (1849-1926) 2089
BURIED TREASURE 1451, 1726, 6010, 7927, 8169, 10050, 11521, 12658,
  12734, 12981, 13427, 14010, 15555, 15869, 16299, 16718, 17426, 17846
BURLINGTON (NEW JERSEY)--history 15210
BURMA 3261, 6609, 6610, 13853
BURNETT, CAROL (1934?-) 3442
BURNEY, FANNY see ARBLAY, FRANCES (BURNEY) D'
BURR, AARON (1756-1836) 4322
BURR CONSPIRACY (1805-1807) 7859
BURUNDI 3045, 3612

BUSES   4015, 4276, 6793, 8694, 9743, 11814, 12081, 15629
BUSHBABIES (ANIMALS)   16300
BUSHMEN   1170, 8977, 11091, 12118, 12991, 13511
BUSINESS   718, 956, 4701, 12115, 12274, 14439, 15146, 16147, 18450
   vocational guidance   7823
BUSINESSMEN   8711
   Toronto--biography   1163
BYZANTINE EMPIRE   3438
   history--Constantine XI Dragases (ruled 1448-1453)   17479
BYZANTIUM   4891

- C -

CABEZA DE VACA, ALVAR NUÑEZ (1490?-1557?)   9728, 16582
CABINET OFFICERS--United States   9267
CABLE CARS   2732, 2805
CABLES, SUBMARINE--Atlantic   12651
CACTUS   10387
CALCULATING MACHINES   1689
   problems, exercises, etc.   13249, 15085
CALENDARS   111, 3825
   Jewish   5309
CALIFORNIA   1275, 2859, 2860, 6644, 17099
   gold discoveries   1867, 6003, 6070, 6643, 11470
   history   11470
      to 1846   1267, 1277, 5872, 13011
   pictorial works   6443
CALL, LOUISE "WEZIE"   2848
CALVERT FAMILY   164
CALVES   3795
CAMELS   2052, 2705, 2783, 3157, 3732, 3856, 5588, 6332, 6971, 7049, 8445,
   9282, 10823, 11123, 11408, 11432, 11793, 17087, 17555, 17727
CAMEROON   2997
CAMOUFLAGE (BIOLOGY)   700, 3805, 4759, 5904, 8584, 8921, 11247, 11908,
   14663, 15282, 15631, 15715
CAMP FIRE GIRLS   9120
CAMPANELLA, ROY (1921-)   15108, 15434, 17217
CAMPGROUNDS--Ohio   12054
CAMPING   433, 857, 858, 1491, 1660, 2252, 3078, 3781, 4847, 5035, 5891,
   6477, 6784, 7276, 7457, 7668, 8330, 8331, 8384, 9132, 9237, 9243, 9685,
   9802, 9963, 11943, 12365, 12810, 13000, 13377, 13390, 13413, 13633,
   14116, 14375, 14841, 15046, 15118, 15425, 16361, 16759, 17302, 17522,
   17538, 18267, 18409, 18501
   anecdotes, facetiae, satire, etc.   11454
CANADA   363, 773, 2674, 4243, 5376, 5864, 5865, 5866, 8671, 11474, 11526,
   14254, 14641
   description and travel   11446, 12657, 14584
   exploring expeditions   804
   history   362, 3994, 4385
      pictorial works   9185
      1755-1763   10984
      to 1763 (New France)   4168, 8094, 16580, 17984
         discovery and exploration   7756, 13332, 16584
      1763-1791   5054

War of 1812 17554
  rebellion (1837) 17067
immigration and emigration 3896
industries 10139
social life and customs 10140, 10141
upper 11277
Western--history 5246
CANADIAN LITERATURE--20th century 11647
CANADIAN POETRY 10480, 10481, 10482
collections 5055
CANALS 1587, 1824, 2466, 2528, 2529, 5013, 6077, 6195, 6202, 9425, 11995,
  12002, 14792, 16086, 18201
England 17481
Ohio 17891
CANCER 1511, 15679; see also TUMORS
CANDLES 6818
CANOES AND CANOEING 1274, 1406, 2029, 5763, 6878, 12313, 13495, 15387
Minnesota 9148
CAPE COD--fishermen of 841
CAPE TRAFALGAR, BATTLE OF (1805) 2723
CAPITALISTS AND FINANCIERS 17674
CAPITALS (CITIES) 6968
CAPYBARAS 13470
CARBON 15315
CAREW, ROD (1945-) 1178, 10771
CARIBBEAN AREA 13096
description and travel--views 5591
CARIBBEAN SEA 4086
CARIBE 697
CARIBOU 14174
CARLISLE (PENNSYLVANIA)--U.S. Indian School--athletics 7612
CARNEGIE, ANDREW (1835-1919) 11577, 15564
CARNIVALS 3284
CAROLS see CHRISTMAS--MUSIC
CAROUSELS 2379, 10102, 13198
CARPENTRY--vocational guidance 10783
CARPETS 13328
CARRIAGES AND CARTS 8679, 9245, 11018, 12207, 12289, 14333, 17045,
  17347
CARSON, CHRISTOPHER "KIT" (1809-1868) 1352, 2887, 6636, 7176, 16275
CARSON, RACHEL LOUISE (1907-1964) 10316, 16244
CARTIER, JACQUES (1491-1557) 804, 16579, 16963
CARTOGRAPHY--history 8227
CARTOONS AND CARICATURES 450, 2105, 2106, 2233, 5415, 6925, 8219,
  9586, 15338, 16289
CARUSO, ENRICO (1873-1921) 9027
CARVER, GEORGE WASHINGTON (1864?-1943) 313, 5498, 7151, 11999,
  12390, 16274, 16812, 16950, 17783
CASALS, PABLO (1876-1973) 215
CASALS, ROSEMARY (1948-) 9074
CASH, JOHNNY (1932-) 2026, 16698
CASSATT, MARY (1844-1926) 11440, 12602, 18073
CASTILLO DE SAN MARCOS (ST. AUGUSTINE, FLORIDA) 16508
CASTLES 1392, 1489, 1825, 4360, 7037, 11201, 12852, 17149, 17154, 17960
CASTLETON (VERMONT) 3713
CATHAL CROBHDHEARG (KING OF CONNAUGHT), (d. 1224) 13795
CATHEDRALS 9036, 11202, 14508

CATHER, WILLA (SIBERT), (1873-1947) 1886, 6203
    portraits, etc. 15860
CATHOLIC CHURCH 4774, 5967
CATLIN, GEORGE (1796-1872) 7858, 14519
CATS 163, 167, 265, 274, 275, 506, 613, 803, 805, 806, 807, 818, 1302,
    1357, 1612, 1661, 1665, 1770, 1845, 1862, 1934, 2189, 2297, 2305, 2402,
    2484, 2581, 2600, 2639, 2645, 2791, 2804, 2830, 2846, 2847, 2924, 3106,
    3107, 3245, 3247, 3401, 3572, 3644, 3645, 3648, 3673, 3674, 4067, 4223,
    4671, 4673, 4678, 4720, 4898, 5421, 5746, 5884, 5897, 6078, 6213, 6386,
    6465, 6543, 6659, 6952, 7046, 7071, 7378, 7505, 8063, 8177, 8301, 8513,
    8518, 8775, 8799, 9261, 9295, 9457, 9593, 9595, 9598, 9657, 9695, 9946,
    10216, 10243, 10265, 10447, 10512, 10961, 11678, 11929, 12185,
    12187, 12299, 12456, 12772, 12773, 12864, 12983, 13159, 13268, 13476,
    13533, 13779, 13842, 13900, 13903, 14448, 14537, 14649, 14799, 15074,
    15088, 15130, 15262, 15286, 15355, 15368, 15481, 15628, 15804, 15832,
    15833, 16128, 16258, 16887, 17145, 17186, 17322, 17369, 17371, 17531,
    17660, 17822, 17951, 18002, 18303, 18364, 18392, 18457, 18577
    pictorial works 9089
    poetry 5340, 5920, 16692
CATTAILS 18222
CATTARAUGUS COUNTY (NEW YORK) 18382
CATTLE 664, 4617, 4618, 5049, 14176, 14775
    drives 6867
    parturition 3795
    Texas 4937, 15887
    trade 2659
    The West 17513, 17723
        history 11221
CAUCASUS--history 8564
CAVALRY 390
CAVELL, EDITH LOUISA (1865-1915) 4698, 5355, 7343, 17316
CAVES 5791, 10148, 10430, 13058, 13814, 17505
    animals 2293
    drawings 1204, 1234, 2755, 8552
    dwellers 15439
    Europe 1204
    United States 7623
        directories 15835
CAXTON, WILLIAM (1422?-1491) 7737
CAYUSE INDIANS 10221
CELLS 18497
CELTS 16529
CENTRAL AMERICA--description and travel 11691
CEPHALOPODS 3959
CERAMICS 12547
CEYLON 9833
    history 16098
    social life and customs 16078
    See also SRI LANKA
CHAD 2348, 2999, 8643
CHAGA (AFRICAN PEOPLE) 10542
CHAIRS 9605
CHAKA (ZULU CHIEF), (1787?-1828) 9588, 15232, 18269
    drama 12549
CHAMBERLAIN, WILTON NORMAN (1936-) 5570, 7986, 14748
CHAMELEONS 2925, 8123, 11803, 12980
CHAMPLAIN, SAMUEL DE (1567-1635) 16580

CHAN, MARIE 14235
CHANG-AN (ANCIENT CHINESE CAPITAL) 1378
CHANTS 3746
    Africa 132
CHAPLIN, CHARLES (1889-1977) 9034
CHAPMAN, JOHN (1774-1845) 310, 5034, 8751, 8755, 10635, 12387, 12899
CHARITIES 7708
CHARLES, RAY (1932-) 11816
CHARLESTON (SOUTH CAROLINA) 1836, 7654
CHARMS 216, 1394, 3628, 3745, 5481, 7326, 7913, 11627, 17949
CHAUTAUQUA COUNTY (NEW YORK) 18382
CHAVEZ, CESAR ESTRADA (1927-) 5151, 6198, 16765, 17798, 18447
CHEADLE, WALTER BUTLER (1835-1910) 7768
CHEETAHS 3158, 3944, 15038
    pictorial works 70
CHEMICAL REACTIONS 4115
CHEMICAL WARFARE 2109
CHEMISTRY 6287, 6289, 6301, 6516, 7278
    experiments 12605, 14632, 15406, 15737, 16363
    medical and pharmaceutical 17451
CHEMISTS 7278, 11437
CHENNAULT, CLAIRE LEE (1890-1958) 618
CHER (1946-) 9058
CHEROKEE INDIANS 1248, 1347, 1747, 2870, 3113, 5142, 6021, 8541, 8542,
    8951, 9369, 9370, 9769, 14543, 14544, 16172, 16177
    biography 5782, 13389
    legends 15026, 16968
CHEROKEE OUTLET (OKLAHOMA) 909
CHERRY 13583
CHERRY VALLEY (NEW YORK)--social life and customs 16610
CHESAPEAKE AND OHIO CANAL 6195
CHESAPEAKE BAY 2650
CHESS 9783, 10502
CHESSMEN 3094
CHEYENNE INDIANS 1544, 4912, 10499, 13491, 14773, 14901, 16423, 16508
    legends 13492, 18355
CHI, PAI-SHIH (1861-1957) 11591
CHICAGO (ILLINOIS) 5638, 9422
    description 9820
    fire (1871) 6189, 12625, 13620, 15893
    history 943, 9820, 11218
    Massacre (1812) 901
    World's Columbia Exposition (1893) 10421
CHICKENS 2189, 2605, 2930, 4672, 6064, 6844, 6867, 7371, 8838, 9174,
    9213, 9704, 9786, 10117, 10794, 10844, 10996, 11752, 12180, 12834,
    13226, 13742, 13941, 13978, 14416, 16875, 17101, 17590, 17950
    embryos 3796
CHILD CARE CENTERS 18264
CHILD, LYDIA MARIA (FRANCIS), (1802-1880) 12049
CHILDBIRTH 3209, 4622, 5062, 7652, 13827
CHILDREN 2688, 4517, 12283, 12660, 13420
    abuse 1216, 8749, 14436, 14839, 17477
    in Africa 914, 1939, 1940, 3376, 4409, 4491, 5465, 5475, 5753, 9781,
        11719, 15013, 15774, 16532
        East 9410
        West 1566, 9413, 15212
    in Agadez (Niger) 5458

anecdotes, facetiae, satire, etc. 13350
in Arctic Regions 4490
in Armenia 4289
as artists 177, 12829, 13485, 15353
  Canada 7381
  Israel 18576
  Terezin (Czechoslovakia) 10714
  United States 7381
as authors 21, 131, 177, 1233, 2667, 2814, 3362, 3364, 3458, 3965, 4239,
  7446, 9382, 9392, 9999, 10275, 10716, 10717, 10723, 10777, 12841,
  13485, 15521, 18576
  Canada 7381
  Russia 10714
  United States 7381
in Bali (Island) 4494, 16080
in Bangladesh 10366
in Benin 10286
in Bora-Bora 8447
in Brazil 14237
in Brooklyn (New York City) 17336
in Canada 10141, 10142
care and hygiene 15709, 17651
in Ceylon 16078
in China 2492, 10327, 10330, 10331, 10332, 10335, 11756, 18227
in Colombia 14914
in Czechoslovakia 531, 9159
and death 4155, 7444
in Denmark 2652
development 7790
in Egypt 5476
employment 2806
in Ethiopia 1060, 5455, 6124
in foreign countries 17174
in France 9457
in Ghana 5457, 5540, 6797, 15080
growth 10619
in Haiti 5312
in Hawaii 11185
in Honduras 11599
in Hong Kong 4493, 15078, 15410
in Hungary 15341, 15342
in India 7618, 9029, 15084, 18624
in Israel 5287
in Italy 13780
in Japan 8154, 9854, 11825, 11827, 15079, 16251, 17094, 17097, 18368,
  18369, 18370
in Kashmir 6125
labor 17477
in Lapland 4548
legal status, laws, etc.--United States 5018, 15172
in Lesotho 16201
in Liberia 15077
in Libya 5227
medical examinations 1508
in Mexico 1059, 3652, 3689, 4495, 11599, 15076, 16375
in Morocco 4293, 5589, 10755
in Nepal 4959, 8110, 10287

in New Guinea 13768
in Nigeria 1584, 2501
pictorial works 7615, 11318, 15489
as poets 9382, 10274, 10723
  New York (City) 15001
  Russia 12495
in Poland 5341
portraits 3609
in Portugal 1016, 6794
in Puerto Rico 2500, 5342, 11624, 15081, 15789, 15790
in Rhodesia 968
in South Africa 9410, 16200, 16323
in South Asia 9411
in Switzerland 3386
in Tanzania 14609
in Thailand 6802, 15083, 16079
in the Ivory Coast 1570
in the Sahara 4492
in the United States 2981, 5202
  Appalachian Region 15617
  Dallas (Texas) 3362
  New England 11210
  New York (City) 7446, 9537
in Tunisia 13129
in Turkey 7003, 15082
in Vietnam 3363, 10793
in Wales 17249
in Yugoslavia 5842
Zaire 5343, 5398
in Zambia 4446, 17520
CHILDREN'S LITERATURE--history and criticism 12364
CHIMBU (NEW GUINEA PEOPLE) 13768
CHIMPANZEES 413, 1301, 3945, 8267, 9283, 12642, 17548, 17549, 17550,
  17551
  habits and behavior 10393, 16732
  See also MONKEYS
CHINA 2483, 3394, 3550, 3637, 3671, 4675, 5991, 6020, 7271, 7689, 9808,
  9834, 10328, 10333, 10334, 10336, 10337, 10340, 10341, 10698, 10950,
  14144, 14228, 16989, 17036, 17455, 17577, 17870, 18011, 18214, 18422,
  18584
  art 1182
  civilization 12759, 13680
  commerce--with United States 3052, 16640
  description and travel 3550, 7755
  history 588, 609, 2272, 12540, 15033
    Yuan dynasty (1260-1368) 14758
    War of 1840-1842 3052
    1949- 15204, 15654
  mythology 1657
  poetry 1378
  social life and customs 3325, 5214, 8700, 10756, 11163, 12619
CHINATOWN (NEW YORK CITY) 14235
CHINCOTEAGUE ISLAND 8076, 8077
CHINESE AMERICANS 481, 482, 1008, 1325, 2559, 3436, 5039, 5580, 6087,
  6357, 9336, 9422, 9591, 10586, 10706, 11757, 12333, 12801, 12837, 12982,
  13782, 13783, 16508, 18396, 18397
  California--San Francisco 18395

history 16503
New York (City) 13704, 14235
social life and customs 16503
CHINESE LANGUAGE 9395
writing 17872, 18207
CHINESE NEW YEAR 16838
CHINESE POETRY 10718
CHINOOK INDIANS 10227
CHIPMUNKS 3573, 11258
habits and behavior 17037
CHIPPEWA INDIANS 577, 1009, 1579, 1640, 1748, 2246, 2753, 4242, 4838,
8953, 9727, 12806, 12807, 13118
biography 4856, 10005
legends 1568, 1578, 7418, 10501, 14218, 14452, 16047, 17392, 17448
music 4837
CHIPPEWA NATIONAL FOREST (MINNESOTA) 340
CHIRINOS, LITO (1962?-) 11599
CHISHOLM, SHIRLEY (1924-) 2442, 7821, 8155
CHISHOLM TRAIL 11219, 16701
CHIVALRY 1067, 2548; see also KNIGHTS AND KNIGHTHOOD
CHOCOLATE INDUSTRY AND TRADE 11582
CHOCTAW INDIANS 1994, 3963
CHOTA (VIRGINIA)--history 16177
CHOUTEAU, RENE AUGUSTE (1749-1829) 18257
CHRISTIAN ART AND SYMBOLISM 4559
CHRISTIAN LIFE 1938, 2268, 2595, 2603, 8115, 8116, 8691, 8928, 11325,
12243, 12244, 13554, 15402, 15499
poetry 13744
CHRISTIAN SAINTS 4536, 13586
Spain 4916
CHRISTIANITY 4421, 6873
Africa--Sub-Saharan 12535
CHRISTMAS 40, 148, 176, 229, 230, 412, 438, 546, 743, 775, 853, 903,
1015, 1132, 1376, 1673, 1722, 1742, 1864, 1912, 2167, 2233, 2242, 2314,
2392, 2398, 2422, 2486, 2602, 3095, 3106, 3245, 3259, 3402, 3493, 3678,
3689, 4059, 4061, 4375, 4515, 4638, 4881, 4977, 5187, 5228, 5525, 5547,
5569, 5577, 6088, 6214, 6233, 6410, 6451, 6524, 6552, 6907, 7613, 7650,
7749, 7931, 7950, 7956, 8047, 8265, 8281, 8286, 8499, 8515, 8518, 8540,
8798, 8839, 8926, 9135, 9168, 9290, 9297, 9326, 9328, 9394, 9455, 9456,
9703, 9817, 9912, 10020, 10061, 10068, 10070, 10103, 10108, 10252, 10744,
10833, 10834, 10843, 10985, 11034, 11113, 11154, 11335, 11340, 11594,
11600, 12111, 12207, 12221, 12304, 12358, 12384, 12731, 12974, 13258,
13366, 13379, 13380, 13471, 13784, 13785, 13786, 13895, 13996, 14129,
14422, 14456, 14498, 14504, 14967, 14971, 14974, 15101, 15102, 15217,
15221, 15343, 15378, 15580, 15648, 15889, 16076, 16392, 16424, 16719,
16772, 16782, 16790, 16791, 16807, 16876, 16913, 17029, 17092, 17177,
17191, 17210, 17407, 17463, 17608, 17732, 17769, 17796, 17885, 17947,
18468, 18486, 18598
cards 13539
decorations 4181, 4428, 6907, 12124, 13589, 16865
legends 3232
literary collections 1929, 14203, 14580
music 4995, 5291, 9710, 15238
carols 974, 5291, 6579, 8257, 8611, 9600, 12862, 13398, 14970, 15528,
15825, 17033, 17547, 17741, 17770
English 10250, 10253
Old English 972

Polish 4994
songs 1897
poetry 1133, 1376, 2215, 2384, 2412, 2449, 3623, 5228, 5229, 8601,
11154, 11339, 14312, 15400, 17019
Poland 16923
Sweden 1691, 17854
symbols 1136
trees 10070
Venezuela 3091
Wales 16808
CHRISTOPHE, HENRI (KING OF HAITI), (1767-1820) 7990
CHRONOLOGY 2471
CHUMASH INDIANS 5647
CHURCH MUSIC 11961
CHURCHILL, SIR WINSTON (1874-1965) 5507
CIBOLA (NEW MEXICO) 13014
CIMARRON (NEW MEXICO) 3964
CINCINNATI (OHIO) 11988, 13537
CINEMATOGRAPHY see MOTION PICTURES
CIPHERS 851, 6585, 10185, 10208, 12621, 13579, 14921, 15192, 15193
CIRCUS 572, 1150, 2956, 3928, 4372, 4918, 5079, 5084, 5728, 6164, 6543,
6561, 6562, 6563, 6709, 6711, 6713, 8347, 8354, 9228, 10086, 10811,
11353, 11533, 12299, 12427, 12556, 13231, 13612, 14698, 16395, 17244,
17752, 18275, 18490
biography 9850
performers 7479, 13869
pictorial works 17916
poetry 3275, 13884, 15379
Ringling Brothers 2719, 3928, 6898
vocational guidance 9666
CITIES AND TOWNS 2424, 2731, 6700, 17281
Iraq 17676
Mesopotamia 17676
pictorial works 8745, 10726
planning 15138, 15144
Rome 11203
ruined, extinct, etc. 2711, 7596, 17784
United States--Wyoming 12217
Spain 9229
United States 6968
Colorado 18215
Ohio 13212
views 14257
CITIZENSHIP 5771
CITY AND TOWN LIFE 53, 160, 258, 538, 776, 862, 944, 980, 988, 1009,
1479, 1488, 1502, 1652, 1654, 1804, 1892, 1957, 2309, 2317, 2408, 2433,
2557, 2737, 2784, 2862, 3359, 3392, 3582, 3621, 3640, 3656, 3860, 3968,
4015, 4147, 4488, 4767, 4770, 4866, 4880, 5186, 5295, 5592, 5638, 5671,
5738, 5771, 5855, 5856, 5859, 6175, 6179, 6459, 6553, 6718, 6781, 7134,
7186, 7285, 7363, 7446, 7615, 7647, 7650, 7705, 7807, 7808, 7900, 8004,
8101, 8209, 8247, 8260, 8449, 8823, 8828, 8829, 9163, 9592, 9594, 9618,
9818, 10002, 10009, 10036, 10184, 10329, 10338, 10592, 10733, 10735,
11098, 11102, 11109, 11182, 11318, 11359, 11612, 11617, 12104, 12112,
12116, 12170, 12241, 12315, 12324, 12588, 12609, 12610, 12766, 12846,
13031, 13713, 13856, 13875, 14048, 14126, 14197, 14212, 14241, 14394,
14443, 14619, 14888, 15042, 15043, 15044, 15050, 15052, 15184, 15243,
15258, 15326, 15481, 15588, 15731, 15997, 16032, 16057, 16234, 16743,

16807, 16817, 16818, 16959, 17008, 17214, 17336, 17384, 17503, 17600, 17657, 17797, 17886, 17951, 18056, 18431, 18628
  England 11480, 11481
    history--pictorial works 7045
  poetry 6405, 8588, 8602, 9054, 9943, 10275, 10277, 10562, 11334, 11671
CITY PLANNING 8198
CITY SERVICES 11205
CIVIL ENGINEERING 16467, 16476
  Rome (Italy) 11203
CIVIL RIGHTS 634, 2964, 3771, 5841, 5871, 5931, 6480
  drama 8044
  United States 18136
CIVIL SERVICE POSITIONS 10928
CIVILIZATION 996, 8399, 17202
  African 1030
  ancient 13915, 16522, 17784, 18110
  Assyrio-Babylonian 1208, 17676
  Egyptian 5815
  Greek 2049, 5636, 5816, 13916, 14034
  medieval 1068, 1698, 1825, 6181
  Mesopotamian 5641
  Minoan 4192
  Mycenean 1209
  Roman 5637
CLAIRVOYANCE 3931
CLARINETS 1512
CLARK, EUGENIE (1922-) 11362
CLARK, GEORGE ROGERS (1752-1818) 4699, 10493, 11014, 12227, 12877, 12885, 15339, 16821, 17933
CLARK, ROSE B. (1852-1942) 3522
CLARKE, BOBBY (1949-) 11859
CLARK'S EXPEDITION TO THE ILLINOIS (1778-1779) 12879, 15339, 16821
CLAY 7895
CLAY, CASSIUS see ALI, MUHAMMAD
CLEANLINESS 1991, 15469
CLEMENS, SAMUEL LANGHORNE (1835-1910) 4529, 11468, 13436, 18232
CLEMENTE, ROBERTO WALKER (1934-1972) 11901, 12085, 13110, 14747, 17141, 17382
CLEOPATRA (QUEEN OF EGYPT), (d. 30 B.C.) 4263, 4587, 10521, 12288
CLERGY 7191, 7818
  homes 16113
  United States--Southwest 3777, 6095
CLERKS 9730
  vocational guidance 8630
CLIFF DWELLERS AND CLIFF DWELLINGS 11662
  United States
    Arizona 5806
    Colorado 17979
CLIMATOLOGY 2006, 2009, 15763
CLOCKS AND WATCHES 1421, 1529, 8832, 11057, 12072, 12548, 12695, 15990, 16857, 18024
CLOTHING AND DRESS 1079, 1167, 1247, 1610, 2451, 4716, 6545, 8307, 12801, 14265, 16607, 17467, 17553
  industry and trade 12709
  protective 3710
CLOUDS 1426, 4717, 11863, 12842
CLOWNS 23, 10019, 13779

CLUBS (SOCIAL) 291, 1906, 5860, 5861, 8328, 12621, 15181
COACHING (ATHLETICS) 923, 4592, 5574, 6648, 7810, 12520, 12780, 15106, 17615, 18492
    autobiographies 6000
COAL MINES AND MINING 112, 1226, 2655, 2702, 4016, 5031, 5315, 9239, 10015, 10563, 12689, 14362, 16678, 17913
COBBLERS 16325
COCHISE (APACHE CHIEF), (d. 1874) 9260, 18331
COCHRAN, JACQUELINE (1910?-1980) 5955, 17616
COCHRANE, ELIZABETH (1867-1922) 5148, 7197, 7559, 12860, 17620
COCHRANE, GORDON STANLEY (1903-1962) 17217
COCOA 213, 17164
CODY, WILLIAM FREDERICK "BUFFALO BILL" (1846-1917) 4547, 16272
COELACANTH 305, 1354
COINS
    American 2328, 2874
    collectors and collecting 8312
COLD 9558, 15747
    physiological effect 3710, 9555
    therapeutic use 9555
COLLAGE 1255, 11688, 17688
COLLECTIVE SETTLEMENTS 8147
    Israel 5287, 5750, 17600
COLLECTORS AND COLLECTING 1711, 4528, 6184, 7955, 11110, 11232, 15867
COLLEGES AND UNIVERSITIES 1056, 6036, 8669, 9584, 16500
    students 705
COLOMBIA 12562, 17207, 17208
    social life and customs 14914
COLOMBO, CRISTOFORO see COLUMBUS, CHRISTOPHER
COLOR 101, 936, 1871, 2867, 3447, 4291, 4759, 5178, 5413, 6257, 7456, 7995, 8236, 9401, 9402, 9403, 10612, 10882, 11168, 11725, 13131, 13658, 13981, 14117, 14225, 16882, 18479
    of animals 11247, 11908, 15715
    of people 125, 936, 3447, 3770, 7456, 10609
    poetry 11347, 14669
COLORADO 207, 884, 2424, 2736, 3000, 3589, 5358a, 15625, 18215
    biography 11737
    description and travel 6219
      views 9371, 11595
    gold discoveries 207
    history 5052, 5509, 6218, 11595, 15770
      pictorial works 11737
      1876-1950 207
COLORADO RIVER 2538, 4308
COLUMBUS, CHRISTOPHER (1446?-1506) 4456, 4549, 5166, 6145, 6147, 7938, 8018, 8317, 9427, 9533, 10422, 11348, 12900, 14892, 15440, 15593, 16581, 17279
COLUMBUS (OHIO)--history 11724
COLUMBUS DAY 15593
COMANCHE INDIANS 1267, 5654, 8547, 13718, 18038
    biography 11900
COMANECI, NADIA (1961-) 12161
COMEDY FILMS--history and criticism 11588
COMETS 747, 18539
COMIC BOOKS, STRIPS, ETC. 2105, 2106, 15134
    United States--history 6925

COMMERCIAL ART 15773
COMMERCIAL PRODUCTS--testing 1514
COMMUNES see COLLECTIVE SETTLEMENTS
COMMUNICABLE DISEASES 5004, 6494, 10604, 10607, 10608, 12960, 18187
COMMUNICATION 113, 9968, 14393, 14836, 15173, 16312, 17304
   biography 16198
   history 12694
   psychological aspects 13793
   See also NONVERBAL COMMUNICATION
COMMUNISM 13241
   Cuba 2815
   Russia--history 9268
COMMUNITY LIFE 1014, 1433, 2483, 2642, 3925, 3926, 4237, 4870, 6737,
   11099, 11448, 11613, 11743, 12020, 12897, 16706
COMMUNITY ORGANIZATION 1501
COMPASS 2139
COMPETITION 5894, 18475
COMPOSERS 918, 3267, 3912, 5593, 5609, 7719, 8817, 9033, 10295, 12702
   Austrian 6975
   Russian 13832
   United States 13831
COMPOSITION (MUSIC) 12321
COMPUTERS 1513, 1528, 4752, 9368, 10686, 11383, 14766, 16107
   vocational guidance 948, 14157
CONCENTRATION CAMPS 3973, 10714
   United States 4317, 16013
CONCEPTS 2390, 4496, 6824, 7997, 8302, 8616, 11837, 14100, 14491, 14992,
   15493, 15840, 15842, 17500, 17889, 18586
CONCORD, BATTLE OF (1775) 1400, 3790
CONCORD (MASSACHUSETTS) 1245
CONDORS 12450
CONDUCTING (MUSIC) 18472
CONDUCTORS (MUSIC) 5608, 18472
CONFECTIONERY 7918, 13393, 17011
CONFEDERATE STATES OF AMERICA--Army--Stonewall Brigade--biography
   6390
CONFLICT OF GENERATIONS 2071
CONFORMITY 9679
CONGO see ZAIRE
CONNECTICUT 7914
   history 16050
     colonial period (ca. 1600-1775) 12351
     Revolution (1775-1783) 4452
CONSERVATION 1952, 13422, 13967
   of natural resources 568, 4506, 5265, 8048, 12175, 12424, 12501, 13340
   poetry 7969, 15863
   United States--history 8224
   vocational guidance 1477
CONSERVATIONISTS 10316
CONSTELLATIONS 2114
CONSTITUTION (FRIGATE) 14337
CONSUMERS
   credit 8179
   education 6697, 14945
   protection 1514
CONTAGIOUS DISEASES see COMMUNICABLE DISEASES
CONTESTS 5860

CONTINENTAL DRIFT 452, 9784, 17703
CONTINENTAL SHELF 17556
  United States 2937
CONTRES I Y RAMIREZ DE ARELLANO, ROBERTO (1791-1825) 4077
CONVERSATION 1018, 16446, 18288
CONVICT LABOR 13217
COOK, JAMES (1728-1779) 1944, 8612, 10315, 15301, 16072, 16578
COOKERY 51, 795, 1081, 1721, 1949, 1950, 2929, 3210, 3515, 3705, 3708,
  3709, 3792, 4089, 4301, 4727, 4913, 4953, 4956, 5387, 6294, 6782, 6870,
  6908, 6990, 7290, 7857, 8261, 8560, 9134, 9278, 9969, 9974, 10028, 10245,
  11296, 11377, 11593, 12123, 12124, 12125, 12386, 12389, 12788, 13053,
  13318, 13391, 13393, 13394, 13515, 13523, 13790, 13996, 14590, 15160,
  15455, 16973, 18263, 18516, 18631
  African 14898
  American 7945, 13490, 13526, 13528
    history 17439
    Michigan 5243
    Nebraska 7111
    The West 13524
  Armenian 8415
  Basque 14253
  Czech 852
  European 13520
  Indian 8127, 8727
  international 15436
  Jewish 679, 6420, 14000
  Mediterranean 13527
  Puerto Rican 4913
  Rumanian 16139
COOLIDGE, ELLEN WAYLES (RANDOLPH), (1796-1876) 12338
COOPERATION 281, 2196, 2503, 9122, 16904
COPENHAGEN (DENMARK) 4131
COPERNICUS, NICOLAUS (1473-1543) 17269
COPPER MINES AND MINING 2247, 2708, 3274
COPPERSMITHS 10698
COPYING PROCESSES AND MACHINES 6024
CORAL REEFS AND ISLANDS 2649, 3525, 5836, 9092, 11905
CORALS 9092, 11905, 14593
CORN 298, 4723, 5399, 10815, 13790
CORONADO, FRANCISCO VASQUEZ DE (1510-1554) 933, 9202
CORSICA 4768
CORTES, HERNANDO (1485-1547) 9080, 9302
COSBY, WILLIAM H. "BILL" (1937-) 13103
COSTA RICA 3002, 3491
COSTUME 1156, 2456, 3328, 4358, 4603, 5053, 5339, 6819, 13288, 13997
  history 4064, 11131, 17467
  Southwest, New--history 4911
COTTON 7669
COUGARS 9285
COUNSELING 12493, 12683
COUNTERFEITS AND COUNTERFEITING 14445, 18101
COUNTING 64, 570, 1054, 1196, 1231, 1494, 1495, 2368, 2928, 3277, 3372,
  3457, 4295, 4366, 5191, 5297, 5749, 5752, 5953, 6161, 6326, 6370, 7272,
  7342, 7345, 7998, 8292, 8298, 8309, 8450, 8912, 9496, 9603, 10027, 10058,
  10084, 10251, 10297, 10620, 10621, 10754, 10946, 10963, 11309, 11403,
  11449, 11533, 11759, 12011, 12070, 12104, 12401, 12870, 13223, 13402,
  13498, 13581, 13659, 13662, 14226, 14490, 14718, 14978, 14989, 14994,

15333, 15396, 15879, 16143, 16215, 16443, 17023, 17032, 17335, 17415, 17915, 18224, 18393, 18414, 18583
COUNTRY LIFE 1070, 2601, 2852, 3081, 3090, 3685, 4142, 4681, 5266, 5354, 5838, 5840, 5935, 9619, 10183, 10567, 11077, 11079, 12117, 14044, 14878, 15262, 16852
  Spain 9227
  United States
    Indiana 9040
    Kansas--Maple Hill 17066
    Middle West 17623
    New York (State)--Cherry Valley 16610
COURAGE 565, 627, 687, 790, 2180, 3163, 3445, 3642, 5583, 5726, 8461, 9688, 9839, 10066, 11795, 13472, 13491, 13830, 15531, 16017, 16174, 16989, 17862, 18377
COURTS 2255
COUSTEAU, JACQUES (1910-) 8959
COVERED BRIDGES 16510
COWHANDS 544, 664, 1733, 2021, 3508, 4937, 5372, 5594, 5773, 5784, 5785, 6052, 6054, 6093, 6632, 7264, 9123, 9125, 10035, 10591, 11219, 11575, 14697, 14707, 14771, 14772, 15002, 15887, 17513, 17723
  in art 195
  poetry 11039
  songs and music 5774, 11039, 14848
  United States--The West 11221, 15661
COWS 303, 3855, 8244, 9442, 10034, 10443, 11800, 12009, 18302
COYDOGS 6174
COYOTES 1235, 6172, 6734, 7935, 9629, 13422, 13444, 14553, 16811, 17197
  control 13951
CRABTREE, LOTTA (1847-1924) 13720
CRAFT, ELLEN (1826?-1897?) 6244
CRAFT, WILLIAM 6244
CRAFTSMEN 13878
CRANDALL, PRUDENCE (1803-1890) 18378
CRANES (BIRDS) 2787, 2853, 8866, 10894
CRANES, DERRICKS, ETC. 18569, 18581
CRAYON DRAWING 15190
CRAZY HORSE (OGLALA INDIAN), (ca. 1842-1877) 2431, 4908, 6633, 7170, 11989, 11994
CREATION 398, 10391, 10544, 17659
CREATURES see MONSTERS
CREE INDIANS 15387
CREEK INDIANS 16423
CREOLES 7820
CRETE 6119, 14827
  antiquities 1209, 4192
CRIME AND CRIMINALS 2426, 7833, 9814, 11461
  investigations 1523, 12245
  laboratories 1523
  United States--The West 16515
CRISTIANI, ARMANDO 13869
CROCKETT, DAVY (1786-1836) 1712, 6103, 8434, 15429, 16168
CROCODILES 5176, 5177, 7223, 12830, 15418, 17361, 17365, 17366, 17367, 17368, 17611, 18495, 18535
CRONKITE, WALTER (1916-) 16700
CROW INDIANS 1296, 1749, 10224, 10828, 11375, 14897, 15991
CROWS 1740, 5205, 13962

CROWTHER, SAMUEL ADJAI, BP. (1806?-1891) 12255
CRUSADES 2516, 17150, 18017
CRUSTACEA 6097, 7888, 8493, 14794, 16228, 18564
CRYOBIOLOGY 9557
CRYPTOGRAPHY 851, 9977, 10185, 10208, 14921, 18538
CRYSTALLOGRAPHY 4560, 6540, 14891
CSONKA, LARRY (1946-) 2618, 7517
CUBA--history 13186
CUBAN AMERICANS 13938
CUFFEE, PAUL (1759-1817) 9310
CULTS 5968
CULTURE see CIVILIZATION
CURAÇAO 17209
CURIE, MARIE (SKLODOWSKA), (1867-1934) 32, 1647, 4705, 8058, 8060,
    8960, 11437, 16844
CURIOSITIES AND WONDERS 7713, 9926, 14401, 14402, 17581
CUSTER, ELIZABETH (BACON), (1842-1933) 14108
CUSTER, GEORGE ARMSTRONG (1839-1876) 14280
CUTHBERT, SAINT (d. 687) 17760
CZECH, BOOKS IN 8262
CZECH AMERICANS 14691
    social life and customs 8262
    in Texas 852
CZECHOSLOVAKIA 531, 2644

- D -

DNA 17567
DAIRYING 303, 532, 10792, 12125, 18302
    vocational guidance--United States--Maine 7007
DAKIN FAMILY 16610
DAKOTA INDIANS 1764, 3254, 4838, 4921, 5219, 7360, 8952, 10269, 11354,
    12023, 14633, 14782, 15948, 15949, 15950, 16278, 16336, 17268
    biography 7170, 17345
    language 3496
    legends 5747, 5847, 9354
    poetry 18256
    social life and customs 14903
    War
        (1862-1865) 15946
        (1890-1891) 1884
DALLAS (TEXAS)
    description and travel 16879
    history 16879
DAMASCUS (SYRIA) 15553
DAMS 5662
DANCERS 4704, 7354, 11584, 11950, 16762, 16895
    biography 781, 1636, 7354, 7732
    Canadian 4503
DANCING 1241, 1636, 4714, 7812, 8936, 9118, 11937, 11950, 16799
    Africa--Sub-Saharan 17536
    pictorial works 5845
    poetry 13747
    Russia 14871

See also BALLET
DANIEL (THE PROPHET) 1857
DANISH AMERICANS 11845
D'ARBLAY, FRANCES see ARBLAY, FRANCES (BURNEY) D'
DARE, VIRGINIA (b. 1587) 16281
D'ARUSMONT, FRANCES (WRIGHT), (1795-1852) 16317
DARWIN, CHARLES (1809-1882) 15420
DATING (SOCIAL CUSTOMS) 5612, 5615, 5616, 14606
DAVID, CONNIE (1954-) 18195
DAVID (KING OF ISRAEL) 1858, 7130, 17782
DA VINCI, LEONARDO see LEONARDO DA VINCI
DAVIS, FRANCES ELLIOTT (1882?-1965) 13711
DAVIS, OSSIE (1917-) 6442
DAVIS, VARINA (HOWELL), (1826-1906) 14109
DAY 2152, 8210, 10121, 10297, 12614, 15611, 17007, 17008, 17009
DAYAN, MOSHE (1915-) 16664
DAYDREAMS see IMAGINATION
DAYTON (OHIO)--Flood (1913) 5248, 6362
DEAD SEA SCROLLS 4392, 8537, 13259
DEAF see PHYSICALLY HANDICAPPED--DEAF
DEATH 18, 219, 312, 536, 565, 568, 1027, 1146, 1572, 1573, 2064, 2312, 2387,
    2480, 2786, 2986, 3068, 3152, 3156, 3577, 3580, 3593, 3603, 3716, 3731,
    3733, 4126, 4213, 4710, 4722, 4927, 5009, 5011, 5271, 5638, 5658, 5683,
    5713, 5759, 6576, 6601, 6869, 6880, 7071, 7258, 7282, 7444, 7533, 7605,
    7734, 7759, 8785, 9489, 9492, 9691, 9695, 9914, 9948, 10120, 10235, 10498,
    10936, 11124, 11127, 11175, 11616, 12176, 12178, 12266, 12440,
    12539, 13165, 13214, 13367, 13655, 13952, 14291, 14499, 14550,
    15512, 15548, 15553, 15748, 15766, 15882, 16202, 16262, 16348, 16416,
    16430, 16903, 17322, 17334, 17512, 17816, 18563
    psychological aspects 10618
DEATH VALLEY (CALIFORNIA AND NEVADA) 973
DEBATES AND DEBATING 5837
DEBORAH (JUDGE OF ISRAEL) 9192
DECISION MAKING 1671, 3332, 8606, 11278, 11543, 14414, 15168, 17685
DECKER, MARY (1958-) 9070
DEER 1348, 1389, 1844, 2986, 3084, 4757, 5242, 8568, 8806, 9190, 10895,
    11256, 12146, 12565, 13056, 13772, 14154, 14752, 14866, 16858
DEERE, JOHN (1804-1886) 1072
DE FOREST, LEE (1873-1961) 4941
DELAWARE--history 4391, 14019
    Colonial period (ca. 1600-1775) 3395, 14184
    Revolution (1775-1783) 3395
DELAWARE INDIANS 1750, 4961, 7758, 15210
    captivities 14346, 14347
DELLUMS, RONALD V. (1935-) 5963
DENDUR (EGYPT)--Temple 9635
DENETSOSIE (1891-1969) 9247
DENMARK 2652, 9204, 13800, 16027
    history
       1448-1660 7850
       German occupation (1940-1945) 660, 18329
DENTISTRY 1092, 6611, 7268, 7671, 13304, 13808, 17583
    vocational guidance 9481
DENTISTS 14533
DENVER, JOHN (1943-) 9068
DENVER (COLORADO)--history--pictorial works 9371
DE PALMA, RALPH (1884-1956) 13089
DEPARTMENT STORES 3647, 4765, 7778, 15966

employees 7778
DEPRESSIONS, ECONOMIC (1929) 2606, 3540, 3838, 4964, 5066, 5811,
    8750, 8752, 9505, 12039, 12051, 12256, 12266, 12686, 13537, 14049,
    16043, 16694, 16852, 16853
DESERT ANIMALS see ANIMALS--DESERT
DESERT LIFE 5227
DESERTION AND NONSUPPORT 7436
DESERTS 1236, 1243, 2195, 2540, 2544, 3175, 3480, 4295, 5251, 5486, 6416,
    6964, 7050, 7490, 7842, 10292, 10602, 11762, 12219, 14881, 16392, 17417,
    17810, 18218
    pictorial works 788
    wildlife 3480, 3500
    Wyoming 5521
DESIGN 5045, 5048, 15802
DE SOTO, HERNANDO see SOTO, HERNANDO DE
DETECTIVES 485, 12245
DETROIT (MICHIGAN)
    description and travel--guide-books 9646
    Siege (1760) 5427
DEVIL 840, 1600, 8418, 9209, 17076, 18436
DIABETES AND DIABETICS 2110, 3969
DIAMONDS 4483, 18540
DIAZ DE BIVAR, DON RODRIGO (ca. 1043-1099) 6714, 7020
DICKEY, BILL (1907-) 17217
DICKINSON, EMILY (1830-1886) 1137, 1460, 5933, 11050
DICKINSON, SUSANNA (1814-1883) 11547
DICKINSON FAMILY 5933
DICTIONARIES 4415, 7996, 13039, 13079, 13263, 17445, 17446
    polyglot 7854, 7855
DIDRIKSON, BABE see ZAHARIAS, MILDRED "BABE" (DIDRIKSON)
DIEGO, JOSE DE (1866-1918) 16245
DIEGO, JUAN (1474-1548) 17404
DIET 1854
    United States--history 13524
DIGESTION 5490, 15604
DiMAGGIO, JOE (1914-) 5880
DINKELSBUHL (GERMANY)--history 6674
DINNERS AND DINING 5923, 12811, 13364, 13527, 17714, 18234
DINOSAURS 309, 527, 1797, 3516, 3753, 3798, 4108, 4466, 8349, 8350,
    8676, 8919, 8922, 9468, 9542, 9906, 10110, 10229, 11365, 13201, 13289,
    13953, 15304, 15430, 15641, 16568, 16787, 18541
    food 14664
    poetry 3811
DIOGENES, THE CYNIC 299
DIPHTHERIA 486
DISARMAMENT 7300
DISCOVERIES (IN GEOGRAPHY) 5189
    Portuguese 14893
DISCRIMINATION 9440, 16291
DISNEY, WALT (1901-1966) 5870, 7674, 12366, 17619
DISPLACEMENT 4121
DISSENT
    Russia 819
    United States 17684
DISTRICT OF COLUMBIA--police 6358
DIVINATION 828
DIVING 16459

DIVING, SUBMARINE 1035, 1505, 3736, 3824, 6058, 6348, 7961, 8627, 11771, 12425, 18034, 18089

DIVORCE 92, 257, 1220, 1541, 1596, 1807, 1819, 2808, 2810, 4135, 4258, 6590, 6972, 7445, 7649, 8773, 9338, 9509, 9911, 10737, 10907, 11372, 11376, 11611, 11968, 11972, 12683, 12783, 13529, 13595, 13737, 13738, 14328, 14341, 14561, 15112, 15116, 15854, 16355, 16814, 18209, 18241
  pictorial works 14003

DIX, DOROTHEA LYNDE (1802-1887) 983, 5336, 11579, 12031, 17616

DOCK, CHRISTOPHER (d. 1771) 4640

DOCTORS see PHYSICIANS

DODGE, MARY (MAPES), (1831-1905) 11794

DODGE CITY (KANSAS) 3127

DOGHO (KING OF NIGERIA) (d. 1932) 8889

DOGS 18, 280, 486, 552, 654, 701, 722, 937, 1026, 1152, 1153, 1388, 1502, 1618, 1622, 1655, 1769, 1926, 1953, 2202, 2203, 2225, 2226, 2227, 2228, 2298, 2397, 2484, 2849, 2893, 2968, 3068, 3072, 3110, 3112, 3170, 3287, 3379, 3399, 3506, 3558, 3638, 3800, 3923, 4127, 4309, 4379, 4518, 4672, 4676, 4678, 4917, 5027, 5082, 5088, 5089, 5090, 5124, 5163, 5225, 5349, 5378, 5548, 5691, 5983, 5987, 6129, 6171, 6175, 6178, 6260, 6396, 6445, 6451, 6455, 6457, 6458, 6466, 6528, 6864, 6866, 7030, 7142, 7143, 7144, 7374, 7377, 7487, 7501, 7505, 7597, 7604, 7605, 7607, 7608, 7619, 7638, 8201, 8214, 8347, 8357, 8451, 8821, 9178, 9188, 9516, 9572, 9598, 9606, 9607, 9658, 9875, 9878, 9879, 9937, 10107, 10344, 10355, 10675, 10677, 10731, 10897, 10934, 11041, 11042, 11117, 11242, 11397, 11398, 11799, 12191, 12420, 12428, 12429, 12432, 12523, 12542, 12865, 13204, 13244, 13426, 13477, 13568, 13642, 13655, 13693, 14107, 14155, 14201, 14420, 14468, 14469, 14526, 14705, 15041, 15287, 15331, 15338, 15393, 15470, 15471, 15622, 15743, 15791, 15804, 15814, 15871, 16191, 16192, 16205, 16263, 16346, 16414, 16547, 16656, 16706, 16748, 16768, 16786, 17061, 17143, 17146, 17188, 17262, 17413, 17440, 17588, 17660, 17671, 17776, 17777, 17827, 17923, 17948, 17953, 18053, 18058, 18158, 18253, 18379, 18588, 18589, 18590, 18592, 18606
  breeds 8061, 8118
    Chu 1306
  poetry 13508
  shows 7602, 8118
  sled 486
  training 2282, 2283, 14008, 16571, 17144

DOLLHOUSES 867, 6955, 14494, 15828

DOLLS 687, 717, 812, 861, 907, 1295, 1395, 1630, 2263, 2275, 2566, 2670, 3164, 3667, 5851, 6937, 6950, 6951, 6954, 6974, 6976, 7040, 7222, 7321, 7322, 8940, 8995, 9345, 9739, 10369, 10745, 11172, 11173, 11336, 11619, 11677, 11678, 11758, 12491, 12999, 13441, 13676, 13787, 15067, 15117, 15518, 15811, 16075, 16572, 16990, 17028, 17406, 17407, 18052, 18086, 18301, 18327, 18629

DOLPHINS 1409, 3128, 3525, 4573, 5284, 7092, 8423, 9701, 10348, 12462, 12636, 13751, 17579

DOMESTIC ANIMALS 5177, 5807, 6725, 6780, 7803, 7903, 8352, 12637, 13555, 13979, 13982, 18488
  history 4607

DONKEYS 269, 554, 1265, 1343, 3122, 5114, 5589, 5660, 6321, 7146, 7330, 8067, 8445, 8923, 10333, 10689, 12745, 13016, 13242, 13849, 13907, 16193, 16196, 17236, 18057, 18102
  Death Valley Region 10628

DONNER PARTY 16542

DOUGLAS, STEPHEN ARNOLD (1813-1861) 9671, 12883

DOUGLASS, FREDERICK (1817?-1895) 639, 1918, 4569, 5036, 7193, 13382, 16246, 18093
DOVE (SLOOP) 7145
DOWN'S SYNDROME 999
DRAGONS 1785, 2325, 3071, 4236, 4484, 4619, 4805, 6398, 6532, 7153, 7636, 8507, 9210, 9714, 9996, 10091, 11552, 12608, 12647, 12730, 12934, 13402, 13806, 14231, 14516, 14883, 14974, 16643, 16785, 18011
  pictorial works 15254
DRAMA 5099, 13657
  technique 11506
DRAWING 721, 8937, 18163, 18485
  study and teaching 400, 401, 1965, 2869, 5410, 5411, 5415, 5418, 8515, 17700, 18484
  technique 5409, 5412, 17545, 18484
DREAMS 2076, 4291, 4735, 6188, 8034, 8370, 8453, 9621, 13402, 13403, 15699, 16286, 17748, 18446, 18512
DRESSMAKING 4166, 14622
DREW, CHARLES RICHARD (1904-1950) 1608, 7720, 16252
DROUGHTS 6014, 16404
DRUG ABUSE 801, 1091, 1590, 1808, 2765, 3373, 3767, 3829, 5338, 7082, 7257, 7651, 8478, 8653, 10781, 11520, 11696, 12163, 12667, 15608, 17774, 17990, 18248, 18295
  case studies 1590
DRUGS 5338, 5613, 7993, 8653, 12300, 16434, 17774, 18248, 18291, 18295, 18546
DRUIDS AND DRUIDISM 8788, 13824
DRUM 2697, 6447, 8192, 13921, 15018
  African 2734
  methods 14687
DRUMMERS 12243
DU BOIS, WILLIAM EDWARD BURGHARDT (1868-1963) 7665, 10177, 16243
DUCKS 342, 605, 3382, 4510, 5151, 5757, 5991, 6215, 6376, 6756, 6779, 6844, 6996, 8804, 9150, 10647, 11239, 12192, 13843, 14089, 14350, 14729, 15497, 17923, 17925
  habits and behavior 4075
DUNBAR, PAUL LAURENCE (1872-1906) 7100, 15129
DUNCAN, WILLIAM (1832-1918) 17742
DUNHAM, KATHERINE (1910-) 1636, 7732
DUNKIRK (FRANCE), BATTLE OF (1940) 17053
DUNNING, EMILY see BARRINGER, EMILY (DUNNING)
DURYEA, CHARLES E. (1861-1938) 9013
DURYEA, JAMES FRANK (1869-1967) 9013
DUST 102
DUTCH AMERICANS 8932
  history 16738
  New York (City) 8738
    history 5425
  New York (State) 4905
DUTCH POETRY 16092
DWARFS 3747, 4664, 7843, 15609
DWELLINGS--poetry, 10595
DYE, JACOB (1875-1961) 5195
DYER, MARY (d. 1660) 4253
DYES AND DYEING 4716

- E -

ESP see EXTRASENSORY PERCEPTION
EADS, JAMES BUCHANAN (1820-1887) 18358
EAGLES 140, 340, 1407, 4842, 5217, 9577, 10388, 10851, 15560, 18471
EARHART, AMELIA (1898-1937) 4586, 4707, 7963, 8684, 11605, 13334,
  15246, 17620
EARP, WYATT BERRY STAPP (1848-1929) 8437
EARS 122
EARTH 751, 2113, 2117, 2144, 9930, 10357, 14152, 14187, 14742, 15157,
  18559
  crust 11832
  internal structure 11487
  rotation 2152
EARTH SCIENCES 933, 10210, 14787
EARTHMOVING MACHINERY
  operators--vocational guidance 6281
  pictorial works 8299
EARTHQUAKES 2331, 11381, 11834, 11913, 13464, 15738
EARTHWORMS 4509, 10347
EASTER 1019, 1139, 1473, 2511, 3076, 5910, 7745, 7932, 7959, 8271, 8305,
  11153, 12205, 13381, 14637, 15222, 15992, 17011
  eggs 46
  poetry 8589
EASTMAN, CHARLES ALEXANDER (1858-1939) 5219
EASTMAN, SETH (1808-1875) 11295
EATON, TIMOTHY (1834-1907) 1163
ECLIPSES 2124
ECOLOGY 157, 731, 1415, 1417, 1433, 1507, 1649, 1952, 2649, 4310, 4506,
  5249, 5368, 5856, 6110, 6343, 6739, 6750, 7050, 7119, 7328, 7796, 8226,
  8346, 8425, 8503, 8811, 9285, 9470, 9923, 10292, 10896, 10923, 11160,
  11250, 11382, 12175, 12294, 13474, 13802, 13947, 13949, 13954, 13956, 13958,
  13961, 13964, 14299, 14417, 14787, 14875, 15274, 16996, 16997, 17560,
  17609, 17834, 18222, 18223, 18230, 18313
  Arctic 141
  Africa--grasslands 2365
  jungle 1179
  North America 13959
  poetry 25
  ponds 2740
  United States--history 8224
  wetlands 2470, 2473
ECONOMICS 642, 643, 11543
  policy 13522
EDEOGU (OKLAHOMA) 2501
EDDY, MARY (BAKER), (1821-1910) 7907
EDINBURGH (SCOTLAND) 5137
EDISON, THOMAS ALVA (1847-1931) 4211, 6547, 7514, 11760, 12928, 15445
EDMUNDSON, SARAH EMMA (1841-1898) 16637
EDUCABLE MENTALLY HANDICAPPED see MENTALLY HANDICAPPED
EDUCATION 4157, 4290, 7614, 13829, 16169
  anecdotes, facetiae, satire, etc. 9641
  careers 1478
  elementary--Puerto Rico 12839
  experimental methods 729
  United States
    Georgia--history 13616

history   11019
   urban   3617
value of   3115
EDUCATORS   see   TEACHERS
EELS   6357
   electric   6045
EGGS   3796, 4175, 8651, 11153, 11888, 15279
   decoration of   4182
   experiments   12202
EGYPT   3003, 3670, 6645, 8042, 8665, 8877, 10556, 11298, 11549, 11992,
   12269, 12531, 12699, 13262, 15667, 17570, 17940
   antiquities   307, 1212, 9121, 13229, 16567, 17200
   civilization   10453, 11204, 11371, 11373, 11990, 12288, 13681, 15395
      Middle Kingdom (ca. 2000 B.C.)   11123
      to 332 B.C.   7791, 7792, 7794, 11623, 13908, 14459, 15192, 15193,
         16567, 17201
   description and travel   17465
   history   739, 5815, 12627, 15063
   immigration and emigration   7137
   social life and customs   12997, 17804
EGYPTIAN LANGUAGE--writing, hieroglyphic   11623
EIELSON, CARL BENJAMIN (1897-1929)   3258, 8112
EISENHOWER, DWIGHT DAVID (1890-1969)   7835, 12451, 15549
EL CAMPO (TEXAS)--social life and customs   852
EL SALVADOR   3004, 16509
ELEANOR OF AQUITAINE (CONSORT OF HENRY II), (1122?-1204)   9992
ELECTIONS   5963, 10847, 13613
ELECTRIC BATTERIES   18381
ELECTRIC ENGINEERING   4390, 6286
ELECTRIC INDUSTRIES   12711
   workers   12711
ELECTRIC MOTORS--amateur's manuals   14251
ELECTRICITY   748, 752, 3096, 4123, 5491, 6303, 12436, 13762, 17377, 18381
   experiments   2001
   power   4390, 5504, 15451
      conservation   5504
ELECTRONIC APPARATUS AND APPLIANCES   7327
ELECTRONIC DATA PROCESSING   see   COMPUTERS
ELECTRONICS   1446, 13835, 16468
ELEPHANTS   707, 1149, 1207, 1486, 3261, 4259, 4425, 4645, 4646, 4647,
   4648, 4649, 4650, 4840, 5238, 5744, 6607, 6899, 7093, 7260, 7491, 7492,
   8137, 8234, 8294, 8360, 9394, 9395, 9396, 9842, 10855, 10856, 11499,
   11533, 11704, 12141, 12506, 12545, 13557, 13834, 13853, 13931, 14036,
   15015, 15363, 15376, 15377, 15537, 16265, 16792, 17418, 17489
   African   3946
   pictorial works   14873
   poetry   14873
ELEVATORS   7966, 13176
ELIOT, GEORGE (1819-1880)   17327
ELIZABETH I (QUEEN OF ENGLAND AND WALES), (1533-1603)   1283, 1648,
   7694, 15521, 16527
ELIZABETH II (QUEEN OF ENGLAND AND WALES), (1926-)   10965
ELIZABETH OF HUNGARY, SAINT (1207-1231)   7785
ELK   11432
ELLESMERE ISLAND   2535
ELLINGTON, DUKE (1899-1974)   12362
ELLIS ISLAND (NEW YORK)   7980

ELVES see FAIRIES
EMBRYOLOGY 11877, 15268, 18497
  birds 1967, 15279
  human 15592
EMIGRATION see IMMIGRATION AND EMIGRATION
EMOTAN (NIGERIAN WOMAN) 13121
EMOTIONS 431, 1080, 1082, 1324, 1337, 1537, 1542, 1631, 1722, 1820, 1822,
  1955, 1988, 2100, 2183, 2414, 2592, 3389, 3982, 3983, 3984, 3985, 4945,
  5139, 5293, 5379, 5634, 6979, 7072, 7376, 7970, 8259, 8873, 8964, 9488,
  9637, 10109, 10244, 10486, 10619, 10664, 10741, 11555, 11940, 12136,
  12465, 12748, 13418, 13793, 14560, 14620, 15727, 15729, 16199, 16386,
  16753, 17585, 17587, 18167
EMPLOYMENT
  of men 13482
  part-time 10543
  temporary 10543, 13604
ENAMEL AND ENAMELING 5324
END OF THE WORLD 2125
ENDANGERED SPECIES 10895
ENERGY 103, 2153
  atomic 100
  conservation 5504, 11711, 15646
  policy--United States 8949
  See also specific types of energy, e.g., SOLAR ENERGY
ENGINEERING 15093, 17702
ENGINEERS 10528
ENGINES 17697, 18557
ENGLAND 181, 187, 323, 518, 621, 685, 810, 977, 1217, 1220, 1970, 1977,
  1978, 2724, 3212, 3248, 3455, 3528, 3548, 4082, 4084, 4085, 4087, 4088,
  4398, 4925, 5282, 5674, 5678, 5743, 6252, 6253, 6573, 6575, 6605, 7069,
  7202, 7220, 7378, 8176, 8737, 9189, 10444, 10954, 10957, 11108, 11317,
  11428, 11485, 11958, 12055, 12194, 12437, 12941, 13427, 13599, 13601,
  15557, 16411, 16598, 16600, 16668, 16954, 16955, 16958, 17073, 17481,
  17604, 17717, 17760, 17957, 17958, 17959
  biography 5507
  civilization 13194
  colonization 3153
  description and travel 201, 6379, 14926
  history 2549, 2722, 2725, 4836, 5877, 13799, 14926, 17610
    to 499 6570
    to 1066 13715, 16985
    to late 15th century 760, 1310
    to mid-19th century 2728
    Roman Period (55 B.C.-A.D. 449) 8144, 16521, 16526, 16528
    Anglo-Saxon period (499-1066) 4318, 4320, 8144, 16519, 16525
    7th century 6571
    11th century 18270
    Norman period (1066-1154) 4836, 13081, 16530
    medieval period (1066-1485) 1068, 2311, 4318, 11028, 16982, 18047
    Henry II (1133-1189) 9217
    Plantagenets (1154-1399) 9992
    13th century 16979
    14th century 3452
    Edward III (1312-1377) 4633
    Henry IV (1367-1413) 14013
    15th century 7737, 7739
    Tudors (1485-1603) 17952, 17961

    Elizabeth I (1533-1603) 1283, 1284, 15521
    Civil War (1642-1649) 2726, 2727, 7847, 17671, 17955
    George III (1738-1820) 6384
    20th century 17478, 17759
    World War (1939-1945) 3126
  poetry 190, 238, 1920, 2439
  politics and government 5282
  queens 16983
  social conditions 4501
  social life and customs 591, 1376, 5110, 6796, 7038, 12194, 17152
    16th century 5743
    pictorial works 7045
ENGLISH LANGUAGE
  dictionaries 14997
  etymology 84, 753, 766, 767, 768, 769, 770, 5822, 5969, 6626, 6627,
    9979, 10195, 12969, 15392, 16156
  foreign words and phrases 768
  homonyms 1157, 7534, 7536, 17204
  lexicography 10051
  semantics 5822, 6627
  slang 10402
  study and teaching 362
  synonyms and antonyms 8303, 16087
  terms and phrases 7534
    polyglot 6230
ENGLISH LITERATURE 1289, 3099, 11604
ENGLISH POETRY 190, 238, 1309, 1363, 1376, 1717, 1774, 1920, 2236,
  3100, 3180, 3181, 3182, 3309, 3808, 3809, 3817, 3819, 3820, 3821, 3880,
  4071, 6228, 7123, 7152, 7201, 7231, 7251, 7252, 7253, 7254, 7585, 8108,
  8731, 8734, 9610, 10467, 11306, 12247, 12249, 12252, 13311, 13577, 13747,
  14202, 14207, 14292, 14666, 14669, 15404, 15405, 15529, 15872, 15904,
  15914, 16297, 16742, 16809, 17157, 17462
  collections 4685, 4686, 4688, 4689, 4691, 4692, 6221, 7333, 7696, 7698,
    8957, 10278, 10279, 10976, 11935, 12509, 13450, 14183
  history and criticism 1718
  20th century 10717, 16956
ENGRAVING 8516
  technique 17699
ENTERTAINERS 231, 1915, 3442, 3841, 10046, 17619, 17673
  actors and actresses 9076, 9244, 13466
  comedians 3442, 9034, 11588, 13103, 15514, 16696
  singers 1070, 1623, 3185, 4161, 5134, 7309, 9001, 9027, 9058, 9068,
    9072, 9073, 11284, 12483, 12487, 12599, 12799, 13101, 16514, 16698,
    16909
ENTERTAINING 2182, 4696, 14421, 17364
ENVIRONMENTAL ENGINEERING 7560
ENVIRONMENTAL POLICY 13, 72, 12198, 12209
  vocational guidance 1519, 16209
  See also CONSERVATION
ENZYMES 1516
EPIC POETRY 6714, 16517
EPILEPSY 15682
EPISCOPAL CHURCH 5331
EQUIANO, OLAUDAH (b. 1745) 9699
EQUIPMENT AND SUPPLIES 10605
ERICSON, LEIF (d.ca. 1020) 1396, 4553, 7177, 9203, 15565
ERVING, JULIUS (1950-) 2164

ESCAPES 385, 4131, 7677, 13798, 17991, 17992
ESKIMO POETRY 10713, 14136
    collections 5846, 8660
ESKIMOS 1344, 1751, 2170, 2209, 2259, 2447, 2746, 3049, 3470, 3659, 3662,
    3902, 4092, 4272, 4349, 4475, 4490, 5366, 5767, 5900, 6137, 6138, 6740,
    7187, 7547, 7962, 8109, 8655, 9981, 11922, 13299, 13513, 13683, 14485,
    15186, 15411, 16566, 16867, 17215, 17473, 17631, 17873
    Alaska 9194, 9195, 11746, 16184, 18200
    art 6926
    Canada--Northwest Territories--legends 12121
    children 17172
    legends 6828, 6829, 8659, 8661, 8662, 8663, 11288, 11545, 12056, 12781,
    14137
ESPOSITO, PHIL (1942-) 2622
ESSAYS 5426, 9838
ESTEVAN (d. 1539) 13280, 15534
ESTHER (QUEEN OF PERSIA), (2nd century B.C.?) 648, 2251
ESTHETICS 17499
ESTIMATION THEORY 10869
ETHICS 848, 1087, 1693, 3307, 6351
ETHIOPIA 42, 1720, 1839, 2074, 6646, 7885, 9550, 12890, 13519, 15554,
    15555, 15772, 17571
    history 5258, 10306, 15062
    social life and customs 5455
ETHNOLOGY 5581, 5582, 10393, 10758, 11663, 13510, 13767, 15541
    Africa 9184, 12589
      West 13912
    Australia 940, 8698
      legends 14692
    Hawaiian Islands 13882
    Niger Valley 9193
    Nigeria 9193
    Sierra Leone 7084, 7085
    United States--Southwest, New 12838
ETIQUETTE 330, 608, 1312, 1313, 6216, 8279, 8419, 9398, 9400, 9436, 9751,
    10497, 12659, 15166, 15846, 18288
EUROPE 8498, 14780
    description and travel--guide-books 16564
    history--A.D. 392-814 48891
    pictorial works 571
EVE (BIBLICAL CHARACTER) 14181
EVERGLADES (FLORIDA) 5690, 7815, 8927
    history 1728
EVERT, CHRIS (1954-) 2634, 7692, 9059, 11862, 15905
EVIL see GOOD AND EVIL
EVOLUTION 4174, 7266, 11875, 11876, 11949, 12641, 14148, 15420, 18496
EXCAVATIONS (ARCHEOLOGY) 17784
    Palestine 7722
    United States 1002, 1006
EXCHANGE 4748, 10254, 12323, 14407
EXECUTIVE POWER 17681
EXERCISE 584, 5451, 10712, 17483
EXPERIMENT (SLOOP) 2984
EXPERIMENTS 15736
EXPLORERS 31, 383, 1258, 1583, 1730, 1737, 2524, 2976, 2979, 4608, 4848,
    5189, 8018, 9080, 9082, 9083, 9202, 9391, 9427, 9589, 9728, 9939, 12228,

12900, 13719, 14318, 14758, 15895, 16578, 16579, 16580, 16581, 16582,
16583, 16584, 16586, 16588, 16589, 16590, 16594, 16595, 16689, 16933,
17167, 17938
  to America 9203
  English 5742
  to Iceland 9203
  Norse 7177
  Spanish 2866, 17279
EXPLOSIVES 7567
EXTINCT ANIMALS 528, 3811, 5282, 11866, 15665
EXTRASENSORY PERCEPTION 829, 1619, 4893, 5122, 5123, 9765, 12576,
12789
EYE 8886, 15600
  diseases and defects 12681, 14127
  surgery 15987
EYEGLASSES 5527, 5896, 7057, 11066, 14905, 18138, 18205

- F -

FABLES 379, 380, 1865, 2842, 3260, 3307, 3461, 4531, 4551, 5588, 6183,
6497, 6499, 6508, 6510, 7493, 7894, 8610, 9709, 9713, 10122, 10189, 10190,
10191, 11820, 12278, 12279, 14007, 14036, 14199, 14205, 14306, 16334,
17155, 17778
  Akan 4454, 4487
  East Indian 6461
  English 14204
  Hebrew 16045
  Spanish 14872
FABRICS 9949
FACE 2188, 2190, 5412
FACTORIES 6450
FAIRIES 147, 1190, 2230, 2833, 3747, 4049, 4550, 4558, 4719, 4977, 6554,
7098, 7230, 8779, 9327, 9679, 9680, 10842, 10843, 11390, 11962, 12263,
12733, 13304, 13376, 13408, 13929, 14062, 15610, 15993
  poetry 3819, 11767, 14667
FAIRS 4920, 5566, 7095, 8352, 10757, 11135, 11729, 12924, 13516, 17566,
17910
FAIRY TALES 22, 148, 264, 268, 270, 271, 273, 275, 276, 277, 360, 379,
380, 434, 435, 436, 437, 438, 439, 440, 441, 442, 443, 444, 445, 446,
447, 448, 449, 499, 576, 656, 713, 714, 715, 716, 919, 1051, 1259, 1297,
1318, 1634, 1868, 1869, 1995, 2194, 2485, 2833, 2840, 2922, 3122, 3218,
3243, 3272, 3384, 3693, 3837, 3858, 3874, 4188, 4240, 4357, 4384, 4550,
4558, 4620, 4652, 4685, 4719, 4737, 4738, 4745, 4882, 5112, 5121, 5313,
5472, 5579, 5676, 5678, 5679, 5680, 5795, 5867, 6111, 6128, 6163, 6324,
6467, 6498, 6506, 6582, 6583, 6591, 6613, 6614, 6617, 6968, 7219, 7236,
7237, 7291, 7292, 7369, 7386, 7387, 7388, 7390, 7391, 7392, 7393, 7394,
7395, 7396, 7397, 7398, 7399, 7401, 7402, 7403, 7404, 7405, 7406, 7407,
7408, 7409, 7410, 7429, 7497, 7636, 7679, 7717, 7747, 7841, 7869, 7870,
7871, 7872, 7873, 7874, 7875, 7876, 7877, 7878, 7879, 7880, 7881, 7958,
8103, 8180, 8233, 8371, 8413, 8605, 8654, 8665, 8864, 8899, 8941, 9043,
9044, 9045, 9046, 9048, 9049, 9050, 9053, 9155, 9183, 9349, 9690, 9697,
9706, 9776, 9808, 9831, 9869, 9941, 10218, 10239, 10291, 10372, 10373,
10374, 10395, 10396, 10474, 10495, 10496, 10796, 10888, 10948, 10990,
11004, 11032, 11078, 11299, 11301, 11302, 11303, 11304, 11305, 11431,

11554, 11629, 11632, 11634, 11638, 11640, 11641, 11642, 11828, 11829,
11840, 12017, 12258, 12373, 12419, 12608, 12730, 12744, 12746, 12751,
12867, 12946, 12973, 12976, 12978, 13155, 13264, 13425, 13532, 13651,
13652, 13653, 13667, 13905, 13975, 13980, 13990, 13991, 14006, 14007,
14012, 14018, 14204, 14208, 14438, 14450, 14488, 14510, 14778, 14968,
15005, 15058, 15113, 15265, 15371, 15427, 15456, 15775, 15781, 15784,
15819, 15969, 16074, 16298, 16315, 16559, 16625, 16654, 16772, 16826,
16855, 16912, 17078, 17128, 17138, 17140, 17240, 17381, 17488, 17515,
17598, 17754, 17755, 17787, 17876, 17898, 17926, 17943, 17944, 18007,
18010, 18012, 18013, 18016, 18020, 18022, 18023, 18025, 18026, 18027,
18028, 18043, 18334, 18404, 18410, 18411, 18412, 18416, 18504, 18584
  African   1539
  Chinese   8400
  Danish   4167
  German   6468
  Russian   151, 17839, 17840, 17841
  Slavic   4742
  Spanish   10188
  Swedish   13077
FAITH   3163
FALCONRY   6181, 6749, 9545, 14408, 18047
FALCONS   13803, 15037
FAMILY LIFE   92, 125, 137, 161, 221, 222, 223, 224, 240, 405, 419, 425,
    426, 429, 538, 559, 592, 603, 606, 614, 692, 702, 810, 826, 855, 874,
    977, 1096, 1108, 1173, 1197, 1215, 1216, 1218, 1220, 1292, 1320, 1390,
    1692, 1709, 1710, 1772, 1794, 1810, 1821, 1943, 1957, 2057, 2062, 2064,
    2065, 2157, 2200, 2221, 2265, 2266, 2267, 2313, 2510, 2596, 2602, 2603,
    2606, 2641, 2658, 2678, 2692, 2724, 2771, 2782, 2786, 2809, 2835, 2839,
    2843, 2857, 2858, 2877, 2959, 3065, 3169, 3173, 3283, 3357, 3390, 3392,
    3393, 3479, 3491, 3562, 3565, 3566, 3567, 3575, 3580, 3584, 3601, 3626,
    3632, 3684, 3688, 3860, 3864, 3870, 3916, 3930, 3931, 3978, 4091, 4127,
    4141, 4153, 4256, 4257, 4278, 4279, 4284, 4288, 4439, 4448, 4498, 4499,
    4500, 4517, 4520, 4523, 4525, 4632, 4642, 4887, 5010, 5062, 5064, 5130,
    5235, 5246, 5271, 5277, 5293, 5354, 5371, 5386, 5463, 5467, 5468, 5511,
    5512, 5513, 5514, 5515, 5536, 5550, 5551, 5552, 5559, 5612, 5617, 5634,
    5644, 5649, 5687, 5712, 5738, 5981, 6069, 6071, 6076, 6182, 6206, 6237,
    6316, 6397, 6470, 6619, 6690, 6710, 6764, 6893, 6953, 7067, 7096, 7210,
    7242, 7284, 7286, 7289, 7290, 7306, 7308, 7312, 7373, 7380, 7432, 7433,
    7472, 7587, 7646, 7648, 7656, 7660, 7680, 7729, 7801, 7913, 7953, 7957,
    7968, 8019, 8041, 8108, 8216, 8323, 8372, 8373, 8416, 8467, 8474, 8540,
    8631, 8642, 8704, 8750, 8752, 8757, 8760, 8761, 8887, 8942, 8946, 8967,
    9159, 9231, 9243, 9321, 9322, 9323, 9342, 9376, 9379, 9383, 9429, 9432,
    9506, 9509, 9731, 9788, 9818, 9889, 9904, 9905, 9908, 9910, 9913, 9918,
    9961, 9985, 10079, 10114, 10182, 10219, 10339, 10340, 10404, 10406,
    10407, 10427, 10546, 10560, 10563, 10565, 10568, 10569, 10570, 10573,
    10581, 10582, 10586, 10587, 10751, 10832, 10853, 10865, 10867, 10936,
    10939, 10941, 10942, 10943, 10944, 10951, 10981, 11094, 11126, 11208,
    11234, 11240, 11395, 11401, 11405, 11419, 11474, 11494, 11531, 11557,
    11815, 11818, 12012, 12018, 12019, 12055, 12089, 12117, 12132, 12173,
    12174, 12185, 12287, 12433, 12507, 12525, 12661, 12678, 12684, 12912,
    12914, 12945, 12955, 13049, 13317, 13320, 13331, 13410, 13413, 13424,
    13446, 13451, 13530, 13594, 13602, 13604, 13605, 13606, 13635, 13637,
    13714, 13736, 13854, 13862, 14044, 14045, 14049, 14095, 14102, 14120,
    14147, 14304, 14307, 14328, 14343, 14390, 14498, 14538, 14616, 14623,
    14781, 14836, 14837, 14840, 14842, 14847, 14877, 14948, 14971, 15069,
    15187, 15244, 15245, 15402, 15517, 15562, 15579, 15580, 15588, 15626,
    15655, 15724, 15727, 15729, 15731, 15891, 15919, 15968, 16019, 16037,

16059, 16113, 16114, 16232, 16343, 16344, 16350, 16358, 16381, 16398, 16408, 16409, 16497, 16516, 16574, 16602, 16605, 16690, 16703, 16704, 16705, 16707, 16708, 16752, 16753, 16819, 16833, 16851, 16852, 16947, 16948, 17094, 17147, 17148, 17212, 17227, 17228, 17231, 17248, 17295, 17296, 17326, 17360, 17441, 17501, 17517, 17539, 17545, 17713, 17795, 17816, 17900, 17903, 17904, 17905, 17906, 17907, 17908, 17913, 17954, 18036, 18176, 18186, 18208, 18231, 18354, 18464, 18533, 18607
  Africa 132
  England 3528, 12731
  Japan 17093
  Mexico 17533
  pictorial works 14167
  poetry 3626
  Russia 13531, 17457
  Sweden 8033
  United States--North Dakota 14579
  See also BROTHERS AND SISTERS; DIVORCE; FATHERS--AND DAUGH-
    TERS; FATHERS--AND SONS; MOTHERS--AND DAUGHTERS; MOTHERS
    --AND SONS; SINGLE PARENT FAMILY; STEPBROTHERS; STEPPAR-
    ENTS; STEPSISTERS; TRIPLETS; TWINS
FAMILY LIFE EDUCATION 15931
FAMINES 1984
FANTASY 4, 169, 185, 192, 261, 262, 264, 265, 266, 268, 270, 271, 272, 273, 368, 417, 540, 596, 786, 846, 867, 869, 870, 929, 1055, 1061, 1066, 1108, 1113, 1117, 1118, 1199, 1200, 1225, 1228, 1404, 1498, 1503, 1611, 1672, 1675, 1828, 1833, 1846, 1876, 1877, 1880, 1881, 1883, 1971, 1973, 1974, 1975, 2000, 2092, 2099, 2177, 2201, 2271, 2273, 2289, 2361, 2421, 2472, 2661, 2679, 2756, 2795, 2804, 2861, 2943, 3098, 3105, 3156, 3280, 3286, 3312, 3388, 3477, 3536, 3537, 3593, 3672, 3677, 3694, 3765, 4080, 4100, 4281, 4283, 4287, 4291, 4339, 4342, 4370, 4373, 4381, 4393, 4396, 4400, 4401, 4402, 4405, 4418, 4440, 4441, 4444, 4445, 4459, 4484, 4542, 4619, 4664, 4687, 4712, 4725, 4729, 4733, 4735, 4855, 4892, 4895, 5074, 5083, 5084, 5086, 5087, 5088, 5089, 5090, 5091, 5095, 5171, 5183, 5184, 5185, 5186, 5187, 5188, 5192, 5198, 5199, 5201, 5280, 5330, 5347, 5357, 5469, 5474, 5537, 5538, 5543, 5554, 5620, 5668, 5694, 5697, 5699, 5700, 5708, 6022, 6038, 6066, 6136, 6178, 6258, 6408, 6444, 6474, 6571, 6659, 6789, 6950, 6951, 7069, 7086, 7096, 7153, 7154, 7211, 7217, 7218, 7260, 7323, 7434, 7538, 7579, 7983, 7984, 8005, 8049, 8182, 8287, 8288, 8290, 8295, 8353, 8501, 8502, 8505, 8640, 8726, 8790, 8816, 8836, 8902, 8909, 8917, 8931, 8932, 8998, 9141, 9142, 9143, 9145, 9158, 9200, 9250, 9251, 9300, 9314, 9339, 9341, 9343, 9346, 9437, 9510, 9511, 9623, 9679, 9711, 9712, 9787, 10003, 10021, 10027, 10102, 10132, 10192, 10259, 10263, 10264, 10368, 10415, 10423, 10440, 10469, 10514, 10516, 10517, 10596, 10659, 10688, 10689, 10690, 10691, 10692, 10693, 10694, 10704, 10797, 10800, 10804, 10809, 10810, 10824, 10825, 10831, 10836, 10931, 10982, 11020, 11021, 11022, 11025, 11026, 11027, 11068, 11172, 11173, 11183, 11212, 11213, 11235, 11300, 11307, 11368, 11395, 11410, 11423, 11427, 11429, 11430, 11551, 11559, 11670, 11775, 11939, 11955, 11956, 11957, 12057, 12063, 12194, 12246, 12248, 12251, 12263, 12325, 12379, 12443, 12563, 12575, 12591, 12634, 12692, 12733, 12734, 12774, 12791, 12793, 12822, 12918, 12933, 12936, 12939, 12946, 12947, 12948, 12949, 12950, 12993, 13048, 13123, 13168, 13230, 13232, 13409, 13430, 13455, 13477, 13542, 13704, 13733, 13896, 13983, 14062, 14096, 14121, 14380, 14399, 14474, 14548, 14768, 14856, 14857, 15161, 15332, 15334, 15337, 15367, 15376, 15377, 15378, 15379, 15380, 15385, 15614, 15701, 15778, 15961, 15962, 15966, 15972, 16155, 16160, 16161, 16310, 16383, 16636, 16883, 16915, 16918, 16972, 16990, 17021, 17059, 17176, 17255, 17259, 17261,

17275, 17280, 17287, 17399, 17414, 17450, 17654, 17750, 17776, 17792,
17794, 17845, 17854, 17897, 17965, 18049, 18183, 18217, 18319, 18320,
18355, 18417, 18425, 18478, 18511
FANTIS 10491
FAR EAST see MIDDLE EAST
FARFAN, ARMANDO (1970?-) 10086
FARGO (NORTH DAKOTA) 2097
FARM LIFE 663, 838, 1148, 1330, 1641, 1664, 1665, 1666, 1696, 2590, 2596,
2597, 2789, 2986, 3155, 3650, 3836, 3997, 4617, 4618, 5128, 5179, 5471,
5646, 5707, 5725, 5918, 5938, 6013, 6015, 6073, 6775, 7007, 7083, 7934,
8244, 8341, 8429, 8517, 8915, 9005, 10142, 10443, 10485, 10559, 10561,
10564, 10583, 10587, 10792, 10842, 11030, 11109, 11517, 12308, 12423,
12582, 12684, 13007, 13210, 13453, 13569, 13979, 13982, 14046, 14155,
14196, 14657, 14716, 14795, 14991, 15004, 15890, 16028, 16372, 16722,
16729, 16827, 16995, 17007, 17009, 17225, 17338, 17590, 17645, 17777,
17901, 18060, 18160, 18408, 18488
  Australia 4751, 13641
  Canada 10141
  Hungary 15342
  Prince Edward Island 17441
  Spain 9227
  Sweden 10835
  United States
    Florida 13874
    Maine 14323
    Middle West 17623, 17624
      pictorial works 8017
    Missouri 14045
    Texas 11565
FARM TENANCY 7614, 8783, 10565, 10589
FARMERS 12866, 17245
FARMS 8918, 12637
FASTS AND FEASTS 6059, 12170
  Catholic Church--Spain 17264
  Judaism 94, 1291, 1628, 3918, 3920, 3927, 5485, 6805, 7303, 8237, 10097,
  12478, 14000, 14001, 14053, 15407, 15446
FATHER FLANAGAN'S HOME, BOYS TOWN (NEBRASKA) 7191
FATHERS 5298, 8456, 10581, 16311, 18601
  and daughters 688, 2676, 2810, 2843, 3205, 3565, 3579, 3676, 3742,
  3812, 5840, 6616, 6869, 7657, 8908, 9812, 11175, 11441, 15216, 16814,
  17972, 18406, 18465, 18508
  and sons 427, 945, 1219, 2088, 2767, 3417, 3558, 3619, 4128, 4442,
  5869, 6177, 6185, 6813, 6981, 7134, 7741, 8087, 8269, 8530, 8533, 9242,
  9744, 10116, 10129, 10738, 11071, 11616, 11967, 12438, 13454, 13664,
  14046, 14080, 14081, 14677, 15469, 15505, 16620, 16624, 16670, 16730,
  16793, 16957, 17864, 18231, 18396, 18397
FEAR 1080, 2070, 2289, 2416, 2498, 3441, 5061, 5104, 6456, 9306, 9312,
  10040, 10747, 11064, 11111, 11364, 11553, 12400, 13120, 14620, 15813,
  16346, 16642, 16769, 16989, 17263, 17333, 17375, 17586, 17713
  of dark 847, 3934
  of storms 2993
FEMINISM 1794, 4437
  United States 9982
    history 11979
FEMINISTS 9081, 12861, 13576, 16317, 18059
FERMI, ENRICO (1901-1959) 5492
FERTILIZATION OF PLANTS 8574, 14084

FESTIVALS 8881, 9397, 11639, 12829, 13998, 16734
    Europe 5493
    Japan 2533
    Jews 17663
    Mexico 11661
    United States--Indiana--pictorial works 11625
    Venezuela 12868
FETTERMAN FIGHT (1866) 6944
FEUDALISM 1825, 17152
FEVER 1593
FICTION--technique 13729
FILMS see MOTION PICTURES
FINANCE, PERSONAL 17318, 18450
FINGER PLAY 7228, 7345, 9222, 9223, 9224
FINK, MIKE (1770-1823?) 5780
FINLAND 871, 1586, 2564, 2994
FINNISH AMERICANS 45, 12229, 16373, 16379
FIRE see FIRES
FIRE DEPARTMENTS 13071, 13552
    equipment and supplies 3786, 5946, 7156, 7293
    New York (City) 1252
FIRE ENGINES 10575
FIRE FIGHTERS 1336, 5772, 7269, 7293, 10575, 13071, 13548, 14316, 16940
    vocational guidance 8187, 13552
FIREARMS 607, 2204, 3779, 3788
    history 13571
FIRES 2435, 2464, 7568, 8439, 15207, 15874, 15927
    extinction 3786, 16225
    prevention 13552
    The West (U.S.)--pictorial works 526
FIRESTONE, HARVEY SAMUEL (1868-1938) 13276
FIREWORKS 6059
FIRST AID 1416, 7078, 17193
    handbooks, manuals, etc. 7238
FISHER (ANIMAL) 13957
FISHERIES 6206, 6724, 13892, 18565
    vocational guidance 14644
FISHERMEN 1016, 10328, 10705, 13776, 15584, 16793
    poetry 841
FISHES 697, 2091, 2450, 2478, 5379, 6045, 6047, 6739, 8000, 8622, 8911,
    9461, 10875, 10885, 10886, 11672, 12434, 12757, 13134, 13339, 13353,
    13643, 13963, 14299, 15299, 15318, 15496, 15764, 17183, 17917
    eggs 6044
    habits and behavior 6044
FISHING 417, 524, 2031, 2393, 2771, 3767, 3769, 3782, 3806, 4826, 5578,
    6060, 6739, 6973, 8384, 8810, 9517, 9686, 10267, 11538, 12411, 13308,
    13847, 14153, 15224, 15382, 15576, 15584, 15586, 16337, 16338, 16819,
    16937, 17523, 17658
    commercial 9883
    equipment and supplies 14004
    Ghana 5456
    United States 5578
FISHING INDUSTRY--Maine 11457
FISK, CARLTON (1947-) 9012
FITZPATRICK, THOMAS (1799-1854) 6630
FLACK, ROBERTA (1940-) 9073, 12487
FLAGS 5395, 5587, 10033, 13463

United States   1736, 4326, 6297, 11924, 13341
   Louisiana   2222
FLAMINGOES   12591
   fables   14043
FLANAGAN, EDWARD JOSEPH (1886-1948)   7191
FLANNIGAN, KATHERINE MARY (O'FALLON), (1891?-1954)   6243
FLEAS   3799
FLEMING, PEGGY (1948-)   12486
FLIES   3951
FLIGHT   1239, 5699, 5892, 6248, 12871, 15963
FLIGHT CREWS   14156
FLOODS   2332, 2832, 3667, 4450, 5248, 5656, 5995, 6211, 8863, 8914, 10568,
   12186, 16652, 18383
   control   157
FLORENCE (ITALY)--social life and customs   17151
FLORIDA   885, 4189, 5354, 8474, 10404, 10407, 10589, 10896, 17426, 17869,
   18315
   history--Spanish Colony (1565-1763)   7943
FLORIDA KEYS   1028, 3321, 8550, 11905, 16354
FLOUR MILLS--Ohio--history   6548
FLOWER GARDENING   8402
FLOWERS   242, 339, 1391, 4465, 5042, 5210, 7424, 9616, 12022, 12253,
   12739, 13162, 14084, 15319, 16691, 17115, 17213
   arrangement   12558
   drying   6157
   Illinois   5301
   pictorial works   17415
FLUTE   6365, 16549, 17230
FLYING SAUCERS   2115, 9936, 16035, 18143
FOG   14830, 15115, 17000
FOLK ART   9837, 18595
   Mexico   14661
   Ukraine   11153
   United States   6876, 6934, 8637, 9836, 12693
FOLK DANCING   13911
   Africa   17536
FOLK DRAMA   10252
FOLK LITERATURE   10721
FOLK MUSIC   1930, 17195
   history and criticism   1527
   Puerto Rico--history and criticism   11056, 12840
FOLK SONGS   302, 304, 771, 1899, 2096, 4734, 5404, 5405, 7904, 7964,
   10246, 10247, 10249, 10256, 10258, 12216, 13920, 15000, 18114, 18515,
   18523
   African   11564, 14566
   Armenian   8664
   Chinese   4903
   English   9498, 9710, 13923, 17921
     in the United States   10248
   Japanese   4903
   Kenyan   9983
   Korean   4903
   Latin American   4653
   Scottish   12816, 12818, 14301
   Spanish   13940, 14411, 14523
   Spanish American   14293
   Ugandan   15356

United States   29, 302, 1773, 1898, 2979, 3300, 3304, 10248, 14022,
   14024, 14028, 14029, 14031, 15236, 15237, 15238, 15239, 16086, 16088,
   17022, 17351
   New York (State)   16831
   Ohio   5252
   Utah   8703
   The West   11039
FOLKLORE   269, 656, 777, 919, 1046, 1132, 1138, 1211, 1214, 1375, 1382,
   1606, 1787, 2012, 2326, 2465, 2864, 3086, 3089, 3734, 3874, 3881, 4071,
   4200, 4628, 4804, 4861, 4862, 4868, 4888, 4936, 4998, 5001, 5348, 5404,
   5432, 5737, 5796, 6467, 6498, 6500, 6501, 6502, 6509, 6511, 6612, 7292,
   7718, 7774, 7793, 7840, 8027, 8407, 8858, 8859, 8974, 9047, 9049, 9050,
   9097, 9101, 9706, 9708, 10391, 10447, 10448, 10452, 10666, 11164, 11390,
   11627, 11628, 11630, 11631, 11633, 11635, 11638, 11640, 11644, 11820,
   11964, 12097, 12109, 12139, 12258, 12476, 12498, 12530, 12975, 13050,
   13384, 13501, 13893, 14014, 14489, 14517, 14570, 15140, 15779, 15788,
   16315, 16328, 16867, 17239, 17380, 18164
   Acoli   1487
   Africa   1, 2, 3, 6, 7, 8, 80, 210, 586, 631, 673, 676, 677, 1158, 1539,
      1577, 1696, 1995, 2347, 2457, 2459, 2734, 3050, 3231, 3353, 3472,
      3534, 3541, 3712, 4197, 4206, 4267, 4436, 4470, 4483, 4628, 4772, 4989,
      4990, 5351, 5359, 5360, 5361, 5362, 6080, 6083, 6159, 6314, 6317, 6319,
      6320, 6322, 6323, 6612, 7070, 7104, 7237, 7478, 7497, 7582, 7641, 7724,
      7725, 7726, 9443, 9467, 9546, 9781, 9822, 10001, 10004, 10488, 10623,
      10629, 10736, 10813, 10984a, 11130, 11315, 11739, 12762, 12966, 12971,
      13052, 13648, 14352, 14454, 14455, 14493, 14525, 14962, 15015, 15017,
      16335, 16340, 16420, 16421, 16433, 16438, 16613, 16671, 17185, 18065,
      18251, 18280, 18596
      Central   1792, 17025
      drama   18127
      East   4347, 7973, 7975, 7979, 9561, 11819, 13042, 13043, 18111
      North   6839, 8443
      West   10, 595, 630, 631, 1077, 1214, 1544, 4206, 4434, 5015, 7474,
         7498, 7814, 8973, 11566, 12077, 12572, 13852
   Algeria   14360
   Arabia   2376, 3874, 7679, 9864, 10239, 10289, 10290, 12867, 17787
   Armenia   8409, 8414, 8546, 16660, 16661
   Ashanti   589, 593, 594, 4208, 11289
   Asia   730, 2165, 9434
      drama   18127
   Australia   13313
   Austria   17246
   Aztec   12275
   Bantu   677, 8113, 8463, 13927, 14956, 14958, 14961, 14964
   Basuto   11738, 14957
   birds   3315
   Black American   1581, 3211, 3217, 4203, 5729, 7773, 8723, 10629, 10630,
      10631, 17817, 18210
   Botswana   2353, 9780
   Brazil   14515
   Brittany   12142
   Bukusu   7724
   Burma   796, 9614, 12113
   Canada   4982
   Caucasus   6855
   Celtic   8334, 9052, 11323, 12142
   Central America   3124

China   27, 260, 1657, 3054, 3260, 3326, 4822, 8472, 8740, 9681, 9861,
    9865, 10821, 12114, 12499, 14406, 17012, 17241, 18211, 18297, 18352,
    18406, 18584
collections   1045, 1369, 1374
Congo   9862, 9866, 14959
Cornwall   11642, 18513
Czechoslovakia   2644, 5867, 5868, 6464, 7870, 14041
Denmark   1162, 1548, 7463, 7837, 7871, 9705, 9707, 13024
East Indian   9674, 9675
Egypt   7249, 11623, 12531, 18482
England   2374, 3307, 3894, 3942, 4319, 5879, 6959, 7872, 8157, 8158,
    9044, 9045, 9046, 9051, 9053, 14016, 15364, 15393, 15616, 16422, 16980,
    18513
Eskimo   6828, 6829, 11545
Estonia   11196, 18161
Ethiopia   2358, 4207, 4613, 5349, 7384, 11675
Europe   2548
Finland   1968, 2023, 2949, 3533, 4860, 5868, 16601
France   1598, 1600, 2373, 2382, 3218, 3272, 4061, 5579, 6163, 6506, 8510,
    11431, 11807, 13533, 13652, 14520, 14527
French Canadian   2970, 7425
Friesland   16077
Germany   1297, 2922, 6468, 6674, 7386, 7387, 7388, 7389, 7390, 7392,
    7393, 7394, 7395, 7398, 7399, 7400, 7401, 7402, 7403, 7404, 7406, 7407,
    7409, 7843, 7873, 8864, 10948, 13653, 16654, 17240, 18026
Ghana   30, 76, 173, 575, 590, 591, 593, 4485, 4486, 9613, 13019, 13191,
    16121, 16122, 16976, 18387
Greece   300, 5696, 7874, 8524, 8525
Haiti   4199, 9273, 16798
Hausa   1581
Hawaii   2370, 2545, 2546, 3879, 4983, 12307, 16839, 16840
Hopi   16616
Hottentot   11657
Hungary   391, 392, 1663, 3879, 6858, 11641, 15344
Iceland   11350, 15056
Igbo (African people)   13054
India   1044, 4750, 4984, 6717, 7215, 7875, 9048, 13922, 14036, 15235,
    15574, 16946
Indians of North America   2022, 2371, 3524, 4644, 4979, 4980, 4981,
    4986, 4987, 5220, 5824, 6504, 6941, 6942, 6943, 8656, 10380, 15104
    Iroquois   13072
    Mexico   5590
    Navaho   3315, 9248, 17173
    Ojibway   2324
    United States--Southwest   5590
Indonesia   1844, 4196
    Java   9809
Iran   5474, 12017, 13656, 18213
Ireland   1834, 3878, 4384, 4478, 4945, 4978, 5606, 6382, 7236, 7876,
    8784, 11455, 13026, 13671, 13796, 14206, 16422, 16523, 16524
Islands of the Pacific   8447
Italy   3468, 4726, 8324, 8326, 14504, 18520
Jahdu   7663, 7664
Jamaica   15543
Japan   1047, 1147, 1155, 2194, 3053, 3535, 5256, 5263, 7877, 8236, 8336,
    8941, 10794, 10801, 10802, 11199, 11293, 11826, 11830, 12541, 13667,
    14859, 14977, 16137, 16615, 16893, 17091, 17096, 17100, 17103, 18212,

18360, 18403, 18525
Jewish   679, 802, 7447, 7878, 8231, 8232, 8238, 8944, 8945, 11287, 15359,
  16449, 18524
Kenya   2355, 5704, 7724, 7725, 7726, 8905, 9443, 9983, 10167, 11561,
  13044, 13045, 13195, 13858, 13859, 13860, 14760, 14960, 15994, 17035
Kikuyu   11811, 12854, 17510
Korea   3055, 8896, 9219
Laos   18212
Lapland   16131
Latin America   1084, 9221
Latvia   5164, 8714
Lebanon   15821
Liberia   4273, 7813, 8056, 11801
Lithuania   18597
Majorca   12016
Malagasy Republic   2349
Malawi   14960
Malaya   5003
Masai   9, 6792
Matabele   10220, 14963
Mayan   12275
Mexico   5, 1014, 1084, 1267, 2179, 4935, 4985, 5590, 7032, 9384, 10010,
  10438, 10859, 11188, 13668, 14660, 14726, 16382, 16936, 16969, 18212,
  Jalisco   2890
Middle East   3051, 4988, 5727
Mongolia   13202
Morocco   1602
Mossi   7498
Near Eastern   5727
Nepal   8258
Nigeria   85, 202, 1031, 1546, 2357, 4205, 4628, 5619, 6771, 12076, 13054,
  13125, 15014, 16612, 16800, 17179, 17180, 17289, 17290, 17291, 17429,
  17569
Norway   713, 714, 715, 4515, 4550, 4555, 4556, 4558, 6510, 10242, 11409,
  12164, 17877, 17883, 10266
Nso   10266
Nyasaland   14960
Oceania   6874
Orient   9434, 12633, 16938
Pakistan   15653
Persia   12017
Philippines   699
Poland   4993, 4997, 4999, 17076
Portugal   1015, 1016
Puerto Rico   249, 253, 1367, 1368, 1369, 1370, 1371, 1372, 1374, 3276
Rhodesia   7731
  Southern   16967
Romania   14749
Russia   150, 152, 695, 1561, 1695, 2372, 2508, 2918, 2919, 4480, 6507,
  6845, 6847, 6848, 6849, 6851, 6852, 6853, 6854, 6856, 6857, 7879, 8171,
  9126, 9127, 10862, 11286, 12494, 13804, 14007, 14114, 14115, 14211,
  14271, 14396, 14397, 14422, 15781, 15861, 16884, 16921, 17839, 17840,
  17841, 18349, 18518
San   8025, 13630, 15226
Scandinavia   2277, 9349, 16074
Scotland   7880, 8787, 12815, 12817, 12819, 12820, 18064
  Orkney Island   4348
Senegal   2354

Siberia 6850
Sierra Leone 2352, 18372
Slovenia 6846
Sotho 10812
South Africa 1995, 6308, 11503, 13861, 15226
South America 6229, 6231, 11537
Spain 4609, 9221, 9235, 12422
Spanish American 9098
Sudan 17025
Sweden 7881, 18516
Switzerland 5190, 8822
Tanzania 1632
Thailand 10111, 10112
Tibet 8740
Tunisia 1603, 1607
Turkey 5056, 5313, 17234, 17428, 17430, 17431, 17432, 17433, 17434,
 17436, 17437, 17438
Udmurt 6854
Uganda 1158, 1159, 2350, 15356
Ukraine 1784, 14743, 16575, 18363
United States 1713, 1732, 2020, 2021, 2334, 2335, 2844, 3301, 3303,
 3734, 4186, 4391, 4703, 4706, 5407, 5432, 5433, 5434, 5729, 5772, 5773,
 5779, 5784, 5785, 6004, 6013, 6015, 6016, 6061, 6496, 6868, 7599, 7882,
 7978, 9385, 9597, 10131, 10449, 10630, 11093, 11271, 11272, 11392,
 11548, 11569, 14139, 14425, 14701, 14969, 15143, 15149, 15419, 15421,
 15422, 15423, 15424, 15426, 15533, 15712, 16266, 16390, 16391, 16552,
 17074, 17337, 18210, 18242
 Appalachian Mountains 3507, 17022
 Blue Ridge Mountains 3302, 4270
 Indiana 16554
 Kansas 14849
 Middle Atlantic states 9105
 Missouri 12957
 New England 9100
 New Mexico 7029
 New York (City) 9096
 North Carolina 7240
 Northwest, Old 9104
 Ohio 11668
 South Carolina 1856
 Southern states 9095
 Southwest, New 2866
 Texas 1268
 Tombigbee River 1048
 Wisconsin 6572
Upper Volta 7498
Venezuela 378, 14412
Vietnam 7126, 9776, 14438, 16644, 16686, 17331
Wales 6615, 9350, 12977, 13986, 13987, 14424, 16826
West Indies 2458, 3125, 15544, 15546, 15547
Xosa 14965
Yiddish 10908
Yoruba 4202, 6430
Yugoslavia 4382
Zaire 2356, 11292
Zambia 2351
Zimbabwe 16967

Zulu   14966, 15228
See also LEGENDS
FOOD   104, 1582, 3643, 8035, 9278, 9293, 9902, 10032, 10297, 10603, 12123,
    12664, 13527, 13561, 14802, 15167, 15866, 16649, 17464, 17566, 18140
    additives   15680
    contamination   15680
    dietetic--recipes   7910
    poetry   168
FOOD CHAIN (ECOLOGY)   13948
FOOD INDUSTRY AND TRADE   12710, 16648
FOOD SERVICE--vocational guidance   6273
FOOD SUPPLY   8643, 13522, 13968, 13992, 16648
    United States--history   13524
FOOLS   1162, 5358, 10254
FOOTBALL   474, 475, 476, 583, 949, 1533, 1536, 1684, 1729, 2295, 2987,
    2988, 3215, 3415, 3417, 3419, 3430, 3432, 4002, 4028, 4225, 4713, 4778,
    4789, 4791, 4864, 4972, 5167, 5168, 5196, 5574, 6168, 6678, 6686, 6692,
    6695, 7518, 8860, 8983, 8985, 9017, 9493, 9627, 9749, 9954, 10767,
    10773, 10774, 11069, 11070, 11777, 11841, 11856, 11864, 11873, 11882,
    11889, 11894, 11899, 11902, 12393, 12780, 14158, 14241, 14242, 14384,
    14734, 14735, 15106, 15532, 15571, 16463, 16474, 16477, 16479, 16480,
    16481, 16482, 16487, 16492, 16764, 17047, 18492
    defense   475
    dictionaries   10912, 13079
    history   7612, 8487, 8488, 10477, 10919, 10921, 12156, 12779
        addresses, essays, lectures   8486
    players   949, 1177, 2161, 2607, 2615, 2618, 2620, 2624, 2632, 2635,
        2636, 3215, 3846, 4592, 4788, 5167, 5168, 6168, 7517, 7518, 7521,
        7526, 7809, 7810, 8189, 9017, 10767, 10773, 10774, 10893, 10915, 10919,
        11870, 11871, 11880, 11881, 11895, 12488, 13106, 14093, 14094, 14734,
        15433, 15877, 15906, 15911, 16130, 16473, 16485, 16845, 16846, 16847,
        17615, 18438
FORCE AND ENERGY   1441, 2153, 7798, 8398, 8930, 10510, 13682, 13761,
    14741, 15924
FORD, GERALD R. (1913-)   14, 12083
FORD, HENRY (1863-1947)   198, 1128, 2816, 9670, 12363, 12812, 13113,
    13277
FOREST FIRES   3113, 4449, 5379, 5382, 12182, 13964, 16036, 16687, 16794,
    17182, 18193
    California   6706
    prevention and control   17506
FOREST RANGERS   15583
FOREST RESERVES   18226
FORESTS AND FORESTRY   950, 2277, 5041, 8815, 9923, 12591, 13114, 14106,
    15156, 15179, 15274, 15354, 16997
    Kenya   986
    miscellanea   10923
    North America   10923
FORMOSA   see TAIWAN
FORT DEARBORN (ILLINOIS)   901
FORT DIX (NEW JERSEY)   11984
FORT SNELLING (MINNESOTA)   13465
FORTEN, CHARLOTTE L. (1838-1914)   5037, 11051
FORTEN, JAMES (1766-1842)   5038, 9305
FORTIFICATION   4360, 11201
    United States   7163, 13570
        Northwest, Old   11223

Wisconsin 4615
FORTS 6704, 7413, 7919, 7925, 9669, 11852, 14374, 17554, 18530
FORTUNE, AMOS (1709 or 1710-1801) 18376
FOSSEY, DIAN 9768
FOSSILS 301, 397, 398, 527, 528, 550, 666, 910, 2730, 4505, 4578, 5396, 5473, 5502, 5804, 8440, 8624, 8676, 9541, 11835, 11907, 11949, 14187, 14288, 15025, 15414
collectors and collecting 8826, 17775
England 1711
living 305
North America 916, 3776
pleistocene 3802, 8512
United States 17786
    Michigan 8511
    New Mexico--Rio Arriba County 17775
FOSTER, ABIGAIL (KELLEY), (1810-1887) 863
FOSTER HOME CARE 219, 1027, 1192, 2790, 2955, 5136, 5373, 5620, 5788, 10936, 12000, 13323, 13368, 14322, 14839, 16403, 17350, 18109
FOUND OBJECTS see RECYCLING (WASTE)
4-H CLUBS 4920, 8366, 18060
FOURTH OF JULY 4458, 7192, 7544, 13615, 18595
FOX, GEORGE (1624-1691) 18407
FOXES 1187, 2487, 2657, 2789, 4443, 5136, 5891, 5892, 5893, 6173, 6226, 6523, 6550, 6753, 8068, 8411, 8838, 9213, 9307, 9326, 9786, 9881, 9941, 10647, 12182, 14404, 14417, 14427, 16404, 16930, 17239, 17566, 18370
folklore 6851
FOYT, A. J. (1935-) 5444, 10137, 11853, 13089, 13100
FRACTURES 18204
FRANCE 1387, 2285, 2755, 2956, 2967, 3444, 5278, 5716, 5718, 5722, 10867, 15455, 16886, 17051, 17423, 17747, 18246
colonies--America 8431
history
    German occupation (1940-1945) 1679, 14845
    Revolution (1789-1799) 2727
politics and government (1945-) 5489
FRANCIS OF ASSISI, SAINT (1182?-1226) 2571, 13788
FRANKLIN, ARETHA (1942-) 13101
FRANKLIN, BENJAMIN (1706-1790) 306, 752, 2001, 4210, 4534, 4545, 5007, 5233, 6040, 6391, 9418, 10419, 11986, 12106, 12348, 14983
FRANKS--history (to 768 A.D.) 373
FRAUD 5345, 5358
FRAZIER, JOE (1944-) 13061
FRAZIER, WALT (1945-) 2638, 10918
FRECKLES 1817
FREDERICKSBURG (TEXAS)--history 7686
FREE SPEECH 2728
FREE WILL AND DETERMINISM 3332
FREEDOM 1783, 6141, 8322, 9240, 11471, 11839, 15009, 16357, 16385, 18005
FREEMAN, ELIZABETH (1744-1829) 5781
FREIGHT AND FREIGHTAGE 16472, 18567
FREMONT, JESSIE (BENTON), (1824-1902) 17388
FREMONT, JOHN CHARLES (1813-1890) 2714, 2976
FRENCH AMERICANS 5513, 5850, 8431
history 10134
FRENCH AND INDIAN WAR see UNITED STATES--HISTORY--FRENCH AND INDIAN WAR
FRENCH, BOOKS IN 368a, 2924, 4078, 9899, 10372, 10373, 10374, 10884

FRENCH CANADIANS 2961, 2962, 8431, 9995, 11474
FRENCH EQUATORIAL AFRICA 12991
FRENCH LANGUAGE 16213
  dialects--Louisiana 14311
FRENCH LITERATURE 1007
FRENCH POETRY 4062, 4656, 4657, 6228, 15939
FRENCH SUDAN 7488
FRENCH WEST AFRICA--description and travel 13068
FRESH WATER ANIMALS 8792, 15154
FRESH WATER BIOLOGY 1143, 9470, 14219
FRESH WATER PLANTS 8405
FRIEDRICH II (EMPEROR OF GERMANY), (1194-1250) 8465
FRIENDS, SOCIETY OF 327, 328, 815, 3207, 4641, 5335, 5918, 8758, 8759,
  11043, 12354, 17056, 17060
  England--biography 18407
FRIENDSHIP 81, 91, 221, 258, 293, 353, 507, 508, 536, 538, 555, 623, 681,
  693, 694, 703, 855, 988, 997, 1025, 1031, 1034, 1185, 1219, 1221, 1279,
  1326, 1345, 1403, 1540, 1908, 1909, 1961, 2094, 2101, 2290, 2292, 2406,
  2415, 2416, 2420, 2502, 2552, 2570, 2591, 2781, 2790, 2884, 2965, 3284,
  3310, 3360, 3383, 3413, 3425, 3555, 3557, 3560, 3561, 3576, 3579, 3583,
  3624, 3637, 3694, 3741, 3759, 3764, 3807, 3863, 3925, 3938, 3939, 3941,
  3976, 3983, 3984, 3985, 3988, 3994, 4058, 4140, 4145, 4251, 4292, 4368,
  4369, 4408, 4448, 4449, 4452, 4524, 4526, 4531, 4678, 4718, 4799, 4814,
  4817, 4820, 4821, 4857, 4880, 4921, 4925, 5010, 5103, 5182, 5188, 5227,
  5479, 5521, 5522, 5533, 5549, 5564, 5646, 5709, 5716, 5750, 5895, 5979,
  6355, 6455, 6457, 6783, 6813, 6904, 7031, 7073, 7074, 7114, 7120, 7154,
  7220, 7243, 7261, 7285, 7286, 7287, 7290, 7299, 7385, 7430, 7441, 7483,
  7532, 7543, 7558, 7600, 7606, 7607, 7654, 7662, 7695, 7721, 7783, 7833,
  7851, 8007, 8039, 8049, 8129, 8149, 8273, 8293, 8340, 8355, 8365, 8369,
  8396, 8478, 8548, 8549, 8609, 8736, 8827, 8842, 8966, 9161, 9167, 9240,
  9327, 9334, 9440, 9447, 9487, 9517, 9602, 9638, 9660, 9735, 9961, 9991,
  10006, 10039, 10041, 10042, 10116, 10338, 10400, 10487, 10515, 10615,
  10667, 10740, 10797, 10826, 10882, 10937, 10939, 10940, 10986, 10991,
  10992, 10994, 11079, 11098, 11099, 11101, 11102, 11103, 11104, 11105,
  11106, 11107, 11120, 11169, 11193, 11386, 11528, 11538, 11556, 11622,
  11669, 11709, 11710, 11713, 11716, 11717, 11817, 12063, 12095, 12120,
  12152, 12167, 12171, 12176, 12453, 12480, 12490, 12508, 12522, 12662,
  12682, 12683, 12908, 12909, 12911, 12913, 13000, 13166, 13205, 13251,
  13367, 13409, 13460, 13473, 13480, 13525, 13638, 13640, 13655, 13876,
  13942, 13945, 14009, 14035, 14052, 14111, 14121, 14379, 14387, 14388,
  14395, 14462, 14474, 14497, 14499, 14562, 14563, 14572, 14755, 14757,
  14825, 14833, 14844, 15045, 15048, 15119, 15175, 15180, 15183, 15221,
  15224, 15267, 15363, 15459, 15460, 15461, 15466, 15468, 15474, 15475,
  15476, 15478, 15515, 15516, 15520, 15531, 15621, 15701, 15707, 15765,
  15793, 15816, 15842, 15857, 15858, 15859, 15882, 15923, 15945, 15964,
  16025, 16050, 16194, 16213, 16241, 16262, 16285, 16287, 16290, 16303,
  16358, 16404, 16516, 16665, 16668, 16674, 16712, 16756, 16758, 16785,
  16815, 16942, 16948, 17013, 17021, 17051, 17111, 17213, 17237, 17246,
  17276, 17321, 17333, 17364, 17370, 17454, 17456, 17459, 17460, 17468,
  17670, 17715, 17720, 17728, 17791, 17867, 17924, 17949, 17964, 18087,
  18132, 18170, 18171, 18208, 18240, 18413, 18418, 18420, 18468, 18490,
  18521, 18602, 18605, 18609, 18611, 18620, 18621, 18622
  caricatures and cartoons 15135
FROGS AND TOADS 22, 2895, 3088, 3318, 4118, 4526, 4527, 4712, 5522,
  5523, 5524, 5525, 5992, 6337, 6473, 7889, 7890, 7891, 8039, 8639, 9622,
  10246, 10875, 10991, 10992, 10993, 11250, 11806, 11927, 11933, 12268,
  12628, 12643, 13086, 13227, 13740, 13741, 14518, 14530, 15718, 15741,

16998, 18521
FRONTIER AND PIONEER LIFE 310, 327, 403, 500, 519, 1076, 1277, 1282,
  1296, 1466, 2264, 2266, 2275, 2690, 2712, 2794, 3174, 3479, 3697, 3886,
  3996, 4058, 4268, 4457, 4618, 4660, 4708, 4709, 4710, 5511, 5512, 5513,
  5514, 5515, 5526, 5535, 5604, 5644, 5646, 5847, 5850, 5883, 6070, 6169,
  6199, 6201, 6237, 6388, 6866, 6896, 6931, 7165, 7728, 7928, 7936, 7981,
  8427, 8430, 8618, 8619, 8670, 8672, 8674, 8759, 8762, 8819, 8820, 9272,
  10224, 10268, 11314, 11563, 11575, 11785, 11790, 11792, 11795, 11797,
  11798, 11800, 11981, 11988, 11998, 12308, 12340, 12387, 12433, 12526,
  13189, 13295, 14320, 14372, 14374, 14621, 16170, 16179, 16181, 16182,
  16263, 16306, 16396, 16401, 16622, 16670, 16676, 16721, 16790, 17040,
  17270, 17348, 17439, 17601, 17722, 17757, 17890, 17900, 17901, 17902,
  17903, 17904, 17905, 17906, 17907, 17909, 17933, 17938, 18037, 18082,
  18258, 18309, 18377, 18435, 18441
  biography 13722
  Saskatchewan--Russell Lake Region 13731
  United States 2269, 8010, 11222, 12526, 13717
    Great Plains 14708
    Iowa--Waterloo 7987
    Kansas 8939, 18040
    Louisiana 12824
    Middle West 7861
    Minnesota 12459
    Missouri Valley 17908
    Nebraska 17735
    North Dakota 14578
    Ohio Valley 11214
    Oklahoma 9625
    South Dakota 13228
    Southern states 16178
    Texas 6629, 17634
    Utah 7727
    The West 1691, 6635, 9348, 10644, 10646, 13333, 14654, 15127, 17513,
      18072
    Wisconsin 7868
FRUIT 4407, 4625, 5808, 7469, 8038, 8208, 8239, 15272, 16186
FUEL 10509
  United States 8949
FULAHS 2039
FULANIS 9858, 17970, 18003
FULTON, ROBERT (1765-1815) 8188, 14061
FUNERAL RITES AND CEREMONIES 3733
FUNGI 9560, 14805
FUR TRADE AND TRADERS 3900, 4846, 9669, 14320
  Canadian 5490
    Northwest 389
  United States
    Michigan 9279
    The West 6896
FURNITURE 7714
FYNN, HENRY (d. 1861) 15229

- G -

GABON 3005
GAITHER, ALONZO S. (1903-) 1729
GALAXIES 741
GALDIKAS BRINDAMOUR, BIRUTE 9768
GALILEI, GALILEO (1564-1642) 3711, 14614
GALLIPOLIS (OHIO)--history 971
GAMA, VASCO DA (1469-1524) 9718, 14893, 16594
GAMBIA 3006, 4604, 4605, 4606
GAME
   and game-birds--Louisiana--Vermilion Parish 9150
   preserves 14597
   protection 9878, 11089, 11274
   Minnesota 5954
GAMES 399, 1042, 1123, 1907, 2086, 2696, 2894, 2945, 3333, 4568, 4715,
   4727, 5416, 5814, 5835, 6241, 6564, 6565, 6566, 6905, 7029, 7339, 7711,
   7989, 8763, 10074, 10158, 10207, 10258, 10379, 10642, 11049, 11060,
   11505, 12546, 13421, 13836, 13940, 14170, 14421, 14509, 14916, 15145,
   15237, 15515, 15573, 15771, 16432, 16532, 16992, 16993, 17174, 17314,
   17383, 17690
   board 2086, 11451, 11697
   England 13146
   history 13146
   indoor 1286, 3149
   Mexico 259
   number 106, 6161, 6586, 7338
   Ping-Pong 16460
   poetry 9032
   singing 1773, 3304, 4653, 6161, 9335, 10257, 10258, 13940, 17756, 18115,
   18120
   United States 10257
   word 16190, 16992, 16993
GANDHI, INDIRA (1917-1984) 17894
GANDHI, MATHATMA (1869-1948) 5230, 9029, 14283
GANGS 1263, 1785, 2408, 2992, 4693, 5611, 5674, 6002, 7373, 8216, 9918,
   11480, 11613, 13639, 14389, 14484, 15927, 17073, 17604, 17790
   United States--history 7831
GANNETT, DEBORAH (SAMPSON) see SAMPSON, DEBORAH
GARDENING 987, 2671, 5074, 5250, 5325, 5798, 5800, 5802, 6529, 7945,
   9636, 9958, 10075, 10384, 11592, 11679, 12189, 12208, 12267, 15289,
   17476, 17855, 18185
   vegetables 8708
GARDENS 12739
   Canada--Toronto 10240
   miniature 12208
GARFIELD, JAMES ABRAM (1831-1881) 5765
GARRISON, WILLIAM LLOYD (1805-1879) 5625
GAS, NATURAL 12849, 14363
GAS AND OIL ENGINES 4120, 17169
GAS INDUSTRY AND TRADE--employees 12711
GASES 3706
GASPE PENINSULA (QUEBEC) 9995
GAULLE, CHARLES DE, (1890-1970) 5489
GAUTAMA BUDDHA see BUDDHA
GAUTIER, FELISA RINCON DE see RINCON DE GAUTIER, FELISA

GAZELLES 1069
GEESE 568, 1571, 4817, 5183, 5184, 5185, 5186, 5187, 5188, 5756, 6068,
    6271, 6495, 6859, 7549, 7934, 8082, 8517, 9150, 11112, 12573, 13901,
    15196, 15463
GEHRIG, LOU (1903-1941) 11150
GEMINI PROJECT 7509
GENEALOGY 996
GENERALS--United States 6390, 7182, 13335
GENERATION GAP see CONFLICT OF GENERATIONS
GENETICS 12475, 13811, 15681
GENGHIS KHAN (1162-1227) 1210, 4560
GEOGRAPHICAL DISTRIBUTION OF ANIMALS AND PLANTS 8582, 11876,
    15677
GEOGRAPHY 4732, 5395
    ancient 833
    Antarctic Regions 744
    See also under countries with the subheading "Geography"
GEOLOGY 397, 6086, 6526, 9784, 11832, 11833, 14187, 16366, 18336, 18559
    North America 13037
    vocational guidance 7008
GEOMETRICAL DRAWING 5385
GEOMETRY 114, 1436, 1448, 3292, 3371, 4904, 6292, 6378, 6399, 11142,
    11143, 13626, 13627, 13759, 14227, 14798, 15800, 17017, 17491
GEOPHYSICS 8869, 10357, 15094
GEORGE III (KING OF ENGLAND), (1738-1820) 6384, 12342
GEORGIA 13862, 17945, 17946
    description and travel--views 15209
    history 1248, 12906
        Colonial period (ca. 1600-1775) 1702, 2359
GERBILS 4950, 8553, 13274, 13424, 15685, 16903, 17656
GERMAN AMERICANS 1393, 4378, 6699, 8476, 9297, 9625, 12349, 13993,
    15797, 18169
    history 10135
    Texas 5986
GERMAN POETRY 12448, 13746
GERMANY 1391, 6352, 13584, 18175
    foreign relations (1933-1945) 7021
    history
        20th century 16569
        1933-1945 6113, 6114, 6120, 14349
        1945-1950 1390
        Allied occupation (1945-) 4800
    politics and government (1933-1945) 7021, 12045
    social life and customs 7376
GERMANY (WEST)--1949- 9847
GERONIMO (APACHE CHIEF), (1829-1909) 7173, 16585, 18070, 18332
GETTYSBURG, BATTLE OF (1863), 1273, 6676, 9484, 12337
GHANA 154, 411, 412, 590, 2159, 3007, 4661, 4662, 4663, 4665, 4695, 5197,
    9578, 9579, 9580, 9613, 10491, 13521, 14860, 16973, 16974, 16976, 17852,
    18528
    biography 75
    description and travel 9873, 11010
        views 16533
    education 12590
    history 18133
        19th century 10165
    social life and customs 591, 592, 1861, 5456, 5462, 6797, 7460, 9576,

15080
GHOSTS   197, 355, 497, 836, 1066, 1401, 1835, 1856, 2181, 2237, 2238,
   2240, 2798, 2799, 3446, 3476, 3749, 4101, 4106, 4117, 4881, 5634, 5949,
   6006, 6062, 6472, 6475, 6603, 6604, 7206, 7746, 7927, 8587, 8876, 8925,
   9097, 9131, 9361, 9759, 9934, 10451, 10452, 10955, 11363, 11415, 11428,
   11602, 11726, 11958, 12810, 13213, 13384, 13408, 13448, 14122, 14418,
   14425, 14430, 15241, 15520, 15746, 16051, 16118, 16129, 16781, 16782,
   16789, 18108
   United States
      Alabama 18107
      Georgia 18106
GIANNINI, AMADEO PETER (1870-1949) 7673
GIANTS 1859, 2235, 4221, 4738, 5083, 5469, 7984, 10092, 10995, 12263,
   14354, 15550, 15838, 17881, 18408, 18409
   miscellanea 14917
GIBBONS 1945, 15039
GIBSON, ALTHEA (1927-) 6787
GIBSON, BOB (1935-) 6788, 10892
GIDEON, CLARENCE EARL (1910-1972) 10687
GIFTS 1057, 1278, 2422, 4428, 6309, 7856, 8015, 9394, 10845, 10950,
   14935, 16424, 17769, 18608
GILA MONSTER 8249
GILBRETH, FRANK BUNKER (1868-1924) 6822
GILBRETH, LILLIAN EVELYN (MOLLER), (1878-1972) 6822
GIOTTO DI BONDONE (1266?-1337) 14506
GIRAFFES 3998, 5182, 7107, 14261, 15066, 17405
GIRL SCOUTS 4700, 6870, 6871, 8165, 14058
GIRLS 393, 711, 1814, 2341, 4262, 5745, 6445, 9208, 11069
GISH, DOROTHY (1898-1968) 6872
GISH, LILLIAN (1896-) 6872
GLACIAL EPOCH 11906, 16633
   Great Lakes Region 8512
GLACIERS 10349, 11011, 16633
GLANDS 14365
GLASS
   manufacture 2521, 3531, 5943
   painting and staining 18238
GLENN, JOHN HERSCHEL (1921-) 205, 13663
GLIDERS (AERONAUTICS) 9758
   models 9540
GLIDING AND SOARING 7575, 14335, 18216
GLOBES 8223, 15157
GNADENHUTTEN (OHIO)--Massacre (1782) 8146
GOATHERDS 12640
GOATS 1040, 1058, 1597, 3722, 4932, 6318, 6735, 7951, 9617, 15195, 15652,
   16824, 17104, 17589
   mountain 3097
   Niger--Agadez 5458
GOBI DESERT 12540
GOD 4410, 5102, 5103, 5965, 5967, 5968
GODDARD, ROBERT HUTCHINGS (1882-1945) 12385, 17294
GOGH, VINCENT VAN, (1853-1890) 4947
GOLD HILL (CALIFORNIA) 17102
GOLD MINES AND MINING 143, 2866, 6439, 9242, 13014, 13870
GOLDFISH 4073
GOLDMAN, EMMA (1869-1940) 15619
GOLDWATER, BARRY MORRIS (1909-)--art collections 7025
GOLF 6685, 9061, 11897, 11909, 14150, 15926

GOLFERS 4786, 5328, 9026, 9069, 11897, 13102, 13193, 17219
GOOD AND EVIL 687, 4084, 4085, 4087, 4088, 4883, 5590, 5638
GOOLAGONG, EVONNE (1951-) 8098, 9062, 12484
GOPHERS 11160
GORGAS, WILLIAM CRAWFORD (1854-1920) 9430, 17987
GORILLAS 1301, 1961, 1977, 4817, 5789, 6897, 8356, 9238, 11283, 15036
GOTHIC REVIVAL (LITERATURE) 11604
GOULD, SHANE (1956-) 7102, 9075
GOVERNMENT
    local 5299, 17975
        vocational guidance 11450
    resistance to 6113
GOVERNORS--United States 8556
GRAHAM, MARTHA (1893-) 16762
GRAND CANYON 17123
GRANDFATHERS 95, 312, 1942, 2057, 2071, 2480, 2495, 2781, 2787, 3322,
    6672, 7707, 8033, 8632, 8655, 9849, 10119, 10120, 10301, 10616, 11170,
    11970, 13801, 14048, 14470, 16102, 16357, 16416, 18109, 18610
GRANDMOTHERS 92, 288, 1001, 1146, 1219, 1805, 2184, 2496, 2499, 3152,
    3212, 3584, 4722, 4728, 5616, 5658, 6973, 7005, 7552, 8019, 8102, 9154,
    9211, 9637, 9888, 9889, 10106, 10183, 10302, 11080, 11541, 15812, 16016,
    16424, 17112, 17332, 17862, 17978, 18235, 18395
GRANDPARENTS 4093, 4163, 4521, 4522, 4728, 11815, 12329, 12505, 17400,
    18132, 18160
    pictorial works 14166
GRANT, ANNE (MacVICAR), (1755-1838) 1826
GRANT, JULIA (DENT), (1826-1902) 6028
GRANT, ULYSSES SIMPSON (1822-1885) 7182, 9485, 13080, 14195, 14245,
    16280, 16813
GRAPHIC METHODS 6241, 6401, 11121
GRAPHOLOGY 830, 11615
GRASSES 14385
GRASSLANDS 6965
    Africa 2365
GRAVITATION 735, 1429, 1517, 2129, 2151, 5449, 17181
GREAT BRITAIN see ENGLAND
GREAT-GRANDMOTHERS 1192
GREAT LAKES 1126, 1127, 2013, 7866, 8492, 8673, 13892, 16553
    discovery and exploration 11444
    history 2013, 2014, 2015, 2042, 2043, 2044, 2045, 2046, 6823, 7865,
        14140
    See also individual lakes, e.g., LAKE SUPERIOR
GREAT LAKES REGION 7838
    antiquities 4872
    description and travel 5323, 5384, 5389, 11442, 13208
    history 794, 5384, 7422, 13208
GREAT PLAINS 10142
    description and travel 10346
GREAT SMOKY MOUNTAINS 3585, 3586
GREECE 3683, 4018, 4022, 10117, 12640, 18509
    antiquities 13916, 14034
    civilization 10454
    history 5353, 5636, 5816
        Persian Wars (500-449 B.C.) 14238
        1944-1949 6118
    modern 17543
        history--occupation (1941-1944) 18507

   social life and customs 14034
GREEK AMERICANS 6731, 9358
GREEK POETRY--collections 10719
GREENE, JOE (1946-) 2636
GREENFIELD, ELOISE (1929-) 7313
GREENHOW, ROSE O'NEAL (1814-1864) 5631
GREENLAND 3686
GREENWICH VILLAGE (NEW YORK) 3842
GREETING CARDS 5533, 13999
GRETTIR ASMUNDARSON (996-1031) 12790
GREY OWL (NATIVE AMERICAN), (1888-1938) 13792
GRIMKE, ANGELINE EMILY (1805-1879) 18059
GRIMKE, ARCHIBALD HENRY (1849-1930) 16294
GRIMKE, SARAH MOORE (1792-1873) 18059
GRISSOM, VIRGIL I. "GUS" (1926-1967) 3271
GROCERY TRADE 7273, 13030
GROOMING, PERSONAL 5469, 5896, 14944
GROUNDHOGS 9740
GROWTH 579, 2475, 2849, 3494, 4138, 4189, 5710, 7790, 7971, 8002, 8114,
   8958, 9446, 9531, 9608, 10076, 10260, 12013, 14721, 15601, 16641, 16960,
   17582, 18318, 18616
GROWTH (PLANTS) 14087
GUADALUPE, NUESTRA SEÑORA DE 13281, 17404
GUARNERI, GIUSEPPE (b. 1686?-?) 17847
GUATEMALA--social life and customs 9196
GUATEMALAN INDIANS 3494
GUAYMI INDIANS 6544
GUESTS 17099
GUIANA 6046
GUIDE DOGS 3602, 7721, 8093, 14008, 14118, 18195
GUIDED MISSILES 3778, 4040
GUINEA 3008, 9789
GUINEA PIGS 1874, 1875, 1882, 5766, 15885
GUION, CONNIE M. (1882-) 2889
GUITARS 8193, 8633
GULF STREAM 2256
GULLS 859, 1130, 1403, 3069, 4511, 7091, 15114, 15199
GYMNASTICS 951, 1305, 1895, 3544, 4875, 6478, 9071, 9415, 14074, 14730,
   17373
GYMNASTS 5585, 15909, 16505
   Romania 12161
   United States 9067
GYNECOLOGISTS--Canada--Ontario 18088
GYPSIES 5537, 6949, 9971, 17232, 17245
GZOWSKI, SIR CASIMIR STANISLAS (1813-1898) 15525

                              - H -

HACHIHOKI 3717
HAIDA INDIANS 7357, 7766
   legends 11965
HAIL 2142
HAIR 6997, 7001
   care and hygiene 6265, 11137

sculptured--African 1227
HAITI 4951, 5312, 7146, 10857, 16511
 history 7990
  Revolution (1791-1804) 16426, 16593
HALE, NATHAN (1755-1776) 12345
HALE, SARAH J. (1788-1879) 2710
HALL, GLENN (1931-) 5573
HALLOWEEN 48, 496, 1138, 1142, 1151, 1186, 1564, 1963, 2018, 2069, 2243,
 3075, 4015, 4081, 4871, 4953, 5420, 6270, 6958, 9454, 10062, 10709,
 10934, 11363, 11677, 12223, 12414, 13316, 13383, 13728, 14503, 15120,
 15185, 15503, 15847, 17247, 17580, 18153, 18469, 18621
 decorations 6908
 poetry 1384, 8593, 12402, 13886
HAMER, FANNIE LOU (1917-1977) 9378
HAMIL, HAROLD (1906-) 7644
HAMILL, DOROTHY (1956?-) 17223
HAMILTON, ALEXANDER (1757-1804) 3349, 4322
HAMILTON, HENRY (1796-?) 7867
HAMILTON (ONTARIO) 6123
HAMSTERS 1771, 14767, 14768, 15686
HANCOCK, CORNELIA (1840-1926) 11261
HANCOCK, JOHN (1737-1793) 6395
HAND 10100
 pictorial works 872
HANDICAPPED see MENTALLY HANDICAPPED; PHYSICALLY HANDICAPPED
HANDICRAFT 216, 218, 317, 365, 366, 406, 516, 1789, 2281, 2947, 3094,
 3327, 3328, 3329, 3330, 3333, 3705, 3792, 3901, 3902, 3915, 4182, 4427,
 4471, 4472, 4473, 4727, 4761, 4900, 4953, 5006, 5324, 5326, 5478, 6130,
 6816, 6820, 6821, 6907, 6908, 7118, 7856, 7857, 8030, 8031, 8338, 8410,
 8764, 8765, 8766, 8767, 8768, 9468, 9667, 9837, 9840, 9916, 9966, 10778,
 10806, 10808, 10871, 11059, 11060, 11322, 11509, 11778, 12126, 12128,
 12204, 12491, 12492, 12632, 12802, 12893, 12952, 13285, 13296, 13297,
 13589, 13590, 13591, 13608, 13610, 13689, 13878, 13998, 13999, 14001,
 14169, 14170, 14494, 14532, 15490, 15753, 15771, 16008, 16247, 16649,
 16733, 16734, 16735, 16736, 16865, 17285, 17309, 17447, 17497, 17504,
 17604, 17686, 17689, 17695, 17708, 17745, 17942, 17983, 18149, 18150,
 18151, 18448
 Africa 4471, 9726
 Asia 16124
 Latin America 3903
 study and teaching 10094
 United States 9835, 9836, 12127, 17284
  Appalachian Region 8638
  history 8560
HANDWRITING see GRAPHOLOGY
HANDY, WILLIAM CHRISTOPHER (1873-1958) 12367
HANNIBAL (247-183 B.C.) 1207, 8234, 9079
HANUKKAH (FEAST OF LIGHTS) 1627, 1742, 3262, 3351, 3758, 8235, 12477,
 14500, 15726, 16708
 poetry 4090
HARBORS--North Carolina 16129
HARLEM (NEW YORK CITY) 7532, 7622, 11227, 12089, 12613, 16235, 17356
 history 18442
 social conditions 11211
HARMONY 16099
HARPER, VALERIE (1940-) 9076
HARPS 12796

HARRELSON, BUD (1944-) 10760
HARRIS, FRANCO (1950-) 2635
HARRISON, WILLIAM HENRY (1773-1841) 13462, 18473
HARVEY, CHARLES THOMPSON (1829-?) 14142
HATS 723, 1114, 2850, 8460, 9162, 9165, 9596, 12560, 12866, 13943, 16783
HAUSAS 5314, 5317, 13057, 18361
HAVASU INDIANS 3481
HAVASUPAI INDIANS 9119
HAVLICEK, JOHN (1940-) 2163
HAWAII 1057, 6440, 12835, 16096, 16609, 16838
   description and travel 13882
   history 11581
   social life and customs 11185
HAWKS 1239, 10389
HAYDN, JOSEPH (1732-1809) 10295
HAYES, BOB (1942-) 10893
HEALTH see HYGIENE
HEALTH CARE see MEDICAL CARE
HEALY, KATHERINE (1969?-) 10089
HEART 11120, 15596, 18561
   catheterization--in infancy and childhood 3368
   disease 10816, 15687
      diagnosis 3365
   surgery 3365, 3366, 3367, 15792
HEAT 115, 1012, 1423, 3710, 5819, 15207, 17299
   experiments 15747
HEATING 17168
HEAVEN 11948
HEBREW, BOOKS IN 603, 11665
HEBREW POETRY 1549
HEBRIDES 320
HEDGEHOGS 1832, 7372
HEIN, PIETER PIETERSZOON (1578-1629) 12350
HEISMAN, JOHN WILLIAM (1869-1936) 17222
HELENA, SAINT (ca. 246-326?) 4539, 7786
HELICOPTERS 4812, 10681
   military 4811
   piloting 4041
HENNEPIN COUNTY (MINNESOTA) 9367
HENRIQUE, O NAVEGADOR, INFANTE OF PORTUGAL see HENRY THE
   NAVIGATOR
HENRY, DAN (1860-?) 5526
HENRY, PATRICK (1736-1799) 2888, 6392
HENRY THE NAVIGATOR (1394-1460) 2524, 9082
HENSON, JOSIAH (1789-1883) 3186
HENSON, MATTHEW ALEXANDER (1866-1955) 537, 12225, 14403
HERBS 5043
HERCULANEUM (CITY) 4802
HEREDITY 1425, 1439, 12475, 13811, 17567
HEROES AND HEROINES 820, 1165, 2087, 2180, 4057, 5071, 5632, 8009,
   10120
   Spanish 820
HEROIN HABIT see DRUG ABUSE
HERONS 1094, 9220, 14574, 16721
HERSHEY, MILTON SNAVELY (1857-1945) 11582
HEYERDAHL, THOR (1914-) 1258, 1737
HI JOLLY see JOLLY, HI

HICKOK, JAMES BUTLER (1837-1876) 451, 6640, 8436
HIEROGLYPHICS 15192, 15193
HIGH FIDELITY SOUND SYSTEMS 13093
HIGHWAYS 2057
HIKING 2032, 6652, 7795, 11321
HILL, JAMES JEROME (1836-1916) 3898
HILLARY, SIR EDMUND (1919-) 16435
HILLIARD, MARION (1902-1958) 18088
HILLS 12010
HINCKLEY (MINNESOTA)--Fire (1894) 16557
HINDUISM 5260, 15795
HIPPIES 10166, 15183
HIPPOPOTAMUSES 334, 1470, 2378, 3145, 3793, 5180, 5181, 5192, 10849,
    11174, 11934, 12593, 13315, 15402
HIROSHIMA (JAPAN)
    bombardment (1945) 2446
    personal narratives 12635
HISPANIC AMERICANS 6210, 16627
    biography 820
    See also MEXICAN AMERICANS
HISTORIC BUILDINGS
    United States 16427
        Minnesota 8519
        Nebraska--Lincoln 11412
HISTORIC SITES 2205, 3783
    Ontario 13137
    United States
        guide-books 16854
        Minnesota 5575
HISTORICAL MARKERS--Michigan 12151
HISTORY 12442
    ancient 17153
    feudal period 8943
    local 15194
        guide-books 17675
    miscellanea 8573
    modern 6143, 6144, 6146, 6147, 6148, 6151
        19th century 6140, 6149, 6150
    Ohio 17892
    See also under specific countries or areas with subheading "History"
HITLER, ADOLF (1899-1945) 15568
HOBBIES 14863, 15141, 18499; see also specific activities, e.g., GARDEN-
    ING
HOCKEY 3433, 4029, 4112, 4113, 4781, 4782, 4783, 4784, 5092, 5541, 5899,
    6235, 6679, 6809, 8527, 8892, 8893, 8894, 9015, 10910, 10920, 11071,
    11847, 12553, 12717, 12990, 13135, 13180, 13181, 13183, 13302,
    14159, 14240, 14358, 15852, 16456, 17486, 17814
    defense 6808
    dictionaries 10914, 17446
    pictorial works 12989
    players 2612, 2622, 5273, 5573, 5898, 7524, 10910, 11492, 11859, 11860,
        11861, 12449, 12990, 13181, 16465, 18491
HODGES, ANN (1952-) 4094
HOFFMAN, ABBY (1936-) 11319
HOLIDAYS 2666, 3189, 3358, 4727, 4869, 4871, 4938, 4942, 4953, 5505,
    5792, 5905, 5910, 5913, 6462, 9230, 10070, 10245, 10852, 10854, 11639,
    13297, 14000, 15223, 16081, 16509, 16734

decorations 3792, 14935
drama 1471
Mexico 11661
poetry 54, 1381, 2218, 10280, 10973, 15219
songs and music 14025
United States 11508, 13335
   New England 17034
see also specific days, e.g., THANKSGIVING DAY
HOLLAND see NETHERLANDS
HOLMES, OLIVER WENDELL (1841-1935) 13574
HOLY WEEK 13085
HOME 8180, 10073, 11169, 13041
   and school 1080, 1082, 4516, 10296
HOME ECONOMICS 7857, 10028
   equipment and supplies 15089
HOMESTEADING see LAND SETTLEMENT
HOMOSEXUALITY 8469
HONDURAS--social conditions 11599
HONESTY see TRUTHFULNESS AND FALSEHOOD
HONEY 6484
HONEYMAN, JOHN (fl. 1776) 18146
HONG KONG 3198, 15841
   description and travel 9405
      views 14927
   social life and customs 8111, 15078, 15410
HOOPER, BEN (1857-1957) 2334
HOOPLE, MARY (WHITMORE), (1769?-1860?) 8561
HOOVER, HERBERT (1874-1964) 3897
HOPE, LESLIE TOWNS "BOB" (1903-) 16696
HOPI INDIANS 637, 922, 5391, 7025, 9115, 9116, 9118, 14021, 15413, 16617,
   16619
   legends 4195, 4198
   rites and ceremonies 876, 6122, 16618
HOPPER, ISAAC T. (1771-1852) 864
HORMONES 14365
HORNSBY, ROGERS (1896-1963) 5880
HOROMBO (AFRICAN CHIEF) 10542
HORROR 8417, 9459
HORSE RACING 874, 6660, 8066, 8071, 8079, 17911
HORSEBACK RIDING 467, 989, 990, 1024, 1685, 4079, 4867, 4886, 6419,
   8078, 10088, 12034, 14276, 14639, 14711, 15263, 15826, 16455, 17912,
   17989, 18306, 18451
   South Africa 16164
HORSES 158, 244, 390, 455, 456, 457, 458, 459, 460, 461, 462, 463, 464,
   465, 466, 467, 468, 469, 470, 471, 472, 553, 560, 564, 909, 989, 992,
   993, 994, 1450, 1552, 1629, 2063, 2080, 2344, 2345, 2544, 2552, 2575,
   2654, 2676, 2836, 3296, 3314, 3481, 3484, 3497, 3766, 3768, 3884, 3996,
   4016, 4126, 4128, 4466, 4507, 4574, 4675, 4696, 4825, 4831, 4832, 4833,
   4834, 4886, 4909, 4949, 5026, 5028, 5029, 5294, 5383, 5520, 5521, 5566,
   5654, 5688, 5689, 5690, 5692, 5735, 5823, 6136, 6310, 6372, 6656, 6881,
   7225, 7226, 7375, 7379, 7380, 7423, 7540, 7544, 7598, 7600, 7601, 7707,
   8065, 8066, 8069, 8070, 8072, 8073, 8075, 8076, 8077, 8078, 8120,
   8124, 8167, 8348, 8364, 8380, 8404, 8586, 8675, 8829, 8920, 9124,
   9474, 9921, 10088, 10102, 10126, 10184, 10365, 10381, 10390, 10551,
   10688, 10998, 11186, 11342, 11565, 11875, 11964, 12302, 12334, 12375,
   12431, 12433, 12477, 12578, 13049, 13198, 13445, 13472, 13596, 13601,
   14050, 14051, 14052, 14076, 14176, 14275, 14330, 14413, 14543, 14638,

14694, 14702, 14705, 14706, 14710, 14712, 14828, 14889, 14890, 14897,
14901, 14950, 14951, 14952, 15263, 15303, 15394, 15483, 15827, 15837,
15888, 15935, 15970, 16563, 16670, 16676, 16783, 16994, 17301, 17442,
17468, 17911, 17912, 17989, 18060, 18273, 18276, 18306, 18496, 18630
  breeds 989, 992, 16536
  law and legislation 17683
  pictures, illustrations, etc. 8062
  poetry 8600, 9181
  shows 14639
  South Africa 16164
  training 388, 7224, 15264, 18451
  United States 2078
HORTON, WILLIE (1942-) 2751
HORTON (KANSAS)--description and travel--views 8017
HOSPITALS 386, 703, 3297, 3505, 3707, 3837, 4180, 4230, 4785, 5101, 5327,
  5736, 7632, 9567, 11159, 11311, 12580, 13023, 13329, 14264, 14723,
  15388, 15509, 15709, 15792, 15900, 15987, 16204, 16378, 16630, 16642,
  17611, 17638, 17737, 17738, 17739, 17740, 18532
  emergency service 1251, 9563, 16157
  vocational guidance 6276
  volunteers 3882
HOTELS, MOTELS, ETC. 2831, 2862, 3563, 3740, 15963
  vocational guidance 18172
HOUDINI, HARRY (1874-1926) 5529, 9682, 10046, 10047, 17619, 17803,
  17985
HOUSE PLANTS see PLANTS--HOUSE
HOUSEBOATS 1983, 10570, 13345
HOUSEHOLD APPLIANCES, ELECTRIC 14750, 18188
  maintenance and repair 9611
HOUSEHOLD EMPLOYEES 232, 815, 5850, 12194, 12519, 16972
HOUSEHOLD EQUIPMENT AND SUPPLIES 8370
HOUSES 633, 2862, 3654, 4424, 5107, 5906, 6056, 8795, 12172, 14708,
  14879, 15071, 15817, 15975, 17735
  cleaning 17888
  historic 2718
  painting 5178
HOUSTON, SAMUEL (1793-1863) 9303, 10317, 10318
HOWE, GORDIE (1928-) 1176, 5898
HOWE, JULIA (WARD), (1819-1910) 17389
HOWE, SAMUEL GRIDLEY (1801-1876) 12044
HUALAPAI INDIANS 6774
HUDSON, DAVID ROCK (1957?-) 9851
HUDSON, HENRY (d. 1611) 2982, 9390
HUDSON VALLEY 12618
  description and travel--views 14185
HUGHES, LANGSTON (1902-1967) 5133, 7817, 12043, 12601, 17427
HULL HOUSE (CHICAGO) 9420
HULL, ROBERT MARVIN "BOBBY" (1939-) 11860, 18491
HUMAN
  behavior 289, 325, 658, 998, 1772, 2051, 2087, 3288, 3322, 4440, 4715,
    4935, 5081, 5345, 5530, 5567, 5599, 5682, 5710, 6543, 6708, 7710, 8378,
    9295, 9306, 9376, 9466, 9573, 9694, 9827, 9917, 10008, 10054, 10069,
    10164, 10326, 10650, 10931, 11004, 11040, 11192, 11297, 11337, 11407,
    11580, 11614, 11799, 11931, 12615, 12680, 12742, 12750, 12994, 13049,
    13154, 13897, 13902, 14560, 15167, 15551, 15618, 15689, 15841, 16142,
    16446, 16511, 16752, 16957, 17098, 17325, 17594, 17728, 17733, 17923,
    17968, 17977, 18517, 18526, 18600, 18613, 18626, 18629

biology 835, 9745
ecology 7328, 14681
mechanics 834
relations 281, 296, 3191, 3935, 7200, 7213, 7245, 8636
rights 11839
skeleton 1013
HUMBOLDT, ALEXANDER, FREIHERR VON (1769-1859) 16822
HUMOR see WIT AND HUMOR
HUMORISTS--American 4623, 4624
HUNDRED YEARS WAR (1339-1453) 17108
HUNGARIAN AMERICANS 7113
HUNGARIANS 7677
HUNGARY 14967, 15341, 15342
HUNS 4891
   folklore 15344
HUNTER, JIM "CATFISH" (1946-) 16132
HUNTING 551, 559, 600, 1026, 1219, 1348, 1353, 2598, 4445, 4926, 4964,
   5380, 5691, 6669, 6863, 7484, 7546, 7741, 7766, 8865, 9790, 9878, 11460,
   11538, 11704, 12068, 12184, 12341, 13290, 13352, 15803, 16171, 16552,
   17522, 17923
   Africa 17420
     East 204
       Kenya 5035
       Transvaal 5983
       Zaire 6666, 6667
   primitive 1204
HUPA INDIANS 5643
HURON INDIANS 974, 3665, 7893
   missions 7919
HURRICANES 495, 2527, 8617, 10407, 12852, 16288, 16620
HURSTON, ZORA (NEAL), (1903-1960) 12581
HUTCHINSON, ANNE (MARBURY), (1591-1643) 4253, 5623
HYDRAULIC ENGINEERING 1264
HYENAS 11842
HYGIENE 1422, 2701, 5004, 12234, 12838, 15928, 18139
HYPERACTIVE CHILDREN 6592

- I -

IBIBIOS (AFRICAN TRIBE) 5557
ICE 665
ICE HOCKEY see HOCKEY
ICE SKATERS 9066, 10089, 12486
ICE SKATING 4674, 4783, 4792, 4966, 9064, 10089, 16457, 17223, 17224
ICEBERGS 501, 6538, 10349, 15125
ICELAND 16185
   history 9825
ICHTHYOLOGISTS 11362
IDAHO 988, 2265, 12229
IDEALISM 14846
IDENTIFICATION 12743
IDENTITY 11653
IGBO (AFRICAN PEOPLE) 1753
ILLINOIS 886, 1741, 1775, 3009, 4309, 6192, 12119, 14147

description and travel 14011
history 5535, 7702, 9669, 13881, 14011
  Civil War (1861-1865) 8891
  miscellanea 18199
  pictorial works 12335
ILLITERACY 16658
ILLUSTRATORS 1768, 14902
IMAGINATION 278, 279, 545, 572, 574, 626, 2564, 2843, 3458, 5357, 5564,
  5679, 6596, 7308, 7666, 7965, 9514, 9702, 9816, 10081, 10260, 10262,
  10475, 10614, 10738, 10862, 10997, 11166, 11169, 12306, 12749, 13076,
  13362, 13567, 14216, 14435, 15366, 15475, 15513, 15575, 15839, 17056,
  17413, 17761, 18620, 18625, 18626
IMMIGRATION AND EMIGRATION 362, 519, 539, 541, 615, 1030, 1076, 1393,
  1782, 1867, 3168, 3187, 5295, 7678, 7980, 8185, 8341, 8342, 9272, 9426,
  10569, 10668, 11526, 11845, 11959, 12229, 12308, 12654, 12907, 13794,
  14354, 14370, 15627, 15797, 16027, 16497, 16676, 16708, 17014, 17315,
  18128
personal narratives 1010
Russian 3515
IMPOSTORS AND IMPOSTURE 8634
INCAS 1754, 3495, 9501, 13685
INDENTURED SERVANTS see HOUSEHOLD EMPLOYEES
INDEPENDENCE 16780
INDIA 681, 1167, 1983, 1985, 3250, 5893, 6171, 6492, 7480, 7618, 8239,
  9472, 9845, 10391, 10856, 12018, 12019, 12543, 14112, 15819, 16439,
  16774, 17572
description and travel 11086
history 5077
Kashmir 1989
poetry 3148
social life and customs 6798, 7167, 15084, 15561, 18624
INDIAN FIGHTERS 387
INDIAN POETRY--collections 8660
INDIANA 359, 887, 2693, 2694, 3010, 5034, 5534, 6351, 6364, 8756, 11563,
  12881, 13828, 13829, 14636, 16552, 16853
birds 7550
description and travel 10173, 10293, 13466
  views 11625
history 606, 607, 3611, 5288, 5982, 10173, 10471, 11790, 12917, 16554,
  16835, 16836
social life and customs 9040, 16723
INDIANAPOLIS (INDIANA)--history 11573, 12880
INDIANS OF CENTRAL AMERICA 1757, 4963, 6544
games 10379
Guatemala--social life and customs 9196
legends 12416
INDIANS OF INDIA see "East Indians" under appropriate headings, e.g.,
  FOLKLORE
INDIANS OF MEXICO 16894
art 4963, 6916
legends 2871, 13668, 14726, 16969
religion and mythology 14726
INDIANS OF NORTH AMERICA 21, 28, 780, 878, 917, 933, 935, 994, 1004,
  1009, 1261, 1406, 1407, 1410, 1551, 1579, 1642, 1687, 1690, 1764, 1789,
  1840, 1955, 2038, 2210, 2554, 2753, 2851, 2870, 2971, 2972, 2973, 3097,
  3216, 3251, 3254, 3255, 3314, 3315, 3380, 3470, 3485, 3608, 3642, 3653,
  3885, 3924, 4005, 4006, 4008, 4012, 4072, 4250, 4328, 4329, 4332, 4338,

4457, 4845, 4848, 4909, 4912, 4967, 5014, 5219, 5381, 5479, 5517, 5519,
5521, 5544, 5545, 5643, 5644, 5645, 5652, 5703, 5730, 5793, 5857, 6051,
6115, 6240, 6371, 6372, 6373, 6374, 6638, 6758, 6762, 6776, 6790, 6945,
6946, 6948, 7164, 7346, 7351, 7359, 7362, 7466, 7502, 7543, 7546, 7554,
7742, 7936, 7981, 7993, 8146, 8358, 8380, 8394, 8428, 8490, 8606, 8699,
8950, 8951, 8952, 8953, 9086, 9087, 9393, 9520, 9856, 9944, 9953, 10179,
10205, 10227, 10228, 10230, 10231, 10234, 10322, 10473, 10499, 10577,
10638, 11013, 11087, 11152, 11322, 11330, 11354, 11416, 11466, 11698,
11728, 11742, 11749, 11770, 11789, 11849, 12377, 12378, 12547, 12623,
12685, 13013, 13018, 13070, 13290, 13293, 13298, 13339, 13404, 13440,
13453, 13461, 13514, 13677, 13709, 14180, 14543, 14544, 14545, 14621,
14633, 15213, 15442, 15540, 15656, 15773, 15933, 15943, 15947, 15950,
15991, 16044, 16049, 16172, 16416, 16423, 16537, 16649, 16679, 16721,
16832, 17041, 17170, 17243, 17540, 17772, 17993, 18079, 18159, 18385
  agriculture 7945, 10383
  Alaska 7361
  anthropometry 9853
  antiquities 5397, 6091, 15023, 15024, 15414
    collectors and collecting 7740
  art 218, 597, 1023, 3729, 4963, 6929, 6935, 8381
    exhibitions 4963
  biography 235, 487, 491, 494, 577, 657, 666, 4008, 4012, 4249, 4611,
    4827, 4856, 4859, 4908, 5245, 5247, 5276, 5430, 5653, 5776, 5782,
    6639, 7117, 7168, 7170, 7173, 7178, 7179, 7180, 7347, 7348, 7352,
    7658, 7941, 8011, 8012, 8133, 8879, 9247, 9309, 9519, 9520, 10005,
    10530, 11904, 12328, 12701, 12727, 13389, 14222, 14571, 16508, 16585,
    16592, 17171, 17344, 17345, 17508, 17617, 18070, 18071
  British Columbia 1707
  Canada 1578
    legends 1568, 11458
  captivities 347, 2280, 3606, 6580, 6866, 8013, 8561, 9348, 10233, 13621,
    14346, 14347, 15946, 16925, 18004, 18112, 18168, 18271
  children 10187, 17172
  cliff dwellers and cliff dwellings 2541, 7554
  costumes and adornment 8383, 8765, 8768, 11778, 16104
  culture 13314
  dances 5519, 5824, 8765, 8768, 13868, 16104
  dwellings 8392
  education 3486, 10187, 14021
  fishing 7565, 8384
  food 298, 7411, 7945, 8127, 10383
  games 1003, 8385, 10379
  government relations 9519, 18039
  Great Lakes region 4872, 10124
    art 6932
    legends 5518
  handicraft 218, 1285, 4473, 8382, 8764, 8766
  history 646, 1002, 2339, 4827, 5531, 6094, 6729, 9519, 12769
  hunting 8386, 9088, 14782
  implements 7740
  industries 218, 1469, 4473, 6935, 8381, 8764, 8766, 14864
  legends 921, 1379, 1576, 1638, 2020, 2336, 2338, 2445, 2509, 3233, 3538,
    3914, 4306, 4328, 4397, 4413, 4644, 4760, 4979, 4980, 4981, 4986, 4987,
    5934, 6232, 7349, 7754, 7922, 7976, 8170, 8184, 8329, 9099, 9259, 9354,
    9356, 11177, 11178, 11288, 11413, 11458, 11643, 11822, 11823, 13444,
    14133, 14137, 14452, 14465, 14765, 15103, 15104, 15105, 15491, 15578,
    15829, 16849, 16909, 16910, 17274, 17337, 17341, 17469, 17820

medicine 8387
Mexico 9198
money 12330
museums 6091
music 1637, 1640, 4413, 4837, 6885, 8379, 8388, 13666, 14864
Northwest, Old--wars 8879
Northwest Pacific 1762, 2258, 3719, 6888, 7357, 7766, 8438, 8658, 11260,
   11823, 13396, 14765, 18284
  art 6930
  legends 7762, 7763, 7764, 7765, 7767, 7882, 11732, 13985
origins 4232, 9117, 11857
pictorial works 2246, 3729, 4411, 5443, 7353, 15035
picture-writing 8389
poetry 3234, 11046, 11544, 17165
  collections 1380, 1383, 1639, 8543, 9357
portraits 10105
pottery 18272
pre-Columbian 1002
religion 216, 597, 877, 912, 1242, 8337, 10380, 17306
rites and ceremonies 15598
sign language 414, 3723, 3724, 8390, 16927, 16928
social life and customs 5174, 5219, 5519, 7353, 12893, 12894, 14864,
   14979, 15126, 18284
transportation 8393
treatment 2907, 4797, 6021, 10644, 18039
United States
  Arizona 1233, 5824
    rites and ceremonies 16618
  Atlantic Coast 16638
  California 1188, 1575, 1576, 1578, 1888, 2543, 4397, 5872, 5934, 8701,
     10105, 17197
    Southern 18531
  Great Plains 414, 5519, 7427, 8220, 9088, 11700
    legends 11703, 18386
    religion 11703
  Kansas 17194
  Maryland 11587
  Michigan 7316, 7419, 7420
  Minnesota 4838, 10640
    legends 16047
  Mississippi 1994
  New Mexico 5173, 5824, 6075
  New York (City)--Manhattan Island 1410
  New York (State)--antiquities 16441
  North Carolina 17765
  Ohio 17892
    antiquities 13855
  Oklahoma 8933
  Pennsylvania 17469, 17470
  Southern states 16178
  Southwest--art 16650
  Southwest, New 780, 877, 878, 930, 1005, 1244, 3524, 5173, 9362,
     9363, 11413, 11477, 14232, 17306
    antiquities 16639
    art 6933, 8975
    costumes and adornment 8975
    food 12838

textile industry and fabrics 4773, 5174, 9114
  trading posts 9114
  Texas 13718, 17532
  Utah 8778
  The West 7858, 11699, 13333, 14054, 15127
    biography 16539
    history 6729
  wars 2339, 4008, 5050, 6888, 8391, 12461, 17724
  women 7347, 10828, 17508
  See also specific tribes, e.g., HOPI INDIANS
INDIANS OF SOUTH AMERICA 1205, 1754, 11598, 13236
  Andes Mountains 12415
  art 4963
  Peru--art 6917
  legends 9386, 12415, 12416
INDIANS OF THE WEST INDIES
  legends 12416
  Puerto Rico 251, 252
INDIVIDUALITY 33, 344, 2662, 3191, 3195, 3205, 3283, 3663, 3929, 3931,
  3933, 4803, 4813, 4817, 4922, 5357, 5739, 5827, 5935, 7317, 9171, 9994,
  10067, 10883, 11127, 12557, 13696, 14117, 14774, 15734, 17385, 18004
INDONESIA 2820
  civilization 17626
  description and travel 16675
  history 17626
  social life and customs 9473
INDOOR GAMES see GAMES
INDOOR GARDENING see PLANTS--HOUSE
INFANTS 432, 533, 2262, 2413, 4622, 8373, 8666, 10981, 11126, 11614,
  11651, 12752, 13365, 14309, 15069, 15601, 16208
  care and hygiene 14874
  growth 14874
INHERITED TRAITS see HEREDITY
INOUYE, DANIEL (1924-) 7055, 8906
INSECT-PLANT RELATIONSHIPS 7119
INSECTS 336, 1053, 1054, 1798, 2296, 2879, 2923, 2933, 3171, 3635, 3797,
  3948, 3950, 3951, 3953, 3958, 3961, 3962, 4361, 4626, 4883, 4968, 4969,
  5208, 5351, 5607, 5715, 6191, 6326, 6732, 6733, 7081, 7162, 7366, 7884,
  7886, 7887, 8121, 8502, 8578, 8793, 8824, 8830, 8845, 8846, 8847, 8850,
  8852, 8853, 8857, 9638, 9724, 9793, 9922, 9931, 9967, 10222, 10238, 10876,
  11165, 11246, 11249, 11660, 11673, 11683, 12064, 12276, 12620, 13167,
  13356, 13582, 13777, 13950, 14784, 14788, 14829, 14878, 15258, 15262,
  15302, 15309, 15310, 15320, 15522, 15523, 15630, 15637, 15691, 15716,
  15717, 15719, 15739, 15896, 16237, 16239, 16259, 16724, 17308, 17359,
  17884, 17964, 18220, 18548
  aquatic 11244
  behavior 3805
  collecting 3943, 5607
  development 8849
  Ghana 575
  habits and behavior 8623, 13355, 17238
  hives--poetry 1317
  Illinois 18305
  injurious and beneficial 3179, 8403
  metamorphosis of 3948, 13225, 15281, 16837
  Nigeria 18437
  pictorial works 13581, 16545

poetry 5666, 8306
INSTINCT 6249, 15285
INTERNATIONAL GEOPHYSICAL YEAR (1957-1958) 8869
INTERPERSONAL RELATIONS 14615, 15165, 15169, 15171, 15173
INTERPLANETARY VOYAGES 3527
INVENTIONS 4009, 6556, 8555, 9436, 11705, 12571, 13880, 15445
  history 17649
  United States 8874
INVENTORS 3725, 4211, 4941, 5657, 7911, 8874, 10017, 11590, 11760, 12652,
  12928, 13113, 13880, 14057
INVERTEBRATES 6104, 15316, 15754
IOWA 888, 2340, 3011, 7109, 11851, 14443
  history--addresses, essays, lectures 7570
IRAN 227, 10555, 13849, 17746
  description and travel 16672
IRELAND 521, 522, 1867, 2098, 3194, 3484, 3701, 3878, 4948, 10863, 11419,
  11453, 13308, 16409, 17227, 17232
  famines 5939
  history 10651
  rebellion of 1798 4148
  social life and customs 3484
IRISH AMERICANS 5939, 8475, 9280, 9424, 11313, 12570, 15627, 16497,
  17632
IRON AGE 14033
IROQUOIS INDIANS 790, 1755, 2445, 3234, 5544, 7350, 14557, 15540, 18166
  legends 9356, 13867, 14133, 14507, 16103
IRRIGATION 116
ISABELLA D'ESTE (CONSORT OF FRANCIS II, MARQUIS OF MANTUA),
  (1474-1539) 12129
ISHI (d. 1916) 10104
ISLAM 5259, 5964
ISLANDS 1000, 3074, 3160, 3247, 3606, 4846, 5284, 5844, 6469, 7423, 9144,
  9656, 10302, 10405, 10406, 10889, 11241, 13095, 15275, 16187, 16544,
  16620, 18048, 18428
  Indian Ocean 15548
ISLANDS OF THE PACIFIC 9412, 11850
  discovery and exploration 8612
ISRAEL 3917, 3918, 7501, 7678, 10126, 10219, 12967, 14325, 16048, 17600,
  17662
  biography 4570
  description and travel 6831, 8448, 9406, 14928
    views 14812
  history 4952, 12857, 17602
    1917-1948 7528
  social conditions 6988
  social life and customs 603
ISRAEL-ARAB WAR
  1948-1949 6116
  1967 12968
  1973 13028
  See also JEWS
ISRAELI POETRY--collections 18576
ISTANBUL (TURKEY) 17829
  history 9037, 16518
  Siege (1453) 17479
ITALIAN AMERICANS 2379, 7458, 10193, 10617, 11597, 11680, 13776
  in Baltimore (Maryland) 14899

ITALIAN CANADIANS 14254, 17464
ITALIAN WIT AND HUMOR--pictorial works 12557, 12560
ITALY 541, 5294, 7846, 8071, 12343, 14212, 15967
   history
      medieval 3284
      18th century 866
   social life and customs 5214
IVORY COAST 1565, 7494, 13521
   description and travel 15212
   history 18134
IWO JIMA, BATTLE OF (1945) 10476

- J -

JACKALS 2371
JACKSON, ANDREW (1767-1845) 3774, 5602, 11187, 16165
JACKSON, JESSE (1941-) 7621
JACKSON, MAHALIA (1911-1972) 4161, 5134, 9001, 11284
JACKSON, RACHEL (DONELSON), (1767-1828) 7108
JACKSON, REGGIE (1946-) 2623
JACKSON, THOMAS JONATHAN "STONEWALL" (1824-1863) 4482, 6390
JACKSON, WILLIAM HENRY (1843-1942) 9372
JACKSON 5 (MUSICAL GROUP) 10196, 12485
JAGUARS 1303
JAMAICA 5949, 9860, 12834, 13252, 13253, 13254, 13255, 13256
JAMESTOWN (VIRGINIA)--history 2873, 4939, 5959, 7629, 10320
JAPAN 2464, 2482, 3066, 3202, 4474, 4958, 6036, 6074, 7203, 7636, 8940,
   9300, 10329, 10705, 10711, 10799, 10800, 12636, 13369, 14976, 15848,
   17092, 17097, 17104, 17105, 17256, 18148, 18366, 18368
   art 228, 785
   civilization 16064
   to 1600 12761
   description and travel 5253, 9107, 12001, 13883, 17573
   festivals 11758
   foreign relations--United States 7022
   history
      Heian Period (794-1185) 2953, 13371
      Gempei Wars (1180-1185) 13370
      1941 7022
   holidays 11748
   poetry 1315, 1319
   social life and customs 2533, 6799, 14272, 15079, 16251, 17573
JAPANESE AMERICANS 3427, 4317, 5040, 5429, 7851, 7901, 9147, 10472,
   13781, 17095, 17099, 17101, 17102
   Washington (State) 16013
JAPANESE CANADIANS
   evacuation and relocation (1942-1945) 16614
   in British Columbia 16614
JAPANESE POETRY 4654, 8954, 8955, 10715, 10718, 10720, 12293
JAQUES, FRANCIS LEE (1887-1969) 9149
JARLAIT, PATRICK DES (1921-1972) 4856
JAZZ MUSIC 3839, 4420, 4957, 5528, 8086, 8719, 9620
JAZZ MUSICIANS 16514
JEANNE D'ARC, SAINT see JOAN OF ARC, SAINT
JEFFERS PETROGLYPH SITE (MINNESOTA) 11084

JEFFERSON, THOMAS (1743-1826)   1115, 3349, 9433, 12338, 12497
JEKRI (AFRICAN PEOPLE)   8890
JELLYFISHES   15536, 17559
JEMISON, MARY (1743-1833)   6580, 10572
JERUSALEM (ISRAEL)   5068, 8268
    views   1473
JESUITS   7919
JESUS CHRIST   649, 12027, 15992, 16048
    art   13556, 15353
    childhood   1680, 5966, 13130, 13556, 16681, 18180
    nativity   1265, 2122, 2449, 7131, 7330, 8377, 9414, 10140, 12079, 12537,
        12929, 13397
JET PLANES   17293
JEWELERS   953
JEWELRY   4900
    amateur's manuals   4582
JEWS   1709, 3242, 3926, 5358, 6764, 7528, 8943, 9730, 10036, 12582, 12967,
    13506, 15780, 15783, 17661, 17662
    Arab relations   598, 611, 5750, 17013, 17599
    biography   12196, 13544
    in Canada   17311
    in Czechoslovakia   16709
    in Eastern Europe   8683, 16447
        history   12052
    in France   14845
    in Germany   9574
        history (1933-1945)   9731, 10660, 14348
        persecutions   12045
    handicraft   1291
    history   12441
    in the Netherlands   6220, 4670, 14224
        social conditions   14223
    in Poland   6883, 15782, 17311
        persecutions   18534
    in Russia   819, 2699, 2700
        history   8141, 16210
    in the Ukraine   14053, 16450
    in the United States   94, 1341, 2776, 3737, 3738, 3739, 3754, 6993, 7262,
        7690, 8101, 8942, 8946, 9504, 9985, 10145, 10732, 10937, 11525, 12763,
        14370, 15517, 16703, 16704, 16705, 16707, 16708
        biography   5308, 10601
        history   12046
        pictorial works   16444
        social conditions   12048
    rites and ceremonies   3262, 5485, 10665
    social life and customs   7006
    See also   ISRAEL
JEWS AND GENTILES   9506, 14910
JOAN OF ARC, SAINT (1412-1431)   3450, 4541, 5635, 5917, 11774, 14655,
    18035
JOB SATISFACTION--United States   12859
JOCKIMO, PAUL   18196
JOGGING   724
JOHN, ELTON (1947-)   12787
JOHNNY APPLESEED   see   CHAPMAN, JOHN
JOHNSON, JAMES WELDON (1871-1938)   5290, 5777, 16243
JOHNSON, LYNDON BAINES (1908-1973)   11181, 12800, 13075, 14949

JOHNSON, RAFER LEWIS (1935-) 5882
JOKES 1532, 3221, 3814, 5030, 8363, 9639, 9641, 9642, 15150, 15365,
  16843, 16966, 17130, 17875, 17878
JOLIET, LOUIS (1645-1700) 9880, 16590
JOLLY, HI (1828?-1903) 9282, 9882
JONAH (BIBLICAL PROPHET) 2560, 11207
JONES, CASEY (1864-1900) 14696
JONES, CLEON (1942-) 18439
JONES, DEACON (1939-) 10766
JONES, MARY (HARRIS), (1830-1930) 17753
JONES, PARNELLI (1933-) 10768
JONES, PATTIE (RIDLEY), (1884-) 7313
JOPLIN, SCOTT (1868-1917) 5593
JORDAN 13816
JOSEPH (BIBLICAL PATRIARCH) 2561, 13559
JOSEPH (NEZ PERCE CHIEF), (1840-1904) 4611, 7168, 12360
JOSEPHINE (CONSORT OF NAPOLEON I), (1763-1814) 12512
JOUETT, JOHN (1754-1812) 7580
JOURNALISM 1444, 3932, 3940, 10900, 11180, 18316
  vocational guidance 6279, 7011, 10611,
JOURNALISTS 3966, 7197, 16198
  United States 12604
JOY AND SORROW 9249, 12596, 13411, 15464, 17317, 17355, 18613
JUAREZ, BENITO PABLO (1806-1872) 36, 782, 4576, 16587
JUDAISM 5967, 6285, 14665
JUDGES 12453, 13574
  Canada--biography 9110
JUDO 2444, 7752, 7753, 12704, 12708
JUNEAU, SOLOMON LAURENT (1793-1856) 10418
JUNGLES 602, 2310, 2462, 2695, 4818, 6171, 7480, 7481, 7482, 7489, 9254,
  9725, 9843, 11534, 12544, 14505, 15418, 17257, 17629, 17928
  ecology 1179
  fauna 1964
JUNK FOOD 13699
JUSTICE, ADMINISTRATION OF 2255, 16570
JUVENILE DELINQUENCY 1895, 2807, 3595, 6002, 6180, 7608, 12318, 12423,
  14390, 16773

- K -

KABBARLI (AUSTRALIAN ABORIGINES) 1174
KADEN, AMELIA ROSEA 6167
KAFKA, FRANZ (1883-1924) 4254
KAHTAHAH 13396
KAINAN INDIANS 3314
KALAHARI DESERT 1170, 8314, 8678
KALINE, ALBERT WILLIAM (1934-) 2747
KANGAROOS 4512, 5082, 13405, 16214
  habits and behavior 8807
KANSAS 889, 2834, 3013, 3697, 9324, 18040
  description and travel
    guide-books 18324
    views 11179

historic houses, etc. 17843
history 1098, 8739, 17843
  anecdotes, facetiae, satire, etc. 8939
  pictorial works 12236
  1854-1861 1125, 5914, 18037
  Civil War (1861-1865) 1125, 7557
  1866- 10238, 12308
KARANKAWA INDIANS 49
KARATE 3385, 7751, 10012, 10013, 10014, 12705, 12706, 12707, 17278,
  18152
KARTS AND KARTING 2763, 14067, 14068
KASHMIR
  description and travel 6125
  social life and customs 1983, 6125
KATCHINAS 876, 7025
KATSUSHIKA, HOKUSAI (1760-1849) 14400
KAUNDA, BETTY (1928-) 12533
KAUNDA, KENNETH DAVID (1924-) 13770, 16737
KEINO, KIPCHOGE (1940-) 12905
KELLER, HELEN ADAMS (1880-1968) 1646, 2410, 4571, 4572, 7116, 8150,
  8151, 9645, 13433, 14336, 16864, 17416, 17616, 17934
KELP 10354
KEMBLE, FRANCES ANNE (1809-1893) 15206
KENNEDY, JOHN FITZGERALD (1917-1963) 7195, 11751
KENNEDY, ROSE (FITZGERALD), (1890-) 5329, 7892
KENSINGTON GARDENS 1118
KENTON, SIMON (1755-1836) 17938
KENTUCKY 3174, 15579, 18231
  history 12340, 15806
KENYA 3043, 3240, 3376, 4298, 4409, 6134, 6439, 8213, 9499, 9738, 9807,
  13518, 13933, 14259, 14759, 14760, 16300, 16324, 17248, 17375
  description and travel 5035, 8897, 9721
  education 17743
  forests and forestry 986
  history 4421
  social life and customs 14671, 14672, 14673, 17374
KEOGH, MYLES WALTER (1840-1876) 10522
KESTRELS 13803
KETTERING, CHARLES FRANKLIN (1876-1958) 18506
KEYES, LEROY (1947-) 18438
KHAMA (AFRICAN CHIEF), (ca. 1830-1923) 4433
KIDD, WILLIAM (d. 1701) 10420
KIDNAPPING 322, 1223, 4930, 5127, 8652, 9452, 9797, 10545, 11973,
  12972, 13325, 13634, 14618, 15967, 16229, 16380, 16801, 16975, 17890,
  18100, 18101, 18361
KIEP, OTTO (1886-1944) 3590
KIKUYUS 1947, 3376, 6873, 9497, 9723, 14673, 17230
KILLIAN, ELIZABETH (19th century) 16100
KILMER, BILLY (1939-) 7519
KINDERGARTEN 1653, 15345
KINETIC ART 8030, 11689
KING, BILLIE JEAN (1943-) 2611, 3441, 11858, 13104
KING, CORETTA SCOTT (1927-) 16697
KING, MARTIN LUTHER, JR. (1929-1968) 1933, 3547, 4683, 7797, 11411,
  12212, 13386, 18066, 18454
  iconography 14719
  poetry 12099

KING ARTHUR (fl. 6th century) 726, 2579, 5877, 8144, 8158, 11291, 14017, 17084
KING PHILIP'S WAR (1675-1676) 16226
KINGS AND RULERS 817, 3794, 3878, 5345, 5347, 6384, 7431, 9318, 11633, 12863, 16440, 16749, 16858, 17246, 18423
KINGSLEY, MARY HENRIETTA (1862-1900) 16576
KIOWA INDIANS--legends 11700, 11702
KISHINEV MASSACRE (1903) 16210
KITCHENER (ONTARIO) 5130, 9956
KITCHENS 4343
KITES 823, 2829, 5046, 6020, 6162, 7208, 13496, 13939, 14270, 14573, 17105, 17414, 17870, 18311, 18406, 18423, 18429
KLAMATH INDIANS 16371
KLONDIKE GOLD FIELDS (ALASKA) 6200, 13870
KNIEVEL, EVEL (1938-) 10046, 14982
KNIGHTS AND KNIGHTHOOD 1007, 1067, 1715, 2579, 3308, 5414, 6938, 8156, 8158, 8470, 11291, 12791, 12794, 14208, 15055, 15057, 15983, 17016, 17108; see also CHIVALRY
KNITTING 3915
KOALAS 5079, 5080, 9972, 12869
KOBAYASHI, ISSA (1763-1827) 6435, 10720
KOM (AFRICAN PEOPLE) 5834
KORBUT, OLGA (1955-) 1305, 5585, 9071, 15909, 16505
KOREA 512, 2489, 3521, 7508, 8886, 12906, 14190
    history--Korean War (1950-1953) 3521, 8886, 13241, 13924
    poetry 1099
    social life and customs 6800
KOYA CHIEFDOM (SIERRA LEONE)
    history 8885
    kings and rulers 8885
KU KLUX KLAN 343
KUBLAI KHAN (1216-1294) 1210
KUNG (AFRICAN PEOPLE) 1170

- L -

LABOR AND LABORING CLASSES 7744
    biography 10000
    United States 12859
        history 12038
            pictorial works 14900
LABOR DAY 11694
LABOR UNIONS 6254, 9239
    history 6584, 12038
LABORATORIES 1511, 1514
LACANDON INDIANS 13914
LAFAYETTE, MARIE JOSEPH PAUL YVES ROCH GILBERT DU MOTIER, MARQUIS DE (1757-1834) 1674, 7088
LAFITTE, JEAN (1782-1854) 16632
LA FLESCHE, SUSETTE (1854-1900) 18071
LA GUARDIA, FIORELLO HENRY (1882-1947) 9534
LAKE ERIE 10405
    Battle of (1813) 1124, 11779
LAKE MICHIGAN 17766, 17767

LAKE MINNETONKA (MINNESOTA) 9367, 18069
LAKE SUPERIOR 2277
  region--description and travel 10930
  views 16219
LAKES 6966
  Minnesota 9148
LAMONT, BARBARA (1925-) 7011
LAMU ARCHIPELAGO (KENYA) 14671
LAND SETTLEMENT 3977
LANDLORD AND TENANT 11556, 11848, 12613
LANDMARKS--United States 2463
LANDSCAPE PAINTING 12550
LANGO LANGUAGE, BOOKS IN 13046
LANGUAGE AND LANGUAGES 109, 4567, 5356, 6520, 10077, 10119, 11158;
  see also under specific languages, e.g., SPANISH
LAPLAND 1984, 4841, 7619, 9818
LA SALLE, RENE ROBERT CAVALIER, SIEUR DE (1643-1687) 350, 7121,
  9083, 11444, 13332, 16588
LASERS 7799
LATIN AMERICA 792
  foreign relations--United States 4216
LATIN AMERICANS--Southwest, New 10364
LAUNDRY 1325
LA VERENDRYE, PIERRE GAULTIER DE VARENNES, SIEUR DE (1685-1749)
  7756
LAW 3114, 16570, 18118
  miscellanea 8875
  United States 8875, 12953, 15365
LAWICK-GOODALL, JANE, BARONESS VAN (1934-) 9768
LAWRENCE, THOMAS EDWARD (1888-1935) 11443
LAWYERS 5728, 6170, 10670, 13109, 17722
  United States--biography 16030
  vocational guidance 7009
  women 5146
LAXALT, PAUL DOMINIQUE (1922-) 10428
LEADERSHIP 3445, 7099
LEARNING AND SCHOLARSHIP 12915
LEARNING DISABILITIES 2428, 4129, 13419, 13594, 16550
LEASE, MARY ELIZABETH (CLYENS), (1853-1933) 16318
LEAVES 3178, 6525, 8855, 15321, 18173
LEBANON 2172, 14755, 14756, 14757
LEE, ROBERT E. (1807-1870) 3908, 4481, 9485, 13335
LEFT- AND RIGHT-HANDEDNESS 10606
LEGENDS 377, 1007, 1138, 1375, 1377, 4021, 5400, 5603, 6638, 10446, 17161
  Africa--West 12762
  Alaska 14137
  Australia--aborigine 800
  Celt 4395, 7464
  China 16820
  France 12652
  Germany 2438, 6674, 13653
  Hawaii 2545, 13882
  Hungary 15344
  Indians of North America 4397
  Ireland 16523
  Japan 11199
  Mexico 2871, 9384, 12417, 16969

Michigan--Mackinac Island   7418
Morocco   3377
Nigeria--Northern   7122
Orient   4204
Polynesia   16071
Scandinavia   9349
Scotland   12819, 18064
Spain   3146, 9233, 9235
United Nations   6411
United States   1713, 10449
   Texas   6840
   Wisconsin   4616
See also FOLKLORE
LEGISLATION   16570, 17683
LEGISLATORS   372, 5622, 6035, 7816, 7818, 7821
United States   7055, 10377
vocational guidance   10377
LEMMINGS   632, 12575, 12805
LEMON   16363
LENINGRAD (RUSSIA)--Siege (1941-1944)   16746
LENSES   2257, 15159
LEONARDO DA VINCI (1452-1519)   9993
LEOPARDS   38, 248, 4915, 7486, 12239, 15038, 15868
LEPRECHAUNS   2837
LESOTHO   3014
history   14895
LETTER WRITING   4340, 14233
LETTERING   5940, 7106
LETTERS   9798
LEUKEMIA   3731
LEVY, URIAH PHILLIPS (1792-1862)   5308
LEWANIKAS (SOUTH AFRICAN KING), (ca. 1842-1916)   11433
LEWIS, C. S. (CLIVE STAPLES), (1898-1963)   672
LEWIS, ELEANOR PARKE CUSTIS (1779-1852)   1998
LEWIS, JOHN LLEWELLYN (1880-1969)   10000
LEWIS AND CLARK EXPEDITION (1804-1806)   4533, 4699, 12753, 15247
LEXINGTON (MASSACHUSETTS)   1245
Battle of (1775)   1400, 1408, 3790
LIBERIA   3015, 3256, 3257, 3258, 3613, 4264, 6647, 7134
biography   8055, 8057
description and travel   12270
social life and customs   15077
LIBERTY BELL   1853, 7627, 12408, 14558
LIBRARIANS   939, 1911, 2735
LIBRARIES   1911, 3556, 7319, 10945, 10946, 12574, 14513, 14939, 15973,
   17342
LIBRARY SCIENCE   12518
LIBYA   3016, 4095, 5227, 11367
LIEOU-LIN (CHINA)   12619
LIFE   789
   origin   11868
   on other planets   5439, 10048, 13233, 16321
LIFESAVING   4351, 6053, 7597
   England--Lynmouth   8320
LIGHT   2132, 6288, 6300, 8706, 15096, 15137, 16417, 17089
LIGHTHOUSES   165, 188, 3160, 4448, 7276, 9677, 12288, 14938, 16560,
   16797, 17526

LIGHTNING 2127, 18545
LILIUOKALANI (QUEEN OF THE HAWAIIAN ISLANDS), (1838-1917) 11581,
    12798, 16370, 18080
LINCOLN, ABRAHAM (1809-1865) 484, 2563, 3140, 3714, 3883, 4023, 4530,
    4543, 5303, 5535, 5921, 6139, 6140, 6149, 7743, 7930, 9417, 9570, 9571,
    9671, 11122, 11351, 11467, 11486, 11741, 12153, 12158, 12337, 12344,
    12813, 12872, 12883, 12901, 12920, 13200, 14110, 14884, 15437, 17339
    homes 14178
    iconography 6236, 7704
    journeys--Washington (D.C.) 13617
    monuments, etc. 12224, 12240, 14178
    museums, relics, etc. 12224, 14178
LINCOLN, MARY (TODD), (1818-1882) 490, 17936
LINCOLN, NANCY (HANKS), (1784-1818) 10637, 16277
LINCOLN, ROBERT TODD (1843-1926) 492
LINCOLN, SARA BUSH (JOHNSON), (1788-1869) 879
LINCOLN, THOMAS (1853-1871) 6377, 12337, 12344
LINCOLN, WILLIAM WALLACE (1850-1862) 12344
LINCOLN (NEBRASKA)
    buildings 11412
    history 11412
LIND, JENNY (1820-1887) 3185, 12599
LINDBERGH, CHARLES AUGUSTUS (1902-1974) 4460, 5961, 6152, 10822
LIONS 65, 66, 67, 68, 69, 1302, 1922, 3955, 4217, 4531, 4895, 5716, 5717,
    5718, 5719, 6259, 7484, 7489, 8253, 8803, 9299, 10064, 11784, 12892,
    13473, 13932, 15038, 17419
LITERATURE--collections 5595, 6423, 6655, 13485, 16659, 16662
LITHOGRAPHY 8229
LITTLE, LESSIE JONES (1906-) 7313
LITTLE, MALCOLM see X, MALCOLM
LITTLE BIG HORN, BATTLE OF THE (1876) 6947, 10226, 14280
LITTLE PEOPLE 12938, 16563, 17661, 17662, 18123
LITTLE TURTLE (MIAMI CHIEF), (ca. 1752-1812) 3057
LIVINGSTONE, DAVID (1813-1873) 669, 7184, 10312, 14005
LIZARDS 497, 2195, 3949, 6335, 7972, 11061
LLAMAS 3957
LOBIS 7495
LOBSTERS 3070, 3992, 15261, 16682
LOCAL GOVERNMENT--Michigan 10702
LOCKS AND KEYS 10324
LOCKWOOD, BELVA ANN (BENNETT), (1830-1917) 5146, 6170
LOCOMOTIVE ENGINEERS 7280
LOCOMOTIVES 13098, 13708
LOGAN COUNTRY (COLORADO) 7644
LOGGING see LUMBER AND LUMBERING
LOGIC, SYMBOLIC AND MATHEMATICAL 6773
LOMBARDI, VINCE (1913-1970) 5574, 15106, 18492
LONDON (ENGLAND) 1219, 1222, 2429, 4404, 4693, 6262, 6605, 9814, 14420,
    15707, 16599, 16977, 17597, 17673
    fire (1666) 4885
    history--16th century 6271, 7204
    police 15191
    social life and customs 11374
LONDON (ONTARIO) 4385
LOONS (BIRDS) 341, 7637
LOS ANGELES (CALIFORNIA) 13782
    Simon Rodia Towers 11518

LOUISIANA 2957, 3017, 3187, 7062, 10325, 10558, 15898
   description and travel 5218
   history 2222, 11511
LOVE, NAT (1854-1921) 5783
LOVE 549, 1121, 4475, 5678, 7233, 7245, 8594, 10367, 10974, 12259
   pictorial works 12168
   poetry 12295, 18362
LOW, JULIETTE (GORDON), (1860-1927) 8165, 14058
LOYALTY 15548
LULLABIES 304, 5461, 9180, 18476, 18523
LUMBER AND LUMBERING 402, 1641, 5925, 6254, 7415, 7496, 8997, 14317,
   15894, 16377
   Canada 10139
     Ottawa Valley 2178
   United States
     Great Lakes region 13385
     Michigan 11921
       history 5195
     Minnesota 14818, 14819, 14862
LUMBERJACKS 10139, 13385
LUNAR BASES 1504
LUNAR PETROLOGY 2141, 6526
LYNN, FRED (1952-) 2608
LYNN, JANET (1953-) 9066, 11879

- M -

McADOO, BOB (1951-) 17080
MACCABEES 8235
McCARTHY, JOE (1887-1978) 17221
McCARTHY, JOSEPH RAYMOND (1908-1957) 7018
McCAULEY, MARY (LUDWIG) HAYES (1754-1832) 16276
McCORMICK, CYRUS HALL (1809-1884) 9428, 12652
McDONALD, FLORA (1722-1790) 3668
McGILLICUDDY, CORNELIUS see MACK, CONNIE
McGRAW, JOHN JOSEPH (1873-1934) 17221
McGUFFEY, WILLIAM HOLMES (1800-1873) 17982
MACHINE SHOPS--vocational guidance 10784
MACHINE TOOLS 18570
MACHINERY 831, 7685, 8036, 9111, 9532, 9665, 13691, 14514, 14942, 15089
   pictorial works 8299
McJUNKIN, GEORGE (1851-1922) 6093
MACK, CONNIE (1862-1956) 17221
MACKENZIE, WILLIAM LYON (1795-1861) 14173, 17067
MACKINAC BRIDGE (MICHIGAN) 7414, 14737, 16220
MACKINAC ISLAND (MICHIGAN) 11386
   history 4844, 12806
     pictorial works 13551
McLAUGHLIN, SAM (1871-1972) 13585
MacNAB, SIR ALLAN NAPIER (1798-1862) 1164
MACRAME 10808, 12128
MACROPHOTOGRAPHY 11083
MACY, ANNE (SULLIVAN) see SULLIVAN, ANNE
MADAGASCAR see MALAGASY REPUBLIC

MADISON, DOLLEY (PAYNE) TODD (1768-1849) 4576, 7171, 11745, 12028,
  12356, 12875
MAGELLAN, FERDINAND DE (d. 1521) 5450, 9716, 13815, 16589
MAGI 1722
MAGIC 265, 938, 978, 1022, 1360, 1361, 1394, 1976, 2472, 2796, 3122, 3269,
  3334, 3341, 3343, 3345, 3346, 4056, 4107, 4109, 4274, 4286, 4339, 4401,
  4445, 4664, 4814, 4976, 5198, 5199, 5200, 5201, 5471, 5537, 5694, 5844,
  6018, 6019, 6466, 6503, 6553, 6712, 7097, 7200, 7326, 7412, 7832, 7908,
  8180, 8791, 9211, 9258, 9340, 9342, 9344, 9715, 9761, 10049, 10090,
  10091, 10206, 10475, 10516, 10680, 10959, 11047, 11062, 11363, 11550,
  11932, 11939, 12552, 12732, 12735, 12736, 12739, 12794, 12796, 12913,
  12996, 13006, 13318, 13324, 13429, 13807, 13837, 15122, 15181, 15259,
  15362, 15389, 15391, 15552, 15847, 15968, 16332, 16914, 16916, 16917,
  17813, 17941, 18019, 18321, 18341, 18343, 18344, 18417, 18426
  biography 9683
  history 9197
MAGICIANS 849, 5419, 5529, 6791, 7246, 10047, 10049, 11623, 13820, 17188,
  17622, 17803
MAGNA CARTA 8318
MAGNETIC RECORDERS AND RECORDING 13773
MAGNETISM 2153
MAGNETS 117, 5820, 6295, 13757, 13762, 14850
MAIDU INDIANS--legends 1576
MAIGUMER, CHARLES 8053
MAINE 3666, 3680, 5850, 10179, 11240, 11241, 14322, 14324, 14574, 18079
  birds 4511
MAJORS, ALEXANDER (1814-1900) 454
MAKAH INDIANS 9856
MAKE-UP, THEATRICAL 1156, 2456, 4220
MALAGASY REPUBLIC 880, 3046, 11708
MALAWI 881, 3018, 3594, 9584, 9777
  social life and customs 8928
MALAYA 15556
MALAYSIA 9582, 10519
MALCOLM X see X, MALCOLM
MALLORY, SIR THOMAS (15th century) 8332
MALLOY, VIVI (1967?-) 10088
MAMMALS 325, 2494, 5206, 8710, 10350, 13141, 15322, 16728, 18055
  Australia 4327
  Canada--Ontario 4435
  fossil 3802, 4578, 8512
  habits and behavior 6983, 13674, 15633, 16732
  migration 12805
  physiology 6983
  Tanzania--Serengeti Plain 15038
  United States--Michigan 12147
MAMMOTHS 314, 2203
MAN
  influence on nature 7328, 8028, 8425, 9199, 13754, 14681
  origin 3641
  prehistoric 523, 910, 1316, 3264, 3405, 4232, 4889, 5396, 5597, 7048,
    7266, 7741, 7805, 8362, 8397, 9790, 9876, 11516, 11869, 12327, 14033,
    15439, 15706, 16984, 17065, 17482
    North America 15023
    Tanzania 13512
    United States 17786
MANDAN INDIANS 8366, 8367

MANTLE, MICKEY (1931-) 11648, 11887, 15673
MANUFACTURERS 3854, 12115, 12598, 16470
MAO TSE-TUNG (1893-1976) 612
MAORIS 942, 11385
  education 729
  legends 14524
MAP DRAWING 2366, 3138
MAPLE 15293, 17003
MAPLE HILL (KANSAS)--social life and customs 17066
MAPLE SUGAR 6726, 17592
MAPS 3138, 3765, 5494, 6284, 13083
  history 5189
MARCIANO, ROCKY (1923-1969) 10770
MARCONI, GUGLIELMO MARCHESE (1874-1937) 3725
MARDI GRAS 10558
MARIETTA (OHIO) 18298
MARINE
  animals 346, 4304, 9039, 9090, 11254, 15030, 15154, 15261, 15271, 15307,
    18144
  aquariums 15313
  biologists 10545
  biology 1085, 1592, 5804, 6748, 7002, 18034
  ecology 11276
  plants 8405
  pollution 11276, 12144
  resources 2364, 5799, 11276, 12144
MARION, FRANCIS (1732-1795) 2409
MARKETING 10032
  vocational guidance 7589
MARKETS 11135
MARMOTS 11491
MARQUETTE, JACQUES (1637-1675) 9880, 16590
MARRIAGE 1172, 6735, 7284, 8408, 8773, 9483, 9732, 11105, 11975, 13644,
    14341, 15767, 16027, 16666, 18522
  customs and rites 11842, 11974, 14887
    medieval 10298
MARS (PLANET) 9927, 13543
  exploration 6723
MARSHALL, THURGOOD (1908-) 5787, 18456
MARSHES 4954, 6097, 6098, 6343, 15880, 15892
MARSUPIALS 4327, 9190, 10385
MARTIN, VICTORIA CLAFLIN (WOODHULL), (1838-1927) 11979
MARTIN DE PORRES, SAINT (316-401?) 1676
MARTINEZ, ANTONIO JOSE (1793-1867) 1563
MARTINEZ, MARIA (MONTOYA), (1881?-) 12724
MARTINIQUE 14852
MARY, VIRGIN 4538
MARYLAND 161, 162, 164, 1838
  biography 14586
  history 11586, 14588
    Colonial Period (ca. 1600-1775) 5881, 7510, 11780
    exhibition 8140
    Revolution (1775-1783) 5881
    20th century 2969
MASAI 1756, 1981, 5005, 7625, 7635, 14907, 17422
MASKS (FACIAL) 317, 2456, 4220, 4359, 14653
  Africa--West 13912

MASKS (SCULPTURE) 8754, 13919
MASON, JOSEPH (1807-1883) 2198
MASS MEDIA--biography 2024
MASSACHUSETTS 1288, 6777
   history
      Colonial Period (ca. 1600-1775) 2072, 3473, 10585
      New Plymouth (1620-1691) 7438, 9085, 15884
      Revolution (1775-1783) 3532
         campaigns and battles 14783
   social life and customs--Colonial Period (ca. 1600-1775) 11017
MASSEY, HART (1823-1896) 3854
MATHEMATICAL RECREATIONS 3290, 9445, 10207, 13249, 14314, 15085, 18342, 18343
MATHEMATICIANS 16362
MATHEMATICS 105, 756, 1101, 2689, 4828, 5821, 6773, 8522, 9112, 9331, 12134, 15563, 16106, 17563
   history 8399
MATHIUS, ROBERT BRUCE (1930-) 5882
MATTER--properties 1437
MAURITANIA 3020
MAURY, MATTHEW FONTAINE (1806-1873) 10321
MAY DAY 10634
MAYAS 1757, 8535, 9502, 13686, 13937, 14285
MAYFLOWER (SHIP) 7628, 7931, 11355
MAYO, CHARLES HORACE (1865-1939) 7058, 7675
MAYO, WILLIAM JAMES (1861-1939) 7058, 7675
MAYO, WILLIAM WORRELL (1819-1911) 7675
MAYORS 17975
MAYS, WILLIE (1931-) 5305, 5506, 7701, 11916, 15110, 16491
MBUNDU (AFRICAN PEOPLE) 16555
MEAD, MARGARET (1901-1978) 3443, 11976, 12481
MEAT INDUSTRY AND TRADE 9956
MEDICAL CARE 3707, 3837, 9530, 9567, 13486, 14534, 14996, 15987, 16157, 17584, 17638, 17737, 17738, 17739, 17740, 18192, 18532
MEDICAL CENTERS 1251, 6403, 9562
MEDICAL INSTRUMENTS AND APPARATUS 10605
MEDICAL TECHNOLOGISTS 13486
MEDICAL TECHNOLOGY 6272
   vocational guidance 6276
MEDICINE 835, 1592, 2841, 14534, 17584
   biography 984, 2025
   cultural 3492
   dictionaries 4415
   discoveries 9530
   professions 4230
   vocational guidance 4597, 5452, 6277, 11786, 16012
MEDICINE MEN 8368, 8387
MEDIEVAL LIFE see CIVILIZATION--MEDIEVAL
MEDITERRANEAN SEA 9952
MEEKER, NATHAN COOK (1814-1879) 13211
MEIR, GOLDA (MABINOVITZ), (1898-1978) 4570, 4952, 11607, 12464, 12857
MEITNER, LISA (1878-1968) 4255
MEKONG RIVER--description and travel 10916
MEKONG VALLEY--social life and customs 10916
MELVILLE, HERMAN (1819-1891) 8646
MEMORY 10748, 12965
MENDEL, GREGOR (1822-1884) 13811

MENDELSSOHN-BARTHOLDY, FELIX (1809-1847) 8817
MENELIK II (NEGUS OF ETHIOPIA), (1844-1913) 4502
MENNONITES 4636, 4640, 4643, 5130, 9383, 14722, 16398, 18040, 18333
  Pennsylvania 2095, 8629
MENSTRUATION 5337
MENTAL HEALING 3830
MENTALLY HANDICAPPED 217, 999, 2426, 2427, 2792, 2993, 2994, 3058,
  3423, 3581, 4246, 4873, 5369, 5614, 5633, 5634, 5711, 5714, 6366, 6592,
  6601, 7662, 7735, 7824, 8002, 9218, 9894, 9990, 10667, 10944, 12036,
  12756, 13736, 14276, 14324, 14379, 14550, 15727, 15880, 15897, 15920,
  15988, 17452, 17834, 18322
MERCHANT MARINE 5392
MERCHANTS 10378
MERCURY, PROJECT 205, 13663
MERMAIDS 13771, 17493, 18418
MERRITT, WILLIAM (1793-1862) 1166
MESOPOTAMIA
  antiquities 1208
  history 5641
METABOLISM 1011
METAL FOILS 4430
METALWORK 4430, 13611
METEORITES 6085
METEOROLOGICAL INSTRUMENTS 16135
METEOROLOGY 6519, 8130, 9933, 12675, 13692, 13764, 14824, 18545
METEORS 18551
METLAKAHTLA 17742
METRIC SYSTEM 1327, 1688, 2134, 2149, 4824, 6521, 8228, 10214, 10457,
  14086, 15070, 16394, 18571
  history 7561
METROPOLITAN AREAS 15138
MEXICAN AMERICANS 44, 839, 1563, 1811, 1896, 2916, 3862, 4228, 4655,
  4712, 4955, 5149, 5150, 5153, 5307, 5559, 6126, 6437, 6493, 6652, 6705,
  7279, 8132, 8540, 10223, 11527, 11744, 11761, 11763, 13012, 13035, 13483,
  13675, 13778, 13784, 13786, 13790, 14761, 16680, 16714, 16727, 16905,
  17198, 18445
  biography 4876, 12666, 12784, 17798
  Rio Grande Valley--social conditions 18197
  social life and customs 3493, 12332, 12665
  Texas 18197
MEXICO 663, 1320, 1629, 2547, 2568, 2820a, 3062, 3192, 3652, 3678, 3691,
  3871, 4754, 5063, 5561, 5562, 5569, 5660, 6059, 6127, 6621, 7548, 8104,
  9198, 9475, 9867, 10244, 10729, 11747, 11997, 12138, 12479, 12664, 12771,
  13016, 13625, 13787, 14662, 16010, 16326, 16347, 16353, 16658, 16908,
  17646, 17828
  antiquities 6916
  description and travel 5495, 6486, 7027, 16565
  Gold Rush 1463
  history 782, 3823, 5495, 7027, 11473, 11763, 16587, 16727
    Conquest (1519-1540) 9080, 9302
    War of Independence (1810) 10232
    1910-1946 16597
  presidents 36, 4756
  social life and customs 3192, 5063, 5214, 8994, 15076, 17260, 17305
MEZADA FORTRESS (ISRAEL) 18357
MIAMI INDIANS 3057, 6961, 18112
MICE 159, 297, 1398, 1604, 1841, 1842, 1843, 2081, 2084, 2101, 2104, 2300,

2301, 2380, 2412, 2420, 2921, 3563, 3570, 5075, 5270, 5994, 6262, 6266, 6291, 6321, 6327, 6328, 6329, 6333, 6838, 6956, 6957, 7576, 7770, 8137, 8454, 8455, 8799, 9653, 9695, 10068, 10071, 10353, 10868, 10872, 10877, 10878, 10879, 10887, 11000, 11113, 12219, 12220, 12221, 12222, 12223, 12574, 12851, 12910, 12974, 12983, 12984, 12985, 12986, 12987, 12992, 13173, 13937, 14129, 14419, 14495, 14799, 15262, 15485, 15486, 15521, 15694, 16187, 16189, 16342, 16352, 16825, 16886, 16887, 16888, 16889, 16890, 16891, 16892, 17210, 17369, 17394, 17408, 17591, 17741, 17793, 18392, 18489, 18594
  poetry 15504, 17535
MICHIGAN 890, 915, 995, 3021, 3299, 5840, 5925, 6759, 7297, 7417, 7424, 9727, 12979, 13871, 13936, 14721, 16373, 16376, 16377, 16549
  biography 6106, 6760, 6761
  boundaries--Ohio 6755
  description and travel 6107, 7298, 10703, 12776
    guide-books 16419
    views 13196
  economic conditions 10700, 10701, 10703
  history 16, 1664, 3063, 4617, 4618, 4852, 5118, 5828, 6760, 6761, 7416, 7426, 9279, 10700, 10701, 10703, 14189
    to 1837 18082
    19th century 7415
    War of 1812 7643, 11852
    Civil War (1861-1865) 17994
  politics and government 7839, 10699, 10702
MICHOACAN (MEXICO) 17305
MICROELECTRONICS 5454
MICROORGANISMS 10707, 15155
MICROSCOPES AND MICROSCOPY 1308, 15155, 15280, 18179
MIDDLE AGES 4376, 9661, 11026, 13654, 15822, 18018
MIDDLE EAST 754, 2825, 13907
  description and travel 8202
  history 10947
  See also individual countries, e.g., ISRAEL
MIDDLE WEST 7864, 7866, 13448
  description and travel 6027, 18228
  industry and trade 10598
  poetry 6027
  social life and customs 11351, 17623
MIDWAY, BATTLE OF (1942) 8647
MIGRANT LABOR 2221, 6126, 6658, 7642, 10197, 10223, 10573, 11761, 13942, 14434, 15590, 15923, 16372, 16403, 16680, 16714, 17509, 17865, 18197, 18447
  California 17666
MIKASUKI INDIANS 8046
MILAN (ITALY)--history--to 1535 9993
MILITARY 390, 3059
  art and science--history 12656
    miscellanea 14402
  posts 7163
  service 2762, 7512
    compulsory 8084
      Russia 9133
MILK 303, 6483
MILKWEED 7119
MILLAY, EDNA ST. VINCENT (1892-1950) 7504
MILLER, CINCINNATUS HEINE "JOAQUIN" (1839-1913) 14636

MILLIONAIRES   13030
MILTON, WILLIAM FITZWILLIAM, VISCOUNT (1839-1877)   7768
MINERALOGY   5805, 13437, 14386, 15638
  collectors and collecting   15756
  Canada--Ontario   8136
  United States   11052
    Michigan   8024, 12150
MINERS   16796
MINES AND MINERAL RESOURCES   2529, 3236, 4394, 4466, 4483, 11692
  history--United States   3274
  Canada--Ontario   8136
  United States--Colorado   18215
MINNEAPOLIS (MINNESOTA)
  description and travel   5996
  history   5996
MINNESOTA   891, 2260, 2467, 2468, 2469, 3022, 9385, 11098, 11106
  art   3728
  biography   12459, 13753
  description and travel   9148, 9151
    addresses, essays, lectures   13753
    views   12502, 17242
  history   8519, 9274, 13752
    addresses, essays, lectures   13753
    local   5575, 12459
    pictorial works   8014
    20th century   10822
MINNOWS   13963
MINORITIES
  literary collections   2308, 17069
  United States   9522, 9523, 9524, 9525, 9526, 18307
    Minnesota--addresses, essays, lectures   13753
MISSIONS   14162, 16327
  Africa   1633, 4970
  Christian   9207
  foreign   15499
  Nigeria--Calabar   16591
MISSISSAUGA (ONTARIO)   13547
MISSISSIPPI   9426, 16399
MISSISSIPPI RIVER   530, 1026, 2553, 3900, 4265, 4848, 5644, 6155, 7159,
  8491, 10352
  art   11295
  discovery and exploration   9880, 13332
MISSISSIPPI VALLEY--description and travel   9590
MISSOURI   892, 1349, 1351, 3023, 3591, 12132, 17083
  history   18259
  social life and customs   12957
MISSOURI VALLEY--description and travel   17908
MITCHELL, ARTHUR (1934-)   16895
MITCHELL, MARIA (1818-1889)   985, 12032, 17620, 17935
MITCHELL, WILLIAM "BILLY" (1879-1936)   2660, 12380
MITTENS   9573, 9656, 17004
MOBILES (SCULPTURE)   8523, 13285
MOÇAMBIQUE   11704
MOCHICA INDIANS   1480
MODEL AIRPLANES   12575
MODELING (ART)   7895, 10503, 13406, 13836, 14368, 15205, 15251, 15823,
  17687

MODELS AND MODELMAKING   4360, 11539, 14249
MODELS, FASHION   14478
   vocational guidance   17443
MODERN DANCE   16762
   pictorial works   5845
MODOC INDIANS   10231
   Wars (1873)   11161
MOHAVE INDIANS   1005, 7344
MOHAWK INDIANS   234, 8947
MOHAWK RIVER   8251
MOHAWK VALLEY (NEW YORK)   8251
   history--Revolution (1775-1783)   5268
MOLDAVIA   17206
MOLDS (BOTANY)   9975
MOLECULES   110
MOLES (ANIMALS)   4374, 6743, 8286, 9327, 10368, 10425, 12033, 12585,
   14023
MOLLUSKS   7730
MONASTERIES   2952
   Buddhist   660
MONETARY POLICY--United States   13278
MONEY   1107, 1167, 2192, 5350, 10659, 14940, 16657, 18117
   history   18116
MONGOLISM   see   DOWN'S SYNDROME
MONGOLS   8464
   history   10209
MONGOOSE   2965, 9860, 11684
MONKEYS   348, 1304, 4690, 5349, 6719, 7039, 7844, 8804, 9320, 9582, 9725,
   9940, 10080, 14145, 14261, 14262, 14263, 14264, 14265, 14266, 14267,
   14269, 14270, 14490, 15849, 16314, 16436, 16970, 18547
   China--folklore   18297
   See also CHIMPANZEES
MONOTREMES   9191
MONROE, EARL (1944-)   9011
MONROE, JAMES (1758-1831)   7703
MONSTERS   349, 641, 832, 1362, 1430, 1719, 1890, 2229, 2860, 2876, 4220,
   4330, 5254, 6421, 8732, 8770, 9653, 11068, 11482, 11635, 11930, 12067,
   12843, 12870, 13705, 13724, 14919, 15336, 15337, 15477, 16520, 16896,
   17131, 17320
   poetry   13887, 17461
MONTANA   1282, 4136, 4143, 4930, 7655, 10228, 11432, 14952
MONTEZUMA, CARLOS (1866-1923)   657, 666
MONTFORD, SIMON OF (EARL OF LEICESTER), (1208?-1265)   16979
MONTGOMERY (ALABAMA)--race relations   12090, 16291
MONTHS--poetry   17162
MONTREAL (QUEBEC)   16049
   description and travel--guide-books   15824
MONUMENTS   2463, 2718, 6311, 13335, 13387
MOODY, LADY DEBORAH (1600-1659)   4253
MOON, CHARLOTTE "LOTTIE", (1840-1912)   12357, 16501
MOON   1557, 2135, 2136, 2509, 4628, 11775, 12303, 12563, 13097, 15032,
   15448, 15634, 15855, 16856, 17133
   exploration   1504
   poetry   8731, 15178
   rocks   2141
MOOSE   563, 4352, 6336, 11474, 13697, 16379, 18155, 18156
   legends   1595

MORAVIAN INDIANS 8146
MORAVIANS--history 15011
MORELIA (MEXICO) 17305
MORGAN'S RAID (1863) 7860
MORMONS AND MORMONISM 2704, 2707, 2720, 9246, 9352, 9879, 11845, 17972
MOROCCO 3024, 3199, 3200, 4467, 5589, 8445, 10755, 14670, 16025
   description and travel 15542, 16067
   history 16067
   social life and customs 6801
MORRISON, GEORGE (1919-) 10005
MOSAICS--technique 15250
MOSES, ANNA MARY (ROBERTSON) "GRANDMA" (1860-1961) 647, 7194
MOSES (BIBLICAL PATRIARCH) 13562, 14911
MOSHESH (BASUTO CHIEF), (d. 1870) 14895
MOSLEMS see MUSLIMS
MOSSES--Louisiana 11765
MOSSI (AFRICAN PEOPLE) 7498
MOTHERS 998, 2177, 2443, 5235, 5922, 7558, 9154, 11682, 12296, 13344, 15074, 15465, 17134, 17320, 17981
   and daughters 3191, 3288, 3566, 4740, 5617, 5896, 7321, 8268, 9909, 10752, 11843, 13348, 18614, 18625
   employment 1710, 10299, 11094, 11843, 13864, 15919, 17296
   and sons 4426, 4816, 5712, 8597, 11616, 13443, 13903, 16322, 18582
MOTHERS' DAY 13618
MOTION 1429, 10510, 14741, 15744
MOTION PICTURE PHOTOGRAPHY 17692
MOTION PICTURES 450, 832, 1443, 2481, 3388, 5254, 5870, 6558, 6559, 6560, 8635, 11589, 12366, 16862
   history 9034
   vocational guidance 9507
MOTOR VEHICLES 960, 6875, 7685, 8691, 9998, 12289
   maintenance and repair--vocational guidance 10785
   operators 12081, 12112
      vocational guidance 6280, 7280
MOTORBOATS 5763, 13346, 13438, 13439
   safety measures 12670
MOTORCYCLE RACING 3416, 6683, 13989, 14071, 15136
MOTORCYCLES 3563, 3570, 4039, 5262, 5762, 10410, 12674, 14326, 14679, 14861, 14982, 18399
   maintenance and repair 13092, 15917
MOTT, LUCRETIA (COFFIN), (1792-1880) 2668, 5627, 16240
MOTTA, DICK (1931-) 12520
MOUNDS AND MOUND BUILDERS 7742, 10636, 15024, 15213, 15668, 16163
   Ohio Valley 12624
MT. KILIMANJARO 10840
MOUNTAIN LIFE 1352, 2154, 2155, 2156, 2158, 3097, 3172, 4269, 4406, 5064, 6752, 10559, 11476, 12003, 12183, 12184, 13177, 16174, 17058
MOUNTAINEERING 7099, 15567, 17122
MOUNTAINS 1356, 3110, 6967, 9955, 10840, 12424, 13177, 16102, 16435, 16935, 17781
MOVING, HOUSEHOLD 1090, 1334, 1341, 1402, 1556, 1585, 1659, 2417, 2557, 2578, 3242, 3868, 4708, 5481, 5906, 6184, 6354, 6813, 7317, 7914, 8148, 8149, 8340, 8365, 8427, 8474, 8729, 8860, 8895, 9439, 9440, 9486, 10732, 10733, 10866, 12185, 12490, 12539, 12588, 13474, 13640, 15117, 15477, 15625, 16841, 16902, 17601, 17606, 17863
MOZART, WOLFGANG AMADEUS (1756-1791) 4336, 9984, 12343

MUHAMMAD (ca. 570-632) 13669
MUHAMMAD ALI see ALI, MUHAMMAD
MUIR, JOHN (1838-1914) 3513, 4910, 5132, 7196, 12898, 15666a, 16308
MULES 2192, 4269, 7165
MULTILINGUAL BOOKS see BOOKS--POLYGLOT
MUMMIES 11393, 13229
   Egypt 307
MUNICIPAL ENGINEERING 3265, 8745
MUÑOZ MARIN, LUIS (1898-) 11610, 16245
MUÑOZ RIVERA, LUIS (1859-1916) 14274, 16245
MURDER 13447
MURPHY, EMILY (FERGUSON), (1888-1933) 9110
MUSEUMS 2882, 3760, 6266, 9989, 11389, 17679
MUSHROOMS 3947, 5300, 14805, 16531
MUSIAL, STANLEY FRANK (1920-) 14483
MUSIC 2189, 4336, 5673, 6434, 7898, 8677, 8913, 9756, 10559, 10879, 13271,
   13975, 14623, 14725, 16063, 16636, 17190, 17326, 17651, 18440
   Africa--history and criticism 17534
   almanacs, yearbooks, etc. 4346
   analysis, appreciation 15266, 15659
   economic aspects 10780
   history and criticism 2270, 8126
   Jewish--history and criticism 5311
   poetry 13747
   quotations, maxims, etc. 4346
   theory 5724
   Ukrainian--history and criticism 13145
   vocational guidance 10780, 12003
MUSIC, POPULAR (SONGS, ETC.) 5528
   Puerto Rico--history and criticism 12840
   United States 9737
      Michigan 12277
   writing and publishing 9106
MUSICAL FORM 3912
MUSICAL INSTRUMENTS 1017, 5363, 6836, 7277, 7898, 7899, 9764, 10136,
   10174, 11176, 11238, 11456, 13833
   Africa 4902, 13921
   construction 18149
   methods 5556
MUSICIANS 272, 353, 1071, 2026, 4960, 5145, 5275, 5528, 6825, 7270, 7661,
   7811, 7830, 8935, 10531, 10990, 11816, 12362, 12485, 15041, 15793, 15865,
   16514, 18068
   Black American 9353, 9620
   country--history and criticism 8040
   jazz 8085
   vocational guidance 3840, 7010
   See also individual types of musicians, e.g., PIANISTS
MUSKRATS 6514, 8282, 13082
MUSLIMS 4421
   children of 914
MUSS, SULTAN OF MALI (fl. 1824-) 10678
MUSTANGS (ANIMALS) 991, 8074
MYSTERY AND DETECTIVE STORIES 138, 142, 143, 194, 319, 322, 403,
   407, 423, 429, 509, 599, 684, 843, 844, 943, 976, 988, 1043, 1063, 1201,
   1217, 1221, 1222, 1224, 1293, 1391, 1412, 1559, 1614, 1836, 1837, 1891,
   1892, 1893, 1903, 1904, 1905, 1906, 1972, 1985, 1986, 1987, 2247, 2278,
   2427, 2428, 2556, 2797, 2798, 2799, 2856, 2882, 2883, 2884, 3061, 3062,

3161, 3177, 3194, 3204, 3248, 3306, 3445, 3704, 3730, 3857, 3861, 3884,
3889, 3900, 4102, 4103, 4104, 4105, 4110, 4119, 4139, 4260, 4261, 4307,
4370, 4393, 4394, 4398, 4399, 4483, 4668, 4843, 4847, 4849, 4850, 4851,
4853, 4880, 4893, 4919, 4925, 5013, 5078, 5084, 5085, 5094, 5125, 5137,
5163, 5314, 5468, 5546, 5553, 5598, 5599, 5600, 5634, 5686, 5976, 5980,
6043, 6092, 6105, 6205, 6264, 6350, 6415, 6601, 6879, 6980, 7107, 7250,
7421, 7540, 7557, 7603, 7659, 7730, 7738, 7739, 8008, 8167, 8168, 8173,
8174, 8175, 8177, 8178, 8179, 8255, 8534, 8535, 8536, 8550, 8573, 8670,
8682, 8704, 8712, 9030, 9130, 9186, 9198, 9218, 9319, 9365, 9375, 9508,
9602, 9803, 9823, 9945, 9987, 10022, 10152, 10153, 10268, 10334, 10363,
10401, 10407, 10413, 10479, 10673, 10674, 10740, 10829, 10830, 11091,
11371, 11373, 11389, 11396, 11420, 11484, 11583, 11714, 11769, 11809,
11952, 11960, 12055, 12319, 12382, 12502, 12527, 12852, 12853, 12981,
13009, 13262, 13286, 13294, 13419, 13452, 13517, 13598, 13642, 13734,
13735, 13739, 13806, 13819, 13821, 13825, 13894, 13992, 14023, 14097,
14105, 14125, 14128, 14228, 14408, 14437, 14445, 14469, 14470, 14542,
14595, 14596, 14803, 15472, 15473, 15479, 15557, 15705, 15808, 15870,
15886, 15912, 15913, 15952, 15965, 15976, 15977, 15978, 15979, 15980,
15981, 15982, 16033, 16114, 16115, 16116, 16117, 16118, 16119, 16120,
16223, 16384, 16891, 16892, 16944, 16954, 16977, 17072, 17075, 17086,
17093, 17120, 17209, 17288, 17395, 17411, 17424, 17507, 17519, 17524,
17526, 17527, 17528, 17530, 17757, 17790, 17829, 17830, 17831, 17832,
17833, 17835, 17836, 17837, 17838, 17960, 18008, 18085, 18097, 18100,
18125, 18260, 18265, 18266, 18285, 18316, 18328, 18389, 18430, 18433,
18466
MYTHOLOGY 1377, 2548, 8337, 11421, 12795
  African 673
  Babylonian 5737
  Celtic 8334
  Chinese 1657
  classical 1481, 4020, 7906
  dictionaries 13263
  Egyptian 11294
  Greek 768, 3877, 4019, 4546, 5696, 5698, 6661, 6662, 6664, 7247, 7248,
    8335, 11445, 13973, 13974, 15347, 15348, 15349, 15350, 15352, 16922,
    17077
  Norse 1132, 3876, 4555, 5333, 5740, 8327, 8640, 9815
  San 15226
  Spanish 3146
  Yoruban 6892

- N -

NADER, RALPH (1934-) 13109
NAIMBANA (KOYA CHIEF) 8885
NAMATH, JOSEPH WILLIAM "JOE WILLIE" (1943-) 1535, 2615, 9017, 11880,
  13106
NAMES, GEOGRAPHICAL 12664
  United States 381, 6048, 13716
    Colorado 6219
    Nebraska 5984
    Ohio 13212
NAMES, PERSONAL 287, 2320, 5448, 6775, 10212, 10953, 11074, 12499,
  12536, 12664, 16173, 17358, 17993

NAMIBIA 10823
  history 15227
NANSEN, FRIDTJOF (1861-1930) 1583
NANTUCKET (MASSACHUSETTS) 7244, 17060
NAPOLEON I (1769-1821) 14423
NARANJO, MICHAEL (1944-) 12725
NARCOTIC HABIT see DRUG ABUSE
NASCIMENTO, EDSON ARANTES DO see PELE
NASR, AL-DIN, KHWAJAH 9674
NASR, AL-DIN, MULLA 9675
NASSAU (BAHAMAS) 5788
NAST, THOMAS (1840-1902) 17273
NATIONALISM--Africa 8496
NATURAL DISASTERS 4627, 14528, 14807
NATURAL HISTORY 365, 366, 655, 831, 833, 1027, 1264, 1414, 1415, 1493,
  1801, 1943, 1951, 1954, 2477, 2737, 2738, 3080, 3082, 3698, 4065, 4159,
  5480, 5922, 6738, 6960, 6982, 8096, 8685, 9173, 9482, 10967, 12220,
  13116, 13171, 13592, 13949, 14355, 14432, 14444, 14648, 14788, 14790,
  14943, 15031, 15159, 15288, 15306, 16809, 18235, 18627
  Africa 12298
  Canada 9923
    Northwest Territories 2535
      Bathurst Island 16541
  collectors and collecting--technique 8825
  conservation 9199, 11541
  Great Lakes region 352, 5249
  guide-books 17942
  miscellanea 9926
  New Zealand 4621
  North America 1706
  Ontario 9415, 13117
  outdoor books 7118
  pictorial works 784, 8300, 9149, 9152, 10791
  poetry 47, 784, 1095, 1317, 2394, 3083, 3478, 4299, 5908, 5911, 5915,
    5916, 6488, 7698, 8955, 9054, 10281, 11532, 11727, 12292, 12397, 13153,
    16611, 16725
  United States 2476, 2477
    Maryland 1552
    Michigan 12149
    Minnesota 8569, 8570, 8571, 9923, 13115, 13117
    Okefenoke Swamp 13802
    Ozark Mountain region 14290
    Virginia 1552
    Wisconsin 17942
NATURAL RESOURCES 13967, 13968, 16364
  Michigan 13550
NATURALISTS 1738, 2198, 3513, 3664, 4910, 5132, 7196, 8224, 15666a,
  16169, 16308, 16723
  correspondence 15360
  England 15420
NATURE IN LITERATURE 5661
NATURE PHOTOGRAPHY 8300, 9852, 15031
NAVAHO INDIANS 39, 166, 356, 515, 564, 636, 637, 638, 1005, 1058, 1171,
  1468, 1469, 1594, 1642, 1759, 1789, 1840, 2038, 2539, 2557, 2974, 2975,
  2978, 3315, 3481, 3490, 3492, 4328, 4329, 4331, 4967, 5174, 5422, 5424,
  6776, 6837, 7358, 8166, 8374, 8539, 9362, 10225, 10370, 11087, 11626,
  11742, 11754, 12178, 12282, 12334, 12775, 13015, 13534, 13535, 14098,

14232, 14463, 14477, 14800, 17980, 18198
art 7315
biography 8375, 9247, 12723
handicraft 7315
history 11033, 18384
language 3501, 4328, 4329, 12446, 12892
  books in 7593
legends 4980, 7754, 9248, 12446, 14553
poetry 11544
religion 18384
social life and customs 9248
textile industry and fabrics 4773, 9114
trading posts 9114
NAVAL BATTLES 1124
NAVIGATION 10304, 10313, 16870, 16871, 16873
Polynesia 13689
NAYLOR, PHYLLIS (REYNOLDS), (1933-) 12679
NEAR EAST see MIDDLE EAST
NEBRASKA 893, 1076, 3522, 4880, 8642, 16622
biography 16401
history 4880, 16401, 18128
  pictorial works 12832
NEEDLEWORK 8338, 10657, 10807, 12128, 13267, 13327, 16009, 17352, 18076
NEHRU, JAWAHARLAL (1889-1964) 11773
NEIGHBORS see COMMUNITY LIFE
NELSON, CINDY (1955-) 9060
NEPAL 4959, 14177
  description and travel 8110
  social life and customs 8110, 10287
NEPTUNE (PLANET) 759
NEPTUNE'S CAR (CLIPPER SHIP) 10300
NERVOUS SYSTEM 9471, 17625
NETHERLANDS 3772, 4674, 4677, 4680, 4682, 4966, 5995, 7239, 7443, 8688, 11037, 16093, 18029
history 4669, 4670
  War of Independence (1556-1648) 12350
  German occupation (1940-1945) 5601, 6220, 9140, 14224, 15530, 16750, 17226
  1945- 14223
social conditions 14223
NEUROSES 8283
NEVADA 18202
history 12370
NEW, CHARLES (1879-1957) 6102
NEW CASTLE (DELAWARE) 4333
history 12015
NEW DENVER (BRITISH COLUMBIA)--Relocation Center 16614
NEW ENGLAND 223, 224, 236, 1568, 3669, 4119, 7584, 7730, 17125
history 16154
social life and customs--Colonial Period (ca. 1600-1775) 11352
NEW GUINEA 941, 11400, 16073
social life and customs 13768
NEW HAMPSHIRE 1793, 5479, 5583, 11985
NEW JERSEY 4449, 6242, 14440
history
  Colonial Period (ca. 1600-1775) 4367, 12626
  Revolution (1775-1783) 12626, 12728

NEW MEXICO   3493, 3497, 3964, 5423, 7466
   history--to 1848   12650, 14820
NEW ORLEANS, BATTLE OF (1815)   11187, 16632, 17849
NEW ORLEANS (LOUISIANA)   416, 419, 1993, 6154, 11012
   history   3298, 7630, 7820, 9673
   streets   3298
NEW YEAR'S DAY   7437, 9292, 10340, 10756, 11163, 15463
   Chinese   3325
NEW YORK (CITY)   1001, 1251, 1252, 3841, 4130, 4638, 5295, 6731, 6734,
   7318, 8230, 8828, 10615, 10667, 10669, 11414, 11416, 11612, 12170, 12507,
   12609, 12765, 13270, 14973, 15260, 15627, 16621, 16623, 16703, 16704,
   16705, 16707, 16708, 16804, 17361, 17795, 17796, 17797, 17986, 18505
   description and travel   6032, 14929
   history   3182, 4588, 5889, 11002
     Colonial Period (ca. 1600-1775)   3703, 5425, 7590, 11585
     Revolution (1775-1783)   3982, 7590, 14027
   mayors   9534
   poor   12130
   social conditions   7446, 9537
   social life and customs   8738, 14235
     Colonial Period (ca. 1600-1775)   5425, 12504, 16090
   underground areas   10376
   Zoological Park   15197
NEW YORK (STATE)   3690, 6242, 12409
   antiquities   16441
   description and travel   5874
   history   5271, 11620, 18382
     Colonial Period (ca. 1600-1775)   3396, 4905
     18th century   1585
NEW ZEALAND   942, 2822, 4621, 9549, 9551
NEWSPAPERS   364, 7610, 7924, 10611, 11180
NEWTON-JOHN, OLIVIA (1948-)   9072
NEZ PERCE INDIANS   992, 1752, 14897
   biography   7168
   legends   7978, 11731
   wars (1877)   6117, 13726, 14104
NIAGARA (ONTARIO)--historic houses, etc.   16341
NIAGARA FALLS   3096
NICKLAUS, JACK WILLIAM (1940-)   4786, 17219
NICKNAMES   11074, 14002, 14303
NIGER   3025
   social life and customs   5458
NIGER RIVER   5888
NIGERIA   37, 79, 674, 675, 1031, 1333, 1584, 1617, 2039, 2040, 2041, 2302,
   2341, 2501, 3633, 5115, 5321, 5322, 6112, 6346, 6770, 7709, 8967, 9689,
   10308, 11138, 13063, 13124, 15128, 16269, 16800, 16801, 16934, 17574,
   17970, 18003, 18361
   biography   4809
   description and travel   4808, 9722, 9873, 13069
     poetry   17252
   history   5315, 5365
     1851-1899   8882
     1865-1898   5315, 5320
     19th-20th century   8889
   native races   7642
   Northern--history
     addresses, essays, lectures   7122

English occupation 5317
politics and government 17576
social life and customs 5314, 5317, 9193, 9325, 17121, 17576
social problems 5557
NIGERIAN POETRY 17250, 17251
NIGHT 847, 1240, 2070, 2152, 2383, 2389, 2400, 3389, 3682, 3784, 3934,
    4729, 5060, 6188, 8591, 9214, 9490, 9587, 10058, 10059, 12059, 12614,
    14813, 15098, 16896, 17114, 18619, 18628
    poetry 5915
NIGHTINGALE, FLORENCE (1820-1910) 3887, 8741, 12876, 18348
NIKOLAEVA, VALENTINA VLADIMOROVNA TERESHKOVA (1937-) 15488
NILE VALLEY 12627
NKRUMAH, KWAME (1909-1972) 13857
NOAH (BIBLICAL CHARACTER) 8863
NOATICA INDIANS--legends 3639
NOBEL PRIZES 13399
NOGUCHI, HIDEYO (1876-1928) 4474
NOGUCHI, ISAMU (1904-) 16898
NOISE 256, 6460, 6531, 11364, 11490, 11963, 12669, 16722, 16787, 18077
    pollution 9337
NONVERBAL COMMUNICATION 5568, 6698
NOOTKA INDIANS 16423
NORSEMEN see VIKINGS
NORTH AMERICA--antiquities 15023
NORTH CAROLINA 1356, 3110, 4267
    description and travel 1359, 14431
    history 17475
        Colonial period (ca. 1600-1775) 2672, 10175, 13863
        Revolution (1775-1783) 10175
    social life and customs 7240
NORTH DAKOTA 894, 2097, 2205, 3026, 6089, 14577, 16602, 16603, 16604,
    18061
    biography 14576, 14578
    farm life 14575
NORTH POLE 537
NORTHMEN see VIKINGS
NORTHWEST
    Old 3139
        history 7862, 7863, 11223, 16677, 17933
            Revolution (1775-1783) 10493, 11014
    Pacific--history 928
NORWAY 725, 871, 996, 4550, 4556, 4558, 7681, 11510
    social life and customs 4556
NORWEGIAN AMERICANS 4437, 4438, 4554, 7868, 8195, 8430, 8526
NOVA SCOTIA 4070
NOVELISTS--American 2490
NUBIA 5073
NUMBER GAMES see GAMES--NUMBER
NUMBER THEORY 93, 97, 106, 118, 119, 351, 750, 756, 1431, 1447, 2926,
    3291, 3370, 6375, 6402, 7338, 10121, 10356, 10523, 11139, 11141, 11144,
    11146, 11147, 11148, 11536, 12994, 13758, 14168, 14801, 15799, 15873,
    16112, 17415, 17823
    poetry 9031, 13132
    See also SET THEORY
NURSERY RHYMES 73, 238, 304, 548, 1230, 1767, 1769, 1770, 2234, 2303,
    2304, 2407, 2696, 2811, 2812, 2813, 3387, 4060, 4062, 4629, 4639, 4684,
    4810, 4995, 4996, 5406, 5416, 5462, 5902, 6432, 6505, 7016, 7112, 7251,

7253, 8016, 8412, 8924, 8934, 9181, 9182, 10283, 10595, 10861, 12235, 12374, 12422, 12512, 12513, 12514, 12515, 12516, 12517, 12747, 13147, 13148, 13149, 13499, 13563, 13838, 13977, 14055, 14217, 14292, 14569, 14668, 15330, 16084, 16091, 16095, 16145, 16739, 17026, 17027, 17564, 17918, 17998, 18242, 18243, 18300
  Chinese 18351
  Danish 1830
  English 238, 6228
  French 6228
  Japanese 4654
  Mexican 14659
  Russian 18519
  Spanish 259, 6485, 6487, 17495
NURSERY SCHOOLS 287, 8800, 12421, 14535, 18190
  music 1773, 12281, 18510
NURSES AND NURSING 982, 983, 1786, 1931, 3249, 3847, 3887, 6205, 7265, 7271, 8116, 8741, 8742, 10198, 10199, 10200, 11436, 12272, 12580, 12876, 12884, 13711, 14607, 15059, 16378, 17353, 18348
  biography 3847, 3849, 4697, 4698, 5355, 7169
  history 4697, 4698
  vocational guidance 9564, 9568
NUTRITION 9355, 17707
NUTS 5213
NZINGA (QUEEN OF MATAMBA), (1582-1663) 16555

- O -

OAK 16997
OAKLEY, ANNIE (1860-1926) 231, 3834, 7188, 10046, 17620, 18074
OAKVILLE (ONTARIO) 2249
OATMAN, OLIVE ANN (1838?-1903) 10233
OBASEKI, AGBO 8882
OBEDIENCE 4055, 6703
OBESITY 1815, 1854, 2781, 16005
O'BRYANT, TILMON B. (1920-) 6358
OBSERVATION 12096, 18371
OBSTETRICIANS--Canada--Ontario 18088
OCCULT SCIENCES 7569, 10658, 13906, 17581
OCCUPATIONS see VOCATIONAL GUIDANCE
OCEAN 9932
  bottom 6995
  currents 3598
  travel 2903, 3679, 7848, 8253
  waves 18555
OCEANIA--discovery and exploration 15301
OCEANOGRAPHY 734, 1085, 1522, 2048, 2231, 2232, 3121, 4035, 5105, 6651, 10820, 11382, 11884, 14010, 18041
  experiments 15757
  vocational guidance 14644, 17562
OCRACOKE ISLAND (NORTH CAROLINA)
  description and travel 6962
OCTOPUS 3959, 10060, 15498, 17363
  habits and behavior 8580
OFFICE MANAGEMENT 1106

OGLETHORPE, JAMES EDWARD (1696-1785) 1702
O'HARA, DEE (1935-) 3847
OHIO 895, 3027, 6004, 12501, 12588, 14243, 15766, 16827
  antiquities 13855
  biography 7105
  boundary dispute (1835) 6755
  description and travel 6193, 13536
  drama 5247
  governors 7110
  history 387, 971, 1641, 4325, 4708, 4710, 4711, 5604, 6158, 6193, 7105,
    8690, 9924, 9944, 12002, 12945, 14457, 14610, 15248, 17891, 18298
    anecdotes, facetiae, satire, etc. 14248, 15249
    examinations, questions, etc. 18287
    local 8968
    1784-1813
      drama 5247
    Western Reserve--pictorial works 2752
  social life and customs 8689
OHIO RIVER 5099
OHIO RIVER VALLEY--history 12878, 16726
OIL WELLS see PETROLEUM
OILFIELDS see PETROLEUM
OILS AND FATS 17378
OJIBWAY INDIANS 7594
OKEFENOKEE SWAMP 4157, 13802
OKLAHOMA 896, 909, 1193, 3028, 6981, 7062
  description and travel 8933
  history 3977, 9625
OLD AGE 1805, 1942, 2605, 3584, 3859, 4135, 5664, 7552, 8222, 8462, 9488,
    11970, 13801
OLD NORTHWEST see NORTHWEST--OLD
OLYMPIC GAMES 11896, 17484
  ancient 6939
  Revival (1896-) 4863, 5653, 5882, 5887, 6721, 8161, 13395, 16475, 17485
  winter 11917
OMAHA INDIAN RESERVATION (NEBRASKA) 10187
OMAHA INDIANS 10187, 18071
  biography 4249
O'MEARA, WALTER (1897-) 13119
ONASSIS, JACQUELINE (1929-) 11750
ONEIDA INDIANS 12727, 14329
ONONDAGA INDIANS 16925
ONTARIO 2307, 4244, 4274, 4385, 4579, 7757, 13136, 13142, 16113
  description and travel 16926
    guide-books 13138
    views 13139
  history 517, 519, 974, 11324
    miscellanea 13137
    pictorial works 12159
  police 1088
  See also under other terms with subheading "Ontario", e.g., HISTORIC
    SITES--ONTARIO
OPERAS 6291, 13168, 16284, 17163
  history and criticism 6653
  librettos 12080
  stories, plots, etc. 2565, 2576, 2577, 4336, 12373, 17283

OPERATIONS 13329
OPOSSUMS 1599, 3155, 3934, 3936, 3937, 11251, 12186, 12297
OPTICAL ILLUSIONS 574, 1307, 13279, 15752
ORAIBI (ARIZONA)--description and travel 9115
ORANGE 16502
ORCHESTRA 1017, 3912, 5363, 10136, 13833
ORDNANCE--manufacture 5404
OREGON 3556, 11376
OREGON TRAIL 6138, 7933, 13333, 14808, 16263
ORGANICULTURE 5798, 9974
ORIENTEERING 2033
ORIGAMI 604, 7712, 14912, 16849, 18373
ORKNEY ISLANDS 4429, 10648, 10649
ORNITHOLOGY 14972
ORPHANS 180, 183, 219, 258, 328, 560, 689, 690, 704, 866, 1623, 2177,
    2280, 2489, 2584, 2604, 2721, 2960, 2967, 2968, 3323, 3519, 3826, 4017,
    4070, 4369, 4371, 4401, 4497, 4583, 4873, 4887, 5281, 5577, 5583, 5614,
    5743, 5788, 6004, 6049, 6469, 6602, 6663, 7066, 7484, 7496, 7937, 8466,
    8468, 9252, 9591, 9805, 10405, 10408, 10546, 10839, 11108, 11120, 11184,
    12002, 12238, 12428, 12906, 12927, 13217, 13320, 13603, 13625, 13655,
    13828, 13924, 14287, 14324, 14564, 15820, 15957, 16353, 16376, 16381,
    16411, 16428, 16573, 16621, 16622, 17225, 17231, 17865, 17868, 17886,
    17957, 18044, 18178, 18282
ORR, BOBBY (1948-) 2612, 5273, 9015, 10910, 11861
ORTIZ, JUAN (d. 1543?) 16180
OSCEOLA (SEMINOLE CHIEF), (1804-1838) 235, 3511, 7178, 7355, 7595,
    11479, 16592
OSTRICHES 5907, 6550, 8581
OTTAWA (ONTARIO) 15903, 16229
    history 4154
OTTAWA INDIANS 5828
    biography 7179, 7941, 13461, 17344
OTTERS 346, 561, 1281, 1405, 2780, 7766, 7781, 8281, 9304, 9773, 10354,
    10790, 11903, 12188, 15524, 18135
OUTDOOR LIFE 366, 11322, 13116, 13171, 13203, 14163, 17869
OUTDOOR RECREATION--vocational guidance 11226
OUTER BANKS (NORTH CAROLINA) 16717, 16718
OUTER SPACE--exploration 3527, 6522, 6723, 15758
OVERLAND JOURNEYS TO THE PACIFIC (U.S.) 613, 1589, 2712, 7933,
    11280, 11314, 14703, 16307
OWENS, JESSE (1913-1983) 9535, 13216
OWLS 2082, 2241, 2865, 6347, 6594, 6615, 6751, 7639, 7962, 8422, 8576,
    8808, 10067, 11003, 11200, 12525, 13501, 13650, 15009
OXFORD (OHIO)--history 8669
OZARK MOUNTAIN REGION--description and travel 14290
OZARK MOUNTAINS 3383, 3589
OZETTE INDIAN VILLAGE 9856

- P -

PACIFIC COAST INDIANS--wars with (1847-1865) 6888
PACIFISM 863, 5510
PACKAGING 16471
PAGE, ALLAN (1945-) 1177

PAIGE, LEROY "SATCHEL" (1906?-1982) 14738
PAINTERS
  biography 12719
  United States 10525, 12602
PAINTING 1386, 2076, 2868, 3294, 8516, 9700, 11729, 11753, 12241, 12395,
  17963
  Belgian 4234
  Chinese 10718
  history 226, 329, 1180, 1181
  Japanese 10718
  technique 3087, 7896, 7897, 11690, 15190, 15252, 16097, 17474, 17698
PAIUTE INDIANS 5857, 7806, 9086, 17124, 18202
  legends 8329, 13266
  music 13666
PAKISTAN--description and travel 10294
PAKISTANIS--in the United States 873
PALEO INDIANS 9117
  Washington (State) 9853
PALEOBOTANY see PLANTS--FOSSIL
PALEONTOLOGY see FOSSILS
PALESTINE--civilization 12760
PALMER, ALICE ELVIRA (FREEMAN), (1855-1902) 6026
PALMER, ARNOLD (1929-) 13102
PALMER, WILLIAM JACKSON (1836-1909) 17893
PALMISTRY 16842
PANAMA 12347
  history 14383
PANAMA CANAL 14383
PANDAS 1901, 5239, 7448, 10065, 13540, 14143, 17966
PANKHURST, DAME CHRISTABEL (1880-1958) 12855
PANKHURST, EMMELINE (GOULDEN), (1858-1928) 12855
PANKHURST, ESTELLE SYLVIA (1882-1960) 12855
PANTOMIME 4368, 4372, 6650, 11658, 14653
PAPAGO INDIANS 3480, 3483, 3488, 3499, 6240
  legends 921
PAPER CRAFTS 199, 316, 406, 604, 3328, 10504, 10779, 11560, 13406,
  13539, 13609, 13626, 13627, 14643, 15253, 15753, 16735, 16736; see also
  ORIGAMI
PAPER MAKING AND TRADE 2520, 3773
PAPIER-MACHE 9289, 9468
PARACELSUS (1493-1541) 14613
PARACHUTES 5193
PARADES 5053, 8457, 11555, 16941
PAREJA, JUAN DE (1606-1670) 4755
PARENT AND CHILD 1543, 1941, 2058, 3191, 3352, 3872, 3985, 4153, 7284,
  7428, 7445, 7857, 8628, 9733, 9908, 10074, 10182, 12678, 12956, 15170,
  15931, 16208, 17134, 17981
  pictorial works 14167
PARICUTIN (VOLCANO) 10729
PARIS (FRANCE) 200, 997, 1388, 1677, 2958, 6213, 10217
  description and travel 14930
  history
    1589-1789 9672
    1940-1945 17330
PARK, BRAD (1948-) 2633
PARK, MUNGO (1771-1806) 17167
PARK CITY (UTAH) 13928

PARK RANGERS 14915
  vocational guidance 8186
PARKER, ELY SAMUEL (1825-1895) 5776
PARKER, QUANAH (1854-1911) 491, 8547, 11900
PARKER, WILLIAM 865
PARKS, GORDON (1912-) 7733, 17055
PARKS, ROSA (1913-) 7310, 12090
PARKS 4932, 9855, 12197, 13934, 14791, 14862, 14915, 17979
  Canada 13140, 13141, 13143, 13144
  city 997
  rangers 3785
  vocational guidance 11226
PARODIES 10976
PARROTS 1670, 4277, 4418, 18549
PARSONS, JOHNNIE (1918-) 13089
PARTIES 4746, 5388, 6196, 11681, 13872
PASSOVER 15612, 15730
PASTEL DRAWING 15190
PATERNO, JOE (1926-) 12780
PATRICK, SAINT (373?-463?) 14281
PATRIOTIC POETRY 18225
PATRIOTISM 1625, 17618, 18225
PATTEN, JOSHUA A. (1826 or 1827-1857) 10300
PATTEN, MARY ANNE (BROWN), (1837-?) 10300
PAUL, WESLEY (1970?-) 6087
PAVLOVA, ANNA (1881-1931) 11584
PAWNEE INDIANS 9684
  legends 9354
PEA PATCH ISLAND 4391
PEACE 5510, 5750, 6365, 13507, 18576
PEACE CORPS (U.S.) 10201
  Ecuador 4216
  Ghana 4695
PEACOCKS 18170
PEAFOWL 11734
PEALE, CHARLES WILSON (1741-1827) 5502
PEARL DIVING AND DIVERS 13010
PEARL HARBOR, ATTACK ON (1941) 7022, 16710
PEARY, ROBERT EDWIN (1856-1920) 537
PECCARIES 8248
PEDDLERS AND PEDDLING 6075, 8672, 11981, 12112, 13217, 14512, 15849
PELE (1940-) 2637, 6677, 7527, 7825, 11898, 16699
PELICANS 1399, 15203, 18170
  poetry 10467
PEN DRAWING 18485
PENCIL DRAWING 17700
PENGUINS 719, 783, 4801, 5720, 5721, 6267, 9311, 10599, 12291, 13493
  habits and behavior 16828
PENN, WILLIAM (1644-1718) 311, 4992, 6146, 7205, 7883, 16596, 17939
PENNEY, JAMES CASH (1875-1971) 8711
PENNSYLVANIA 897, 3029, 6077, 6381, 10553, 12207, 17338
  foreign population 17471
  history 12024, 16398
    Colonial period (ca. 1600-1775) 10554, 12696, 16270
    18th century 815
    French and Indian War (1754-1760) 2280
    Revolution (1775-1783) 5428, 6675, 10554

social life and customs--Colonial period (ca. 1600-1775) 17044
PENNSYLVANIA DUTCH   2095, 3061, 4636, 4640, 4643, 8926, 12204, 12205,
    12677
PERADE, MME. FARIEU DE LA   see   VERCHERES, MARIE MADELEINE
    JARRET DE
PERCEPTION   88, 1432, 10025, 14732, 14733, 14975
PERCUSSION INSTRUMENTS--construction   9756
PERIODICITY   14787
PERLEY, HELEN MEWER   9256
PERRY, JAMES ALEXANDER (1801-1881)   11779
PERRY, MATTHEW GALBRAITH (1794-1858)   8878, 10128
PERRY, OLIVER HAZARD (1785-1819)   11044, 11779
PERSHING, JOHN JOSEPH (1860-1948)   6153
PERSIA   see   IRAN
PERSONALITY   4731
PERU   3495, 4276, 16512
    antiquities   1205, 6917
    natural history   8971
    social life and customs   11598
PETERS, PHILLIS   see   WHEATLEY, PHILLIS
PETERS, THOMAS (1738?-1792)   8052
PETIGRU, JAMES LEWIS (1789-1863)   5285
PETROLEUM   2522, 3980, 3999, 10561, 12697, 12849, 14364
    industry and trade   5033, 12711, 14364
    workers   12711
PETROLOGY   13437
    Canada--Ontario   8136
    United States   11052
        Michigan   12150
PETS   161, 284, 497, 621, 1018, 1373, 1650, 1943, 2196, 2641, 2913, 3141,
    3177, 3435, 3949, 4373, 4648, 5138, 5152, 5423, 6433, 6452, 7320, 7515,
    8000, 8965, 9391, 9489, 9602, 9604, 9651, 9652, 9655, 9732, 10566, 10940,
    11757, 13261, 13301, 13763, 13772, 14213, 15174, 15636, 15915, 16206,
    16224, 16264, 16314, 16430, 16744, 17118, 17119, 17639, 18239; see also
    specific animals, e.g., DOGS
PHARO (EGYPT)   12288
PHILADELPHIA (PENNSYLVANIA)   4388, 6071, 12206
    description and travel   7591
    history   4641
        Colonial period (ca. 1600-1775)   7591, 12197
        Revolution (1775-1783)   7591
PHILANTHROPISTS   3854
PHILIP, KING (METACOMET), (SACHEM OF THE WAMPANOAGS), (d. 1676)
    5276
PHILIP, SCOTTY (1858-1911)   17268
PHILIPPINES, REPUBLIC OF THE   2816, 9677
    description and travel   16939
    history--1812-1898   14220
PHILLEO, PRUDENCE CRANDALL   see   CRANDALL, PRUDENCE
PHILLIPS, JOHN (d. 1883)   453
PHILOSOPHERS   299
PHOENICIA--civilization--10th century B.C.   9719
PHOTOGRAPHERS   6312, 7479, 7733, 11595, 14854, 17055
    war   8545
PHOTOGRAPHY   361, 787, 1643, 4431, 6361, 8480, 8686, 9284, 9980, 10375,
    10431, 10507, 12088, 12896, 14444, 15620, 16490, 17694, 17969
    of animals   5035

artistic 4749, 6924, 9372, 10777
   of children 4749
   Colorado--history 11595
   of rocks 12559
PHOTOSYNTHESIS 8706
PHOTOTHERAPY 8706
PHYSICAL EDUCATION AND TRAINING 584, 5451, 7824
PHYSICAL FITNESS 584, 5451, 5503, 10712, 15099, 17483
PHYSICALLY HANDICAPPED 212, 512, 518, 540, 560, 635, 649, 976, 1224,
   1265, 1342, 1646, 2392, 2671, 2853, 2900, 2987, 3165, 3197, 3321, 3322,
   3398, 3428, 3602, 3995, 4571, 4572, 4659, 4757, 5354, 5659, 5895, 6367,
   6471, 6599, 6638, 7224, 8006, 10564, 10594, 10935, 10938, 10940, 11162,
   11186, 12079, 12552, 12587, 12916, 13632, 14015, 14275, 14638, 14953,
   14954, 14955, 14972, 15620, 15623, 15935, 16011, 16042, 16068, 16203,
   16322, 16325, 16428, 16493, 16530, 16757, 16806, 17063, 17124, 17228,
   18130, 18178, 18253, 18270, 18418
   biography 6716, 6825
   blindness 2744, 2745, 3429, 5316, 5896, 7116, 7721, 8006, 8093, 8150,
     9218, 9645, 11310, 14825, 14975, 16747, 17190, 17192, 17704, 17835,
     18158, 18195, 18255, 18422
   cerebral palsy 9788
   deafness 4132, 7116, 10653, 11401, 13578, 14486, 15934, 16060, 17402,
     18194, 18249, 18299
     means of communication 3281, 5568, 6992
   hearing impaired 10929
   rehabilitation 18196
PHYSICIANS 427, 657, 666, 3607, 4484, 5147, 5490, 5611, 5786, 7058, 7265,
   7440, 10810, 12003, 12092, 12271, 13057, 14996, 16252, 18192, 18475
   Ontario 15500
   United States 10527
PHYSICISTS 5492, 14614
PHYSICS 834, 1012, 2128, 2130, 2206, 3305, 6302, 6530, 13684, 13754,
   16369, 18091
   experiments 5817, 5957, 11687, 12199, 12200, 14250, 16365, 17805
PHYSIOLOGY 9530, 9531, 11357, 11387, 11463, 11464, 14151, 18558
   history 14366
   See also ANATOMY
PIANISTS 5673, 7437, 13597
PIANKHI (KING OF ETHIOPIA), (c. 751-710 B.C.) 9255
PIANO
   methods 2896
   music 8664
   tuning 6978
PICASSO, PABLO (1881-1973) 7302
PICCOLO, BRIAN (1943-1970) 12458
PICNICS 10323
PICTURE-WRITING--Indian 4872, 11326, 11327
PIEGAN INDIANS 5730
PIGEONS 505, 506, 6957, 7114, 10805, 11132, 12543, 13846, 16359, 18544
PIGS 791, 1218, 1678, 2319, 2852, 4528, 5093, 6511, 7035, 8269, 8585, 9201,
   11005, 12922, 13210, 13224, 13407, 13703, 14164, 14165, 15624, 15712,
   16188, 16193, 16195, 16349, 17212, 18486
   wild 6745
PIKE, ZEBULON MONTGOMERY (1779-1813) 680, 16283
PIKE'S PEAK (COLORADO)--gold discoveries 5358a
PILGRIMS (NEW ENGLAND COLONISTS) 1288, 2558, 3473, 5623, 6042, 7180,
   7438, 7628, 7931, 7940, 11017, 11355, 15658

PIMA INDIANS 17630
  legends 921, 15491
  social life and customs 15492
PIÑATAS 2279
PINKERTON, ALLAN (1819-1884) 485, 1956
PIONEERS see FRONTIER AND PIONEER LIFE
PIRATES 418, 2679, 3322, 4101, 6005, 6807, 6833, 7183, 7927, 8837, 9752,
  9952, 10050, 12347, 12418, 14255, 14408, 14823, 16129, 16299, 16330,
  16859, 17596, 17773, 17846
PITCHER, MOLLY see McCAULEY, MARY (LUDWIG) HAYS
PLAGUES 9204
PLAINS INDIANS 1544, 14695, 14979
PLANETS 759, 761, 2118, 2138
PLANTATION LIFE 14020
  Chesapeake Bay region 17043
  Louisiana 11511, 12930
PLANTE, JACQUES (1929-) 5573
PLANTS 242, 576, 1697, 1799, 2143, 2932, 3801, 5207, 7017, 7119, 7324,
  7468, 8405, 8504, 8854, 10093, 10342, 11133, 11592, 13356, 13822, 13960,
  14082, 15123, 15295, 15298, 15300, 15324, 15769, 17664, 18593
  in art 7896
  climbing 15298
  collection and preservation 18550
  cultivated 2477
    history 7945
  diseases 2272
  edible 1287, 14083
  fossil 4177, 14664
  house 2555, 5325, 5800, 5802, 10029, 12208, 13392, 15289, 16034
  poetry 12510
  poisonous 2739, 10814, 10817
  propagation 17635
  rare--United States 8402
PLASTICS 7562
PLATE TECTONICS 9784
PLAY 279, 282, 1238, 1699, 1902, 1908, 1910, 1913, 2173, 3630, 4741, 5679,
  5812, 5978, 6494, 6671, 6701, 7016, 8908, 8996, 9216, 9257, 10079, 10110,
  10738, 11519, 12116, 12261, 15839, 16143, 17761, 18006, 18131, 18191,
  18277, 18461, 18467, 18579
  poetry 9032, 12280
PLAYGROUNDS 12845
PLAYS 40, 188, 193, 203, 292, 1323, 1471, 1645, 2073, 2159, 2286, 2944,
  2946, 2948, 3285, 3348, 3374, 3375, 4359, 4485, 5170, 5417, 5924, 6313,
  6319, 6450, 6657, 8044, 8262, 8680, 8735, 9312, 9868, 10001, 10252,
  10795, 11230, 11567, 11821, 12006, 12226, 12572, 13062, 13063, 13219,
  13220, 13250, 13541, 13644, 13895, 14414, 14552, 15922, 16335, 16437,
  16534, 18127
  Christmas 9477
  collections 13127
  production and direction 8681
  school 43, 2418, 16437
  Spanish 18503
PLUMBING 4389, 18572
PLUNKETT, JIM (1947-) 7521
PLUTO (PLANET) 759
PLYMOUTH (MASSACHUSETTS) 3791, 6393
  history 17678

POCAHONTAS (d. 1617)   2567, 4557, 5626, 10416, 11755, 13628, 15397, 17409, 17937
POETICS   4183, 12101
POETRY   168, 238, 239, 772, 773, 799, 1097, 1318, 1321, 1322, 1850, 2691, 2696, 3067, 3101, 3102, 3279, 3459, 3460, 3461, 3462, 3463, 3464, 3465, 3466, 3467, 3634, 3692, 3808, 3809, 3810, 3811, 3813, 3815, 3816, 3817, 3818, 3819, 3820, 3821, 3827, 4463, 4658, 4688, 4689, 4691, 4725, 4744, 4747, 4890, 5012, 5055, 5106, 5116, 5141, 5340, 5675, 5839, 5849, 5852, 5854, 5878, 7697, 8376, 8733, 8969, 9031, 10163, 10257, 11092, 11265, 11346, 11723, 12410, 12468, 12469, 12472, 12494, 13133, 13260, 13312, 14018, 16952, 17535
    African   354
        Ghanaian   5462
    animals   13309
    anthologies   17818
    bilingual   6488
    city and town life   1804
    collections   128, 149, 1097, 1133, 1309, 1920, 3808, 3813, 4299, 6030, 6715, 7229, 8183, 8599, 8603, 8924, 10281, 10721, 10970, 10974, 10977, 11209, 11281, 11306, 12405, 12466, 12489, 13310, 13745, 13893, 14172, 14334, 15178, 16149, 16861, 17015, 17156, 17157, 17159, 17160, 17710, 17956, 18162, 18242, 18362
    deserts   3175
    ecology   25
    friendship   5140, 16692
    girls   8590
    Haiku   784, 1315, 1319, 3147, 3166, 8954, 8955, 9276
        technique   785
        United States   11532, 12292
    humorous   56, 2217, 2219, 3100, 3459, 3462, 3463, 3816, 8310, 9055, 9639, 10979, 11270, 12510, 13163, 13888, 14612, 15703, 15863, 15938
    Indians of North America   357, 1380, 1383, 1639, 3658
        Navaho   2974, 2975
    Japanese   1099, 1315, 1319, 3147
    Korean   1099
    limericks   2212, 2216, 2219, 10465, 10470, 17496
    modern   2250
        20th century   5155, 10641, 12404
    nonsense verses   1365, 1829, 1831, 1900, 2326, 2646, 3101, 3103, 3459, 3463, 3816, 3817, 4345, 4748, 5106, 5433, 6489, 7081, 8774, 9518, 9659, 9698, 10461, 10462, 10463, 10464, 10465, 10466, 10467, 10468, 10480, 10481, 10482, 11804, 12648, 13732, 13889, 14292, 14376, 15027, 15148, 15368, 15372, 15374, 15938, 17015
        United States   13164
    of places--Nigeria   17252
    running   130
    Russian   2940
    Scottish   2691
    seashore   4239
    seasons   1656, 3626, 3818, 5928, 7960, 8734, 8880, 10155, 13311
    Sijo   1099
    sky   5848
    Spanish   3092
    Spanish American   1449
    spring   1381
    United States--Great Plains   3504
    Yoruban   1332

See also under other headings with subheading "Poetry"; see also Poetry
  by language, e.g., ENGLISH POETRY
POETS 7688, 12600, 12601
  English 1459, 17158
  United States 1137, 1458, 1459, 1460, 5131, 5133, 6438, 7817, 10533,
    12030, 15129, 17158, 17312, 17427
    (20th century) 14886
  women 14229
  See also names of specific poets, e.g., DICKINSON, EMILY
POINTE DE SABLE, JEAN BAPTISTE (1745?-1818) 7148
POLAND 15782, 15836
  history 9662
    Casimir IV (1447-1492) 9661
    occupation (1939-1945) 16448, 18326
  social life and customs 5341
POLAR REGIONS 8097, 8614, 9298
POLICE 1088, 1250, 2765, 3266, 4876, 5149, 5150, 7012, 9187, 13547,
  14458, 15843, 17976, 18119
  pictorial works 6099
  Rhodesia 13209
  vocational guidance 5801, 7012, 11764, 14160
POLIOMYELITIS 3321, 6350, 7224
POLISH AMERICANS 4642, 5295, 5549, 5621, 9918, 10593, 13670, 18356
POLITICAL PARTIES 12703, 16318
POLITICIANS 1609, 12917, 17516
  Israel 4570
  United States 306, 2453, 3350, 6040, 6391, 6392, 7818, 11986
POLITICS, PRACTICAL 5618, 11693, 12140
POLK, LEONIDAS, BISHOP (1806-1864) 5331
POLLUTION 71, 2176, 2675, 2798, 3265, 4721, 5367, 5368, 6110, 6902,
  7328, 7535, 7573, 7581, 8153, 8206, 8346, 12198, 12209, 13340, 13478,
  13754, 13755, 13967, 15632, 15924, 16795
  poetry 12066
  research 1524
POLO, MARCO (1254-1323?) 2532, 9717, 13898, 13926, 14758
POLTORATSKY, ELLEN SARAH (SOUTHEE), (1819-1908) 374
POLYNESIA 16071
POLYNESIANS 13689
POMO INDIANS 2432, 18283
PONDS 11250, 14875, 15519, 16996, 17560, 18223
  ecology 2740, 4310
PONTIAC (OTTAWA CHIEF), (d. 1769) 7179, 7356, 7941, 8497, 13461, 17344
PONTIAC'S CONSPIRACY (1763-1765) 7053
PONY EXPRESS 62, 2569, 3252
POOR--rehabilitation 16953
  addresses, essays, lectures 9527
  pictorial works 12040
POPULATION 6223, 11248, 13966, 13968
PORCUPINES 2880, 2881
PORPOISES 5284, 8423
PORTER, COLE (1891-1964) 5609
PORTUGAL 7556
  history--period of discoveries (1385-1580) 2524
  social life and customs 6794
POSTAGE STAMPS 3228, 4732
  collectors and collecting 13067, 16945, 18502
  topics

astronautics 9633
United Nations 9634
POSTAL CARDS--Ontario--Toronto 5866
POSTAL SERVICE
employees 954
letter carriers 11843
vocational guidance 6278, 13553
POTATOES 10988, 15296, 15692
POTAWATOMI INDIANS 13070
POTTER, HELEN BEATRIX (1866-1943) 241, 11923, 13840
POTTERY 2281, 3489, 5326, 6821, 8367, 8867, 15205, 16820, 17107, 17686
history 13909
United States
Arizona 18272
New Mexico 18272
POULTRY 11405
POVERTY 155, 225, 244, 652, 1402, 1996, 2547, 2655, 5638, 5813, 6354,
10370, 10573, 13038, 13787, 14878, 15624, 16010, 16358, 16402, 16623,
16953, 17187, 17651, 17828
POWELL, ADAM CLAYTON (1908-1972) 7816
POWELL, JOHN WESLEY (1834-1902) 2538, 2979, 13719, 17123, 17853
POWER (MECHANICS) 2126, 8398, 8930, 13682, 15924, 17697
POWER RESOURCES 2126, 3096, 5032, 7529, 7571, 8949, 11711, 13522,
13682, 13955, 14690, 15646
POWHATAN (INDIAN CHIEF), (d. 1618) 12701
POWHATAN INDIANS 12701, 13628
PRAIRIE DOGS 382, 3229, 4185, 5240, 11488, 14302, 15174, 15200
legends 925
PRAIRIES 12242
PRAYER 5853, 17030, 17031, 17324, 18380
PRECIOUS STONES 3520
PREHISTORIC ERA see ANTHROPOLOGY; PALEONTOLOGY
PREHISTORIC MAN see MAN--PREHISTORIC
PREJUDICES AND ANTIPATHIES 160, 1154, 1334, 1339, 1341, 1724, 1782,
1809, 2742, 3578, 3581, 3608, 3646, 3861, 3865, 3869, 3871, 3924, 4225,
4242, 4929, 5310, 5429, 5549, 5581, 6356, 6769, 6772, 6949, 7139, 7262,
7283, 7457, 7466, 8521, 8531, 8736, 9506, 9648, 9792, 10234, 10491,
10809, 11514, 12108, 12120, 12490, 12808, 12897, 12970, 13112, 14037,
14102, 14323, 14605, 14844, 14910, 16023, 16162, 16550, 16757, 17126,
17197, 17612, 18249
PRESIDENTS 14, 3140, 3188, 3848, 4023, 4231, 4365, 4543, 4577, 5624,
7182, 7195, 9270, 9558, 10494, 10539, 10540, 10552, 11181, 12083, 12800,
12872, 12883, 12901, 12902, 12920, 13075, 13200, 13335, 13432, 13566,
14195, 14647, 18081
children 14234
elections 7216, 17254
history 17681
wives 488, 492, 1812, 2777, 4575, 4576, 6028, 7171, 9668, 11262, 12029,
12875, 13946, 14647
See also names of specific presidents, e.g., LINCOLN, ABRAHAM
PRIDE, CHARLEY (1938?-) 1070
PRINCE, LUCY TERRY (d. 1821) 9513
PRINCE EDWARD ISLAND (CANADA) 12368, 17441
PRINCES AND PRINCESSES 186, 3122, 3384, 9249, 9693, 11303, 11337,
12552, 13081, 16856, 16857, 16929
PRINTERS 12002
PRINTING 955, 1073, 4316, 4764, 5496, 6024, 7301, 13591

practical 10144
vocational guidance 4599, 6279
PRINTS 7896
technique 14536, 17708
PRISONERS 1091, 3595
of war 7262
PRISONS 8528, 11410
PRIVACY, RIGHT OF 15958
PROBABILITIES 10870
PROBLEM SOLVING 2687, 3559, 3560, 3565, 3649, 4135, 7289, 7532, 8753, 12577, 12764, 13322, 13738, 14278, 14328, 15883, 16351, 16386, 16753, 18240
PROENNEKE, RICHARD 9630
PROGRAMMING (ELECTRONIC COMPUTERS)--vocational guidance 948
PROLL, ANNE MARIE (1953-) 9056
PROPHECIES (OCCULT SCIENCES) 7533
PROSPECTING 16468
PROTECTIVE SERVICES 6275
PROTESTANTISM 5967
PROVERBS 3273, 8514, 9632
Africa 10213, 10625, 13150
PRUDHOMME, DON (1941-) 8163
PSYCHIATRY 9886
PSYCHICAL RESEARCH 9765, 12792, 17581
biography 9760
PSYCHOLOGY 6991, 7586, 7588, 11206, 15684
PSYCHOTHERAPY--residential treatment 18379
PUBLIC HEALTH--vocational guidance 4901
PUBLIC SERVICES see specific types, e.g., POSTAL SERVICES
PUBLIC SPEAKING 12587, 13866
PUBLIC UTILITIES 18573
PUBLIC WELFARE 12612
PUBLISHERS AND PUBLISHING--vocational guidance 6279
PUEBLO BONITO (NEW MEXICO) 5397
PUEBLO INDIANS 21, 933, 1005, 1760, 2276, 2299, 3255, 3489, 3503, 5516, 5517, 8727, 9362, 14477, 14820, 16829
antiquities 5397
art 18272
biography 12724, 12725, 12726
history--Revolt (1680) 6094
legends 3539, 4981, 7754, 11290
rites and ceremonies 3482
PUERTO RICANS 1996, 3413, 3867, 3872, 7982, 16017
biography 372, 7461, 11610, 12785, 14294, 16245, 17024
in New York (City) 1373, 1652, 1992, 2183, 2628, 2886, 5863, 9609, 9739, 10730, 10744, 11211, 11608, 11721, 12314, 12316, 12331, 12649, 15589, 16628, 16805, 16806, 17667, 18505
in the United States 1134, 1254, 1806, 2090, 10146, 10288, 16015, 16623, 16773
PUERTO RICO 1129, 1130, 2016, 2500, 6777, 9739, 11721, 14410, 17647
description and travel 14585
folklore 249, 253
history 250, 252, 2160, 10146, 14295
politics and government 11610
cartoons and caricatures 13158
social life and customs 5342, 11624, 14585, 15081, 15789, 15790
PULITZER, JOSEPH (1847-1911) 12604, 12858

PULLMAN, GEORGE MORTIMER (1831-1897) 12598
PULSARS 1525
PUMAS 11, 1698, 6744, 7564, 8250, 11282, 14763
PUNIC WAR, SECOND (218-201 B.C.) 9079
PUPPETS AND PUPPET-PLAYS 1500, 2050, 2223, 2287, 3331, 3610, 3611,
    3720, 3721, 4146, 4266, 4269, 4386, 5417, 6654, 8197, 9102, 9103, 9601,
    10724, 11078, 11570, 13369, 13783, 14552, 14650, 14651, 14652, 16866,
    17876
PURITANS 12339, 16226
PUZZLES 569, 4362, 4568, 5985, 6050, 6587, 10961, 10962, 13500, 14675,
    14733, 16558, 17135, 17137, 17472, 17643, 17644, 17690, 17920
PYGMIES 1761, 6043, 6666, 6668, 6669, 10267, 13931, 15535
PYLE, ERNIE (1900-1945) 18075
PYRAMIDS 9365, 11204

- Q -

QUAILS 16144
QUAKERS see FRIENDS, SOCIETY OF
QUANAH (INDIAN CHIEF), (1845?-1911) 6524
QUASARS 1525
QUECHUA INDIANS 11598
QUEENS 809, 4602, 4883, 11633, 11937, 12511
QUESTIONS AND ANSWERS 1440, 1714, 2107, 8315, 10082, 10820, 14867,
    15369, 15658, 15732, 15733, 17641, 18338, 18339
QUETICO-SUPERIOR AREA 5954
QUICKSAND 4724
QUILEUTE INDIANS 1281, 9851
QUILTS AND QUILTING 12024, 16009
QUOTATIONS 8702

- R -

RABBIS 5358
RABBITS 46, 57, 905, 1168, 1960, 2396, 2472, 3076, 3108, 4074, 4680,
    4803, 4819, 6360, 6453, 6454, 6463, 6703, 8122, 8143, 8305, 8408, 8682,
    9215, 10880, 10949, 11111, 12082, 12189, 12190, 12773, 13301, 13841,
    13844, 14637, 15015, 15072, 15152, 15177, 15693, 17020, 17397, 17605,
    17815, 17871, 17995, 17999, 18043, 18487, 18608
    legends 7973
    poetry 1290, 5919
RACCOONS 1999, 2085, 2400, 4373, 8117, 9830, 10511, 11497, 11797, 12400,
    12923, 12925, 12926, 14273, 14785, 15559
RACE 11912
RACE RELATIONS 81, 653, 944, 1154, 1818, 2430, 3186, 3206, 3414, 4630,
    4694, 5725, 6578, 7783, 9000, 9648, 12167, 12567, 12713, 15216, 16651
    United States 3617, 3971, 7135, 7136, 7140
       Alabama--Montgomery 12090
RADIATION 6288
RADICALS AND RADICALISM 5016
RADIO BROADCASTING

short wave 3636
vocational guidance 6283, 7011, 11345
RADIOACTIVITY 6515, 12994
RADIOLOGISTS 12027
RADISSON, PIERRE ESPRIT (1620?-1710) 12921
RADIUM 32
RAILROAD ENGINEERS 12598
RAILROADS 517, 793, 2904, 5292, 5394, 6017, 6893, 7294, 8104, 10311,
    10578, 11151, 11498, 12011, 12673, 13418, 13469, 13708, 18268
  history 17725, 18000
  models 17693
  stations 12653
  United States
    history 8435, 11224
      Michigan 5364
        history 5117
  vocational guidance 11978
  yards 4923
RAIN AND RAINFALL 289, 1800, 2142, 5277, 5656, 6014, 6597, 8458, 10158,
    14832, 15615, 17005, 18367
RAIN FORESTS 1964
RAINBOWS 2318, 6268
RALEIGH, SIR WALTER (1552?-1618) 5742
RALEIGH'S ROANOKE COLONIES (1584-1590) 10663
RAMON Y CAJAL, SANTIAGO (1852-1934) 3607
RANCH LIFE 560, 664, 860, 2544, 2848, 3964, 6054, 7513, 7543, 7644,
    7734, 7951, 9720, 10590, 10591, 11054, 11743, 11844, 12376, 13049, 14213,
    14214, 14709, 14710, 14711, 14716, 14772, 15483, 15887, 15973, 16068,
    17865, 17866, 17868, 18005
  Australia 13206
RANDOLPH, ASA PHILIP (1889-1979) 7314
RANDOLPH, MARTHA (JEFFERSON), (1772-1836) 9672
RANSOME-KUTI, JOSIAH JESSE (1855-1930) 4809
RASSIN (CHIEF OF MAFONDA), (1825-1890) 18330
RATS 1605, 4370, 10662, 12193, 12575, 12992, 13805, 13842, 15469, 15694,
    16212, 18552
READING 1701, 3763, 5552, 7305, 7339, 10749, 11756, 14990
  remedial teaching 12583
REASONING 7577, 7578
REBELLIONS see REVOLUTIONS
RECLAMATION OF LAND--Netherlands 16093
RECONSTRUCTION (1865-1876) 2505, 8990, 9376, 9524, 10645, 18274
RECREATION 18314
  centers--Russia 12496
RECYCLING (WASTE) 1253, 2104, 3901, 7563, 12321, 14787, 14882, 15408,
    15771
RED CLOUD (SIOUX CHIEF), (1822-1909) 6637, 6944, 17345
RED LAKE INDIAN RESERVATION (MINNESOTA) 2246
REDUCING 1854, 1990, 2051, 2151, 6815, 7910, 10902, 11718, 13525, 13698,
    14624, 16005, 17435, 18254
REDWOOD 96, 15670
REED, VIRGINIA ELIZABETH B. (d. 1921) 16542
REED, WALTER (1851-1902) 7440
REFERENCE BOOKS--guide-books 17825
REFUGEES 1709, 4670, 4800, 5295, 5583, 7087, 7956a
  Jewish 6988
  political 12951

REFUSE AND REFUSE DISPOSAL   1253, 8206, 10358, 11712, 15408, 15605,
   15644, 18587
REGIONAL PLANNING   15138
REINCARNATION   14056
REINDEER   1948, 4841, 8577
REISS, JOHANNA (deLEEUW), (1929?-)   14223, 14224
RELIGIONS   975, 1814, 3921, 6551, 6709, 7829, 9763, 10392, 10862, 11040,
   14059, 14606, 15234, 17233, 18181, 18182
RELIGIOUS FREEDOM   5623
RELIGIOUS LIFE   3701, 7964, 12538
RELIGIOUS POETRY--collections   6618
REMINGTON, FREDERIC (1861-1909)   13545
RENAISSANCE   6145, 13917
REPORT WRITING   2108
REPORTERS AND REPORTING   979, 1444, 2758, 5148, 5616, 6031, 6033, 6034,
   11180, 12860, 13233, 17682
REPRODUCTION   534, 579, 1439, 1852, 2084, 3795, 3796, 3800, 3804, 4178,
   4753, 7077, 7462, 7652, 8313, 9530, 10355, 11877, 11885, 11886, 11893,
   11947, 12013, 12014, 12844, 13353, 13354, 13827, 13865, 15279, 15527,
   15592, 15607, 15695, 15708, 16207, 16400
REPTILES   338, 2169, 3060, 5809, 8625, 8794, 13144, 13357, 17310, 17538,
   18141, 18575
   fossil   4505
   in Kansas   3852
RESCUE WORK   1464, 7480
RESEARCH   1511, 5008, 8667
RESPIRATION   2140, 11695, 15696
RESTAURANTS, BARS, ETC.   8294, 13697, 18568
RETAIL TRADE--vocational guidance   4765
REVERE, PAUL (1735-1818)   5508, 5951, 6100, 6380, 7198, 10424
REVOLUTIONS   865
   Philippine Islands   14220
REWARDS (PRIZES, ETC.)   5345, 9867
RHINOCEROS   621, 8575, 15704
RHODE ISLAND--history--Colonial period (ca. 1600-1775)   17633
RHODESIA   683, 902, 968, 3030, 3594, 5732, 9494, 12529, 12718
   history--Colonial period   18103
   Southern   9552
RHYTHM   8721
RHYTHM BANDS   7899
RICCI, MATTEO (1552-1610)   13797
RICE, JOAN MOORE (1954-)   9067
RICE   1588, 1848
RICHARDS, LINDA ANN (JUDSON), (1841-1930)   982, 3847, 17616
RICHTHOFEN, MANFRED, FREIHERR VON (1892-1918)   18312
RICKENBACKER, EDWARD VERNON "EDDIE" (1890-1973)   3600
RIDDLES   1668, 1669, 2946, 3220, 3222, 3224, 3449, 3509, 3832, 4362, 4739,
   5030, 6766, 6817, 9639, 9642, 9643, 10448, 10450, 11114, 11115, 11116,
   12058, 12233, 12388, 12467, 13499, 14626, 14689, 14917, 14918, 14919,
   14920, 15147, 15998, 16843, 17127, 17205, 17498, 17879, 17880, 18165,
   18338, 18339
   United States   5433
      Kentucky   16316
RIESEBERG, HARRY EARL (1892-)   10046
RIGBY, CATHY (1952-)   9057
RIIS, JACOB AUGUST (1849-1910)   12130
RILEY, JAMES WHITCOMB (1849-1916)   12284

RINCON DE GAUTIER, FELISA (1897-) 7461, 12917
RIO GRANDE RIVER 4312
RIO GRANDE VALLEY 4312
    social conditions 18197
RITES AND CEREMONIES 1694, 8026, 11516, 17970; see also under various
    cultures with subheading "Rites and ceremonies," e.g., JEWS
RIVER PILOTS 4333
RIVERS 813, 1264, 2939, 4271, 5875, 5888, 8705, 9962, 10345, 10916, 11988,
    12268, 12353, 12629, 12878, 13059, 13969, 14146, 14153, 14451, 16004,
    16014, 16065, 16070, 16166, 17083, 17123, 17271, 17315, 17575, 17668,
    17669, 17780, 17788, 17842, 17874, 18298
    Africa 11435
    Canada 11446
    discovery and exploration 16590
    United States 11472
RIZAL Y ALONSO, JOSE (1861-1896) 14220
ROADS 2716, 9665, 13275, 14529, 14796
    history 4971
    poetry 13152
ROANOKE ISLAND--history 2872, 10663
ROBBERS AND OUTLAWS 174, 814, 1091, 1293, 1556, 2103, 2239, 2291,
    3744, 3803, 4104, 4150, 4664, 4899, 5049, 5315, 5316, 5320, 5321, 6007,
    6017, 6315, 6328, 6644, 6985, 7490, 8343, 8597, 8693, 8834, 9802, 10150,
    10229, 10733, 11992, 12493, 12534, 12699, 12718, 13046, 13292, 13636,
    13654, 14015, 14138, 15554, 15859, 16194, 16515, 16975, 17139, 18431,
    18432
    poetry 1686
    Southwest, New 14252
ROBERTS, SIR CHARLES GEORGE DOUGLAS (1860-1943) 13792
ROBERTSON, OSCAR (1938-) 5570
ROBESON, PAUL (1898-1976) 7309, 7661
ROBINSON, BROOKS (1937-) 2613
ROBINSON, FRANK (1935-) 18443
ROBINSON, JOHN ROOSEVELT "JACKIE" (1919-1972) 3741, 5501, 13105,
    14467, 14745, 15433
ROBOTS 2261, 5640, 15857, 16484
ROCK MUSIC 17196
ROCK MUSICIANS 5275, 18068
    England 12787
    United States 5275
ROCKETRY 7059, 7511
    amateur's manuals 6835
ROCKETS (AERONAUTICS) 2116, 4038, 4040, 6737, 9968
    engines 4038
    models 6835
ROCKNE, KNUTE KENNETH (1888-1931) 4451, 16473, 17220, 17222
ROCKS 1237, 5805, 6526, 7991, 9887, 12559, 13690, 14386, 14740, 15638,
    18347
    collectors and collecting 15756
    painting--Great Lakes region 4872
RODENTS 8119, 15639, 16206
RODEOS 5741, 7544, 14069, 14704, 14711, 14950, 16848
ROEBLING, JOHN AUGUSTUS (1805-1869) 17272
ROEBLING, WASHINGTON AUGUSTUS (1837-1926) 17272
ROGERS, ROBERT (1731-1795) 6673
ROGERS, WILL (1879-1935) 4623, 4624, 17619
ROGERS' RANGERS 15871

ROLE PLAYING   17085
ROLFSRUD, ERLING NICOLAI (1912-)   14579
ROLLER SKATING   668, 2035, 10486, 13074, 14973, 15428
  history   8100
ROMANCE   319, 2278, 2743, 5616, 5738, 6205, 8668, 8670, 11097, 11124,
  12539, 13597
ROMANIA   14256
ROME (ITALY)   4067, 18124, 18125
  antiquities   4363, 11203
  civilization   14461
  description and travel--views   14931
  history   757, 2316, 4363, 5111, 5637, 13799
  social life and customs   4906, 10966
RONNE ANTARCTIC RESEARCH EXPEDITION (1946-1948)   14594
ROOFS   5047
ROOSEVELT, ELEANOR (ROOSEVELT), (1884-1962)   4575, 6811, 7056, 7190,
  14331, 17653
ROOSEVELT, FRANKLIN DELANO (1882-1945)   10309, 10411, 13432, 16498
ROOSEVELT, THEODORE (1858-1919)   394, 3151, 6620, 8696, 12346
ROOT CROPS   15277, 15297
ROPES   11956
ROSE, EDWARD (fl. 1811-1834)   5775
ROSE, ERNESTINE LOUISE (1810-1892)   5308, 16445
ROSE, PETE (1942-)   2621, 10769, 14608
ROSS, BETSY (GRISCOM), (1752-1836)   11924, 17652
ROSS, JOHN (CHEROKEE CHIEF), (1790-1864)   3510
ROSSINI, GIOACCHINO (1792-1868)   6434, 7719
ROTE, KYLE (1950-)   4975
ROWLAND, ANNIE SARAH   14936
ROYAL AIR FORCE COLLEGE (CRANWELL, ENGLAND)   6109
RUBENSTEIN, HELENA (1870-1965)   5621
RUDOLPH, WILMA (1940-)   9077
RUGS   1789
RUNAWAYS   12, 220, 1193, 2058, 2155, 2396, 2510, 2662, 3390, 3519, 3831,
  3871, 3930, 4133, 4369, 5373, 5788, 6747, 7657, 7784, 8197, 8259, 9804,
  9989, 10337, 10341, 10737, 10840, 12955, 13322, 14171, 14472, 14538,
  16043, 16385, 16834, 17403, 17477, 17480, 18259
RUSSELL, BILL (1934-)   4776
RUSSELL, CHARLES MARION (1864-1926)   6631
RUSSELL LAKE REGION (SASKATCHEWAN)--description and travel   13731
RUSSIA   254, 376, 2699, 2700, 3439, 4139, 4946, 6397, 9507, 12582, 12690,
  13531, 13971, 14601, 18508, 18529
  description and travel   3552, 5734, 12691
  history   1781, 9133
    19th century   8564, 9332
    Nicholas II (1868-1918)   8141, 16210
RUSSIAN AMERICANS   5576
RUSSIAN POETRY   11920
  20th century   12495
RUTH (BIBLICAL CHARACTER)   13564
RUTH, GEORGE HERMAN "BABE" (1895-1948)   7819, 17292
RWANDA   3047
RYERSON, ADOLPHUS EGERTON (1803-1882)   4469
RYUN, JIM (1947-)   12722

- S -

SABAH (MALAYSIA) 10519
SABIN, FLORENCE RENA (1871-1953) 13619
SACAGAWEA (1788?-1812) 1734, 5430, 5701, 15247, 15398, 17346
SAFARIS 598, 5035, 8705
SAFETY see ACCIDENTS--PREVENTION
SAGAS 15056
SAGER FAMILY 6238
SAGINAW COUNTY (MICHIGAN)--history 7453
SAHARA DESERT 1765, 3857, 5227, 5457, 6414, 6417
    description and travel 9404, 9408
    social life and customs 6416
SAILING 87, 2329, 2454, 6754, 6785, 8673, 10304, 12312, 12527, 13091,
    13826, 14079, 14186, 14373, 16007, 16871, 17628, 17701
SAILORS 5773, 10304, 14373
ST. AUGUSTINE--Siege (1702) 7943
ST. CROIX (VIRGIN ISLANDS) 12382
ST. LAWRENCE RIVER 9431
    discovery and exploration 804
ST. LOUIS (MISSOURI)
    description and travel 15255
    history 15255, 18257
ST. MARTIN, ALEXIS (1797-1880) 5490
ST. PATRICK'S DAY 1140, 2899
ST. VALENTINE'S DAY 1135, 2574, 4727, 7473, 7944, 7958, 8592, 11107,
    11678, 12204, 14496, 15124
STE. MARIE (ONTARIO) 7893
SAINTS 5635, 5681
    Irish--poetry 8929
    See also names of individual saints, e.g., BERNADETTE, SAINT
SALAI, ANDREA (ca. 1480-ca. 1524) 9993
SALAMANDERS 11257
SALEM (MASSACHUSETTS) 6385
SALISHAN INDIANS--legends 13985
SALOMON, HAYM (1740-1785) 12196
SALOMON, JANET LYNN (NOWICKI) see LYNN, JANET
SALT 2306, 2709, 6998
SALVAGE (WASTE, ETC.)--vocational guidance 14644
SAMARKAND 1378
SAMBURUS 14672
SAMPSON, DEBORAH (1760-1827) 3320, 3475, 11349, 11360
SAN (AFRICAN PEOPLE) 8025, 8314, 8678, 9435, 11762, 13511, 13766, 17764
    folklore 15226
SAN FRANCISCO (CALIFORNIA) 2805, 6234, 11530, 18395
    description and travel 6389, 14932
    history--Civil War (1861-1865) 1269
SAN FRANCISCO BAY 7160
SAN JACINTO, BATTLE OF (1836) 3094, 11546
SAN JUAN (PUERTO RICO) 1129
SAN PASQUAL, BATTLE OF (1846) 13011
SAN SABA MISSION (TEXAS) 6207
SAND 3135
SAND DUNES 11890
SANDBOXES 9160
SANDBURG, CARL (1878-1967) 6197, 12030, 14886

SANDILE (1821-1878) 12025
SANDPAINTINGS 17306
SANDPIPERS 8812
SANDWICHES 167
SANFORD, MARIA LOUISA (1836-1920) 7804
SANGAMON COUNTY (ILLINOIS)--history 1723
SANGER, MARGARET (HIGGINS), (1883-1966) 10180
SANITATION 14502, 18139
SANTA CLAUS 1912, 2233, 4151, 7950
SANTA FE TRAIL 63, 1589, 8495, 16702
SANTEE INDIANS 5219
SANTIAGO see RAMON Y CAJAL, SANTIAGO
SANTO, RON (1940-) 2323
SAŌ PAULO (BRAZIL) 14237
SARGASSO SEA 9038
SATELLITES see ARTIFICIAL SATELLITES
SATIRE 5074, 9679, 9680, 16563
SATURN (PLANET) 759
SAUDI ARABIA--description and travel 13631
SAUK INDIANS 1294, 4845, 10638
SAULT SAINTE MARIE (MICHIGAN) 9425
    history 12806, 12807
SAUND, D. S. (1899-1973) 14941
SAVINGS AND THRIFT 12801
SAVORGNAN DE BRAZZA, PIERRE PAUL FRANÇOIS CAMILLE COMTE
    (1852-1905) 2915
SAWCHUK, TERRY (1929-) 5573
SAXOPHONES 1512
SAYERS, GALE (1943-) 3846, 11871
SCANDINAVIA
    commerce and economic conditions 871
    See also individual countries, e.g., NORWAY
SCANDINAVIAN AMERICANS 8479, 11574
SCARABS 11992
SCARECROWS 5670, 7436, 10799
SCAVENGERS (ZOOLOGY) 5209
SCHALLENBERGER, MOSES (1826-1909) 16307
SCHLIEMANN, HEINRICH (1822-1890) 2168, 5353
SCHOHARIE COUNTY (NEW YORK)--history 13188
SCHOLARSHIPS, FELLOWSHIPS, ETC. 6692
SCHOLL FAMILY 6113
SCHOOLCRAFT, HENRY (1793-1864) 4848
SCHOOLS 37, 211, 325, 364, 421, 422, 429, 478, 674, 809, 1087, 1338,
    1340, 1815, 2101, 2157, 2174, 2341, 2599, 2601, 2669, 2683, 2957, 2963,
    2969, 2971, 3172, 3240, 3555, 3564, 3568, 3759, 3761, 3762, 3763, 3861,
    3866, 3868, 4158, 4252, 4489, 4640, 4694, 5288, 5320, 5321, 5322, 5421,
    5429, 5448, 5549, 5552, 5646, 5673, 5695, 5699, 5746, 5766, 5828, 5837,
    5894, 5971, 5979, 6367, 6814, 6886, 6948, 6986, 7074, 7135, 7212, 7213,
    7614, 7655, 7834, 7851, 7854, 7902, 7914, 7923, 7924, 7947, 7948, 7949,
    8021, 8087, 8115, 8204, 8333, 8372, 8509, 8553, 8693, 8797, 8834, 8860,
    8861, 8907, 8999, 9002, 9094, 9164, 9166, 9175, 9176, 9208, 9264, 9439,
    9490, 9528, 9649, 9734, 9794, 9795, 9796, 9798, 9799, 9800, 9802, 9823,
    9824, 9828, 9999, 10216, 10225, 10230, 10584, 10586, 10657, 10661, 10938,
    11019, 11097, 11101, 11104, 11106, 11107, 11157, 11184, 11191, 11228,
    11462, 11515, 11622, 11686, 11961, 12317, 12529, 12630, 12895, 12918,
    12970, 12981, 13029, 13046, 13060, 13178, 13179, 13372, 13481, 13600,
    13605, 13622, 13704, 13936, 13945, 14197, 14341, 14344, 14372, 14394,

14549, 14605, 14720, 14724, 14904, 14985, 15016, 15047, 15649, 15836,
16051, 16241, 16261, 16758, 16770, 16774, 16934, 17068, 17117, 17248,
17449, 17460, 17502, 17730, 17743, 17791, 17799, 17821, 17945, 17946,
18262, 18365, 18388
  assembly programs 5913
  attendance 5321
  children--transportation 7954
  nurses 17821
  pictorial works 1329
  preparation 82
  segregation and integration 1198, 1809, 2956, 3863, 9002, 13127, 14549,
    16241, 17047, 17425, 17863
   law and legislation 16293
  song books 520
  urban 3828
SCHUBERT, FRANZ PETER (1797-1828) 6975
SCHUMANN, CLARA (1819-1896) 10169
SCHUMANN, ROBERT ALEXANDER (1810-1956) 10169
SCHURZ, CARL (1829-1906) 17079
SCHWEITZER, ALBERT (1875-1965) 789, 4479, 5611, 6208, 11649, 12094,
  15711
SCIENCE 737, 742, 1414, 4324, 5503, 6306, 10282, 10685, 12133, 12137,
  12435, 12825, 15092, 15096, 15159, 15758, 15759, 16018, 17001, 17603
  apparatus and instruments 15771
  experiments 52, 510, 511, 1102, 1103, 1104, 1105, 3708, 3709, 4065,
    4066, 8095, 9444, 12201, 12396, 12412, 13764, 14249, 14250, 14361,
    14631, 15095, 15158, 17129, 17806, 17807, 17808, 17809, 18337, 18340,
    18346
  history and criticism 2008
  methodology 12413, 15761
  miscellanea 17641
  problems and exercises 12853
  study and teaching 17129
  terminology 753, 770
  See also specific aspects of science, e.g., SOUND
SCIENCE FICTION 371, 404, 735, 1262, 1591, 1619, 1635, 2002, 2003, 2004,
  2005, 2007, 2010, 2861, 2863, 2878, 2942, 2951, 3263, 3403, 3404, 3406,
  3407, 3408, 3409, 3410, 3411, 3412, 3448, 3525, 4096, 4169, 4581, 4651,
  4693, 4892, 4894, 4896, 4897, 5058, 5135, 5136, 5215, 5216, 5370, 5401,
  5435, 5436, 5437, 5438, 5440, 5441, 5597, 5640, 5695, 5945, 5960, 5960a,
  5962, 7442, 7800, 8020, 8021, 8022, 8023, 8562, 8563, 8565, 8566, 8707,
  8730, 8998, 9503, 9770, 9772, 9925, 10500, 10513, 10547, 10548, 10549,
  10550, 10811, 11065, 11378, 11706, 11722, 12454, 12931, 12932, 12935,
  12938, 12940, 12942, 12943, 13326, 13478, 13543, 13694, 13702, 14103,
  14277, 15019, 15020, 15021, 15669, 15672, 15831, 16031, 16393, 17568,
  17899, 18021, 18030, 18031, 18032, 18033, 18398, 18425
  collections 764
  Russia 6843
SCIENTIFIC RECREATIONS 1104, 1532, 6588, 15095, 16368, 17806, 17809,
  18339
SCIENTISTS 313, 737, 742, 3711, 4705, 7912, 11999
  France 16822
  Germany 16822
  United States 13719
SCISSORS AND SHEARS 10026
SCOLIOSIS 1816
SCOTCH-IRISH--in the United States 9281

SCOTLAND 502, 4429, 4466, 5135, 5136, 6958, 8781, 8782, 8786, 8791,
     10460, 10864, 11399, 11417, 11418, 11505, 13798, 16301, 16302, 16304,
     16305
    highlands 3379
    history 503, 8780, 8788, 8789, 17595
    immigration and emigration 7128
SCOTT, ANN (HAMILTON), (1774?-?) 6383
SCOTT, ROBERT FALCON (1868-1912) 4608
SCOTTISH AMERICANS 5577, 7128, 8045, 9281, 9419, 11530
SCOUTS AND SCOUTING 5035, 6871, 8165, 11787, 14058
SCRIVENERS 7737
SCULPTORS 11529, 12725, 16898
SCULPTURE 15251, 17687, 17688
    appreciation 13240
    Cameroon 5834
    United States 6876
SEA LIONS 45
SEA STORIES 521, 622, 628, 645, 842, 1975, 2411, 3246, 5942, 7915, 8494,
     11235, 13096, 16715, 16793, 16797
SEAFARING LIFE 5119, 15985
SEAGULLS 859, 6736, 17062
SEAHORSES 12463
SEALS (ANIMALS) 1650, 2367, 3688, 6296, 9964, 13155, 18412
SEAMSTRESSES 10989
SEASHORE 415, 1356, 1705, 2679, 4280, 6595, 10211, 10924, 10925, 12254,
     14779, 14832, 15305, 16158, 16227, 18589
    biology 2474, 3120, 4066
    pictorial works 787
SEASONS 365, 1314, 1951, 2148, 2684, 6413, 4718, 5000, 7902, 8026, 13343,
     13650, 13775, 14648, 17002, 18618
    pictorial works 1656
    See also individual seasons, e.g., SPRING
SEATTLE (CHIEF OF THE SUQUAMISH AND ALLIED TRIBES), (d. 1866)
     12361
SEATTLE (WASHINGTON) 17601
    biography 16013
SEAVER, TOM (1944-) 2625, 3756, 4796, 16488
SECORD, LAURA (INGERSOLL), (1775-1868) 1165
SECRETARIES 956
    vocational guidance 8630
SECURITY 15131
SEEDS 913, 1697, 2932, 7670, 8844, 9373, 14381, 15308, 16186
    dispersal 7974, 9374, 14085, 17636
    germination 2855
SEEING EYE DOGS see GUIDE DOGS
SELF-DEFENSE 7751, 7752, 7753, 12706, 12707, 12708
SELF-IDENTITY see INDIVIDUALITY
SELFISHNESS 14355
SELF-PERCEPTION 696, 1542, 3201, 5102, 5357, 5738, 6074, 6182, 6187,
     6349, 7245, 8644, 9830, 12645, 13073, 13629, 14521, 14688, 15469, 15881,
     15999, 16899, 17211, 17302, 17372, 17868, 18267, 18383
SELF-PORTRAITS 10613
SELF-RELIANCE 8289
SEMANTICS 1157
SEMINOLE INDIANS 1028, 1128, 1763, 2506, 5545, 7359, 12685, 18315
    biography 1731, 7178, 7355, 16592
    folklore 1062

SEMINOLE WAR
   1st (1817-1818) 9360, 12041
   2nd (1835-1842) 235, 7595, 9360, 11479, 12041
   3rd (1855-1858) 9360
SEMMES, RAPHAEL (1809-1877) 15951
SENECA INDIANS 6580
   legends 13306
SENEGAL 3031, 7068
SENSES AND SENSATION 308, 2188, 2190, 3469, 7929, 10133, 10776, 15208,
   15595, 15599, 15745, 16365, 17655, 17789, 18548
   miscellanea 9959
   poetry 1962
SEPOY REBELLION (1857-1859) 5077
SEQUOYAH (CHEROKEE INDIAN), (1770?-1843) 2870, 3715, 9370, 9978,
   11701, 13389, 14063
SERENGETI PLAIN (TANZANIA) 15038
SERVICE INDUSTRIES--vocational guidance 4297
SET THEORY 120, 121, 1431, 6406, 8304, 11145, 16784, 17824; see also
   NUMBER THEORY
SETON, ERNEST THOMPSON (1860-1946) 13792, 15360
SEWING 4165, 4166, 14622, 15995
SEX EDUCATION 1194, 4753, 5745, 7075, 7076, 7077, 7462, 7530, 7652,
   8395, 9262, 9263, 10617, 11886, 11893, 12755, 15527, 16400, 17861
   pictorial works 6001
SEX ROLES 5712, 7077, 7321, 7539, 8225, 10590, 10672, 10708, 10752, 13629,
   13879, 14095, 14415, 14750, 15067, 15113, 15163, 15514, 15723, 16110,
   16495, 16929, 17456
SEXUAL ETHICS 5615
SHACKLETON, SIR ERNEST HENRY (1874-1922) 4608
SHADES AND SHADOWS 4749, 6593, 9593, 13775, 15096, 15137, 17017
SHADOW PANTOMIMES AND PLAYS 2698, 3285, 3720
SHAKERS 5629, 18424
SHAKESPEARE, WILLIAM (1564-1616) 6271, 7204
   adaptations 3454, 10203, 12166
   contemporary England 8615
   criticism and interpretation 3453
   stage history 8321
SHAMAN 931
SHAPE see SIZE AND SHAPE
SHARKS 1813, 3077, 4097, 6045, 10440, 11361, 11366, 15323
   research 11362
SHAWNEE INDIANS 347, 4012, 5245, 16279, 17890
   legends 1640, 15105
SHEA, DON (1925-) 6685
SHEEP 144, 654, 2800, 3675, 6212, 7064, 9462, 11685, 12924, 12927, 13951,
   16211, 17627, 17864
   Ethiopia 2074
   New South Wales 9782
   United States--New England--history 6727
SHELBY, JOSEPH ORVILLE (1830-1897) 11331
SHELLS 17, 3597, 4429, 7094, 9091, 18214
SHEPHERDS 1235, 1265, 3502, 7913, 10113, 12079, 13642, 15003
SHERIDAN, PHILIP HENRY (1831-1888) 14193
SHERMAN, WILLIAM T. (1820-1891) 1739
SHETLAND ISLANDS 18412
SHIPBUILDING 12020
   history 17042

SHIPS AND SHIPPING 89, 645, 2441, 2525, 2650, 3116, 5119, 5392, 6344,
6833, 7235, 7539, 7574, 8128, 8139, 9938, 11444, 12658, 13017, 13494,
13672, 16254, 16711, 17042, 18567
Great Lakes 2013, 2014, 2044, 11500
Mississippi River 1215
SHIPWRECKS 911, 1464, 2015, 2045, 2262, 3429, 3605, 4351, 4798, 7490,
13791, 16098, 16563, 16688, 16712, 17995, 18048
Great Lakes 2042, 2044, 2045, 2046, 14140
SHOES AND SHOE INDUSTRY 1715, 5947, 7086, 9920, 11825, 17135, 14305
SHOOTING 9942
SHOPPING 1328, 14600
SHORT STORIES 182, 184, 185, 191, 196, 197, 254, 293, 567, 773, 774,
776, 778, 779, 833, 908, 1662, 1841, 2056, 2404, 2461, 2486, 2491, 2815,
2891, 3163, 3225, 3227, 3334, 3339, 3355, 3356, 3357, 3358, 3360, 3361,
3696, 3893, 4188, 4380, 4463, 4580, 4651, 4685, 4687, 5162, 5318, 5319,
5441, 5668, 5677, 5679, 5790, 5791, 5792, 5794, 5796, 5797, 6065, 6081,
6082, 6313, 6319, 6454, 6604, 6843, 7015, 7231, 7232, 7291, 7325, 7477,
7553, 7745, 7748, 7749, 7921, 8003, 8106, 8135, 8211, 8255, 8256, 8417,
8418, 8587, 8744, 8779, 8904, 8910, 9249, 9448, 9449, 9459, 9503, 9575,
9579, 9580, 9581, 9583, 9676, 9689, 9779, 9844, 9884, 9986, 9994, 10030,
10093, 10118, 10171, 10592, 10593, 10669, 10725, 11001, 11130, 11138,
11155, 11236, 11300, 11404, 11601, 11602, 11603, 11723, 12026, 12065,
12075, 12326, 12398, 12452, 12494, 12606, 12663, 12735, 12831, 13008,
13020, 13027, 13031, 13047, 13122, 13169, 13218, 13307, 13343, 13366,
13428, 13431, 13488, 13503, 13505, 13568, 13813, 13893, 14053, 14065,
14286, 14307, 14565, 14640, 14865, 15176, 15182, 15359, 15456, 15782,
15785, 16287, 16522, 16721, 16850, 16863, 16985, 17113, 17265, 17266,
17267, 17887, 17954, 17956, 17967, 18154, 18410, 18425, 18477, 18612
African 4835, 8956
Ghanaian 13221
Japanese 14858
Mexican 2890
Spanish 16002, 16006
United States 126
Yiddish 8683, 14053
SHOSHONI INDIANS 15247, 18072
legends 7976
SHREWS 3088, 5926
SHRIMPING INDUSTRY 9426
SIAM see THAILAND
SIBERIA 7485, 9462
description and travel 7853, 16720
SICILY 3161, 5813, 6049, 9819
SICK 1173, 1387, 2100, 11441, 11493, 14836, 14837, 16897
coping with the 856, 1173
SIERRA LEONE 1030, 3032, 3541, 3614, 3616
colonization 8885
history 18330
social life and customs 7084
SIGN LANGUAGE--dictionaries 16928
SIGNALS AND SIGNALLING 3735
SIGNS
and signboards 35, 6441
and symbols 8029, 11134, 14393, 14558
SIJO 1099
SIKKIM 9479, 14177
SIKSIKA INDIANS 15126

SILHOUETTES 12298
SILK 13560
SILKWORMS 16230
SILVER MINES AND MINING 12370
SILVERWORK 5948
SIMON, CARLY (1945-) 12483
SIMPSON, O. J. (1947-) 2620, 4788, 6168, 7526, 8189, 10767, 11895, 18438
SINGAMON (MICHIGAN) 18085
SINGER, ISAAC BASHEVIS (1904-) 15776
SINGING 18588
SINGING GAMES see GAMES--SINGING
SINGLE PARENT FAMILY 854, 2088, 3337, 3979, 5610, 5673, 8268, 9904,
    9909, 15049, 15526, 15657, 16141, 16730, 17539, 18582
SIOUX INDIANS 557, 1249, 5220, 10577, 11768, 14902, 17353
  legends 5747
SISTERS see BROTHERS AND SISTERS
SITTING BULL (DAKOTA CHIEF), (1831-1890) 494, 6639, 9253, 11904,
    13004, 16278
SIZE AND SHAPE 573, 786, 1116, 2390, 2514, 2927, 3289, 3371,
    4218, 5418, 6292, 6378, 6400, 7339, 8297, 8304, 8726, 9461, 9742, 9767,
    9970, 10044, 10045, 13243, 13759, 14152, 14168, 14227, 14236, 15064,
    15091, 15386, 15452, 15453, 15454, 15702, 15798, 15801, 16146, 17919,
    18415
  poetry 1503
SKATEBOARDING 2594, 4566, 14073, 14221
SKATERS 11879, 17223, 17224
SKATING 667, 4674, 11879, 15188
SKELETON 1013, 7449, 10952, 15697
SKIERS 9060
  Austria 9056
SKIN 14793, 15606, 15698
  care and hygiene 11137
SKIN DIVING 1028, 5836, 7852, 15006, 16878, 17767
SKIS AND SKIING 2036, 2830, 3142, 3144, 4030, 5794, 6132, 6696, 9060,
    12310, 12715, 13192, 15582, 16877, 18316, 18325
SKOPJE (YUGOSLAVIA)--earthquakes 5842
SKUNKS 904, 2912, 6338, 11645, 15075, 18193
SKYDIVING 5193, 9565
SKYLAB PROGRAM 5194
SLAVE TRADE 6186, 10632, 11438, 16254
  Africa--West 236, 8680
    history 13706
  history 8695
  North Atlantic region 8680
  Sierra Leone 8885
  United States 236, 10926
SLAVERY 864, 1626, 1924, 2067, 2504, 2627, 3186, 4569, 5036, 5648, 6381,
    7925, 7926, 8322, 9952, 12551, 12587, 12769, 13124, 13799, 17852, 18157
  in Africa 8695
  fugitive slaves 15944
  history 10654, 12047, 13706
  in the United States 8695, 8989, 8992, 9002, 9028, 9308, 9513, 9525,
    10926, 11216, 12050, 16238, 16397, 16562
    anti-slavery movements 3375, 3381, 7208, 7925, 9305, 9885, 16292,
      17529, 17785
    condition of slaves 10632
    Connecticut 18483

Kansas 5914
Louisiana 12930
Maryland 7208
Missouri 17529
personal narratives 10632, 16153
Southern states 7052
SLEDDING 12010
SLEEP 1111, 6188, 8591, 9512, 10655, 12850, 15242, 15284, 15462, 15602, 15699, 15868, 17511, 18156, 18615, 18619
poetry 7967
SLESSOR, MARY (MITCHELL), (1848-1915) 16591
SLOCUM, FRANCES (1773-1847) 18112
SLOTHS 8424
SLOVAK AMERICANS 14691
SLOVENIAN AMERICANS 13972
SLOW LEARNING CHILDREN 10296
SLUMS 7211, 15954, 15997
New York (City) 12130
SMALLS, ROBERT (1839-1915) 12091, 16236, 16246
SMITH, ABIGAIL (ADAMS), (1765-1813) 1997
SMITH, BESSIE (1898-1937) 12383
SMITH, JEDEDIAH STRONG (1798-1831) 2713, 10310, 12228
SMITH, JOHN (1580-1631) 6144, 10416, 16586
SMITH, MARGARET (CHASE), (1898-) 6035
SMITH, NOLLE R. (1888-) 7467
SMITH, VENTURE (1729?-1805) 18483
SMOKING 12667, 14123, 14883, 16904, 18292
physiological effect 11522, 11695, 16020, 16760
SMUGGLING 321, 1467, 3603, 5599, 7098, 11983, 16055, 16801
SNAILS 2788, 8125, 9650, 10874, 14521, 14831, 15721, 17137, 18566
SNAKES 1971, 2068, 2199, 2965, 6349, 7063, 7782, 7992, 9860, 10753, 12403, 13120, 13489, 14555, 15443, 15722, 15742, 17132, 18552
Ontario 11031
United States--Alabama 18096
SNOFRU (KING OF EGYPT) (fl. 2500 B.C.) 11623
SNORRI THORFINNSON (d. 1010) 1411
SNOW 665, 1355, 1404, 2145, 2497, 2741, 4213, 4235, 5120, 5226, 7957, 9326, 9607, 9744, 10024, 10157, 11402, 11426, 13258, 13363, 14139, 14790, 15044, 17010, 17714
SNOWMOBILES 12445
SOAP BOX DERBIES 635, 8986, 8987, 14070, 14247, 17672
SOCCER 558, 4031, 4839, 4974, 6677, 6877, 7788, 7789, 9480, 9848, 10215, 11073, 12318, 12586, 15941, 16962
players 123, 2637, 4975, 6677, 7825, 11898, 16699
Brazil 7527
vocational guidance 13246
SOCIAL ACTION 1501, 14434
SOCIAL ADJUSTMENT 5481
SOCIAL CHANGE 95, 5294
SOCIAL CLASSES 15511
SOCIAL PROBLEMS 1808, 3240, 3540, 3574, 3582, 4017, 5422, 5599, 12682, 12914, 14388, 14838, 16960
literary collections 9392
SOCIAL PSYCHOLOGY 18293
SOCIAL REFORMERS 5483
SOCIAL SCIENCES 13891
SOCIAL SERVICES 15220

vocational guidance 8769, 11055
SOCIAL WELFARE--history 17986
SOCIAL WORK 4797
  workers 7175, 9644, 11055
SOCIALLY HANDICAPPED 8772
  children 1894
SOCIETY OF FRIENDS see FRIENDS, SOCIETY OF
SOFTBALL 1776, 15118, 16458, 16462, 16767
  pictorial works 11279
SOIL CONSERVATION 1189, 8028; see also ECOLOGY
SOIL SCIENCE 9615
SOILS 7977, 9615, 10347, 14531, 14789, 15736
SOILS (ENGINEERING) 4303
SOKOTO (NIGERIAN PROVINCE)--history 2039
SOLAR ENERGY 52, 1434, 1515, 2146, 9929, 15925
SOLAR RADIATION 13775
SOLAR SYSTEM 740, 759, 761, 7090, 9935, 15750
SOLDIERS 2954, 6673, 8433, 9138, 10493, 11360, 12218, 12877, 12885
  Black American 10827
SOLOMON (KING OF ISRAEL), (10th century B.C.) 5352
SONGS 634, 3104, 3354, 3970, 4299, 5406, 5461, 6160, 6161, 6804, 6889,
  7715, 8611, 9495, 9884, 10255, 10258, 10283, 12216, 12281, 13238, 13838,
  14025, 14027, 14559, 15237, 15239, 15335, 17756, 17771, 18120, 18203,
  18510
  African 14454, 14566
  Black American 6884
  Czech 395
  English 13920
  Japanese 8217, 17802
  Jewish 8237, 13920
  Puerto Rican 13350
  Slovak 395
  Spanish 9222, 9223, 9224, 14293, 14523
  United States 1049, 1898, 6628
    national 2436, 11189, 15501
SORCERY 9991, 11636
SOTO, HERNANDO DE (ca. 1500-1542) 2434, 16180
SOUBIROUS, BERNADETTE, SAINT see BERNADETTE, SAINT
SOUND 294, 2130, 2150, 2385, 2386, 2391, 2395, 2399, 2405, 9039, 9928,
  10162, 13040, 13133, 13688, 13760, 14604, 15805, 16085, 16089
  experiments 294
  poetry 1240, 15650
  recording and reproducing 9106
SOUTH AFRICA 1633, 3551, 4302, 5460, 8978, 10727, 11090, 11091, 11655,
  11730, 13272, 13374, 14597, 17419, 17838
  description and travel 8898, 9441, 12786
  history 14487, 16197, 16673
    Kafir Wars (1811-1878) 12025
    Great Trek (1836-1840) 15225
    1836-1909 8092, 8898
    War (1899-1902) 1065, 1946, 8090, 8091
  politics and government 8607
  race relations 8607, 8898, 12286
  social life and customs 16200, 16201, 16323
    addresses, essays, lectures 13347
SOUTH AMERICA 3130, 5826; see also individual countries, e.g., BRAZIL
SOUTH ASIA--description and travel 8202

SOUTH CAROLINA 1835
  history
    Colonial period (ca. 1600-1775) 2673
    Revolution (1775-1783) 1266
SOUTH DAKOTA 898, 3575, 4058, 11465, 17902
  history 13228, 17270
SOUTHERN STATES 343, 1195, 12120, 16816
  race relations 12567, 16693
  see also individual states, e.g., SOUTH CAROLINA
SOUTHWEST
  New 637, 6776, 16044
    antiquities 6095, 11662, 16639
    description and travel 11477, 17417
    discovery and exploration 13014
    history 9882, 10364
    social life and customs 4911
  old--19th century 1272
SPACE AND TIME 267, 274, 323, 371, 416, 502, 503, 504, 507, 522, 686,
  1438, 1499, 1557, 1883, 1969, 1976, 1978, 2098, 2274, 4282, 4286, 4393,
  4395, 4403, 4404, 4406, 4429, 5697, 5889, 5945, 6252, 7329, 7455, 8048,
  8903, 9297, 9333, 9771, 9774, 10259, 10261, 10648, 10649, 10651, 10688,
  10689, 10690, 10691, 10692, 10693, 10694, 10704, 10933, 10954, 10957,
  10958, 11316, 11317, 11376, 11379, 11422, 11559, 11953, 11954, 11972,
  12576, 12732, 12737, 12821, 12934, 12937, 12941, 12944, 13070, 13172,
  13176, 13319, 13326, 13348, 13599, 13643, 14546, 14937, 15844, 15845,
  15971, 16159, 16345, 16573, 16598, 16906, 16961, 17084, 17178, 17717,
  17760, 18014, 18015, 18045, 18126, 18317, 18480
SPACE FLIGHT 1032, 1420, 2116, 2863, 3526, 5393, 6270, 6555, 7059,
  14263, 14868, 14869
  manned 4042
  to Mars 6723
  to the moon 3853, 6305, 6425, 7506, 8191, 15444, 15768, 17549, 17931
SPACE PERCEPTION 9461, 11535
SPACE SCIENCES 3787, 4042, 4043
SPACE STATIONS 2011, 4305, 5194, 6296, 9078
SPACE VEHICLES 2123, 4043
  in art 401
SPAIN 183, 3226, 7023, 10456, 13085, 13373, 16624, 18177
  history 6714, 11016
    1340- 12538
    Ferdinand and Isabella 1479-1516 8613
    1492 13506
  legends and mythology 3146
  social conditions 11838
  social life and customs 9227
SPANISH, BOOKS IN 15, 169, 170, 171, 172, 247, 248, 249, 250, 251, 377,
  378, 379, 380, 407, 408, 409, 410, 682, 1120, 1121, 1456, 1722, 2056,
  2165, 2188, 2244, 2455, 2891, 2892, 2901, 2902, 2903, 2904, 2905, 2914,
  3067, 3091, 3092, 3133, 3146, 3219, 3225, 3227, 3545, 3904, 3905, 3906,
  3907, 3969, 3974, 4170, 4171, 4337, 4340, 4341, 4342, 4345, 4362, 4380,
  4381, 4407, 4408, 4432, 4516, 4517, 4518, 4519, 4520, 4521, 4522, 4523,
  4524, 4525, 4584, 4585, 4645, 4647, 4813, 4877, 4878, 4879, 4913, 5156,
  5224, 5289, 5539, 5542, 5555, 5562, 5749, 5829, 5831, 5832, 5833, 5876,
  6131, 6479, 6482, 6490, 6523, 6528, 6546, 6550, 6554, 6556, 6557, 6558,
  6559, 6560, 6561, 6562, 6563, 6564, 6565, 6566, 6567, 6568, 6569, 6652,
  6655, 6777, 6841, 6842, 7029, 7162, 8107, 8197, 8252, 8253, 9160, 9161,
  9165, 9170, 9171, 9221, 9226, 9227, 9228, 9229, 9230, 9231, 9232, 9233,

9234, 9397, 9398, 10010, 10147, 10148, 10149, 10194, 10244, 10437, 10456, 10475, 10591, 10885, 10903, 11388, 11571, 11572, 11664, 11766, 11810, 11843, 12004, 12005, 12006, 12007, 12074, 12093, 12219, 12250, 12275, 12410, 12419, 12420, 12422, 12450, 12548, 12561, 12659, 12660, 12661, 12662, 12663, 12664, 12750, 12845, 12868, 13064, 13065, 13086, 13197, 13198, 13230, 13231, 13232, 13233, 13234, 13351, 13409, 13410, 13411, 13412, 13413, 13414, 13415, 13416, 13417, 13418, 13419, 13420, 13421, 13488, 13506, 13507, 13710, 13773, 13813, 13937, 13939, 13944, 13990, 13991, 14081, 14089, 14096, 14098, 14255, 14269, 14295, 14353, 14354, 14355, 14356, 14357, 14407, 14411, 14412, 14416, 14450, 14489, 14591, 14592, 14865, 14868, 14869, 14876, 14877, 14990, 15032, 15130, 15345, 15353, 15354, 15355, 15733, 16000, 16001, 16006, 16018, 16031, 16032, 16731, 16863, 16941, 17262, 17263, 17264, 17265, 17266, 17267, 17329, 17487, 17488, 17489, 17490, 17491, 17492, 17493, 17494, 17495, 17496, 17973
  fables 1484
  fall activities 1455
  plays 1485
  rhymes and riddles 1457
  spring activities 1453
  winter activities 1454
SPANISH AMERICAN POETRY 5158
SPANISH LANGUAGE
  alphabet 9226
  conversations and phrases 9399, 14359
  grammar 4076
  reading materials 1555
SPANISH POETRY 1966, 5539, 5829, 6229, 6231, 6427, 6428, 6479, 6482, 6489, 6512, 6841, 6842, 9153, 9225, 11388, 12004, 12005, 12074, 12537, 12561, 13066, 13197, 13199, 13421, 13984, 14398, 14551, 14591, 14592, 14599, 14717, 14754, 14853, 16001, 16626, 17297, 17492, 17494, 17495
  collections 12841
SPEECH 15597
  disorders 3419, 9649, 13736
SPEED 15065
SPENCER, CLARISSA (YOUNG), (1860-1939) 17972
SPIDERS 2254, 3319, 3960, 6341, 6470, 7000, 7141, 15640, 17300
SPIES 428, 1587, 2041, 4698, 5355, 5427, 5428, 5487, 5631, 5979, 7572, 8152, 8256, 8786, 10149, 10397, 10479, 10545, 11803, 11984, 12886, 16513, 17067, 18078
SPITZ, MARK (1950-) 13107
SPOKAN INDIANS 15484
SPONGES 9093
SPORTS 855, 2653, 3305, 4589, 4593, 4595, 6564, 6565, 6566, 8160, 9108, 9628, 13157, 14135, 15099, 15573, 17648, 18397
  anecdotes, facetiae, satire, etc. 4590, 10913, 14674
  biography 1554, 2750, 13904, 15674, 15675
  interviews 1177, 1178
  miscellanea 4595
  New York (City)--history 5172
  poetry 6030, 9032, 12470, 12471
  science of 1105
  vocational guidance 11344
  winter 1659
  See also specific sports, e.g., SOCCER
SPORTS CARDS--collectors and collecting 11452
SPORTS CARS 9023, 15918

SPRING 1196, 3079, 3621, 4383, 5059, 5505, 6748, 6780, 8801, 10841, 13388,
    16999
    poetry 1381, 9747, 10588
SPRINGFIELD (ILLINOIS)--history 1723
SQUANTO (WAMPANOAG INDIAN), (d. 1622) 2558, 2572, 2573, 7117, 7180
SQUIRRELS 904, 2542, 2779, 8208, 10433, 11048, 13845, 15354, 17929,
    18463, 18591
SRI LANKA 12566; see also CEYLON
STABLER, KEN (1945-) 7519
STANLEY, FRANCIS EDGAR (1849-1918) 9024
STANLEY, FREELAN OSCAR (1849-1940) 9024
STANLEY, SIR HENRY MORTON (1841-1904) 15895
STANLEY-BROWN, MARY (GARFIELD) (d. 1947) 5765
STANTON, ELIZABETH CADY (1815-1902) 5628, 9081
STARFISHES 8813, 9090, 11254, 15700
STARGELL, WILLIE (1941-) 10775
STARR, BART (1934-) 11841
STARS 2114, 2120, 2122, 11164
STATE SYMBOLS
    birds 5210
    flowers 5210
    trees 5211
STATES, NEW 17607
STATESMEN see POLITICIANS
STATISTICS 16108
STATUES 5834, 17897
STAUBACH, ROGER THOMAS (1942-) 7519, 16485
STEAM NAVIGATION 17518
    Great Lakes 477
    Mississippi River 530
STEAM SHOVELS 2733
STEAMBOATS 5534, 5644, 7158, 7296, 12353, 17518
    pictorial works 477
STEEL 5936
STEIN, GERTRUDE (1874-1946) 2665
STEINMETZ, CHARLES PROTEUS (1865-1923) 7531
STEINMEYER, FERDINAND (1720-1786) 1624
STEPBROTHERS 17962
STEPPARENTS 17962
    stepfathers 5617, 8773
    stepmothers 2590, 5633, 9492, 12579, 16101
STEPPE (MONGOLIA)--history 1210
STEPSISTERS 5633, 5634, 15767, 17962
STEREOPHONIC SOUND SYSTEMS 13093
STEVENSON, ADLAI E. (1900-1965) 17516
STOCK EXCHANGE 821
STONE AGE 14033
STONEHENGE 2137
STONEMASONS 1310
STOREKEEPERS 7273
STORES--retail 15146
STORIES IN RHYME 125, 175, 243, 640, 845, 903, 1299, 1387, 1490, 1496,
    1611, 1827, 1828, 1871, 2099, 2980, 3235, 3285, 3440, 3624, 3625, 3822,
    4221, 4233, 4245, 4745, 4898, 5002, 5152, 5226, 5346, 5404, 5663, 5664,
    5665, 5667, 5670, 5672, 5904, 5906, 5923, 5930, 6096, 6441, 6463, 6471,
    6495, 6827, 7626, 8301, 8305, 8307, 8309, 8378, 8457, 8473, 8688, 8732,
    8833, 8843, 8915, 9205, 9453, 9454, 9455, 9496, 9912, 9919, 10071, 10155,

10156, 10157, 10518, 10754, 10985, 10999, 11002, 11063, 11075, 11076,
11167, 11168, 11231, 11340, 11766, 12179, 12213, 12214, 12350, 12646,
12720, 12842, 12871, 13402, 13403, 13469, 13471, 13474, 13583, 13588,
13805, 13809, 13879, 13899, 13902, 14130, 14179, 14200, 14706, 15336,
15346, 15367, 15373, 15376, 15377, 15379, 15380, 15381, 15382, 15385,
15613, 15816, 16374, 16507, 16823, 17204, 17398, 17591, 17648, 17712,
17729, 17733, 17896, 18142, 18167, 18393, 18415, 18514
STORIES WITHOUT WORDS   280, 286, 415, 483, 535, 570, 571, 629, 720,
1149, 1202, 1862, 2254 2921, 3106, 3109, 3282, 3286, 4666, 5402, 6407,
7035, 7036, 7037, 7038, 7039, 7040, 7041, 7042, 7043, 7044, 7046, 7086,
7638, 7639, 7759, 7803, 8035, 8406, 8831, 9704, 10018, 10019, 10020,
10021, 10022, 10023, 10024, 10026, 10906, 11496, 11673, 11674, 11925,
11926, 11927, 11928, 11929, 11933, 11934, 11941, 11944, 12135, 12418,
14095, 14350, 14382, 14501, 14656, 15048, 15176, 15708, 16442, 17057,
17119, 17515, 18121
STORKS   2401, 4476, 4682, 15198
STORMS   1526, 2527, 4868, 18617
STORY, NELSON (1838-1926)   17723
STORYTELLING   288, 512, 5678, 6061, 10946, 11103, 13414, 14521, 15803
collections   11034, 16659, 16662
STOUT, PENELOPE (1622-1732)   4253
STOWAWAYS   622, 6003, 6602
STOWE, HARRIET ELIZABETH (BEECHER), (1811-1896)   9308, 14715,
17857, 18147
STRAIT, TREVA (ADAMS), (1909-)   16401
STRATFORD (ONTARIO)--description and travel--guide-books   16127
STREET CLEANING   2729
STREET RAILROADS   7161
Canada--Toronto   5864
STRESS (PSYCHOLOGY)   8205, 8467
STRIKES AND LOCKOUTS   5151, 5153, 6198, 6443, 6986, 11406
vineyard laborers--California   5151, 5153, 16500, 16765, 17798
STRINGED INSTRUMENTS   9764
STRUCTURAL ENGINEERING   8686
STUART, MARY (QUEEN OF SCOTS), (1542-1587)   13730
STUDENTS   11406
STUDY, METHOD OF   9469
STURBRIDGE (MASSACHUSETTS)   2017
STUYVESANT, PETER (1592-1672)   4323, 11002, 11414, 17858
SUBMARINES   3736, 15417, 17287, 17812, 18335
SUBMERSIBLES   15417
SUBURBAN LIFE   9241, 10114
SUBWAYS   2183, 8508, 9678, 13269
SUCCESS   7620, 18450
biography   17444
SUDAN   3033, 8042, 8948
history--Abyssinian Expedition (1868)   8089
SUEZ CANAL (EGYPT)   2643, 14685
SUFFRAGE   3451, 4024, 11788, 16399
SUGAR   7672
SUGER (ABBOT OF SAINT DENIS), (1081-1151)   7672, 14511
SUICIDE   5614
prevention   11523
SUKKOTH   94
SULLIVAN, ANNE (1866-1936)   2410, 4571, 4572, 8151, 11578, 17416, 17934
SULLIVAN, TOM (1947-)   6825
SUMERIANS   8325

SUMMER 366, 1456, 1996, 5464, 5466, 5616, 5682, 5760, 5980, 7292, 9144, 10141, 11099, 13349, 15050, 16816, 17356, 18419
SUN 52, 762, 765, 2147, 3136, 3892, 4628, 8210, 12007, 15449, 18553
SUN YAT SEN (1866-1925) 2488
SUNDIATA (KING OF MALI), (d. 1255)--legends 1609
SUPERMARKETS 3270
  vocational guidance 10610
SUPERNATURAL 345, 1289, 2897, 5122, 6251, 8337, 8682, 8781, 10007, 10960, 11369, 11603, 13174, 13428, 13449, 15830
SUPERSTITION 416, 2272, 4815, 5557, 15140, 16757, 18178, 18474
  poetry 12405
SURFING 3993, 5283, 13173, 15878
  addresses, essays, lectures 9895
  biography 13094
SURGERY 9569
  infancy and childhood 3365, 3367
SURVIVAL 11, 500, 911, 2066, 2429, 2695, 3247, 3429, 3517, 3605, 4798, 5246, 5479, 6345, 6740, 7255, 7681, 7682, 8023, 8657, 9204, 11715, 11969, 12424, 12524, 12903, 13013, 13643, 13791, 14528, 14676, 14678, 14764, 14904, 16039, 16071, 16148, 16187, 16712, 18079, 18168, 18354
SWAHILI LANGUAGE
  alphabet 5751
  books in 4924
SWAMPS 5690, 13802, 13971, 15898, 18494
SWANS 447, 448, 562, 5756, 8851, 11621, 17794
SWAZILAND 3034
SWEDEN 428, 429, 2511, 7428, 7430, 7432, 8033, 10826, 10835, 10843, 12107, 17147, 17468
  social life and customs--pictorial works 14751
SWEDES 7676
SWEDISH AMERICANS 4334, 5520, 5526, 8196, 9429, 9432, 10852, 10853, 10854, 12907
SWEDISH POETRY 17860
SWIMMERS 6890, 9075, 13107
SWIMMING 959, 1339, 1783, 6053, 6971, 7102, 8529, 9063, 9750, 10031, 13036, 13073, 14814, 14815, 14816, 14817, 14821, 15054, 15587, 16260, 16459, 18158, 18267
  training 4194
SWINGS 11654
SWITZERLAND 688, 14807, 16102, 17530
  pictorial works 12550
SWORDS 3788, 9679, 10711
SYMBIOSIS 698, 15635
SYMPATHY 9901
SYRUPS 17592
SYSOEVA, EKATERINA ALEKSEEVNA (1829-1893) 375
SZOLD, HENRIETTA (1860-1945) 3919

- T -

TAILORING 4716
TAIPEI (TAIWAN) 15541
TAIWAN 2819, 3323, 5264
TAKASHIMA, SHIZUYE (1928-) 16614
TAKULLI INDIANS 1707

TALISMANS see CHARMS
TALLCHIEF, MARIA (1925-) 4704, 7354, 16900
TANAINA INDIANS--legends 17253
TANGANYIKA see TANZANIA
TANKA (JAPANESE) POETRY 1098
TANNING 5950
TANZANIA 3035, 7592, 9553, 9823, 11089, 11601, 13518, 14260, 14609,
  16256, 16257, 17277
  description and travel 9407, 13512
    views 7034
  history 7149
TAOS INDIANS 3487, 9612, 18236
  art 177
  poetry 18237
TAPESTRY 4836
TARANTULAS 3960
TARASCAN INDIANS 18171
TARBELL, IDA MINERVA (1857-1944) 3966, 6031
TARKENTON, FRANCIS A. (1940-) 2161, 2607, 10763, 11870, 15906
TASMANIA 3310, 3312, 3313
  native races 3311
TATARS--legends 14397
TAXATION 10927, 18119
TAYLOR, SUSIE KING (1848-1912) 1931
TCHERNAVIN, TATIANA 16720
TEACHER-STUDENT RELATIONSHIPS 1082, 3568, 3617
TEACHERS 728, 1056, 3868, 4252, 4461, 4489, 4640, 5037, 5746, 5828, 7274,
  7307, 7804, 10534, 11578, 13616, 14060
  Black American 11051
  women 2648, 6029
TEALE, EDWIN WAY (1899-1981) 16723
TECHNOLOGY 4324, 8746, 9532, 13677, 13678, 13679, 13680, 13681, 13683,
  13685, 16018
  China--history 15671
  history 17649
  transfer 3787
  United States 10442
  vocational guidance 8649
TECUMSEH (SHAWNEE CHIEF), (1768-1813) 4012, 4275, 5247, 8879, 11217,
  16279
  plays 5247
TEETH 4666, 5177, 7671, 11240, 13808, 14533
  care and hygiene 9746, 14345, 17583
TEJAS INDIANS 14162
TEKAKWITHA, CATHERINE (1656-1680) 2343
TELECOMMUNICATIONS--vocational guidance 6278
TELEGRAPH 3725
TELEPHONE 342, 2150, 3440, 4513, 11846, 13001
  operators 961
  vocational guidance 4600
TELEVISION 1445, 2793, 4125, 14547
  advertising 9586
  broadcasting 7779, 15507
    of news 1444
      biography 16700
    programs 2423, 15942
    vocational guidance 6283, 7011, 9915, 11345, 14161

production and direction 9347
vocational guidance 16407
TELL, WILLIAM (fl. 13th-14th century?) 2536, 6434, 8822
TEMNE (AFRICAN PEOPLE)
    kings and rulers--biography 8885
TEMPERAMENT 705, 1683
TEMPERATURE 1423
TENNESSEE 2584, 16171
    history 16170
       Civil War (1861-1865) 16174
TENNIS 962, 970, 3426, 4032, 4127, 4793, 4794, 4795, 5169, 6787, 6812,
    8098, 8608, 8861, 8984, 9042, 9065, 10394, 10520, 11273, 11666, 11858,
    12122, 13035, 13245, 14371, 15240, 15932, 16947
    players 2611, 2634, 7692, 8098, 8159, 9059, 9074, 10394, 11855, 11858,
       11862, 11980, 12482, 12484, 13104, 15905, 16483
       Australia 9062
TERESA, SAINT (1515-1582) 4916
TEREZIN (CONCENTRATION CAMP) 10714
TERHUNE, ALBERT PAYSON (1872-1942) 17142
TERRARIUMS 8099, 15754, 18221
TERRELL, MARY (CHURCH), (1863-1954) 16243
TETON INDIANS--legends 18386
TEXAS 860, 899, 1268, 1276, 2659, 2795, 4353, 4354, 4355, 5511, 5512,
    5513, 5514, 5515, 5594, 7062, 7165, 7905, 7928, 8342, 8343, 17315
    biography 331, 10123, 11225, 14351
    description and travel 11844, 13156
       views 15060
    East 11124
    geography 14933
    history 11220, 14009, 14933, 16183, 17634
       to 1846 50, 1685, 5051, 5986, 6806, 11328, 17541
       Revolution (1835-1836) 9301, 11546, 16880
    social life and customs 9179
TEXAS RANGERS 8083, 11332, 11333, 13434, 17634
TEXTILE INDUSTRY 1610, 2515, 9949, 15538
TEWA INDIANS 3485
THAILAND 824, 826, 1588, 2824, 7667, 7676, 8263, 13624, 13818, 17578
    social life and customs 6802, 15083, 16078
THAMES RIVER 7159
THANKSGIVING DAY 1021, 1083, 1144, 1323, 3354, 4462, 4869, 5423, 6900,
    7748, 7940, 8915, 9137, 11156, 14499, 15218, 17678, 18350, 18591
    legends 1141
THEATER 4130, 6567, 6568, 6569, 9824, 13593
    Africa 17537
    England 1284
       history 8321
    production and direction 14441
    vocational guidance 850
THEODORE II (NEGUS OF ETHIOPIA), (d. 1868) 15062
THERAPEUTICS--suggestive 3830
THIEVES see ROBBERS AND OUTLAWS
THOMPSON, JOHN ALBERT (1827-1876) 3142
THOREAU, HENRY DAVID (1817-1862) 3891, 14419
THORPE, JIM (1888-1953) 5653, 14222, 15107
THOUGHT AND THINKING 12782, 14476, 16551, 18024
THUNDERSTORMS 2127, 7256, 18545
TIBET 2952, 5537, 10728, 14112

TICONDEROGA, BATTLE OF (1758)   13454, 13458
TIDES   3137, 3598
TIE-DYEING   4874
TIGERS   56, 1055, 2481, 2804, 2911, 6154, 14603, 15007, 15795, 18042,
    18051, 18475
TIGUA INDIANS   16218
TIMBUCTOO   15211
TIME   26, 107, 738, 1314, 1358, 1361, 1421, 3825, 6217, 7802, 9232, 9900,
    10038, 10890, 11338, 12695, 13982, 14727, 15068, 15329, 15666, 17466,
    17706, 18585
    history   3825
    measurements   1053, 1529
TIMIDITY   see   BASHFULNESS
TIMUCUA INDIANS   16180
TLINGIT INDIANS
    biography   13396
    legends   15829
TOADS   see   FROGS AND TOADS
TOBOGGANS   12996
TOGO   3037, 16976
TOKYO (JAPAN)   3975
TOLEDO WAR (1835)   6755
TOLERATION   33, 5549, 5581, 16170, 17838
TOMBIGBEE RIVER--folklore   1048
TONGUE TWISTERS   8645, 13850, 13851, 15148, 15383
TOOLS   90, 108, 14522
TOOTHACHE   17971, 17973
TOPOLOGY   6404
TORNADOES   2527, 4675, 10434, 15579
    Ohio--Xenia (1974)   10186
    poetry   136
TORONTO (ONTARIO)   361, 13548, 15794
    Canadian National Exhibition--pictorial works   11081
    description and travel--views   5864, 5866
    ferries--history   5865
    social life and customs   5864
    theaters   15591
TORONTO ISLANDS (ONTARIO)--history   5865, 8254
TOTEMS AND TOTEMISM   8438
TOUSSAINT-LOUVERTURE, FRANÇOIS-DOMINIQUE (1743-1803)   16593
TOWERS--Ontario--Toronto   2802
TOYMAKERS   9389
TOYMAKING   11060, 12802
TOYS   283, 720, 1346, 1928, 2301, 2379, 3333, 3391, 3536, 4360, 4468, 6067,
    6256, 6258, 7365, 8266, 9351, 9912, 10685, 10704, 11594, 11945, 11963,
    12246, 12250, 12479, 12492, 12638, 13175, 13708, 13896, 15810, 18043,
    18050, 18434
TRACK ATHLETICS   585, 724, 822, 4033, 4244, 6087, 6649, 6891, 7620,
    8532, 8988, 9070, 9077, 9535, 9792, 10489, 11072, 11233, 12714, 13005,
    13216, 14246, 15107, 18130
    poetry   130
TRACKING AND TRAILING   11782, 15288, 17642
TRADE UNIONS   6584
TRADEMARKS--history   2875
TRAFALGAR (CAPE), BATTLE OF (1805)   2723
TRAFFIC
    accidents   8796

engineering 16646
regulations 5770, 15585
signs and signals 11308
TRAILDRIVING 6641
TRAINS 624, 4923, 6017, 7294, 10578, 11498, 12011, 13257, 13469, 13554, 14492, 16645
TRAMPOLINING 8626
TRAMPS 2958, 15121
TRANSPLANTATION OF ORGANS, TISSUES, ETC. 12891
TRANSPORTATION 960, 8037, 13234, 14333, 16472, 17610, 18145, 18481
history 8679, 12289, 17347
vocational guidance 7207
TRANSVAAL--description and travel 5983
TRAPPING 403, 565, 2713, 6896, 8865
TRASVINA, CESAR 14761
TRAVEL 200, 363, 369, 411, 599, 1313, 2419, 2904, 2941, 3168, 3889, 4015, 4271, 4276, 4454, 5227, 5358a, 5537, 5893, 6709, 7840, 8094, 8152, 8194, 8655, 8668, 8694, 8705, 9240, 9244, 9245, 9499, 9743, 9806, 9962, 10326, 10694, 11100, 12268, 12429, 13006, 13059, 13234, 13269, 13417, 13445, 13625, 13839, 14066, 14449, 15211, 15885, 16075, 16166, 16169, 16652, 16800, 16976, 17286, 17315, 17970, 18276, 18298, 18435
TRAVEL AGENTS 963
TRAVIS, WILLIAM BARRET (1809-1836) 11220
TREASURES 1726, 2330
TREEHOUSES 17463
TREES 337, 824, 913, 919, 1389, 2392, 2537, 2578, 2580, 2855, 2892, 3238, 3835, 3845, 4068, 4187, 5041, 5211, 5279, 5532, 5810, 6738, 6902, 7324, 7470, 8027, 8208, 8495, 8856, 9827, 13153, 13161, 13583, 13862, 14141, 14310, 14770, 15293, 15670, 15701, 15761, 16694, 17092, 17116, 17349, 17801
in cities 5279
diseases and pests 15156, 17175
identification of 6525, 12265, 18554
pine 1389
United States
Indiana 4762, 15506
Michigan 12148
Minnesota 12265
in winter 3801
wounds and injuries 17175
TRENTON, BATTLE OF (1776) 7703, 17044
TRENTON (NEW JERSEY)--politics and government 15139
TREVINO, LEE (1939-) 9026, 17219
TRIALS 837, 14132
TRICKS 1101, 2288, 4115, 6018, 6019, 6712, 7908, 9129, 9761, 10206, 10207, 15362, 15847
TRILLIUM (FERRY)--history 5865
TRIPLETS 165
TROLLEY CAR see STREET RAILROADS
TROPICAL FISH 14922, 16907, 18219, 18250, 18542
TROPICS 1964, 6969
TROY 1209, 2168, 5353, 12532, 14209
romances 7247
TRUCK DRIVING 18413
TRUCKS 18459, 18574
models 17696
TRUMAN, HARRY S (1884-1972) 3848, 5624

TRUMPET 1921
TRUTH, SOJOURNER (1797?-1883) 1562, 13187, 13575
TRUTHFULNESS AND FALSEHOOD 1363, 2263, 4924, 5066, 5685, 9376,
    10671, 11827, 12846, 14728, 15459, 16425, 17354, 18468
TSIMSHIAN INDIANS
    legends 8203, 16964, 16965
    missions 17742
TSUNAMIS 8336
TUAREG INDIANS 1765, 5457, 7486
TUBMAN, HARRIET (ROSS), (1815?-1913) 5499, 7174, 8743, 11358, 16246,
    16562, 18104
    plays 3375
    poetry 10399
TUGBOATS 7157, 7158, 7159, 7160, 10303, 13748, 14627
TUMORS
    prevention and control 1511
    See also CANCER
TUNISIA 3042, 10983, 11036, 13129, 14670
TUNNELS 9663
TURKEY (COUNTRY) 3338, 10115
    history--Ottoman Empire (1288-1918) 17479
    social life and customs 7003, 15082
TURKEYS 5423, 11914, 16221
TURKMEDOV, YAKUB ABDUL 9463
TURNBULL, RODERICK 17066
TURNER, NAT (1800?-1831) 7370, 18093
TURQUOISE 8975
TURTLES 77, 78, 1018, 3397, 4508, 6339, 6409, 7047, 7120, 7488, 8270,
    8426, 8491, 9265, 11380, 12564, 13087, 14210, 14445, 15292, 15690,
    17558, 17561, 17971, 18495
TUSCARORA INDIANS 18166
    legends 15578
TUSHKINE (TRIBE) 7485
TUTANKHAMEN (KING OF EGYPT), (fl. 14th century B.C.) 4191, 16567
    tomb 6936
TUTORS 8469
TWAIN, MARK see CLEMENS, SAMUEL LANGHORNE
TWIN LAKES REGION (ALASKA) 9630
TWINS 635, 857, 3562, 3569, 3804, 4144, 5099, 9509, 13038, 13122, 13509,
    17121, 17334, 18001, 18100
TYPHOONS 3198

- U -

UFO see FLYING SAUCERS
UGANDA 3044, 7840, 9254, 9442, 9779, 9794, 9795, 9796, 9797, 9798, 9799,
    9800, 9801, 9802, 9803, 9804, 12630, 13518, 13931
    history 5510, 16810
    kings and rulers 5510
    legends 5510
UKRAINE 1780
UKRAINIAN AMERICANS 10143, 16389
UMBRELLAS AND PARASOLS 2244, 2245, 9777, 18367
UNDERGROUND RAILROAD 328, 2327, 2504, 3186, 3512, 5918, 6364, 8671,

9028, 9366, 10101, 11813, 11987, 12050, 12336, 15944, 16562, 17785, 18323
UNDERSEA RESEARCH STATIONS 6298
UNDERWATER EXPLORATION 1028, 2231, 3736, 4763, 5105, 6227, 8959, 11772, 15417
UNIFORMS, MILITARY 12919
UNITARIANISM 5336
UNITAS, JOHN (1933-) 7295, 11881
UNITED NATIONS 5484, 5605, 9631, 14047, 14947, 16058
  Armed Forces 5758
  biography 7828
  Children's Fund 15120
  pictorial works 10285, 14934
UNITED STATES 8186, 9947, 12157, 15581
  antiquities 7740
  Armed Forces
    Air Force Missile Test Center (Cocoa, Florida) 14925
    Army 1887
      aviation 4811
      Black American troops 5050
      Cavalry
        history 5050
        (10th) 13727
      Military Academy (West Point) 3789
        biography 14191
      Mountain Division--(10th) 3143
      vocational guidance 13247
    Black Americans 12218
    Coast Guard 501, 3913, 10413
      search and rescue operations 7079
    Marine Corps 16991
    medals, badges, decorations, etc. 9736
    Navy
      Submarine Forces 11015
      vocational guidance 13248
    women 7512
  biography 578, 1256, 4063, 4535, 4858, 5632, 7653
    collections 8484
    poetry 1461, 12100
  Bureau of Indian Affairs 12727
  civilization
    Black American influence 5071
    Indian influence 13314
  commerce 3052
    China--history 16640
  Congress 4229, 9269, 17680
    biography 14941
    House of Representatives 10377
    Senate 8557, 13502
      biography 9688
  Constitution 3910, 5871, 12460
    1st-10th amendments 18136
  constitutional history 14894
  Declaration of Independence 2342, 3911, 4458, 13614, 14646
    signers 5873, 18304
  description and travel 2107, 4928, 9020, 14442, 18229
    guide-books 16854

economic conditions (1918-1945)   12039
exploring expeditions   935, 2531
fairs   13516
foreign population   9837, 14134, 16140, 17014
foreign relations
   Japan   7022
   Latin America   4216
Forest Service   18226
history   646, 1935, 3356, 3909, 3990, 4696, 5374, 5731, 5924, 7166, 7332,
   9035, 9266, 11370, 11475, 11991, 12988, 14781, 16945, 17684, 17724,
   18252
   cartoons and caricatures   16608
   literature--New York   2983
   local   381, 6048, 13716, 17711
   Naval   8878
   plays   14653
   pictorial works   3726
   poetry   2213, 3821
   race relations   7332
   wit and humor   16608
   Colonial period (ca. 1600-1775)   164, 2672, 2673, 3681, 4253, 4323,
      4333, 4334, 4454, 4634, 4637, 5269, 5639, 5850, 5941, 5943, 5947,
      5948, 5950, 6040, 6151, 6524, 7185, 7926, 7942, 8428, 10442, 10538,
      10553, 13490, 14134
      biography   6146, 9084, 16175
      social life and customs   860
   French and Indian War (1755-1763)   5427, 5850, 6673, 12519, 15871,
      16049, 17984
   Revolution (1775-1783)   736, 1266, 1311, 1408, 1997, 2077, 2342, 2631,
      2980, 3203, 3320, 3350, 3475, 3660, 3661, 3790, 3844, 3981, 4387,
      4452, 4458, 5126, 5129, 5268, 5286, 5428, 5885, 5886, 5951, 6101,
      6148, 6394, 6670, 6675, 6707, 7580, 7611, 7627, 7703, 7867, 9364,
      9643, 10397, 10408, 10479, 10524, 11038, 11125, 11360, 11781, 11924,
      12345, 12354, 12408, 13458, 14946, 15040, 15087, 15953, 17343,
      17848, 17850
      biography   233, 6100, 6380, 6395, 7198, 8221, 8433, 12196, 14340,
        15984, 16276, 16540
      campaigns and battles   1400, 3989, 16082
      causes   12342, 16716, 18304
      Loyalist-Rebel split   1266
      Minutemen (Militia)   1408
      miscellanea   9643
      personal narratives   11733
      pictorial works   16427
      quotations, maxims, etc.   5944
      refugees   12951
      Secret Service   14135
      women   580
   1783-1815   736, 4322, 4699, 6202
   Constitutional period (1789-1809)   16726
   19th century   14020
   War of 1812   2517, 3216, 4711, 7939, 8668, 9272, 9775, 11982, 16553,
      17851, 18083
      campaigns and battles   7643, 11852
      Naval operations   17849
   1815-1861   3775, 9245

Black Hawk War (1832) 18441
War with Mexico (1845-1848) 924, 5051, 14194
Naval Expedition to Japan (1852-1854) 10128
Civil War (1861-1865) 1269, 1273, 1349, 2629, 2630, 4356, 5267, 5487,
    5999, 6149, 6641, 7583, 7848, 8147, 8339, 8713, 8748, 8891, 8990,
    9323, 9485, 9521, 9626, 10414, 10643, 10679, 11229, 11329, 11330,
    11796, 12344, 12352, 13237, 16110, 16174
    biography 5285, 5631, 16319, 16637
    Black Americans 7214, 11504, 14032, 16319
    campaigns and battles 6390, 6676, 9484
    causes 7019, 7925, 9521
    communications 6138
    medical and sanitary affairs 4697
    Naval operations 13016
    personal narratives--Confederate side 12824
    regimental histories
        Michigan 17994
        Stonewall Brigade 6390
        Wisconsin infantry--8th 15560, 18471
    Secret Service 6138, 14135, 16637
1865-1921 9524
1889- 12020, 12022
War of 1898 3151
1901-1929 9523
1917-1933 5841
Executive Order 9066 (1942) 3973
1960- 13127
immigration and emigration 5306, 12048, 12507, 14134
    history--pictorial works 7691
    personal narratives 1010
industry--history 17038, 17674
National Park Service 3785
occupations 5459
officials and employees 10928
politics and government 5100, 5299, 9267, 11693
    1789-1797 3349
    1797-1801 3349
    20th century 8558
    1933-1945 10411
    1945-1953 10846
    1953-1961 10846
race relations 9522, 9525, 9526
Secret Service 12698
social conditions 4858, 15511
    pictorial works 12040
    1865-1918 9523, 11979, 14900
        addresses, essays, lectures 9527
    1918-1932 9523, 12039
social life and customs 2346, 14170, 18252
    Colonial period (ca. 1600-1775) 232, 1330, 1826, 4370, 4472, 5202,
        5702, 5883, 10442, 11019, 13490, 13528, 14319, 16606, 17038, 17039,
        17235
    1783-1865 4315, 11478, 17046
    19th century 17650, 18464
    1865-1918 231, 932, 3738, 7364, 8207
    1918-1945 3986, 10850
    1945-1970 10846
sources 542

Supreme Court   9271, 10309, 10687
    biography   18456
Volunteers in Service to America   17844
Western Reserve--pictorial works   2752
See also under individual states, e.g., TEXAS
UNIVERSE   1382, 12961
UNMARRIED MOTHERS   9909, 10487
    personal narratives   11667
UPPER VOLTA   30, 38, 7483, 7495
URANIUM MINES AND MINING   1706
URANUS (PLANET)   759
URBAN RENEWAL   2642, 9945, 15954, 16628
URUGUAY   4940
    history   12060
UTAH   2706, 5970, 5972, 5975, 5977, 7727, 9285, 15820, 16026
    history   8778
    songs and music   8703
UTE INDIANS   1955
    Wars (1879)   13211

- V -

VACATIONS   326, 5649, 6318, 6474, 11848, 14375, 14876, 15996, 16118
VACCINATION   3752
VALLEY FORGE (PENNSYLVANIA)   7591, 11993, 16082
VALLEYS   6970, 8811
VALUES   422, 1783, 2437, 2655, 3576, 6354, 13993, 14938
VAMPIRES   11391
VAN GOGH, VINCENT   see   GOGH, VINCENT VAN
VAN LEW, ELIZABETH (1818-1900)   12886
VASA (WARSHIP)   6227
VASQUEZ DE CORONADO, FRANCISCO (1510-1549)   13014, 16583
VATICAN CITY   4774
VEGETABLES   1287, 6476, 6529, 12267, 15277, 15311, 16920
VEHICLES--history   12289, 17045
VELARDE, PABLITA (1918-)   12726
VELAZQUEZ, DIEGO (1599-1660)   4755
VENEREAL DISEASES   8872
VENEZUELA   7063, 16876
    history   13236
VENICE (ITALY)   2375, 4261, 10056
VENTRILOQUISM   8862, 9766
VERCHERES, MARIE MADELEINE JARRET DE (1678-1747)   2248
VERENDRYE, PIERRE GAULTIER DE VARENNES, SIEUR DE LA   see   LA
    VERENDRYE, PIERRE GAULTIER DE VARENNES, SIEUR DE
VERMILION PARISH (LOUISIANA)--Paul J. Rainey Wild Life Sanctuary   9150
VERMONT   2862, 5707, 9859, 10567, 16350
VERRAZANO, GIOVANNI DA (1485?-1527)   16595
VERSALLES, ZOILO (1940-)   16763
VERTEBRATES   10952
    fossils   8511, 8624
VETERINARIANS   2060, 4414, 7263, 11024, 16405, 16418
VETERINARY MEDICINE   1509, 2224, 6832
    vocational guidance   2060, 6832, 7013, 16320

VICE-PRESIDENTS--United States 5755
VICKSBURG (MISSISSIPPI)--Siege (1863) 12352
VICTORIA (QUEEN OF ENGLAND), (1819-1901) 6901, 7909, 16410
VIENNA (AUSTRIA)--history 12954
VIETNAM--history 2534, 7024
VIETNAMESE CONFLICT (1961-1975) 3363, 4311, 5143, 7024, 7127
    children 10793, 13710
    public opinion 2778
VIGILANCE COMMITTEES--history 11524
VIKINGS 1396, 1411, 2582, 3129, 3592, 3686, 7845, 7849, 8452, 9203, 12790,
    13794, 14321, 16518, 16986, 16987, 16988
VILLAGE LIFE 11808, 12287, 15713
VINCENNES (INDIANA)--history--Revolution (1775-1783) 15339, 16821
VIOLENCE 12327, 12596, 14541
    United States 11524
VIOLIN 59, 353, 1029, 1531, 4635, 10668, 11029
VIOLIN MAKERS 17847
VIOLINISTS AND VIOLONCELLISTS 3267
VIRGIN ISLANDS 495, 497, 2377
    description and travel 8432
    history 8432
VIRGINIA 650, 3681, 16535
    history--Colonial period (ca. 1600-1775) 5959, 10176, 10663, 12701
    politics and government--Colonial period (ca. 1600-1775) 16716
VIRGINIA RANGERS 16176
VIRUSES 12962
VISION 11783, 14905, 17704
VITAMINS 9355, 12963, 17707
VOCABULARY 547, 846, 4337, 7994, 11049, 11810, 12101, 13039, 14101,
    14215, 14855, 14995
VOCATIONAL GUIDANCE 424, 430, 939, 946, 947, 948, 949, 950, 951, 952,
    953, 954, 955, 956, 957, 958, 959, 960, 961, 962, 963, 964, 965, 966,
    967, 1092, 1474, 1475, 1476, 1477, 1478, 1479, 1496, 1519, 1520, 1522,
    1523, 1524, 1691, 2027, 2564, 2760, 3193, 3840, 4297, 4601, 5459, 5801,
    5803, 6086, 6273, 6274, 6275, 6276, 6277, 6278, 6279, 6280, 6281, 6282,
    6283, 6557, 6765, 6832, 7007, 7008, 7009, 7010, 7011, 7012, 7013, 7268,
    7274, 7280, 7560, 7744, 7761, 7823, 8186, 9481, 9907, 10299, 10377,
    10610, 10611, 10784, 10785, 10787, 10788, 10904, 11344, 13246, 13247,
    13248, 13482, 13484, 13486, 14880, 14985, 14986, 14998, 15008, 15233,
    16209, 16320, 16418, 17443
    collections 1229
    study and teaching 15008
    women 11682
    See also specific professions, e.g., TEACHERS
VOICE 9766
VOLCANOES 2530, 5076, 10729, 11834, 16509, 17828
VOLUNTEER WORKERS 3882
VON STREETER, JAMES (1941-) 16415
VOTING 13613
    United States 10847
VOYAGES AND TRAVELS 2441, 7145, 9755, 16222, 18046
    around the world 14038, 17286
VOYAGEURS NATIONAL PARK (MINNESOTA) 389
VULTURES 4222, 6330, 13473, 17136

- W -

WABASH RIVER 6363
WAGNER, WILHELM RICHARD (1813-1883) 17163
WAGONS see CARRIAGES AND CARTS
WAITERS AND WAITRESSES 964
WALD, LILLIAN D. (1867-1940) 1786, 5308, 17986
WALES 319, 1215, 1883, 6422, 9811, 12440
  social life and customs 16808
WALKING 2032, 15459
  Minnesota 2467, 2468, 2469
WALLACE, LEW (1827-1905) 14999
WALLACE, WILLIAM ALEXANDER ANDERSON (1817-1899) 6629
WALRUSES 9964
WAMPANOAG INDIANS 808
  biography 7117, 7180
WANGOMBE (KIKUYU CHIEF), (d.ca. 1902) 9723
WANYANLIMAS 16256, 16257
WAR 5074, 5978, 8253, 9138, 9973, 10988, 12957, 13241, 16875, 17401
  miscellanea 14402
  moral and religious aspects 4219
WARD, AARON MONTGOMERY (1844-1913) 981
WARD, NANCY (d. 1822) 5782
WARDROBES 10690
WARM SPRINGS (GEORGIA) 1342
WARNER, GLENN SCOBEY (1871-1954) 17222
WARREN, WILLIAM WHIPPLE (1825-1853) 577
WARSHIPS 13016
WART HOGS 4870, 11730
WASHERWOMEN 18394
WASHINGTON, BOOKER TALIAFERRO (1856-1915) 1925, 7147, 16243, 16271,
  17546, 18137
WASHINGTON, GEORGE (1732-1799) 1998, 2583, 4365, 4552, 4577, 5231,
  6041, 6142, 6143, 6311, 7115, 8471, 9421, 10494, 11993, 12902, 16217,
  18081, 18146
WASHINGTON, MARTHA (DANDRIDGE) CUSTIS (1731-1802) 488, 17189,
  17391
WASHINGTON (DISTRICT OF COLUMBIA)
  Capitol 13976
  history 15901
  social life and customs 10540
  White House 10540, 14234
WASTE PRODUCTS 5478
WATER 616, 1521, 1791, 6542, 8687, 12721, 12814, 14686, 15450, 15762
  conservation 616, 1189
  experiments 510, 14632, 16022
  pollution 616, 1521, 1791, 3336, 9470, 10435, 13170, 13339, 13969, 16795
    experiments 16021
  purification 3336, 16268
  science 2206
  supply 1521
    California--Santee 16268
WATER COLOR PAINTING 7897
WATER SKIING 2037, 9387
WATER SPORTS 14078
  safety measures 6053, 14391

WATIE, STAND (1806-1871) 9626
WATUSI 13931
WAUNEKA, ANNIE (1912-) 12723
WEALTH 10561, 12811, 16250
WEASELS 13359, 13957
WEATHER 1426, 1442, 1526, 2006, 2009, 2127, 4209, 4238, 4962, 9933,
    10276, 11910, 12203, 13764, 14824, 15090, 15763
  control 1849
  forecasting 965, 7609, 16135
  lore 4561, 18206
WEAVING 2692, 4716, 7739, 9667, 10806, 12128
WEEDS 5044, 18313, 18419
WEIGHTLESSNESS 2151
WEIGHTS AND MEASURES 98, 755, 1428, 2131, 2134, 2991, 4824, 4965,
    5843, 6369, 6400, 7337, 8228, 9903, 11140, 11542, 12617, 13687, 13756,
    14804, 15070, 15453, 16105, 16109, 16394, 18571
  instruments 2991
  United States 6521, 7561
WEST, JERRY (1938-) 4787, 5570
THE WEST (UNITED STATES) 923, 1268, 1270, 1272, 1275, 1276, 1278,
    1280, 1350, 1451, 1452, 1691, 2240, 2531, 2663, 3252, 3502, 3732, 4150,
    4514, 6006, 6008, 6009, 6017, 6774, 7553, 7921, 8075, 9004, 9242, 9369,
    9720, 10369, 10439, 10441, 14026, 14327, 14771, 15002, 15034, 16396,
    17568, 18273
  in art 6931, 13545
  biography 493, 7176, 11314, 12526, 16515
  description and travel 13333, 15661, 17910, 18484
  exploration 6635
  history 2711, 10644, 11221, 14054
WEST INDIANS--in the United States 17797
WEST INDIES 34, 3131, 3204, 5591
  description and travel 15545
WESTWARD MOVEMENT 3064
WETLANDS 2473, 15892
WETZEL, LEWIS (1764?-1808) 1847
WHALES 1397, 1403, 2290, 5667, 5956, 8423, 8809, 9821, 10596, 11259,
    11356, 11489, 12290, 13647, 13751, 14297, 14353, 14524, 15029, 16189,
    17579, 18449, 18543
  in art 7381
  Pacific Grey 3954
  poetry 7381
WHALING 4702, 5767, 5942, 6344, 7565, 11996
  New England 6724
WHARTON COUNTY (TEXAS) 852
WHEAT 2272, 18333
WHEATLEY, PHILLIS (1753?-1784) 1958, 6438, 7150
WHEELS 6783, 12232, 12289, 13190, 15012, 17045
WHITMAN, MARCUS (1802-1847) 13721
WHITMAN, NARCISSA (PRENTICE), (1808-1847) 13721, 17521
WHITNEY, ELI (1765-1825) 10319
WHITTIER, JOHN GREENLEAF (1807-1892) 17312
WHITWORTH, KATHY (1939-) 5328
WIGGIN, KATE DOUGLAS (SMITH), (1856-1923) 11791
WILD ANIMALS see ANIMALS
WILD FLOWERS 339, 15325, 16543
  Colorado 14429
  Louisiana 2337

Minnesota--identification 12528
Ohio--identification 9896
Texas 18062
WILDER, ALMANZO J. (1857-1949) 17910
WILDER, LAURA (INGALLS), (1867-1957) 17439
correspondence 17910
journeys--Missouri Valley 17908
WILDERNESS AREAS 4579
Minnesota 5954
Ohio 12054
WILDERNESS SURVIVAL 6747
WILDLIFE 15100, 17257
conservation 13, 709, 1571, 1827, 1945, 2892, 3201, 4775, 4914, 4926,
4931, 6269, 6735, 7065, 7796, 10505, 11128, 11129, 11274, 11488, 11866,
13022, 14597, 15647, 17923, 18230
Africa 706, 707, 4344
Canada--Ontario 4352
poetry 3317
South America 15642
United States--Death Valley region 10628
refuges 7549
watching 2664
WILDLIFE MANAGEMENT--Ontario 12964
WILLARD, ARCHIBALD (1836-1918) 3890
WILLARD, FRANCES ELIZABETH (1839-1898) 11788
WILLIAMS, DANIEL HALE (1856-1931) 5786, 12092
WILLIAMS, ROGER (1604?-1683) 5232, 9084
WILLIAMS, THEODORE SAMUEL "TED" (1918-) 5880
WILLIAMSBURG (VIRGINIA)
description and travel--views 17453
history 10397, 10398, 13565
social life and customs 13565
WILLS 11372
WILSON, JACK see WOVOKA
WIND see WINDS
WIND INSTRUMENTS 9757
WIND POWER 4829
WINDMILLS 4184, 4758, 4829, 5760, 17233
Netherlands 16093
WINDS 1114, 1442, 2207, 5561, 5562, 6625, 11166, 12293
WINGS 18405
WINNEBAGO INDIANS 3972
WINTER, GEORGE (1809-1876) 1023
WINTER 665, 1801, 2405, 2593, 2741, 4179, 4816, 6165, 6779, 7423, 7542,
9946, 10142, 12276, 13337, 13569, 14790, 14904, 18036, 18603
poetry 10571
preparation for 83
WINTER SPORTS 5764
WISCONSIN 900, 2264, 3039, 4849, 4850, 4851, 5128, 5379, 5471, 5520,
5646, 5837, 5838, 6194, 6757, 14372, 14589
description and travel 4769, 4854
history 403, 532, 615, 2266, 2743, 4615, 4616, 4854, 5577, 8043, 11342,
15894
anecdotes, facetiae, etc. 6572
WISCONSIN INFANTRY--8th Regiment--1861-1865 18471
WISHES 513, 978, 2360, 2585, 3268, 3631, 4274, 5431, 7905, 10404, 16893,
16899

WIT AND HUMOR   179, 181, 418, 693, 906, 1064, 1270, 1306, 1700, 1716,
   1821, 2361, 2589, 2663, 2692, 3104, 3176, 3221, 3223, 3241, 3372, 3400,
   3509, 3808, 3814, 4116, 4173, 4219, 4223, 4285, 4342, 4364, 4440, 4441,
   4935, 5076, 5081, 5086, 5091, 5092, 5094, 5095, 5162, 5198, 5356, 5420,
   5432, 5434, 5565, 5684, 5773, 5796, 5862, 5970, 5971, 5972, 5973, 5974,
   5975, 5977, 6003, 6008, 6009, 6010, 6011, 6012, 6013, 6014, 6015, 6016,
   6063, 6477, 6719, 6865, 7061, 7319, 7320, 7577, 7578, 7844, 7952, 8080,
   8152, 8160, 8284, 8504, 8802, 8814, 8836, 9101, 9329, 9452, 9639, 9640,
   9641, 9642, 9692, 9857, 9960, 9999, 10037, 10072, 10159, 10600, 10741,
   10743, 10750, 10838, 11119, 11155, 11236, 11237, 11297, 11670, 11936,
   12073, 12644, 12809, 12810, 12956, 13282, 13283, 13287, 13291, 13300,
   13330, 13694, 13699, 13700, 13701, 14125, 14258, 14471, 14503, 14539,
   14540, 14602, 14699, 14700, 14876, 14987, 14988, 15132, 15147, 15150,
   15375, 15652, 15807, 16147, 16193, 16224, 16249, 16316, 16506, 16549,
   17100, 17109, 17362, 17372, 17399, 17565, 17777, 17875, 17878, 18046,
   18078, 18154, 18164, 18310, 18578
   pictorial works   9585
   Puerto Rican   13158
WITCH DOCTORS   12271, 12272
WITCHCRAFT   1020, 1362, 1970, 2845, 3745, 4111, 4403, 5314, 5554, 5952,
   7234, 7376, 7832, 8421, 8572, 9212, 9997, 10932, 11096, 11537, 12611,
   12687, 12688, 12947, 13906, 15974, 16050, 17064, 17462
   history   9976
   United States   237, 13587, 16151, 16152
WITCHES   48, 685, 1246, 1465, 2156, 2846, 2936, 3342, 3344, 3345, 3346,
   3347, 3418, 3431, 4044, 4045, 4046, 4047, 4048, 4049, 4050, 4051, 4052,
   4053, 4054, 4214, 4804, 4805, 4806, 4807, 4871, 5272, 5420, 5554, 6270,
   8172, 8359, 8572, 8789, 10055, 10362, 10934, 11418, 11448, 11558, 11802,
   12140, 12821, 12833, 13468, 13725, 13728, 15327, 15778, 16309, 17110,
   17247, 17396, 17412, 17580, 18009, 18427, 18469, 18470
   poetry   17462
WIZARDS   9811
WOLTERS, RICHARD A. (1920-)   18216
WOLVES   145, 324, 1131, 3542, 4142, 4931, 5377, 6137, 6176, 6740, 9128,
   10627, 12341, 13025, 13674, 14404, 14527, 15480, 15899, 17065, 17215,
   17239
   habits and behavior   17859
WOMBATS   15902
WOMEN
   in aeronautics   55, 4707, 5595, 6728
   in astronautics   7963, 8697
   athletes   4667, 8482, 8483, 9041, 14822, 14834, 16136, 17224
      Canada   11319
   authors   2665
   in the Bible   1052
   biography   7892, 16683, 17621
   Black Americans   2703, 2715
   in business   1658
   civil rights   863, 1271, 1866, 3530, 6072, 7181, 7503, 8997, 9515, 9826,
      9982, 11979, 12174, 16110, 16111, 16295, 16669
   condition of work   4024
   dancers   4704
   editors   2710
   education   17126
   educators   2648, 6026, 6029, 7804
   employment   9907, 9982, 12102, 13484, 15233, 17444
      pictorial works   12008

ethnologists--biography   9768
golfers   5328
gymnasts   5585
history   4730, 7364, 7771
Jewish   10656
lawyers   5146
legislators   5622
Liberation Movement   2950, 5628
Malawi--biography   8928
in the mass media industry   2024
newspaper reporters   5148
painters   12719
physicians   984, 2025, 2889, 3474, 5147, 7172, 8742, 10314, 12856
poetry   12741
poets   5933, 16861
in rodeos   7693
scientists   4705
social conditions   1282, 4024
social life and customs   4730
spies   4698, 5355, 5631
suffrage   863, 1866, 4501, 5628, 5630, 7503, 7587, 15390, 16599
in the television industry   9915
United States   1658, 12655, 14654, 15921
   biography   55, 2054, 2507, 3657, 3661, 3850, 4504, 4660, 4697, 4704,
      4707, 5144, 6767, 7503, 9317, 14658, 16333, 17444, 17620
   history   8900, 10236, 17544
   Nebraska   12700
      biography   9647
   The West--social conditions   10646
vocational guidance   6786
Zambia   4447
WONDER, STEVIE (1950-)   5275, 7811, 7830, 18068
WOOD   17379
   carving   2551, 12370, 15482, 17687
      history   13910
WOODCHUCKS   11491
WOODHOUSE, CAROLINA AUGUSTA   14791
WOODLAND INDIANS   14409, 14979
WOODWARD, HENRY (1646?-ca. 1688)   16175
WOODWORK   90, 10305
WOOL   3208, 4716
WOOL INDUSTRY AND TRADE--New England--history   6727
WORK   1278, 3968, 4528, 7744, 7982, 10995, 12738, 12859, 13047, 14267,
   14940, 17188, 18117
   night   3784
WORLD HEALTH ORGANIZATION   7676, 15928
WORLD HISTORY   1119, 6141, 9365, 17216
WORLD WAR I (1914-1918)   3150, 5082, 8972, 11100, 11105, 15959, 18160
   aerial operations   7507
      Germany   18312
   biography   4698
   England   5693
WORLD WAR II (1939-1945)   538, 587, 996, 1215, 1887, 2446, 2599, 2725,
   3126, 4083, 4669, 4675, 5375, 5682, 6114, 6119, 7846, 8145, 10478, 11510,
   11984, 13128, 13853, 15351, 15960, 16499, 16713, 17051, 17229, 17478,
   17811, 17812, 18507
   aerial operations   11053, 14279

Arctic Ocean   16711
Austria   12954
Black Americans   3529
Burma   5157
campaigns   8538
  Africa--North   1777
  England   6574, 6623
  Europe--West   1777
  France--Normandy (June 6, 1944)   1779
  Germany   6120
  Italy   3143
  Russia   16746
  Solomon Islands   16991
children   1679, 4215, 16971
China   5157
Crete   14827
Denmark   18329
England   10956, 14279, 16412, 16971, 17480, 17759
evacuation of civilians   16614
France   5375
Jews   1679, 4670, 16448
  Netherlands   5601
Naval operations   16711
Netherlands   15531, 17226, 17233
Pacific Ocean   1778
personal narratives   16971
  American   16991
  Jews   14224, 18534
prisoners and prisons--Germany   17992
refugees   4800, 6623, 10660
regimental histories--United States--10th Division   3143
Ukraine   16450
underground movements
  biography   13873
  Jews   12045
  Netherlands   16750
  Poland   18326
United States   2093
WORMS   10881, 10883, 12740, 13970, 15740, 16779
WORSHIP   5967
WOUNDED KNEE CREEK, BATTLE OF (1890)   1884
WOVOKA (1856-1932)   912
WRESTLERS   212, 5869
WRESTLING   11650, 13467
WRICE, HERMAN (1940-)   1501
WRIGHT, FRANK LLOYD (1869-1959)   14113
WRIGHT, ORVILLE (1871-1948)   6204, 6903, 7199, 9536, 12455, 14030, 14282,
  15986, 16282
WRIGHT, WILBUR (1867-1912)   6204, 6903, 7199, 9536, 12455, 14030, 14282,
  15986, 16282
WRITING   5552, 5634, 11756
  history   4392, 5108, 16685
WYAM INDIANS   11424, 11425
WYOMING   15004
  description and travel   12217
  history   6893
WYOMING VALLEY (PENNSYLVANIA)   3843

- X -

X, MALCOLM (1925-1965)   134, 7826, 17800
X-RAYS--equipment and supplies   17740

- Y -

YACHTS AND YACHTING   16007, 16653
   racing   11854
YAK   368a
YANA INDIANS   10104
   legends   1575
YAQUI INDIANS--legends   4332
YEAST   9975
YELLOWSTONE NATIONAL PARK (WYOMING)   9855
YOGA   3316, 6906
YOKUTS INDIANS--music   13666
YOM KIPPUR   7303
YONKERS (NEW YORK)   9321, 9322
YORKTOWN (VIRGINIA)--Siege (1781)   6039
YORUBAS   85, 2302, 13063, 15016, 16269
YOUNG, ANDREW (1932-)   7818
YOUNG, BRIGHAM (1801-1877)   2704, 17972
YOUNG, WHITNEY M. (1921-1971)   11618
YOUTH   1932, 2807, 2838, 6749, 7288, 10166, 10484, 10617, 11160, 12078,
   15931, 16042, 17751
   biography   14289
   employment   10543, 14913
   health and hygiene   6768
   human behavior   15164, 15818, 15862, 18296
   interviews   8636
   Israel   6988
   Russia   12496
   suicidal behavior   11523
   United States--New York (City)--case studies   11946
   See also BOYS; GIRLS
YUCATAN   1304
YUGOSLAVIA   11619
   social life and customs   5842
YUGOSLAVIAN AMERICANS   9426

- Z -

ZAHARIAS, MILDRED "BABE" (DIDRIKSON), (1912-1956)   4667
ZAIRE   3040, 3231, 4248, 8691, 11325, 11679, 13554, 15402, 15713, 16327
   description and travel   9874, 11312, 17763
   history   610, 4247, 11439
   social life and customs   5343, 5398
ZAIRE RIVER   9951
ZAMBIA   1064, 3048, 3594, 4446, 5067, 6166, 7325, 8705, 11433, 11808,

15537, 16387
history 13770, 14744
women 4447
ZAPATA, EMILIANO (1879-1919) 16597
ZANZIBAR see TANZANIA
ZEBRAS 706, 3162, 8921, 18095
ZENGER, JOHN PETER (1697-1746) 6527
ZION NATIONAL PARK (UTAH) 2707
ZIONISTS 4570, 4952
ZODIAC 14851
ZOOLOGICAL GARDENS 2055, 2223, 2224, 2909, 3378, 4424, 7545, 7634,
   7695, 8138, 8816, 9172, 9261, 10652, 11275, 13268, 13538, 14308, 14567,
   15036, 15197, 15416, 15643, 16745, 17184, 17463
   employees 2223, 7275
ZOOLOGICAL MODELS 9468
ZOOLOGISTS 11362
ZOOLOGY 245, 1191, 1795, 3141, 4174, 4512, 5206, 5310, 6702, 7796, 8792,
   10432, 11136, 14713, 15282
   Africa 6830, 11197, 18094
     East 204, 4775, 7633
     pictorial works 5344
   Arctic regions 9558, 17298
   classification 5310, 15273
   curiosa and miscellany 8442
   ecology 15635
   experimental 10622
   Louisiana 5244
   miscellanea 9959, 14039
   North America 11782, 15202
   North Dakota 12242
   Polar regions 9298
   research 6736
   Rocky Mountains 18402
   South America 15642
   territoriality 3743
   urban 6960
   vocational guidance 2223
ZULU WAR (1879) 17716
ZULULAND 12271, 12272
ZULUS 1766, 3750, 6994, 8444, 8978, 12273, 14716, 15229, 15230, 15231,
   16200, 17088
   history 18269
ZUMARIS, SALLY (1915-) 3847
ZUNI INDIANS 3498, 15412
   legends 8199
   social life and customs 7028